Aquarium Fishes of the World

TS-292

AQUARIUM FISHES OF THE WORLD

Dr. Herbert R. Axelrod, Dr. Warren E. Burgess, Neal Pronek,
Glen S. Axelrod, David E. Boruchowitz

Zebra danios, *Brachydanio rerio*

TS-292

Photography

Many of the photographers in this book were taken by Dr. Herbert R. Axelrod, but numerous other photographers contributed as well. Since a book such as this one, depending as it does on the quality of its photos for much of the information it seeks to convey, owes a great debt to the photographers whose work it includes, we take this opportunity to list them—hoping that we haven't missed any and promising that if we have we'll correct any oversights at the first opportunity.

Hiromitsu Akiyama
Dr. Gerald R. Allen
D. Allison
Takashi Amano
T. Anger
K. Attwood
Glen S. Axelrod
Dr. Hiroshi Azuma
B. M. Barr
B. Baymiller
Friedrich Bitter
M. Brembach
Pierre Brichard
Thierry Brichard
Dr. Martin Brittan
Dr. Warren E. Burgess
Dr. Brooks Burr
M. Chauche
K. Cole
Donald Conkel
C. C. Corcoran
R. de Boer
B. Degen
Dr. G. Dingerkus
Vojtech Elek
J. Elias
Dr. Augustin Fernandez-Yepez
Walter Foersch
Dr. Stanislav Frank
H. J Franke
Dan Fromm
Dr. Jacques Gery
S. Gill
Dr. Robert J. Goldstein
Dr. Myron Gordon
Dr. Harry Grier
H. Hansen
Courtesy I.N.P.A.
K. Jeno
Rodney Jonklaas
J. Kadlec
Burkhard Kahl
Dr. K. Knaack
A. Kochetov
S. Kochetov
Ad Konings
J. Lambert
R. Lawrence
Horst Linke
Ken Lucas, Steinhart Aquarium
Gerhard Marcuse
Dr. Richard L. Mayden

Hans Mayland
G. Meola
Manfred Meyer
Marine Planning (Aqua Life, Japan)
Midori Shobo (Fish Magazine, Japan)
F. P. Mullenholz
New York Zoological Society
Leo G. Nico
Aaron Norman
Dr. Joanne Norton
Anatoly Noznov
Y. W. Ong
Dr. Lawrence M. Page
Klaus Paysan
MP + C. Piednoir, Aqua Press
E. Purzl
Kurt Quitschau
Dr. J E. Randall
Hans-Joachim Richter
Mervin F. Roberts
Erhard Roloff
Andre Roth
M. Sandford
Jorgen Scheel
Gunter Schmida
D. Schneider
Harald Schultz
T. Schulz
L. Seegers
Mark Smith
Dr. Wolfgang Staeck
Rainer Stawikowski
Glenn Y. Takeshita
Kenjiro Tanaka
Donald C. Taphorn
Edward C. Taylor
Dr. D. Terver, Nancy Aquarium
Gerald J. M. Timmerman
Dr. Bruce J. Turner
Arend van den Nieuwenhuizen
Braz Walker
J. Ward
Wardley Products Co.
Franz Werner
Uwe Werner
R. Wildekamp
Willhock
T. Woeltjes
Gene Wolfsheimer
T. Yokoyama (All-Japan Institute for Nishikigoi)
Ziehm
Ruda Zukal

Contents

CELSIUS° = 5/9 (F° − 32°)   FAHRENHEIT° = 9/5 C° + 32°
METRIC MEASURES AND EQUIVALENTS
CUSTOMARY U.S. MEASURES AND EQUIVALENTS

1 INCH (IN)		= 2.54 CM
1 FOOT (FT)	= 12 IN	= .3048 M
1 YARD (YD)	= 3 FT	= .9144 M
1 MILE (MI)	= 1760 YD	= 1.6093 KM
1 NAUTICAL MILE	= 1.152 MI	= 1.853 KM

1 CUBIC INCH (IN^3)		= 16.387 CM^3
1 CUBIC FOOT (FT^3)	= 1728 IN^3	= .028 M^3
1 CUBIC YARD (YD^3)	= 27 FT^3	= .7646 M^3

1 FLUID OUNCE (FL OZ)		= 2.957 CL
1 LIQUID PINT (PT)	= 16 FL OZ	= .4732 L
1 LIQUID QUART (QT)	= 2 PT	= .946 L
1 GALLON (GAL)	= 4 QT	= 3.7853 L

1 DRY PINT		= .5506 L
1 BUSHEL (BU)	= 64 DRY PT	= 35.2381 L

1 OUNCE (OZ)	= 437.5 GRAINS	= 28.35 G
1 POUND (LB)	= 16 OZ	= .4536 KG
1 SHORT TON	= 2000 LB	= .9072 T
1 LONG TON	= 2240 LB	= 1.0161 T

1 SQUARE INCH (IN^2)		= 6.4516 CM^2
1 SQUARE FOOT (FT^2)	= 144 IN^2	= .093 M^2
1 SQUARE YARD (YD^2)	= 9 FT^2	= .8361 M^2
1 ACRE	= 4840 YD^2	= 4046.86 M^2
1 SQUARE MILE(MI^2)	= 640 ACRE	= 2.59 KM^2

1 MILLIMETER (MM)		= .0394 IN
1 CENTIMETER (CM)	= 10 MM	= .3937 IN
1 METER (M)	= 1000 MM	= 1.0936 YD
1 KILOMETER (KM)	= 1000 M	= .6214 MI

1 SQ CENTIMETER (CM^2)	= 100 MM^2	= .155 IN^2
1 SQ METER (M^2)	= 10,000 CM^2	= 1.196 YD^2
1 HECTARE (HA)	= 10,000 M^2	= 2.4711 ACRES
1 SQ KILOMETER (KM^2)	= 100 HA	= .3861 MI^2

1 MILLIGRAM (MG)		= .0154 GRAIN
1 GRAM (G)	= 1000 MG	= .0353 OZ
1 KILOGRAM (KG)	= 1000 G	= 2.2046 LB
1 TONNE (T)	= 1000 KG	= 1.1023 SHORT TONS
1 TONNE		= .9842 LONG TON

1 CUBIC CENTIMETER (CM^3) = .061 IN^3		
1 CUBIC DECIMETER (DM^3)	= 1000 CM^3	= .353 FT^3
1 CUBIC METER (M^3)	= 1000 DM^3	= 1.3079 YD^3
1 LITER (L)	= 1 DM^3	= .2642 GAL
1 HECTOLITER (HL)	= 100 L	= 2.8378 BU

CLASSIFYING AQUARIUM FISHES

All animals, fishes included, are classified by workers in a particular branch of biology called taxonomy, also referred to as systematics. Taxonomists attempt to group fishes with one another according to certain anatomical and physiological criteria that supposedly reveal evolutionary relationships. In so doing, they necessarily have to erect various classifications and subclassifications into which individual fishes and groups of fishes fit. Each separate classification is represented by a different "taxon" (plural: taxa). The highest taxon —that is, the taxon that includes the greatest number of lower taxa— is the kingdom; all fishes belong to the kingdom Animalia. The next most inclusive taxon is the phylum, which for fishes is the phylum Chordata, the animals (mostly) with backbones. Moving down another notch in inclusiveness, we reach the taxon of the class; for almost every freshwater aquarium fish, the class would be Osteichthys, the bony fishes.

The class Osteichthys is broken down into numerous taxa called orders. As far as keepers of freshwater aquarium fishes are concerned, there are only five important orders (*important* here meaning that among them they contain the great bulk of tropical fishes on the market) and another few orders that contain all the rest. The orders are further subdivided into families. The family is above the two lowest classifications, the genus and the species, in the sense that it is bigger, more inclusive; most families include a number of different genera, and most genera include a number of different species. For purposes of clarifying relationships, taxonomists have also devised such taxonomical subcategories as subspecies and subgenera and tribes and suborders and a few others, but they're just refinements of the major taxonomical levels.

The generic and the specific appellations applied to any given fish in effect become the "scientific" name of that fish under the system of binomial classification currently in use. The name of the genus appears first in the binomial pair, followed by the specific name. Both names conventionally appear in italic type (or are otherwise distinguished) when rendered in print, with the generic name (but not the specific name, even if it derives from a proper noun) starting with a capital letter. Thus the taxonomical name of the Guppy, which is in the genus *Poecilia* and distinguished from other members of that genus by the specific name *reticulata,* would be given as *Poecilia reticulata.*

FAMILY RELATIONSHIPS

The point to bear in mind concerning the various fish families and their importance to you is that the placement of species within a given family normally is indicative of certain likenesses among those species. By definition they have to have a sameness of physical characteristics that set them apart from fishes in other families, but those samenesses usually relate to anatomical details that are of no concern to aquarists. Sometimes, however, the anatomical differences are important because they directly relate to the relative ease or difficulty of keeping the species involved. Hobbyists are very reasonably concerned, for example, that all of the fishes of the family Belontiidae are equipped with an auxiliary breathing apparatus that enables them to extract oxygen from the atmosphere as well as from their aquarium water, because that peculiarity bears directly on the keeping of belontids in aquaria.

In general there also is a relatively uniform pattern to the way fishes of a particular family reproduce, and that is an important consideration for hobbyists. But within the families, especially the large families, there is room for divergence from the main familial pattern. The family Cichlidae and the family Belontiidae, for instance, contain both mouthbrooding and non-mouthbrooding species, and there are a number of variations on both of those themes as well. As a matter of fact, there can be significant differences in spawning behavior among species right within the level of the genus. The genus *Betta,* for example, contains some species that are bubblenest builders and some that are mouthbrooders.

The grouping of fishes into their taxonomical niches is not an exact science, so much of it depends on judgment calls. Different taxonomists have different opinions and will classify things in different ways. Additionally, taxonomists can change their opinions as new data bearing on assumed relationships are uncovered. Since the taxonomists are the ones who put the names on the fishes (and who group them into families and orders and such), the names applied to aquarium fishes can easily change from authority to authority and from time to time.

The type of name change that occurs most frequently in aquarium literature results from a fish's having been moved from one genus to another. Recently, for example, many of the fishes of the very popular family Cichlidae have been placed in genera different from the ones in which they had been grouped for many years. The practical result is that many of the cichlids now have new names; those names are reflected in this book, as are the new names of many other species.

The families that contain the great bulk of tropical aquarium fish species are Cyprindae, Cichlidae, Characidae, Belontiidae and Poeciliidae. Various catfishes are also commonly offered to aquarists, but the catfishes form an entire order by themselves, not just a family.

Family Cyprinidae (Order Cypriniformes)

The family Cyprinidae, the carps, includes a wide range of aquarium species, with most of them being small, fast-moving, relatively peaceful species such as the Zebra Danio, White Cloud Mountain Fish, Tiger Barb, and Rasbora, but it also includes some much bigger fishes, such as the Koi, and a number of species that at first look generally are not thought to be especially carp-like. An example of the last-named type would be the Red-Tailed Shark and the other aquarium "sharks." Probably the best-known cyprinid in the world would be the good old Goldfish. The family Cyprinidae is very widely represented geographically, but most aquarium cyprinids come from Asia, especially Southeast Asia.

Zebra Danio, *Brachydanio rerio*

Red-tailed Shark, *Epalzeorhynchos bicolor*

White Cloud Mountain Fish, *Tanichthys albonubes*

Tiger Barbs, *Capoeta tetrazona.* This is a pair, the male being the fish with the red snout and red edging to the dorsal and caudal fins.

Family Cichlidae (Order Perciformes)

The family Cichlidae, which includes all of the fishes commonly known as cichlids, comprises such old favorites as the Angelfish and the Oscar and the Ram, all from the Americas, as well as the more recently popularized African species from Lakes Malawi and Tanganyika and the old-time African favorite the Egyptian Mouthbrooder. The family also has a few Asiatic representatives.

Auratus, *Melanochromis auratus.* The fish shown is a dominant male.

Angelfish, *Pterophyllum scalare*

Steindachner's Dwarf Cichlid, *Apistogramma steindachneri*

Firemouth Cichlid, *Herichthys meeki*

Family Characidae (Order Characiformes)

The family Characidae includes the fishes popularly known as tetras, which group includes such aquarium stalwarts as the colorful and peaceful Cardinal and Neon Tetras and the slightly less colorful and peaceful various Rosy and Serpae Tetras as well as most of the other tetra species, some of which although being a good deal less colorful have other virtues to compensate. Included in this family also are the piranhas, which neither look like nor behave like their colorful little relatives.

This family has been subject to much systematic re-grouping of its genera into different families and subfamilies recently. Until the early 1970s the Characidae had been a sort of superfamily encompassing not only all of the tetras but also the pencilfishes and headstanders and hatchetfishes and a number of other groups. Then it was broken down into close to twenty separate families, but more recently a number of the groups (the piranhas are an example; for a number of years they were considered to be a family by themselves, the Serrasalmidae) that had been raised to full family status have been put into the Characidae and other characiform families. By far the majority of characids in the hobby come from South America, but a few come from Africa.

Red-tailed Chalceus, *Chalceus macrolepidotus*

Cardinal Tetras,
Paracheirodon axelrodi

Red-bellied Piranha,
Pygocentrus nattereri

Bleeding Heart Tetra,
*Hyphessobrycon
erythrostigma*

Family Belontiidae (Order Perciformes)

This family contains the Siamese Fighting Fish and almost all of the fishes popularly called gouramis; the group as a whole contains some of the most commonly seen fishes in the hobby. All of the aquarium species come from Southeast Asia.

Once placed within one very large family, the Anabantidae, and referred to in general as "labyrinth fishes" because of their possession of a many-branched auxiliary breathing apparatus, the perciform labyrinth fishes currently are grouped into a number of different families, of which the family Belontiidae is by far the most important for aquarium purposes.

A male Siamese Fighting Fish, *Betta splendens.*

Popularly called a gourami but not in the family Belontiidae, this is a Kissing Gourami, *Helostoma temmincki* (family Helostomidae).

A male Blue Gourami, *Trichogaster trichopterus*

A male Dwarf Gourami, *Colisa lalia*

Family Poeciliidae
(Order Cyprinodontiformes)

The family Poeciliidae contains all of the aquarium hobby's popular livebearing fishes: the Guppy and the Mollies (both in the genus *Poecilia*) and the Platies and the Swordtails (both in the genus *Xiphophorus*). It also contains a number of other livebearing species that are seen much less commonly than the popular livebearing species. It does not, however, contain all of the livebearing species that are seen in the hobby; examples of non-poecilid livebearers offered at least from time to time in the aquarium trade would be any of the goodeids (family Goodeidae) and the various species of the family Hemiramphidae, generally called Halfbeaks.

Dermogenys pusillus, the Malayan Halfbeak, a livebearing species but more distantly related to the poecilids than the goodeids are.

Male Swordtail, *Xiphophorus helleri*

Male fancy Guppy, *Poecilia reticulata*

A pair (female in foreground, dwarfing the male) of Mosquito Fish, *Heterandria formosa,* representative of a poecilid species much less popular than the fishes of the Guppy/Molly/Platy/Swordtail groups.

The Catfish Families (Order Siluriformes)

Rounding out the most-often-seen families of aquarium fishes are the fishes within the order Siluriformes, which comprises, among other things, all of the many different catfishes sold in the aquarium trade. There are more than twenty different catfish families that have representatives appearing at least occasionally on the market, and two of those families, the Callichthyidae and the Loricariidae, contain species that are stocked by just about every pet shop and tropical fish specialty store.

The catfishes range from completely inoffensive and comical but terribly misnamed "scavengers" to esurient monsters that will happily engulf anything they can cram into their capacious maws.

Like other *Corydoras* species, this *Corydoras axelrodi* is completey peaceful with other fishes.

Rineloricaria parva, one of the loricariid catfishes generally referred to as "suckermouth" catfishes, doing some helpful work in scouring algae off the side of its tank.

Synodontis longirostris, a member of the African catfish family Mochokidae.

Pimelodus pictus, a member of the family Pimelodidae. Like many other pimelodids, this fish poses a danger to small tankmates.

OTHER FAMILIES

Certain species that don't fall within any of the family groups listed thus far have achieved popularity that in many cases exceeds that of many of the fishes in the "important" families. The Arowana species (family Osteoglossidae), for example, are popular—that is, sought after; they are not always in good supply—as are some of the elephantnoses (family Mormyridae), hatchetfishes (family Gasteropelecidae, closely related to the Characidae), pencilfishes (family Lebiasinidae, also closely related to the Characidae), killifishes (family Aplocheilidae), spiny eels (family Mastacembelidae), loaches (family Cobitidae), gobies (family Gobiidae), puffers (family Tetraodontidae), rainbowfishes (family Melanotaeniidae), knifefishes (from a few different families) and some others. Representatives of all of the families listed above are shown below and on following pages.

Brachygobius nunus, one of the bumblebee gobies; family Gobiidae.

Mastacembelus armatus, a spiny eel of the family Mastacembelidae.

Tetraodon fluviatilis,
one of the puffers;
family
Tetraodontidae.

Gnathonemus tamandua,
one of the fishes gener-
ally referred to as
"elephantnoses," even
though not all of them
have an elongated snout;
family Mormyridae.

A killifish, *Epiplatys annulatus;* family Aplocheilidae.

A trio of Clown
Loaches, *Botia
macracanthus;*
family Cobitidae.

Nannostomus beckfordi, one of the pencilfishes; family Lebiasinidae.

Glossolepis incisus, a rainbowfish of the family Melanotaeniidae.

The Arowana, *Osteoglossum bicirrhosum;* family Osteoglossidae.

Eigenmannia virescens, a New World knifefish; family Gymnotidae. (There are other families as well).

Carnegiella strigata, a hatchetfish; family Gasteropelecidae.

LISTING OF GENERA AND FAMILIES

Following is a listing of genera of aquarium fishes presented in the fish catalog section of this book and the families to which those genera belong. The list is arranged alphabetically by genus, with the genus appearing as the second name (the name in *italic* type) in each couplet of names and the family as the first name.

Cyprinidae, *Abramis*
Curimatidae, *Abramites*
Doradidae, *Acanthodoras*
Cobitidae, *Acantopsis*
Cichlidae, *Acarichthys*
Cichlidae, *Acaronia*
Characidae, *Acestrorhynchus*
Achiridae, *Achirus*
Acipenseridae, *Acipenser*
Aplocheilidae, *Adamas*
Cyprinodontidae, *Adinia*
Cichlidae, *Aequidens*
Cyprinidae, *Alburnoides*
Poeciliidae, *Alfaro*
Goodeidae, *Alloophorus*
Doradidae, *Amblydoras*
Goodeidae, *Ameca*
Amiidae, *Amia*
Terapontidae, *Amniataba*
Anabantidae, *Anabas*
Anablepidae, *Anableps*
Loricariidae, *Ancistrus*
Curimatidae, *Anostomus*
Cyprinodontidae, *Aphanius*
Aphredoderidae, *Aphredoderus*
Characidae, *Aphyocharax*

Aplocheilidae, *Aphyosemion*
Cichlidae, *Apistogramma*
Cichlidae, *Apistogrammoides*
Cyprinodontidae, *Aplocheilichthys*
Aplocheilidae, *Aplocheilus*
Apteronotidae, *Apteronotus*
Osteoglossidae, *Arapaima*
Ariidae, *Arius*
Cichlidae, *Astronotus*
Characidae, *Astyanax*
Goodeidae, *Ataeniobius*
Bagridae, *Auchenoglanis*
Cichlidae, *Aulonocara*
Aplocheilidae, *Austrofundulus*
Characidae, *Axelrodia*
Badidae, *Badis*
Bagridae, *Bagrichthys*
Cyprinidae, *Balantiocheilos*
Cyprinidae, *Barbodes*
Atherinidae, *Bedotia*
Poeciliidae, *Belonesox*
Belontiidae, *Belontia*
Belontiidae, *Betta*
Cichlidae, *Biotodoma*
Cichlidae, *Biotoecus*
Gobiidae, *Boleophthalmus*

Cobitidae, *Botia*
Ctenolucidae, *Boulengerella*
Cyprinidae, *Brachydanio*
Gobiidae, *Brachygobius*
Poeciliidae, *Brachyrhaphis*
Mochokidae, *Brachysynodontis*
Callichthyidae, *Brochis*
Characidae, *Brycinus*
Characidae, *Bryconops*
Cichlidae, *Bujurquina*
Gobiidae, *Butis*
Callichthyidae, *Callichthys*
Cichlidae, *Callochromis*
Mormyridae, *Campylomormyrus*
Cyprinidae, *Capoeta*
Cichlidae, *Caquetaia*
Cyprinidae, *Carassius*
Tetraodontidae, *Carinotetraodon*
Gasteropelecidae, *Carnegiella*
Characidae, *Catoprion*
Centrarchidae, *Centrarchus*
Chacidae, *Chaca*
Cichlidae, *Chaetobranchopsis*
Characidae, *Chalceus*
Cichlidae, *Chalinochromis*
Channidae, *Channa*
Clariidae, *Channalabes*
Goodeidae, *Chapalichthys*
Characidae, *Characidium*
Goodeidae, *Characodon*
Characidae, *Charax*
Characidae, *Cheirodon*
Cyprinidae, *Chela*
Curimatidae, *Chilodus*
Cichlidae, *Chilotilapia*
Notopteridae, *Chitala*
Cyprinodontidae, *Chriopeoides*
Cichlidae, *Chromidotilapia*
Bagridae, *Chrysichthys*
Cichlidae, *Cichla*

Cichlidae, *Cichlasoma*
Clariidae, *Clarias*
Cichlidae, *Cleithracara*
Cobitidae, *Cobitis*
Lobotidae, *Coius*
Belontiidae, *Colisa*
Tetraodontidae, *Colomesus*
Characidae, *Colossoma*
Aplocheilidae, *Congopanchax*
Lebiasinidae, *Copeina*
Lebiasinidae, *Copella*
Callichthyidae, *Corydoras*
Characidae, *Corynopoma*
Cottidae, *Cottus*
Atherinidae, *Craterocephalus*
Cichlidae, *Crenicara*
Cichlidae, *Crenicichla*
Characidae, *Crenuchus*
Cyprinidae, *Crossocheilus*
Characidae, *Ctenobrycon*
Ctenoluciidae, *Ctenolucius*
Anabantidae, *Ctenopoma*
Cyprinodontidae, *Cubanichthys*
Gasterosteidae, *Culaea*
Curimatidae, *Curimata*
Cichlidae, *Cyathopharynx*
Cyprinidae, *Cyclocheilichthys*
Aplocheilidae, *Cynolebias*
Aplocheilidae, *Cynopoecilus*
Cichlidae, *Cynotilapia*
Cichlidae, *Cyphotilapia*
Cichlidae, *Cyprichromis*
Cyprinidae, *Cyprinella*
Cyprinodontidae, *Cyprinodon*
Cyprinidae, *Cyprinus*
Cyprinidae, *Danio*
Hemiramphidae, *Dermogenys*
Callichthyidae, *Dianema*
Citharinidae, *Distichodus*
Gobiidae, *Dormitator*

Aspredinidae, *Dysichthys*
Percichthyidae, *Edelia*
Gymnotidae, *Eigenmannia*
Elassomatidae, *Elassoma*
Gymnotidae, *Electrophorus*
Syngnathidae, *Enneacampus*
Centrarchidae, *Enneacanthus*
Cyprinidae, *Epalzeorhynchos*
Aplocheilidae, *Epiplatys*
Cichlidae, *Eretmodus*
Catostomidae, *Erimyzon*
Poplypteridae, *Erpetoichthys*
Erythrinidae, *Erythrinus*
Cyprinidae, *Esomus*
Percidae, *Etheostoma*
Cichlidae, *Etroplus*
Aplocheilidae, *Foerschichthys*
Aplocheilidae, *Fundulosoma*
Cyprinodontidae, *Fundulus*
Poeciliidae, *Gambusia*
Cyprinodontidae, *Garmanella*
Cyprinidae, *Garra*
Gasteropelecidae, *Gasteropelecus*
Gasterosteidae, *Gasterosteus*
Cichlidae, *Genyochromis*
Cichlidae, *Geophagus*
Characidae, *Gephyrocharax*
Poeciliidae, *Girardinus*
Characidae, *Glandulocauda*
Melanotaeniidae, *Glossolepis*
Mormyridae, *Gnathonemus*
Gymnarchidae, *Gymnarchus*
Characidae, *Gymnocorymbus*
Cichlidae, *Gymnogeophagus*
Gymnotidae, *Gymnorhamphichthys*
Gymnotidae, *Gymnotus*
Gyrinocheilidae, *Gyrinocheilus*
Batrachoididae, *Halophryne*
Cyprinidae, *Hampala*
Cichlidae, *Haplochromis*

Characidae, *Hasemania*
Helostomatidae, *Helostoma*
Cichlidae, *Hemichromis*
Cyprinidae, *Hemigrammocypris*
Characidae, *Hemigrammopetersius*
Characidae, *Hemigrammus*
Hemiodontidae, *Hemiodopsis*
Hemiramphidae, *Hemirhamphodon*
Hepsetidae, *Hepsetus*
Cichlidae, *Herichthys*
Cichlidae, *Heros*
Cichlidae, *Herotilapia*
Poeciliidae, *Heterandria*
Heteropneustidae, *Heteropneustes*
Characidae, *Holobrycon*
Balitoridae, *Homaloptera*
Erythrinidae, *Hoplias*
Callichthyidae, *Hoplosternum*
Cyprinidae, *Horadandia*
Characidae, *Hyphessobrycon*
Gymnotidae, *Hypopomus*
Loricariidae, *Hypostomus*
Cichlidae, *Hypselecara*
Gobiidae, *Hypseleotris*
Ictaluridae, *Ictalurus*
Characidae, *Iguanodectes*
Indostomidae, *Indostomus*
Characidae, *Inpaichthys*
Cichlidae, *Iodotropheus*
Melanotaeniidae, *Iriatherina*
Anablepidae, *Jenynsia*
Cyprinodontidae, *Jordanella*
Cichlidae, *Julidochromis*
Cichlidae, *Krobia*
Siluridae, *Kryptopterus*
Kurtidae, *Kurtus*
Cyprinidae, *Labeo*
Cichlidae, *Labeotropheus*
Cichlidae, *Labidochromis*
Cyprinidae, *Labiobarbus*

Characidae, *Ladigesia*
Cichlidae, *Laetacara*
Cyprinodontidae, *Lamprichthys*
Cichlidae, *Lamprologus*
Centropomidae, *Lates*
Pimelodidae, *Leiarius*
Bagridae, *Leiocassis*
Terponidae, *Leiopotherapon*
Characidae, *Lepidarchus*
Cobitidae, *Lepidocephalus*
Lepidogalaxiidae, *Lepidogalaxias*
Lepisosteidae, *Lepisosteus*
Centrarchidae, *Lepomis*
Curimatidae, *Leporinus*
Cypinidae, *Leptobarbus*
Cyprinodontidae, *Leptolucania*
Cichlidae, *Limnochromis*
Auchenipteridae, *Liosomadoras*
Bagridae, *Lophiobagrus*
Cyprinodontidae, *Lucania*
Luciocephalidae, *Luciocephalus*
Cyprinidae, *Luciosoma*
Mastacembelidae, *Macrognathus*
Belontiidae, *Macropodus*
Malapteruridae, *Malapterurus*
Belontiidae, *Malpulutta*
Mastacembelidae, *Mastacembelus*
Cichlidae, *Melanochromis*
Melanotaeniidae , *Melanotaenia*
Cichlidae, *Mesonauta*
Characidae, *Metynnis*
Characidae, *Micralestes*
Anabantidae, *Microctenopoma*
Cichlidae, *Microgeophagus*
Pimelodidae, *Microglanis*
Syngnathidae, *Microphis*
Characidae, *Mimagoniates*
Cobitidae, *Misgurnus*
Characidae, *Moenkhausia*
Gobiidae, *Mogurnda*

Nandidae, *Monocirrhus*
Monodactylidae, *Monodactylus*
Mormyridae, *Mormyrops*
Characidae, *Myleus*
Characidae, *Mylossoma*
Bagridae, *Mystus*
Nandidae, *Nandus*
Cichlidae, *Nannacara*
Citharinidae, *Nannaethiops*
Lebiasinidae, *Nannostomus*
Cichlidae, *Nanochromis*
Cichlidae, *Neetroplus*
Balitoridae, *Nemacheilus*
Characidae, *Nematobrycon*
Ceratodontidae, *Neoceratodus*
Citharinidae, *Neolebias*
Hemiramphidae, *Nomorhamphus*
Scorpaenidae, *Notesthes*
Aplocheilidae, *Nothobranchius*
Siluridae, *Ompok*
Cyprinidae, *Opsaridium*
Cichlidae, *Opthalmotilapia*
Cichlidae, *Oreochromis*
Adrianichthyidae, *Oryzias*
Osphronemidae, *Osphronemus*
Cyprinidae, *Osteochilus*
Osteoglossidae, *Osteoglossum*
Callichthyidae, *Otocinclus*
Eleotridae, *Oxyeleotris*
Cyprinidae, *Oxygaster*
Aplocheilidae, *Pachypanchax*
Loricariidae, *Panaque*
Pangasiidae, *Pangasius*
Cobitidae, *Pangio*
Pantodontidae, *Pantodon*
Notopteridae, *Papyrocranus*
Characidae, *Paracheirodon*
Ambassidae, *Parambassis*
Gobiidae, *Parapocryptes*
Auchenipteridae, *Parauchenipterus*

Hemiodontidae, *Parodon*
Belontiidae, *Parosphromenus*
Loricariidae, *Peckoltia*
Bagridae, *Pelteobagrus*
Cichlidae, *Pelvicachromis*
Gobiidae, *Periophthalmus*
Pimelodidae, *Perrunichthys*
Cichlidae, *Petenia*
Characidae, *Petitella*
Cichlidae, *Petrochromis*
Cichlidae, *Petrotilapia*
Citharinidae, *Phago*
Poeciliidae, *Phallichthys*
Poeciliidae, *Phalloceros*
Characidae, *Phenacogaster*
Characidae, *Phenacogrammus*
Cyprinidae, *Phoxinus*
Pimelodidae, *Phractocephalus*
Phractlaemidae, *Phractolaemus*
Amphiliidae, *Phractura*
Pimelodidae, *Pimelodella*
Pimelodidae, *Pimelodus*
Pimelodidae, *Pinirampus*
Doradidae, *Platydoras*
Aspredinidae, *Platystacus*
Pimelodidae, *Platystomatichthys*
Poeciliidae, *Poecilia*
Poeciliidae, *Poeciliopsis*
Nandidae, *Polycentropsis*
Nandidae, *Polycentrus*
Polypteridae, *Polypterus*
Characidae, *Poptella*
Potamotrygonidae, *Potamotrygon*
Poeciliidae, *Priapella*
Characidae, *Prionobrama*
Cyprinidae, *Probarbus*
Cyprinodontidae, *Procatopus*
Protopteridae, *Protopterus*
Loricariidae, *Pseudacanthicus*
Characidae, *Pseudochalceus*

Characidae, *Pseudocorynopoma*
Cichlidae, *Pseudocrenilabrus*
Doradidae, *Pseudodoras*
Balitoridae, *Pseudogastromyzon*
Atherinidae, *Pseudomugil*
Pimelodidae, *Pseudopimelodus*
Pimelodidae, *Pseudoplatystoma*
Belontiidae, *Pseudosphromenus*
Cichlidae, *Pseudotropheus*
Aplocheilidae, *Pterolebias*
Cyprinidae, *Pteronotropis*
Cichlidae, *Pterophyllum*
Loricariidae, *Pterygoplichthys*
Cyprinidae, *Puntius*
Characidae, *Pygocentrus*
Lebiasinidae, *Pyrrhulina*
Poeciliidae, *Quintana*
Aplocheilidae, *Rachovia*
Characidae, *Rachoviscus*
Cyprinidae, *Rasbora*
Cyprinidae, *Rasborichthys*
Cyprinidae, *Rasboroides*
Melanotaeniidae, *Rhadinocentrus*
Cyprinidae, *Rhinichthys*
Cyprinidae, *Rhodeus*
Loricariidae, *Rineloricaria*
Aplocheilidae, *Rivulus*
Characidae, *Roeboides*
Anabantidae, *Sandelia*
Cichlidae, *Satanoperca*
Cyprinidae, *Scardineus*
Scatophagidae, *Scatophagus*
Schilbeidae, *Schilbe*
Balitoridae, *Schistura*
Osteoglossidae, *Scleropages*
Scatophagidae, *Selenotoca*
Curimatidae, *Semaprochilodus*
Characidae, *Serrasalmus*
Gobiidae, *Sicyopterus*
Cichlidae, *Simochromis*

Pimelodidae, *Sorubim*
Pimelodidae, *Sorubimichthys*
Cichlidae, *Spathodus*
Belontiidae, *Sphaerichthys*
Cichlidae, *Steatocranus*
Gymnotidae, *Steatogenys*
Gobiidae, *Stigmatogobius*
Loricariidae, *Sturisoma*
Cichlidae, *Symphysodon*
Synbranchidae, *Synbranchus*
Mochokidae, *Synodontis*
Plotosidae, *Tandanus*
Cichlidae, *Tanganicodus*
Cyprinidae, *Tanichthys*
Gobiidae, *Tateurndina*
Cichlidae, *Teleogramma*
Atherinidae, *Telmatherina*
Cichlidae, *Telmatochromis*
Aplocheilidae, *Terranatos*
Characidae, *Tetragonopterus*
Tetraodontidae, *Tetraodon*

Characidae, *Thayeria*
Gasteropelecidae, *Thoracocharax*
Cichlidae, *Thysochromis*
Cichlidae, *Tilapia*
Toxotidae, *Toxotes*
Belontiidae, *Trichogaster*
Belontiidae, *Trichopsis*
Aplocheilidae, *Trigonectes*
Characidae, *Triportheus*
Cichlidae, *Tropheus*
Characidae, *Tyttocharax*
Cichlidae, *Uaru*
Belonidae, *Xenentodon*
Notopteridae, *Xenomystus*
Goodeidae, *Xenoophorus*
Tetraodontidae, *Xenopterus*
Goodeidae, *Xenotoca*
Poeciliidae, *Xiphophorus*
Cyprinidae, *Zacco*
Goodeidae, *Zoogoneticus*

CATALOG OF FISHES

The species discussed in the following section are listed in alphabetical order according to their scientific names; the index (page 971) to the fish catalog section cross-references both scientific and common names to enable readers to locate discussions of particular species even if they don't know the scientific name of the fish they're looking for and know only its common name.

A NOTE ABOUT THE ABBREVIATIONS USED

In order to conserve space, always a consideration in a book as far-reaching as this one, we have used boldface initials to stand for the subject headings that appear at the top of each individual fish description in the catalog of fishes. The abbreviations thus used are as follows:

R:=RANGE; the geographical area in which the fish lives in the wild.

For some fishes the range would be very wide, encompassing large parts of a continent or perhaps even more than a single continent. For others it would be very small, perhaps restricted to parts of a single river or river system or even a lake.

H:=HABITS; although concerned primarily with the habits of the species being described as regards its aggressiveness or lack of aggressiveness (especially toward other species), this category of information deals also with other behavioral characteristics such as digging habits and propensity to jump, and it also covers recommendations based on physical characteristics such as size.

W:=WATER; covers water conditions such as temperature, relative hardness and acidity/alkalinity, saltiness and others.

S:=SIZE; in most cases, listed as the maximum size attained.

F:= FOODS; describes, in general terms, foods that are preferred or at least accepted.

C:= COLORS. (Used infrequently.) Deals with colors of wild fishes, occasionally with color differences between sexes.

ABRAMIS BRAMA (Linnaeus)/*Bream*

R: Europe and northern Asia. **H:** Peaceful; a bottom-feeding species that will help clean up food that has been left uneaten by other fishes. **W:** Not critical. A temperate fish that spawns at 15°C or more. **S:** Up to 60 cm. **F:** Will thrive on almost any food.

Occurs in small schools in ponds and sluggish streams in European and northern Asiatic waters, where it is often caught by anglers. Sexes can only be distinguished in fairly large specimens, when the females become heavy with roe. This fish is not a very popular aquarium inhabitant, but young specimens may be kept with other coldwater species such as Goldfish. There are numerous species of this genus and all have similar appearance and habits. They are members of the family Cyprinidae, the carp-like fishes.

ACANTHODORAS SPINOSISSIMUS

ABRAMITES HYPSELONOTUS (Günther)/*Headstander*

R: Upper Peruvian Amazon, Paraguay, Venezuela. **H:** May be aggressive, also nibble plants. **W:** Water should be soft and slightly acid. Temperature 23 to 25°C. **S:** About 12.5 cm; usually smaller specimens are sold. **F:** Living foods are eagerly accepted, and the fish are fond of nibbling algae or a lettuce leaf.

Not a good community fish as it may often become very aggressive. *A. hypselonotus* is very fond of nibbling plants and will sometimes continue this activity on its fellow tankmates, nibbling away at their fins and scales. Fully grown Headstanders may make enemies among their own kind and nip each other to death. If you are daring or foolish enough to keep this species, they should be given a tank with tough-leaved plants and a leaf of lettuce to nibble on if there is not enough algae present. Chances are that if they find algae or a lettuce leaf, the plants and maybe the tankmates will be left alone.

ABRAMIS BRAMA

ACANTHODORAS SPINOSISSIMUS *Spiny Catfish, Talking Catfish*
R: Middle Amazon region. **H:** Mostly nocturnal; will not molest any fish it cannot swallow. **W:** Not critical. Temperatures should range between 24 and 28°C. **S:** Maximum 15 cm; matures at 10 cm. **F:** Prefers living foods, especially daphnia, tubifex or enchytrae.
This is a spiny fish capable of emitting a sound. This is a faint croak, which you would have to listen to very attentively to hear. As with many of the catfishes, they are mostly nocturnal by habit, shunning bright light. For this reason they should be provided with adequate hiding places, such as flat rocks under which they can dig.

ABRAMITES HYPSELONOTUS

ACANTOPSIS CHOIRORHYNCHUS (Bleeker)/*Long-Nosed Loach*

R: Southeast Asia: Thailand, Malay Peninsula, Sumatra, Borneo, Java; occurs in fresh water only. **H**: Mostly nocturnal; in the daylight hours it usually remains buried in the gravel with only its eyes showing. **W**: Neutral to slightly acid water. Temperature between 24 to 30°C. **S**: Wild specimens attain a length of 18-20 cm; in captivity they remain smaller. **F**: Living foods only: tubifex worms, white worms, daphnia, etc.

Although this fish likes to dig in the sand, don't count on it to clean up and eat leftover foods. It may do this when very hungry, but its preference is worms, and these should be wriggling. This species is one which you must search for frequently, and then often without success. Most of the daylight hours are spent buried in the sand, right up to the eyes. For this reason you must provide a fine grade of gravel or injuries may result when they burrow. Small fishes are perfectly safe with *Acantopsis choirorhynchus;* they are seldom molested.

ACARONIA NASSA

ACARICHTHYS HECKELI Müller and Troschel/Elusive Cichid

R: Throughout central Brazil and all the Amazonian tributaries and the Guianas. **H**: A large, beautiful fish that is rarely imported but which exists in quantity in nature. It should have a large aquarium. **W**: Although not sensitive to water conditions, it is in best color when kept in soft, slightly acid water at a temperature of about 24°C. **S**: To about 15-20 cm. **F**: As with most cichlids, they prefer large, bulky live foods such as small garden worms, but they eagerly take pelletized and frozen foods.

While fishing in the Rio Urubu about 32 km north of Itacoatiara, in 1959, the author (HRA) collected this beautiful species. This was one of the few fishes, from the thousands the author collected, that really impressed him. After spending several hours looking for a likely female of the species, the author gave up in vain. In the next river, he caught hundreds of them and shipped them back to the United States alive. They were not the "smash hit" he thought they would be. No one was able to breed them even though some of the finest fish breeders in Florida tried it.

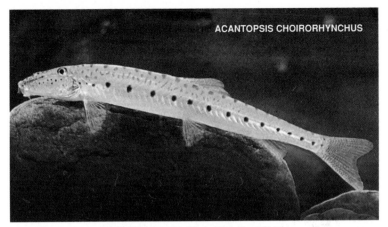

ACANTOPSIS CHOIRORHYNCHUS

ACARONIA NASSA (Heckel)/*Big-Eyed Cichlid*
R: Northern Amazon Region to Guyana. **H**: Nasty, greedy and pugnacious; cannot be trusted in the company of fishes smaller than itself. **W**: Not critical. Temperature about 24°C. **S**: Up to 20 cm. **F**: A heavy feeder; likes food in large chunks. Cut-up earthworms, pieces of raw fish or smaller whole fish are consumed eagerly.

The writer recalls getting two little ones when they came in a shipment of mixed dwarf cichlids. They were small, but their unfriendly attitude toward the other fishes was soon noted and they were given an 80-liter tank of their own. Here they were given large chunks of whatever food was available: pieces of shrimp cut to fit their large mouths, raw fish, fish that had become crippled, and even dog food from cans! Everything went down their capacious gullets, and they got bigger and sassier.

ACARICHTHYS HECKELI

ACIPENSER RUTHENUS

ACESTRORHYNCHUS MICROLEPIS (Schomburgk)/*Pike Characin*

R: Northern South America. **H**: Will eat or damage any other fish put with it. **W**: Requires much room and a good deal of heat, 26 to 28° C. **S**: About 30 cm. **F**: Will take only living foods, preferably smaller fishes.

One look at the torpedo-shaped body, the hungry eyes and barracuda-like teeth of this fellow identifies it as a predatory species of the worst kind. Unlike the pike, which lies quietly half-concealed or cruises along almost motionless like a twig in the water, *Acestrorhynchus microlepis* prefers to pursue its prey, and it is seldom that it cannot overtake it. It is the bane of fish collectors, who get a great many fish damaged or eaten whenever their catch includes one of these. What is more, they must be picked up with caution, or those needle-sharp teeth will tear into the fisherman's hand.

ADAMAS FORMOSUS

ACIPENSER RUTHENUS Linnaeus/*Sterlet*

R: Eastern Europe. **H**: A peaceful fish much given to ceaseless cruising over the bottom. **W**: Not critical. **S**: In nature to one meter. Aquarium specimens seldom exceed 30 cm. **F**: Earthworms, snails, and tubifex worms are preferred. They will also accept frozen foods. **C**: Back and sides blue-gray, underside pale yellow. Fins dark.

The sturgeons are a widely distributed group, ranging throughout Europe and North America. None are suitable for the aquarium when mature, since they attain gigantic proportions (some species up to 4 meters), but young fishes make good aquarium subjects if the aquarium is kept cool. The Sterlet is an extremely graceful fish whose ease of movement is a source of wonder to all who behold it. This species is a bottom feeder. Unfortunately, it is not a voracious feeder and other fishes in the aquarium may consume all the food before the Sterlet finds it. Chances of spawning this species are relatively small. The spawning season in nature is from May through June. The parents deposit the eggs over gravel in rivers. The young are similar to young tadpoles and are black in color.

ACESTRORHYNCHUS MICROLEPIS

ADAMAS FORMOSUS Huber/*Starhead Panchax*

R: Central-southern part of the Republic of the Congo, the old French Middle Congo. **H:** Relatively peaceful but normally is kept in a single-species tank. Young have a tendency toward aggressiveness and cannibalism. **W:** In natural habitat relatively soft, acid (pH 5.8) water at temperatures around 23°C. **S:** Males grow to a length of about 26 mm, females somewhat smaller. **F:** Prefers living foods such as brine shrimp and *Daphnia* of suitable size.

In an aquarium a couple of pairs can easily be housed in a 10-liter tank providing there are sufficient hiding places. This can be accomplished by using plants. Subdued lighting is also recommended. The water should be clean and clear. Like other killifishes, the Starhead Panchax does not take to flake foods or even other prepared foods very well but prefers living foods.

For spawning this little (males 26 mm, females somewhat smaller) killifish add a sunken mop or some German peat (the long-fiber material). The eggs, about I mm in diameter, can be collected at intervals (a week to ten days usual) and stored in damp peat for a period of about four to six weeks.

ADINIA XENICA (Jordan & Gilbert)/*Diamond Killifish*

R: Southeastern Florida to central Texas along the Gulf Coast, mostly in estuarine, brackish, salt marsh areas. **H**: Relatively peaceful. Males may become rough during courtship. Does well with other small brackish water fishes that are not too aggressive. **W**: Prefers brackish water. Can be adapted to pure fresh water, but for full color and vitality they should have salt added to their water. **S**: About 5 cm. **F**: Accepts almost any high quality flake food as well as frozen and freeze-dried foods. Should be offered algae or other vegetable matter such as cooked spinach. The Diamond Killifish is especially fond of mosquito larvae. **C**: Males dark green above, lighter grayish green below. Sides with a series of dark vertical bars alternating with 10-14 pearl-colored bars. Belly yellow; jaw orange. Dorsal and anal fins greenish covered with light (pale blue) spots. Females rather plain.

AEQUIDENS PULCHER

AEQUIDENS APALLIDUS (HECKEL)/*Double-Spot Aequidens*

R: Amazon River near Manaus. **H**: Peaceful, possibly even shy, when not spawning. Makes a good community tank species. **W**: Not critical. Does best in water with a pH close to neutral or slightly acid, up to 10 DH and with a temperature between 24 and 27°C. **S**: Attains a length of up to 15 cm. **F**: Will accept almost any of the normal live or prepared aquarium foods available. A large tank is recommended, the capacity to be not less than 200 liters for fully grown individuals. The water should be neutral to slightly acid, with a hardness of up to 10 DH. The temperature range for best results is 24 to 27°C. The tank decorations can include plants, driftwood and rocks, the last mentioned preferably with some flat surfaces.

ADINIA XENICA

AEQUIDENS PULCHER (Gill) (formerly *A. latifrons*)/*Blue Acara*

R: Panama, Colombia, Venezuela and Trinidad. **H**: Very apt to bully smaller fishes; should be kept only with their own kind or larger fishes. **W**: Not critical; water should be kept well filtered, because the fish are likely to stir up the bottom by digging. Temperature 21 to 26°C. **S**: 15 cm; will begin to breed at 10 cm. **F**: All kinds of live foods, supplemented by chopped beef heart, earthworms, etc.

The Blue Acara may be more apt to be troublesome to keep than the other acaras, but it has to its credit the fact that it is one of the easiest to breed and also one of the least likely to eat its own eggs and fry. It is probably the most robust of all the acaras, and if given the proper attention it will outlive many other aquarium fishes. It spawns like the others, but loves to dig and can be expected to uproot many plants.

AEQUIDENS APALLIDUS

AEQUIDENS SAPAYENSIS

AEQUIDENS RIVULATUS (Günther)/*Green Terror*

R: Peru. **H**: A vicious fish; it will fight with all other fishes, including members of its own species. **W**: Not critical. Temperature 21 to 26°C. **S**: Up to 23 cm. **F**: Will take all standard aquarium fare for large cichlids.

The fishes of the genus *Aequidens* range widely in size, but until recently all of the fishes of the genus were considered to be characterized by a sameness in temperament. They were not the most peaceful of fishes, but for cichlids they were not bad actors at all. The introduction of *Aequidens rivulatus* in 1970 changed that opinion, because here was an *Aequidens* species that was downright mean.

AEQUIDENS TETRAMERUS

AEQUIDENS SAPAYENSIS (Regan)/*Sapaya Cichlid*

R: Northwestern Ecuador. **H:** Relatively peaceful and can be added to a cichlid community tank. **W:** Not critical. Highly adaptable to most W. Prefers a temperature of about 24-27°C. **S:** Attains a length of at least 15 cm. **F:** Will accept a wide variety of foods from live brine shrimp to flake foods.

Spawning this fish is apparently not difficult. It may be a bit hard to distinguish the sexes of younger fish because the fins of the females are just as long and pointed as those of the males. When they get older, however, there is more of a difference because the fins grow longer in the older males.

AEQUIDENS RIVULATUS

AEQUIDENS TETRAMERUS (Heckel)/*Pishuna*

R: Found throughout northern South America from Guyana through Brazil as far south as Rio de Janeiro. **H:** A typical cichlid with typical cichlid behavior. **W:** Insensitive to minor water changes. Appreciates warm water but does well in water from 18 to 30°C. pH of 6.0-7.4; water up to 10 DH. **S:** 15 cm; becomes mature at 10 cm. **F:** Eats all types of bulky foods, whether living or not. Prefers frozen brine shrimp and tubifex.

The distribution of this fish is so large that it has been known under a number of different names from different places. Heckel first described this fish in 1840 as *Acara tetramerus* from the Rio Branco of Brazil. Eigenmann and Bray in 1894 used this species to establish the genus *Aequidens*. In 1891 Eigenmann and Eigenmann called this fish *Astronotus tetramerus* from the Amazon.

ALBURNOIDES BIPUNCTATUS (Bloch)/*Tailor*

R: France eastward to the USSR. Subspecies occur in the Caucasus and Asia Minor. **H:** Usually can be seen near the surface and in small schools. It is best kept with other cold water cyprinids. **W:** A cold water fish needing temperatures from 10°-18° C. Strong aeration is also recommended. **S:** Attains a length of 10-12 cm (rarely over 15 cm). **F:** Prefers small live foods but can be weaned onto prepared foods.

Spawning has occurred in captivity but this is a rare event and only advanced aquarists will probably succeed. The eggs are scattered over the bottom.

ALLOOPHORUS ROBUSTUS

ALFARO CULTRATUS (Regan)/*Knife Livebearer*

R: Costa Rica to Panama and Amazonian region of Brazil. **H:** Generally shy but may be aggressive toward its own kind or nip a few fins from time to time. Not recommended for a community tank. **W:** Not critical. Slightly alkaline water with the addition of a small amount of salt is advisable. Temperature should be 25-28°C. **S:** In central America males grow to 9 cm, females to 10 cm; in Brazil males are 4-5 cm, females 6 cm. **F:** Live foods are almost a must. It is difficult to train these fish to eat flake food, although it has been done.

Alfaro cultratus is one of the more *unusual* livebearers. Males have a gonopodium and females a normal rather short anal fin, but behind these fins and extending to the base of the caudal fin is a sharp keel composed of a row of paired modified scales. It is this feature that led to the common name Knife Livebearer.

ALBURNOIDES BIPUNCTATUS

ALLOOPHORUS ROBUSTUS (Bean)/*Bulldog Goodeid*

R: Lower Rio Lerma basin, Mexico. **H:** Very aggressive and predatory. Cannot be trusted with fry or small fishes. **W:** Favors slightly alkaline, slightly hard water. The addition of a teaspoon of salt per gallon is said to be beneficial. **S:** Normally attains a length of about 12 to 13 cm but is said to reach a length of almost 20 cm total length. **F:** Accepts a wide variety of foods. A varied diet is recommended.

A large tank is recommended, something in the order of 35 gallons or so (about 100 liters) for a small group. At least 25% of the water should be changed weekly. No gravel is necessary on the bottom, which should be dark to bring out the best colors of the fish (a glass-bottomed tank sitting on a dark-colored sheet of construction paper can do the trick). Lots of plants should be used. Not among the most prolific livebearing species.

ALFARO CULTRATUS

AMBLYDORAS HANCOCKI (Valenciennes) *Hancock's Amblydoras*

R: Peruvian and Bolivian Amazon and tributaries, and the Guianas. **H**: Mostly nocturnal; prefers a well-shaded tank. Will seldom uproot plants and does not harm other fishes they cannot swallow. **W**: Temperatures between 24 to 26°C. Water about neutral to slightly alkaline. **S**: To 15 cm. **F**: Small live foods are preferred, such as daphnia, tubifex or white worms.

This attractive catfish is often confused with and sold as *Acanthodoras spinosissimus*. Although it is also spiny, *Amblydoras hancocki* is not in a class with its cousin. It is more peaceful and can be trusted in a community aquarium. When frightened it has the capability of burying itself in the sand with only its large eyes looking out. It can do this so skillfully that the bottom is not roiled, and seldom is there ever a plant uprooted. Sexes may be distinguished quite easily; males have spotted bellies and females do not.

AMIA CALVA

AMECA SPLENDENS Miller & Fitzsimmons/*Butterfly Goodeid*

R: Rio Ameca and its tributaries, State of Jalisco in western Mexico. **H**: Peaceful; good for a community tank. Males aggressive toward females. **W**: Does well with a bit of salt (up to 10%) added to the water; pH about 6.7 -7.4. The temperature R is 23 to 29°C, with an optimum of 25°C. **S**: Attains a length of 9 cm (standard length) in nature. **F**: Will take a wide variety of aquarium foods, but prefers algae, *Daphnia,* live brine shrimp and mosquito larvae.

For spawning, an 80-liter tank with a couple of males and four to six females is best. Some Java moss (for fry) and caves (for protection of the females) are recommended, as males tend to be rather aggressive toward females in the aquarium. Besides the anal fin character, males can be distinguished by color pattern. They have a bright yellow edge to their caudal fin.

Ameca splendens is a community tank species, with a male and two or three females recommended. If young are to be saved, the pregnant females must be moved to a maternity tank. The young usually are not bothered by their parents. The water should have a pH of about 6.6-7.4 and a temperature between 23 and 29°C. At least 25% of the water should be changed weekly. *Ameca splendens* will take a variety of foods but should get some vegetable matter, as in nature it is more of a herbivore. Sufficient aeration and light (for algal growth) sould be provided.

AMBLYDORAS HANCOCKI

AMIA CALVA Linnaeus / *Bowfin, Mudfish, Dogfish*

R: Found in the United States from Vermont to the Dakotas, from Florida to Texas. **H**: A vicious, voracious fish, not to be kept with any fish smaller than itself. **W**: Capable of living in any water that has not been poisoned, though it prefers warm water from 21 to 30°C. **S**: Males grow to 50 cm; females to 75 cm. **F**: This is a fish that will only eat live foods. Small earthworms are acceptable. Larger specimens can be taught to accept beef heart and other meat products. *Amia calva* is of great interest to zoologists because of its relation to many prehistoric forms. The adult coloration is blackish olive with green reticulations on the sides. The lower side of the head has dark spots. The male has a black ocellus (eye-spot) edged with orange at the upper base of the caudal fin. The fish is very common in Florida, especially in the lowland swamps and the larger still pools. The young are very interesting and they poise like snakes above their prey and strike with a fast darting action.

AMECA SPLENDENS

Amia calva skeleton of head.

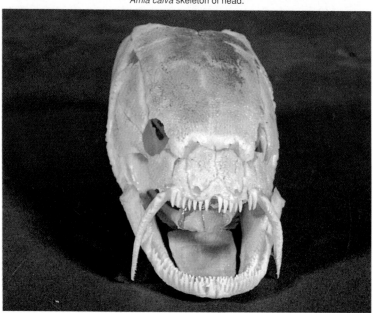

AMNIATABA PERCOIDES

AMNIATABA PERCOIDES (Guenther)/*Black-striped Grunter*

R: Rivers of Australia. **H:** An aggressive and active fish that cannot be kept with fishes much smaller than itself. **W:** Not critical. **S:** Attains a length of only 15 cm. **F:** Will accept most live or frozen foods, especially small feeder fishes.

This pretty fish is known only from the rivers of Australia. It has become quite popular in some regions (for example Singapore) as an aquarium fish, probably because of its hardiness and its coloration, i.e., a yellowish ground color crossed by several blackish vertical bars. The lower portion of the caudal fin is black, and there are some dark stripes running from the eye and below the eye to the tip of the snout. The back may become bluish gray and there may be some blue spots on the tail. The largest specimens tend to lose the stripes. Such fish are often called Silver Perch, at least in Queensland. Other names include Banded Grunter and Tigerfish.

This is an aggressive fish as well as being active, so any tankmates must be large enough to take care of themselves. In fact, small fishes make an ideal food, along with freeze-dried and frozen shrimp or other such delicacies.

Apparently nothing is recorded concerning the breeding habits of the Black-striped Grunter other than they will breed in ponds. This fish is also considered too small to be of any commercial food value even though it does bite on hook and line readily. A variety of baits can be used.

ANABAS TESTUDINEUS (Bloch)/*Climbing Perch*

R: India, Sri Lanka, Burma, Southeast Asia, southern China, Philippine Islands and Malaysia. **H**: Aggressive; should be kept by themselves. Large aquaria should be provided and kept covered. **W**: Not critical. Has a wide temperature tolerance, 18 to 30°C. **S**: Up to 25 cm; becomes mature at 10cm. **F**: Eats almost anything; in the absence of live foods, canned dog food with a high beef content is an acceptable substitute. **C**: Dirty gray to greenish, with a dark spot at the caudal base and another just behind the gill plate.

The Climbing Perch, which incidentally is not a perch, has long been a great curiosity, and it used to be that a show that featured aquarium fishes counted on the antics of this fish to attract many people. A board was placed above an aquarium and one of these fish was netted out and placed on it. It would waddle the length of the board and plop back into the water, to the tireless amusement of the audience. In its native haunts the fish inhabits swampy places where, when the water begins to dry out, it must make its way from puddle to puddle across dry land until it finds another body of water.

ANCISTRUS DOLICHOPTERUS

ANABLEPS ANABLEPS Linnaeus/*Four-Eyes*

R: Northern South America from the Guianas and Venezuela to the Amazon in Brazil. **H**: Surface fish spending most of their time on the surface of the water with their bulging eyes exposed to the air. In nature they move quickly over the surface of the water. **W**: They prefer very hard, warm water. Their natural habitat is usually brackish water canals. They are not found in large rivers or fast moving streams. Temperature 22-26°C. **S**: To about 30 cm in length. **F**: They prefer live food such as small fishes, worms and insects, but they can be tempted to take frozen brine shrimp and bits of beef heart on occasion.

The Four-Eyes is a large fish and has eyes in elevated sockets which give it the ability to see in air as well as water. The pupil is divided by a horizontal cross-partition. This is a livebearing species and gives birth to its young in small non-uniform batches. The young are about 5 cm long when born. The sexes are left- and right-handed, with a right-handed male mating with a lefthanded female. Sexes are easy to ascertain as the male has a gonopodium-like adaptation on his anal fin which is a scaly tube. There is a great preponderance of females in this species. The author (HRA) once collected some 200 *Anableps anableps* in Guyana by laying a net in water less than 5 cm deep. The fish were "herded" onto this shallow bed and the net swiftly lifted. Of the 200 fish collected, only three males were apparent.

ANABAS TESTUDINEUS

ANCISTRUS DOLICHOPTERUS (Kner)/*Bushy-Mouthed Catfish*
R: Northeastern South America. **H**: Peaceful; will not harm even the smallest fish. **W**: Can take a very wide range of water conditions, as long as abrupt changes are not made. **S**: Up to 13 cm. **F**: Accepts all foods and is especially fond of algae.

They spawn in cave-like shelters, which may be duplicated in the home aquarium by rock caves or tubular shelters; of the latter, perhaps bamboo tubes are best, as these have been used on many occasions with good success in the breeding of this bewhiskered species. The male, which sometimes spawns with more than one female at a time, cleans off a space on which to deposit the adhesive eggs. The male guards the eggs and fans them vigorously all during their five- to seven-day incubation period.

ANABLEPS ANABLEPS

ANCISTRUS HOPLOGENYS (Günther)/*Pearl Sucker*

R: Widely dispersed over South America from Guyana to the Rio Paraguay, which separates Paraguay from Brazil. **H**: A nocturnal fish that clings to the glass but prefers "nightwork." **W**: A very hardy species that does well in any type of water as long as it is not too salty. It can be safely maintained in water at a temperature of 19-30°C. **S**: The usual size is under 12.5 cm. **F**: Eats every type of food usually offered aquarium fishes. Should be offered live foods.

The family Loricariidae contains such familiar genera as *Hypostomus, Farlowella,* and *Loricaria,* as well as *Ancistrus.*

This species is one of the most colorful in the genus and though it has a very wide range, it is found in each area in very limited numbers. This should be a very simple fish to spawn as it rarely gets larger than 10 to 12.5 cm. Males have more and longer tentacles than females.

ANCISTRUS HOPLOGENYS

ANCISTRUS TEMMINCKI (Valenciennes)/*Temminck's Bristle-Nose*

R: Upper Amazon, Peru, the Guianas and Surinam. **H**: Generally peaceful toward other fishes, but two individuals cannot always be trusted to get along peacefully. **W**: Clean, well-oxygenated water is essential. Once established in a tank, they should be moved as little as possible. Temperature 21 to 26°C. **S**: About 15 cm. **F**: All small live foods are readily accepted, and an occasional meal of chopped spinach is beneficial.

This species differs from *Ancistrus lineolatus* in that the snout is not so broad and the body has more spots on it. Although the bristles on the fish in the picture are rather small, don't let that fool you! At other times of the year they can be so bristly that you may wonder how they get any food through them. In order to insure that they get their fair share of the feedings, it is well to put in some food before turning out the light. Then the others would not gobble it up before the Bristle-Nose gets it. Care must be taken not to overfeed, though.

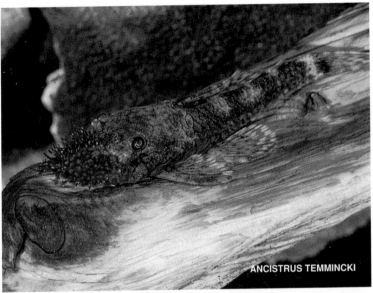

ANCISTRUS TEMMINCKI

Below: *Ancistrus temmincki* surrounded by young.

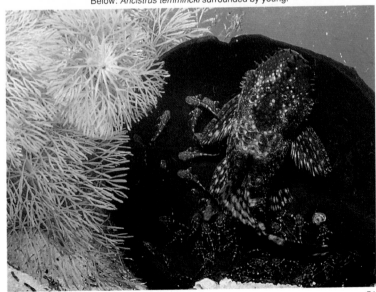

ANOSTOMUS ANOSTOMUS (Linnaeus)/*Striped Headstander*

R: Guyana, Colombia, Venezuela, Amazon River above Manaus. **H**: Mostly peaceful; prefers large aquaria that are well-planted. Likes to nibble algae. **W**: Fairly soft water is preferable, that is neutral to slightly acid. Temperature 24-25.5°C. **S**: 18 cm; usually collected and sold at 8 to 10 cm. **F**: All living foods are preferred, but dried or frozen foods are also taken. The diet should be supplemented with green foods.

A small, pointed head with a mouth that points upwards characterizes this handsome fish. It is a partial vegetarian and occasional feedings of boiled spinach (chopped and sold in little jars as baby food) are eagerly consumed and very beneficial. All efforts at breeding this fish have so far been unsuccessful. Some conditions cannot be duplicated in the aquarium; for instance, a fish may be able to spawn only at greater depths than any aquarium can offer, or it may require more swimming space than it can get in the largest aquaria.

ANOSTOMUS TAENIATUS (Kner)/*Lisa*

R: The Amazon from Brazil to the upper Amazon in Colombia and Peru. **H**: Jumps at the slightest provocation. Its tiny mouth indicates it must have small particled food. **W**: Prefers warm, soft, slightly acid water. Temperature 25°C. **S**: To 12.5 cm. **F**: Small particles of dry food and tiny worms are accepted. Frozen brine shrimp is a favorite food.

This species has been known under nearly every genus in the family! Kner called it *Schizodon taeniatus* in 1859, representing its range as the Rio Guaporé, Barra do Rio Negro and Mato Grosso; Cope, in 1878, called it *Laemolyta taeniata* and said it came from Pebas, Peru; Günther, in 1864, called the fish *Anostomus taeniatus;* Fowler, in 1950, used *Laemolyta* as the proper genus. Because of the mouth's being subcircular in cross-section and because its behavior in an aquarium is absolutely *Anostomus*-like (with upside-down feeding, high jumping and sensitivity to shadows), the author decided to stick with Günther's categorization.

Closeup of head of *A. taeniatus* showing the peculiar mouth.

ANOSTOMUS TERNETZI Fernandez-Yepez/*Red-Mouth Headstander*

R: Guianas, Venezuela, Brazil, Orinoco, Rio Araguaia, and Rio Xingu. **H:** Slightly aggressive, but can he kept fairly well with fishes their own size or larger. They do well in groups. **W:** Not critical. Prefers soft, slightly acid water with a temperature of about 25°C. **S:** Attains a length of ahout 12 cm. **F:** Very undemanding and will eat almost any aquarium foods.

Anostomus ternetzi is very similar in appearance to *A. anostomus* but different enough so that they can be distinguished quite easily. Whereas *A. anostomus* has three dark bands running longitudinally along the body, the middle and lower ones with zig-zag borders, and the interspaces are yellowish; in *A. ternetzi* the upper band is replaced by a brownish zone which has light scale centers forming longitudinal lines, and the middle and lower bands do not have zig-zag edges. In *A. anostomus* the dorsal and anal fins have a good deal of red and there is a suffusion of reddish in parts of the yellowish lines. *A. ternetzi* has paler and narrower lines between the bands and the red is lacking except on the snout.

The mouth of *A. ternetzi* is, as in the other headstanders, upturned and food is most easily captured in middle or upper water levels or at the surface. This does not mean that it will not take food that has fallen to the bottom, as it can flip upside-down to pick up such morsels.

A. ternetzi should be provided with a well-planted aquarium since it is apt to be a bit shy at first when someone approaches the aquarium.

APHANIUS DISPAR

ANOSTOMUS TRIMACULATUS (Kner)/*Three-Spotted Headstander*

R: Amazon Basin, the Guianas. **H**: Moderately peaceful; may be kept safely with fairly large fishes. **W**: Soft and slightly acid water. Temperature 25 to 26°C. **S**: 20 cm; specimens are usually sold at about 10 cm. **F**: Live foods and dried foods, with the addition of occasional green foods such as chopped spinach.

This fish is a bit large for the average aquarium, but it is quite peaceful. It is wise with this type of fish to provide an aquarium that is in a bright location, to encourage a growth of algae, which will be nibbled. With a species like this one, it is also advisable to provide plants that have strong stalks such as *Sagittaria, Cryptocoryne* and the like. These plants will be well cleaned of algae but not chewed.

ANOSTOMUS TERNETZI

APHANIUS DISPAR (Rüppel)/*Long-Finned Arabian Minnow*

R: From northern India westward through Iran, Saudi Arabia, Ethiopia, Israel, Jordan. It not only inhabits both sides of the Red Sea but also has apparently penetrated into the Mediterranean Sea. **H**: Very active, fast fishes. Probably should be kept by themselves because they do better in a brackish water environment. **W**: Prefers brackish water. Temperature 20 to 28°C. **S**: Attains a length of about 8 cm. **F**: The preference is for live foods of all kinds although some vegetable matter in the form of algae, cooked spinach, etc. should be added. **C**: Males and females differ in color. The male is greenish gray or greenish brown with many bluish white spots; the dorsal, anal and pelvic fins are patterned with stripes and spots of similar colors and the caudal fin is yellowish with 2-4 vertical bands. The female is greenish or grayish yellow with a number of vertical dark bars.

ANOSTOMUS TRIMACULATUS

APHANIUS IBERUS (Valenciennes)/*Spanish Minnow*

R: Spain, Morocco and Algeria. **H**: Peaceful and very active. Best to keep two females to one male. **W**: Neutral to slightly alkaline fresh water. Temperature 22 to 24°C. **S**: To 5 cm. **F**: Should be given live foods whenever possible. Other foods are eaten unwillingly or ignored. **C**: Body greenish blue, with about 15 light blue bars. Tail blue with light edge. Females have much less color and colorless fins.

The Spanish Minnow has the distinction of being one of the few aquarium fishes native to Spain. Feeding them is a bit of a problem because they are not easily accustomed to prepared or frozen foods. It is best to have a ratio of two females to each male, as the males are exceptionally vigorous drivers. Eggs are laid near the surface in bushy plants and are not eaten by the parents unless they are driven by hunger. Of course, their safety is assured if they are taken out. Hatching takes place in 6 to 8 days.

APHREDODERUS SAYANUS

APHANIUS MENTO (Heckel)/*Persian Minnow*

R: Iran, Syria, Asia Minor, in strongly brackish to fresh waters. **H**: Will not annoy other fishes, but best kept with only their own kind with similar water requirements. **W**: Slightly hard, alkaline water with one teaspoonful of salt to every 4 liters of water. **S**: To 5 cm. **F**: Live foods with some vegetable matter added.

The difference in coloration in the sexes is very much apparent. The male has brighter, more sparkling colors and, most of all, more than double the amount of blue spots on the sides. Persian Minnows are easy to breed, but if possible two or more females should be used for one male. Eggs are large and easily seen. They can be picked out with tweezers by tearing away the bit of leaf on which they hang and placing the eggs in a hatching tank by themselves. They hatch in 10 to 14 days and the hardy fry are easily raised.

APHANIUS IBERUS

APHREDODERUS SAYANUS (Gilliams)/*Pirate Perch*

R: Atlantic coast of the U.S. from New York to Texas; Mississippi Basin to Michigan. **H**: Nocturnal predator. Will hunt for food at night and will eat any smaller fishes in the aquarium. **W**: Not critical. **S**: Attains a length of about 12.5 cm. **F**: Usually spurns anything but live foods, with minnows its favorites.

The Pirate Perch is an anatomical curiosity. Although it superficially looks quite normal, on closer inspection it is discovered that the vent is not where the vent should be! In juveniles the vent is placed normally (just anterior to the anal fin), but then it migrates anteriorly as the fish grows and winds up beneath the throat just behind the gill openings. Aside from the misplaced vent, the Pirate Perch has two anal spines (most fishes have three) and three dorsal fin spines. It is brownish in color, with some darker brown markings on the head.

APHANIUS MENTO

57

APHYOCHARAX PARAGUAYENSIS

APHYOCHARAX ANISITSI (Eigenmann & Kennedy)/*Bloodfin*

R: Rio Parana, Argentina. **H**: Active, peaceful species that likes to travel in schools and may be trusted in the community aquarium. **W**: Requires clean, well-aerated water that is neutral to slightly acid. Temperature should average about 24°C. **S**: 5 cm; begins to breed when slightly smaller. **F**: Not fussy, as long as there is enough; has tremendous energy and therefore requires frequent feedings.

To breed this fish, prepare an aquarium of about 40-liters capacity with a layer of marbles, about 4 deep, on the bottom. Pour in water from the tank in which they were kept, to which is added one-third fresh tap water of the same temperature until it comes about 15 cm above the marbles. Select the heaviest female and the most active male and place them in this aquarium. A vigorous driving soon takes place, which is punctuated by frequent stops, usually over the same spot. The pair assumes a side-by-side position and with a great deal of quivering a few eggs are expelled and fertilized. The eggs are very small and hatch after only 30 hours.

APHYOCHARAX RATHBUNI

APHYOCHARAX PARAGUAYENSIS Eigenmann/*Rio Paraguay Tetra*

R: Occurs in the Rio Paraguay basin. **H:** A peaceful and easy to keep schooling fish. **W:** Not critical as long as extremes are avoided. A pH of about 6.0 to 7.6 is acceptable with a hardness about 15°dGH. A temperature R of 23 to 28°C is recommended. **S:** Attains a length of about 4 cm. **F:** Will accept a variety of foods including flake food. Small live foods are preferred.

There are several different tetras that have the black and white caudal pattern seen in this species. However, the black and white pattern of the anal fin of this species is not known in other aquarium tetras. Although it was first described back in the early 1900's by Eigenmann it was only sporadically imported along with other similar tetras until 1983.

APHYOCHARAX ANISITSI

APHYOCHARAX RATHBUNI Eigenmann/*Rathbun's Bloodfin*

R: Paraguay basin, South America. **H:** Peaceful and attractive. Does well in a community tank. **W:** Not critical. Temperature 24 to 27°C. **S:** Attains a length of about 4.5 cm. **F:** Not fussy. Prepared foods accepted, but living food should be provided whenever possible.

The courting male is shiny bronze with a similar red color (perhaps more on the anal fin and less on the adjacent part of the body) and the anterior borders of the dorsal, anal and pelvic fins brilliant white (this white may be seen in some specimens on the upper and lower edges of the caudal fin as well). There is also a jet black longitudinal band in the dorsal and anal fins.

Rathbun's Bloodfin is very tolerant of aquarium water conditions. Medium hard to soft water with a pH of 7.0 to 7.6 and a temperature of 24 to 27°C will do nicely. A successful spawning was accomplished at pH 7.4-7.6, total hardness 10 DH, carbonate hardness 2 DH and a temperature of 26°C.

APHYOSEMION AHLI Myers / *Ahl's Lyretail*

R: Tropical West Africa. **H**: Peaceful in the community aquarium. Males sometimes stage "battles" between themselves, but there is seldom any damage. **W**: Soft, slightly acid water. Water used for spawning should have a pH value of about 6.5. Temperature 23 to 25.5°C. **S**: To 6 cm. **F**: Any of the smaller living foods, especially daphnia, are suitable. Frozen foods are taken unwillingly, and dried foods only when hungry.

The fish breeds easily, like most of the egg-hanging *Aphyosemion* species, and two pairs placed in a breeding aquarium can produce about 40 eggs daily for quite a time. It has been found, however, that after two weeks of spawning the eggs prove to be infertile if the sexes are not separated and given at least a week's rest. The practice is a good one to follow with all the *Aphyosemion* species, not only this one. The incubation period is two weeks, give or take a couple of days. Most breeders have stopped using plants when spawning this group and instead are using the "mops" made of nylon.

APHYOSEMION ARNOLDI

APHYOSEMION AMIETI Radda/Amieti *Gardneri*

R: Western Cameroon in the lower course of the Sanaga River. **H**: Not aggressive, although damage to females sometimes occurs in single-pair spawning attempts. **W**: Slightly acid (pH 6-7), moderately hard (5-15 °DH) water at a temperature R of 24-28 °C recommended. Periodic water changes should be made. **S**: Males to 7 cm or more, females to a little less than 6 cm. **F**: Similar to other killifishes; live foods preferred.

This colorful killifish comes from western Cameroon, where it inhabits deep marshy areas lacking stones and, during the rainy season, forest areas. It is a member of the A. *gardneri* group; in fact, the females of A. *amieti* look very much like those of A. *gardneri* so much so that they are said to be difficult to tell apart. The males grow a bit larger than the females, attaining a length of 6 to 7.5 cm to 5.2 to 6.0 cm for the females.

For keeping several pairs a 30- to 40-liter (8-10 gallon) tank with a dark bottom and shallow water is suggested. The water should be clean (filtration and aeration), neutral to slightly acid (pH 6-7) and have a DH of 5-15. The temperature range should be similar to that encountered in their natural habitat—24° to 28°C. Weekly water changes of between 25% and 50% should be made. Since they are not aggressive, the tank can support more than one male as long as shelters (usually plants) are available. An assortment of live foods is necessary for best results, mosquito larvae being closest to their natural diet of insect larvae. The fish will take food from the surface to the bottom.

APHYOSEMION AHLI

APHYOSEMION ARNOLDI (Boulenger)/*Arnold's Lyretail*

R: Niger River Delta, in ditches and swamps. **H**: Should be kept by themselves in a well-planted aquarium. **W**: Provide soft, well-aged water that is acid; pH about 6.5. **S**: About 5 cm; begins breeding at 4 cm. **F**: Living foods such as daphnia, tubifex worms and brine shrimp.

Females do not have the lyre-shaped tail fins and are a comparatively dull brown in color, with some red spots on the body and fins. Well-aged water is almost a must, and a well-established tank that is heavily planted is best. If there is no layer of mulm on the bottom, provide a substitute by putting in a 1-cm layer of well-boiled peat moss from which the water has been poured off. Eggs are laid in this bottom layer and may be found by gently stirring it and then picking the eggs up with a glass tube. They are then placed in a small jar and stored in a dark location. In 30 days the eggs should begin to hatch.

APHYOSEMION AMIETI

APHYOSEMION AUSTRALE

APHYOSEMION AUSTRALE (Rachow) / *Lyretail, Lyretailed Panchax*
R: Southern Cameroon to Gabon. **H**: Peaceful; will not bother other fishes, but will do better if kept by themselves. **W**: Soft, well-aged acid water. **S**: 5 cm; will begin breeding at 2.5 cm. **F**: Daphnia, tubifex worms, enchytrae, brine shrimp, etc.

Probably the most popular of the so-called "panchax" species, which includes genera like *Epiplatys, Aphyosemion, Aphlocheilus, Pachypanchax* and *Aplocheilichthys.* Even while very young, males can be distinguished by their beautiful lyre-shaped tail. Females are comparatively drab brown, with rounded fins and only a few red spots for color. A very easy breeder. Males drive almost ceaselessly, and it is better to use several females for each male. Floating plants may be used to received the eggs, which hang from the leaves by a sticky thread. Eggs are not eaten.

APHYOSEMION AUSTRALE

APHYOSEMION BIVITTATUM (Lönnberg)/*Two-Striped Aphyosemion*
R: Cameroon and Niger Basins, in small streams and swampy areas. **H**: Peaceful, but does better if kept with its own kind. **W**: Well-aged acid water. Temperature about 25°C. **S**: 6 cm; breeds at 4 cm. **F**: Live foods such as daphnia, tubifex worms, enchytrae, brine shrimp, etc. **C**: Body color reddish brown, almost white on the belly. Two dark horizontal stripes. Long red-spotted dorsal and lyre-shaped tail fin.

It deposits its eggs on fine-leaved plants near the surface, but we have also observed that occasionally an egg is buried in the bottom sediment. For this reason, no matter how thoroughly the plants are gone over for eggs, an occasional youngster shows up, seemingly from nowhere. *Aphyosemion* eggs are quite firm, even hard to the touch, and may be handled with little danger of breaking them. However, if hatching time is close at hand, it has been known to happen that an occasional youngster pops out from its shell.

There is some danger of the parents eating their young after they hatch; the trick is to keep them well-fed. The young also learn very early in life that it behooves them to stay away from anything larger than they are. Any fish which does not learn this early in life does not live very long. As with the others, hatching time is 10 to 15 days and the young grow well if started on newly hatched brine shrimp.

Aphyosemion species which do not bury their eggs may be spawned successfully in small aquaria, about four to eight liters. Using these reduces the area in which the eggs may be laid and makes them easier to find. Occurring as they do in small ditches and pools in their native haunts, they do not feel as cramped as a more active fish might. Do not let their leisurely movements fool you, however; they can move rapidly if the occasion demands and are lively jumpers. Never come to the conclusion that because the water level is a bit low they cannot jump out of an uncovered aquarium. Many a good fish has been found on the floor dried up because someone thought they couldn't jump out. A sheet of glass is a small investment and will keep your valuable fish where they belong.

APHYOSEMION BUALANUM (Ahl)/*African Swamp Killie*

R: Eastern Cameroon and the Central African Republic. **H**: Peaceful when kept with fishes its own size. **W**: Varies from soft acid water to hard alkaline water. **S**: To 6 cm; females slightly smaller. **F**: Readily accepts live or prepared foods. **C**: Green on the back, grading to light blue on the flanks with vertical red bars along the body extending to the end of the caudal fin. Blue marginal bands on the caudal fin.

Because of the wide range of habitats in which *A. bualanum* is found, the fish adapts well to nearly any reasonable pH and DH in which they are kept. However, if they are kept in relatively cool (25°C) well-shaded aquaria, their colors appear much richer. This species spawns in plant thickets or near the top in floating nylon mops. They are not as prolific as the majority of their congenerics and under favorable conditions will produce only two to three dozen eggs in a week of spawning activity.

APHYOSEMION CAMERONENSE

APHYOSEMION CALLIURUM (Boulenger)/*Blue Calliurum*

R: Liberia to northern Angola. **H**: Peaceful in mixed company, but they are happier with just their own kind. **W**: Soft, slightly acid water. For spawning, pH value should be about 6.5. Temperature 23 to 25.5°C. **S**: To 6 cm. **F**: Live foods; frozen or dried foods are taken reluctantly.

It is good policy for those who own both *Aphyosemion ahli* and *A. calliurum* to be careful to avoid mixing up the females. Results, if any, of a mating between a male of one variety and a female of another could result in a hybrid that is far inferior in color to either variety, as well as fish that might easily be sterile. Spawning, of course, is the same as in the other egg-hanging species. Eggs are deposited singly near the water's surface in plants or any reasonable plant substitutes given them by their owner. Eggs hatch in 12 to 15 days and the fry begin eating at once. They are hardy and grow rapidly.

APHYOSEMION BUALANUM

APHYOSEMION CAMERONENSE (Boulenger)/*Cameroon Killifish*

R: Southwestern Cameroon, northern Rio Muni, and possibly northern Gabon. **H:** A peaceful species that is usually quite active, including jumping out of the tank if it is not properly covered. **W:** Not critical. Prefers a water temperature from about 21 to 27°C. **S:** A rather small killifish, with males attaining a total length of about 4.5 cm, females about 4 cm. **F:** Prefers live foods, especially such items as mosquito larvae.

This small killifish inhabits small brooks and streams in rainforest areas of the inland plateau of southwestern Cameroon, neighboring Rio Muni, and possibly northern Gabon. It has been divided into several subspecies including *A. c. hassi* from northern Gabon, *A. c. halleri* from around Ambam in southern Cameroon, *A. c. obscurum* from around Yaonde in Cameroon, and of course *A. c. cameronense* from the Dja river in southern Cameroon.

APHYOSEMION CALLIURUM

APHYOSEMION CELIAE Scheel/*Celia's Aphyosemion*

R: Southwestern Cameroon. **H:** Peaceful but very shy. Not recommended for a tank of mixed species. **W:** Tolerant of W. In nature a pH of 6.6-7.0 and a temperature of 24-26°C were found. **S:** Males about 7 cm; females a little smaller. **F:** Prefers *Drosophila* or mosquito larvae but will accept substitutes. Sensitive to pollution due to overfeeding.

Celia's Aphyosemion was discovered by Scheel and Clausen in southwestern Cameroon to the south of the plateau inhabited by a similar appearing species, *Aphyosemion cinnamomeum*. Both of these species have a rounded caudal fin with a distinctive pattern of a reddish to chestnut-colored crescent. It appears in *marigots* (small West African lakes or rivers) and brooks or streams of the forest.

Aphyosemion celiae is tolerant of most water conditions but prefers the pH to be slightly acid to neutral, the hardness slight to moderate and the temperature 24 to 26°C as in nature. It is, however, sensitive to fouled water due to overfeeding.

A pair or trio in a 20- to 30-liter tank is best. The males will show aggression toward other conspecific males, but the battles are generally just ritual displays with the intent of intimidation. Normally, however, it is quite shy, preferring to spend much of its time hiding in a floating spawning mop. As it gets more used to the surroundings the shyness disappears to some extent. If frightened it is apt to jump out of the tank, so a cover and as little commotion as possible are highly recommended. Preferred foods are mosquito larvae and *Drosophila*, but various substitutes are accepted with a little coaxing.

APHYOSEMION CINNAMOMEUM

APHYOSEMION CHRISTYI (Boulenger)/*Christy's Lyretail*

R: Central Congo drainage. **H:** Completely peaceful, but does best in the company of other killies. **W:** For general care old, moderately hard water is preferred. Water for breeding and hatching should be soft and slightly acid. **S:** About 5 cm. **F:** Live or frozen brine shrimp, daphnia, mosquito larvae, etc.

This is one of the species of the genus *Aphyosemion* that develops distinct projections on the dorsal and ventral edges of the caudal fin. The length of these extensions varies greatly from strain to strain, with some showing very little extension while others, such as those from the Kinshasa area of Zaire, develop elegant extensions. A second form, characterized by a large number of red spots on the sides and fins, has been called *A. cognatum,* which is a completely different species. The various color strains and geographical races of *A. christyi* cross readily, but the young are often sterile. This is due in part to the fact that the different populations differ in chromosome numbers.

APHYOSEMION CELIAE

APHYOSEMION CINNAMOMEUM Clausen/*Cinnamon Killie*
R: Western Cameroon, Africa. **H**: Should be kept in a tank of their own. **W**: Slightly acid water about 6 DH. Keep them at about 24°C; spawn them at 24 to 25.5°C. **S**: About 5 cm; females slightly smaller. **F**: Live or freeze-dried foods.

Females are a grayish brown all over and are a little smaller than males. This species belongs to the bottom-spawning group. Their spawning tank should have about 2.5 cm of peat moss on the bottom. When the fish begin to spawn in this, the peat moss is removed with the eggs, carefully pressed out and then placed in a glass jar, which is loosely covered and stored for a month. Then fresh water is poured on the peat moss, and the fry hatch out in a few hours.

APHYOSEMION CHRISTYI

APHYOSEMION COGNATUM Meinken/*Red-Spotted Aphyosemion*

R: Lower Congo River, in the vicinity of Kinshasa. **H**: Peaceful, but best kept by themselves. **W**: Soft, acid, well-aged water. **S**: 6 cm; breeds at 4 cm. **F**: Live foods; daphnia, tubifex worms, enchytrae, etc.

This is one of the top-spawning species. A small aquarium is provided which contains some floating fine-leaved plants or a substitute such as a bundle of nylon yarn that has been tied to a cork. The fish readily accept this substitute and spawn in it. After a few days this mop is removed and the strands separated. Eggs are seen stuck to the threads with a fine sticky string. They may be lifted off by this string with a pair of tweezers to be placed in a jar where they will hatch in about 14 days. Young may be fed on newly hatched brine shrimp.

APHYOSEMION EXIGUUM

APHYOSEMION (DIAPTERON) CYANOSTICTUM Lambert & Gery/*Blue-spotted Killifish*

R: Gabon. **H**: A very peaceful species that is easy to keep and easy to spawn. Males will display toward one another with occasional minor damage being done. **W**: Prefers water that is not too hard and slightly acid. Lighting should not be too bright. **S**: Males to 3.5 cm; females slightly smaller at about 2.5 cm. **F**: Small live foods preferred but will take frozen and freeze-dried foods as well.

This attractive species is one of those killifishes that is attractive, easy to keep, and easy to breed. It was described by Lambert & Gery in 1967 in the genus *Aphyosemion* but some authors prefer to split off this and several other species into *Diapteron* and it may be seen in the literature under either name. *Diapteron* species males lack red spots on the body and fins. The species is quite variable and tail fin colors may range from red to blue.

APHYOSEMION COGNATUM

APHYOSEMION EXIGUUM (Boulenger)/*Exiguum Killie*

R: Cameroon, possibly also extending into the Central African Republic and Republic of the Congo. **H:** Normally shy but aggressive toward members of its own species. Some cover should be provided. **W:** Prefers soft acid water with a temperature of 19 to 24°C. **S:** Attains a length of up to 4 cm. **F:** Live foods are preferred, but it will accept frozen and prepared foods with a little coaxing.

Aphyosemion exiguum is a non-annual killifish which has the reputation of being hard to breed. Males are aggressive and drive the females hard, making it necessary to provide cover for them when attempting to spawn the species. Combinations of one male to two to three females are recommended for best results. Eggs will be deposited on floating plants or nylon mops provided for that purpose. Females lay relatively few large (1.3 to 1.4 mm) adhesive eggs per day which take from 10 to 15 days to hatch. The fry are large enough to be fed newly hatched brine shrimp and are relatively easy to raise. After about eight weeks the sexes can be distinguished.

APHYOSEMION (DIAPTERON) CYANOSTICTUM

·APHYOSEMION FILAMENTOSUM (Meinken)/*Togo Lyretail*

R: Tropical West Africa. **H**: Peaceful in the community aquarium, but better kept with their own kind or similar species. **W**: Water should be soft and slightly acid. Temperature about 24°C. A well-planted or well-shaded aquarium is best. **S**: Males about 5.7 cm; females about 4.5 cm. **F**: Live foods essential; will eat frozen or dried foods.

With most *Aphyosemion* species, the female is about the same size, but here the female is considerably smaller and has far more modest coloration and finnage. Her tail is round, her anal fin is not fringed, and she has only a few red spots on her body. This is one of the top-spawning species, and the male is a very active driver. For this reason it is best (if possible) to give him two or three females so that he can divide his attentions between them rather than run one ragged. Eggs are laid a few each day in the plant thickets near the surface, and hatching time may vary from two weeks to a month.

APHYOSEMION GERYI

APHYOSEMION GARDNERI (Boulenger)/*Steel-Blue Aphyosemion*

R: Coast of Nigeria to the Republic of Congo, where it occurs in small bodies of water. **H**: Should be kept by themselves; males will fight and tear fins if two are kept together. **W**: Well-aged, soft, acid water. **S**: 6 cm; will begin spawning at 4 cm. **F**: Living foods such as daphnia, tubifex worms, enchytrae, etc. **C**: Males are a greenish blue which shades to a deep steel-blue toward the tail. There are many purple dots and markings. Caudal with blue or yellow edges.

This is a bottom-spawner. An aquarium for spawning them may be prepared by putting a layer of peat moss about 1 cm thick on the bottom of a 20-liter aquarium. The peat moss must be well boiled to remove any excess acidity. Soft water is then poured in and when the peat moss settles, the pair of fish is introduced. Some cover, such as floating plants and a few rocks, may also be added to provide an occasional refuge for the female when she is chased too hard. Spawning takes place in the loose peat moss, and close observation will show the preferred locations.

APHYOSEMION FILAMENTOSUM

APHYOSEMION GERYI Lambert/*Gery's Aphyosemion*
R: Sierra Leone. **H**: Peaceful, but better kept in pairs in a small aquarium. **W**: Acid, pH 6.5 to 6.8, and well aged. Temperature 23 to 26°C. Small tanks of 8 to 20 liters capacity seem to be preferred. **S**: Males about 7.5 cm; females about 6.5 cm. **F**: Live food preferred, but will accept freeze-dried foods.

Géry's Aphosemion is an extremely hardy species that can tolerate a wide range and extremes in water conditions. Furthermore, they are not susceptible to many diseases. This, together with the male's bright red coloration (especially during breeding periods), makes this species an excellent aquarium fish. *A.geryi* is not a retiring species and will readily display itself if raised in a well-lit aquarium with open spaces. In nature this fish inhabits pools and slow-moving streams in shaded forest areas. The areas in which they are normally found are usually densely vegetated.

APHYOSEMION GARDNERI

APHYOSEMION KIYAWENSE

APHYOSEMION KIYAWENSE/Seymour's *Killifish*
R: Ghana, primarily around the city of Accra. **H:** Males aggressive among themselves and can be hard on females; other species of comparable size generally ignored. **W:** Not critical as to hardness and alkalinity levels. Temperature of 23 to 26°C. **S:** About 5 cm in captivity; much larger in nature. **F:** Live foods preferred above all others, but meaty prepared foods (especially frozen brine shrimp) accepted.

Aphyosemion kiyawense is one of the killifishes that has not achieved any great degree of popularity in the fish hobby, even among specialists in the keeping of rivulin species. It is a good-looking fish, but it is a very slow grower and a very poor producer. The great German aquarist Erhard Roloff, for example, related that from 40 eggs that were produced by the first pair he kept only six hatched, and they were all belly-sliders. These results were obtained by keeping the eggs in water rather than in damp peat moss; when the peat moss method was used (six to seven weeks is the best length of time to keep the eggs in the peat moss), results were much better but still nowhere near comparable with the number of eggs and fry of many other *Aphyosemion* species. *Aphyosemion kiyawense* will spawn at the age of about four months but has an active life span of only about seven months.

APHYOSEMION LAMBERTI Radda & Huber/Lambert's Killifish

R: Ogowe basin, eastern Gabon. **H:** Very peaceful with its own and other species. Tends to be a bit timid in aquaria. **W:** Very easy to please, accepting a wide variety of W. Collected in nature in waters with a pH R of 5.5 to 7.2. **S:** Reaches a standard length of about 3.5 cm. **F:** Will accept normal aquarium foods readily and particularly loves live foods.

A pair placed in a small tank with no sand, no plants, a small filter, and provided with a spawning medium in the form of a nylon mop or Java moss is all that is needed. A slight increase in the temperature will usually precipitate spawning, or the males and females can be conditioned separately and brought together for spawning. Check for eggs about two or three times per week. The eggs can be hatched by either the wet or the dry method. For the wet method place the eggs in a small container with some water from the spawning tank. Place the container in an area sheltered from light and at about room temperature.

Aphyosemion lamberti can be highly recommended. Unfortunately at this time it is not as readily available in this country as one would like, but hopefully there will be more available in the near future.

APHYOSEMION LIBERIENSE

APHYOSEMION LIBERIENSE (Boulenger)/*Liberian Killie*

R: Liberia. **H**: Not scrappy, but should have their own aquarium. **W**: Soft and slightly acid. Temperature 22 to 26°C. **S**: About 5 cm. **F**: Live, frozen or freeze-dried foods.

This fish will spawn without too much trouble when two or three females are put with one male. The pre-spawning behavior is in typical killifish fashion. Some hobbyists consider this species as a sort of halfway mark between the egg-laying and egg-burying fishes. Given a tank where they have the opportunity of hanging their eggs in bushy plants, they will do so, but when given the opportunity of burying their eggs, they will do this too. It has been observed that eggs left in the breeding aquarium do not hatch on time. Instead of the usual 10 to 12 days, the eggs hatch in upwards of 30 days. It should be noted that if the water in the aquarium is kept clean and free of dirt or peat, the eggs will not exhibit annual characteristics common in killifishes.

APHYOSEMION NIGERIANUM Clausen/*Nigerian Killie*

R: Nigeria, the type locality being a swamp near Arum on the southern foothills of the Jos Plateau, northern Nigeria. **H:** Peaceful and should be kept with peaceful fishes. **W:** Not critical. Apparently not very sensitive to varied W. **S:** Males attain a length of about 7.5 cm, the females only 6 cm. **F:** Will accept an assortment of aquarium foods.

Aphyosemion nigerianum is a colorful killifish that has many favorable attributes. Among the foremost of these is its undemanding nature. It is relatively insensitive to different water conditions, adjusting to varied water composition as long as the changes are not rapid. This characteristic has enabled *A. nigerianum* to occupy a larger than usual geographic range. Yet the variation of the color pattern, size, etc. is very little, the northern Nigeria individuals tending to be a bit larger than the southern ones and having the red bars of the dorsal and upper part of the caudal fins less well defined.

Spawning *A. nigerianum* does not pose a problem. A simple way is to place a pair in a well planted tank (including some floating plants) for about two weeks; inspection of the plants will probably reveal a number of eggs. If the parents are removed there will undoubtedly be some fry swimming around in another week's time. In nature although the eggs do not need a "dry" period they can withstand short periods of being embedded in slightly moist mud. Eggs are deposited in the mud or among the plants.

For more controlled breeding the pair can be placed in a small tank (up to 20 liters) provided only with some spawning mops. Every few days the mops are removed and searched for eggs. These eggs are placed in a separate container with a small amount of fungus remedy. These containers can be used for a week or two's supply of eggs. The newly hatched fry can be offered infusoria for the first few days, after which newly hatched brine shrimp can be provided. Growth is rather rapid.

One should be careful that the temperature does not get too high. Better breeding results are obtained with the temperature in the lower 20's°C than in the middle 20's°C.

75

APHYOSEMION OCCIDENTALE Clausen/*Golden Pheasant*

R: Sherboro Island and Sierra Leone along the coastal lowlands. **H**: Better kept by themselves. This is not a fish for a community aquarium. **W**: Soft, acid water. Temperature 24 to 26°C. **S**: To 10 cm. **F**: Prefers live or fresh foods such as brine shrimp, mosquito larvae or beef heart; will reluctantly adapt to prepared dry foods.

Aphyosemion occidentale is an annual rivulin species. During mating, the male uses his dorsal and anal fins to grasp the female while fertilizing the eggs. After fertilization, the eggs are deposited about one cm below the substrate. The eggs usually need over ten weeks to incubate. It should be noted that peat moss makes a very good substrate medium. After hatching, the fry grow very quickly. The entire cycle of egg-laying, hatching, maturing and mating of the offspring takes roughly 8 months.

APHYOSEMION PUERZLI

APHYOSEMION PETERSI (Sauvage)/*Yellow-Edged Aphyosemion*

R: Ghana, Ivory Coast and Togo. **H**: Peaceful, does better when kept by itself, but may be kept in community aquaria. **W**: Well-aged water of about 8 degrees of hardness. **S**: 6 cm; females 5 cm. **F**: Live foods such as daphnia, tubifex worms, enchytrae.

It is a peaceful species, and the writer recalls keeping a number of them in a community tank for some time. They do not have the gaudy beauty found in many of the *Aphyosemion* species, but rather a quiet charm all their own. This is another top-spawning species; eggs are laid near the surface in bundles of floating plants or their substitutes. Here is another plant substitute that may be used: tie a bundle of Spanish moss (which was previously well boiled) to a cork to keep it near the surface. If you do not care to pick out the eggs and want to save time, simply leave the bundle with the breeders for about 10 days, take it out, snip off the cork and tie it onto another bundle. Eggs hatch in 10 to 15 days like the others, and the youngsters are quite easy to raise.

APHYOSEMION OCCIDENTALE

APHYOSEMION PUERZLI Radda & Scheel/*Puerzl's Killifish*
R: Central and western Cameroon. **H:** Peaceful, but best kept in an aquarium by themselves. **W:** Slightly acid water (pH 6.6-6.8) with a temperature of 21 to 24°C recommended. **S:** One of the larger killifishes, reaching a total length of about 8.5 cm. **F:** Will eat most anything but should receive some live foods whenever possible.

Spawning is no problem. Set up a 20-liter (or larger) tank with slightly acid (pH 6.6-6.8) water at a temperature of 21 to 24°C. A smaller tank is not recommended as there is a great deal of chasing during courtship and spawning and small tanks might not give enough room to the female to escape the male's attacks. The bottom substrate, where the eggs will be deposited, can be either a layer of peat moss or a sunken spawning mop. The peat moss method with a subsequent period in which the eggs are kept "dry" seems to be more successful than the "wet" incubation in the spawning mop.

APHYOSEMION PETERSI

APHYOSEMION SANTAISABELLAE MARMORATUM Radda/*Marbled Killifish*

R: Western Cameroon, the type locality being 16 km northwest of Mbonge and 32 km west of Kumba. **H:** A peaceful species that tends to become shy in open water. **W:** Not critical. Neutral to slightly acid water that is not too hard is sufficient. A temperature of 21° to 26 °C is adequate. **S:** The type material was no more than 5 cm total length, but in the aquarium a length of 7-8cm for the male and almost as much for the female is common. **F:** Will accept a variety of aquarium foods, although live foods are preferred.

A tank about 10 to 12 liters (2 ½-3 gallons) in capacity can house a single pair comfortably. The addition of a spawning mop will provide the fish with not only a place to spawn but also a place to hide when frightened. The male can sometimes be seen in the mop with only his head sticking out before trying to attract a female. During spawning the male will become very dark, almost black sometimes, contrasting sharply with the metallic green parts of the pattern.

APHYOSEMION SJOESTEDTI

APHYOSEMION SCHEELI Radda/*Scheel's Killifish*

R: Niger Delta. **H:** An active killifish that does well in a single-species tank or a community tank of mixed killifishes. May be territorial. **W:** Generally prefers soft and slightly acid (pH 6.6-6.8) water with a temperature of about 24°C. **S:** 3.5 cm SL. **F:** Will eat a wide variety of aquarium foods, but should receive live foods on a regular basis for best results.

In a community tank (about 80 liters or more), the bottom should be covered with peat or similar material and the surface provided with floating plants such as *Riccia, Salvinia natans, Ceratopteris,* or *Lemna.* Their behavior changes somewhat in this situation as they remain in open water more (although near some refuge) and become somewhat territorial, defending a specific area from other fishes by threats and postures. No injuries result. Although they will breed in such a tank, no fry ever survive.

When spawning, about 20 to 30 eggs are deposited every two days by each female. This number dwindles considerably in about a week if the spawners are not provided with proper nourishment.

Aphyosemion scheeli is very hardy and rarely becomes sick when it attains adulthood. The young are sensitive to *Costia,* however, as well as the medications used to combat it.

APHYOSEMION SANTAISABELLAE MARMORATUM

APHYOSEMION SJOESTEDTI (Lönnberg)/*Blue Gularis*

R: Guinea to Cameroon. **H**: Better kept by themselves; definitely not a fish for the community aquarium. **W**: Soft, acid water. Temperature 24 to 27°C. **S**: To 9 cm. **F**: Live foods of all kinds. The Blue Gularis comes from a region in which the dry seasons are exceptionally long. This means that eggs are laid before the waters recede completely. The eggs that have been buried in the mud then go into a sort of resting period from which they are released when months later the rains begin to fall and the areas where the eggs were laid again begin to fill with water. Hatching follows very quickly and the fry grow at a furious rate until they become mature and lay their own eggs in the few months before the evaporating waters leave them stranded. Of all the West African "annuals," this one has the longest incubational period: 3 to 6 months.

APHYOSEMION SCHEELI

APHYOSEMION STRIATUM (Boulenger)/*Five-Lined Killie*

R: Coastal lowlands of Gabon and Equatorial Guinea. **H**: Not scrappy if kept with fishes their own size or a bit larger. **W**: Does well in soft slightly acid water but adapts well to harder, more alkaline conditions. Temperature 19 to 23°C. **S**: 5 to 6 cm; females slightly smaller. **F**: Prefers live or fresh foods such as brine shrimp, mosquito larvae or beef heart, but will adapt to prepared dried foods.

Aphyosemion striatum is a typical plant-spawner that will lay its eggs in either clumps of vegetation or in floating nylon spawning mops. The eggs should be water-incubated and will hatch in 12 to 16 days. The fry are large enough to take newly hatched brine shrimp nauplii as a first food. They grow quickly and will begin spawning in about three months. Like many of the other African killifish species, the fry are particularly susceptible to velvet disease, *Oodinium*. This can be easily avoided by giving them frequent partial water changes and by adding about 1 teaspoon of non-iodized salt to every 4 liters of their water.

APISTOGRAMMA AGASSIZI

APHYOSEMION WALKERI (Boulenger)/*Walker's Killifish*

R: Ghana. **H**: Non-aggressive. **W**: Not critical as long as extremes are avoided. Temperature 23 to 26°C. **S**: 7.5 cm; females 6 cm. **F**: Prefers live foods and prepared meaty foods; will take flake foods but usually not finely granulated dry foods.

As with most other *Aphyosemion* species, adult males are very easy to distinguish from adult females, as the females are much less ornately adorned with color and have less elaborate finnage. Female *A.walkeri*, however, are more liberally sprinkled with red dots than most other *Aphyosemion* females. This is a bottom-spawning species in which the eggs should be stored in peat moss for a comparatively long period before they are ready to hatch; they may alternatively be left in water rather than stored in peat moss, but under such conditions many more eggs will fungus, as the peat moss has a better preservative effect on them.

APHYOSEMION STRIATUM

APISTOGRAMMA AGASSIZI (Steindachner)/*Agassiz's Dwarf Cichlid*
R: Middle Amazon region. **H**: Fairly peaceful except when spawning. **W**: Fairly soft, almost neutral water. Temperature 23 to 25°C. **S**: 7.5 cm; begins breeding at 5 cm. **F**: Live foods, enchytrae and tubifex worms preferred.

Apistogramma agassizi is a very popular fish. One of the big advantages with dwarf cichlids is that they do not require a large aquarium for breeding. Forty liters is ample with this one. Some retreats should be provided, such as a flowerpot laid on its side and a few rocks. The pair should be carefully fed in advance and be in the best of condition. They will soon inspect one particular spot and begin cleaning it carefully. The female then lays row after row of eggs, which the male fertilizes. Then the female suddenly take over. She drives away the male and guards the eggs, which hatch in 4 days. The male should be removed when he is done with spawning, to prevent bloodshed.

APHYOSEMION WALKERI

APISTOGRAMMA BITAENIATA/*Banded Dwarf Cichlid*

R: Central Amazon region. **H:** Usually peaceful, except when spawning; better kept by themselves. **W:** Water quality is important over the long run, especially for spawning. Water hardness should be 8 German degrees or less; the pH should be slightly on the acid side of neutral. Temperature should be about 28°C. **S:** Up to 9 cm; females up to 6.5 cm. **F:** Live foods.

This species is more difficult to breed than most of the other *Apistogramma* species. The pair perform a breeding ritual which culminates in the female laying eggs that stick to a wall or ceiling of a cave. The egg number varies between 60 and 100, depending upon the age of the fish and the spawning conditions. Furthermore, the eggs vary in color, the color depending upon the diet of the female before spawning. Fry hatch in three days and become free swimming four to five days after hatching. The fry can eat newly hatched brine shrimp. The fry reach sexual maturity in six months.

APISTOGRAMMA CACATUOIDES

APISTOGRAMMA BORELLI (Regan)/*Umbrella Dwarf Cichlid*

R: Rio Paraguay Basin. **H:** Males play at being fierce toward other members of the tank. Best kept in a tank of their own. **W:** Water hardness shouldn't exceed 12 DH. Also the pH should remain within the range of 6.0 and 6.5. Temperature between 21 to 25°C. **S:** Up to 7 cm. **F:** Freeze-dried brine shrimp is relished. Will also accept certain dry foods. Must have a varied diet, which should include live foods, especially at spawning time.

Just before the actual spawning time, you will see the female's small nipple-like projection, the ovipositor. In this species the female is the one who takes the initiative in courtship; she gets the male interested by swimming alongside him, and with her body slightly tilted she beats him lightly with her tail. With this movement the edges of her tail caress the belly region of the male, exciting him and creating within him the desire to spawn. He then hypnotically follows her to the selected spawning spot, which is usually the upper part of a cave or flowerpot, if it has been thoughtfully included by the aquarist within the tank setup. The eggs are oval and colored red!

APISTOGRAMMA BITAENIATA

APISTOGRAMMA CACATUOIDES Hoedeman/*Cockatoo Dwarf Cichlid*

R: Peruvian Amazon. **H**: Peaceful, but better kept by themselves. **W**: Soft, slightly acid water. Temperature 24 to 27°C. **S**: Slightly over 5 cm; females about 1 cm smaller. **F**: Live or frozen foods.

The Cockatoo Dwarf Cichlid is a perky little fellow whose aggressive manner is mostly bluff. Given a number of hiding places, several pairs have been known to spawn at the same time and raise the young to the free-swimming stage. Once the female is guarding eggs she develops a bright yellow color and has a mean disposition toward her mate. He becomes a very worried and harassed individual until removed to another tank, and if the female has to rush from her duties with the eggs to keep the male at a proper distance she is likely to get so excited that she will eat her eggs.

APISTOGRAMMA BORELLI

APISTOGRAMMA GIBBICEPS

APISTOGRAMMA GIBBICEPS Meinken/*Gibbiceps*

R: Region of the Rio Negro. **H:** Relatively peaceful but are territorial, especially when spawning. **W:** Normal aquarium conditions for general keeping with temperatures around 23°-28°C. Clean, clear water a must. **S:** Females reach about 6 cm in length, males slightly larger at 8 cm. **F:** Live foods preferred but will accept prepared foods also.

Once settled in a new tank, the female will immediately seek out a cave or hole for her territory. Several females may squabble over the choicest territories but they will settle down shortly. The male will include some or all of the females in his larger territory and will not be chased by them. A female ready to spawn will exhibit a light swollen belly region which is displayed to the male as he passes through her territory. The female courts him by erecting her fins, trembling, and arching her body, trying to lure him to her selected nest site. She swims back and forth to the nest site displaying until he reacts by following her and shows some courting behavior of his own. He may stray at times but returns frequently. When the female starts intensive cleaning of sections of the walls of the cave he does remain in the area. Once satisfied with the clean-up, the female makes some dry runs over the area until finally some eggs are produced. The male follows and fertilizes them. This is repeated until the eggs are all deposited. The male swims away (if he is a bit slow the female may help him on his way) and patrols the periphery of the territory while the female guards and fans the immediate vicinity of the eggs. In three or four days the eggs hatch. Hatching may be assisted by the female by sucking the fry out of the eggshells individually. The fry are then transferred to a hollow or pit in the cave floor. In about four more days the yolk is completely absorbed and the fry are free-swimming. Newly hatched brine shrimp and other suitable fry foods can be offered. The fry grow rapidly and are still tended by the female for several weeks. Cleanliness is important and so frequent partial water changes are recommended.

APISTOGRAMMA MACMASTERI

APISTOGRAMMA MACMASTERI Kullander/*Macmaster's Apisto*

R: The Rio Meta in the environs of Villavicencio State in the Orinoco Basin. **H:** A peaceful species but territorial like other species of *Apistogramma*. A secretive substrate brooder. **W:** Soft, slightly acid water with a temperature R of 23°-30°C recommended. **S:** Attains a length of about 8 cm. **F:** Live foods preferred although will accept prepared foods as well.

The systematics of the species of *Apistogramma* is still quite confused. This is partly due to holotypes of some species being juveniles or females and almost unrecognizable when compared to fully grown, adult living males. Until definitive studies are made the names here reflect the current usage.

Sexes are easily distinguished by both form and coloration. The males are much more ornate and have reddish borders to the upper and lower caudal lobes. They also have more pointed dorsal and anal fins. The females are generally yellowish with dark markings. The females select territories (usually secluded holes or caves) and may fight over choice spots so provision should be made in the tank for as many potential territories as there are females. The male will have a larger territory encompassing several females. Spawning on the flower pot or cave wall follows preliminary courting. About 100 or more eggs are deposited and immediately guarded by the female. The male patrols his larger territory. Hatching occurs in about four days and free-swimming in about a week. The male participates in brood care on occasion but the bulk of the job goes to the female. Newly hatched brine shrimp provides a good first food for the fry and it can be supplemented by a variety of nourishing small sized prepared or live foods. In two months the young fish are about 10 mm long.

APISTOGRAMMA PERTENSIS (Haseman)/*Amazon Dwarf Cichlid*

R: Central Amazon region. **H**: Peaceful in mixed company, but best kept by themselves. **W**: Soft, slightly acid water. Temperature 24 to 27°C. **S**: Males to 5 cm; females somewhat smaller. **F**: Live or frozen foods.

These are probably the best parents of all the dwarf cichlids. They seldom eat their eggs and do not seem to go in for all the hysterical histrionics the others resort to when they imagine their precious eggs are threatened. Even the female does not become quite the tigress that most females of the *Apistogramma* species develop into once there are eggs to be guarded. If the tank where they spawn is not too small she will sometimes tolerate the presence nearby of her mate, and pairs have been known to raise their young in perfect harmony.

APISTOGRAMMA TRIFASCIATUM

APISTOGRAMMA STEINDACHNERI (Regan) *Steindachner's Dwarf Cichlid*

R: Essequibo and Demerara Rivers, Guyana. **H**: Quarrelsome among members of its own species and with other cichlids, but peaceful with most other fishes, especially those that swim at mid-water and top-water levels. **W**: Not critical, except that partial water changes should be made even more frequently than with most other species, as being constantly maintained in "old" water has a pronouncedly bad effect on this fish. Temperature 22 to 26°C. **S**: Males to about 7.5 cm; females slightly smaller. **F**: Takes all standard aquarium foods; especially relishes frozen bloodworms.

This good-looking dwarf cichlid, close in requirements to other *Apistogramma* species, is a dependable breeder and parent, and it is prolific as well. Breeds in typical *Apistogramma* fashion.

86

APISTOGRAMMA PERTENSIS

APISTOGRAMMA TRIFASCIATUM (Eigenmann & Kennedy) *Blue Apistogramma*

R: Bolivia and Paraguay. **H**: Peaceful except when spawning. Best kept in their own tank. **W**: Water hardness should be about 6 to 10 DH. Temperature 22°C. Raise to about 24°C for spawning. **S**: Males to 6 cm.; females slightly under 5 cm. **F**: Live or freeze-dried foods. Will take dried foods only when very hungry.

It is recommended that a tank of about 40 liters in capacity be used with a number of rocks, an empty flowerpot on its side and other retreats. This dwarf cichlid is not very needful of high temperatures, doing quite well at about 22°C. When the female is prepared to spawn she takes on a gleaming yellow body color. A few hours before spawning begins, the female's ovipositor, or breeding tube, becomes plainly visible, and she gives her undivided attention to the spot that has been chosen for her eggs. The male waits patiently until she begins to plaster down row after row of reddish colored eggs, and he follows, fertilizing them.

APISTOGRAMMA STEINDACHNERI

APISTOGRAMMOIDES PUCALLPAENSIS Meinken/*T-Bar Dwarf Cichlid*

R: Peruvian Amazon, specifically a branch of the Rio Ucayali near Pucallpa, Peru. **H:** Generally peaceful and tend to be a little timid, so best kept in a tank by themselves. **W:** Soft, slightly acid water at a temperature between 24 ° and 27°C is recomended. **S:** Attains a length of about 2.5 cm in the wild, slightly larger in captivity. **F:** Live foods such as small *Dapnia*, cyclops, and mosquito larvae are best.

Apistogrammoides pucallpaensis is a small, peaceful dwarf cichlid from small, slow-moving streams feeding the Rio Ucayali near Pucallpa, Peru. The pH there is about 6.0-6.6, but the fish do very well in a pH of 7.0. In the wild the T-Bar Dwarf Cichlid attains a length of about 2.5 cm, yet in captivity it grows a bit larger, perhaps due to a better diet than available to it in its natural habitat. Although this species looks to all intents and purposes like a species of *Apistogramma,* it has been placed in a separate genus by virtue of its 7-9 anal fin spines (3-4 in *Apistogramma),* the position and formation of the lateral line, and other minor differences.

An aquarium to breed this species need be no larger than 20 liters. It should be supplied with sand (about 5 cm is fine) and a flowerpot or slate pieces forming caves as spawning sites. Some water plants such as water sprite, dwarf sword plants, and *Fontinalis* should be added. For filtration a small sponge filter should be sufficient. The water should be slightly soft, neutral to slightly acid, and at a temperature of between 24 ° and 27 °C. For conditioning, small live foods (*Dapnia*, cyclops, mosquito larvae, etc.) are recommended. About a third to half of the water should be changed every month.

The male apparently initiates the courtship by swimming to the female and, with fins erect, parading and shimmying about her. His red-spotted tail fin is spread wide and wagged back and forth to impress the female. If the female is receptive and ready to spawn, her yellow color intensifies and the dark markings become deep black. This color change usually means that spawning is imminent. The female selects and cleans the spawning site, which is normally on the roof of a cave or inside a flowerpot, and soon starts to deposit the eggs, which the male fertilizes. Spawning lasts up to an hour with occasional brief rests, resulting in the deposition of a total of about 120 orange eggs. These are vigorously protected by the female—even the male has to find himself a hiding place. They hatch in about two days and usually are moved to a shallow pit in the sand by the female.

The fry are about 3 mm long and may take very fine cyclops nauplii or may graze on whatever they can find among the plants. They are shortly able to accept newly hatched brine shrimp. With proper feeding and frequent water changes the fry grow quickly (in two weeks they are about 10 mm long), and at six months they can be sexed. At as early an age as nine months to a year they may start to spawn.

The parents may occasionally eat the spawn, but normally they will not if they are well fed. Also, two males in the breeding tank is one too many if it is a small tank. It is interesting to note that female guarding is unusual in the species of *Apistogramma,* another item that makes the T-Bar Dwarf Cichlid stand out from its cousins.

Below: *A. pucallpaensis* tending eggs (left) and during spawning.

APLOCHEILICHTHYS MACROPHTHALMUS (Meinken) *Bigeye Lampeye*

R: Nigeria, near the coast, where they occur in small freshwater streams, swimming against the current. **H**: Peaceful, but should never be kept with large fishes, because of their small size. **W**: Water should be soft and about neutral. Temperature 24 to 25.5°C. **S**: 4 cm; spawns at about 2.5 cm. **F**: Small living foods, as well as dried foods.

When the female is ready, and this can be seen by the eggs which are clearly visible through her body wall, she may be placed with a male that is lively and shows good color in a tank of about 20 liters capacity. A bundle of *Nitella* or a few strands of *Myriophyllum* are placed with them. The pair come together in a plant thicket and an egg is expelled. The egg is amazingly large when compared to the size of the female. Spawnings are small and may last over a period of several days. Eggs hatch in 8 to 10 days, and the fry must be carefully fed on very fine dried food after a week on infusoria. Growth is extremely slow, and full size is not attained until after at least a year has passed.

APLOCHEILUS BLOCKI

APLOCHEILICHTHYS PUMILUS (Boulenger)/*Tanganyika Lampeye*

R: Lake Edward, Kivu, Victoria and Tanganyika and their affluents. **H**: Peaceful, prefer to be kept in a school instead of singly or in pairs. **W**: Water should exceed 10 degrees of hardness; alkalinity about 7.5 pH. Temperature 22 to 25°C. **S**: About 4.5 cm. **F**: Living foods preferred, but it is possible that they may be trained to take frozen or prepared foods.

Contrary to the places where most *Aplocheilichthys* species are found, this one is native to the large lakes of Africa and the streams flowing into them. Even with the best of care these fishes have only a short life span, and an individual that passes the ripe old age of one year is unusual.

The spawning ritual is characterized by interesting courtship behavior and culminates in the production of small clusters of eggs. These clusters are fertilized by the male and then placed on fine-leaved water plants by the female. The eggs hatch in 12 to 14 days.

APLOCHEILICHTHYS MACROPHTHALMUS

APLOCHEILUS BLOCKI (Arnold) *Dwarf Panchax, Green Panchax, Panchax from Madras*
R: Madras, India. **H**: Peaceful, but should not be kept with large fishes. **W**: Well-aged water
that is soft and slightly acid. Temperature 21 to 25°C. **S**: Males 5 cm; females slightly smaller.
F: Will eat dried foods, but this *must* be supplemented with live foods. **C**:
Because of its small size, it can be spawned in a limited space. An 8-liter aquarium will accommodate a pair comfortably, and eggs will be found among the surface plants with a fair amount of regularity. These will hatch in about 2 weeks, but the young will be found to be rather small. Infusoria must therefore be fed at first, but the young will soon be large enough for newly hatched brine shrimp. From here on raising them is easy. Like other members of the group, this species is an accomplished jumper, and the aquarium in which they are kept should be kept covered with a pane of glass.

APLOCHEILICHTHYS PUMILUS

APLOCHEILUS LINEATUS

APLOCHEILUS DAYI (Steindachner)/*Day's Panchax, Singhalese Panchax*

R: Sri Lanka. **H**: Will not annoy anything it cannot swallow. May be kept in company with larger fishes. **W**: Neutral to slightly acid. Temperature 24.5 to 25.5°C. **S**: 8.5 cm; females only a little smaller. **F**: Dried food will be taken, but live food should be given as a supplement at least occasionally.

Unlike *A. blocki,* this fish needs a bit more room in which to spawn, but this is not to say a large tank. One of about 20 liters capacity is enough for spawning purposes; keep it covered. Of course, they may be kept in larger quarters at other times. This fish is a top-spawner, and its eggs will be found at fairly regular intervals in the plants near the surface. There will never be a large spawning at any one time; with this family of fishes only a few eggs ripen each day, and these are the ones that will be laid. They will not be eaten and may be allowed to accumulate for several days before gathering.

APLOCHEILUS PANCHAX

APLOCHEILUS LINEATUS (Valenciennes) *Panchax Lineatus, Striped Panchax*

R: Malabar, India, and Sri Lanka. **H**: Best kept by themselves; although usually peaceful except with small fishes, they sometimes harass other fishes. **W**: Neutral to slightly acid soft water. Temperature 24 to 27°C. **S**: 10 cm; will begin to spawn at 6 cm. **F**: Live foods such as daphnia, tubifex worms, enchytrae and adult brine shrimp. Dried foods may be fed occasionally.

Several pairs may be kept in a 60-liter aquarium. When spawning is desired, separate females and feed them until they become well-rounded. Then select the best male and put them together in an aquarium of about 20 liters capacity, using two females to each male. Provide plenty of floating bushy plants; in a few days they will be festooned with eggs which hang from them by a thread, like balls from a Christmas tree. Then return the breeders to their original aquarium. In 10 to 15 days the good-sized fry will be seen swimming around just below the surface, where they will feed greedily on newly hatched brine shrimp and grow rapidly.

Aplocheilus lineatus normally cruises the upper levels of the tank, patrolling back and forth in an apparently unending search for small living prey—baby livebearers are an example of the type of prey these fish will happily gobble up. Available in a number of color forms slightly different from one another, *A. lineatus* is one of the most commonly available of killifish species.

APLOCHEILUS DAYI

APLOCHEILUS PANCHAX (Hamilton-Buchanan) *Panchax Panchax, Blue Panchax*
R: India, Burma, Malay Peninsula, Thailand, Indonesia. **H**: Will not bother anything they cannot swallow, and may be kept in community aquaria that do not contain small fishes. **W**: Soft,
slightly acid water, preferably well aged. Temperature 24 to 26°C. **S**: 6 to 8 cm; will begin
spawning when three-fourths grown. **F**: Mostly living foods such as daphnia, enchytrae or
tubifex worms. Frozen or dried foods may be given occasionally.

The Blue Panchax spawns like the other species, among floating plants or substitutes such as
nylon mops, bundles of nylon fibers or Spanish moss. A temperature of about 26°C works best
for spawning. If eggs are removed for hatching, they may be handled with the fingers; if tweezers are used, do not grasp the eggs directly with the tweezer points. The concentrated pressure can easily damage the shells. Close the points under the egg and then lift them up. Eggs
hatch in 12 to 15 days.

APLOCHEILUS LINEATUS

APTERONOTUS ALBIFRONS (Linnaeus)/*Black Ghost*

R: Amazon River and Surinam. **H**: A peaceful, friendly fish. **W**: Soft, slightly acid water best, but this is not too important, as variations in water composition are taken in stride. **S**: Up to 47 cm. **F**: Not a fussy eater; will take dry, frozen and live food. Tubifex eagerly accepted.

The Black Ghost is different from the other knifefishes; it is a completely peaceful fish and will not disturb others. What's more, it can be tamed and accustomed to taking food directly from the hand of its owner, like some of the larger cichlids. In a fish as large as *Apteronotus*, this can be a very impressive sight. This, coupled with the fish's very prepossessing appearance, makes the Black Ghost a distinctive attraction, well worth the high price that is asked for the specimens that are occasionally available.

ARIUS JORDANI

ARAPAIMA GIGAS (Cuvier)/*Arapaima, Pirarucu*

R: Entire tropical South American region, usually in the deeper, larger streams. **H**: Because of their size, any more than one to a large tank would be unthinkable. **W**: Water conditions are not particularly important with this species. Temperature 24 to 27°C. **S**: To about 4.5 m in the wild, captive specimens seldom over 60 cm. **F**: In capitivity they will eat nothing but living fishes.

Arapaima gigas belongs to the family Osteoglossidae, which comprises some of the largest freshwater fishes in the world. This family is also known for its many primitive characteristics. For example, *A.gigas* is covered with heavy, bony scales that form a mosaic pattern across its body. This can be very impressive looking when one sees a large specimen, which incidentally can weigh in excess of 200 kg.

The Pirarucu can only be kept in very large aquaria of 200 liters or more. It is important that the tank be well covered as this fish tends to jump.

APTERONOTUS ALBIFRONS

ARIUS JORDANI (Eigenmann & Eigenmann)/*Jordan's Catfish*
R: Panama Bay to Peru, eastern Pacific Ocean. **H:** A peaceful bottom-feeder that normally will not bother other fishes. **W:** Not critical. Can be kept in both fresh or salt water. The temperature R should be 20 to 25°C. **S:** Attains a length of at least 33 cm. **F:** Eats a wide variety of foods. Most of the ariid catfishes are mouthbrooders, and it is expected that this will be the case with Jordan's Catfish. It is the male that incubates the eggs, the brooding taking place in either fresh water or salt water depending upon the species. In the related *Arius felis* the male will brood some 50 or more eggs or almost a month before hatching occurs. Even then he continues to keep the young in his mouth for an additional two months before finally releasing hem. He does not feed during this time.

ARAPAIMA GIGAS

ARNOLDICHTHYS SPILOPTERUS (Boulenger) *Arnold's Characin, Red-Eyed Characin*
R: Tropical West Africa, especially the Lagos region and the Niger Delta. **H**: A peaceful species.
W: Soft, neutral to slightly acid water. Temperature 26 to 28°C. **S**: Seldom exceeds 6 cm. **F**:
Has a good appetite and will eat dried food as well as live foods; some live foods should be
provided, however.

Although it has been known to aquarists since 1907, it has never been reported as having been
bred in captivity. A clue could be taken from its life habits; it is known to swim in large schools
near the surface of open waters. Maybe this fish is one of those that prefer to spawn in more or
less large numbers, and it would be necessary to keep a school of them together in a large
aquarium before results could be expected. Unfortunately, we are not likely to see a large
number of these fish at any one time. They are lively swimmers, and any time the collectors get
them into the seine, they have the exasperating habit of playfully leaping over the top of it.

ASTYANAX BIMACULATUS

ASTRONOTUS OCELLATUS (Cuvier) *Oscar, Peacock Cichlid, Velvet Cichlid*
R: Eastern Venezuela, Guyana, Amazon Basin to Paraguay. **H**: Only very small specimens
may be kept with other fishes; when bigger, they will attack and swallow smaller fishes. **W**: Not
critical. Temperature 22 to 28°C. Breeds at 26°C. **S**: 30 cm; spawns at half that size. **F**: A very
greedy eater which prefers its food in large chunks. Live fish, snails, dog food, raw beef heart,
etc. **C**: Dark brown with light brown to yellow mottled markings. Youngsters go through various
color changes. Red ocellated spot at tail base. Available also in red and albino forms.

A pair will generally get along quite well, but sometimes battles occur. A separation of several
days by placing a pane of glass between them will sometimes calm them down. Usually they
are excellent parents, guarding their eggs and fry, but as so often happens with cichlids, eggs
might be eaten. If this is done frequently, the parents or eggs should be removed and the eggs
hatched artificially by placing an air-stone near them, causing a gentle circulation. Spawns are
generally large and may number as high as 1,000 eggs. Young hatch in 3 to 4 days and grow
rapidly if fed generously. First food should be newly hatched brine shrimp, graduating to larger
foods as the fish grow. Parents should have a large aquarium, and if there are any plants, they
are likely to be uprooted. Provide some large, smooth rocks and deep gravel; they like to dig.

ARNOLDICHTHYS SPILOPTERUS

ASTYANAX BIMACULATUS (Linnaeus)/*Two-Spotted Astyanax*

R: Northeastern and eastern South America south to the La Plata Basin. **H**: Peaceful if kept with other fishes of about the same size. **W**: Water characteristics are not important, if clean. Temperature 21 to 25°C are optimum. **S**: To 15 cm; in captivity usually half that size. **F**: Live or frozen foods preferred, but prepared food also taken if hungry.

Sexes are quite difficult to distinguish with any amount of certainty until the females develop eggs, at which time their rounder contours provide the only certain method of sexing. If it is desired to spawn them, a pair should be given their own tank of at least 60 liters capacity. At a temperature of about 25°C, active driving by the males takes place and soon a great number of eggs are dropped among the plants and haphazardly about the tank. Hatching takes place in 24 to 36 hours, and after 5 days the yolk-sac is absorbed and the fry become free-swimming. Raising them is easy; newly hatched brine shrimp can be fed at once. Growth is rapid.

ASTRONOTUS OCELLATUS

ASTYANAX FASCIATUS

ASTYANAX FASCIATUS (Cuvier)/*Silvery Tetra, Blind Cave Tetra*

R: Texas to Argentina. **H**: Will get along with other fishes of its size; very likely to eat plants. **W**: Not at all critical, but slightly alkaline water is best. Temperature 21 to 24°C. **S**: To 9 cm. **F**: All foods accepted, but there should be some vegetable substances included, such as lettuce or spinach leaves.

The only characin in United States waters is *Astyanax fasciatus.* It is the northernmost representative of a widespread genus that comprises about 75 species all the way down to Argentina. Spawning is very similar to that of most tetra species. The male drives the female through the plants, and eggs are scattered in all directions. The eggs are not very sticky and many fall to the bottom. Once the pair has finished, an egg-hunt is begun, and if they are not removed most of the eggs will be eaten. Hatching takes place in 24 to 36 hours, but it is not until 5 days later that the fry absorb their yolk-sacs and begin to swim freely. They are able to tear up newly hatched brine shrimp at once and are easily raised.

One of the most interesting examples of natural adaption is the Blind Cave Tetra, *Astyanax fasciatus.* The Blind Cave Tetra previously was known as *Anoptichthys jordani,* also known as *Astyanax mexicanus.* Here we have a fish that has lived for countless generations in total darkness; over the years the eyes have gradually been lost. To compensate for this it has a strange sense that prevents it from bumping into things and hurting itself. The sense of smell is also very keen, and it can find food every bit as well as sighted fishes. To spawn this fish, it is advisable to give it an aquarium of 40 to 60 liters capacity, with a double layer of pebbles or marbles on the bottom. Eggs are expelled in a more or less haphazard fashion, and if there is no means of keeping the parents away from them, they will be gobbled up almost as quickly as they are laid.

ATAENIOBIUS TOWERI

ATAENIOBIUS TOWERI (Meek)/*Blue-Tailed Goodeid*

R: Rio Verde in San Luis Potosi, Mexico. **H:** Peaceful and rather active, but it does well with other fishes its own size. **W:** The pH is not critical, but alkaline water is preferred; hard water is necessary. A temperature range of 20-29°C. is adequate. This species is sensitive to water quality. **S:** Attains a length of 10 cm. **F:** Omnivorous and accepts a wide variety of aquarium foods. A vegetable based flake food or other source of greens is recommended.

The tank for keeping Blue-Tailed Goodeids need not be too large, one with a 40-liter capacity being sufficient. The bottom can be covered with gravel or, to help keep the pH on the alkaline side, dolomite (a mixture of gravel and dolomite can be used). Sufficient plants for shelter for a harassed female or babies should be added. Filtration can be fairly simple, and dolomite can be added to the filter box as well. Feeding is not difficult, for *Ataeniobius toweri* will accept most aquarium foods. A variety of foods, including some with vegetable matter, can be given. Flake foods, frozen and live brine shrimp, tubificid worms, etc., can be alternated in the daily feedings (twice or three times a day is best).

Sexual dimorphism is similar to that of the other goodeids: the male's first five or six rays of the anal fin are shorter, stiffer, and compacted to form a gonopodium. This cannot be seen at birth but starts to develop when the males attain a length of about 2.5 to 3 cm. What is unusual about this species is that the usual trophotaenia (cord-like embryonal appendages) are absent. Instead the fry have conspicuous embryonic fin folds and the yolk sac is larger than in the other members of the family. Because of this, *Ataeniobius toweri* is placed in its own subfamily called Ataeniobiinae.

The fry of this livebearer are capable of eating newly hatched brine shrimp and crushed flake food. The female appears heavily swollen when about to give birth but doesn't show any dark gravid spot. It is best to check the tank for fry when you suspect she might be ready to deliver. Well-fed parents do not usually eat the young, but a few might disappear now and then. Several generations may even be kept in a single tank, and the population will level off at a stable number.

AUCHENOGLANIS OCCIDENTALIS (Cuvier & Valenciennes)/*Giraffe-Nosed Catfish*

R: Widespread throughout the central part of Africa from the Niger River to the Congo River and Blue Nile, as well as Lakes Chad, Bangwelu, Mweru, and Tanganyika. **H:** A voracious predator which cannot be kept with smaller fishes. **W:** Not critical as long as extremes are avoided. Optimum temperatures are about 24 to 28°C. **S:** Attains a length of just over 50 cm. **F:** Live foods of all kinds preferred. Voracious feeders, so plenty of food must be available.

At first glance one might mistake this fish for one of the synodontids. On closer inspection, however, the differences can be seen. For example, the gill membranes are free or only narrowly attached to the isthmus rather than strongly attached as in the synodontids. The mouth is built differently from the more sucker-like type of the synodontids, and the barbels are not fringed like those of the synodontids. All these features place *Auchenoglanis occidentalis* in the family Bagridae along with the likes of *Chrysichthys, Leiocassis, Mystus,* etc. The color pattern is quite variable but basically consists of a reticulated pattern as shown. The black spot on the upper corner of the gill cover may be joined by others along the body and on the upper edge of the caudal peduncle.

Since this species attains a relatively large size (about 51 cm), only the younger ones are kept in home aquaria. Because of the attractive color pattern and the pleasing shape of the large fins (especially the adipose fin), this species makes a welcome addition to large tanks of public aquaria.

The tank that will house *Auchenoglanis occidentalis* should be very large for obvious reasons. It should have a sandy base material where the catfish can grub for food and should be provided with suitable hiding places where *Auchenoglanis* can retire when disturbed or frightened. Since this species shies away from bright lights, only dim illumination should be provided. The proper temperature is in the range of from 24 to 28°C. The Giraffe-Nosed Catfish is a voracious feeder, and any small fishes that are in its tank might well be mistaken for food. Live food is preferred, and lots of it. It will accept anything from earthworms to beef heart and rolled oats, however, so feeding should not be a problem as long as there is enough available.

Sex differences are not known, and spawning this species has not been reported as yet.

AULONOCARA JACOBFREIBERGI Johnson/*Jacobfreibergi*

R: Lake Malawi, Africa. **H**: Relatively peaceful if kept with other African lake cichlids of its own size; plenty of rocky caves should be provided. **W**: Hard and alkaline with a pH of 7.6 or higher. Temperature 22 to 28°C. **S**: About 12 cm. **F**: Not critical; like most Malawi cichlids, they will take a wide variety of fish foods and will do very well on a good flake food and brine shrimp (frozen or live).

Spawning is accomplished in typical fashion with the male displaying before the female with fins spread, swimming in circles around her, and shimmying in front of her with his colors greatly intensified. The eggs are laid and fertilized and are immediately picked up by the female. The male may pick up some too, but that's the last you will see of those eggs. If the female strays off before spawning is completed, the male will quickly drive her back to the spawning area. After an hour spawning is generally finished and the female is left to wander away.

AUCHENOGLANIS OCCIDENTALIS

AULONOCARA JACOBFREIBERGI

AUSTROFUNDULUS LIMNAEUS Dahl/*Myers' Killifish*

R: Northern Colombia. **H:** Apt to be nasty to other fishes; best kept with their own kind. **W:** Soft and slightly acid. Temperature 24 to 26°C. **S:** Slightly over 12 cm. **F:** All sorts of living foods preferred; if not available, frozen foods or beef heart.

Like the Guppy breeders, the aquarium hobby has given birth to another highly specialized group, the killifish breeders. These people make a specialty of keeping and propagating cyprinodonts. There are about 25 genera in this group, the species of some of which can be divided into two general spawning groups: the plant-spawners and the egg-buriers. Our *Austrofundulus limnaeus* is a member of the latter, the egg-burying class. It occurs in ditches and small bodies of water in northern Colombia, and collectors who want mature fish must hunt for them when the waters have receded considerably. At this time they spawn and bury their eggs in the soft bottom mud. Eventually the water dries up, leaving the parent fish stranded and gasping, shortly to die. The eggs live on in an almost-dry state until the downpours of the rainy season fill the bodies of water once more and the eggs hatch.

AUSTROFUNDULUS LIMNAEUS

AXELRODIA RIESEI Géry / *Ruby Tetra*

R: Rio Meta, Colombia. **H:** Excellent aquarium fish. Pert, lively, but not at all aggressive. Shouldn't be kept with large fishes that will take advantage and keep it in constant hiding. **W:** Especially clean water conditions are necessary. Best colors will appear when water is on the soft side with a pH slightly on the acid side, about 6.5. Temperature 22 to 26°C. **S:** Up to 2 cm. **F:** Will accept freeze-dried feedings. Certain flake foods are also willingly taken. Live foods should be included in their diet.

Dr. Herbert R. Axelrod and Mr. William Riese, after whom the species is named, were the lucky gentlemen who first collected this South American fish. Everyone on this expedition was astonished at finding such an incredibly tiny species. *A. riesei* will undoubtedly prove to be one of the smallest aquarium fishes on record. But regardless of its diminutive proportions, it is still an eye-opener. *Axelrodia riesei's* eye coloring is most unusual, ruby-red above, golden with blue iridescence below.

AXELRODIA RIESEI

BADIS BADIS BURMANICUS (Ahl)/*Burmese Badis*

R: Burma. **H**: Peaceful, but will hide a great deal if kept in the community aquarium. **W**: Not critical; should have a well-planted aquarium with a number of hiding places. **S**: About 6 cm. **F**: Small live foods only.

In body form it resembles *Badis badis,* but the colors differ considerably. The sides are covered with numerous rows of red dots, interspersed in the upper half with blue ones. At times there are 6 to 9 dark bars which extend halfway down the sides. The colors do not change as drastically and startlingly as *Badis badis,* but the spawning procedure is exactly the same for both. The female Burmese Badis carries the same colors as her mate, but they are not as bright.

BAGRICHTHYS HYPSELOPTERUS

BADIS BADIS BADIS (Hamilton-Buchanan) *Badis, Dwarf Chameleon Fish*

R: India. **H**: Peaceful, but will hide a great deal when kept in a community aquarium. **W**: Not critical; a well-planted aquarium should be provided, with several small flowerpots laid on their sides. **S**: Up to 8 cm; will begin breeding at 5 cm. **F**: Live food only, in sizes tiny enough for their small mouths.

When kept by themselves in a small aquarium, they breed readily. A rock or leaf surface, or the inside of a flowerpot if one has been provided, will be cleaned scrupulously by the male. The female is then coaxed to the spot and, if she is ready to spawn, will hang 50 to 60 eggs on the surface. Sometimes a plant leaf or the corner of the aquarium is selected. Eggs hatch in 2 to 3 days, and the fry are very small and helpless at first. Not until 2 weeks have passed do the youngsters become independent of their parents. Infusoria should be fed initially, and when the fry become large enough to handle newly hatched brine shrimp, growth becomes rapid.

BADIS BADIS BURMANICUS

BAGRICHTHYS HYPSELOPTERUS *(Bleeker)/Black Lancer Catfish*
R: Sumatra, Java, Borneo. **H:** Tends to be territorial as well as light shy. Its aggressiveness is directed more toward members of its own kind than toward other species. **W:** Does well in a variety of conditions as long as extremes are avoided. Water temperatures should be within normal limits for tropical fishes.**S:** Attains a length of more than 40 cm. **F:** Will accept a wide variety of aquarium foods but does best with meaty live and frozen foods.

The Black Lancer Catfish is a species that does not appear for sale very often. Its rich, deep black body with a white stripe tinged with bluish or purple overlying the lateral line from the rear of the head to the tail makes it a very attractive species to aquarists, and it is generally snatched up very quickly (in spite of its usually high price) when it does appear.

BADIS BADIS BADIS

BARBODES CALLIPTERUS

BALANTIOCHEILOS MELANOPTERUS (Bleeker)/*Bala Shark*

R: Thailand, Sumatra, Borneo and Malaysia. **H**: Active and peaceful. A skilled jumper that requires a covered tank. **W**: Neutral to slightly alkaline. Temperature 24 to 26°C. **S**: To 36 cm; in the aquarium it seldoms exceeds 13 cm. **F**: All sorts of live foods are preferred. Also fond of boiled oatmeal.

Do not let the popular name "Shark" fool you into thinking that this is a ferocious, predatory fish. The sole reason for the name is a superficial resemblance of the dorsal fin's shape to that of the oceanic marauder. It goes over the bottom frequently and thoroughly, picking up bits of food that were overlooked by others. This is done without a great deal of stirring up of the gravel and sediment. Add to this useful trait the facts that it is attractively colored and easily fed, and you have the reasons for its popularity.

BARBODES FASCIOLATUS

BARBODES CALLIPTERUS (Boulenger)/*Clipper Barb*

R: Niger River and Cameroon, West Africa. **H**: Usually peaceful, but some specimens are fin nippers. **W**: Soft, slightly acid water preferred. Temperature 21 to 30°C. **S**: Up to 8 cm. **F**: Live foods are preferred, but dry foods and frozen foods are accepted if not fed exclusively.

One difficulty in breeding the Clipper Barb is the fish's insistence on spawning under different conditions at different times. One time it may spawn in water of pH 6.6 and DH 6, whereas at some other time of the year it will reject these conditions and force the breeder to work out alternative water compositions. Like many of its relatives, the Clipper Barb likes a well-planted tank; some of the plants should be of the soft variety, which will enable the fish to add some vegetable matter to its diet.

BALANTIOCHEILOS MELANOPTERUS

BARBODES FASCIOLATUS (Günther)/*African Banded Barb*

R: Zimbabwe (Rhodesia) area. **H**: Active and fairly peaceful. **W**: Neutral to slightly acid water. Hardness not too important, as long as extremes are avoided. Temperature 21 to 30°C. **S**: 6 cm. **F**: Takes all foods, but live foods are accepted much more readily.

The spawning substrate should consist of fine-leaved plants. The water should be mature and slightly acidic (pH about 6 or 6.5). The addition of fresh water will sometimes help to stimulate spawning. The spawning tank should be positioned so that it will catch the morning sunlight. If the mating pair is placed in the breeding tank in the evening, there is a good chance that they will spawn the following morning. After a period of active driving, adhesive eggs are produced that stick to the plants and also fall to the bottom of the aquarium. The eggs will hatch in one or two days depending upon the temperature of the water.

BARBODES LATERISTRIGA (Cuvier & Valenciennes) *T-Barb, Spanner Barb*
R: Java, Borneo, Sumatra, Thailand, Malay Peninsula. **H**: Peaceful at smaller sizes, but inclined to bully smaller fishes when it reaches full size. **W**: Soft, slightly acid water. Temperature 21 to 29°C. **S**: 20 cm, but usually seen much smaller. **F**: Takes all foods, particularly live foods.
The T-Barb is no longer considered one of the really common aquarium fishes, but it still has a following with hobbyists who like to maintain at least one tank of large fishes; it is well suited to this use. As is to be expected with so large a fish, many eggs are laid. These eggs are scattered in and around plant thickets, and the parents, although not averse to eating their eggs, are not to be counted within the ranks of the really avid egg-eaters.

BARBODES PENTAZONA

BARBODES MELANAMPYX (Day)/*Swamp Barb*
R: Burma, eastern India. **H**: Peaceful and active; becomes less active when confined to small tanks. **W**: Soft, slightly acid water. Temperature 21 to 27°C. **S**: Up to 12 cm. **F**: Accepts all live and frozen foods and most dry foods.
The Swamp Barb is so named because in its home waters in Asia it is encountered most often in low-lying, swampy areas with much small vegetation. It is frequently found in land given over to rice culture, and this would almost lead one to the conclusion that the fish likes or is at least able to stand dirty water for long periods. This is definitely not so! Like most of its relatives, the Swamp Barb, despite its name, feels best in large clean, well-filtered tanks. The Swamp Barb is not difficult to breed, as it quite readily scatters its eggs among the plants.

BARBODES LATERISTRIGA

BARBODES PENTAZONA (Boulenger)/*Banded Barb, Five-Banded Barb*
R: Malay Peninsula, Borneo. **H**: Active and fairly peaceful. **W**: Soft, slightly acid water. Temperature 23 to 26°C. **S**: 5 cm. **F**: Accepts all foods, especially small live foods.
Barbodes pentazona is relatively easy to coax into spawning. *B.pentazona* spawns in the customary barb manner, but the mating act is accompanied by more "dancing" and less chasing from one end of the tank to the other than with its relatives. Sexing adult specimens is not difficult, as the female is fuller in form and is less colorful; in the female the pectoral fins are also clear.

BARBODES MELANAMPYX

BARBODES PENTAZONA RHOMBOOCELLATUS Koumans/*Ocellated Barb*

R: Borneo. **H:** Active and fairly peaceful. **W:** Not critical, however soft water with a pH of about 7.0 preferred for spawning. Temperature range 24 to 30°C. **S:** Reaches a length of about 5 to 6 cm. **F:** Not very choosy. Will accept most types of aquarium foods.

This distinctive little barb is only occasionally seen in aquarium stores. It is easily recognized by the light centers to the body bands (at least anteriorly) forming the pattern from which the name was derived. It also possesses a dark spot at the posterior base of the dorsal fin, as mentioned by Koumans in his description.

BARBODES VIVIPARUS

BARBODES SCHWANENFELDI (Bleeker)/*Tinfoil Barb*

R: Sumatra, Borneo, Malacca, Thailand. **H:** Peaceful and very active; a very good jumper and a plant eater. **W:** Soft, slightly acid water; sediments should be kept to a minimum. Temperature 23 to 26°C. **S:** Up to 35 cm. **F:** Takes all foods, but should have plenty of vegetable matter in its diet.

This fish grows rapidly and is soon too big for all but the largest tanks. As it grows older the body continues to deepen. Even at its full size, however, the Tinfoil Barb does not lose all of its attractiveness, for the orange coloring of the fins is heightened with age, which is the reverse of the usual procedure, as most fishes lose their bright colors as they increase in age and size. The general spawning pattern of large barbs is adhered to, but the large adult size of the fish demands that only very large aquaria be used.

BARBODES PENTAZONA RHOMBOOCELLATUS

BARBODES VIVIPARUS Weber/*Viviparous Barb*

R: Southeast Africa. **H**: Peaceful and very active; a good jumper. **W**: Soft, slightly acid water. Temperature 23 to 26°C. **S**: To 6 cm. **F**: Accepts all foods, but prefers live or frozen food.

Little is presently known about the reproduction of this species as it is not a widespread fish in the hobby. Weber, the describer of this fish, named it *"viviparus"* because he thought it was a livebearing fish. He came to this conclusion through dissection of specimens and never actually saw the fish spawn in the wild or in captivity.

When feeding this fish, any good prepared aquarium food can form the basis of their diet. It is a good ida, however, to offer some live foods once or twice a week. In general, barbs are heavy eaters and one can see their abdomens swell if they are given too much food.

BARBODES SCHWANENFELDI

BEDOTIA GEAYI Pellegrin/*Madagascar Rainbow*

R: Madagascar. **H**: Peaceful and active; never molest their tankmates. **W**: Somewhat alkaline water required, about pH 7.3 or 7.4. Temperature 24 to 26°C. **S**: 6 to 7 cm. **F**: Not a fussy eater; will eat dried foods readily, but should get live food occasionally. **C**: Body greenish with a dark stripe running from the eye to the caudal base. Dorsal, anal, and caudal fins have dark edges. This fish usually makes an immediate hit with all who see it for the first time. *Bedotia geayi* prefers alkaline water, and it is not at all happy when placed in the slightly acid water to which most egg-laying species are usually relegated. Given water that ranges from neutral to slightly alkaline, however, they soon feel very much at home. They spawn near the surface in closely-bunched plants, dropping only a few brown eggs every day. Eggs and fry are not usually eaten, and the youngsters are easily raised on brine shrimp.

BELONTIA HASSELTI

BELONESOX BELIZANUS Kner/*Pike Top Minnow, Pike Livebearer*

R: Southern Mexico, Honduras, Costa Rica, Nicaragua, and Guatemala. **H**: Very vicious; cannot even be trusted with smaller members of their own species. **W**: A roomy tank that has been heavily planted is ideal. Water should have an addition of salt, 1 tablespoonful for every 4 liters. **S**: Males about 15 cm; females about 20 cm. **F**: **C**: Sides are grayish to olive-green, with numerous tiny black dots on the sides.

Females that are ready to deliver young, as their swollen bellies would indicate, should be place in their own well-planted quarters at a temperature of about 29°C. The youngsters are quite touchy at first and must also be protected from their greedy mother. *Daphnia* is a good food for them to start with, followed by fully grown brine shrimp or baby Guppies. Keeping this fish fed is the greatest problem.

BEDOTIA GEAYI

BELONTIA HASSELTI (Cuvier)/*Java Combtail*

R: Malay Penninsula, Java, Bali, Borneo, Sumatra. **H**: Peaceful for a large anabantoid. **W**: Composition of water not critical, but temperature is; the temperature should not be allowed to fall below 24°C. **S**: Up to 10 cm in the aquarium; probably larger in the wild. **F**: Accepts all standard aquarium foods. **C**: The spot at the base of the rear of the dorsal fin on males varies in size and intensity from fish to fish; overall body color ranges from golden to light brown.

Much more deep-bodied and less aggressive than *Belontia signata, B. hasselti* has a subdued appeal. It is not colorful, but the lacy effect achieved by the markings in the tail, dorsal, and anal fins of the male is very pleasing. *Belontia hasselti* spawns like *B. signata* by blowing a very sketchy bubblenest to hold the floating eggs together. Males and females are easily differentiated; the females do not have the dark spot at the rear of the body below the dorsal fin, nor do they have the lacy markings in the fins.

BELONESOX BELIZANUS

BELONTIA SIGNATA (Günther)/*Combtail*

R: Sri Lanka. **H**: Vicious toward smaller fishes; should be kept only with those that are able to take care of themselves. **W**: A large tank is required. Water not critical. Temperature should be at least 25°C. **S**: 12.5 cm. **F**: Very greedy; will take coarse dried foods, but prefers chunky foods such as pieces of earthworms or lean raw beef. **C**: Sides are a reddish brown, lighter in the belly region, outer edge of the tail is fringed.

This fish builds a bubblenest in which a great number of eggs are placed. Sometimes a pair will share parental duties in guarding the eggs and fry, but more often one or the other will be constantly driven away. If this happens, take out the fish that is being chased. When they become free-swimming, the youngsters have no further need of parental attention. There is always the chance that the appetite of the parents might overcome their affection, and they should also be removed. This is a not a fish for the community aquarium.

BETTA COCCINA

BETTA BELLICA Sauvage/*Slender Betta*

R: Perak, in Malaysia. **H**: Not a good fish for the community tank. Although there is not the aggressiveness between males as in *B. splendens,* they are best kept alone. **W**: Not critical, but a high temperature (25 to 30°C) must be maintained. **S**: About 10 cm. **F**: Should get living foods, with occasional supplements of dried foods.

B. bellica is more beautiful than the wild *B. splendens.* Would aquarium-bred specimens yield the wide variety of colors and huge fins that *B. splendens* has? We will not know the answer for a long time to come. This attractive fish is longer and more slender-bodied than *B. splendens,* and the males can be distinguished by their longer ventral fins. Unfortunately, they have proven to be not quite as active as their illustrious cousins. They spawn by building bubblenests.

BELONTIA SIGNATA

BETTA COCCINA Vierke/*Red Fighting Fish*

R: Central Sumatra. **H:** A particularly shy bubblenest builder that does not do well in a communiy tank of aggressive fishes. **W:** Prefers soft water with a slightly acid to slightly alkaline pH and a temperature between 22° and 28°C. **S:** Attains a length of about 4.5 cm. **F:** Small-sized live foods preferred but will eventually accept other fare including crushed flake food.

The spawning set-up does not differ markedly from the normal tank where they are maintained, with one major exception. It was discovered by one aquarist that spawning did not occur until the fish were provided with hollow tubes (about 4-6" in length) that floated just below the surface. The bettas occupied these tubes and in a short time spawned in them. The bubblenest was built inside the tubes and spawning proceeded in a normal fashion. Initial spawnings produced up to 30 milk-white eggs but these were young fish in their first attempts at spawning so older, more experienced spawners may produce more. The male appeared to guard the tube, the female guarding the outside area. Hatching occurs within a day or two and in three days feeding should commence. In another two days they become free swimming. First foods offered may be liquid fry food, *Euglena* culture, or other suitable material. Soon microworms and newly hatched brine shrimp can be substituted.

BETTA BELLICA

BETTA IMBELLIS Ladiges/*Peaceful Betta, Crescent Betta*

R: Malaysia.**H**: Peaceful among themselves or toward other species. **W**: Neutral water of moderate hardness. Temperature 23 to 27°C. **S**: About 5 cm. **F**: Will take a variety of live, frozen, or prepared foods. **C**: Males dark brown with a bright red-orange border along the posterior edge of the caudal fin and on the distal tips of the anal and pelvic fins. Females are a dull mottled brown with orange pelvic fin tips and a less intense red-orange border on the caudal fin.

In nature, *Betta imbellis* is found in shady habitats in thickets of vegetation or under submerged roots. In captivity is it also predisposed toward dwelling in dark or shady places. Therefore, the fish will show its best colors by providing it with plants having large overhanging leaves or floating vegetation such as *Riccia* or water sprite.

It breeds in the fashion of a typical bubblenest builder with the male offering all of the parental care.

BETTA PUGNAX

BETTA MACROSTOMA Regan/*Brunei Beauty*

R: Sarawak, Borneo. **H**: Should be kept in a species tank. Males should be separated. **W**: Needs well-planted tank. Temperature 23-27°C, pH 6.5-7.2 **S**: 10 cm **F**: Live foods preferred. Spawning proceeds in typical Betta style until a batch of eggs are laid. The female comes out of the nuptial embrace first and gathers up the eggs. When the male revives she maneuvers so that they are head to head and then starts spitting the eggs out towards his mouth. Eventually he gets the idea and accepts the eggs, picking up those that have dropped to the bottom. The sequence is repeated until the female is depleted of eggs; she then moves off, leaving the male to care for the brood. This he does in normal mouthbrooder fashion for about a week or so. The fry have so far been difficult to raise.

BETTA IMBELLIS

BETTA PUGNAX (Cantor)/Penang *Betta*

R: Penang (Malaysia) and possibly Sumatra. **H:** Generally peaceful and may be a bit shy. **W:** In nature found in clear water with a slightly acid (6.4) pH. Temperature range around 22° to 28°C. **S:** Attains a length of about l0 cm. **F:** Will take a variety of aquarium foods, but prefers *Daphnia* and mosquito larvae.

The female responds by becoming very active and posturing near the male until the first attempts at an embrace are seen. After a few false runs, there is a real embrace that produces eggs. A complete spawning embrace apparently is accomplished only after a trip to the surface for air. The embrace lasts for several seconds. At first a single egg is released, then up to 20 or so eggs about 1.5 mm in diameter are released. These fall off the anal fin of the male (or even onto the aquarium gravel). The female recovers from the embrace and picks up whatever eggs she can find. As the male recovers the female will spit the eggs out in front of him until he gets the idea that he should pick them up in his mouth. He may even pick some off the bottom. Up to about 120 eggs are thus transferred over a period lasting up to eight hours.

BETTA MACROSTOMA

BETTA SMARAGDINA

BETTA SMARAGDINA Ladiges/*Peaceful Betta*

R: Korat, near the Laotian border. **H**: Peaceful for a *Betta* species; males do not attack one another except when vying for attention of females. **W**: Neutral, soft water suitable. Temperature should be kept from 22 to 27°C. **S**: To about 6 cm for both males and females. **F**: Takes all prepared and frozen meaty foods and all regular live foods; especially relishes tubifex worms. *Betta smaragdina* might someday replace *Betta splendens* as the most commercially important *Betta* species. In addition to its less combative nature, it also is able to withstand maintenance at slightly cooler water temperatures, and the fry are easier to raise than Siamese Fighting Fish fry. Males do not fight.

BETTA SPLENDENS

BETTA SPLENDENS

BETTA SPLENDENS Regan/*Betta, Siamese Fighting Fish*

R: Thailand, Malaysia, Southeast Asia. **H**: Usually peaceful with other fishes of its own size, but two males in the same aquarium will fight until one retreats. **W**: Not critical; breathing atmospheric air as they do, they can be kept in very small containers. Temperature should not go below 25°C. **S**: 5 to 6 cm. **F**: Will take dried foods, but should get an occasional meal of live foods. **C**: Many colors have been developed: red, green, blue and combinations of these colors.

Next to the ubiquitous Guppy and Goldfish, this is probably the most popular of all aquarium fishes. Their brilliant colors are a monument to the fish-breeder's art and have been developed by selective breeding from a rather nondescript greenish, short-finned fish that is still bred in Thailand today for fighting. Fish fighting is as much of a sport in Thailand as cockfighting is in many other parts of the world. The procedure is simple: two males are placed in a small aquarium and wagers are made and taken as to the outcome. The fish tear away at each other furiously until one or the other is overcome by exhaustion or weakness. The vanquished is then fished out by its owner, who either disposes of it or nurses it back to health, and the winner's owner collects his money. *Betta splendens* is a bubblenest builder and is easily bred.

BETTA TAENIATA Regan/*Striped Betta*

R: Originally known only from Sarawak, Borneo, but later discovered in Sumatra and Thailand.
H: Males will fight to the death if kept together. **W:** Not critical, but frequent changes are recommended. Temperature 24 to 27°C. **S:** Reaches a total length of about 8 cm. **F:** Will readily accept a variety of live foods and will eventually take some of the prepared aquarium foods, frozen or dry, as well.

The four specimens used by C. Tate Regan in his original description of *Betta taeniata* were collected by Mr. A. Everett in the Senah River, Sarawak, Kalimantan (Borneo). The species was later reported from Sumatra and Thailand, with the first major influx into the aquarium world coming in 1956. They did not create a big stir at that time and disappeared until Walter Foersch and Edith Korthaus brought more back to Germany in 1978. With the strong interest in *Betta* species today, *B. taeniata* is getting another chance. It is hoped it will remain for a while. The aquarium should be as large as possible. Richter uses a tank of approximately 30 gallons for breeding. The water he uses has a carbonate hardness of 7 and a total hardness of 21. The water temperature ranges between 24 and 27°C. He recommends frequent water changes as long as the fish are disturbed as little as possible. Under these conditions the fish bred quite readily, so *Betta taeniata* is therefore said to be easy to breed. For better viewing of the animals, the tank should be planted heavily in the sides and rear, leaving sufficient swimming space in the middle. A single plant, usually a large-leaved *Cryptocoryne,* may be selected as a favorite haunt and spawning place.

It is best to place only a single pair in the breeding tank. They will be shy at first but will eventually settle down and come out for their feedings of *Daphnia*, *Cyclops*, and mosquito larvae. In a pinch well-cleaned tubifex can be used. At 7 cm, the males are about a centimeter longer than the females and the head is blunter than the pointed head of the female. The males are also usually more brightly colored with stronger markings. Males will darken when confronting one another in a fight. The body of the loser will first show some stripes and then turn light brown. He will flee but may come back for a rematch before long. Females ready to spawn also show this light color and their abdomens will be swollen with eggs.

The female nudges the male on his side repeatedly as he shows his dark brown color. As he assumes a striped pattern the female attracts him toward the spawning site (possibly on the bottom in the shelter of the *Cryptocoryne* leaves). Early attempts by the male to embrace her meet with failure but eventually succeed. Some eggs and sperm are extruded and, as the male remains rigid, the female frees herself and picks up the eggs. As the male recovers, the female approaches him and spits the eggs out in front of him so that he can pick them up. This may take a few trials before succeeding, and as the spawning goes on the pair get more proficient. Up to 30 white eggs a little over a millimeter in size are laid. Spawning will continue for about four to seven hours, after which the egg-laden male seeks out a quiet place to brood his progeny. The fry are released in about nine to 12 days, are about 6 mm in length, and are ready for newly hatched brine shrimp or similar food. The young grow very quickly.

Above and below: *Betta taeniata*

BETTA UNIMACULATA (Popta)/*One-Spot Betta*

R: Borneo. **H:** Generally peaceful. Males are aggressive toward one another, but fighting is mostly ritualistic. **W:** Not critical. Neutral water of about 7 DH at a temperature range of 23 to 28°C should be used. Regular partial water changes are recommended. **S:** Attains the rather large size for a *Betta* of 11 cm in males (females reach only 9 cm). **F:** Should be given a well-rounded diet of live foods including mosquito larvae, brine shrimp, *Daphnia*, etc.

Betta unimaculata is said to occur in Borneo near the headwaters of forest streams where the streams consist of small pools connected by mere trickles of water (if connected at all). It is expected that *Betta unimaculata* repopulates some of these pools after torrential rains and the ensuing runoff reduce the population. To do this the One-Spot Betta must be an accomplished jumper-and so it is. According to Richter, they are active jumpers (with the male more so than the female) and their aquarium must be kept covered to prevent loss of the fish. Even so, he relates that the males will still jump even after many attempts fail due to their bouncing off the cover. They were observed spreading their fins and throwing their body into an "S" shape before leaping.

BIOTOECUS OPERCULARIS

BIOTODOMA CUPIDO (Heckel)/*Cupid Cichlid*

R: Middle Amazon Basin and western Guyana. **H:** Extremely quarrelsome. **W:** Not critical. **S:** 12.5 cm. **F:** Like most other large cichlids, this species requires large amounts of animal-based foods.

The Cupid Cichlid does not appear to be a species destined for great popularity except with the most dedicated cichlid enthusiasts. This species is suitable for community aquariums only when its companions are as large or larger, with temperaments that match that of *B. cupido*. This species is reported to be an open substrate spawner, but it is seldom bred. Any aquarium used for breeding this species should be large and have ample hiding places. The pair should be watched carefully and separated if love-making becomes too rough.

BETTA UNIMACULATA

BIOTOECUS OPERCULARIS (Steindachner)/*Green Dwarf Cichlid*
R: The Rio Negro in Brazil. **H**: Typically nocturnal; hugs the bottom of the aquarium and hides among plants and any other nook it can find. **W**: Temperatures between 21 to 29°C and acid conditions, a pH of 6.0-6.8 best. **S**: Under 10 cm. **F**: Prefers worms to anything else, but eagerly takes frozen brine shrimp and beef heart.

The fish spawns rather easily if properly fed on live foods such as small earthworms, tubifex worms, and frozen brine shrimp. The pair seeks seclusion, sometimes even going into a darkened flowerpot, where about 60 eggs are laid in a small circle. They exercise extreme parental care and zealously guard their young until a week after they are free swimming. It is advisable to remove the parents as soon as the young are free swimming and able to take freshly hatched brine shrimp.

BIOTODOMA CUPIDO

BOEHLKEA FREDCOCHUI

BOEHLKEA FREDCOCHUI Géry / *Cochu's Blue Tetra*

R: Peruvian Amazon region, near Leticia, Colombia. **H**: Peaceful but very sensitive; best kept with other fishes with similar characteristics. **W**: Soft, slightly acid water is highly important in this species. The addition of peat moss (for acidity) in the filter is beneficial. Temperature 23 to 26°C. **S**: Up to 5 cm. **F**: Live or frozen foods; dried foods only when there is nothing else at hand.

Like many of the tetras from the Upper Amazon region, Cochu's Blue Tetra is not seen at its best unless it has water that is to its liking. In the region where this fish occurs, the water has very little mineral content and there is an influx from other streams where the humic acid content is high, plus a great deal of rain water at certain times of the year, so we must approach these conditions by using water that is soft and has a certain amount of acidity.

BOLEOPHTHALMUS PECTINIROSTRIS

BOLEOPHTHALMUS PECTINIROSTRIS (Linnaeus) *Comb-Toothed Mudskipper*
R: Japan and China to Malaysia, the East Indies, and Burma. **H**: Rather territorial, requiring roomy, specialized aquarium with bottom that slopes from a water depth of not over 15 cm to dry land to allow the fish to leave the water. Rocks and pieces of driftwood should be provided for resting places. **W**: Water should be brackish. Salinity should range from a tablespoon of sea salt for every 4 liters of fresh water to a mixture of half fresh water and half sea water. Tank must be covered tightly and kept warm to maintain high humidity. Temperature 25 to 28°C. **S**: Up to 20 cm in nature. **F**: Small worms, *Drosophila* (fruit flies), other insects, or live foods. Substitutes, such as small pieces of beef heart, are sometimes accepted.
Among the truly unusual fishes of the world are the large gobies known as mudskippers. Obviously so-named because of their habit of springing or "hopping" over the tropical mudflats where they live, seeming almost more like insects than fishes. In some cases they even seem to prefer jumping away from an enemy than swimming away. The Comb-Toothed Mudskipper, like others, has "bugged" eyes that are perfectly adapted to aerial vision. This is unusual, since most fishes' eyes would be no more useful out of water than ours are under water without the aid of a face mask.

127

BORARAS UROPHTHALMOIDES

BORARAS UROPHTHALMOIDES (Kottelat)/*Ocellated Dwarf Rasbora, Exclamation-Point Rasbora*

R: Sumatra. **H**: Peaceful; because of their diminutive size, they should not be kept with larger fishes. **W**: Soft water, no more than 5 DH, with an acidity of pH 6.5. Temperature 23 to 27°C. **S**: 3 cm. **F**: Smaller live foods preferred, but dried foods also accepted; they are also fond of picking at algae.

Spawning may be accomplished in a small aquarium of 12 to 20 liters, which should be planted with one or two broad-leaved plants like *Cryptocoryne* species and a bunch of fine-leaved plants like *Myriophyllum*. Temperature should be gradually raised to 27°C. Driving is not at all vigorous.

BOTIA ALMORHAE

BOTIA ALMORHAE Gray / *Almora Loach*

R: Pakistan, India. **H**: A typical loach with bottom-dwelling habits. **W**: Prefers very soft, slightly acid water with temperatures in the high 20's (°C). **S**: Seldom larger than 10 cm in length. **F**: This species often starves in an aquarium, for they must have worms in their diet, preferably tubifex.

This loach has never been exported from Pakistan in commercial quantities only because there are so few exporters in that small country. The Indian variety is probably a subspecies, if not a separate species, as it is very much lighter in color and much smaller, but there is so much variability from population to population that it is impossible to determine the differences between the two varieties without a statistical analysis of the validity of certain meristic differences.

BOTIA BEAUFORTI Smith/*Beaufort's Loach*

R: Thailand. **H**: Generally peaceful toward other fishes; mostly nocturnal. Will remain mostly in the darker portions of the aquarium. **W**: Soft, slightly acid water, well-aerated. Tank should have a number of hiding places and be dimly lighted. Temperature 23 to 26°C. **S**: 20 cm. **F**: Live foods, especially tubifex or white worms preferred; frozen and prepared foods also eaten, as well as food left by other fishes.

Don't try to keep *Botia beauforti* unless you have a large tank. The 20 cm size given is a maximum, but 15 cm specimens are not at all unusual. This species has a double spine under the eye. *B. beauforti* should not be kept singly, but rather in a group. If kept singly, they may develop a nasty attitude toward their tankmates; on the other hand, if kept in a group, a sort of "pecking order" is established among themselves, and they should be provided with a number of hiding places for the protection of the weaker ones.

BOTIA HYMENOPHYSA

BOTIA BERDMOREI Blyth/*Berdmore's Loach*

R: Burma. **H**: Peaceful toward other fishes if kept in a group; mostly nocturnal. **W**: Soft, slightly acid water, well-aerated. Tank should have a number of hiding places and be dimly lighted. Temperature 23 to 25°C. **S**: To 8 cm. **F**: Live foods, especially tubifex and white worms, preferred; frozen and prepared foods also eaten, and food left by other fishes.

BOTIA BEAUFORTI

BOTIA HYMENOPHYSA (Bleeker)/*Banded Loach*

R: Malaysia, Thailand, Java, Sumatra, and Borneo. **H**: Occurs in flowing streams of fresh water. Mostly nocturnal; shuns light and stays in the darker portions of the aquarium. **W**: Should be given clean, well-oxygenated water. Temperature 24 to 27°C. **S**: In captivity about 15 cm; wild specimens are said to attain 30 cm. **F**: Will take any living foods, including small fishes. Will also rummage around the bottom for uneaten leftovers.

This loach is found in flowing streams, so it is best provided with clean, well-filtered and well-aerated water. For some unexplained reason, they will sometimes dash madly from one end of the aquarium to the other, stirring up the bottom sediment and anything else that is loose. Perhaps this is sheer playfulness. Sex differences have never been fully determined, and if they have ever spawned in captivity it has never been observed or reported.

BOTIA BERDMOREI

BOTIA LOHACHATA

BOTIA LOHACHATA Chaudhuri /*Pakistani Loach*
R: Pakistan. **H:** A typical loach with bottom-dwelling habits. **W:** Prefers very soft, slightly acid
water with high temperatures in the high 20's (°C). **S:** Seldom larger than 10 cm in length. **F:**
This species often starves in an aquarium, for they must have worms in their diet, preferably
tubifex.

The Pakistani Loach is famous only because it is one of the very few fishes from Pakistan
which have made aquarium history. The Pakistani people are very active in the aquarium field
and their aquarium in Karachi must be applauded as a major contribution to "living museums of
the world." *Botia lohachata* often is confused with *Botia almorhae* because of their great similarity of appearance; some, in fact, consider the first two species to be just subspecies. Young
B. lohachata and *B. almorhae* also are confused with *B. sidthimunki*, but when fully grown the
former are easily distinguishable from *B sidthimunki*.

132

BOTIA MACRACANTHA (Bleeker)/*Clown Loach*

R: Sumatra, Borneo, and the Sunda Islands. **H:** Peaceful, not quite as nocturnal as some of the other species. **W:** Clean, well-aerated water. Temperature should not exceed 24°C. **S:** 30 cm maximum, but most specimens do not exceed 10cm. **F:** They like to grub for leftover morsels at the bottom, but should also get some living foods.

This is a very active species that often swims up and down the glass sides of the aquarium for no apparent reason. There have been no successful spawnings observed in the aquarium except perhaps by accident. Some day some fortunate aquarist will be successful, and a very desirable aquarium fish will become more available at a lower price. At the present time it is also not known what the external sex differences are, and it is impossible to tell the males from the females without killing them.

BOTIA MODESTA Bleeker/*Orange-Finned Loach*

R: Thailand, Vietnam, Malaysia. **H**: Peaceful, a community aquarium fish. Nocturnal. **W**: Does best in water at a pH of 6.6 in very soft water. Prefers high temperatures of about 28°C. **S**: To 10 cm. **F**: Prefers tubifex worms, but as a scavenger it probes the bottom for almost any kind of food. **C**: The orange fins may become yellow if they do not have insects or shrimp in their diet. This is a rarely imported loach that frequently accompanies shipments from Thai (Siamese) exporters. The fish is very sensitive to chemicals and it should not be treated with dyes such as malachite green or methylene blue unless the fish is dipped into a bath and quickly removed. They prefer a place to hide during the day and should be given a cave or half coconut shell under which they can escape bright light.

BOTIA SIDTHIMUNKI

BOTIA MORLETI Tirant/*Hora's Loach*

R: Thailand. **H**: Peaceful, mostly nocturnal. Will remain mostly in the darker portions of the aquarium. **W**: Soft, slightly acid water, well-aerated. Tank should have a number of hiding places and not be brightly lighted. Temperature 23 to 25°C. **S**: To 10 cm; usually smaller. **F**: Live foods, especially tubifex or white worms, preferred; frozen and prepared foods also eaten, and food left by other fishes may be accepted.

The *Botia* species all have a protective device that is shared by only a few other fishes. There is an erectile spine, sometimes two, under each eye. This inflicts a painful but non-venomous sting when the fish is handled. This has proven to be the downfall of many a bird or larger fish that caught a *Botia* and did not spit it out quickly enough. The loach lodges in their throat and they eventually choke on it.

BOTIA MODESTA

BOTIA SIDTHIMUNKI Klausewitz/*Dwarf Loach*

R: Thailand. **H**: Peaceful, playful, seems to be less nocturnal than the other species. **W**: Soft, alkaline water, well-aerated. Temperature 23 to 25°C. **S**: 4 cm. **F**: Small live foods preferred; other foods accepted.

B. sidthimunki is the smallest known member of a group in which some species get rather big. The writer had some that were not yet full-grown when he got them. They were about 2 cm in length. Once day there was only one when there were formerly three. After a thorough search it was found that the other two had squeezed into the intake tube of the outside filter, where they were found happily grubbing around in the glass-wool. It was some time before they became too large to squeeze through the narrow openings, and they frequently had to be netted out of the filter. It is doubtless the most active and playful of the *Botia*.

BOTIA MORLETI

BOTIA STRIATA

BOTIA STRIATA Rao/Zebra Loach

R: Southern India. **H:** Peaceful and lively; likes to be in a group of its own species. **W:** Soft, slightly acid water best, but does well in a variety of conditions. Temperature 20 to 25°C. **S:** Attains a length of about 6 cm in the aquarium; grows larger (10 cm) in nature. **F:** Live foods, especially tubificid worms, are preferred, but it will accept normal aquarium substitutes.

Botia striata is a very attractive loach that, unfortunately, is seen only rarely in the aquarium trade. It was for a long time thought to be just a pretty color variety of *Botia hymenophysa,* but eventually it was regarded as a separate species. Early reports had the two species occurring together in nature, while in fact *Botia hymenophysa* comes from Thailand, Malaya and the Greater Sunda Islands and *Botia striata* comes from southern India. They are easily separable by color pattern so that aquarists should have no difficulty in distinguishing one from the other. In its early days in the hobby the Zebra Loach was called erroneously *Botia strigata* and was also known by the trade name *Botia* "weinbergi."

The Zebra Loach is quite inoffensive and can be kept in a community tank without problems. It is very lively once it gets over its initial timidity. To help accomplish this the tank housing this loach (and others for that matter) should be dimly lit and provided with a number of hiding places in the form of caves, flowerpots, coconut shell halves, driftwood, etc. The loaches will hide at first but will eventually come out and swim around the tank searching for food among the gravel grains. Zebra Loaches do best when kept in a group.

Spawning of the Zebra Loach has not been reported, but it is expected to follow the pattern of the known species. In many cases spawnings happen unobserved and the first indication that it has occurred is a group of babies swimming around. What is known is that when a pair of loaches swims around the tank side by side as if they were attached (and perhaps they are by the hooked spines located below the eyes), spawning is to be expected.

BOULENGERELLA MACULATA

BOULENGERELLA MACULATA (Valenciennes)/*Spotted Pike Characin*

R: Amazon basin. **H:** Predatory on small fishes. Should be kept with larger fishes or with members of its own kind. **W:** Not critical. A pH of between 6.0 and 7.5, a hardness of 6 DH or less and a temperature between 24 and 27°C are recommended. **S:** Attains a length of 35 to 40 cm. **F:** Small live fishes such as goldfish and livebearers (guppies may be too small) are preferred. *Boulengerella maculata* is easily recognized by its spotted pattern. It may exhibit a lateral dark band as in *B. Lateristriga,* but that species lacks the spots. In addition, the Spotted Pike Characin has a small cylindrical cartilaginous appendage on the upper jaw colored bright red. In the other species of *Boulengerella* this appendage is the same color as the snout. The function of this appendage is not known, but in the Spotted Pike Characin its bright red color might act as a lure to prey animals that might mistake it for a small red worm. Since *B. maculata* is a predator that lurks in the vegetation waiting for small fishes to come close enough to strike, this lure might give it an added advantage in obtaining food.

Heavy filtration is not needed as the waste is in the form of small pellets that are easily siphoned off. Live foods are a must. Small goldfish and large livebearers are recommended. Fishes with spiny fins should be avoided. A small (2.5-3 cm) fish two or three times a day is sufficient for pike characins of about 12.5 cm, a 2.5-5 cm prey fish is enough for one 12.5-30 cm and one 7.5-10 cm prey fish every other day can be fed to the largest Spotted Pike Characins of over 30 cm.

The Spotted Pike Characin can be kept in a community tank of larger fishes. When kept with other pike characins it usually is the dominant species, guarding a territory from the others. Its aggression is directed mostly toward other species rather than members of its own kind. There is no information on spawning or sexual dimorphism.

BOULENGERELLA LATERISTRIGA

BOULENGERELLA LATERISTRIGA (Boulenger)/*Striped Pike Characin*
R: Rio Negro. **H:** Predatory; cannot be kept with small fishes. **W:** Moderately soft with a pH of 4.0-6.8 and a temperature of 24 to 27°C suitable. **S:** Reaches a length of about 25 cm. **F:** Prefers small live fishes like goldfish and livebearers.

By shape and temperament one might consider the pike characins as the barracudas of fresh water. They are long and slender with numerous close-set teeth in each jaw. These teeth point backward toward the interior of the mouth, helping prevent prey from escaping and aiding in guiding the prey down the gullet. The Striped Pike Characin will lurk near the top of the water column, camouflaging itself among the aquatic vegetation or whatever happens to be handy. As prey nears it will wait for the opportune moment to strike or will slowly approach its intended victim until it can capture it with a quick dart.

The Striped Pike Characin at 25 cm is one of the smallest of the pike characins and is somewhat rare in the wild compared to the others. It is easily distinguished by the incomplete lateral line (in *B. lucia* it is complete) and color pattern (not spotted like *B. maculata*). It has a cylindrical, cartilaginous appendage at the tip of its upper jaw which is the same color as the jaw. This appendage is also present in the other species and is the same color as the jaw in *B. lucza* but bright red in *B. maculata*. Its function is still not known.

A large aquarium should be provided for the Striped Pike Characin, 200 liters or bigger. It should also be well planted and in a place where there is little disturbance. When frightened the Striped Pike Characin will dash about and ram into the sides of the aquarium, usually damaging the jaw appendage and leaving a blunted sore spot. It may well be that at the time of purchase the fish will be in this condition from its actions during shipment. The pH should be within the range of 4.0-7.1 (with 6.8-7.1 optimal) and the hardness should be about 4 DH or less. The best temperature should be 26°C, but anywhere from 24 to 26°C is acceptable. Live fishes which it can stalk are the best foods. Choose the soft-finned species like goldfish and livebearers over the spiny-finned forms such as cichlids to prevent injury from the spines. The decorations should be adequate to provide shelter for the Striped Pike Characin but should not be so much that the prey can easily escape. For a 12.5 cm or smaller *B. lateristriga* two to three 2.5-4 cm fish per day are sufficient. For larger fish (up to 25 cm) a 5 cm prey fish is enough. Nothing is known about the spawning of the pike characins and no one has been able to find any sexual dimorphism.

BRACHYDANIO ALBOLINEATUS

BRACHYDANIO ALBOLINEATUS (Blyth)/*Pearl Danio (golden variety known as Gold Danio)*
R: Moulmein Region of India, Burma, Thailand, Malacca, and Sumatra. **H**: Very active swimmer; likes sunny tanks with clean, well-aerated water. Likes to swim in schools with others of its own kind. **W**: pH and hardness not critical. Aquaria need not be large, but should provide a good amount of open space for swimming. Temperature 22 to 25°C. **S**: 6 cm. **F**: A good eater like most active fishes. Will thrive on dry as well as living foods, but some living foods should be included occasionally.

This little fish has all the attributes of a good aquarium inhabitant. It is above all peaceful; it does not outgrow a small aquarium; it eats all foods and besides is one of the most easily bred egglayers. A small school of these fish with the sun playing on them in a well-planted aquarium is a very pretty sight. The approved way of spawning them is to place them in a long aquarium with about 10 cm of half fresh and half aged aquarium water. The bottom should be covered with several layers of large pebbles or glass marbles.

BRACHYDANIO FRANKEI Meinken/*Leopard Danio*

R: Not definitely known, probably India. **H**: Peaceful and very active. Prefers to swim in small schools. **W**: Not critical, as long as the water is clean and well aerated. Temperatures 24 to 26°C. **S**: About 6 cm; females slightly larger. **F**: A good eater, accepting prepared as well as live or frozen foods.

Mr. Franke expressed the opinion that this was a genuine newcomer, which was confirmed by Hermann Meinken, who named it in Franke's honor. The *Brachydanios* have long been very popular because of their attractive colors, ceaseless activity, small size, and ease with which they are bred. The Leopard Danio spawns in the same manner as the Zebra Danio, by laying non-adhesive eggs, but the female does not become depleted in one spawning; eggs are laid daily until there are as many as 1,000.

BRACHYDANIO NIGROFASCIATUS

BRACHYDANIO KERRI (Smith)/*Kerr's Danio*

R: Koh Yao Yai and Koh Yao Noi Islands, Thailand. **H**: Peaceful, active, best kept in a group. **W**: Not critical; water should be clean and well-aerated. **S**: 4 cm. **F**: Small live foods preferred; frozen and prepared foods also taken willingly.

This is one of the lesser-known species of this popular genus. Why it has not "caught on" is one of those unsolved mysteries. It is every bit as peaceful, active, and hardy as the Zebra or Pearl Danio, and its colors are certainly far from unattractive. It is as easy to breed as the others, and raising the young presents no problems either. Maybe some day some breeder will make a great "discovery" and suddenly everybody will wonder why they have been passing them up all these years. Like the other danios, the best way to keep them is in a school of about a dozen, with enough swimming space to suit their active nature.

BRACHYDANIO FRANKEI

BRACHYDANIO NIGROFASCIATUS (Day)/*Spotted Danio*

R: Upper Burma to Rangoon and the Moulmein region. **H**: Active swimmer; does not require a large aquarium, but some open space should be provided. **W**: Clean, well-aerated water; pH and hardness not critical. Temperature should be between 22 to 25°C. **S**: Slightly under 5 cm. **F**: Dried and frozen foods as well as living foods are eagerly eaten, but should not be too coarse.

This fish was once known as *Brachydanio analipunctatus,* but it got its present name back in 1869. Being a smaller and not quite as strikingly colored fish, we do not see it as often as *B. rerio* or *B. albolineatus,* but it is every bit as satisfactory in the aquarium. Rather than keep it in pairs, it is better to put about 6 to 12 together, as they like to congregate in schools. Both sexes are very similar in coloration, but the females may be distinguished by their fuller, heavier bodies. Like the other *Brachydanio* species, this one lays non-adhesive eggs that should be allowed to fall between layers of pebbles or glass marbles to prevent their being eaten by the parents.

BRACHYDANIO KERRI

BRACHYDANIO RERIO (Hamilton-Buchanan)/*Zebra, Zebra Danio, Striped Danio*
R: Coromandel Coast of India, from Calcutta to Masulipatam. **H**: Peaceful, active, likes to travel in schools. **W**: pH and hardness not critical. Prefers clean, well aerated water, being native to flowing streams. **S**: About 5 cm. **F**: A heavy eater, like all active fishes. All foods are accepted, but some live foods should be included.

The Zebra Danio is hardy, always active, and will never attack any of its tankmates. Besides, it is easily bred, easily fed, and will withstand much abuse without serious consequences, making it just about the perfect aquarium fish. Many advanced breeders remember it as the first egglayer they ever spawned, and in almost all cases many of the fry were raised successfully. There are many methods of breeding the Zebra Danio, which like the other *Brachydanio* species lays a non-adhesive egg. All of these methods have the same purpose, to keep the parents from eating their spawn. Of course, the layer of pebbles or marbles technique described for other *Brachydanio* species is still the most popular, because it gives the breeders the most swimming area. Another is a bag of nylon mesh, wide enough to let through the eggs but not the breeders, which is suspended in the breeding aquarium. This species also exists in a long-finned form.

BRACHGOBIUS DORIAE

BRACHYGOBIUS AGGREGATUS Herre/*Philippine Bumblebee Goby*
R: Philippine Islands. **H**: A typical goby that spends most of its time "hopping" from one spot to another, often attaching itself to the glass with modified ventral fins. **W**: Hard, alkaline water is preferred, with very high temperatures in the 20's (°C) being necessary. **S**: Under 5 cm. **F**: Live food is a necessity; small worms are best.

This is a bottom fish that should be kept in mildly brackish water. They can sometimes be induced to spawn with partial water changes. A varied diet and an abundant amount of live foods are also important considerations. Relatively large eggs are laid in flowerpots or under stones and number between 75 and 140. Depending upon the temperature of the water, the young will hatch in 4 to 5 days. They will be guarded by the male for at least one week.

BRACHYDANIO RERIO

BRACHYGOBIUS DORIAE (Günther)/*Doria's Bumblebee Goby*
R: Borneo and the Malay Archipelago. **H**: Should be kept by themselves in a small aquarium. Hiding places should be provided. **W**: Water should have an addition of one heaping teaspoonful of table salt per 4 liters. Temperature 24 to 26°C. **S**: Up to 2.5 cm. **F**: Small live foods exclusively.

Brachygobius doriae spawns in a very similar manner to many of the cichlids. The male cleans off a patch in a secluded spot, such as the inside of a flowerpot. The eggs are laid here and then the male guards them. Hatching time varies greatly from one egg to the other, but at the end of 5 days the fry should all be out. Two days later they are free-swimming. All this time the male is guarding them fiercely, but there is no point in leaving him there when the young are able to take care of themselves, and they could be eaten.

BRACHYGOBIUS AGGREGATUS

BRACHYPLATYSTOMA JURUENSE

BRACHYPLATYSTOMA JURUENSE (Boulenger)/*Golden Tigerstriped Catfish*
R: Amazon River system in Brazil and Peru. **H:** Sits quietly during day but is a nocturnal predator. **W:** Normal aquarium conditions sufficient as long as extremes are avoided. **S:** Attains a length of about 60cm to 90cm (2-3 feet). **F:** Feeds on live foods (feeder goldfish) at night.

The Golden Tiger-striped Catfish, *Brachyplatystoma juruense,* has only recently been seen in the aquarium trade. Several specimens were imported and there was a flurry of activity as the search for the proper name commenced. It was not long in coming as the way was paved by a similar catfish, the Tiger-striped Catfish, *Merodontotus tigrinus.* A comparison of the two species reveals substantial differences in color and pattern but also a great similarity, and the question has been raised whether these fishes really should be placed in separate genera.

The Golden Tiger-striped Catfish grows rather large, to almost a meter, so that only young individuals may be kept by the average aquarist. Because of its size it is routinely caught in its range by natives and used for food. They are fished for by gill net during July and August in the Rio Madeira, Brazil. It apparently migrates upstream in schools, perhaps with its own species or with a close relative, *B. flavicans.* It is captured at the Teotonio rapids in small numbers when the water is low and the floods are about to start. The recent imports came from the headwaters of the Amazon in Peru.

It needs a very large tank (150 gallons or more depending upon its size) with good aeration and filtration. It is very quiet during the day, sitting on the bottom on its ventral and anal fins so that the pectoral fins are not touching the substrate. Food added at this time goes unnoticed. Feeder goldfish placed in the tank are not touched but are no longer evident the next morning, indicating that this is, like many other catfishes, a nocturnal predator. The sitting position, shape of the body, and long trailing filaments of the caudal fin seem to indicate that this is a moving water species, seemingly confirmed by its presence in the Teotonio rapids.

This is not the fish for the average aquarist. It is for the advanced hobbyist and particularly for the catfish enthusiast. The price is still considerable, with prospects of it dropping very much in the near future very slim.

BRACHYRHAPHIS EPISCOPI (Steindachner)/*Bishop*

R: Both slopes of central Panama. **H:** Fin nippers that are best kept in a tank with their own kind, and even then they need plants for protection. **W:** Not critical about water chemistry, but nitrogenous wastes should be kept to a minimum by frequent water changes. **S:** Attains a length of about 3-3.5 cm (males) to 4-5 cm (females). **F:** Not fussy about food, but should receive at least occasional feedings of live foods, especially insect matter.

The Bishop is not a difficult fish to maintain as long as it is provided with clean, clear water. This can best be accomplished by good filtration and aeration as well as water changes on a daily basis (30-60% has been recommended). It is not fussy about food, but since it is an insect predator as much insect material (preferably live) as can be found should be offered. A temperature of about 20° to 25°C is preferable.

Two forms of the Bishop have been discovered, one with the usual lateral spots seen in other members of the genus and another with a lateral stripe, a pattern not seen in any of the other species of the genus. In the spotted form the male shows his intentions toward the female by an intensification of the lateral spots; the striped form intensifies the stripe. The male then nuzzles the courted female and postures in front of her with his fins erect and his tail beating. Females of the spotted form will usually respond by attacking the courting male. The tank should be well planted so that there are areas of refuge for such beset males. On the other hand, the striped form female will usually swim away, the male in swift pursuit. Nuzzling males may even bite the female at the vent and hang on like bulldogs for several seconds. A male performs a "bobbing" dance for the female as he circles her, occasionally stopping to impress the female with a lateral display, fins erect, and violent tail-beating. The spotted males do not "dance" for the females but do exhibit lateral displays. Once the females have dropped their young they apparently give off a chemical signal that the males interpret as an okay to start courting again.

To save the young, females that are ready to give birth should be placed in a livebearer trap with sufficiently large mesh.

Although the striped form is less aggressive toward other fishes than the spotted form, these fish are not candidates for a community tank; it has been reported that the spotted form chewed the tails of even *Corydoras* catfishes kept in the same tank.

BRACHYRHAPHIS HOLDRIDGEI Bussing/*Red-Finned Bishop*

R: Atlantic slope of Costa Rica and Nicaragua. **H:** Aggressive fin nippers like *Gambusia*. Best kept by themselves with plenty of cover. **W:** Not critical, but sensitive to nitrogenous wastes. A temperature of 20° to 25°C is acceptable. **S:** Males about 4-4.5 cm, females 4.5-5.5 cm. **F:** Not fussy about food. Will eat any decent aquarium foods offered.

This small poeciliid is reminiscent of the genus *Gambusia* so familiar to aquarists as fin nippers. In fact, *Brachyrhaphis holdridgei* has this same nasty habit and may even carry it out to a greater extent, much to the detriment of other species of fishes that are forced to share quarters with it. However, it is somewhat more colorful than the species of *Gambusia* and has been welcomed by connoisseurs of livebearing fishes as a fine addition to their tanks. It is relatively easy to keep, being not too particular about the water chemistry of its tank. However, it is best to keep the water relatively clear and clean, for a buildup of nitrogenous wastes may be detrimental to the fish or at least inhibit it from mating.

BRACHYSYNODONTIS BATENSODA

BRACHYRHAPHIS TERRABENSIS (Regan)/*Upland Livebearer*

R: Pacific slope of southern Costa Rica and western Panama, at higher elevations. **H:** Fairly peaceful, but females are antagonistic toward males. **W:** Not important. Temperature 16 to 24°C. **S:** Males 2.5 cm; females 3 cm. **F:** Accepts dried food.

There are at least 20 genera of livebearing fishes, but most are rarely seen in the aquarium. For the most part, these livebearers are drab fishes with few markings and little or no color. A substantial number, for example the Upland Livebearer, are attractively but modestly colored. Even at their best, however, these livebearers are drab when compared to platies, swordtails, and mollies. Because of this, species like *Brachyrhaphis terrabensis* are rarely imported.

BRACHYRHAPHIS HOLDRIDGEI

BRACHYSYNODONTIS BATENSODA (Rüppell)/*Mustachioed Upside-Down Catfish*
R: Tropical Africa. **H:** A truly upside-down catfish; not nocturnal like most *Synodontis* species. Peaceful. **W:** Not critical, but seems to prefer water that is slightly alkaline and moderately hard. **S:** Attains a length of at least 20 cm. **F:** Not fussy about food, but the particles should be relatively small.

Brachysynodontis batensoda is THE upside-down catfish. It is most probably the one that is depicted in Egyptian hieroglyphics in an upside-down position, for it spends almost all of its time inverted as opposed to many species of *Synodontis* that will invert only on occasion. This species starts out rightside-up, but early in life it will make some attempts at swimming in the inverted position. These reversals of position become more and more frequent until it remains inverted for almost all of its swimming time. In contrast to *Synodontis* species that will swim upside-down only in the protection or seclusion of ledges or plant leaves, this species will swim back and forth right out in the open in this position in the tank. As might be expected, this species is countershaded; that is, it has a darker belly than back, so that when it is in the inverted position it matches normally swimming fishes that have a darker back than belly.

BRACHYRHAPHIS TERRABENSIS

147

BROCHIS MULTIRADIATUS

BROCHIS MULTIRADIATUS Orces-Villagomez/*Hog-nosed Brochis*

R: This species was discovered irt the Upper Napo River system of Ecuador. **H:** A peaceful species much like *Corydoras* species that scour the bottom looking for food. **W:** Slightly acid to neutral pH (6.0-7.0) and moderate hardness (about 15°GH) with a temperature of 21-25°C is acceptable. Some current should be supplied and regular water changes implemented. **S:** Attains a length of about 8-10 cm. **F:** A variety of live, freeze-dried, frozen, and flake foods are accepted. Some green vegetable matter should be included.

Brochis multiradiatus is a peaceful species that is constantly rummaging over the bottom searching for food with its barbels. For this reason sharp-edged bottom material should be avoided as the barbels could be damaged. For the same reason, plants that are added to the tank should be well anchored and with good root systems to prevent the catfish from uprooting them as they forage. The Hog-nosed Brochis can be added to a community tank that would be acceptable to species of the genus *Corydoras*.

For a single-species tank a 20-gallon size is recommended. The bottom material can vary from relatively fine to coarse-grained material as long as there are no sharp edges. Bunch plants and well-rooted plants should be relegated to the back and sides of the tank leaving an open place for swimming. A power filter can be used to provide some current and to help oxygenate the water. Partial water changes are necessary because in poor quality water (high in organic compounds) the barbels seem to deteriorate. In addition to topping off after siphoning, water changes of approximately l/2 to 2/3 (depending upon ammonia and nitrite readings) should be made every two to three weeks. The pH should be neutral to slightly acid (6.0-7.0) with a moderate hardness (about 15°GH), and a temperature of 21°-25°C.

BROCHIS SPLENDENS

BROCHIS SPLENDENS (Castelnau)/*Common Brochis*

R: Upper Amazon; also in the Ambiyacu River, a tributary in Peru. **H**: Peaceful, feeds on the bottom, where it is useful in picking up uneaten foods left by other fishes. Seldom uproots plants. **W**: Not critical; sensitive to only one thing: there must be no salt in the water. **S**: About 6 cm. **F**: Eats any kind of prepared foods, but should get an occasional feeding of tubifex worms, of which it is very fond.

At first sight, this fish looks like a stubby *Corydoras aeneus,* but there are enough important anatomical differences to put it into another genus. The body is much higher and more compressed; the adipose fin is considerably larger and has one ray which is spiny and gives the fin a pointed appearance; the armor plates on the head also extend onto the snout. There are no known external sex differences, with the possible exception that the armor plates in female specimens may not meet as closely as in the males, which would probably be more noticeable in females with eggs.

BRYCINUS CHAPERI (Sauvage)/*Chaper's Characin*

R: West Africa, Upper Guinea, Gold Coast to the Niger River. **H**: Peaceful if kept with fishes of its own size. **W**: Water should be soft and slightly acid. Temperature 24 to 26°C. **S**: Attains a length of 9 cm. **F**: Dried food is taken when hungry, but any kind of live food is preferable.

This is one of the African characins which we do not see very often, but due to increased facilities from that area we may see it a bit more frequently and also get better acquainted with it. Distinguishing the sexes and spawning are similar to that of the Long-Finned African Tetra, *Brycinus longipinnis.*

BRYCINUS NURSE

BRYCINUS LONGIPINNIS (Günther)/*Long-Finned African Tetra*

R: Tropical West Africa, Sierra Leone to Zaire. **H**: Timid; an active swimmer that remains in the middle reaches of the aquarium. **W**: Water should be soft and slightly acid, preferably filtered through peat moss. Temperature 24 to 26°C. **S**: To 12.5 cm. **F**: Larger sized live foods; can be accustomed to frozen foods or beef heart.

Sexes can be distinguished by the shape of the anal fin, rounded in the male and with a straight edge in the female. Besides, the male has a high, pointed dorsal fin while that of the female is considerably smaller and round. Both sexes have a horizontal stripe that begins in the middle of the body at a point above the end of the anal fin and is carried by the middle rays through the fork of the tail. The eye is another attractive feature, being bright red.

BRYCINUS CHAPERI

BRYCINUS NURSE (Rüppel)/*Nurse Tetra*

R: Widely distributed in tropical African waters, Nile to Senegal. **H**: Somewhat shy, very active. Prefer to swim in groups in the middle reaches of the aquarium. **W**: Water should be soft and slightly acid, preferably filtered through peat moss. Temperature 24 to 26°C. **S**: To 25 cm.; usually offered for sale at 8 to 10 cm. **F**: Large live foods such as cut-up earthworms or fully grown brine shrimp; can be accustomed to frozen foods.

Probably because of their large size and active nature, there have been no recorded spawnings in captivity, although their wide distribution in African water indicates an active as well as prolific nature. Sexes can be easily distinguished even while they are young. The females have an anal fin that is straight at the edge, while the males have one with a rounded edge.

BRYCINUS LONGIPINNIS

BRYCINUS TAENIURUS (Günther)/*Narrow-Lined African Tetra*

R: Central Africa. **H**: Peaceful and active; may be a fin nipper due to its teeth. Relatively unknown. **W**: Soft, acid water with a pH close to 6.0 or even lower. Temperature should be above 24°C. **S**: Up to 10 cm.; may grow larger if properly cared for. **F**: Accepts all live foods and a wide variety of dried and frozen foods.

Dr. Jacques Géry, one of the world's leading experts on characins, collected, photographed and identified this specimen for us. Previously, we only knew this fish from small ones that were shipped intermingled with other fishes as this is not a recognized aquarium species. Chances are that it would be difficult to spawn, as are most African tetras, because they are so badly handled prior to reaching our aquaria. Even this beautiful specimen, collected and photographed in Africa, lost a few scales during handling, as can be seen above the vent.

BUJURQUINA MARIAE

BRYCONOPS MELANURUS (Bloch)/*Jumping Anchovy*

R: Amazon River and Guianas. **H**: A school fish that jumps from the water to catch flying insects. Very peaceful but requires a large tank with a great deal of swimming space. **W**: Prefers moving water or water that is heavily agitated. Temperature should be 25°C and the softer the better. A pH of 6.6 is best. **S**: Up to 13 cm. **F**: Prefers live food such as wingless *Drosophila* flies, which can be sprinkled onto the surface of the tank, but they do well on dried foods and frozen brine shrimp.

The Jumping Anchovy is a delicate species that is difficult to keep in the aquarium. Possibly for this reason, *Bryconops melanurus* is seldom seen in the aquarium hobby. This species prefers slightly acid water with warm temperatures between 25 to 28°C. The tank must be very well covered because, as its common name states, this fish likes to jump. It is best kept in its own company of a dozen or so tankmates and will school almost continuously. Because of this activity, a large aquarium is required. Live food is preferred.

BRYCINUS TAENIURUS

BUJURQUINA MARIAE (Eigenmann)/*Maria's Cichlid*

R: Upper Amazon, Peru and Colombia. **H**: Fairly peaceful with fishes its own size, a bit danger-ous when spawning. **W**: Not too sensitive to water conditions. Does best in water from 24-28°C, with a pH of 6.8 and as soft as possible. **S**: To 12.5 cm. **F**: Prefers live foods such as tubifex worms, earthworms and small fishes. Willingly accepts frozen brine shrimp, dried foods, espe-cially those which are pelletized, and bits of beef.

A very colorful cichlid with interesting spawning habits if offered the proper environment. Set up a 60- or 80-liter aquarium in which the water has been darkened a little by peat filtration. Be careful that the pH doesn't go below 6.8. Since this fish likes dark water, use black gravel on the bottom to make the aquarium even darker and let the top grow thick with floating plants. These are the conditions under which the fish will become extremely colorful and active.

BRYCONOPS MELANURUS

BUJURQUINA VITTATUS (Heckel)/*Green Acara; Banded Aequidens*

R: A widespread species occurring from the Guianas to Paraguay. **H:** Relatively peaceful. May be somewhat aggressive when spawning. A delayed mouthbrooder. **W:** Not critical. A neutral to slightly acid pH and moderately hard water are acceptable. Temperature should be between 23° and 27°C. **S:** Attains a length of about 15 cm. **F:** Prefers live foods of all kinds but readily accepts frozen, freeze-dried, and even flake foods.

Bujurquina vittatus is a wide-ranging species occurring over much of tropical South America from the Guianas and Venezuela to southern Brazil and Paraguay.

Any species that is found over such a wide area usually is not demanding as far as aquarium conditions are concerned. A pH near neutral and medium hardness are acceptable. Temperatures in the range of 22° to 27°C also suit this fish. The tank need not be too large as this fish attains a length of only about 15 cm. It should have aquarium sand or gravel, plants, rocks, and driftwood. The set-up should provide an open expanse of sand where a flat rock or broad leafed plant *(Echinodorus) is* positioned as these are favorite spawning sites of this fish. Feeding is no problem as a variety of standard aquarium foods is accepted. Live foods should be offered on a regular basis, especially if the fishes are to be spawned.

There is no sexual dichromatism, but the male may be larger than the female. Spawning probably will occur shortly after a water change. It is not preceded by any elaborate courtship and you may be aware that something is about to happen only by their interest in cleaning a potential spawning site and their reluctance in allowing other fishes in the tank to approach this site. Cichlids are kept further away than non-cichlids. Spawning is similar to other egg-laying substrate spawners, with the female making a few dry runs over the site first before actually depositing some eggs. The male follows, fertilizing the eggs as he passes over them. However, instead of laying the eggs in straight rows they may be deposited in circles, the fish rotating in a counterclockwise direction. Spawning is accomplished relatively quickly, with about 200 or so eggs deposited in approximately half an hour. The eggs are whitish to amber. They are guarded and fanned by the parents (both take part alternately) for 24 to 36 hours. After that time the fry are "chewed" out of their eggshells and retained in the mouth like a mouthbrooder. Although the male is usually the one who does most of this brooding, the female will take her turn. The exchange takes place at regular intervals at secluded spots. The parent holding the fry spits them out onto a smooth surface and the other parent quickly takes them up. With time, the fry become more active and the length of time they are allowed out becomes longer as the time they are in the parents' mouth becomes shorter. Once free swimming the parents start to lose interest in their care. While the black and white banded fry are out they are actively searching for food. Normal food for such fry is accepted.

BUTIS BUTIS (Hamilton-Buchanan)/*Crazy Fish, Ca Bong*

R: Found from India to the Solomon Islands. **H**: A typical goby which clings upside down to plants and rocks and swims upside down as well. **W**: Not very particular about water conditions, but since it is found in some brackish water areas, it is assumed that it has a tolerance for hard water. **S**: About 15 cm. **F**: Prefers live foods, but is an active scavenger and cleans rocks and plants of algal growths incessantly.

The author entered the aquarium depot of Lee Chin Eng in Djakarta, Indonesia in 1959 and was greeted with the exclamation: "Dr. Axelrod, I've discovered a new fish!" The author quickly investigated the fish and remarked, "I doubt that it's new, but it sure is acting crazy." That night Lee wrote a letter to a German importer and said he had "Axelrod's new Crazy Fish." The name stuck in Europe and in the United States, and the Crazy Fish became a very popular scavenger. The Crazy Fish, even with its big mouth, doesn't seem to be too dangerous to smaller fishes, but this may have been because it was so well fed.

BUJURQUINA VITTATUS

BUTIS BUTIS

CALLICHTHYS CALLICHTHYS (Linnaeus)/*Slender Armored Catfish*

R: Eastern Venezuela, Trinidad to Buenos Aires. **H**: Quite active for a catfish; in its native waters it prefers quiet water and a muddy bottom. **W**: Not critical. Temperatures should not exceed 24°C. Well-rooted plants should be used lest they be uprooted. **S**: 18 cm; tank-raised specimens do not usually exceed 13 cm. **F**: A very greedy eater. Prefers living foods, up to and including small fishes.

This fish has a huge appetite and should not be trusted with small fishes or his appetite will extend to them. If kept in a large aquarium that is to their liking, they live to a ripe old age. If it is desired to spawn this fish, a very large aquarium is required. In the summer months a pool might be given them, although we have not heard of this procedure being used. Sex differences are very slight, but the females have slightly duller colors and a deeper, more rounded body. The male is said to build a bubblenest in which he keeps and guards a huge number of eggs.

CAMPYLOMORMYRUS TAMANDUA

CALLOCHROMIS PLEUROSPILUS (Boulenger)/*Pastel Cichlid*

R: Lake Tanganyika, Africa. **H**: Not exceptionally quarrelsome, but will eat fishes that they can swallow. **W**: Hard, alkaline water. The addition of one teaspoon of non-iodized salt per 4 liters of water is beneficial. Temperature 24 to 27°C. **S**: Rarely exceeds 9 cm. **F**: Not a picky eater. Easily adapts to dry food or tubifex worms.

Recent first-hand observations of some of the breeding techniques of lacustrine (lake-dwelling) cichlids in nature have revealed that there are apparently a number of different breeding schemes followed by different species, most resulting in maternal mouthbrooding. One such scheme, used by *Callochromis pleurospilus,* is group spawning.

CALLICHTHYS CALLICHTHYS

CAMPYLOMORMYRUS TAMANDUA (Günther)/*Worm-Jawed Mormyrid*
R: Volta, Niger, Tchad, Shari, and Zaire Basins. **H**: Inhabits quiet pools that have their bottoms covered with fallen logs and trees. This is a very sensitive fish that prefers privacy, quiet, and darkness. **W**: Prefers warm water at a temperature of about 26°C with a pH of 7.2 and as soft as possible. **S**: Aquarium specimens are under 20 cm. **F**: A true bottom-feeding scavenger that eats worms, pelletized dry foods, and frozen brine shrimp.

Go to any small lake or pool in Africa and find yourself a pile of logs, rocks, or fallen branches and you are almost certain to find one of the mormyrids. There are at least one hundred different members of this very interesting family. All have highly specialized mouths and most have dorsal and anal fins that are set back on the last third of the body. Most have a thin caudal peduncle and have the general body shape of a submarine. They are very delicate fish and do best in an aquarium that has been set up and designed especially for them. Their aquarium should have a minimum of light and a maximum of privacy.

CALLOCHROMIS PLEUROSPILUS

CAPOETA HULSTAERTI (Poll)/*Butterfly Barb*

R: Central Zaire region. **H**: Peaceful, almost shy; should be kept only in company with very small fishes or their own kind. **W**: Soft, clean, highly acid water. Temperature about 26°C. Should be moved from tank to tank as little as possible. **S**: 2.5 cm; mostly a little smaller. **F**: Small live foods preferred.

Original shipments contained only males, which are easily distinguished by their yellow dorsal, anal, and ventral fins. As the specimens at hand died and were dissected, the truth finally dawned and African shippers began to collect females as well as males and ship them out. Nevertheless, although the fish has been with us for many years now, it is seldom bred. The few successful breeders tell us that it breeds like the other barbs by depositing its eggs in bushy plants. The fry are tiny and spawnings are small. Raising them is quite a task.

CAPOETA OLIGOLEPIS

CAPOETA FASCIATUS (Jerdon)/*Ember Barb*

R: India. **H**: Peaceful and active; a good jumper. **W**: Soft, slightly acid water. Temperature 23 to 26°C. **S**: 8 cm. **F**: Takes both live and prepared foods.

The male, when in condition, takes on a beautiful red color accentuated by the dusky black of the fins. Luckily, the red coloring is kept throughout the year, even outside spawning time, but it is most bright during the spawning period. The female, normally plain in color, also takes on a red hue at this time, but she is never as intensely colored as the male. The Ember Barb spawns in the usual barb manner, but the males are very hard drivers, and harm might come to the females if sufficient hiding space is not provided.

CAPOETA HULSTAERTI

CAPOETA OLIGOLEPIS Bleeker/*Checker Barb*

R: Sumatra. **H**: Peaceful and active. **W**: Soft, slightly acid water is desirable, but small variations in water composition are easily withstood. Temperature 23 to 26°C. **S**: About 5 cm. **F**: Takes all foods.

The Checker Barb is small, hardy, peaceful, easy to breed, and active; although by no means brilliant, it is an attractive fish. In prime condition, the fins of the male take on a pleasing red-orange hue, and the coloring of the upper portion of his body becomes darker, providing a handsome contrast. When in good condition, it is very easy to tell the sexes apart, but even when the male has not assumed his courting dress there is little difficulty, for the female is fuller and the black edging of her dorsal fin is less pronounced. For so small a species, the scales are quite large and distinct, which adds to the attractiveness of the fish. The Checker Barb spawns in typical barb fashion.

CAPOETA FASCIATUS

CAPOETA SEMIFASCIOLATUS (Günther)/*Half-Striped Barb*

R: Southern China. **H**: Peaceful. **W**: Soft, slightly acid water; tank should be densely planted. Temperature 21 to 27°C. **S**: 7 cm. **F**: Takes live, frozen, and dry foods.

Prefers a medium to large aquarium (larger than 50 liters) that is placed in a sunny position. Although it will stand temperatures in the range given above, 22 to 24°C is ideal. The tank should contain some plants but not enough to cramp the overall swimming area.

The male *Capoeta semifasciolatus* is slimmer than the female and more colorful. This is most noticeable around spawning time. During the pre-spawning courtship the male approaches the female with his dancing body in an oblique position. He tries to coax her into the plants where the eggs will be laid.

CAQUETAIA KRAUSSI

CAPOETA TETRAZONA (Bleeker)/*Tiger Barb, Sumatra Barb*

R: Sumatra, Borneo. **H**: A very active fish and a fast swimmer; inclined to nip the fins of slower species. **W**: Soft, slightly acid water. Temperature 21 to 29°C. **S**: Up to 8 cm. **F**: Takes both live and prepared foods. Should also have vegetable matter included in diet. **C**: Sides brassy yellow, interrupted by four black stripes. Bottom portion of dorsal fin black, upper portion trimmed in red; upper and lower lobes of tail and ventral fins red; snout red. A number of varieties, including an albino, are also available.

The Tiger Barb has much to recommend it. It is flashily colorful, hardy, easy to breed, and usually in good supply. About the only drawback the fish has is that it is inclined to nip its tankmates. Long-finned fishes are usually the victims in these cases, but the Tiger Barb is not particular in its choice and other fishes are also pursued. Oddly enough, some schools of Tiger Barbs are kept in a community tank without ever doing any damage; in this regard, one or two *C. tetrazona* are likely to do more fin nipping than six or seven, presumably because the barbs in the larger group are so busy chasing each other that they don't have time to bother other species. For spawning *C. tetrazona,* which spawns in typical barb fashion, use water that is softer than the water in which they are customarily maintained. For example, if their regular tank water is 8 DH, they will spawn more readily in water of 6 DH. The fry are small at first but grow rapidly.

CAPOETA SEMIFASCIOLATUS

CAQUETAIA KRAUSSI (Steindachner)/*Sharpheaded Cichlid*
R: Northern Colombia and northwestern Venezuela from the Rio Atrato to around Maracaibo.
H: Very aggressive; has been compared in temperament to *Hemichromis fasciatus*. **W**: Not
critical. **S**: To about 26 cm total length. **F**: Will eat almost any aquarium fare including small
fishes, beef heart, brine shrimp, etc. Heavy feeders.
Spawning is fairly typical. The pair will cooperate in cleaning a flat rock, piece of slate, or
flowerpot that has been put into the tank for that purpose. The immediate area will also be
cleaned up, which means the removal of any plants or other fishes in the vicinity. A number of
pits are dug in the gravel as well. Immediately before egg deposition the male will tap or nudge
the female repeatedly in the area of her vent. When the female is ready she will lay a string of
eggs on the flat surface and the male will follow along to fertilize them. This continues until all
the eggs are laid and fertilized. Be prepared for a large spawn, as there are reports of more
than 1,000 eggs being deposited at one time, covering a large surface area.

CAPOETA TETRAZONA

CARASSIUS AURATUS

CARASSIUS AURATUS (Linnaeus)/*Goldfish*

R: Originally from China, now introduced into temperate waters the world over. **H**: Peaceful; large-finned specimens should not be kept with other fishes that might nip their fins. **W**: Water characteristics are not critical, but it should be clean and well aerated. Best temperatures 10 to 21°C. **S**: Sizes vary with breeds. Average size in the aquarium 8 to 10 cm. **F**: Prepared and frozen foods taken just as eagerly as live foods. **C**: Has been bred into various colors and color combinations of red, black, white, yellow, etc.

The hobby of fish-keeping owes its popularity more than anything else to the Goldfish. They are mentioned as early as 970 A.D. by the Chinese, and in the sixteenth century the care and breeding of Goldfish, which were at first playthings of the nobility, became commonplace and a number of fancy breeds were developed. Because of their innate love for beauty and living things, the Chinese and Japanese have remained the world leaders in the development and production of the many fancy breeds of Goldfish available today. We see such freakish fish as the Lionheads, Pompons, Telescopes, Celestials, Eggfish, and many others too numerous for this small space. There are fish with short single fins and others with long flowing fins. Some breeds have double fins; some have large, sail-like dorsal fins; and others have no dorsal fin at all. Some are pure white; others are midnight black.

A pair of lilac orandas.

FANCY GOLDFISH VARIETIES

It seems that the lessened popularity of the common Goldfish has come about as a result of the recognition on the part of hobby newcomers of the advantages the true tropical fishes have over Goldfish. However, warm-water fish tanks within the home have not greatly affected the interest in fancy Goldfish varieties. Really good Goldfish of the hard-to-get varieties are eagerly sought after and command high prices.

Red oranda.

Peacock (Jikin).

Azumana shiki.

Female edonoshiki.

Goosehead redcap.

Two views of high back calico ryukins.

U.S.A. bred ranchu goldfish.

Award-winning show oranda goldfish.

Calico oranda Goldfish.

Red and white fantail Goldfish.

CARINOTETRAODON LORTETI

CARINOTETRAODON LORTETI (TIRANT)/*Somphongs' Puffer*
R: Tachin River system of Thailand. **H:** Peaceful toward fishes other than puffers. **W:** For best results the water should be neutral to slightly alkaline and moderately hard. The recommended temperature range is 23 to 26°C. **S:** Attains a length of at least 7 cm in aquaria, possibly larger in the wild. **F:** Live foods, especially snails, are preferred, but pieces of frozen foods are accepted.

This pufferfish is often called Somphongs' Puffer. As in the case of most puffers, it is able to inflate its body to form a sphere when in trouble. It is rather aggressive toward members of its own species as well as other puffers, and its direct attack on the target usually means the demise of the slow-reacting puffers, especially if they are kept together in a relatively small tank. On the other hand, Somphongs' Puffer is relatively peaceful when kept with fishes other than puffers and can be an ideal addition to a community tank.

This species is relatively easy to keep. The water should be moderately hard and with a neutral or slightly alkaline pH. The temperature range should be between 23 and 26°C. Feeding is no problem, although live foods are preferred (especially snails). They accept frozen foods when nothing better is offered. Although puffers are often considered brackish water or even marine fishes, some species, including Somphongs' Puffer, are best kept in pure fresh water.

The color is highly variable, with the dark and light areas changing from time to time. The bright red color of the keel adds to the attractiveness of this species, as does the blue color of the inner part of the caudal fin. All in all this would be an attractive addition to a community tank (as long as no other puffers are kept with it).

CARNEGIELLA MARTHAE Myers/*Black-Winged Hatchetfish*

R: Peru, the Brazilian Amazon, Rio Negro, and the Orinoco in Venezuela. **H**: Active jumpers; have to be kept in a covered tank, preferably a long one. Peaceful; may be kept with other non-aggressive species. **W**: Soft, slightly acid water. Temperature 24 to 27°C. **S**: 4 cm; usually a bit smaller. **F**: Floating prepared foods eaten when very hungry, but live foods like mosquito larvae or wingless fruitflies are best.

The Black-Winged Hatchetfish is the smallest known member of the genus *Carnegiella*. The name *marthae* was given to this species in 1927 by Dr. George S. Myers because they were favorites of his wife Martha. They are easily distinguished from the other hatchetfishes not only by a black ventral edge to the belly, but also a black area inside the long pectoral fins.

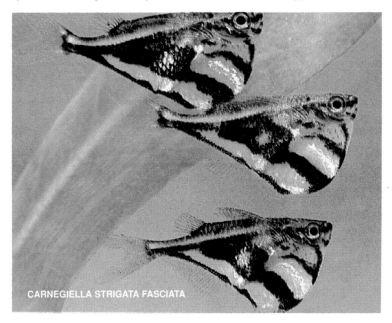

CARNEGIELLA STRIGATA FASCIATA

CARNEGIELLA STRIGATA STRIGATA (Günther)/*Marbled Hatchetfish*

R: Guyana, middle and upper Amazon region, especially in jungle streams. **H**: Occurs in schools near the surface. In the aquarium they are peaceful, but are likely to jump if a cover is not provided. **W**: Soft, slightly acid water. Temperature about 26°C. **S**: About 8 cm. **F**: Will readily accept dried food that floats on the surface, but anything that falls to the bottom cannot be picked up.

Most works say that it has never been bred, but the fact is that it has happened, but only rarely. The sexes can be distinguished by looking at the fish from above; the females are slightly wider in the body. The rare descriptions of the spawning say that tiny eggs are laid in plant clusters at the surface, and to the best of our recollection very few if any of the fry were hatched and raised. One of the obvious assumptions as to why the fish will not spawn readily is that there is some food, possibly winged, that the fish devour in their natural habitat and that the aquarist cannot duplicate.

CARNEGIELLA MARTHAE

CARNEGIELLA STRIGATA FASCIATA (Garman)/*Marbled Hatchetfish*

R: Guyana. **H**: Found in shaded pools where it leaps from the water for insects flying very close to the surface. **W**: Very sensitive to temperature and water changes. Prefers very soft, slightly acid water. Temperature 23 to 26°C. **S**: Under 8 cm. **F**: This species must have small live food. Dropping wingless *Drosophilia* flies onto the surface of the water is an ideal way to feed this species. They also take small amounts of floating foods containing brine shrimp.

It is generally accepted that the hatchetfishes of the subfamily Gasteropelecinae are the only true "flyingfish" that move their pectoral fins to aid in their flight. The other so-called flyingfishes, such as the marine Exocoetidae and the freshwater African *Pantodon,* do not voluntarily move their pectorals in flight but probably use them for stabilization while in "flight." Probably the best food would be mosquito larvae, because these spend a great deal of time at the surface and, being insects, would be the food most relished by a fish that gets its food at the surface.

CARNEGIELLA STRIGATA STRIGATA

CATOPRION MENTO (Cuvier)/*Wimple Piranha*

R: Lower Amazon, Bolivia, Guianas. **H**: Peaceful, but will attack small fishes. **W**: Soft, slightly acid water in a well-planted tank. Temperature 23 to 26°C. **S**: About 10 cm. **F**: Larger live foods are best. Otherwise, frozen foods or bits of fish, shrimp, clams, or oysters.

Catoprion mento has all the ferocious appearance of a true piranha as well as an attractive set of colors of its own, which makes it an interesting aquarium fish capable of being kept in a community tank without danger to its tankmates, unless they are small. They resemble a piranha so convincingly that even the natives who collect them are sometimes fooled. Although the Wimple Piranha cannot compete with the real piranhas in dental equipment, they *do* have small teeth which they will not hesitate to use on something as small as a Guppy or Neon Tetra. In nature the fish is a scale-eater.

CHACA CHACA

CENTRARCHUS MACROPTERUS (Lacépède)/*Flier*

R: Southern United States; Texas to Virginia and the Mississippi Valley. **H**: An aggressive territorial fish that is best kept with other fishes of equal size or larger. **W**: Neutral to alkaline water of moderate hardness. Temperature 15 to 22°C. **S**: To 18 cm in nature but rarely exceeds 10 cm in captivity. **F**: Earthworms, crickets, and small crayfish, but will accept guppies and small chunks of beef.

At least partly because of its small size, the Flier readily adapts to a captive existence. It should, however, be kept only with other temperate species, as it does not adapt well to warmer water that most tropical species are kept in. The Flier can usually be found in weedy ponds or near weed beds along the sandy shores of lakes and rivers. It is best to start with young fish about 3 cm in length, as the young ones will more readily adapt to aquarium foods.

Being a temperate-water fish, *Centrarchus macropterus* spawns on a seasonal basis, usually once in the spring and often again in the late summer. It should be kept fairly cool between spawnings, as the cooler water will amplify its coloration.

CATOPRION MENTO

CHACA CHACA (Hamilton-Buchanan)/*Frogmouth Catfish*

R: India. **H**: Nocturnal, sedentary. Should not be kept with smaller fishes. **W**: Not critical. Temperatures around 24°C are best. **S**: Reaches 20 cm. **F**: Will eat any living or frozen food, but prefers earthworms.

This bizarre catfish is one of three members of its family, the Chacidae. The tough skin, numerous barbels, fleshy processes on the head, broad mouth, and tadpole-like shape combine to make this a unique fish. Flattened fish are usually found on the bottom, and *Chaca* is no exception.

The Frogmouth is a nocturnal catfish, coming out to feed only at night. It requires a heavily shaded aquarium with many plants or caves in which to hide during the day. The gigantic mouth enables it to swallow large fishes, so it should never be put in a tank with smaller fishes.

CENTRARCHUS MACROPTERUS

CHAETOBRANCHOPSIS BITAENIATUS (Ahl)/*Two-Striped Cichlid*

R: Middle Amazon basin and Guianas. **H**: Said to be peaceful and not grub up the bottom. **W**: Not critical. Temperature 24 to 27°C. Once they have become established, they should be moved as little as possible. **S**: To 12 cm. **F**: Seem to prefer the larger live foods, but can be acclimated to chunks of beef heart.

This is a fish which is rarely collected, but a few young specimens sometimes come in masquerading as either "unknown" species or something else. When mature, most of them get such a ragged appearance on the anal fin that they look as if they came out second best in battle. This is a normal characteristic, however, and actually the species is said to be quite peaceful in the few accounts we get. Personally the author is of the opinion that Mother Nature did not give them such a big mouth for nothing and would hesitate to put one in mixed company or with a number of others unless the tank were heavily planted and contained a number of hiding places.

CHALINOCHROMIS BRICHARDI

CHALCEUS MACROLEPIDOTUS Cuvier/*Pink-Tailed Chalceus*

R: Guyana, Surinam and French Guiana. **H**: Peaceful if kept in a school with no small fishes in the same tank. **W**: Not critical; best temperature about 25°C. Once they have become established, they should be moved as little as possible. **S**: To 25 cm. **F**: Generous feedings are necessary, using earthworms, tubifex worms or chopped beef heart.

This is another fish which is often offered by dealers while it is still very young, and it grows and grows until it has become too big for all available tanks. If given an aquarium of at least 200 liters capacity which is well planted and aerated, a group of about a half-dozen *Chalceus macrolepidotus* makes a very attractive picture. They are active and always on the move, and their big scales have a highly metallic gleam. When in particularly good condition, the fins as well as the tail become bright red. They are excellent jumpers, and when being seined in their native Guyana waters most of them will leap nimbly over the net rather than let themselves be caught. A glass cover on their aquarium is therefore essential if one does not want to find them on the floor some morning. When in Guyana, the author noticed that the Indians were always quick to pounce upon these fish when their large size made it advisable to discard them. They considered them a delicacy which they seldom got otherwise, because their slender shape and active habits made it difficult to shoot them with a bow and arrow, the Indians' accepted method of catching fish.

CHAETOBRANCHOPSIS BITAENIATUS

CHALINOCHROMIS BRICHARDI Poll/*Brichardi*

R: Lake Tanganyika, Africa. **H**: Not especially vicious. A good aquarium fish when kept with species of its own size. **W**: Hard, alkaline water, DH 10 to 20; pH 7.5 to 9.0. Temperature 24 to 26°C. **S**: 15 cm in nature; slightly smaller in the aquarium. **F**: An omnivorous feeder requiring some vegetable matter in its diet. Will readily take frozen and prepared dry foods.

Although these fish are substrate spawners, they do not lay their eggs out in the open, as do some of their substrate spawning relatives. Rather, they prefer to spawn in the dark recesses of caves and crevices. Accordingly, they should be provided with plenty of rocks or inverted clay flowerpots with small openings cut in them. Once they have spawned, usually one parent at a time performs the brooding duties while the other stands guard outside the spawning area. Since the eggs are concealed, it is not known exactly how long it takes them to hatch. The fry make their first appearance at about one cm in length when the parents guide them out of the cave for their first foraging experience. They are usually abandoned by their parents when they reach two cm in length. These fish go through several color phases as they mature.

CHALCEUS MACROLEPIDOTUS

CHANDA BURUENSIS (Bleeker)/*Siamese Glassfish*

R: Thailand, Malaysia, Sumatra, Celebes, and the Philippines. **H**: Best kept by themselves. Even then, two males in the same tank might pick on each other. **W**: Native to brackish waters, which must be duplicated in the aquarium by adding 2 teaspoonsful of salt to every 4 liters of water. Temperature about 26°C. **S**: Aquarium-raised specimens usually under 5 cm. **F**: Small living foods such as newly hatched brine shrimp and small worms. Dry foods taken only when starving.

Males are likely to have little disagreements, and for this reason a tank that affords some opportunity for concealment where the defeated ones can escape the bullying of their victors is recommended. They spawn readily, but the resulting fry are very small and getting them to a size where they can handle larger foods is a real problem. A good rotifer culture would be the answer, but these are not always very easy to come by.

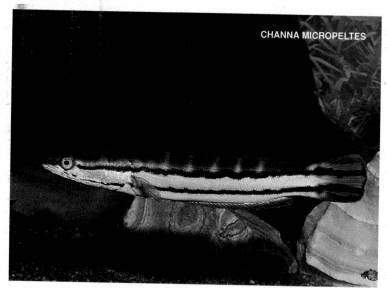

CHANNA MICROPELTES

CHANNA MICROPELTES (Cuvier)/*Red Snakehead*

R: Southeast Asia, into India. **H**: A voracious, greedy species, but not everything that it kills is destined to serve as food, as it often kills without eating the fishes it has destroyed. **W**: Not critical; this is a very hardy and adaptable fish. **S**: Up to 1 meter; usually offered for sale at 8 to 10 cm. **F**: Eats most meaty (living and non-living) foods when young; in large sizes it prefers live fishes and amphibians but will take large chunks of meat. **C**: As the fish grows older the red stripe becomes much less intense, gradually fading to a muddy tan or into blotches instead of an uninterrupted stripe.

Channa micropeltes, formerly called *Ophiocephalus micropeltes,* has been offered in the aquarium hobby more frequently over the last few years than it has been in the past, even though it has been known to aquarists for a long time from sporadic importations. In one way at least it is a very satisfactory aquarium fish, because it is one of the most hardy known. Possessed of an auxiliary breathing apparatus, it is capable of withstanding exceedingly foul water conditions in its aquarium, being sensitive on only one point of aquarium management, water temperature; the species is highly susceptible to bad effects caused by chilling. Despite its hardiness and the obviously colorful appearance of young specimens, however, the Red Snakehead definitely is a fish to avoid for someone with limited facilities, for it is one of the greatest killers known among aquarium fishes. If its habit of destruction were reserved only for fishes that are intended to serve as food, the situation wouldn't be as bad, but the fact is that the Red Snakehead often kills and just ignores its victim, leaving it lying around the tank to rot. In its smaller sizes the fish is necessarily less destructive than when it has begun to put on real growth, but many a community tank of small fishes has been quickly wiped out after the tank's unsuspecting owner had innocently introduced a seemingly harmless and attractive Red Snakehead. As the fish grows it becomes a menace to just about everything that can get within its reach, and it is entirely willing and capable of literally biting the hand that feeds it. In its home waters in Asia fully grown meter-long individuals guarding their young have been known to attack people entering the water.

A *Channa* species on the prowl.

CHANNALLABES APUS (Günther)/*Eel Catfish*

R: Zaire and Angola regions. **H**: Mostly nocturnal. Young specimens will not bother the other fishes, but it is best to keep larger ones by themselves. **W**: Not critical. Temperature 21 to 24°C. **S**: Up to 30 cm. **F**: Greedy eaters that will consume great amounts of tubifex worms. Other foods may be substituted, such as beef heart or pieces of fish.

The body is laterally compressed and the dorsal, caudal, and anal fins form an unbroken line from the back to the anus. The ventral fins are missing completely. The head is very small and at first sight one might be led to believe that a large brown worm had somehow gotten into the aquarium. They are very hardy and long-lived, and because of an accessory breathing organ they are not dependent upon the oxygen in their aquarium water. They get to be about 30 cm long and have never to our knowledge been spawned in captivity.

CHARACIDIUM FASCIATUM

CHAPALICHTHYS PARDALIS Alvarez/*Polka-dot Goodeid*

R: Spring-fed upper tributary of the Rio Balsas, Rio Lerma basin, Mexico. **H**: A very active, non-aggressive goodeid that could make a decent community species as long as it is not housed with a slow-moving long-finned species such as fancy guppies. **W**: Not critical, but water that is on the hard, alkaline side is best. A teaspoon of sea salt per gallon may be added. Temperatures of 26° to 28 °C are suggested. **S**: Females attain a length of up to about 6 cm, males slightly smaller. **F**: Will accept a wide variety of aquarium foods. No problems with feeding should be encountered.

The Polka-dot Goodeid is not very shy and in fact is very active. They always seem to be on the move chasing each other—especially males chasing females. Unfortunately, males chasing females all the time does not mean that insemination occurs every time. In fact, it probably occurs on average only twice a month. That, coupled with the inability of females to store sperm and the 45-day gestation period, makes these fish less prolific than most of the more common poeciliids wherein the gestation period is only 30 days or so and the females are able to store sperm for future release of young. An average of about 15 fry are dropped each time. These fry are about 15-20 mm in length and generally are ignored by the parents.

CHANNALLABES APUS

CHARACIDIUM FASCIATUM Reinhardt/*Banded Characidium*
R: South America, Orinoco region in the north to La Plata region in the south. **H**: Comes from streams where there is some current; therefore requires fresh, clean water in an uncrowded aquarium. **W**: Clean, well-oxygenerated water, about neutral. Temperatures should not exceed 24°C. **S**: 6 cm. **F**: Not a fussy eater, but prefers living foods.

The Banded Characidium stays mostly in the lower reaches of the aquarium and often digs into the gravel for bits of food. Males are recognizable by their larger fins, which are yellowish in color. Spawning is accomplished in the lower parts of the tank, and as many as 150 eggs may result. The very tiny eggs hatch in 30 to 40 hours, and the fry begin to swim in 3 days. Remaining near the bottom as they do, they often are undetected until they have grown considerably.

CHAPALICHTHYS PARDALIS

CHARACODON LATERALIS Gunther/*Rainbow Goodeid*

R: Lowland streams from Central America north to Jalisco in Mexico. **H:** Should be kept in a single-species tank rather than a community tank. The males may be a bit aggressive toward females. **W:** Needs very clean water with a pH of not less than 7.4. A temperature range of 23° to 27°C is sufficient. **S:** The male attains a length of about 45 mm; the female grows larger, reaching a length of about 55 mm. **F:** Will generally eat typical aquarium fare, but prefers a goodly amount of live foods.

Males are a bit aggressive toward females, but there is rarely any serious damage done. Males also fight among themselves, so it is best to keep only one male for up to three females. For spawning, two or three males should be placed with six to eight females. Normally the bottom cover of Java moss will suffice for protection of the fry and adults, but this livebearer is extremely cannibalistic on its fry and it is usually necessary to trap the female in order to save as many of the four or five young produced as possible.

CHEIRODON KRIEGI

CHARAX GIBBOSUS (Linnaeus)/*Glass Headstander*

R: Guianas, lower and middle Amazon region, and Rio Paraguay. **H:** Perfectly peaceful and harmless. **W:** Not critical. Temperature should average about 24°C. **S:** 15 cm; aquarium specimens are usually much smaller. **F:** Prefers live foods, but dried foods may be fed when others are not available.

Because of its lack of colors, this is a fish that is not often imported and still more seldom bred. Males are slightly smaller than their mates and have a more slender build. Because of their size, a large aquarium is required if spawning is desired. If some bundles of bushy plants are provided, the fish soon lose much of their accustomed sluggishness and courtship begins. Eggs are released among the plants, and the spawning is apt to be quite large. The incubation period is 30 hours, and the resulting fry are very small. The first days are critical, and an abundance of infusoria is essential.

CHARACODON LATERALIS

CHEIRODON KRIEGI Schindler/*Three-Spot Tetra*

R: Upper Guaporé River, Brazil. **H**: Perfectly peaceful and not a bit shy. **W**: Not critical; best is slightly acid, soft water. Temperature 24 to 27°C. **S**: 5 cm. **F**: Not a fussy eater; dried foods are accepted equally as well as live or frozen fare.

In a tank of mixed species it quickly makes itself at home, and I have never seen one attack another fish. In the photograph the lower fish is the male and the upper the female. The fact that there is a black spot in the same place as the "gravid spot" of the livebearing species is no indication that the fish is ready to spawn, and if there have even been any spawnings we have not heard of them. This is not a popular aquarium fish, and there have been few importations of them into the United States or Europe.

CHARAX GIBBOSUS

CHELA CAERULEOSTIGMATA (Smith)/*Siamese Hatchetfish*

R: Thailand. **H:** Peaceful and should be kept only with non-aggressive species. It is a jumper, so the tank should be well covered. **W:** The water chemistry is not critical. There should be sufficient aeration, and a temperature range of 25° to 28°C is recommended. **S:** Attains a length of 7 to 8 cm. **F:** Will accept any good aquarium foods, but prefers live foods such as mosquito larvae, *Daphnia*, and brine shrimp.

For spawning, a long tank of at least one meter is necessary and must be supplied with nylon mops or clumps of Java moss as spawning sites. Plump females should be separated and conditioned for three or four days on a highly nutritious and varied diet. The male should be added in the evening, and the tank should be inspected closely for eggs for the next two days. If none are present, remove the male and continue to condition the female until the next try. Siamese Hatchetfish like highly oxygenated turbulent water and may decide to spawn close to the stream of air bubbles from the airstone, so it may be advantageous for observation to move the airstone to the center of the tank. The adults are not reported to be egg-eaters, but for safety's sake it is best to remove them once spawning has occurred or to remove the spawning mops to a smaller tank where the eggs can be hatched under more controllable conditions. An average spawn may be in the neighborhood of 100 to 300 eggs. It is recommended that the free-swimming fry be moved to a tank of about 20-40 liters, as it is not advisable to feed in a tank with unhatched eggs. The first foods should be infusoria and microworms. After about a week, newly hatched brine shrimp and small daphnia can be tried.

CHELA LAUBUCA

CHELA DADIBURJORI Menon/*Dadio*

R: Vicinity of Bombay, India. **H:** Active fish that, if possible, should be kept in a small group; a jumper, so keep their tank covered. **W:** soft to medium-hard water. temperature 22 to 25°C. S: 3 cm. **F:** Accepts dried foods as enthusiastically as live or frozen foods.

The Dadio is never likely to win any prizes for its coloration alone, but it has everything else to recommend it. It is active, gregarious, and will accept anything in the food line that comes its way. It is not particularly sensitive to water conditions and seems to breed readily. The specific name honors its discoverer, Shri Sam J. Dadyburjor of Bombay, India. In June, 1960, we received a few specimens and sent them to Mr. E. Roloff in Karlsruhe, Germany. He gave them a long tank of their own, such as is used for spawning the *Danio* species. In one corner he placed a nylon "mop," which is merely a tassel of nylon yarn attached to a cork to make it float. The tank was otherwise bare and the fish had no choice but to spawn in the nylon threads. Mr. Roloff thinks, however, that they normally attach their eggs to the underside of a broad plant leaf. There were less than 100 eggs laid, and the parents were removed immediately afterward. Hatching began on the next day, but the fry did not begin to swim until the sixth day.

CHELA CAERULEOSTIGMATA

CHELA LAUBUCA (Hamilton-Buchanan)/*Indian Hatchetfish*

R: India, Burma, Sumatra and Malaysia. **H**: Peaceful fish that prefers the upper reaches of the aquarium; active swimmers and skilled jumpers, so keep their aquarium covered. **W**: Neutral to slightly acid, soft water for spawning; otherwise water conditions are unimportant. Temperature 24 to 27°C. **S**: Up to 6 cm. **F**: Will eat any food; being top-feeders, they prefer a food that does not sink rapidly.

Here we have a fish that is quite attractively colored, easily fed, not difficult to spawn, and easy to keep; still, hobbyists never seem to get excited about it. This is a paradox that exists with some species. Sometimes, suddenly, a fish "catches on," and people who have known and avoided a particular species for years suddenly fall all over each other to get them. The spawning act of *Chela laubuca* is interesting. An aquarium with a large water surface is best. There need be no precautions against the eating of eggs by the parents; if well-fed they show little inclination to do so. Males are distinguished by their thinner bodies and brighter colors, and little attention is paid to the females until about dusk. After an active pursuit the male embraces the female from the left with his fins, and a large number of eggs result. They hatch in about 24 hours at a temperature of 26°C.

CHELA DADIBURJORI

CHILODUS PUNCTATUS

CHILODUS PUNCTATUS Müller & Troschel/*Spotted Headstander*
R: Northeastern South America between the Amazon and the Orinoco. **H**: Very peaceful; pays little attention to the other fishes. Rather shy, and should be moved as little as possible. **W**: Slightly acid to neutral water, very soft. Temperature should range between 24 to 27°C. **S**: About 9 cm. **F**: Diet should be largely vegetarian; lettuce or spinach leaves are nibbled frequently. Some dried food and live food also.

The Spotted Headstander swims in a normally head-down position and is very fond of nibbling algae from rocks and plants. Females are about 1 cm longer than the males, and the body is considerably heavier. A large aquarium is preferred, with much clear space for swimming. During spawning a remarkable change in coloration takes place. The horizontal line disappears and a large, round, dark shoulder spot, which is visible at no other time, shows up. Non-adhesive eggs are released near the surface and sink unmolested to the bottom.

CHILOTILAPIA RHOADESI (Boulenger)/*Rhoades' Chilo*

R: Endemic to Lake Malawi. **H:** Aggressive toward members of its own species. Should be kept with similar large cichlids. **W:** Needs hard, alkaline water with a pH of 7.2 to 8.6. Temperature range 23 to 28°C. **S:** Reaches a length of about 22 cm. **F:** A snail-eater in nature, but will accept most aquarium foods eagerly.

Chilotilapia rhoadesi is an African cichlid from Lake Malawi and in general should do well in tanks suitable to other species from that lake. It was first discovered by Captain E.L. Rhoades in Lake Nyasa (Lake Malawi) and brought back to the British Museum, where Boulenger named it in his honor.

Chilotilapia rhoadesi is a large fish attaining a length of more than 20 cm, and it should be housed in a suitably large tank (preferably 400 liters or more). In nature it seems to prefer areas with sandy bottoms, and its aquarium should have a layer of sand or gravel as well. Large robust plants can be used for decoration along with a scattering of rocks which are arranged to provide some protection to other fishes if and when needed. It is not necessary to set up the tank with a great deal of rockwork as one would for mbunas. Most aggression is directed against members of its own species (especially males against males), but *C. rhoadesi* will generally tend to dominate other fishes as well. A single male with several females is recommended.

Chilotilapila rhoadesi has not been bred in the aquarium (possibly due to its large size), but a female with a mouthful of eggs has been kept successfully. The differences between the sexes outside the breeding season are difficult to see, but breeding males can be easily recognized since they lose the lateral pattern and take on an overall sky blue color.

This species is the only member of its genus and is probably related to certain members of the genus *Haplochromis* (for example *H. placodon).* It is widespread in the lake, occurring in the southern parts as well as the northern.

CHITALA ORNATA

CHITALA ORNATA (Gray)/*Clown Knife Fish*

R: Mekong, Chao Phraya, and Meklong River basins. **H**: Mostly nocturnal, and peaceful at small sizes but distinctly predatory at larger sizes; will usually not bother other fishes about equal to them in size, but will quarrel with members of their own species. **W**: Soft, acidic water preferred; temperature should be maintained at 24 to 27°C. **S**: In nature, to about 90 cm at the maximum; never seen this large under aquarium conditions. **F**: Live foods, worms especially, are readily accepted, as are most frozen foods; dry foods are not always accepted by fish over 10 cm long.

Chitala attaches masses of eggs to upright structures such as large plants. The male devotedly guards the eggs, which hatch within six days at a temperature of about 32°C according to Dr. Hugh M. Smith. This abnormally high temperature might not be too much out of line when you consider the tropical areas the fish inhabit and the fact that the waters in which they live are usually slow-moving or stagnant, allowing the temperature to build up.

CHRIOPEOIDES PENGELLEYI

CHRIOPEOIDES PENGELLEYI Fowler/*Jamaican Pupfish*

R: Southwestern Jamaica. **H:** Peaceful and easily spawned. Does best in a single-species tank with 2 males and 4 females. **W:** Not critical, but prefers harder, alkaline water with a bit of salt added. Cannot stand sudden changes. **S:** Males to 6 cm, females to 5 cm. **F:** Eats almost any normal aquarium foods.

The Jamaican Pupfish was named by Fowler in 1939. The generic name was selected because of the fish's supposed resemblance to the Rainwater Killifish, *Lucania goodei*, which at that time was called *Chriopeops goodei*. Parenti suggested that *Chriopeoides* should be synonymized with *Cubanichthys*, the name becoming *Cubanichthys pengelleyi*

This species has a fairly good disposition and is easy to breed. Sexes are readily distinguishable. Males grow faster than females and are correspondingly larger (to 6 cm as opposed to 5 cm for females) as well as deeper bodied. Some males also develop a nuchal hump or gibbosity. The lateral stripe of males is also broader and more diffuse, with the portion from the snout to just behind the head very dark and distinct; the dusky anal stripe seen in the female is also absent. If seen in the proper reflected light, males have a delicate greenish to bluish iridescent sheen on their sides.

The Jamaican Pupfish is a continual spawner and is usually most alive in the early morning hours. Males will dance around the females and dart off to challenge other males, the dominant males winning the right to court the females. The courting males try to entice the females into the fine-leaved plants. If a female is ready to spawn she will comply and maintain a position in the plants. The male will react immediately by "plastering" himself against the side of the female. After a short interval they break apart with a sudden jerk, releasing eggs and sperm as they do. The eggs, about 1.2-1.5 mm in diameter, are adhesive, sticking to the plants. If you wish a large percentage of healthy fry, collect the eggs daily and hatch them separately. Hatching occurs in anywhere from 9 to 14 days depending upon temperature. The fry will accept a wide variety of suitably sized foods. Infusoria, rotifers, and newly hatched brine shrimp are suggested. The fry grow quickly and are ready to spawn in about three months.

CHROMIDOTILAPIA GUENTHERI (Sauvage)/*Günther's Mouthbrooder*

R: West Africa, Sierra Leone to Cameroon. **H**: Aggressive, especially to others of its own species. **W**: Hard, alkaline water preferred and best for spawning. Temperature 24 to 27°C. **S**: 15 cm; smaller specimens most usually offered for sale. **F**: Accepts all meaty live, frozen, and freeze-dried foods.

After the spawning pair has established a territory within the tank, male and female join in scooping out a depression in the gravel bottom. After the eggs have been laid and fertilized, the male picks them up and carries them mouthbrooder fashion during the incubation period and until they are able to fend for themselves. During this time, the female is very zealous in helping the male drive off intruders into their territory, and she helps shepherd the free-swimming fry on the occasions that they leave the male's mouth. In this species the female is slightly more colorful than the male, exhibiting a reddish area around the belly that is completely missing in the male.

CICHLA OCELLARIS

CHRYSICHTHYS ORNATUS Boulenger/*Ornate Congo Catfish*

R: Central Africa, particularly Congo to the Cameroons. **H**: Not aggressive with larger fishes, but not to be trusted with smaller ones. **W**: Not critical. **S**: Attains a length of up to 26 cm or more. **F**: Will accept a wide variety of aquarium foods and will benefit from regular feedings of live foods.

The Ornate Congo Catfish does well in captivity until it starts to outgrow its tank. It is not aggressive and may be included in a community tank as long as the fishes there are large enough to take care of themselves. Smaller fishes are generally looked upon as potential food, even those half its own length. There may be an occasional difference of opinion with the larger fishes, but these usually are settled quickly and without damage to either party. The water chemistry is not critical although a pH on the acid side would be closer to the natural habitat. Temperatures can be in a range normally used for tropical fishes. Feeding the Ornate Congo Catfish is no problem. Although in the wild the diet of the smaller individuals includes insect larvae and small crustaceans, with the larger individuals adding fishes to this menu, most typical aquarium foods are accepted. Brine shrimp, bloodworms, and other frozen foods are good, and if a feeder fish is added once in a while there should be no problem in keeping this catfish.

190

CHROMIDOTILAPIA GUENTHERI

CICHLA OCELLARIS (Bloch & Schneider)/*Peacock Cichlid, Lukanani*

R: Widely distributed throughout tropical South America, except in the La Plata System. **H**: A predatory fish that cannot be kept with smaller species; it will even attack others of its own size. **W**: A large, well-aerated aquarium is an absolute necessity. Temperature about 25°C. **S**: To 75 cm. **F**: Will eat only living things like large earthworms, smaller fish, dragonfly and other large insect larvae, tadpoles, etc.

In nature *Cichla ocellaris* spawns in shallow water. As spawning time approaches, mature males develop a hump behind the head and their coloration intensifies. Holes are dug in the mud and several nests are formed. The female lays over eight thousands eggs. After the eggs hatch, both parents guard the young fry for about three weeks; the male then chases the female away so that he can guard the young on his own. This fish can be recommended only for extremely large aquaria, pools, or ponds.

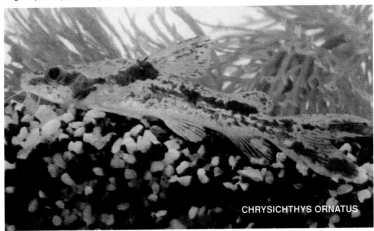

CHRYSICHTHYS ORNATUS

CICHLASOMA BIMACULATUM (Linnaeus)/Two-Spot Cichlid

R: The Guianas. **H**: Typical cichlid, but not as nasty as some. Should not be kept with smaller fishes. **W**: Not critical; slightly alkaline is best, but not too hard. Temperature 23 to 26°C. **S**: To 20 cm; in the aquarium it seldom attains 15 cm. **F**: Live or frozen foods, or substitutes like beef heart, pieces of raw clam, mussel, shrimp, etc.

This is not one of the brilliantly colored cichlids. As the fish gets older most of the colors fade to a silvery gray and the two spots on the sides that were scarcely noticeable become very prominent. Once a pair have become accustomed to each other they get along well and usually make excellent parents. Of course, the best way to assure good breeding pairs is to raise about a half-dozen young ones together and then allow them to make their own selections.

CLARIAS ANGOLENSIS

CICHLASOMA PORTALEGRENSIS (Hensel)/Port Acara, Black Acara

R: Santa Catarina, Rio Grande do Sul, Bolivia, Paraguay, Rio Uruguay. **H**: Moderately peaceful, but should not be kept with smaller fishes. Will do some digging, and some plants may be uprooted. **W**: Not critical. Temperature 22 to 24°C. Large aquaria are recommended because spawns are often large. **S**: 12.5 cm; attains maturity at 7.5 cm. **F**: Has a robust appetite, and to the usual menu of live foods may be added such items as chopped beef heart, canned dog food, etc. **C**: Body greenish brown; each scale has a dark border. Dorsal, anal and caudal fins have a reticulated pattern.

A popular cichlid species, and one of the easiest to breed. Sexes are fairly easy to distinguish. Females are slightly smaller, and males have long, flowing dorsal and anal fins. This species is likely to do some digging, and therefore plants with a firm root-stock, such as the Cryptocoryne species or Sagittaria, should be preferred. A rock with a flat surface should also be provided. When the parents are ready to spawn, and with a healthy pair this will be quite often, they will clean off this rock and deposit on it a great many eggs. Parental caring is usually very tender, and a family of these fish is an intriguing thing to watch. Young hatch in four to five days, as is usual with cichlids, after which time the parents dig a number of shallow depressions in the bottom gravel. The fry are moved from one to the other of these depressions, and any youngster with the temerity to try to swim away is promptly gobbled up by the parent and spat back into the protection of the depression.

CICHLASOMA BIMACULATUM

CLARIAS ANGOLENSIS Steindachner / *Brown Clarias*

R: Widespread through western central Africa. **H**: A voracious catfish not to be trusted with smaller fishes. **W**: Needs warm water, 24 to 30°C, but is not otherwise demanding as to water characteristics. **S**: Up to 36 cm. **F**: Takes all meaty foods; live tubifex worms are preferred by small individuals of the species.

CICHLASOMA PORTALEGRENSIS

CLARIAS BATRACHUS Linnaeus/*Pla Duk Dam, Albino Clarias*

R: India, Sri Lanka, Burma, Malaysia, East Indies, Philippines, Indochina, and Thailand. **H**: An amazing fish that jumps out of aquaria and walks for long distances without dying. **W**: Hardy and tolerant to any water that is not too salty or too cold. Can tolerate temperatures from 10 to 32°C. **S**: Grows to at least 46 cm in nature. **F**: Eats anything usually offered to aquarium fishes. The catfishes of the genus *Clarias* are an extremely interesting group of fishes, for they have a huge accessory breathing organ in the branchial cavity that enables them to utilize atmospheric oxygen in the same way that higher animals do. As a result, their gills have atrophied to the point where they are practically useless and it has been demonstrated that if they are maintained in an aquarium with a floating glass cover, so that they are unable to reach atmospheric air to breathe, they die of suffocation.

COBITIS TAENIA

CLEITHRACARA MARONI (Steindachner)/*Keyhole Cichlid*

R: Surinam, Demarara River, Guyana. **H**: Very peaceful, has been known to breed in community aquaria without molesting the other fishes. Seldom uproots plants. **W**: Clean water, neutral to slightly acid. Temperatures should be a bit higher than for other cichlids of its type, about 28 to 30°C. **S**: begins to breed at 6.5 cm. **F**: Live foods of all kinds, but not too large.

Sexes are not easy to distinguish, as both develop long filaments on the dorsal and anal fins. This is a beautiful, highly desirable cichlid; the only thing which can be said against it is that it is not very easy to spawn. Sexes are not easy to distinguish, as both develop long filaments on the dorsal and anl fins. However, when they are ready to spawn and the breeding tubes begin to project from the vent, it will be noticed that the female's tube is heavier. A well-mated pair will spawn in the usual cichlid manner: a smooth surface is cleaned off and the eggs are placed there and fertilized. Both fish usually take turns fanning and mouthing the eggs, which can number up to 300 but are usually less. Hatching takes place in 5 days, and the parents usually take excellent care of their offspring, but of course there are exceptions.

The "Keyhole" part of the common name of course derives from the dark mark running vertically down the sides of the fish shortly behind mid-body. This mark is not entirely constant and varies in size and intensity not only from fish to fish but also from time to time on the same fish.

CLARIAS BATRACHUS

COBITIS TAENIA Linnaeus/*Weatherfish, Spined Loach*

R: Extremely wide, covering parts of both Europe and Asia. **H**: Peaceful and inclined toward shyness. **W**: Water conditions for this species are not of special importance, as long as extremes of pH and DH are avoided. Can take temperatures lower than 16°C, but a range in the low 20's (°C) is best. **S**: Up to 10 cm. **F**: Takes all foods, but particularly likes living foods that congregate near the bottom, such as worms.

The range of this fish is so wide that many authorities, no doubt working at least in part on the theory that no single animal should be allowed to cover so much territory, have broken the species up into at least seven subspecies according to geographical origin. No matter where it comes from, this little loach is a peaceful addition to the community tank, where it is most often kept as a scavenger under the mistaken notion that the fish lives by choice on leftover food particles. It is said that weather can be predicted from the actions of this fish.

CLEITHRACARA MARONI

COIUS MICROLEPIS (Bleeker)/*Siamese Tiger Fish*

R: Thailand, Sumatra, and Borneo. **H**: Peaceful; will not harm any fish it cannot swallow. **W**: Neutral to slightly acid. Temperature 23 to 26°C. **S**: To 38 cm in its natural waters; much smaller in the aquarium **F**: Larger live foods or chunks of shrimp or raw lean beef. **C**: Body yellow to cream or pinkish, with black vertical bars.

We have had reports that when a *C. micolepis* is displeased with its surroundings it not only sulks but loses its yellow coloring and becomes almost entirely black. Feeding is not much of a problem. Smith, in his book *The Freshwater Fishes of Siam, or Thailand*, mentions keeping them in an aquarium where they thrived on shrimp and raw meat. They have not yet been bred in captivity, and it still remains to be seen if they attain maturity at the smaller sizes attained in the aquarium.

COLISA CHUNA

COIUS QUADRIFASCIATUS (Sevastianov)/
Many-Barred Tiger Fish

R: Thailand, India, Burma and the Indo-Australian Archipelago. **H**: Peaceful, will not molest other fishes, but will swallow those that are small enough to be eaten. **W**: Neutral to slightly acid. Temperature 23 to 26°C. **S**: To 38 cm in their natural waters. **F**: Larger live foods, chunks of shrimp, or raw fish. **C**: Yellowish to coppery in color with 8 to 10 dark brown bars, some of which unite as the fish grows older.

Adult *C. quadrifasciatus* look much like *C. microlepis*. One of the ways of telling them apart is that *C. micolepis* has much smaller scales, 105 in the lateral line, while *C. quadrifasciatus* has only 70. We turn again to H.M. Smith as our authority with the statement that there may be as many as 8 to 10 vertical bars, some of which remain distinct at all ages. The genus was revised by Roberts and Kottelat in 1994, who changed the name from *Datnioides* to *Coius*.

COIUS MICROLEPIS

COLISA CHUNA (Hamilton-Buchanan)/*Honey Gourami*
R: India. **H**: Peaceful and shy. **W**: Soft, slightly acid water desirable. Temperature 24 to 28°C. **S**: 6 cm. **F**: Will accept some dry foods, but prefers small living foods, especially crustaceans. *Colisa chuna* is a bubblenest builder that spawns like the Dwarf Gourami, but *C. chuna* uses less vegetable matter in the construction of its nest. Also, the male Honey Gourami is inclined to be more tolerant of the hesitancy of the female to spawn, whereas the male *Colisa lalia* will damage the female if she is not provided with enough refuge. Like the Dwarf Gourami, *Colisa chuna* does best at a temperature between 24 and 28°C.

COIUS QUADRIFASCIATUS

COLISA FASCIATA (Bloch & Schneider)/*Giant Gourami*

R: India: Coromandel Coast, Northwest and North Provinces, Assam. **H**: Peaceful, a good community fish. **W**: Not critical; they like warm water. Temperature 25 to 26°C. **S**: Males about 12 cm; females a little smaller. **F**: They eat anything and have tremendous appetites.

Breeding is very easily accomplished, and a well-mated pair may easily make a nuisance of themselves by breeding too often. Like the other *Colisa* species, they prefer to anchor their bubblenest to a floating plant, and a few should be provided. When they are ready to spawn, the water should be reduced to only 8 to 10 cm deep. After a number of false tries, the pair will eventually produce as many as 800 eggs, which hatch in about 24 hours. They fry become free-swimming in two more days, at which time the male may be removed; the female should be removed when she is finished laying eggs.

COLISA LALIA

COLISA LABIOSA (Day)/*Thick-Lipped Gourami*

R: India and Burma. **H**: Peaceful and rather shy; a good fish for the community aquarium. **W**: Requires warmth, otherwise not critical as to water conditions if extremes are avoided. Temperature about 25°C. **S**: 10 cm; usually somewhat smaller. **F**: Live foods preferred, but in the absence of these prepared foods are acceptable.

The males seem to get a kick out of making bubblenests and are less likely to get rough when a female is not ready for spawning. Care must be taken not to combine this or for that matter any other thread-finned fish with a nippy species such as some of the barbs, or in a very short time the long, thin ventral fins will be reduced to stumps. In time the fins grow back, but the new fin is often a bit crooked at the point where growth began.

COLISA FASCIATA

COLISA LALIA (Hamilton-Buchanan)/*Dwarf Gourami*
R: India, Bengal and Assam. **H**: Very peaceful; likely to be shy and retiring if kept with fishes that annoy it. **W**: Water should be neutral to slightly acid; enjoys a tank that gets a good amount of sunlight. Temperature 24 to 27°C. **S**: Largest males never exceed 6 cm; females 5 cm. **F**: Not a fussy eater. Dried foods accepted, but should be alternated with live foods.

The Dwarf Gourami is one of the beloved hardy perennials of the aquarium fish world. The Dwarf Gourami is unusual among the bubblenest builders in that it includes bits of plants, twigs and other debris in its nest. The result is a firm bundle that holds together for a long time after the fry are hatched. The eggs are tiny, and if not provided with fine infusoria at first the fry are likely to starve. Once past the critical stage, however, when they are large enough to handle newly hatched brine shrimp, they prove hardy and growth is rapid.

COLISA LABIOSA

COLOMESUS ASELLUS (Müller & Troschel)/*South American Puffer*

R: Venezuela, Guianas, the upper Amazon, Rio Branco and Rio Araguaia. **H**: Generally peaceful but may occasionally nip a fin or two. **W**: Neutral to slightly alkaline hard water. Temperature 24 to 26°C. Tank should be well planted. **S**: To 15 cm; usually smaller. **F**: Especially fond of snails or will take the larger-sized foods. Probably could be trained to take strips of raw fish.

Most of the puffers we keep in the aquarium are from the East Indies and there are also a few from Africa and Thailand. The saltwater species are, of course, native to the warm and temperate waters of most of the world. But for one to come from South America, and far upstream in the Amazon at that, is highly unusual. They have been seen only occasionally among the dealers. You will find that this puffer is not quite as nasty as some of the others and that you can keep them in a community aquarium if you do not put them with such juicy morsels as smaller fishes.

COPEINA GUTTATA

CONGOPANCHAX MYERSI (Poll)/*Myers' Lampeye*

R: Zaire. **H**: Peaceful, but because of their tiny size they cannot be put in community aquaria with any other fishes. Happiest in a school of 12 or more. **W**: Soft, slightly acid water. Temperature 23 to 25°C. **S**: 2.5 cm or slightly less. **F**: Small live foods exclusively.

The eggs are placed onto fine-leaved plants where they will hatch in about two weeks, depending upon the temperature. Although the female has the same color pattern as the male, her fins are usually colorless, while those of the male are pigmented. It is not essential to remove either parent fish after the eggs hatch. If the fish are well fed, there is little cannibalism and many of the young ones can be raised right with the parents. The newly hatched fry are minute and should be given infusoria as a first food. They are hardy but grow slowly at first.

COLOMESUS ASELLUS

COPEINA GUTTATA (Steindachner)/*Red-Spotted Copeina*
R: Central Amazon region. **H**: Peaceful; good community tank fish if not kept with others much smaller than themselves. **W**: Not critical; a wide range of temperatures is tolerated, with optimum temperatures around 24°C. **S**: Wild specimens attain a size of about 10 cm; in captivity 15 cm. **F**: Heavy eaters that will take prepared foods, but they should also be given live foods whenever possible.

Copeina guttata becomes larger in captivity than it does in the wild. The same has been observed with trout and other fishes that occur in habitats where there was a food shortage. The fish matured but remained much smaller. *Copeina guttata* has another claim to being unusual. It is a true characin but does not spawn in a manner usual for characins; their behavior is more like that found among the cichlids. The male scoops out a depression in the gravel in an open spot, and a large number of eggs are deposited into this depression. Here they are guarded and fanned by the male. Fry hatch after 30 to 50 hours and are easily raised. *Copeina* are jumpers, so be sure to keep their tank covered at all times.

CONGOPANCHAX MYERSI

COPELLA ARNOLDI (Regan)/*Splash Tetra, Jumping Characin*

R: Amazon River, in the region of Rio Para. **H**: Very peaceful, but should always be kept in a covered aquarium because of its jumping habits. **W**: Neutral to slightly acid. Temperature between 24 to 26°C. **S**: 8 cm; females about 6 cm. **F**: Live foods preferred, but will take dry food when hungry.

In nature, a pair will seek out an overhanging leaf and together leap out of the water and cling to this leaf long enough to paste several eggs there. They then drop back, to repeat the process again and again until there are more than 100 eggs in a closely packed mass on the underside of the leaf. The eggs do not hatch until 3 days later, during which time the male remains under the leaf and every 15 minutes or so splashes water on them with his tail to keep them from drying out.

COPELLA VILMAE

COPELLA NATTERERI (Steindachner)/*Spotted Copella*

R: Amazon Basin. **H**: Peaceful; a good community fish. Should be kept in a covered tank. **W**: Soft, slightly acid water. Temperature 22 to 28°C. **S**: Up to 8 cm. **F**: Not too particular, but not all dry foods are accepted.

Distinguishing the sexes is easy with mature specimens, because the male's dorsal fin is very definitely longer and more tapered; also, he is more elongated in shape. Although *Copella nattereri* closely resembles *Copella arnoldi,* its breeding pattern is quite different. Instead of jumping from the water to lay its eggs, the Spotted Copella deposits its eggs on submerged plants, usually broad-leaved plants such as Amazon sword plants. At a temperature of 25°C the eggs hatch in about a day.

COPELLA ARNOLDI

COPELLA VILMAE Géry/*Rainbow Copella*

R: Brazilian Amazon. **H**: A very typical member of the *Copeina-Copella* group. Keep in covered tank as this species may jump. **W**: Prefers warm, slightly acid, soft water. Temperature 24 to 28°C. **S**: To about 6 cm. **F**: Eats any small particle food, especially dried pelletized foods. Also requires some live foods or frozen brine shrimp in order that the male will keep his beautiful colors.

These fish prefer to spawn on broad-leaved, submerged plants. The male prepares the spawning site by cleaning the prospective spawning area for up to several hours, then he coaxes the female toward the spot. He does this by swimming around the female and occasionally nudging her with his mouth. The male cares for the spawn, which hatches in about 24 hours. The fry are very small and should be fed infusoria. They move to the surface of the water soon after they have hatched. The adults should be removed from the breeding tank.

COPELLA NATTERERI

CORYDORAS ACUTUS Cope /*Blacktop Catfish*

R: Upper Amazon. **H:** Peaceful. **W:** Soft, slightly acid water desirable. Temperature 23 to 26°C. **S:** 6 cm. **F:** Accepts all foods.

Although this little catfish is rarely seen, it makes a good aquarium subject, as it is peaceful and hardy. Specimens of this fish are usually found among importations of more popular *Corydoras* species. In dealers' tanks they are almost always mixed in with other *Corydoras,* as there have been no direct attempts at importing this fish as a separate species, for it is little known and has no following among the aquarium public in general. For the casual tropical fish store browser, *Corydoras acutus* has no special charm, and when purchased it is usually the last, or one of the last, specimens to be chosen from the general "scavenger" tank.

CORYDORAS ARCUATUS

CORYDORAS AENEUS (Gill)/*Aeneus Catfish*

R: Widely distributed over South America from Trinidad to the La Plata. **H:** Very peaceful; constantly going over the bottom for scraps of leftover food. Useful in keeping the tank clean. **W:** Neutral to slightly alkaline; water should have no salt added to it. These fish come from absolutely fresh water. Temperature 22 to 26°C. **S:** 7 cm; usually a bit smaller. **F:** All dried foods are accepted, but to keep them in really good shape an occasional feeding of tubifex worms should be given.

These fish have little to fear from any enemies; they have sharply spiked anal and dorsal fins that would make a large fish feel as though it were biting into a pincushion. His armor plates, which he wears on his body in place of scales, give a hard, bony surface to a smaller fish that might feel inclined to nibble on him. With such protection, who needs teeth? The natives have an odd way of catching these fish. They choose a small pond where the ripples tell them that there are catfish there surfacing for air. Then they build a dam where the water enters and they let the pond run dry. This leaves the catfish flopping about in the mud. There are about 100 different species of *Corydoras* sold in pet shops.

CORYDORAS ARCUATUS Elwin /*Skunk Catfish, Tabatinga Catfish*

R: Amazon region, above the city of Tefe. **H:** Peaceful; being a bottom-feeder makes it especially valuable for finding and eating leftover food. **W:** Neutral to slightly alkaline water; it is important to leave out any salt. Temperature about 25°C. **S:** About 4.5 cm. **F:** Besides food left by other fishes, an occasional feeding of live food should be given.

Probably the most important reason why the common *Corydoras* species are so seldom bred is because most hobbyists consider them as strictly scavengers and will put one into each of their tanks to eat any food left by the other fishes in that tank. If two are used, no attention is paid to whether they are a pair or not. We would doubtless hear of many spawnings if pairs were given their own tanks and were well fed with living foods. Sexing is not the near impossibility it once was considered. Looking at a group of mature fish from above, it will be seen that some of them are wider in their body than the others; these are the females. These catfish do not eat their eggs; all that is required is that there are no other fish in the tank to eat eggs or fry.

CORYDORAS BARBATUS (Quoy and Gaimard) /*Banded Corydoras*

R: Brazil (Southeast). **H:** Peaceful. **W:** Soft, slightly acid water desirable. Temperature 22 to 28°C. **S:** Up to 13 cm. **F:** Takes all foods. **C:** Light brown body covered by large black markings. Belly color pink.

While *Corydoras barbatus,* because of its size, is not considered to be one of the better catfishes for the community tank, the fish is occasionally brought into the country and put on the market. Usually only young specimens are sold, and many purchasers are amazed to find that their catfish, which they originally supposed would grow no larger than the popular *C. aeneus,* is soon outgrowing its tank. For hobbyists with big tanks this is no problem, but for the hobbyist who buys a couple of *Corydoras* just to fit into the general framework of a small community tank, *Corydoras barbatus* is best left alone.

CORYDORAS ELEGANS

CORYDORAS CAUDIMACULATUS Rossel/*Tail-Spot Corydoras*

R: Rio Guapore, Brazil. **H:** Peaceful; will not disturb fishes or plants. **W:** Slightly alkaline water is best. Avoid sharp edges on rocks or gravel, as the mouth is easily damaged. Temperature 22 to 27°C. **S:** About 5 cm. **F:** All food which falls to the bottom is eaten, but there should be some live as well as prepared food.

As a general rule, *Corydoras* species are not easy to breed. The sexes can be distinguished most easily when the fish are ripe. The females are larger and fuller, with larger bellies. The dorsal fin is often pointed in the male while rounded in the female. One ripe female should be mated with two or three males. This fish has a typical *Corydoras* spawning ritual, where the males nudge and push against the female. After a period of time the female begins to swim about the tank with the males in hot pursuit. Several potential spawning sites are cleaned during this process and actual spawning can take place in several locations.

CORYDORAS BARBATUS

CORYDORAS ELEGANS Steindachner / *Elegant Corydoras*

R: Amazon Basin (Upper). **H:** Peaceful. **W:** Slightly acid to slightly alkaline medium-soft water. Temperature 23 to 28°C. **S:** 5 cm. **F:** Accepts all foods, but is particularly fond of small worms. The "Elegant" in this fish's popular name is derived from its specific scientific name, not from any special coloring or markings that would entitle it to such a fancy name. It is certainly a lot plainer than many of the other *Corydoras* species, some of which have been extracted from the "scavenger" category and are now being kept for their good looks alone. However, it is a good community catfish, and its desirability is enhanced by the fact that it is small, seldom reaching over 5 cm in length. Breeding has not been observed, although attempts have been made to spawn this fish.

CORYDORAS CAUDIMACULATUS

CORYDORAS GRISEUS

CORYDORAS GRISEUS Holly/*Gray Catfish*

R: Brazilian Amazon region, in small tributary streams. **H:** Peaceful. Will not bother other fishes, even very small ones. **W:** Slightly alkaline water is best, with no salt content. Temperature about 25 °C. **S:** About 5 cm. **F:** Although dried foods are picked up eagerly from the bottom, live foods should also be fed regularly.

It is possible that this rare little catfish has often been passed up by collectors who considered them a little plain for the average hobbyist's tastes. However, their greatest charm lies in their simplicity of color. It seems that there are never enough aquarists who are interested in the *Corydoras* species to propagate them in quantity. Catching these fish seems like simplicity itself: schools numbering in the hundreds can be seen browsing over a flat sandy bottom. A long seine is spread out and held in place, and then the fish are driven into this with another seine which is pulled along the bottom. A goodly amount of them are seen swimming ahead of the seine, and a large haul is anticipated. Then when the stationary net is approached and the fish see that they are about to be trapped, suddenly they seem to vanish into thin air (or should it be thin water?). They quickly bury themselves in the sand and let the net pass over them, coming up again and swimming away when the danger has passed.

CORYDORAS HABROSUS

CORYDORAS HABROSUS Weitzman/Habrosus

R: The Rio Salinas, a tributary of the Rio Pao Viejo, El Baul, State of Cojedes, Venezuela. **H:** A peaceful dwarf *Corydoras* that is quite suitable for most community tanks of non-aggressive fishes. **W:** Not critical as long as extremes are avoided. Normal temperatures for tropical species should prevail. **S:** A dwarf or pygmy species of no more than about 20 mm standard length. **F:** Accepts aquarium foods that other corys accept, but make sure it is small enough for their tiny mouths.

Keeping this dwarf species is usually no more difficult than with the other species as long as their size is considered when choosing tankmates. These small corys cannot compete well with larger, more aggressive fishes that might not only harass them but snap up all the food before the catfish could get to it. Clean water of normal aquarium parameters suits them fine. A temperature in the normal range is also recommended. The tank should be well planted, while other decorations are optional. Feeding the Habrosus is no problem as long as you make sure they get enough and that the food particle size is small enough to fit their tiny mouths.

Corydoras habrosus can be spawned in relatively small tanks (down to 5 gallons or 20 liters). A small group is best. Conditioning with newly hatched brine shrimp and microworms works well, and they can even handle whiteworms. As the females fill with eggs they are easily distinguishable by their "plump" appearance. Spawning is in typical cory fashion, and the eggs deposited are light yellow and about 0.8 mm in diameter. As the embryo develops the color darkens. The spawnings reported indicate only about 20 or so eggs are laid and that the fry that hatch out are tiny. This means that for the first few days they should be fed with infusoria. Eventually they can graduate to microworms and baby brine shrimp. A 20% water change every two to three days is sufficient. In a couple of months the fry are 5-7 mm long and look very much like their parents. Happily the parents do not seem to take an interest in eggs or fry and if they are well fed can be left with them. The parents spawn at about monthly intervals.

CORYDORAS JULII

CORYDORAS JULII Steindachner/*Leopard Catfish*

R: Small tributaries of the lower Amazon. **H:** Very peaceful and active. Constantly poking on the bottom for bits of food which were overlooked by the others. **W:** Not critical; best water is slightly alkaline and not very hard. **S:** To 6 cm. **F:** All sorts of foods are taken, but enough should be fed so that the catfish will get his share.

One of the most popular and attractive members of the *Corydoras* group is *Corydoras julii* Fortunately the supply is usually good. It is a strange thing about the *Corydoras* catfishes: practically all of the fish we see for sale have been caught wild in South America and imported into this country. The *Corydoras* species are not as difficult to spawn as many others which our hatcheries produce, but nobody wants to spawn *Corydoras*. Like the Neon Tetra, it is cheaper to import them than it would be to raise them. If we were ever cut off commercially from South America (Heaven forbid!) our breeders would soon bend their efforts to producing *Corydoras*, and as a result the collectors would lose a good-sized chunk of business when things were straightened out again.

CORYDORAS MELANISTIUS Regan/*Black Sail Catfish*

R: Guyana to Venezuela. **H:** Peaceful. A bottom-feeder endlessly rooting about for a tidbit of food (and stirring up bottom debris if not siphoned out). **W:** Not critical. Has spawned in water of pH 6.8-7.6 and hardness of about 150 ppm. Temperature should be in the mid 20°sC. **S:** Attains a length of almost 8 cm. **F:** Will take a wide variety of foods. Remember that they do feed off the bottom and floating foods would be a poor choice.

The Black Sail Catfish can be placed in a community tank, where it will do very well as long as enough food is added so that some reaches the bottom where the catfish can find it. The tank can be decorated with plants and rocks as long as some open space is available for the catfish to move around in. The breeding tank can be much simpler with only a few plants (plastic or real) and some bottom gravel. A few pieces of slate or rocks with flat surfaces should be added. The tank itself can be as small as 40 liters in capacity and the water should have a pH between 6.8 and 7.6, a hardness between 80 and 120 ppm and a temperature between 24 and 26°C. A group of *C. melanistius* can be added to the tank with males and females about roughly equal in number. The group can be anywhere from 6 to 8 or 10 for best results. The spawners should be at least a year old. They should be conditioned on the best foods. Spawning is a group affair and starts when males chase the females and nip at their ventral fins. Eventually the female stops and turns toward the male. As she nudges him she expels 2 to 8 eggs into a pocket formed by her ventral fins. She then leaves the male and places the adhesive eggs on a predetermined spot. This spot is first gone over with her barbels and mouth. The selected site may be plants, rocks, the glass sides of the aquarium, or even an inside filter. The process is repeated until all eggs are deposited. The catfish then settle back to their normal bottom activities. Although some *Corydoras* species lay as many as 300 eggs, the reports on *C. melansistius* varied from 30 to 90. Of course the number depends upon the number of females used, their age, etc. The 30 eggs were from a single female. The eggs hatch in about 72 hours but have enough yolk to last for several days. Initial feeding can be small foods such as microworms or newly hatched brine shrimp. Be careful that there is no salt added to the baby tank with the brine shrimp as the fry are very sensitive to salt.

211

CORYDORAS METAE Eigenmann /*Masked Corydoras, Bandit Catfish*

R: Rio Meta, Colombia. **H:** Peaceful and active. **W:** Medium soft water; pH slightly acid to slightly alkaline. Temperature 23 to 29°C. **S:** 6 cm. **F:** Accepts all foods, particularly tubifex worms.

This pretty catfish looks a lot like *C. arcuatus* and *C. rabauti,* and the three are often confused by hobbyists. Unfortunately, while *C. metae* must be given the nod over the other two in good looks, it is seen less frequently and is therefore less often available to the hobbyist who would like to own some relatively pretty catfish. *Corydoras metae* will take part in a mass spawning activity in which the males and females gather round a central location and begin the ritual of laying, fertilizing and finally depositing the eggs. As with *Corydoras paleatus,* the females are more aggressive than the males in initiating the reproductive maneuvers; at the end of the courting actions the male lies passively on his side and allows the female to make contact between her mouth and the male's genital pore. Then the female swims to the place to deposit the eggs, usually a spot on the glass sides of the aquarium, cleans the spot with her mouth and in so doing deposits some of the sperm which she has taken from the male. With C. *metae* the eggs are deposited singly, and they soon become tough and tightly bound to the surface on which they're laid. The fry, which hatch in about five days, are large.

CORYDORAS PALEATUS

CORYDORAS NATTERERI Steindachner /*Blue Catfish*

R: Brazil, Rio de Janeiro to Sao Paulo. **H:** Peaceful. **W:** Neutral, medium soft water. Temperature 22 to 28°C. **S:** Up to 8 cm. **F:** Accepts all regular foods.

Corydoras can very definitely be attractive, and their attractiveness is usually achieved through markings, such as stripes and spots, rather than through general body color. Although *Corydoras nattereri* does possess a stripe, this is not its distinctive feature, because stripes are not rare on the catfish, but color is. Unfortunately, the color of this fish is not always at its brightest, and it takes a while for this catfish to show up at its best. Rarely will *Corydoras nattereri* live up to its potential in the tanks of dealers, who have neither the time nor the space to give the fish the conditions it needs. In the tanks of a hobbyist who is willing to provide this little catfish with more than the bare essentials, however, it soon rewards its owner by assuming the coloration that sets it apart from all other *Corydoras* species.

CORYDORAS METAE

CORYDORAS PALEATUS Jenyns/*Peppered Corydoras*
R: Southern Brazil and parts of northern Argentina. Habiu: Peaceful. **W:** Neutral, medium soft water. Temperature 21 to 27°C. **S:** Up to 8 cm. **F:** Accepts all regular aquarium foods; especially likes worms.
Color Variations: Original type was a dark gray fish with mottled patches of black on the body and spots on fins. An albino variety now exists.
Corydoras paleatus is a comparatively dark species with many dark blotches, irregularly joined, on its sides. This original variety was one of the first of the *Corydoras* species to become popular in this country, but it has fallen by the wayside and is no longer as popular as it once was. However, the fish has maintained at least a small degree of its past popularity in Germany, where the albino form was developed. One of the first *Corydoras* species to be bred (and one of the easiest), *C. paleatus* follows the pattern whereby the male, after an attentive courtship of the female, lies on his back or side and allows the female to lie across him, her mouth in contact with his underside. She then swims away from him and attaches her eggs, which have been expelled during the "contact" position, to a spot which she has cleaned with her mouth. This spot may be a leaf, a rock or a part of the aquarium glass. The first eggs are usually deposited singly, but as the process is repeated more eggs are deposited at each trip.

CORYDORAS NATTERERI

213

CORYDORAS PYGMAEUS Knaack/*Dwarf Corydoras, Pygmy Corydoras*
R: Amazon Basin, Mato Grosso, Paraguay. **H:** Very peaceful and inoffensive. **W:** pH and hardness values not of great importance, as long as extremes are avoided. Temperature 21 to 29°C. **S:** 4 cm. **F:** Accepts all regular foods.

Here is a little catfish which represents a departure from normal *Corydoras* body shape and behavior. First of all, it is a good bit smaller and more streamlined than other *Corydoras,* the difference in body shape being so marked as to lead to this fish's being placed by some authorities into a separate genus, *Microdoras.* Whatever its scientific standing, the Dwarf Corydoras is an interesting addition to a community tank. Contrary to the actions of its relatives, *Corydoras pygmaeus* swims mainly in the middle reaches of the water; it spends little time on the bottom, or at least much less than the other *Corydoras.* Generally considered as one of the easiest catfishes to spawn and raise, the Dwarf Corydoras goes through the rather frenzied mating procedure of the other catfishes, but the fish is much more likely to choose plants for the site of egg deposition; the fry are large for so small a fish.

CORYDORAS RABAUTI

CORYDORAS RABAUTI Lamont/*Rabaut's Catfish*

R: Small tributaries of the Amazon above the mouth of the Rio Negro. **H:** Very peaceful and active; harmless to all but the smallest fry. **W:** Neutral to slightly alkaline. Temperature about 25°C. **S:** To 6 cm, usually a little smaller. **F:** All kinds of food are taken, but enough should be fed if other fishes are present to give the catfish their fair share.

Corydoras rabuati is frequently sold in this country as *Corydoras myersi*, but *C. myersi* is now considered to be not a valid species, but just a synonym of *C. rabauti. C. rabauti* is one of the few *Corydoras* species which the author has been privileged to observe in the act of spawning. There is a great deal of hustle and bustle, which ends with one of the males lying on his side on the bottom. The female swims up to him and nuzzles him in the region of the vent, at the same time releasing two or three eggs into a pocket formed by her ventral fins. She then swims up to a spot on the glass which was previously cleaned off and rubs her mouth against this spot. Then she pushes her belly against the same spot and the sticky eggs are pasted against the glass. A very interesting color change comes over the young: until they are about I cm long they are real beauties. The front half of the body, including the head, is green and the after half is red! Unfortunately these colors are not permanent and a remarkable thing happens: the green becomes darker and forms the stripe, while the red fades and covers the rest of the body.

215

CORYDORAS RETICULATUS

CORYDORAS RETICULATUS Fraser-Brunner /*Network Catfish*

R: Amazon Basin. **H:** Peaceful. **W:** Neutral to slightly alkaline, medium soft to slightly hard water. Temperature 22 to 28°C. **S:** About 5 cm. **F:** Takes all common aquarium foods, but not so fond of worms as other *Corydoras*.

Although this catfish is very rarely seen, it would make a nice addition to a collection of *Corydoras*, for it is an attractive fish. The vermiform markings covering the body and head give a striking appearance to the fish; luckily, these markings are not subject to appearance or disappearance depending on the mood or physical condition of the fish. The markings are always there in fairly distinct form, although it is possible that they can become less clear when the fish is kept under extremely poor conditions. *Corydoras reticulatus* does, however, have one prominent marking which is not present at all times, although, again, this is not subject to mood or to physical condition. Rather, it is dependent on age; the spot is present in the dorsal fin of young specimens but absent in the dorsal fin of older fish. Older fish, instead of having the spot, have a pattern of small dark dashes similar to the markings in the tail, but less dense.

CORYDORAS SCHWARTZI

CORYDORAS SCHWARTZI Rossel /*Schwartz's Corydoras*

R: Brazil, near the mouth of the Purus River. **H:** Peaceful in any kind of company. **W:** Not critical as long as the water is clean. Temperature 22 to 26°C. **S:** About 5 cm. **F:** Will scavenge uneaten food, but should be given their own tank if they are to be fed properly. Live or freeze-dried tubifex worms are ideal and should be alternated with good prepared foods.

Identifying the *Corydoras* species is becoming a constantly more difficult, almost impossible task. At the present time there are over 80 species known to the scientific world, with many more, no doubt, to be added. An interesting thing which is common to most *Corydoras* species which are kept in the hobbyist aquarium is how difficult they are to catch in the wild. When frightened, they quickly and expertly cover themselves with the bottom silt, allowing the seine that was meant to trap them to pass harmlessly over their heads. *Corydoras schwartzi* comes from an area around the mouth of the Rio Purus, which empties into the Amazon a little ways upriver from Manaus.

CORYDORAS SIMULATUS Weitzman & Nijssen/*Copy Catfish*

R: Colombia's Rio Meta river system. **H:** Peaceful and active. **W:** Medium soft water; pH slightly acid to slightly alkaline. Temperature to 29°C. **S:** 6 cm. **F:** Accepts all foods, particularly tubifex worms.

This little catfish looks very much like *Corydoras metae* and for many years was thought to be just that. Its name is derived from the Latin word *simulare,* meaning to imitate. This is due to the similarity in color pattern between this fish and *C. metae.*

C. simulatus spawns in mass. This activity takes place in a central location around which the males and females gather. Here they begin a ritual that includes egg laying, fertilizing and final depositing of the fertilized eggs. The females are more active than the males at initiating the reproductive behavior. When the courting is complete, the male lies passively on his side and allows the female to make contact between her mouth and the male's genital pore. After this action, the female leaves the male to find a suitable surface on which to lay her eggs. She first cleans the site with her mouth and simultaneously deposits the sperm from the male. Eggs are deposited one at a time and become tightly bound with the surface on which they are laid. The fry are large and hatch in four to five days.

CORYDORAS UNDULATUS

CORYDORAS TREITLII Steindachner/*Long-Nose Corydoras*

R: Eastern Brazil. **H:** Peaceful. **W:** Neutral water desirable, but pH may vary slightly above or below this value; soft water not necessary, but advisable. Temperature 22 to 28°C. **S:** Up to 8 cm. **F:** Takes all regular aquarium foods.

Although this fish has been known to ichthyologists since 1906, when it was classified by Steindachner, it has never appeared in quantity on the American market, or at least not under its correct name. However, it was seen in Germany in the early 1930's, but it did not attract much attention there, even though German hobbyists worked with it for a while in an effort to breed it. It defied these efforts and soon dropped out of circulation, but not before it had stirred up a little controversy regarding its correct taxonomic status. This was mainly because of the peculiarly shaped head which was different from the head shape of *Corydoras* species known to hobbyists at that time, being much more elongated. Because of a similarity in coloring, it was also supposed for a short time to be a variety of *Corydoras elegans,* but this point was later resolved.

CORYDORAS SIMULATUS

CORYDORAS UNDULATUS Regan/*Wavy Catfish*
R: Eastern South America, La Plata region. **H:** Does not grub into the bottom like most other species; peaceful. **W:** Temperature 23 to 25°C. Tank should be clean, with no sediment on the bottom. **S:** Females 5 cm; males slightly smaller. **F:** This fish is not a scavenger, so it should be given generous quantities of live foods.

Corydoras undulatus has not been introduced in any numbers until quite recently, although it was first imported in 1909. So far there have been no accounts of their having been bred in captivity, but there is no doubt that their breeding procedure is no different from that of other members of the genus. Males are easily distinguished from the females: they are considerably smaller and much more slender. This species is very active and once they have become accustomed to a tank will live for a long time.

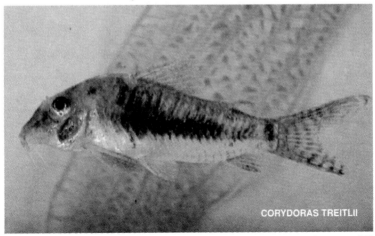

CORYDORAS TREITLII

CORYNOPOMA RIISEI Gill/*Swordtailed Characin*

R: Trinidad, Colombia, and Venezuela. **H**: Peaceful and hardy; a good community fish. **W**: Not critical. Temperature between 22 to 28°C. A sunny, well-planted tank and clear water show it at its best. **S**: Males 6 cm; females 5 cm. **F**: Will take prepared foods. Best foods are daphnia, tubifex worms, and especially white worms, of which they are very fond.

What first strikes the eye is the magnificent finnage of the males and also a peculiar paddle-like extension of the gill plates, which reaches more than halfway down the sides of the males. What the exact function of these extensions is has been argued back and forth for many years. They are kept folded back except during courtship, when the male swims toward the female with these paddles extended at right angles. Strangely enough, there seems to be some sort of internal fertilization, because females that have been separated from their mates for some time have surprised their owners by laying eggs that hatched!

CRATEROCEPHALUS STERCUSMUSCARUM

COTTUS BAIRDI Girard/*Mottled Sculpin*

R: North America from about the Tennessee River system of Alabama and Georgia to Labrador, west to Lake Manitoba in Canada. A second area of distribution includes parts of Washington, Oregon, Idaho, Montana, and adjacent regions of southwestern Canada. **H**: Because of the temperature needs, the Mottled Sculpin should be given a tank by itself. **W**: Best to use water from the stream it was collected in. Needs clean, clear water with a temperature of 5 to 18°C. **S**: Reaches a length of over 13 cm. **F**: Prefers live foods such as stonefly nymphs, chironomids, aquatic crustaceans, etc.

Spawning has been accomplished in an aquarium. An 80-liter tank with the bottom covered with about 5 cm of well-washed river sand and gravel was used. The water was filtered water from the area where the fish were captured. Strong aeration and filtration were provided, with the temperature around 15-18°C (spawning in nature was seen when the temperature was as low as 10°C). A wide flat stone set at an angle can provide the fish with shelter (normally they hide under rocks). The male should be placed in the aquarium first and then the female shortly after. The male will court the female, sometimes resorting to a nip or two to hurry things along, until she decides to follow him to his chosen nest site (which is usually under the flat rock). The eggs are deposited on the roof of the cave and fertilized there, after which the female leaves or is driven off.

CORYNOPOMA RIISEI

CRATEROCEPHALUS STERCUSMUSCARUM Günther/
Fly-Specked Hardyhead

R: East coastal drainage system of Queensland, Australia. **H**: Fairly peaceful; a good jumper and fast swimmer. **W**: Soft, slightly acid water. Temperature 24 to 27°C. **S**: To 13 cm. **F**: Not a choosy eater. Will take prepared as well as live or frozen foods.

This fish is seldom seen in this part of the world because it is rarely imported. With the exception of rainbowfishes, atherinids are seldom kept in the aquarium hobby. These fish typically produce large eggs that have many long filaments. These filaments are adhesive and cause the eggs to become attached to the surrounding vegetation in the water.

COTTUS BAIRDI

CRENICARA FILAMENTOSA Ladiges/*Checkerboard Lyretail*

R: Rio Negro area of the Amazon Basin. **H**: Peaceful with other species, but somewhat combative among themselves. **W**: Not critical. **S**: Up to about 8 cm for males; slightly smaller for females. **F**: Does best on live foods, especially small crustaceans, but will accept most prepared foods.

The species spawns on broad leaves or flat rocks, and the eggs are guarded very jealously by the female, who will actively attack intruders, including the male. Usually there is no male-female confrontation, because the male makes no attempt to get involved with the eggs and stays well clear of the female. *Crenicara filamentosa* shows to its best advantage when maintained only in the company of its own species, but it will live well with other dwarf cichlids if the fishes are accommodated in a tank large enough to allow the establishment of territories without fighting. It is not a very timid species and will remain within view unless housed in tanks that contain bigger and more aggressive fishes.

CRENICARA PUNCTULATA

CRENICARA MACULATA (Steindachner)/*Checkerboard Cichlid*

R: Central Amazon region. **H**: Fairly peaceful, but should have their own tank. **W**: Soft, neutral to slightly acid water. Temperature about 25°C. **S**: Males 10 cm; females to 5 cm. **F**: Varied live foods. **C**: Body yellowish with two rows of alternate square spots on the sides. Male's ventral fins have blue and orange streaks.

A pair will produce a beautiful spawning and the next time under identical conditions everything will go wrong. Possibly the time of sexual ripeness varies between spawnings in this fish, and a pair that achieves this state once may not come due again at the same time. Keeping several pairs and observing them closely would probably do the trick, but good pairs are quite expensive and not easily come by.

CRENICARA FILAMENTOSA

CRENICARA PUNCTULATA (Günther)/*Hercules Cichlid*

R: Upper amazon and Peru. **H**: Very sensitive for a cichlid; prefers hiding in dark corners. **W**: Prefers warm, soft, slightly acid water. **S**: To 10 cm. **F**: Prefers small earthworms, bits of beef, and frozen brine shrimp. Eats coarse grained dry foods, especially pelletized foods. **C**: During spawning the males become very colorful.

Cichlids are, as a general rule, among the most popular fishes to keep in one's aquarium. But when they want to spawn, they will tear up all the plants and attack fishes that come near the nest. This species acts more like a non-mouth brooding African cichlid than a South American cichlid. It hides on the bottom and prefers dark corners to an open stone. Every time we saw a pair spawn it ate its eggs, so not much information about their spawning is available. At any rate, fishes of the genus *Crenicara* spawn very readily, so it shouldn't be anticipated that there will be any trouble with this species.

CRENICARA MACULATA

CRENICICHLA GEAYI Pellegrin/*Half-Banded Pike Cichlid*

R: Central Amazon region. **H**: Predatory and vicious. Can only be trusted with fishes with similar habits in large aquaria. **W**: Not critical. Temperature 23 to 25°C. **S**: To 20 cm; imported specimens usually much smaller. **F**: Large living foods, preferably live smaller fishes.

Picture this fish almost motionless in a clump of aquatic plants. The resemblance to a slime-covered twig with shadows of plant leaves on it would be close enough to deceive any smaller fish and lull it into a very false sense of security. When the prey gets close enough a rush of that torpedo-shaped body, followed by a gulp of that big mouth, reduces the small fish population by one and the Pike Cichlid is already thinking about how good the next victim will taste. As is the case with most predators, at spawning time they usually become the best of parents.

CRENICICHLA NOTOPHTHALMUS

CRENICICHLA LEPIDOTA Heckel/*Pike Cichlid*

R: From the Amazon south to northern Argentina. **H**: A predator that cannot be trusted with other fishes, especially those of a size it can swallow. Tank should be well-planted and afford a number of hiding places. **W**: Not critical. Temperature 23 to 25°C. **S**: To 20 cm. **F**: Large living foods, preferably smaller fishes.

As is usually the case with "nasty" cichlids, a well-mated pair almost always proves to be good parents. Spawning takes place in a depression in the gravel, and a great number of small white eggs result. When the fry hatch the male takes charge of the brood, but the female need not be removed. She soon realizes that she must keep her distance, and does so. While guarding eggs and fry, they should be fed heavily to lessen the temptation to eat their own eggs and fry.

CRENICICHLA GEAYI

CRENICICHLA NOTOPHTHALMUS Regan/Eye-Spot Pike Cichlid

R: Amazon River and its tributaries near Santarem and Manaus. **H**: Slightly more peaceful than the other *Crenicichla* species, but cannot be trusted with other fishes. Should be provided with a number of hiding places as retreats for any that are attacked. **W**: Not critical. Temperature 24 to 26°C. **S**: Up to 20 cm in their native waters. **F**: Generous feedings of live foods are necessary. They take dried foods only when very hungry.

Many beautiful fishes are shunned by hobbyists because of their vicious, predatory habits. This is often the case with the *Crenicichla* species. Without a doubt they are handsome fishes, but to keep them in company with other fishes would be placing the lives or at least the fins of their tankmates in jeopardy.

CRENICICHLA LEPIDOTA

CRENICICHLA SAXATILIS (Linnaeus)/*Spangled Pike Cichlid*

R: Trinidad, Guyana, and Venezuela to the central and eastern Amazon. **H:** Definitely a predator, it should not be kept with small or weak fishes. The males are combative. **W:** Not critical. The temperature is best between 21 and 26°C **S:** Reaches a length of up to 28 cm. **F:** Not choosy. It will eat a wide variety of aquarium foods including small goldfish, guppies, or anything else that will fit into its mouth.

A large tank is a must, especially considering the size this fish reaches. It should be well-planted as the Spangled Pike Cichlid likes to hide, especially when waiting for prey to come by. The bottom should be covered with a layer of sand or gravel, but be prepared for some redecorating by the inhabitants. Males are combative, and the smaller of two placed in a tank usually winds up battered and bruised. A pair seems to get along better together, but make sure there are plenty of refuges just in case. Males generally are slightly larger than females, have the dorsal and anal fins produced into long points, and have many more spangles on the body. Females are slightly smaller, a bit more robust, have fewer spangles, have a rosy flush ventrally, and may have the edge of the dorsal fin and upper part of the caudal fin adorned with black and white markings. Spawning is accomplished in typical egg-laying cichlid fashion, the eggs being placed in a pit in the sand or in a cave (one spawned on the roof of a cave).

CROSSOCHEILUS SIAMENSIS

CRENUCHUS SPILURUS Günther/*Sailfin Tetra*

R: Guyana and central Amazon region. **H:** Probably a predator; do not keep them with any smaller fishes. **W:** Soft, definitely acid water is required. Temperature 24 to 26°C, never lower. **S:** To 6 cm. **F:** All sorts of live foods, preferably larger ones like cut-up earthworms and young livebearers.

One authority says they are peaceful, but the consensus seems to be that they are predatory and may not be trusted in mixed company. Judging by the size of the mouth, we are inclined to side with the latter school of thought. There are also two camps on the question of spawning habits. All authorities agree that the fry have never been raised, but some say that they spawn characin-fashion among plant leaves while others have them laying their eggs on rocks and large-leaved plants. According to one source, the eggs are bright red and are guarded cichlid-fashion by the male.

CRENICICHLA SAXATILIS

CROSSOCHEILUS SIAMENSIS (Smith)/*Siamese Flying Fox*
R: Thailand. **H**: Peaceful; can be kept with any other fishes. **W**: Neutral to slightly alkaline water. Temperature 23 to 26°C. **S**: To 14 cm. **F**: Omnivorous; diet should be supplemented with vegetable substances.
This is a rare fish not only in the aquarium but also in its home water. The fisherman in the region of Thailand from where it comes call it *pla lab mue nang* or "lady's fingernail fish" and say it is good to eat. Where the resemblance lies between the fish and a lady's fingernail is not made clear; perhaps the scales look like a Siamese lady's fingernails, or it may be that the gill-covers have this appearance. We can do nothing but wonder. In the aquarium the Siamese Flying Fox does not have the beautiful fins sported by its close relative *Epalzeorhynchos kalopterus,* but its body colors almost make up for it.

CRENUCHUS SPILURUS

CTENOBRYCON SPILURUS (Valenciennes)/*Silver Tetra*

R: Northern South America from Surinam to Venezuela. **H**: Peaceful with fishes of its own size or larger, but likely to pick on smaller ones. **W**: They prefer clean water, and their tank should be large. Temperature may range from 20 to 25°C. **S**: About 8 cm. **F**: Greedy eaters, they may extend their appetites to some of the plants. Will also take all kinds of dried foods.

Breeding them does not present much difficulty; given enough room and a partial change of water, driving is apt to be vigorous and some plants uprooted. A large female may produce as many as 2,000 eggs. Mating is accomplished by the pair swimming with tilted bodies in tight circles. As with most of the tetra family, the parents must be removed as soon as they have finished spawning or they will find most of the eggs and eat them. Fry emerge after 50 to 70 hours and become free-swimming after the third or fourth day.

CTENOPOMA ACUTIROSTRE

CTENOLUCIUS HUJETA (Valenciennes)/*Blunt-Nosed Gar, Hujeta*

R: Tropical South America. **H**: Aggressive; eats small fishes and flying insects. A jumper, so keep the tank covered. A nocturnal fish. **W**: Not sensitive to changes in water conditions. Does well in water from 21 to 29°C with a pH from 6.0 to 7.6. Prefers soft water, but doesn't suffer too much in hard water. **S**: Up to 25 cm. **F**: Loves floating insects or live baby Guppies.

The author (HRA) collected a specimen in the northern Rio Branco, Brazil. The specimen was 20 cm long. It was collected at night with a dip net as the fish was swimming on the surface of the water. The snout is very interesting and there is an external flap of skin projecting from the lower jaw. The upper jaw folds over the lower jaw giving this harmful-looking fish a disadvantage of having an inferior mouth. Its teeth are relatively small and it either swallows its prey whole or jumps for small flying insects.

CTENOBRYCON SPILURUS

CTENOPOMA ACUTIROSTRE Pellegrin/*Leopard Ctenopoma*
R: Middle and lower Zaire River tributaries. **H**: Predatory; should never be kept with fishes they can swallow. Peaceful with larger fishes; inclined to be shy in small tanks. **W**: Not critical. Temperature 25 to 28°C. **S**: To 15 cm; usually much smaller in captivity. **F**: Any food with a high meat or fish content; very fond of smaller live fishes, pieces of earthworm, etc. Frozen brine shrimp is excellent.

This fish is a predator that hunts and consumes smaller fishes in its native waters, where it is a very hardy and durable fish inhabiting bodies of water that frequently become quite foul in the dry season.

This species builds a loose bubblenest. The *Ctenopoma* species may well be described as the "gouramis" of Africa, but they are much less popular than the Asiatic gouramis.

CTENOLUCIUS HUJETA

CTENOPOMA KINGSLEYAE

CTENOPOMA KINGSLEYAE (Günther)/*Kingsley's Ctenopoma*
R: Widely scattered from Senegal to the Congo region. **H**: Very predatory and nasty; should not be kept with other fishes. **W**: Not critical, but temperature should be high, about 25°C. **S**: Will eat just about everything, but prefers living fish.
This unusual group of fishes occurs in places where the water sometimes partly dries out. They are able to cover considerable distances over land and through wet grass, thanks to their air-breathing ability. When the pool in which they are living dries out, they hop out and flop along until they locate another pool.

230

CTENOPOMA OCELLATUM

CTENOPOMA OCELLATUM Pellegrin/*Chocolate Bushfish*

R: Congo region. **H:** Not scrappy, but is a nocturnal predator on small fishes. Requires subdued lighting and plenty of cover. **W:** Fairly tolerant of most aquarium conditions. Prefers soft, acid water with temperatures from 22-28°C. **S:** Attains a length of about 14 cm. **F:** Live foods best, but can be coaxed onto frozen and freeze-dried foods as well as flake foods.

The Chocolate Bushfish is a very attractive anabantoid from the Congo. It occurs in rapidly flowing streams and probably also in the immediate vicinity of waterfalls, implying of course that it prefers habitats with a high oxygen content. It is a nocturnal predator, usually lurking in the vegetation waiting for small prey animals to approach.

Spawning has not been described, although it apparently has occurred in captivity. This seems to be one of the species of the genus that does not prepare a bubblenest and spawns near the bottom. No parental care is shown. The fry should be raised like gouramis—one to two weeks of infusoria, then *Daphnia* and newly hatched brine shrimp. Remember that when the labyrinth organ is developing the surface should be exceptionally clean and no cold drafts should strike the surface.

Sexual differences are hard to spot in this species. Just posterior to the eyes and on the caudal peduncle there are areas where the scales terminate in small spines. In the males the spines are much more pronounced. It is said that these spines are helpful in holding the female securely while in the nuptial embrace.

Aquarists who wish to try spawning this fish should be patient for they apparently take several years to mature.

CTENOPOMA WEEKSI

CTENOPOMA WEEKSI Boulenger/*Mottled Ctenopoma*

R: Tributaries of the lower Zaire River. **H**: Peaceful with fishes of the same size of larger. **W**: Not critical, but temperatures should be kept high, 26 to 29°C. **S**: To 10 cm. **F**: Larger live foods preferred, especially living fishes.

The females are distinguished by their more rounded fins. This species does not build a bubblenest like the others, nor is one needed. The eggs have an oil content which makes them lighter than water and causes them to float to the surface. During this time the tank should be tightly covered. Like the other *Ctenopoma* species, this one also requires warm water. Breeding temperatures should be 28 to 29°C. Eggs hatch in 24 to 32 hours and the fry become free-swimming in 2 to 3 days. Having a large mouth, they are easily fed and grow rapidly.

CUBANICHTHYS CUBENSIS

CUBANICHTHYS CUBENSIS (Eigenmann)/*Cuban Minnow*

R: Western Cuba. **H**: Will do well in an uncrowded and well-planted aquarium; although it sometimes occurs in brackish waters, an addition of salt is unnecessary. **W**: Should be kept in a sunny location. Temperature 24 to 26°C. **S**: About 4 cm; usually smaller. **F**: This species will seldom eat dried foods unless very hungry. All sorts of living foods are taken.

This fish shares a breeding habit with a few of the other cyprinodonts. Instead of a few single eggs being expelled at a time and hung on plants, the female expels the eggs in a bunch, and they hang like a tiny bunch of grapes on a string from her vent. This string is quite durable, and she may swim around with it for hours before it is torn off, leaving the eggs hanging on a plant leaf or anything she might brush against. The fry hatch after 10 to days and are very small at first. The water should be kept warm, about 25°C, and for the first week infusoria should be fed.

CULAEA INCONSTANS (Kirtland)/*Brook Stickleback, Five-Spined Stickleback*

R: Northeastern and north-central United States into southern Canada. **H:** A mildly aggressive fish except during the breeding season, when the males become extremely pugnacious. **W:** Neutral to slightly alkaline, moderately hard water. Temperature 5 to 18°C. **S:** 8 cm. **F:** Strictly carnivorous, preferring live foods, but will adapt to bits of fresh meat.

The male stakes out a territory and begins to build a bullet-shaped nest constructed of bits of dead plant leaves, threads of algae, and particles of fine sand. This material is cemented together into a hollow tubular shape with a material that is secreted by the male's kidneys. The male then lures a ripe female into the nest. As part of their highly ritualized spawning behavior the male gently nudges the posterior end of the female that remains just outside the nest. This seems to be the releaser that causes the female to expel her eggs in the nest. The female then breaks through the opposite end of the nest as the male swims into the nest behind her to fertilize the eggs.

CYCLOCHEILICHTHYS APOGON

CYATHOPHARYNX FURCIFER (Boulenger)/*Furcifer*

R: Endemic to Lake Tanganyika. **H:** It shows at least some of the aggressiveness of the lake cichlids. **W:** Hard, alkaline water is preferred. The temperature range recommended is from 23 to 27°C. **S:** In nature it attains a length of about 20 cm. **F:** Not choosy. Adapts well to normal aquarium foods.

Cyathopharynx furcifer occurs in mid-water schools near rocky slopes. Breeding is accomplished when the male constructs a sand nest on the highest boulders by bringing up the sand mouthful by mouthful. The strongest male gets the best position (highest point), with the lesser males relegated to the lower boulders. The nest is about 5 cm deep and up to 30 cm across. The male will try to attract females from the hovering school (hence the highest position being best) with looping motions and enhanced colors. Sperm is apparently released into the nest and the male departs as the female arrives. The female picks up sperm as she follows the male into the nest. It is suspected that (1) she is attracted by the bright spots of the pelvic fins of the male and (2) she releases the eggs and catches them in mid-water. The spots on the pelvic fins would then represent eggs she has missed and should chase after to collect, bringing her into the sperm-laden nest. The eggs are brooded in the female's mouth, and the fry are finally released in the comparative safety of the shallow shore.

CULAEA INCONSTANS

CYCLOCHEILICHTHYS APOGON (Valenciennes) *Skin-Head Barb*
R: Java, Borneo, Sumatra, and other islands of the East Indies to Malaysia, Burma, and Thailand. **H**: Peaceful, does well in a community aquarium with fishes its own size. **W**: Not critical. Temperature 21 to 24°C. **S**: To about 25 cm, but not reaching quite that size in aquaria. **F**: Will take most aquarium foods that are "wet" (brine shrimp, beef heart, etc.) or live. Not particularly fond of dried foods.
Cyclocheilichthys apogon, when kept alone, is a peaceful, quiet fish moving sedately around the aquarium in contrast to the other barbs that seem always to be on the move. When more active fishes are added to the aquarium *C. apogon* increases its activity also, perhaps caught up in the motion of the others or just to get its share of the food. It has been said that it becomes very quiet in confined quarters, perhaps as a result of the reduced oxygen supply.

CYATHOPHARYNX FURCIFER

CYNOLEBIAS ADLOFFI

CYNOLEBIAS ADLOFFI Ahl/*Banded Pearl Fish*

R: Southeastern Brazil. **H**: Should be kept by themselves. Males become scrappy. **W**: Tank should have a layer of about an inch of peat moss on the bottom. Temperature 22 to 25°C. **S**: Males to 5 cm; females a little smaller. **F**: Live foods of all kinds that are small enough for easy swallowing.

There is no problem distinguishing between males and females in the Banded Pearl Fish, or for that matter any other *Cynolebias* species. The female has almost no color, and the male often seems to have enough for both. Spawning them is an easy matter. A layer of peat moss on the bottom and a healthy pair is all that is needed. After the female has become considerably thinner the peat moss is netted out and stored in a slightly moist state for three to five months. Eggs hatch in a few hours after the peat moss is put back in the water.

CYNOLEBIAS ANTENORI

CYNOLEBIAS ANTENORI Myers'/*Red-finned Pearlfish*

R: Ceara, Rio Grande do Norte, Brazil. **H:** Peaceful toward other fishes, but best kept by themselves. **W:** Soft, slightly acid water. Temperature about 72-76°F. best. **S:** Reaches a length of
about 2-2 1/2 inches. **F:** Prefers live foods. Will take frozen foods also but will only take dried
food if very hungry. **Color Variations:** Grayish blue anteriorly, more purplish posteriorly, the
body spotted with white. White spots in vertical fins and reddish to orange stripe in anal fin
fading posteriorly; anal fin also with black border.

Cynolebias antenori has been successfully spawned using the same methods as those used
with other species of *Cynolebias*. A small tank (as small as 3-gallon capacity) can be used. The
floor of the tank should be covered with a layer of peat some 3/4 to 1 inch deep and there may
be a spawning mop floating in the water (mainly for the protection of the female). A ripe trio is
added to the tank and fed heavily with live foods for about two weeks. The females should look
noticeably slimmer at this time. After the two weeks the peat is removed from the tank and the
excess water removed. The peat is then stored for four to six months making sure that it is
properly labeled. The date on the label is a big help when trying to remember if the fry are ready
to hatch out. After this long period of storage of the eggs within the peat, the peat can be placed
in a small container (a plastic shoebox has been used successfully) to which water is then
added. Some people prefer to add microworms at this stage. The newly hatched young will be
able to eat microworms as well as some newly hatched brine shrimp.

It appears that the eggs are more likely to hatch when no bright light is turned on them. This
means that the eggs cannot be safely separated from the peat under a bright light—but you
cannot really see the eggs except under adequate lighting. So it is best to move peat and eggs
together and hope that the fish have spawned. It would be very discouraging to wait five months
only to find that there was no spawning.

CYNOLEBIAS ALEXANDRI Castello and Lopez/*Entre Rios Pearl Fish*

R: State of Entre Rios, Argentina. **H**: Pugnacious with members of its own species; generally peaceful with other fishes. **W**: Not critical. **S**: To about 5 cm. **F**: Accepts most meaty foods.

Cynolebias alexandri is an annual fish that lays its eggs at the bottom of ponds that dry out during the South American summer; when the ponds again fill up, the fry are liberated and take up their short lives, repeating the spawning process before they die when the ponds dry up again. Under aquarium conditions, *C. alexandri* spawns in a peat substrate, with both parents actually submerging themselves in the peat while the eggs are individually expelled and fertilized.

CYNOLEBIAS BOITONEI

CYNOLEBIAS BELLOTTI Steindachner/*Argentine Pearl Fish*

R: La Plata region. **H**: Should have a good-sized aquarium to themselves. **W**: Not critical; tank should stand in a sunny spot. A wide variety of temperatures is tolerated, but 22 to 24°C is best. **S**: 7 cm; female a little smaller. **F**: A heavy eater; should be generously fed with live foods whenever possible, but will also accept dried foods occasionally.

This is one of the amazing group known as "annual" fishes. They occur in water holes which evaporate in the course of the dry season, eventually to dry out altogether. Naturally all the fish have already laid their eggs in the mud on the bottom. When the rains begin the eggs hatch and the little fish appear in swarms, eating greedily and growing at an amazing rate until they attain maturity in a few months and lay their eggs in the mud, completing this unique life-cycle.

A pair will spawn readily, using a layer of peat moss as a substitute for the mud bottom. Then the eggs are taken out with the peat moss which is allowed to dry out, but not completely, for a few months. The eggs are then replaced in the aquarium to hatch. The fry grow with amazing rapidity and become mature in six to seven weeks. This fish is seldom seen on sale, and those few that are usually offered are old and far beyond their prime.

CYNOLEBIAS ALEXANDRI

CYNOLEBIAS BOITONEI (Carvalho)/*Brazilian Lyrefin*

R: Near Brasilia, Brazil at altitudes of 1000m. **H**: A typical "annual" species that prefers muddy water holes that may dry out during the dry season. A good jumper, so keep the tank covered. **W**: The temperature of the water in its native habitat ranges from 5 to 37°C. It is found only in rain water with a pH of about 5.8 to 7.2. **S**: Very small; not much larger than 2.5 cm; males larger than females. **F**: Prefers mosquito larvae, freeze-dried worms, and brine shrimp.

Discovered by José Boitone, the Director of the Zoo in Brasilia, the capital of Brazil, the first specimens were sent to Dr. Saturnino de Carvalho of the Museu Nacional in Rio de Janeiro for identification. Carvalho, a student of the great ichthyologist Dr. George Myers, was well qualified to recognize a new fish and originally put *boitonei* in a new genus, *Simpsonichthys,* in honor of his California friend, Charles J. Simpson. Most people now feel *Simpsonichthys* should be placed in *Cynolebias.*

CYNOLEBIAS BELLOTTI

CYNOLEBIAS CONSTANCIAE Myers/*Featherfin Pearlfish*

R: State of Rio de Janeiro in Brazil. **H:** Not quite as aggressive as its relatives. Should best be kept in a single-species tank. **W:** Not critical, but soft and slightly acid water preferred. Usually peat is included in the aquarium for spawning purposes. **S:** Males attain a length of up to 5 cm, females to about 4 cm. **F:** Does well on a variety of foods; has been kept on diet of brine shrimp and *Daphnia*.

If spawning of the Featherfin Pearlfish is desired, a container filled with well-washed peat moss can be placed in the bowl. Such containers may vary in size, success being achieved in containers of a half gallon to one gallon in size. The peat is left in with the breeders for about a week to ten days, after which it is removed and replaced with fresh peat. The egg-laden peat that has been removed is damp-dried (it feels damp but does not drip water when squeezed) and stored. The peat is normally sealed or partially sealed in plastic bags in such a way as to retain some moisture. This can be checked periodically during the developmental period. After approximately three to four months the peat with the eggs can be placed in a small aquarium (8-12 liters is sufficient) with 2.5-5 cm of water on the bottom. The young should hatch out within a short time (at least within 48 hours) or the peat should be dried and tried again after a week or two. The newly hatched fry can be fed rotifers, vinegar eels, microworms, and even newly hatched brine shrimp. After a few weeks the water level can be increased gradually, giving the young fish more room to grow. The fry grow slowly and possibly unevenly depending upon their ability to catch and utilize the food. In about two to three months the largest young will be about 2 cm long and sexual differences may be seen. Usually the males are the largest. Shortly after this time these young fish can be set up as breeders. Our photo shows a female.

CYNOLEBIAS NIGRIPINNIS

CYNOPOECILUS MELANOTAENIA (Regan)/*Fighting Gaucho*

R: Southeastern Brazil. **H:** Do not put two males in the same tank or they will fight until one or both are badly mutilated or dead. **W:** Occurs in ditches and water holes, some of which dry out in the hot season; can adapt to almost any water. **S:** Males about 5 cm; females slightly smaller. **F:** Should be given live food of all kinds. Dried foods are accepted, but not willingly.

Like all *Cynolebias* species, the fighting gaucho is a fish that is short-lived and therefore not often found in the tanks of dealers, who prefer fishes that they can keep over a period of time if they cannot sell them quickly. These fish occur in a variety of conditions, which leads one to wonder just exactly what their breeding habits are. One authority says that they lay their eggs in the mud like the other *Cynolebias* species and that the eggs undergo a drying-out process. Then there is another authority who says that they lay their eggs in bushy plants near the surface. We consider the first authority correct.

CYNOLEBIAS NIGRIPINNIS Regan/*Black-Finned Pearl Fish*

R: Panama River region in Argentina, above Rosario. **H**: Peaceful toward other fishes, but does best when kept with only their own kind. **W**: Soft, slightly acid water. Temperature 22 to 25°C. **S**: To 4 cm; females smaller. **F**: Small live foods are best. Frozen foods are accepted, but only as a second choice.

Males are eager breeders, and they are constantly seeking out the females and trying to coax them to the bottom, which should have a layer of peat moss. They assume a side-by-side position, then almost stand on their heads and push into the peat moss to deposit their eggs. The peat moss is then removed and stored in a slightly damp condition for three or four months. Water is then added and the young hatch in short order.

CYNOPOECILUS MELANOTAENIA

241

CYNOLEBIAS WHITEI Myers/*White's Pearl Fish*

R: Savannah ponds of the Mato Grosso region, Brazil. **H**: Peaceful toward other fishes, but best if kept by themselves. **W**: Soft, slightly acid water. Temperature 22 to 24°C. **S**: To 8 cm; females slightly smaller. **F**: Live or frozen foods. Dried foods accepted only when very hungry. Like the other annual fishes, it occurs in ponds that disappear in the dry months, to fill up again when the rainy season gets under way. Naturally, such a fish has a very short life span and most dealers shy away from them, but a fish with so much beauty generally finds takers in short order, and if the fish is still fairly young when the dealer gets it, it will not be old when he sells it. The usual method of spawning is the same as for the other *Cynolebias* species, with peat moss as the spawning medium, but it has been found by breeders who have spawned this fish that it will also accept fine-grained sand for their purpose.

CYNOTILAPIA AFRA

CYNOLEBIAS WOLTERSTORFFI Ahl/*Wolterstorff's Pearl Fish*

R: Southeastern Brazil. **H**: Aggressive and pugnacious. Not adaptable for community tanks. Should be given their own well planted tank. **W**: Neutral to slightly acid. Temperature 24 to 26°C. **S**: Males to 10 cm; females slightly smaller. **F**: Frequent feedings with live or freeze-dried foods.

Cynolebias wolterstorffi occurs in temporary water holes in southeastern Brazil. It is found in places where it would never be suspected that fish life could be supported, places where the water disappears completely in the hot dry season. The eggs survive for months in the mud where they were buried by the parents, and when the rains begin to fill up the holes again, the eggs hatch and release ravenous fry. Tiny animalcules and, later, insect larvae are gobbled up at a great rate, and in an amazingly short time the former fry are capable of producing and fertilizing eggs.

CYNOLEBIAS WHITEI

CYNOTILAPIA AFRA (Günther)/*Dogtooth Cichlid, Dwarf Zebra*

R: Likoma Island, Lake Malawi, Africa. **H**: A quarrelsome fish. Best kept to themselves in large tanks. **W**: Requires hard alkaline water at temperatures of 24 to 26°C. **S**: About 8 cm. **F**: An omnivorous fish requiring some vegetable matter in its diet. Adapts well to dry prepared foods. *C. afra* breeds in a manner similar to most of the other Malawian mbuna, being a maternal mouthbrooder. It does, however, produce a smaller clutch size than most other mbunas. There are some behavioral differences between this fish and most of the other mbuna which suggest that *C. afra* may be either evolving in a different direction or may be evolving toward the "typical" mbuna. For instance, the fish tends to form schools of up to 100 in number, and it has been observed feeding on plankton. It has a fairly long jaw gape which equips it for feeding on larger planktonic organisms and smaller fishes.

CYNOLEBIAS WOLTERSTORFFI

243

CYPHOTILAPIA FRONTOSA (Boulenger)/*The Frontosa*

R: Lake Tanganyika, Africa. **H**: Peaceful, especially in consideration of its size. **W**: Hard, alkaline water preferred; temperatures 24 to 28°C. **S**: To about 30 cm. **F**: Accepts most standard aquarium foods.

Cyphotilapia frontosa is a mouthbrooder; the female, which normally is not too roughly treated during the pre-spawning period, holds the large eggs for 2 $\frac{1}{2}$ to 4 weeks. The most important factor in determining the length of incubation time is the temperature; at the lower range of spawning temperatures, 26°C, incubation takes longer. For a fish of its size, the number of eggs produced at each spawning is small. When released, the fry are large even for mouthbrooder fry, and they are not difficult to feed. Sexing of mature fish can be done fairly reliably according to the size of the hump on the head, which is much larger on males than on females.

CYPRINELLA LUTRENSIS

CYPRICHROMIS LEPTOSOMA (Boulenger)/*Slender Cichlid*

R: Endemic to Lake Tanganyika, Africa. **H**: Generally peaceful for a lake cichlid, but more aggressive toward its own kind. **W**: Hard, alkaline water is recommended. A temperature range of 24 to 28°C is best. **S**: Attains a length of about 14 cm. Females are only slightly smaller than males. **F**: Will accept almost any type of aquarium fare, including flake foods, but prefers small live foods that can be plucked from the water column.

The male, upon seeing a possibly receptive female, will begin his courting dance with fin and body movements. He eventually swims down to her with his fins close to his body and squeezes some eggs from the female. The eggs are quickly retrieved by the female, and there is a cloud of white sperm released by the male. This species is a pelagic mouthbrooder. The eggs are 3 to 4 mm in diameter, gray-white in color, and relatively few in number (15 were reported in one spawning). In about 24 days the young are ready to be released and will accept newly hatched brine shrimp or other similar foods immediately. The young will usually gather in a small school near the surface of the aquarium water. In the wild the fry are generally brought up from the deep water and released near the surface.

CYPHOTILAPIA FRONTOSA

CYPRINELLA LUTRENSIS (Baird & Girard)/
Red Horse Minnow, "Asian Fire Barb"

R: Illinois and South Dakota south to Louisiana and Texas. **H**: Peaceful; will not molest its tankmates at any time. **W**: Water must be clean and well aerated, and fish should never be crowded. Temperature may go as high as 26°C, but nearer 21°C is better. **S**: 8 cm. **F**: Prepared foods as well as live foods are eaten, but there should be a preponderance of live or frozen foods.

A trio kept in a community aquarium that also contained tropical species spawned right in the center of the tank. The male fanned away the fine gravel in a small area and then spawned for more than an hour, first with one female and then with the other. Since there were other fishes in the tank the eggs were eaten. Since the fish is plentiful in the Dallas, Texas area, no further attempts were made to isolate and spawn them again. Unfortunately, the bright colors of the male only appear for a few months each year.

CYPRICHROMIS LEPTOSOMA

CYPRINODON MACULARIUS Baird & Girard/*Desert Pupfish*

R: Salton Sea, Colorado delta, and Rio Sonoyata, southwestern United States. **H**: Usually peaceful, but best kept by themselves because of their water requirements and spawning type. **W**: Hard, alkaline water with temperatures from 24 to 32°C. Some salt may be added to the water. **S**: Up to about 6 to 8 cm. **F**: Prefers live foods like tubifex and brine shrimp but can be coaxed onto frozen, flake, or other types of foods.

Spawning can be left to occur naturally by placing several pairs or trios (more females than males) in an aquarium, feeding them well, and waiting for developments. It can be speeded up a little by separating males and females and conditioning them with a heavy diet of live foods. The male will display before the female, circling around her and in general trying to entice her into a suitable spawning site. This will be a clump of fine-leaved or bushy plants or, if continuous egg retrieval is desired, nylon spawning mops.

CYPRINUS CARPIO

CYPRINODON NEVADENSIS Eigenmann & Eigennmann/*Amargosa Pupfish*

R: Nevada. **H**: Usually peaceful, but best kept by themselves because of their high temperature requirements. **W**: Water should be somewhat alkaline and warm, about 29°C. **S**: Up to 6 cm. **F**: Live foods preferred, but they can probably be trained to accept frozen foods.

This species was most likely widespread during the period when, many years ago, this entire area was covered with water. Since that time, however, the fish has become isolated in many small bodies of water. Because of this isolation, six different subspecies of this fish have evolved. Due to man's constant tampering with the fragile Nevada ecosystem at least two of these subspecies are thought to be extinct.

CYPRINODON MACULARIUS

CYPRINUS CARPIO Linnaeus/*Carp*

R: Originally from the temperature waters of Asia, now widespread. **H**: Young specimens are peaceful, but constantly stir up the bottom in search of food. **W**: Will adapt to any water; best is slightly alkaline. Temperature 5 to 24°C. **S**: In natural waters they sometimes exceed a meter in length. **F**: Will eat anything edible. **C**: Entire body and fins olive green to reddish, with some dark brown markings on sides.

Cyprinus carpio has been introduced into many ponds and streams in temperate waters, where it adapts quickly, often living a good many years and, if food is sufficient, growing to a large size. Most small to medium-sized fish are shot with a bow and arrow, and larger ones are speared. The Carp is much more respected in Europe and the Asiatic countries than in the United States. Only young specimens can be kept in the home aquarium. These are useful in that they keep the bottom free of all leftover food; the trouble is that they stir things up very vigorously.

CYPRINODON NEVADENSIS

CYPRINUS CARPIO Linnaeus var./*Koi, Japanese Colored Carp*

H: Peaceful with all but the smallest fish. **W:** Slightly alkaline water is best. Temperature from 5 to 24°C. **S:** To about 50 cm. **F:** Omnivorous; should get and will eat a variety of foods, live, frozen, or dried. **C:** Wide range of color varieties from almost all black to pure white.

Koi are highly developed forms of the common Carp in a similar way that fancy-tail Guppies are highly developed forms of the common Guppy. The Koi is particularly well suited to keep in a garden pool, where its touch of brilliant colors would add a great deal of decorative effect. The Koi was produced by Japanese breeders. The results came in a great variety of color variations, and selective breeding did the rest. At the present time there are at least 19 recognized varieties, with the possibility of many more to come. For many years finnage was very close to that of the original Common Carp species, but a long-finned form now has been produced. Whether that long-finned form will be produced in quantity sufficient to fill the demand for it (assuming that there *will* be a demand for it) remains to be seen.

KOI VARIETIES

Although the greatest degree of enthusiasm for Koi in the United States is centered in Hawaii and California, these extremely variable and interesting fish have fans all over the country.

Because of their size, Koi are basically pool fish and do best in an outdoor environment. They are able to withstand a wide temperature range and are undemanding as to water composition, provided that their water is richly supplied with oxygen. In an outdoor pool, suitable filtration and aeration can easily be provided through the use of the pool filters designed specifically for use with garden ponds. Feeding Koi presents no great problems, as they are heavy eaters and accept a wide variety of foods. Worms, shrimp, insects and insect larvae form the major portion of the Koi diet, but vegetable materials in the form of chopped terrestrial and aquatic plants must be included as regular portions. Although Koi are heavy eaters, they will not eat food that is left to stagnate in their pool, so all uneaten foods should be removed immediately. After they become accustomed to their surroundings Koi are quite willing to accept food right from their owner's fingers.

Koi breed substantially the same as goldfish, scattering their eggs into the fine leaves or root systems of plants (water lettuce and water hyacinths are ideal) after a vigorous chase by the males of the females. Normally, more than one male per female is used. Sex differences among mature Koi are easily distinguishable; viewed from directly above, females will be seen to be much stockier from behind the head to just behind the dorsal fin.

Kohaku

Kohaku

Taishô Sanke

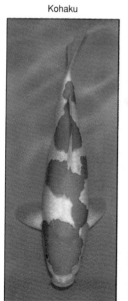

Kohaku

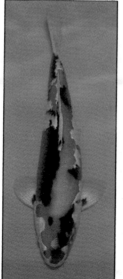

Shôwa Sanshoku

Utsurimono

Shôwa Sanshoku

Utsurimono

Kohaku

A-Ginrin

Kohaku

Taishô Sanke

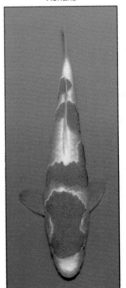

Shôwa Sanshoku   Utsurimono   A-Ginrin

Taishô Sanke   Shôwa Sanshoku   Utsurimono

Taishô Sanke

Shôwa Sanshoku

Utsurimono

Taishô Sanke

Shôwa Sanshoku

Shôwa Sanshoku

Kohaku

Taishô Sanke

Taishô Sanke

Kohaku

Taishô Sanke

Utsurimono

Kohaku

Taishô Sanke

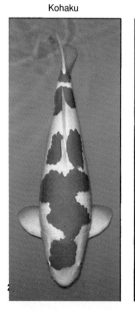

Kohaku

Taishô Sanke

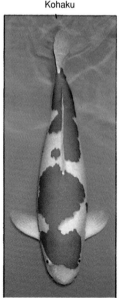

Kohaku

Kohaku

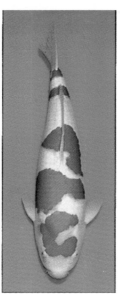

Kohaku

Taishô Sanke

Kohaku

Taishô Sanke

Taishô Sanke

Taishô Sanke
Taishô Sanke
Shôwa Sanshoku

Taishô Sanke
Shôwa Sanshoku
Utsurimono

DANIO AEQUIPINNATUS (McClelland)/*Giant Danio*

R: Quite common on the west coast of India and Sri Lanka. **H**: Peaceful in the community aquarium; will not bother anything it cannot swallow. **W**: Prefers clean, sunny water; pH and hardness not important. Temperature 24 to 26°C. **S**: Wild specimens are said to attain 15 cm; in the aquarium they seldom exceed 10 cm. **F**: Will consume dried as well as live foods; like any active fish, it should be generously fed.

This is one of the old favorites among aquarium hobbyists. It has a good reason to be popular: it is peaceful, active, easy to breed and colorful. It is at home in any aquarium, as long as it is not too small for its size and active habits. Unless it is abused pretty badly, it is seldom attacked by disease. Unlike the *Brachydanio* species the Giant Danio lays adhesive eggs in the manner of the barb species. A thicket of bushy plants is placed at one end of a large aquarium (about 80 liters or more). The water should always be fresh and clear, and the bottom may be covered with glass marbles or pebbles, because the fish sometimes will spawn in the open areas and the eggs could be eaten. Fry hatch in one to two days, but some will take a little longer. For the next three to five days, until the yolk-sac is absorbed, the youngsters will be seen hanging from the glass sides and plants. Then when they begin swimming, food must be provided. Tha males and females are colored similarly to one another, with the males showing a greater intensity of the coloration. Fully adult fish in good condition, however, can easily be told apart because the females, in addition to being much heavier in build are also more deep-bodied.

257

DANIO DEVARIO (Hamilton-Buchanan)/*Bengal Danio*

R: Northwest India, Orissa, Bengal, and Assam. **H**: Peaceful, very active; should not be combined with nervous, slower-moving fishes. **W**: Not critical; water should be near neutral, clean, and not too hard. **S**: To 10 cm. **F**: A hearty eater; will take dried as well as live or frozen foods.

Danio devario is a slightly smaller fish than *Danio aequipinnatus,* the well-known Giant Danio. It would probably be every bit as popular, but its colors are not nearly as brilliant. Like the Giant Danio it is a very active species and could easily cause a tankmate with more sluggish habits to become very nervous. It is always a good policy when mixing fishes in a so-called "community aquarium" to pay attention not only to whether the fishes will hurt each other or not but also whether they have almost equal dispositions. There is no place, for instance, for a nervous, timid fish in the same tank as such ever-active fellows as the danios.

DIANEMA LONGIBARBIS

DERMOGENYS PUSILLUS van Hasselt/*Malayan Halfbeak*

R: Malaysia, Sumatra, Borneo, and Thailand. **H**: Should be kept by themselves; if more than one male is put into a tank, they will fight continually. **W**: Water should have an addition of one quarter teaspoon of salt to every liter of water. Temperature 23 to 26°C. **S**: Males to 5 cm; females to 6.5 cm. **F**: Living foods like daphnia or mosquito larvae.

Males often indulge in battles that result in injury to the beak, the result of which is death. Females will give birth once or twice to a dozen or so young, and then most subsequent young are premature or are born dead for some other reason. Another possibility that comes to mind is that there might be some tiny trace element that is native to their home waters but which is absent in the aquarium. Perhaps some day we will have the answer or someone will take extra pains with them and produce a healthy strain that will be hardy and fertile.

DANIO DEVARIO

DIANEMA LONGIBARBIS Cope/*Porthole Catfish*
R: Peru (Rio Ambyiacu) and Brazil (Amazon system). **H**: Peaceful. **W**: Not critical. **S**: Attains a length of about 10 to 12 cm. **F**: Live foods preferred although they can be trained to accept prepared foods.

The Porthole Catfish has been misidentified as a species of *Hoplosternum, H. thoracatum,* but catfish experts quickly set everybody straight as to its proper name. Its common name apparently originated from the generally straight line of spots along the side of the fish, although there are often more spots present and they are not always aligned in a regular row.

DERMOGENYS PUSILLUS

DIANEMA UROSTRIATA Miranda-Ribeiro/*Stripe-Tailed Catfish*

R: Vicinity of Manaus, Brazil. **H**: Peaceful; somewhat timid. **W**: Not critical; water about pH 7.5 with a hardness of about 10 degrees. Temperature around 24°C. **S**: Up to 15 cm. **F**: Live foods of all kinds accepted and will also take prepared foods.

To the layman this species looks like a Hoplo or Porthole Catfish that has been decorated with a striped tail. We had one in our office aquarium and it was a bit of a "shrinking violet." We didn't often see it without searching first. It seemed to disregard his tankmates and generally spent most of its time hiding among the plants.

DISTICHODUS FASCIOLATUS

DISTICHODUS AFFINIS Günther/*Silver Distichodus*

R: Lower Zaire region. **H**: Peaceful; can be trusted with other fishes, but requires a large aquarium. **W**: Soft, slightly acid water. Temperature 24 to 27°C. **S**: To 13 cm. **F**: Large amounts of live or frozen foods, with an addition of vegetable matter like lettuce or spinach leaves.

Distichodus cannot be trusted in a planted tank as they have strong vegetarian tendencies. This must also be remembered when they are in an unplanted tank; their feedings should be augmented with an occasional lettuce or spinach leaf. This interesting group has never been spawned in captivity, and it is doubtful if this feat will ever be accomplished unless an exceptionally large tank or pool is used for the purpose. It must also be remembered that *Distichodus* are shy fishes, and although the tank cannot be planted it is also possible to arrange rocks, roots, etc. in such a manner that hiding places are provided.

DIANEMA UROSTRIATA

DISTICHODUS FASCIOLATUS Boulenger/*Shark-Tailed Distichodus*
R: Zaire basin and Angola. **H**: Peaceful with other fishes, but requires a large aquarium. **W**: Soft, slightly acid water. Temperature 24 to 27°C. **S**: Up to 30 cm. **F**: Large amounts of live or frozen foods, with the addition of vegetable matter such as lettuce or spinach leaves.

In contrast to the oddly-shaped, deep-bodied members of the group, the Shark-Tailed Distichodus has a body that is a little longer and slimmer than the others. Besides, it has the *Distichodus* habit of plant-eating, which might be tolerated in a more highly colored species but not in an Ugly Duckling like this one. Besides its vegetarian tendencies, this species has the added disadvantage to home aquarists that it gets altogether too large for the average aquarium. The caudal base of young specimens is covered with dark spots, a characteristic that disappears when the fish gets older.

DISTICHODUS AFFINIS

DISTOCHODUS LUSOSSO Schilthuis/*Long-Nosed Distichodus*

R: Upper and middle Zaire River including Khinshasa; Angola. **H**: A docile fish, but tends to nibble plants. **W**: Neutral to slightly acid water of moderate hardness. Temperature 24 to 26°C. **S**: To 40 cm in nature, but smaller in the aquarium. **F**: In nature it feeds on worms and other bottom-dwelling invertebrates as well as on soft vegetation. It will adapt to most aquarium fare, but should be given small amounts of soft lettuce or spinach as a dietary supplement.

This species is an active riverine fish that spends most of its time in the lower water layers. Rather large aquaria should be provided for this fish due to its large size and active nature. Plants are not recommended with any *Distichodus* species because these fish love to nibble at the new shoots and leaves. This fish prefers medium hard water. It should be provided with a number of hiding places, which may include rock caves and hanging branches. Little is known about their breeding habits.

DISTICHODUS NOBOLI

DISTCIHODUS SEXFASCIATUS Boulenger/*Six-Barred Distichodus*

R: Lower Zaire region. **H**: Peaceful toward other fishes, but will nibble plants. **W**: Neutral to slightly acid. Temperature 24 to 27°C. **S**: To 25 cm. **F**: Large amounts of live or frozen foods, supplemented with greens like lettuce or spinach leaves. **C**: Body pinkish to white with six dark bands. Fins are brilliant deep red.

As with the other *Distichodus* species, this one should also get a generous proportion of green foods in its diet and will supplement these with any plants it may find. Some hobbyists who wish to have a planted tank and also keep a plant-eater like this one should set up a background of plants and then insert a glass pane in front of them. This robs the tank of some of its area but it is a good way to keep the fish and plants separated. If the fish are fed a good amount of green foods, they will not feel frustrated if they cannot get at the growing plants.

DISTOCHODUS LUSOSSO

DISTICHODUS NOBOLI Boulenger/*Nobol's Distichodus*
R: Lower Zaire River system. **H**: Peaceful; a good community tank fish, but requires a large aquarium. Nibbles plants. **W**: Soft, slightly acid water. Temperature 24 to 27°C. **S**: To 10 cm. **F**: Large amounts of live or frozen foods, with an addition of vegetable matter like lettuce or spinach leaves. Will occasionally accept flake food.

The genus *Distichodus,* which is endemic (exclusively native) to Africa, includes riverine fishes that live in the lower levels of the water. *D. noboli* is a peaceful species that, because of its very active nature, needs a large aquarium in which to live. Because this fish has a great appetite for shoots and fine leaves, heavy aquarium planting is not recommended. Sex distinctions are not obvious.

DISTCIHODUS SEXFASCIATUS

DORMITATOR MACULATUS (Bloch)/*Spotted Sleeper*

R: Atlantic coastal waters from the Carolinas to Brazil. **H**: Inactive and predatory; should not be kept with smaller fishes. **W**: Water should have a salt content, about a quarter teaspoon per liter. Temperature 21 to 24°C. **S**: To 25 cm. **F**: Eats anything and everything; bits of raw fish are especially relished.

This species has been spawned in captivity. They spawn very much like many species of the cichlid family. Both fish clean off a rock, and a large number of eggs are deposited by the female and fertilized by the male. The tiny fry hatch in a day at 24°C, and when the fry begin to swim it is best to remove the parents. Infusoria should be fed at first, followed by newly hatched brine shrimp and later by larger foods. Not a very satisfactory aquarium fish, the Spotted Sleeper is as inactive as its name indicates and spends most of its time in hiding.

EDELIA VITTATA

DYSICHTHYS CORACOIDEUS (Cope)/*Two-Colored Banjo Catfish*

R: Throughout Brazil and as far west as Ecuador and south to Uruguay. **H**: A bottom-dwelling catfish that is nocturnal in habit and ugly in appearance. **W**: Tolerant of any water with a pH of from 5.0 to 8.0 and a temperature between 16 and 29°C. **S**: About 15 cm. **F**: A true scavenger that ingests everything to be found at the bottom of the aquarium whether or not it is digestible. Sex is easily distinguished because females are much fatter and fuller than males. After selecting an active pair, feed them heavily on tubifex or small earthworms. Spawning usually is easier in the spring. If you have the pair well conditioned after a month on live foods, you can induce spawning by changing 50% of their water with *fresh* tap water of the same temperature. In 48 hours the pair will spawn. Sometimes they spawn under a fallen leaf, but other times they spawn on a large rock and incubate their eggs by sitting on them!

DORMITATOR MACULATUS

EDELIA VITTATA (Castelnau)/*Australian Pygmy Perch*

R: Western Australia. **H**: Peaceful; will not harm other fishes or plants. **W**: Water should be clean and have an addition of a quarter teaspoon of salt to each liter of water. Temperature 16 to 24°C. **S**: To 8 cm. **F**: Live or frozen foods; they can be taught to take dried foods, but do not like them.

In Australia the breeding season occurs between the months of July and January, at which time the fish takes on brilliantly intense colors. There is a black area on the back that gives way to an orange stripe from the forehead to the caudal base, and below this an orange area that covers the entire belly region. Eggs are laid in plants near the bottom, eight to ten being laid each day until a total of about 60 is attained. They hatch in 62 to 74 hours.

DYSICHTHYS CORACOIDEUS

EIGENMANNIA VIRESCENS (Valenciennes)/*Green Knife Fish*

R: Widely distributed all over northern South America. **H**: Mostly nocturnal; very greedy eaters that are best kept by themselves. **W**: Water should be well aged and clean. Temperature 24 to 27°C. This fish is very sensitive to fresh water. **S**: To 45 cm. **F**: Almost any food is taken greedily; preferred of course are the larger live foods, but they also eat chunks of beef heart and oatmeal.

The knife fishes are a very interesting group because of their unusual shape and manner of swimming. Most of them are nocturnal. Their swimming motions are most interesting, and it is difficult to understand how a fish which is equipped with only pectoral fins and an anal fin can swim so rapidly and maneuver so well. Propulsion is accomplished by a rippling motion of the anal fin. If the fish is swimming forward and wishes to reverse direction, it simply reverses the rippling motion and swims backward just as easily.

ELECTROPHORUS ELECTRICUS

ELASSOMA EVERGLADEI Jordan/*Everglades Pygmy Sunfish*

R: Florida and Georgia. **H**: Very timid with other fishes; should be kept by themselves in a small aquarium. **W**: Slightly alkaline water. Room temperatures, about 18 to 20°C, are perfect. **S**: About 3 cm; females a little smaller. **F**: Small live foods are best, like sifted *Daphnia,* newly hatched brine shrimp, etc.

Coming from the Everglades in Florida, they can withstand a variety of temperatures. Because of their tiny size, a pair can be kept quite comfortably in a 4- or 8-liter aquarium. Eggs are usually placed on a plant leaf and hatch in two to three days. Spawnings vary from 30 to 60 eggs. Parents guard the eggs and young, which are easily fed in their first days on dust-fine foods. This fish has at times an odd manner of propelling itself along the bottom: the long ventral fins are alternately swished back and forth along the bottom, giving the fish the appearance of "walking."

EIGENMANNIA VIRESCENS

ELECTROPHORUS ELECTRICUS (Linnaeus) *Electric Eel*

R: Middle and lower Amazon basin. **H**: Because of this species' electric properties it is not suitable as a community tank fish. More than one specimen can sometimes be kept in a tank, but this is risky. **W**: Soft, slightly acid water is optimal, but not important. **S**: Up to 1.8 meters; aquarium specimens much smaller. **F**: Live fishes are preferred; small specimens will take worms and may be taught to accept liver and similar foods. **C**: Young specimens olive-brown with yellowish markings. Adults olive-brown with orange throat. Eyes emerald green.

Although there are several species of fishes that possess electric organs, *E. electricus* has developed them to the greatest extent, with approximately four-fifths of the length of the body being occupied by these elements. The eel does not discharge when at rest, but as it starts to move it emits impulses at the rate of about 50 per second at a strength of up to 1 ampere. The impulses apparently perform the dual functions of navigating device and defensive-offensive mechanism. It is said that the eel stuns its prey before eating it. Electric Eels kept in the same aquarium frequently fight by assuming a head-to-tail position and engaging in tail-slapping, biting, and discharging electricity.

ELASSOMA EVERGLADEI

ENNEACAMPUS ANSORGEI (Boulenger)/*African Freshwater Pipefish*

R: Zaire region in Africa. **H**: Peaceful. **W**: Should be maintained in slightly salty to brackish water. Temperature about 25°C. **S**: 10 cm. **F**: Usually refuses to eat anything but small living fishes, although floating frozen foods may be picked at; aquatic crustaceans and baby livebearers are preferred.

This species has the peculiar breeding pattern of the family Syngnathidae, whereby the male carries the eggs in a brood pouch until they hatch. Fry are equally difficult to raise.

ENNEACANTHUS GLORIOSUS

ENNEACANTHUS CHAETODON (Baird)/*Blackbanded Sunfish*

R: New Jersey south to northern Florida, coastal. **H**: Usually peaceful, but should not be trusted with smaller fishes. Also shy and gets nervous when with very active fishes. **W**: Water should be kept alkaline and a part of it frequently changed. Temperature around 21°C. **S**: 8 cm. **F**: Live foods only; it might be possible to induce them to eat frozen foods, but they will seldom take dried foods. **C**: Body silvery to light yellow, with a number of dark bars running vertically. First ventral rays are orange.

The Blackbanded Sunfish is found in ponds and cypress swamps along the Atlantic Coast from New Jersey down to Northern Florida. The best time to hunt them (after having first checked the fish and game regulations, of course) is early summer, when the young ones have left the nest and are found along the shore in shallow water. These youngsters are best able to make the change to aquarium life, and there are fewer losses. There may be a great temptation to catch some adult specimens, but if you do this be prepared to lose some of your catch, as they do not acclimate themselves as easily to the aquarium. When transporting them do not crowd the containers; remember, a few live healthy fish are better than a lot of dead ones! This is a great favorite with European hobbyists.

The males build a nest by digging out a depression in the gravel. The females are then lured to this nest and a great many eggs are expelled. These eggs are sticky and adhere to the gravel. Females are driven away and should be removed. Males guard the eggs and later the young but should be removed when the young leave the nest.

ENNEACAMPUS ANSORGEI

ENNEACANTHUS GLORIOSUS (Holbrook)
Diamond Sunfish, Bluespotted Sunfish

R: Eastern coastal United States from New York to Florida. **H**: Peaceful when kept with fishes of its own size. **W**: Slightly alkaline water which is kept unheated, at room temperature. **S**: To 8 cm. **F**: Variety of live or frozen foods. Dried foods are accepted unwillingly.

Enneacanthus gloriosus is doubtless one of the most beautiful of our American sunfishes, as well as one of the most peaceful. Occurring as it does in the eastern coastal states of the United States, it should be rated as a cold-water species and should not be kept in a heated aquarium unless there is danger of the water freezing. Spawning takes place among fine-leaved plants. At this time the male may treat the female with excessive roughness. The female should be taken out when finished. Fry hatch in three days and are very easy to raise.

ENNEACANTHUS CHAETODON

ENNEACANTHUS OBESUS (Girard)/*Banded Sunfish*

R: Eastern United States from Massachusetts to northern Florida, coastal. **H**: Because of the cooler temperatures enjoyed by this species it should probably have a tank all to itself. **W**: Not critical. Should have partial periodic water changes. Temperature for breeding a cool 20°C. **S**: About 8 cm. **F**: Feed a wide variety of live foods such as daphnia, cyclops, chironomid larvae, brine shrimp, etc., and perhaps some frozen or freeze-dried prepared foods.

Spawning it is not difficult. As the temperature is raised, the male's colors will intensify if he's in good condition and ready to spawn. He will select a spawning site among the plants (if not enough plants are available he will use a shallow pit in the sand). The male will wait at his chosen spawning site for the female and at her approach will swim toward her in his most vivid coloration and with fins spread. He will prod her with his snout and lead her to the preferred site. There, with some quivering, the spawning process occurs. As the eggs are laid the male will create a strong current with his fins and sweep the eggs into the plants, where they become attached.

EPALZEORHYNCHOS FRENATUS

EPALZEORHYNCHOS BICOLOR Smith/*Red-Tailed Shark*

R: Thailand. **H**: Apt to be a bit scrappy among themselves, but peaceful toward other fishes. **W**: Slightly alkaline water and a hardness of about 10 DH. Temperature 24 to 26°C. **S**: To 12 cm. **F**: All kinds of live foods, besides some vegetable matter like lettuce or spinach leaves. **C**: Deep brown to black body color ending in a red caudal base and tail.

The person who first referred to this group of fishes as "sharks" certainly had a healthy imagination. True, the species has a rather high dorsal fin, but its shape does not even faintly resemble the sickle-shaped dorsal fin of the real sharks that are seen so frequently in marine waters. There is no other resemblance either between the shy, mild-mannered Red-Tailed Shark and its vicious, ever-hungry namesake. The only time the Red-Tailed Shark gives any inkling of a "chip on its shoulder" is when one male intrudes into another's territory.

ENNEACANTHUS OBESUS

EPALZEORHYNCHOS FRENATUS Fowler/*Rainbow Shark*

R: Thailand, Mekong River. **H**: Peaceful toward other fishes; tend to fight among themselves if not given enough tank room. **W**: Water 10 DH and slightly alkaline. Temperature 24 to 27°C. **S**: To 12 cm. **F**: Does best with live or frozen foods and will sometimes accept flake foods; vegetable matter should be included in the diet.

The Rainbow Shark is very much like its close relative the Red-Tailed Shark. Their aquarium should not be given much light and should be provided with an ample amount of hiding places. Although *Epalzeorhynchos frenatus* is generally peaceful toward other species, it tends to be belligerent with its own kind. *E. frenatus* is generally slimmer than *E. bicolor*.

Vegetable matter should be included in its diet in addition to the usual flake and frozen foods. If the Rainbow Shark does not get enough greens, it will tend to pick at the aquarium plants.

EPALZEORHYNCHOS BICOLOR

EPALZEORHYNCHOS KALOPTERUS (Bleeker)/*Flying Fox*

R: Sumatra and Borneo. **H**: Peaceful, even toward smaller fishes. **W**: Not critical. An active fish; therefore aquarium should be of a good size. Sunny location best as it provides algae. **S**: Said to attain 14 cm, but specimens in captivity do not usually exceed 10 cm. **F**: Omnivorous; should have some vegetable substances in its diet, such as is provided by algae.

Most of our so-called "scavenger" fishes are only tolerated because of their useful habits. They keep a tank bottom clear of uneaten food, and many of them also clear the rocks and plants as well as the glass sides of an aquarium of algae. Here we have a fish that does all these things and is beautiful and active as well.

EPIPLATYS CHAPERI CHAPERI

EPIPLATYS ANNULATUS (Boulenger)/*Clown Killie*

R: West Africa, Sierra Leone to Liberia. **H**: Peaceful but must be kept by themselves because of their small size, lest they be eaten. **W**: Water should measure 8 DH or less; pH 6.5 to 7.0. Temperature 23 to 25°C. **S**: Males 4 cm; females 3.5 cm. **F**: Small living foods.

First described by Boulenger in 1915, this species was not brought alive into Europe until 40 years later, when the water offered them proved to be wrong and they all died. Then they simultaneously showed up in shipments from three West African countries and were successfully introduced into Europe. We are greatly indebted to Mr. E. Roloff, who made an expedition into Sierra Leone in 1965, for much of the information we now have on this species. He collected them in water that had a temperature of 25°C, a hardness that measured 5 DH and a pH of 6.7. This information makes it easy to duplicate conditions of their home water or at least to approximate them closely.

Epiplatys annulatus is a very small species and it would never be proper to keep it in a community aquarium for the obvious reason that any of the larger species would regard it as a tasty meal. They breed among the leaves of floating plants, the eggs hatching in two weeks. The tiny youngsters must be started with the finest infusoria. When they can consume them, newly hatched brine shrimp may be substituted. This is probably the most colorful member of the genus. Unfortunately, breeding stock degenerates after a few generations and in-bred lines tend to die out.

EPALZEORHYNCHOS KALOPTERUS

EPIPLATYS CHAPERI CHAPERI (Sauvage)/*Chaper's Panchax*

R: West Africa, Sierra Leone to Ghana. **H**: Peaceful; will not bother anything it cannot swallow. **W**: Prefers soft, acid water and a certain amount of sunlight. Temperature 23 to 25°C. **S**: Males slightly under 5 cm; females a little smaller. **F**: Will eat dried foods when hungry, but prefers live foods of all kinds.

A pair can be put into a small aquarium with a few floating plants. Only a few eggs will be laid each day, and they can be picked out with the fingers. They are quite hard and do not break readily. These are then placed separately in small containers, where they will hatch in about 14 days. The young fry are free-swimming at once, and food must be provided. The best way to feed them is with small amounts of newly hatched live brine shrimp. The fry spend almost all of their time at the surface.

EPIPLATYS ANNULATUS

273

EPIPLATYS CHAPERI SHELJUZHKOI Poll/*Sheljuzhko's Panchax*

R: West Africa, in the region of Abidjan, Ivory Coast. **H**: Peaceful toward any fish they cannot swallow. **W**: Soft, slightly acid water. Temperature 22 to 26°C. **S**: To 6 cm. **F**: Live foods of all kinds; can be trained to eat frozen foods. **C**: Males have a brownish body with rows of red spots on the sides. Females have less color and fewer spots.

Epiplatys chaperi sheljuzhkoi has been confused with a great many other *Epiplatys* species that it resembles very closely, and the mistakes are quite understandable. The distinguishing characteristic here, we are told, is that the horizontal rows of red dots are nice and regular in the lower half of the body as well as the upper half. It is an attractive as well as a very hardy species that spawns readily in the manner of the other *Epiplatys* species.

EPIPLATYS DAGETI

EPIPLATYS CHEVALIERI (Pellegrin)/*Chevalier's Panchax*

R: Zaire. **H**: Relatively peaceful; should be treated like other species of *Epiplatys*. **W**: Slightly acid (pH 6.0-6.5) water with a DH of about 7-10. Temperature of at least 24°C. **S**: Attains a length of about 6.5 cm. **F**: Live food of all kinds preferred; can be coaxed onto prepared foods. During the actual spawning the eggs are deposited among the roots of floating plants or the leaves of plants like *Myriophyllum*. These eggs are usually larger (about 1.1-1.3 mm) and less numerous than those of most other species of *Epiplatys*. Chevalier's Panchax is not particularly an egg-eater, so it is safe to leave the eggs in with the parents (providing they are properly fed). However, if you are desirous of rearing all the young it is always a good idea to separate parents from eggs to prevent any accidents from happening. The young are also safe from their parents. The eggs hatch in about two weeks at a temperature of 26°C or about 19 days at 24°C.

EPIPLATYS CHAPERI SHELJUZHKOI

EPIPLATYS DAGETI Poll/*Red-Chinned Panchax*

R: Southwestern Liberia to southeastern Ghana. **H**: Energetic and active; aggressive toward fishes its own size and smaller. **W**: Slightly acid, soft water is preferred. Temperature 24 to 26°C. **S**: To 5.5 cm. **F**: For this species live foods are best, but it will accept freeze-dried foods. These pretty fish, regardless of their complicated historical origins and troublesome taxonomic considerations, require relatively uncomplicated aquarium maintenance procedures. Floating plants will serve them well, since they remain at the surface of the aquarium water most of the time. In their natural habitat they live in still, murky water, such as pools. Consequently, if their aquarium water is kept in constant movement, this condition is likely to be very uncomfortable for them. Spawning this species is not too difficult, since they are typical of the genus *Epiplatys*.

EPIPLATYS CHEVALIERI

EPIPLATYS DUBOISI Poll/*Dubois' Killifish*

R: Stanley Pool area of Congo. **H:** Relatively peaceful; usually best kept with similar species. **W:** Not critical; will do well in water that is slightly hard or slightly soft. Temperature should be about 22 to 26°C. **S:** One of the dwarf species attaining a length of about 2.5 cm. **F:** Newly hatched brine shrimp are best, but tubificid worms and flake foods are also accepted.

Although the specific name *duboisi* has remained with this fish, the generic name varies depending upon the person who is dealing with them at the time. You will probably see references to this fish under the names *Aphyoplatys duboisi*, *Aplocheilus duboisi* and of course the name adopted here, *Epiplatys duboisi*. This is mostly due to its intermediate position between *Epiplatys*, *Aplocheilus* and even *Aphyosemion*.

For spawning the plants can be dispensed with and replaced with either floating or bottom spawning mops. The small (less than one mm in diameter) adhesive eggs are deposited in the mops and hatch out in about one week or even less. For best results they can be removed and placed in shallow dishes of water to hatch. The fry are very small but are able to handle newly hatched brine shrimp right away. Growth is relatively slow, and maturity is reached only after several months.

EPIPLATYS GRAHAMI

EPIPLATYS FASCIOLATUS (Günther)/*Striped Panchax*

R: Sierra Leone, Liberia to Nigeria. **H:** Not safe with smaller fishes; should be kept in a covered tank to prevent them from jumping. **W:** About neutral and not very hard (10 to 15 DH) with a quarter teaspoon of salt added for every liter. **S:** To 8 cm. **F:** Prefers the larger sizes of live foods, but can be trained to take frozen foods.

Epiplatys fasciolatus are easily spawned as a rule, laying their eggs in the plants near the upper reaches of the aquarium. The eggs in the female ripen only a few at a time, and for this reason spawning is extended over a prolonged period. As a result the young hatch a few at a time as well. With such assorted sizes growing up together it would naturally follow that once the biggest of the lot got big enough to swallow the smallest it would do so, and for this reason the hobbyist who wants to raise the most fish possible has to have a number of well-planted tanks ready and must periodically grade his youngsters as to size.

EPIPLATYS DUBOISI

EPIPLATYS GRAHAMI (Boulenger)/*Graham's Panchex*

R: Southern Nigeria. **H**: Lively and peaceful with others of about its own size. **W**: Soft, slightly acid water is best. Temperature 24 to 26°C. **S**: To 5.5 cm; females slightly smaller. **F**: Live foods in variety; dried foods only in an emergency.

They are skillful jumpers, so their aquarium should be kept covered at all times. You will find that if a pair or more are kept in their own tank, a few youngsters will be found every once in a while swimming at the surface; they can be lifted out with a spoon to a tank of their own where they are not in constant danger of being eaten. Of course, if more young are desired the eggs must be hunted out and hatched in a tank of their own. Hatching time is 10 to 14 days, and the young are able to swim and eat at once. Raising them is no problem, as they have sharp eyes and are skilled at hunting for their food. They should be sorted frequently to prevent cannibalism. Our photo shows the female of the species.

EPIPLATYS FASCIOLATUS

EPIPLATYS HUBERI

EPIPLATYS HUBERI Radda & Purzl/*Huber's Killifish*

R: Southwestern Gabon. **H:** Peaceful with its own kind and with other species. Males may chase each other occasionally. **W:** Not critical; a pH of 7, a hardness of 5-15 dGH, and a temperature of 20 °to 27°C are recommended. **S:** Attains a length of about 7 cm. **F:** Any available small live foods (insect larvae and fruit flies are especially welcomed).

For spawning, an aquarium of 8 to 16 liters is suffficient. The temperature should be near the high end of the range, and the pH is best lowered a bit (6.3-6.8 for example). It is suggested that the potential breeders be conditioned apart from each other and then brought together for spawning. The conditioning foods must be of the live types mentioned previously. The tank should be supplied with a suitable spawning substrate such as Java moss, although other fine-leaved plants are acceptable and artificial spawning mops in the lower third of the tank can be used.

The spawning pair should be brought together for a matter of two to three hours at intervals of three days for best spawning results. The spawning corresponds to that of the well-known aquarium favorites *Aplocheilus lineatus* and *Epiplatys dageti,* wherein the male herds the female into the plants where the eggs are released and fertilized. About five to ten eggs are released per spawning. These are adhesive and remain stuck to the plants. The eggs are about 1.1 to 1.2 mm in diameter and translucent at first, becoming darker (tea color then rusty brown) as the embryo develops. Hatching takes place in approximately one to three weeks depending upon temperature (nine days at 29°C, 20-25 days at 21°C).

Epiplatys huberi is quite cannibalistic, with the larger fry eating their smaller brothers and sisters. It is therefore necessary to segregate them constantly according to size. At the age of about a month the first signs of the pattern (dark crossbars) can be seen. At three months of age they should be about 30 to 35 mm in length, at which time the dark crossbars fade and the yellow color of the males becomes evident. At the age of four to five months the fish can reach sexual maturity although they may not be fully grown.

EPIPLATYS LAMOTTEI Daget/*Lamotte's Rivulin*

R: Region of the source, Niger River, particularly around the border between northwestern Liberia and Guinea. **H:** A peaceful fish that could be housed in a community tank. Stays near the surface. **W:** Not critical. Can tolerate hardness up to 20°dGH, pH values from 6.0 8.0, and temperatures between 22° and 26°C. **S:** Attains a length of 7cm. **F:** Live foods are best but will accept substitutes occasionally.

Lamotte's Rivulin comes from shallow, shady rain forest waters where it finds shelter among roots and the dense growth of aquatic plants. It was originally considered a subspecies of *Epiplatys fasciolatus*, but Col. Scheel regarded it as a valid species.

Sexes are easily distinguished, with the male sporting bright colors, the female being rather drab. Ripe females exhibit a pale, swollen belly area. For best results in spawning this species, a single pair or one male with two females should be placed in a 20-gaillon tank furnished as mentioned above. They should be well conditioned on live foods. The male initially courts the female with closely pressed fins as he swims around and around her. He tries to direct her to where the aquatic plants are located. If the female is ready to spawn she at first follows him, then takes the initiative when the plants are reached by searching for a suitable spawning site. Once this is found she stays there and presses close to the plants. The male immediately swims to her side and with intense trembling the pair assume an "S" shape and release the eggs and sperm simultaneously. With a sudden dart they part, the resulting water currents forcing the fertilized eggs into the plants. The eggs become attached to the plants by adhesive filaments. The eggs are sturdy enough so that they can be removed each evening with your fingers or, if the spawners are well fed, they can be left in the tank for about a week whereupon the egg-laden plant(s) can be removed and replaced for the next week's spawn. About 70-80 eggs can be expected for a week's spawning. In about two weeks (12-18 days) the eggs hatch. The fry will stay close to the surface and should be fed immediately. Newly hatched brine shrimp is a good starter. Cleanliness must be maintained, so siphon often and make partial water changes regularly.

EPIPLATYS LONGIVENTRALIS (Boulenger)/*Banded Panchax*

R: Tropical West Africa, principally southern Nigeria. **H**: Peaceful toward any fish it cannot swallow. **W**: Soft, slightly acid water. Temperature 24 to 27°C. **S**: To 5.5 cm. **F**: Live foods preferred; dried foods only when nothing else is available.

E. longiventralis is definitely not a fish which could be combined with smaller specimens in a community aquarium. Those which it could swallow would be stalked and engulfed, and others which would be a little too large for these attentions would be bullied. It is also a mistake to keep two large males together. Even if there are enough females to keep them both busy, there would be a constant struggle for supremacy.

A healthy pair will spawn readily, hanging their eggs in fine-leaved plants near the surface. The so-called "spawning mops" of nylon yarn are also accepted in lieu of plants. Eggs hatch in 12 to 14 days and during the incubation period should not be exposed to bright light. While they are growing, fry should be sorted frequently to keep the same sizes together; otherwise there will be many losses among the smaller ones from being eaten by the larger ones.

EPIPLATYS SEXFASCIATUS

EPIPLATYS MACROSTIGMA (Boulenger)/*Spotted Panchax*

R: Zaire tributaries near its mouth, Africa. **H**: Peaceful toward any fish it cannot swallow. **W**: Slightly acid, soft water. Temperature 24 to 26°C. **S**: To 6 cm. **F**: Living foods; accepts prepared or frozen foods only when very hungry.

This attractive little fish is likely to be very shy in an aquarium which is sparsely planted, and for this reason it should be kept in a tank which is not too strongly lighted and is well planted. Like other *Epiplatys* species, it is a fairly ready spawner and keeping two or three females to one male not only reduces the wear and tear on the female but also results in more eggs. These hatch in just two weeks' time and have a fairly hard shell, making them easy to handle. If the owners desires, he can mail them by air for quite a distance, as long as they are placed in water again before they hatch. The best way to pack them is in a small box, which is then put in a larger one with paper towels for insulation against temperature shocks.

EPIPLATYS LONGIVENTRALIS

EPIPLATYS SEXFASCIATUS (Gill)/*Six-Banded Panchax*

R: West coast of Africa from southern Liberia to the mouth of the Zaire River. **H**: Fairly peaceful with fishes of their own size. **W**: A well-established, well-planted tank that is not too small is preferred. Water should be soft and slightly acid. Temperature 24 to 26°C. **S**: Large specimens attain a length of 10 cm; average is smaller. **F**: Any kind of living food is preferred; frozen or dried foods are usually passed up.

Males take up a position under the leaves, and when a female or another male swims by, they scoot out with flashing colors. It is advisable once they are established in an aquarium that is to their liking to move them as little as possible. This is of course good advice with any fish, but some adapt to varying conditions more easily than others, and the Six-Banded Panchax is not one of these. When spawning this fish it is best to use a ratio of two or even three females to one male.

EPIPLATYS MACROSTIGMA

ERETMODUS CYANOSTICTUS Boulenger/*Striped Goby Cichlid*

R: Lake Tanganyika, Africa. **H**: Generally inoffensive with other species, although combative among themselves. **W**: Hard, alkaline water preferred. Temperature 23 to 26°C. **S**: Up to 8 cm. **F**: Accepts all standard aquarium foods; the size of the fish's mouth should be considered when selecting foods.

E. cyanostictus is a bottom-dweller that moves from place to place in the tank by a goby-like "hopping" motion rather than a more normal swimming motion. When maintained without other species, it will be less of a bottom-hugger and will make regular visits to other levels in the tank, especially upon introduction of food, but when kept with rough species in a deep tank it will usually stay almost entirely at the bottom.

This is a mouthbrooding species; the female broods the eggs for between five to six weeks and is much more temperamental in her handling of the eggs than many other mouthbrooding females. A slight upset during the brooding period often causes her to eat or expel the eggs, which usually number no more than 25 regardless of the size of the female. The sexes are very hard to distinguish, as there are no reliable indicators of sex. The slight hump-headed appearance of mature males is often a characteristic of females as well, and coloration can not be used at all to differentiate the sexes.

ERPETOICHTHYS CALABARICUS

ERIMYZON SUCETTA (Lacépède)/*Lake Chubsucker*

R: Eastern North America to midwest, from southern New York to Florida, west to Texas and north to Minnesota, Michigan, and Wisconsin. **H**: A specialty fish that should be kept in cool water aquaria. **W**: Variable except that temperatures higher than 21°C usually cause problems. **S**: Reaches a length of about 25 cm. **F**: Will usually take daphnia, brine shrimp, chironomid larvae, copepods.

The tank needs good filtration as the fish stirs up the bottom quite regularly. The tank should also be covered to prevent the fish from jumping out. In nature these fish spawn in early spring (although they can spawn as late as early July). The male cleans an area amid the gravel for egg deposition (although in some cases the eggs are simply scattered). The female lays up to 20,000 eggs over a two-week period. In about six to seven days they hatch out if the temperature is in the upper range, about 22°C or more.

ERETMODUS CYANOSTICTUS

ERPETOICHTHYS CALABARICUS (Smith)/*Rope Fish*

R: Niger Delta, Cameroon. **H**: Largely nocturnal; spends most of its time on the bottom. Best kept only with its own kind. **W**: Not critical; it is not entirely dependent upon the oxygen content of the water for breathing. **S**: Up to 40 cm; tank-raised specimens do not attain this size. **F**: All living foods that are not too large to be swallowed are accepted; also strips of lean beef, beef heart, or earthworms.

It looks more like a snake, an illusion which is further enhanced by its motions. In its habitat it occurs in pools that sometimes dry out in the dry season. Like the lungfishes, it is capable of burying itself in the mud and leaving only a tiny hole for breathing. The dorsal fin of this fish is interesting: it is broken up into a series of small finlets like those found in the mackerel family of oceanic waters. The swim-bladder is paired, with one much larger than the other. This acts as an accessory breathing organ.

ERIMYZON SUCETTA

ERYTHRINUS ERYTHRINUS (Schneider)/*Short-Finned Trahira*

R: Northern and central South America. **H**: A predatory fish with pike-like habits; it will lie motionless and wait for prey to pass by before striking. The species becomes more active at night. **W**: Soft to medium hard water; neutral water (pH 7.0). Temperature 24 to 25°C. **S**: Up to 20 cm. **F**: Live food recommended.

This fish requires a large aquarium with dense vegetation and dim lighting. As this fish is predatory, it can only coexist with other large fishes if it is to be kept in a community aquarium. The males have large dorsal fins with a yellow edge. The females have shorter dorsal fins, which are rounded. *Erthrinus erythrinus* has not yet been bred in captivity.

ETHEOSTOMA CAERULEUM

ESOMUS DANRICA (Hamilton-Buchanan)/*Flying Barb*

R: Singapore and parts of India; numerous in ditches of rice paddies. **H**: Peaceful; spends most of its time at or near the surface. **W**: Not critical, as long as the water is clean. **S**: Said to attain 13 cm in native waters; in the aquarium about 6 cm. **F**: Should have food that floats or stays near the top, such as daphnia (which will gather under a light) or mosquito larvae (which come up for air).

The *Esomus* species have a distinguishing characteristic: a pair of long "whiskers" extend from the corners of the upper lip underneath the body. These barbels are almost half the entire length of the body. A small school of Flying Barbs is attractive in a tank where most of the other fishes are found in the middle and lower reaches, and they provide some action in the upper reaches. Males are smaller and slimmer than the females. They are very prolific spawners, usually in floating plants in the corners.

ERYTHRINUS ERYTHRINUS

ETHEOSTOMA CAERULEUM Storer/*Rainbow Darter*
R: Western New York to Tennessee and Louisiana to Wisconsin and southeastern Minnesota. Southern Missouri and northern Arkansas. **H:** Somewhat shy bottom fish. Best kept in a tank of their own kind or even other darters. **W:** Clean water possibly with a current recommended. Cooler temperatures (not higher than 24° C) are necessary. **S:** Attains a length of about 7-8 cm. **F:** Will eat almost anything but live foods are preferred.

Spawning starts when a ripe female looks for a suitable spot to deposit her eggs. This is usually an open gravel area. The male will closely follow her driving away any male rivals that come too close. The female finds a spot and the male sets up a territory that he defends. The female dives into the gravel and the male positions himself directly above her and starts vibrating. The female vibrates also, with the vibrations of both increasing in intensity for about seven seconds or so with the gravel flying in all directions. The two part and rest as 0 to 7 eggs are deposited. The spawning may be interrupted by other males having to be chased away. Too many interruptions and the female may look for another mate. The eggs can be retrieved with a gravel-cleaning siphon. They are round, transparent with a small oil droplet, and just under 2 mm in diameter. The hatching tank can be smaller (a half-full 10-gallon tank has been recommended) and should be provided with filtration (a couple of sponge filters will do) and perhaps an algae-covered rock or two. The eggs are placed in a glass dish in this tank. In about two weeks the 6 mm long fry hatch out. At first they are relatively inactive as they are absorbing nutrition from their yolk sacs. After about two days a good starting food should be offered and after four days newly hatched brine shrimp should be provided as by this time they are free swimming. In about a month the fry are about 13 mm in length and are starting to color up.

ESOMUS DANRICA

ETROPLUS MACULATUS (Bloch)/*Orange Chromide*

R: India and Sri Lanka. **H**: Fairly peaceful with fishes of its own size, but cannot be trusted completely. **W**: Water should be fresh and clean, with about a quarter teaspoon of salt added to each liter. **S**: About 8 cm. **F**: Should be provided with living or frozen foods; dried food taken only when very hungry.

In form these fish greatly resemble the sunfishes of North America, and their breeding habits are very similar. Although a rock or wide plant leaf may be selected, this fish prefers to find an open space and dig there until it reaches the aquarium bottom, which it will then clean meticulously. The female usually provides little help, leaving this job to the male. The eggs are attached to this bottom surface and carefully tended by both parents. Young hatch in four to six days, and about a week later they begin to swim free.

EXODON PARADOXUS

ETROPLUS SURATENSIS (Bloch)/*Banded Chromide*

R: India and Sri Lanka; in the mouths of streams and bays. **H**: Somewhat quarrelsome; should be trusted only with fishes its own size or bigger. **W**: Requires a generous addition of salt to the water, a tablespoon for every 4 liters or the equivalent of 10% sea water. **S**: Wild specimens may measure up to 40 cm, but we seldom see them more than 8 cm in length. **F**: Should be generously fed with a variety of live foods or frozen full-grown brine shrimp.

This fish is better known to the natives of India as an article of food than as a candidate for the average aquarium. They are usually found in brackish river mouths and sometimes ascend the rivers into fresh water, like the scats that come from the same area. They seem to prefer these brackish waters to marine environments and are seldom found in pure salt water. Occasionally some small specimens come in with shipments as a rarity, but their "chip-on-the-shoulder" attitude with their tankmates, along with their inability to do well in fresh water, will always keep them from becoming favorites among aquarium hobbyists.

ETROPLUS MACULATUS

EXODON PARADOXUS Müller & Troschel/*Miguelinhos*
R: Guyana and Brazil **H**: Small specimens are mostly peaceful toward other fishes; bigger ones are likely to fight among themselves. **W**: Should have a large, sunny tank with plenty of vegetation. Rather high temperatures are required, not under 25°C. **S**: Attains a size of about 15 cm, but specimens in an aquarium seldom exceed 10 cm. **F**: Should get mostly live foods, but will also take frozen foods and pieces of fish, shrimp, etc.

The native women have a warm affection for this little fish and come to look upon them almost as pets. South American aquarists tell us that a number of these little beauties can be raised together and never cause any trouble. The sad truth is that if a number of grown specimens are put in the same tank, in many cases they soon injure each other. However, there have been a few accounts of them spawning in the aquarium. According to these accounts, they spawned in the usual tetra fashion; that is to say, they scattered eggs in bushy plants. The eggs hatched and the fry were of good size and easy to raise.

ETROPLUS SURATENSIS

FOERSCHICHTHYS FLAVIPINNIS (Meinken)/*Yellowfinned Lampeye*

R: Lagos, Nigeria. **H:** Peaceful; best kept in a group of at least a dozen. Because of their small size, they should be given their own quarters. **W:** Soft, slightly acid water is best. Temperature 23 to 26°C. **S:** About 3 cm. **F:** Small live foods only are accepted.

If a number of Yellowfinned Lampeyes are put together, males and females pair off and in a short time a small cluster of eggs is seen hanging from the vent of some of the females. The eggs are soon brushed off when the female swims through some plants, and in 12 to 18 days the very small fry hatch. The tiny fry are a problem to feed. Only the smallest infusoria can be handled, and growth is extremely slow. Once they have been brought to a size where they can eat newly hatched brine shrimp, then things become more normal and growth speeds up.

FUNDULUS CHRYSOTUS

FUNDULOSOMA THIERRYI Ahl/*Ghana Killifish*

R: Northern Togo (type locality) and northern Ghana. **H:** Does well with fishes its own size but is best kept in a tank of its own. **W:** Does best at a pH of about 7, hardness 10 to 15 DH (German), and a temperature of 20°-22°C. A teaspoon of salt per 10 liters of water is recommended. **S:** Attains a length of 3.5 cm. **F:** Not demanding. Will take any suitable small-sized food, but prefers fruit flies *(Drosophila)* and newly hatched brine shrimp. It may be best to separate the sexes for at least two weeks before the spawning attempt. After spawning, the fish are removed, the water is drained, and the peat is gently squeezed until it is damp and breaking apart. It can then be placed in plastic bags and stored for two to three months.

The Ghana Killifish is easily spawned. The tank need be no larger than five liters for a trio of one male and three females. The bottom can be covered with silica sand of the proper consistency or with peat moss, the majority of breeders preferring the latter, to a depth of 2 cm. The water should be softer (3-4 German DH) and more acid (pH 6.5) than the regular tank water and at the warm end of the temperature range. It may be best to separate the sexes for at least two weeks before the spawning attempt. After spawning, the fish are removed, the water is drained, and the peat is gently squeezed until it is damp and breaking apart. It can then be placed in plastic bags and stored for two to three months.

FOERSCHICHTHYS FLAVIPINNIS

FUNDULUS CHRYSOTUS (Günther)/*Golden Ear, Golden Topminnow*
R: Southeastern United States from South Carolina to Texas. **H**: Peaceful if kept with fishes of its own size. **W**: Although it sometimes comes from brackish water, it greatly prefers fresh water. Temperature 23 to 26°C. **S**: To 8 cm. **F**: Has an excellent appetite and will eat dried as well as live or frozen foods. **C**: Sides greenish with rows of red dots. Females have less color and fewer dots. Bright golden spot on each gill-cover.

At spawning time it is not advisable to keep too many males together or there may be fights. It is also a good idea (in the interest of the females) to use two or three females for each male when spawning this fish because the males are hard drivers. Eggs are laid in bushy plants at the rate of a few each day. They hatch in eight to fifteen days, and if they are not removed daily the parents will eat every egg they find.

FUNDULOSOMA THIERRYI

FUNDULUS CINGULATUS Valenciennes/*Banded Topminnow*

R: South Carolina, Georgia, Florida; found in standing water near the coastline. **H**: Peaceful when kept with fishes its own size. **W**: It is advisable to add one teaspoon of salt to every 20 liters of aquarium water. Temperature 23 to 25°C. **S**: To 7 cm. **F**: Will eat most aquarium fish foods, including dried flake food, freeze-dried food and live food.

Fundulus cingulatus should be given an aquarium with plenty of swimming space. The tank should be well planted (although not to the extent that it impedes the fish's swimming) and put in a location where it can get plenty of sunshine. This species is usually peaceful with other species, although the males may sometimes fight among themselves. Sexing is easy, as the males are more brightly colored than the females and also have a more robust body and longer fins.

Fundulus cingulatus is not a difficult species to breed. The fish lay their eggs on the plants during a spawning period which lasts several days. After spawning, the parents should be removed from the breeding tanks before they have a chance to eat their eggs. The young will hatch in one or two weeks and should be fed at once. The fry grow slowly.

FUNDULUS NOTATUS

FUNDULUS HETEROCLITUS (Linnaeus)/*Zebra Killie, Mummichog*

R: Atlantic Coast from Canada to Florida. **H**: Fairly peaceful, but may pick on smaller fishes. **W**: Water should be alkaline and hard (about 20 DH), with some salt added, at least a teaspoonful to every 4 liters; will take full salt water. Should be kept at room temperature. **S**: To 20 cm. **F**: All kinds of live foods, also dried foods that have a vegetable content, such as the so-called "Molly food."

The Zebra Killie is among the most common small fish along the Atlantic Coast, ranging from Canada down to Florida. It prefers the brackish waters of bays and river mouths but is occasionally found in fresh water. During the summer months most of the establishments that sell live bait along the New Jersey coast have a supply of these live "killies" at all times. In the aquarium they are peaceful if not very colorful citizens that thrive very well once they have become established. Tanks are best left unheated. Males are vigorous drivers. The eggs are laid in plant thickets near the bottom. Incubation period is six to twelve days.

FUNDULUS CINGULATUS

FUNDULUS NOTATUS (Rafinesque)/*Blackstripe Killifish*
R: Texas, Louisiana, and Mississippi north to Wisconsin. **H**: Fairly peaceful unless kept with fishes it can swallow. **W**: Should be kept in unheated aquaria at room temperatures. **S**: About 8 cm.; fish from the northern part of the range are smaller. **F**: Should get live foods only; they take dried foods only when very hungry.

Fundulus notatus is distinguished by a black stripe which is indistinct in young specimens, becoming distinctly defined with age. The stripe is especially distinct in mature males. It must be remembered when keeping this and other *Fundulus* species that they are native to much cooler waters than the tropical species and should be kept in an unheated aquarium at room temperature. Eggs are laid in bushy plants and hatch in about ten to fourteen days.

FUNDULUS HETEROCLITUS

FUNDULUS NOTTI (Agassiz)/*Star-Head Topminnow, Masked Minnow*

R: South Carolina to Iowa and Texas. **H**: Best kept only with their own kind, as they are likely to attack other species kept with them. **W**: A good-sized tank should be provided, with thick vegetation and good aeration. Should be kept at room temperature. **S**: 6 cm. **F**: Live foods are preferred; dried foods taken only as a last resort.

Most males of the *Fundulus* species are vigorous drivers at breeding time, and it is best to provide each one with several females in order to prevent them from getting hurt. Eggs are deposited on bushy plants and are usually left alone by the parents. It is best to leave the parents in the breeding tank for a week to ten days, as there are only a few eggs deposited each day. Hatching takes place in twelve to fourteen days. The young are free-swimming at once.

GARMANELLA PULCHRA

GAMBUSIA AFFINIS (Baird & Girard)/*Mosquito Fish*

R: Southern United States from eastern Texas to Virginia; widely introduced. **H**: Aggressive and pugnacious; not for the community aquarium. **W**: Will tolerate a wide variety of water conditions, with temperatures ranging from almost freezing to about 29°C. **S**: Males to 3 cm; females to 5.5 cm. **F**: Wide variety of foods is eaten greedily, especially live foods.

Gambusia affinis is a livebearing fish that is particularly adaptable. It can make itself at home in fairly dirty waters and is as much at ease in tropical temperatures as it is in the sometimes near-freezing waters of its native climes. Its appetite is enormous; a healthy fish can consume it own weight in mosquito larvae every day. It is prolific and the young grow very rapidly.

FUNDULUS NOTTI

GARMANELLA PULCHRA Hubbs/*Yucatan Pupfish*

R: Yucatan, Mexico. **H**: Relatively peaceful with species of the same size, but males are aggressive toward females of their own species. **W**: Accepts a wide range of water conditions; slightly brackish is best. **S**: To about 3.5 cm. **F**: Accepts all standard aquarium foods and will also eat loose algae; this species is a heavy eater.

H.J. Richter, in an article in the February 1975 issue of *Tropical Fish Hobbyist* magazine, described the spawning behavior as follows: "The mating ceremony is opened by the male's swimming around the female. Circling around is followed by aggressive driving, with the male attempting to get near the female from all sides. To start with the female tries to escape, but once it is ready to spawn it allows the male to swim alongside it. The latter now lays its dorsal fin over the back of the female, and a slight trembling can be observed in both animals as the single egg is expelled and fertilized. Abruptly the fish draw apart. The glass-clear egg with a diameter of about 1 mm disappears in the spawning wool. The whole process is repeated fairly frequently."

GAMBUSIA AFFINIS

293

GARRA CAMBOGDIENSIS (Tirant)/*Siamese Stone-Lapping Fish*

R: Thailand. **H**: Peaceful toward even the smallest fishes. **W**: Slightly alkaline water with a good amount of sunlight. Tank should be well-planted and afford some hiding places. Temperature 20° to 25°C. **S**: To 15 cm; becomes mature at half that size. **F**: Accepts all foods, but should be allowed to browse occasionally in an aquarium that has a growth of algae. **C**: Back reddish brown, belly silvery; deep black horizontal line from gill covers to caudal base. All fins reddish. It used to be a problem to get rid of algae in the aquarium, but now with the many algae-eating fishes that have become available the situation reverses itself. Some of these fishes, which include *Epalzeorhynchos, Gyrinocheilos,* and others, do their clean-up jobs so well that the hobbyist often wonders if they are getting *enough* algae. *Garra cambodgiensis* is well known to the natives of Thailand, who call it *pa lia hin,* or "stone-lapping fish."

GASTEROPELECUS STERNICLA

GASTEROPELECUS MACULATUS Steindachner/*Spotted Hatchetfish*

R: Panama and western Colombia. **H**: Peaceful surface fish that may be combined with other non-aggressive fishes in the community aquarium. **W**: Clean, fairly soft water. Temperature 24° to 26°C. Tank should be well planted, but the water surface should be mostly clear. **S**: To 9 cm; mostly smaller. **F**: Difficult to feed; should get live food that remains at or near the surface. **C**: Sides bluish silvery with rows of vertical dark spots. Females have a deeper body with less distinct colors.

Their main article of diet, as can be seen by the shape of the mouth, is insect life that swims at the surface or flies just above it. Mosquitoes are a perfect example of this sort of life. Their larval and pupal stages are spent in the water, where they must make frequent trips to the surface for air. The adult winged form flies close to the water when laying eggs. However, feeding mosquito larvae in the home aquarium has its attendant difficulties, and some hobbyists have used wingless fruit flies *(Drosophila)* with success, but there are still no records of the Spotted Hatchetfish being spawned in captivity.

GARRA CAMBOGDIENSIS

GASTEROPELECUS STERNICLA (Linnaeus)/*Silver Hatchetfish*
R: Peruvian Amazon, Guianas, and the Orinoco Basin in Venezuela. **H**: A top-feeder that spends most of its time waiting quietly for a passing insect. **W**: Prefers warm, soft water with a pH of about 6.4. Temperature 24 to 26°C. **S**: About 6 cm maximum. **F**: Floating foods, wingless *Drosophila* flies, and floating bits of frozen brine shrimp.

Because of this fish's propensity for jumping, the Silver Hatchetfish should be kept in a long, well-covered aquarium. The water should be from 24 to 26°C, soft, and slightly acidic (pH of about 6.4). Live foods are most appreciated, including small crustaceans, midge larvae, fruit flies, and small cockroaches. The Silver Hatchetfish is peaceful and well suited as a member of a community aquarium. Although this is not an impossible fish to spawn, little is known about its breeding habits. Apparently spawns like *Carnegiella strigata*.

GASTEROPELECUS MACULATUS

GASTEROSTEUS ACULEATUS Linnaeus/*Three-Spined Stickleback*

R: Most of Europe, both coasts of North America, northern Africa and northern Asia. **H**: Inclined to be pugnacious toward other fishes, and therefore should have their own tank. **W**: Water should be slightly alkaline with a salt content of about a quarter teaspoonful of salt per liter. Temperature 16 to 18°C. **S**: Up to 10 cm. **F**: Living foods only, such as daphnia, tubifex worms, and white worms.

The nest is built in the shape of a ball with a hole through the middle. As building materials bits of plants, etc., are used. These are held together by a sticky secretion from the male's kidneys. After she has laid her eggs, the female is driven out of the nest and, frequently, one or two more females will add their eggs to the nest as well. The eggs hatch in 10 to 14 days, and the fry are carefully guarded.

GEOPHAGUS BRASILIENSIS

GENYOCHROMIS MENTO Trewavas/*Malawian Scale-Eater*

R: Lake Malawi, Africa. **H**: Aggressive, dangerous to other fishes; a scale-and-fin eater. **W**: Neutral to hard alkaline water preferred, but not strictly necessary. Temperature 22 to 26°C. **S**: To 18 cm. **F**: Accepts all standard aquarium foods, but will also eat scales and fins of other fishes kept with them.

Genyochromis mento is the only mbuna (rock-dwelling cichlid of Lake Malawi) known to eat scales; it also eats fins. Both male and female *G. mento* regularly attack other fishes' scales and fins; it is not necessary, though, to provide *G. mento* with long-suffering tankmates in order to maintain the species in good health, because they will accept and do well on more normal aquarium fare. This mouthbrooding species has not been spawned with the degree of regularity attained with other mbunas.

GASTEROSTEUS ACULEATUS

GEOPHAGUS BRASILIENSIS (Quoy & Gaimard)/*Brazilian High-Hat, Pearl Cichlid*
R: Eastern coastal regions of South America from Bahia to the La Plata. **H**: Fairly peaceful for a cichlid. Larger specimens should be kept only with their own kind or with other cichlids their own size. **W**: Not critical. Temperature should be about 26°C. A pair should have a well-planted tank of about 80 liters. **S**: In their native waters, about 30 cm; about half that in captivity. **F**: Live foods preferably; can be accustomed to pieces of fish or shrimp.

A preferred spawning site is a cleft between two rocks, which could be replaced by an empty flowerpot standing upright. Eggs and young are seldom eaten. The young, which hatch in four or five days, are carefully tended by the parents, who keep moving them from place to place in pits dug for them. When the fry have begun to swim, it is best to separate them from their parents who might at anytime forget their affection for their babies and eat them.

GENYOCHROMIS MENTO

GEOPHAGUS STEINDACHNERI Eigenmann & Hildebrand/*Redhump Geophagus*
R: Northern Colombia from the Rio Magdalena and Rio Cauca. One specimen was collected in the Rio Sinu. **H**: Peaceful, although the male might get rough with the female at times. **W**: Not critical. Temperatures should be in the mid 20's (°C). **S**: From about 10 to 12 cm; spawns at 6 cm. **F**: Not fussy; will eat whatever aquarium-type food is available.

Spawning is not difficult to achieve with the Redhump Geophagus. The aquarium (40 liters or bigger is best) should have gravel, some flat rocks (maybe even the usual flowerpots), and can be planted to provide shelter to one of the partners should the spawning become too combative. The pair can be conditioned with proper feedings in the spawning tank. The lightening of the colors and the dancing displays coupled with the extensions of the breeding tubes are the immediate precursors of egg laying.

GEPHYROCHARAX CAUCANUS

GEOPHAGUS SURINAMENSIS (Bloch)/*Surinam Geophagus*
R: Amazon Basin and the Guianas. **H**: Slightly aggressive; typical diggers and earthmovers. **W**: Not critical; a pH of 7.0 or slightly on the acid side, and hardness 15 to 30. Temperature in the mid 20's (°C). **S**: To 24 cm. **F**: Will accept almost any aquarium food including brine shrimp (frozen or live), beef heart, flake food, etc. (but prefers to take them from the bottom).

The Surinam Geophagus has become one of the more popular species of *Geophagus* recently, and information on its habits and breeding behavior has become available. The tank size should be adequate, at least 80 liters or more, and supplied with a layer of bottom gravel. The decorations should be selected with the habits of these fish in mind; they are earthmovers and, at least at breeding time, plant destroyers. Therefore a few rocks would be best although plants can be used if you are so inclined and are willing to see them torn apart by the Surinams. The temperature should be within the normal limits of tropical fishes, spawning temperatures a few degrees higher. A pH of somewhere around neutral is recommended, although it has been reported that its native waters are on the acid side. Perhaps if you are having trouble spawning this fish you might try dropping the pH down to between 6.2 and 6.5 to see if it will help. The hardness is apparently not important; anywhere from 15 to 30 seems to be acceptable and perhaps the tolerance may even go further.

GEOPHAGUS STEINDACHNERI

GEPHYROCHARAX CAUCANUS Eigenmann/*Arrowhead Tetra*
R: Rio Cauca, Colombia. **H**: In constant motion; active to the point of always having to do something, including bothering its tankmates. **W**: Temperature should range between 24 to 26°C. They prefer water that is somewhat soft and a pH that is slightly on the acid side. **S**: Up to 6 cm. **F**: Live foods best, but will accept freeze-dried feedings; dry food will be accepted if very hungry.

In 1965, when Dr. Axelrod and his special T.F.H. Colombian expedition collected some of these fishes, the aquarium world was able to receive more information and a more critical review of this species. Jacques Géry's critical redescription of these same fishes was highly praised by the scientific world. This species is best kept in a tank that has plenty of elbow room, since they are in constant motion. Also, keeping groups of them, besides being more attractive to the eye, is very practical, since there is less of a tendency for them to quarrel among themselves.

GEOPHAGUS SURINAMENSIS

GIRARDINUS METALLICUS Poey/*The Girardinus*

R: Cuba. **H**: A livebearing fish that greedily gobbles its young if they are not protected with a heavy planting of fine-leaved plants. **W**: Does best in hard water with a slightly alkaline pH of 7.4. **S**: Females reach 7.5 cm; males about 5 cm. **F**: They eat everything, but they should have some frozen brine shrimp or live foods in their diets from time to time.

A very heavily planted aquarium with hard water is necessary to have these fish at their best. The German aquarists feed them with mosquito larvae, probably their natural food, and enjoy much sucess with them, but only the very serious aquarist would consider having them at all, as they are relatively colorless.

The males have an unusual double-pointed gonopodium which is very long proportionally compared to most livebearers. Females are much larger, sometimes being twice as large as the males. The female will drop about 20 to 30 fry per month on a very predictable schedule if conditions are uniform. Unfortunately neither this little fish nor the very similar Yellow Belly *(Girardinus falcatus)* is commonly imported any longer.

GLOSSOLEPIS INCISUS

GLANDULOCAUDA INEQUALIS Eigenmann/*Croaking Tetra*

R: Southeastern Brazil, Rio Grande do Sul. **H**: Peaceful and active; does not disturb plants. **W**: Should be kept in a roomy aquarium at a temperature slightly lower then most tropical species, 21 to 24°C. **S**: Males about 6 cm; females about 5 cm. **F**: Not a fussy eater; besides live foods, will also eat dried foods. **C**: Body brownish above, silvery white below. Front and upper edge of eye bright red. Dorsal and anal edged yellow, with black below.

This species, like the other tetras in its group, has the power to make tiny croaking noises. The fish ingest a gulp of air at the surface of the water. When they release it below the surface, a croaking noise is also emitted.

Not a great deal is known about the breeding habits of this species. Courtship involves active driving and terminates in the laying of eggs.

GIRARDINUS METALLICUS

GLOSSOLEPIS INCISUS Weber/*New Guinea Rainbowfish*

R: Lake Sentani, Irian Jaya, New Guinea. **H**: Peaceful, a schooling fish that requires a large aquarium. **W**: Slightly alkaline water with a hardness of 18 to 25°DH. Temperature between 24 to 26°C. **S**: Up to 15 cm. **F**: Accepts flake foods but prefers such live foods as daphnia, mosquito larvae, and cyclops; also accepts lean beef.

Courtship involves a good deal of chasing. When the male finally catches the female, the two come together over bushy vegetation where the eggs are laid and then fertilized. It should be noted that this species should be given Java moss on which to spawn. The Java moss should be removed (and replaced) from the breeding tank about once a week and transferred into an incubator aquarium with a temperature of about 27°C. The eggs are very adhesive and should be clear. The eggs will hatch about two weeks after they are laid.

GLANDULOCAUDA INEQUALIS

GNATHONEMUS PETERSI (Günther)/*Peter's Elephant-Nose*

R: Central Africa. **H**: Soft, slightly acid warm water preferred. Temperature 24 to 27°C. **W**: Generally peaceful and shy. **S**: About 23 cm. **F**: Small live foods, especially tubifex worms; will not take coarse-ground dry food.

Gnathonemus petersi has always been one of the more popular mormyrids, partly because it shares the interesting habits of its relatives within the family, partly because of its attractive coloration, and partly because it has a good long "nose," which is a real point of attraction to those who appreciate the out of the ordinary appearance of a fish.

GYMNOCORYMBUS TERNETZI

GYMNARCHUS NILOTICUS Cuvier/*Aba Aba*

R: Upper Nile through Chad and Niger to Senegal. **H**: A predator with an electric potential but generally shy; should be treated like the elephant-noses (Mormyridae). **W**: Soft, slightly acid warm water is preferred. Temperature should be in the mid 20's (°C). **S**: Grows to a length of about 150 cm and a weight of more than 12 kilos. **F**: Small live foods including fishes.

Gymnarchus niloticus, like the mormyrids, possesses electric organs in the posterior part of its body. The weak electrical discharges set up an electrical field that can be used for navigation in the dark, murky or silty waters of the native swamps, or flood plains at night, or to aid in the location of food. The small eyes apparently are not adequate for these functions.

GNATHONEMUS PETERSI

GYMNOCORYMBUS TERNETZI (Boulenger)/*Black Tetra*

R: Paraguay and Rio Guaporé Basins in southern Brazil, Argentina, and Bolivia. **H**: A fast moving fish that is responsible for some fin nipping, but it cannot do real damage to fishes larger than itself. **W**: This is not a warm water fish as so many people think. It does best in temperatures in the low 20's (°C). **S**: In nature specimens as large as 8 cm are found; tank-raised specimens rarely grow larger than 4 cm. **F**: To be at its best this fish requires live food, but it can live for years with nothing but pelletized dry food and a bit of frozen brine shrimp now and then.

Breeding in captivity is not a difficulty for this species. An aquarium planted with thick bunches of fine-leaved plants will prove an excellent spawning tank. Soft, clear, acidic water should be used for spawning. Only gravid females should be placed in the spawning tank. The spawning ritual is a vigorous affair. Pairs actively dive together into the dense plant growth and then press their sides together. The female passes her eggs while quivering. The male then fertilizes them.

GYMNARCHUS NILOTICUS

GYMNOCORYMBUS THAYERI Eigenmann/*Straight-Finned Black Tetra*

R: Upper Amazon, Bolivia and Colombia in warmer waters. **H**: A fast swimming fish that should be well fed at all times if kept in a community aquarium. **W**: Prefers warmer, softer, and more acid waters than its much blacker cousin, *G. ternetzi*. Temperature 24 to 26°C. **S**: Not larger than 5 cm. **F**: Prefers copious feedings of live foods, but does equally well if fed frozen brine shrimp and a varied diet of prepared foods. Some live food should be offered weekly.

Undoubtedly many of the black tetras swimming around in aquaria now under the name of *Gymnocorymbus ternetzi* are *G. thayeri*. This fish is much smaller than its cousin, reaching 5 cm maximum in nature. *G. thayeri* may represent a new subspecies. *G. ternetzi* is relatively deep-bodied, the depth going 1.6 into body length while *thayeri* has a length that is twice its depth; thus, this is the real test.

Spawning of this species is very simple and is merely a matter of separating the sexes and finding enough live foods to bring them into the peak of condition. Any live foods can do it, though daphnia and tubifex worms seem to be best.

GYMNOGEOPHAGUS RHABDOTUS

GYMNOGEOPHAGUS BALZANII Perugia/*Paraguay Mouthbrooder*

R: Paraguay (Rio Parana). **H**: Peaceful; timid. **W**: This species is tolerant of a wide range of water conditions varying from very soft to medium-hard, pH 6.5 to 7.5, and water temperature of 20 to 27°C. **S**: To about 18 cm for males; females slightly smaller. **F**: Takes all standard aquarium fare, both living and prepared; pieces should not be too small.

In a tank containing a lot of gravel that could have a tendency to become fouled by becoming a repository for organic matter, *Gymnogeophagus balzanii* will serve as an active cleaner of the tank — provided, of course, that the tank is equipped with suitable filtration for removing the debris stirred up by the fish. *G. balzanii* is a mouthbrooder. The female broods the eggs for a week to ten days after picking them up in her mouth, and when she releases them they are easily large enough to accept newly hatched brine shrimp.

GYMNOCORYMBUS THAYERI

GYMNOGEOPHAGUS RHABDOTUS Hensel/ *Pearl-Striped Geophagus*
R: Southern Brazil (Rio Grande do Sul) through Uruguay to at least Buenos Aires in Argentina.
H: Generally peaceful. Not a real "earth-mover" as are some species of *Geophagus*. **W:** Not
critical. Resistant to low temperatures (12 to 14°C), but should be kept around 22 to 26°C. **S:**
Said to attain a length of 18 cm, but will breed at half that size or even smaller. **F:** Will accept
almost any type of good aquarium food, including flake food.
The sexes are not easily distinguished until the breeding tube appears (blunt and 2 mm in
diameter in the female, pointed and directed backward in the male). Both sexes scour a rock
surface in preparation for the eggs. The male courts the female with spread fins and does little
dances in front of her as he becomes darker in color and shows six to nine irregular vertical
bars. The dorsal and anal fins are edged with black. Spawning is normal for an egglayer, with
the female making a few false passes over the spawning site before actually depositing around
200 rather small, translucent eggs over the next four hours.

GYMNOGEOPHAGUS BALZANII

GYMNORHAMPHICHTHYS RONDONI Miranda-Riberio/*Mousetail Knife Fish*

R: River systems of Venezuela. **H**: Peaceful and shy; should not, however, be put with very small fishes. **W**: Soft, slightly acid water. Temperature 24 to 27°C. **S**: Up to 15 cm; usually 10 cm. **F**: Small live or frozen foods.

The flesh of this fish is semitransparent with the gill chamber and peritoneum silvery. The fish has a dorsal series of irregular blotches and a dark line from the snout to the eyes.

When swimming, *Gymnorhamphichthys rondoni* uses its long anal fin for locomotion as it moves back and forth in an undulating manner. Most of the time, however, it remains burrowed in the sand or mud.

GYRINOCHEILUS AYMONIERI

GYMNOTUS CARAPO Linnaeus/*Banded Knife Fish*

R: Guatemala south to the La Plata. **H**: Mostly nocturnal; a predatory species best kept by itself. **W**: Not critical. Temperature 24 to 26°C. **S**: Is said to attain 58 cm; imported specimens seldom over 15 cm. **F**: Pieces of beef heart, fish, or shrimp; prefers small fishes above all.

The knife fishes are extremely interesting oddities in the aquarium. There is no dorsal fin or caudal fin; where a fish would normally have a tail, the body simply comes to a point. There are pectoral fins, but they contribute little to the fish's locomotion and simply serve to steer it. It propels itself by means of a rippling motion of the long anal fin. This rippling motion can be reversed instantaneously and the fish can swim backward with the same ease as forward. *Gymnotus carapo* is not adapted for keeping in a community aquarium. Its favorite food is smaller fishes, on which it generally feeds while the tank is in almost darkness. These fish do not congregate in schools when in their natural water; the author (HRA) saw them caught in Guyana, and at no time were there more than three or four among a netful of other fishes.

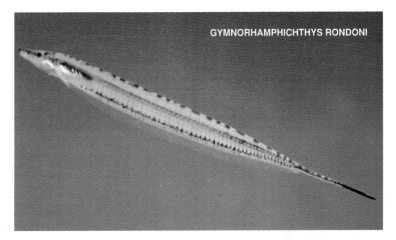

GYMNORHAMPHICHTHYS RONDONI

GYRINOCHEILUS AYMONIERI (Tirant)/*Chinese Algae-Eater*

R: Widely distributed throughout Thailand. **H**: Small specimens usually peaceful. **W**: Clean, well-aerated, slightly alkaline water. To promote algal growth, a generous amount of sunlight should enter the tank. **S**: Seldom exceeds 13 cm in the aquarium. **F**: Vegetarian; grazes on algae much of the time. Will also take dried foods or a piece of crushed lettuce or spinach leaf. *Gyrinocheilus aymonieri* has an underslung mouth which forms a sucking disc. With this it is able to anchor itself to a rock in swiftly moving water. It has been observed also that it is not entirely loath to use its mouth to attach itself to other fishes in the tank—not a very endearing trait . This interesting fish has heavily vegetarian habits and will do an excellent job of cleaning up algae in a surprisingly short time. If no algae are available, a crushed lettuce or spinach leaf will do nicely. So far nothing is known of their reproductive habits.

GYMNOTUS CARAPO

307

HALOPHRYNE TRISPINOSUS (Günther)/*Toadfish, Freshwater Lionfish*

R: India to Thailand, Java, Borneo, Sumatra, Malaysia. **H**: A voracious species that is not safe to keep with any small fishes. **W**: Not critical; can do well in semi-brackish water. **S**: Over 30 cm in the wild; usually seen much smaller in the aquarium trade. **F**: Prefers whole fish as food; most individuals will take either live or frozen fish. Smaller individuals will accept smaller non-fish foods.

This species dislikes bright light and usually seeks caves and other hiding places in which to lurk, making only occasional forays around the tank. Larger fish of the species will bully smaller individuals and keep them from food, although even smaller individuals are greedy eaters. *Halophryne trispinosus* has been spawned under aquarium conditions, but fry have not been successfully reared. Large yellowish eggs were laid in a cave and guarded by the female.

HAPLOCHROMIS (PROTOMELAS) ANNECTENS

HAMPALA MACROLEPIDOTA van Hasselt/*Sidebar Barb*

R: Java, Sumatra, Borneo, Malaya, Burma, Indo-China, and Thailand. **H**: A large, aggressive species that must be kept with fishes it cannot swallow. **W**: Not critical as long as extremes are avoided. Water temperatures should be in the range of 22° to 28°C. **S**: Reaches a length of at least 70 cm. **F**: Not fussy about food and will consider small fishes in the aquarium as part of its diet. Feeder goldfish can be used.

The Sidebar Barb is a fairly large barb (it attains a length of at least 70 cm in parts of its range) inhabiting streams and lakes where there is clear water (although some specimens are found in turbid water occasionally) and usually a bottom of sand, gravel, or rocks. In turbid waters the bottom may be more silty. The natural food of small individuals seems to be insects (according to stomach content analyses), while that of the larger fish seems to be mostly other fishes.

The Sidebar Barb undergoes some changes in color pattern with age. Young individuals have the lateral bar reduced to an oblong spot or short bar, and there may be a bar across the middle of the caudal peduncle and another at the base of the caudal fin. With growth the posterior bars fade and the anterior bar elongates to come into contact with the dorsal fin base. In some parts of the range, however, there are variations in the posterior bars (one or both missing or reduced to a spot), but in all cases the bar below the dorsal fin is always present and helps identify this species.

HALOPHRYNE TRISPINOSUS

HAPLOCHROMIS (PROTOMELAS) ANNECTENS (Regan)/*Annectens*
R: Lake Malawi, Africa. **H**: Relatively aggressive (especially during spawning time), but can be kept with other Malawi cichlids that are not timid or easily dominated. **W**: Hard, alkaline water. Temperature 24 to 28°C. **S**: To about 20 cm. **F**: Takes all of the usual aquarium foods.
Haplochromis annectens spawns like most of the Malawi mouthbrooders. The male will set up a territory of sorts and start shifting the bottom gravel around until the whole tank is upset and he is eventually satisfied. The female is enticed to the spot where spawning occurs, the female winding up with a mouthful of pale beige eggs some 2 mm in length. When the bulging gular area of the female is noticed, wait a day or two and then move her to more secluded quarters.

HAMPALA MACROLEPIDOTA

HAPLOCHROMIS (ASTATOTILAPIA) BURTONI (Günther)/*Burton's Mouthbrooder*
R: Widespread in Africa south of the Sahara. **H**: Usually too aggressive to be kept with smaller fishes; should have a tank of their own. **W**: Neutral to slightly acid. Temperature 24 to 26°C. **S**: About 10 cm; females slightly smaller. **F**: A greedy eater; some vegetable substances should be given.

H. burtoni is a maternal mouthbrooder. The spawning rituals include chasing and whirling movements. The pair end up above shallow pits or rock ledges. Fifty to a hundred eggs are laid and then immediately picked up by the female. They develop in ten days to two weeks. The eggs are fertilized when the female nibbles at the anal fin of the male soon after she picks up her eggs.

HAPLOCHROMIS (DIMIDIOCHROMIS) COMPRESSICEPS

HAPLOCHROMIS (ASTATOTILAPIA) CALLIPTERUS (Günther) *Callipterus*
R: Lake Malawi, south to southern Mozambique. **H**: Very quarrelsome. **W**: Hard and alkaline. Temperature 24 to 26°C. **S**: About 10 cm. **F**: Live or frozen foods, with an addition of foods with a vegetable origin.

H. callipterus is a maternal mouthbrooder. A close eye should be kept on the females; separate them when there is a mouthful of eggs in evidence. Like the others of this Malawi group, their habitat provides a great deal of algae that is eaten in addition to their normal diet, and if we can provide some hair algae for nibbling purposes, all the better.

HAPLOCHROMIS (ASTATOTILAPIA) BURTONI

HAPLOCHROMIS (DIMIDIOCHROMIS) COMPRESSICEPS (Boulenger)/*Malawian Eye-Biter*

R: Lake Malawi, Africa. **H**: A predator that will eat any small fishes that it can completely engulf. **W**: Similar to most Malawi fishes, the water for this species should be hard and alkaline with a pH of 7.6 or higher. Temperature should be about 22 to 28°C. **S**: Reaches a maximum length of about 25 cm. **F**: Eats small fishes in nature but will take many of the standard foods for other cichlids.

The Malawian Eye-Biter is a maternal mouthbrooder and spawns in a manner similar to other species of Lake Malawi *Haplochromis*. The eggs and fry are tended for about three weeks, after which they are released and are on their own. Fry can take newly hatched brine shrimp or fine flake food.

HAPLOCHROMIS (ASTATOTILAPIA) CALLIPTERUS

HAPLOCHROMIS ELECTRA

HAPLOCHROMIS ELECTRA Burgess/*Deep Water Hap I*

R: Lake Malawi. **H:** Fairly peaceful for an African Lake cichlid; aggressive when guarding territory during spawning periods. **W:** Hard, alkaline water as in almost all African lake cichlid tanks with optimum pH of 8.0 and DH of 7. The temperature should be about 78°F. (26°C.). **S:** Attains a length of about 6 inches. **F:** Not critical, will take any of the common foods given to African lake cichlids.

Of the many new species of *Haplochromis* being imported into the United States the Deep Water Hap I, *Haplochromis electra*, is at the present time the most popular. The color pattern is distinctive and bright, which perhaps is the cause of much of this popularity. Most noticeable is the vertically elongate dark blue or blackish shoulder bar in both sexes. This is actually the first major bar and is followed by half a dozen or more similar bars of decreasing intensity, the posterior-most often barely visible.

Spawning *H. electra* is not difficult. It follows the pattern of most previous *Haplochromis* species. A flat rock is cleaned or a pit dug in the sand by the male and he ventures about the tank in his brightest colors trying to attract one of the females to it. He is basically a bright shimmering light blue with silvery white background body color. A band or patch below the eyes and the area from the chin to the pelvic fins are black. The females are similarly patterned but the colors are very much subdued.

As the female enters the spawning area the pair circles over the rock or pit for a while until she makes an actual egg-depositing run. As she swings around to pick the eggs up in her mouth the male, which was following her, fertilizes them. The female picks up the eggs in her mouth and sets about depositing a few more. This procedure continues until all the eggs are laid, although there may be interruptions due to other fishes interfering and having to be evicted by the male or the female may wander off and have to be coaxed back by further displays and posturing by the male. Once the eggs are all safely in the female's mouth she may be removed to a maternity aquarium to wait out the approximately three-week incubation period. If possible it is best to delay this move for a day or two or until the brooding instinct is set.

About 50 to 100 fry may be released from a single spawning. They can be easily raised on newly hatched brine shrimp and crushed flake food. In about six weeks they are normally about an inch in length.

Spawnings seem to occur shortly after water changes as is the case for many of the Malawi cichlids.

HAPLOCHROMIS (CHEILOCHROMIS) EUCHILUS Trewavas/*Euchilus, Big-Lips*
R: Lake Malawi, Africa. **H**: Fairly peaceful for a Malawi cichlid; somewhat less aggressive and territory-minded than other Malawi cichlids. **W**: Prefers hard, alkaline water. Temperature 24 to 26°C. **S**: To 33 cm. **F**: Much prefers live foods but will accept frozen foods and freezed-dried foods, also good flake foods. **C**: Color and pattern vary greatly according to the age of the fish. Adult specimens show a lot more blue on both body and fins and have other highlights not present in younger fish.

H. euchilus is not a very easy fish to spawn. If not conditioned properly and put into the best possible health, it will refuse to propagate. Luckily, it is not an overly temperamental species as to water and food requirements. The species does not like cool water and is very intolerant of abrupt changes in temperature, even more so than most other species. *H. euchilus* is a mouthbrooding species in which the female cares for the eggs and fry. Upon release by their mother, the fry are able to take newly hatched brine shrimp immediately. The fry grow comparatively quickly, but only if they receive regular and substantial changes in their tank water. Tank-raised *H. euchilus* are much less likely to disturb plants than wild fish are.

Haplochromis euchilus, commonly called Euchilus or Big-Lips, is a usually peaceful Malawian cichlid that is less territorial (except when breeding) than most other Rift Lake cichlids of its size. Growing up to 33 cm in the wild, this fish lives in the rocky littoral zone (shallow enough to allow photosynthetic flora to exist) of the lake.

Here *Haplochromis euchilus* grazes on the heavy algae carpeting the rocks, feeding largely upon the insects that in turn live off the algae. Juvenile specimens lack the large lips of the adults. Adults are of a blue-silver color and have two dark bands running along the flanks and back. Sexing live specimens is usually difficult.

In the aquarium, this species will accept freeze-dried and frozen foods, although it usually prefers and thrives on live foods. It is often difficult to get this fish to accept flake foods.

HAPLOCHROMIS FUSCOTAENIATUS Regan/*Fuscotaeniatus*

R: Endemic to Lake Malawi, Africa. **H:** A predatory, aggressive cichlid. It is best kept with comparably large cichlids in a spacious tank. **W:** Requires hard, alkaline water with a temperature of about 25 to 26°C. **S:** Reaches a length of about 25 cm. **F:** Will eat almost any aquarium foods as well as any small fishes placed in the aquarium.

For those who like the larger Rift Lake cichlids, *Haplochromis fuscotaeniatus* should be considered for the community tank. It is closely related to some already established favorites such as *Haplochromis polystigma* and *H. livingstonii,* and its care and breeding are very similar to that for these species.

The blotch pattern is characteristic of the young fishes and the females. As the males mature after about a year (at a size of about 10 cm) they start to become more colorful. The brown pattern starts to weaken and change to a more bluish color. The background remains silvery. The fins become marked with orange spots and dashes, and the anal fin becomes mostly orange with silvery or bluish spots. As spawning time approaches the colors intensify and there is much more blue on the head and body obscuring the blotch pattern.

Spawning follows the pattern of the other Malawi *Haplochromis* species. The male displays before the female to attract her to his spawning site, which may be depressions in the gravel. There is the usual circling and eventual laying of the eggs. The female picks them up in her mouth to incubate. When spawning is completed she should be removed to a separate tank where she can quietly care for the eggs until they hatch and the fry are released in about three weeks' time. Broods are said to number up to 150 or more, and the newly released fry are about 12 mm long. The young Fuscotaeniatus look like their mother.

HAPLOCHROMIS LABROSUS

HAPLOCHROMIS (CTENOCHROMIS) HOREI (Günther)/*Spothead Haplochromis*

R: Found only in Lake Tanganyika. **H:** Aggressive and generally predatory on smaller fishes. **W:** Hard and alkaline. Temperature 23 to 28°C. **S:** Attains a length of over 18 cm. **F:** Will accept almost any type aquarium food, including small fishes.

These are definitely shore fish. They keep very close to the coastline and even penetrate up the estuaries of some of the rivers that empty into the lake. *H. horei* does not venture into deep water and is more likely to be found at depths of less than one meter. In its natural habitat it will feed on higher plants and fishes; Poll found stomachs filled with clupeids (mostly likely *Limnothrissa).* In an aquarium, however, it accepts almost any type of suitable foods, live or prepared. Since it is a predator, make sure you choose the tankmates with care.

HAPLOCHROMIS FUSCOTAENIATUS

HAPLOCHROMIS LABROSUS Trewavas/*Labrosus*
R: Lake Malawi, Africa. **H**: Typical of most Malawi cichlids; aggressive (especially with members of its own kind) but does well in a community situation with other Malawi cichlids. **W**: Hard, alkaline water. Temperature near 26°C. **S**: To about 13 cm. **F**: Easy to feed; will take most of the common live or prepared foods generally available for cichlids.

Spawning occurs in typical fashion, with the male sporting his best colors, displaying in front of the female and trying to entice her into his territory. As the female fills with eggs she is more likely to succumb to his "charms" and follow him, whereupon spawning commences. The female picks up the eggs in her mouth and incubates them. It is best to remove her from the community tank and let her brood the eggs in peace. It has been reported that she might spit the eggs out if moved immediately.

HAPLOCHROMIS (CTENOCHROMIS) HOREI

HAPLOCHROMIS (NIMBOCHROMIS) LINNI Burgess and Axelrod
Elephant-Nose Polystigma; Linn's Haplochromis

R: Lake Malawi, Africa. **H**: Not too aggressive; well suited to a community tank of larger African lake cichlids. **W**: Prefers hard, alkaline water. Temperature between 23 and 28°C. **S**: Reaches a length of at least 35 cm. **F**: Will eat a wide variety of larger sized aquarium foods as well as small fishes.

In almost all respects the Elephant-Nose Polystigma resembles the other members of the blotched-spotted group (*Haplochromis (Nimbochromis) polystigma, H. livingstoni*, etc.), requiring a relatively large tank, plenty of rocks and artificial plants with perhaps a small open sandy space. Two things have been reported as different for this fish. It is less aggressive than the others and fits very well into a community tank. Secondly, it is more sensitive to dissolved waste buildup and the water has to be more carefully monitered.

Spawning follows the pattern of the blotched-spotted group of *Haplochromis* species. The female will carry up to 200 or more eggs for about three weeks. When the fry are released they are about 10-15 mm in length and resemble the female closely.

HAPLOCHROMIS (CYRTOCARA) MOORI

HAPLOCHROMIS (NIMBOCHROMIS) LIVINGSTONI (Günther)/*Livingstoni*

R: Lake Malawi, Africa. **H**: Aggressive. **W**: Hard, alkaline water. Temperature 23 to 28°C (breeding occurs at upper end of range). **S**: Over 30 cm, but usually does not attain this extreme size in aquaria. **F**: Will take a variety of foods including small fishes.

Spawning can be accomplished in a community tank (the male will keep all other fishes at bay during the spawning), and best results are obtained by using one male and two or more females. Spawning itself follows the normal circling pattern with the female at times mouthing the male's vent, possibly ensuring fertilization of the eggs. Up to 200 eggs are laid and brooded by the female for about three weeks. When released, the fry look very much like the female. They can be fed with newly hatched brine shrimp, crushed flake food, or other suitably small and nutritious fare. *Haplochromis (Nimbochromis) livingstoni* is very similar to and often confused with its close relative, *H. (Nimbochromis) polystigma*. Both have the typical large blotches, but *polystigma* has, in addition, many small spots over the body and fins.

HAPLOCHROMIS (NIMBOCHROMIS) LINNI

HAPLOCHROMIS (CYRTOCARA) MOORI (Boulenger)/*Blue Lumphead, Blue Moori*
R: Lake Malawi, Africa. **H**: Peaceful for a comparatively large cichlid, but not completely inoffensive; the degree of aggressiveness is very variable from individual to individual. **W**: Prefers hard, alkaline water. Best temperature around 24°C. **S**: Up to 23 cm. **F**: Takes all normal aquarium foods, especially live and frozen. **C**: both sexes have an over-all blue color, but individuals vary greatly in the amount of black markings on the fins and back according to their geographical origin.
Haplochromis moori is a mouthbrooding species in which the female alone incubates the eggs; the length of time the female holds the eggs in her mouth is variable, depending on temperature and the age and condition of the fish, but in most cases incubation lasts three to four weeks. The fry at the time of release by their mother are able to take newly hatched brine shrimp right away.

HAPLOCHROMIS (NIMBOCHROMIS) LIVINGSTONI

317

HAPLOCHROMIS (NIMBOCHROMIS) POLYSTIGMA Regan/*Polystigma, Polly*

R: Lake Malawi. **H**: Aggressive; highly territorial. **W**: Hard, alkaline water preferred but not strictly required. Temperature 23 to 27°C. **S**: Over 26 cm; usually seen much smaller. **F**: Accepts all meaty foods.

This large, aggressive Malawian cichlid is a greedy eater and fast grower; it is in fact, one of the fastest-growing of all African cichlids. Because of its size and potential for being a bullying killer when maintained in close quarters with other fishes, it should be housed in a large tank that is generously provided with hiding places.

H. polystigma is a mouthbrooding species in which the female broods the young. At a temperature of around 27°C the young can be released from her mouth within ten days; at lower temperatures the hatching/release process takes longer. The female is fiercely protective of the young for a short time after their initial release but generally loses interest in them (and they in her) in about five days. *H. polystigma* is among the most prolific of Lake Malawi mouthbrooders, spawns often numbering over 100.

During feeding the color patterns are very different from that of breeding. The hunting fish are dark brown and have a similar appearance to cowering males. The fish is known to lie on the bottom of the aquarium, feigning unobtrusiveness with its dark coloration. When the prey comes within range, however, the predator strikes out, engulfing the unsuspecting fish.

HAPLOCHROMIS SIMILIS

HAPLOCHROMIS (FOSSOROCHROMIS) ROSTRATUS (Boulenger)/*Rostratus*

R: Lake Malawi, Africa. **H**: Aggressive. Does fairly well with other Malawi cichlids of comparable size. Needs a large aquarium. **W**: Hard, alkaline, very clean water. Temperature 22 to 28°C. **S**: To about 33 cm. **F**: Takes all normal aquarium foods.

They spawn over the sand, usually (but not always) in a depression. The female and male can be seen going in circles over the selected spawning site with the female laying her eggs and the male following after. The female will pick up the eggs on the next go-round and apparently mouth the area of the male's vent. This continues until she has deposited all her eggs. The male tolerates the female in the same tank while she is incubating the eggs and early fry.

Sexing *Haplochromis (Fossochromis) rostatus* is easy with adult fish, because the males take on a bluish color with maturity. the dominant male is darker than the subordinate males and becomes very dark, almost black, with a blue-black head. The females and juviniles retain the spotted pattern.

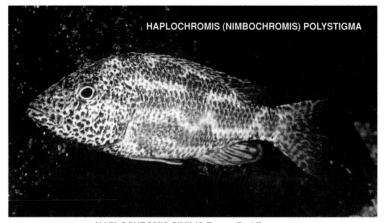

HAPLOCHROMIS (NIMBOCHROMIS) POLYSTIGMA

HAPLOCHROMIS SIMILIS Regan/*Red Empress*

R: Endemic to Lake Malawi. **H:** Typically aggressive *Haplochromis* species. An easy mouthbrooder to spawn. **W:** Hard, alkaline water is a must, with the minimum pH about 7.8-8.0. The temperature should be around 26°C. **S:** Attains a length of about 17 cm. **F:** Will accept a variety of aquarium foods. Should receive vegetable matter as part of its diet.

The Red Empress spawns much like other species of *Haplochromis*. Depressions dug out of the substrate are utilized for the nest. Once the depression is selected and prepared the pair circle it in ever-tightening circles. This action may be broken off as the male chases intruders away. Eventually the female makes some dry runs in the depression to be followed by actual egg-laying. As the eggs are deposited the male follows and fertilizes them. The female picks the eggs up in her mouth (she may not do this after every pass but eventually gets to them). The first spawning may yield only a dozen or so eggs, but this should increase as the female grows older and larger. Incubation is about three weeks. The female can be isolated during this period of time or left in the community situation for a week or two.

HAPLOCHROMIS (FOSSOROCHROMIS) ROSTRATUS

HAPLOCHROMIS VENUSTUS Boulenger/*Venustus*

R: Lake Malawi, Lake I'Aalombe. **H:** Should be kept with fishes its own size. **W:** Requires hard, alkaline water for best health and spawning. Temperature 68-75°F. for general maintenance, 75-82°F. for spawning. **S:** Attains a length of more than 8 inches. **F:** Will eat almost any good aquarium foods including flake foods.

Haplochromis venustus is one of the more popular of the Lake Malawi *Haplochromis* species and may even be considered to be a "standard." It has been bred to the point where many young fish are available at a reasonably low price.

The blotchy pattern makes one think of the *H. polystigma-H. livingstoni* group. It has been confused with one or another of those species at times, but it is easily distinguished from them once one is familiar with the different patterns. Large males are especially attractive, with a sulphur-colored blaze on the nape extending from between the eyes to the dorsal fin, where it extends as a yellow outer portion of the fin. The females and young fish have the pattern of regular blotches; adult males generally start to lose these blotches when reaching sexual maturity (at about 5 inches in length).

H. venustus can be housed in a community tank of Lake Malawi cichlids as long as they are not too large. If so the Venustus tend to become dominated and unable to spawn.

Haplochromis venustus spawns in a manner similar to the other cichlids of Lake Malawi. A pit is dug in the sand and the male courts the female to entice her to his nest. The pair will circle one another as egg-laying proceeds, and occasional direct mouthing of the male's vent by the female occurs. The eggs are tan in color, about 3 mm in length, and about 200 in number. The female will incubate these eggs in her mouth (buccal cavity) for about three weeks. She should be placed in a separate tank with no other fishes to bother her during this incubation period.

The young when released are about 10 mm in length, a bit smaller than the *polystigma-livingstonii* group, but well able to handle the same foods, namely newly hatched brine shrimp and crushed flake food.

HELOSTOMA TEMMINCKI

HASEMANIA NANA (Reinhardt)/*Silver-Tipped Tetra*

R: Rio S. Francisco, southeastern Brazil. **H**: Very peaceful; should be kept in a school of not less than six. **W**: Slightly acid and soft water. Temperature 24 to 26°C. **S**: To 5 cm. **F**: Prepared foods accepted. But live or frozen foods are preferred.

This is not a very popular fish, although several specimens have found their way into the aquarium trade.

HAPLOCHROMIS VENUSTUS

HELOSTOMA TEMMINCKI Cuvier/*Kissing Gourami*
R: Thailand, Indonesia, Sumatra, Borneo, Java, Malay Peninsula, and Cambodia. **H**: Prefer a large aquarium. Plants are not necessary though they do enjoy "chomping" on them to remove whatever has fallen onto them or grown over them. They are easily overcrowded and unless they are given plenty of room their growth is stunted, they develop a "hollow belly," and they die. **W**: The water conditions are not critical, but they do much better in slightly hard water with a pH of 7.0. Temperature 26°C. **S**: Up to 30 cm. **F**: A greedy eater that never tires of looking for food. Their major diet should consist of frozen brine shrimp and worms now and then. They seem to get along very well on salmon eggs (the dried prepared form available as a fish food) and shredded shrimp, though this usually fouls the water.

The Kissing Gourami can be a very annoying article to its tankmates. These fish have broad lips that are widely extended. They press these lips against the aquarium rocks, glass, plants, and also the sides of other fishes so that they may ingest the slime that covers them. These fish also have the habit of touching one another and temporarily locking lips. Some researchers postulate that this behavior pattern is a form of threat display.

HASEMANIA NANA

HEMICHROMIS FASCIATUS Peters/*Five-Spotted Hemichromis*

R: West Africa, widely distributed from Senegal to the Congo. **H**: Very quarrelsome toward other fishes; should be kept by themselves. **W**: Occurs in both fresh and brackish waters. In the aquarium they adapt to any water conditions. **S**: Fully grown about 30 cm. **F**: Will consume any unwanted fish or will settle for chunks of fish or beef heart.

The five large spots on the side often turn into bands, and when they decide to spawn, a startling transformation in color takes place: the entire body becomes suffused with blood-red, the bands become deep black, and the dorsal fin develops stripes of red, yellow and white. Sexes are difficult to distinguish; males have slightly more pointed dorsal and anal fins.

HEMICHROMIS PAYNEI

HEMICHROMIS GUTTATUS Günther/*Jewel Cichlid*

R: Cameroons to eastern Ivory Coast. **H**: Besides being very pugnacious, it has the nasty habit of digging up plants. **W**: Not critical. Temperature should be quite high, about 27°C. **S**: To about 15 cm; usually smaller. **F**: Live foods preferred; frozen foods accepted.

Once a pair has mated, there is seldom any trouble with them afterwards, but selecting a well-mated pair sometimes presents a problem. If you get a male that is ready to spawn and a female that is not, very often the result is a dead or mangled female. Always make sure that when a pair is introduced into a tank there is plenty of refuge such as rocks and plant thickets. A flowerpot placed in a dark corner will usually be the preferred site for spawning, which takes place in the usual non-mouthbrooding cichlid manner.

HEMICHROMIS FASCIATUS

HEMICHROMIS PAYNEI Loiselle/Payne's *Jewel Cichlid*

R: Guinea, Sierra Leone, and Liberia. **H:** Generally peaceful when not ready to spawn. **W:** Not critical. Low hardness and slightly acid pH with a temperature between 25° and 28°C are adequate. **S:** Attains a length of at least 10 cm. **F:** Accepts almost any kind of aquarium food. The spawning male turns slightly lilac with his throat and chest bright red; the entire body is sprinkled with iridescent turquoise spots. The upper part of the body of the female becomes somewhat paler, while the throat and abdominal area become fiery red. As the male begins his courtship, the female seeks out and selects a spawning site, usually a flat rock surface that is protected by some overhang, and begins to clean it. At this time her ovipositor is visible, as is the male's genital papilla. After additional courtship, spawning eventually occurs in typical cichlid fashion with the female laying a string or two of eggs and the male following her fertilizing them. Most spawnings seem to occur during the evening hours. The female guards the eggs as the male guards and patrols the larger territory surrounding the spawning site. The eggs hatch in approximately two days and are immediately hidden away by the female. By this time she has altered her colors, with the upper part of her body changing to light red. In about six days the female emerges with a swarm of fry. With adequate feedings of newly hatched brine shrimp and other comparable types of fry foods, in about two months they may reach a length of up to 5 cm.

HEMICHROMIS GUTTATUS

HEMIGRAMMOCYPRIS LINI Weitzman & Chan/*Garnet Minnow*

R: Southeastern China. **H**: Peaceful and fast-swimming; always active. **W**: Not a truly tropical species, so can take much cooler water than most; tolerates a wide range of pH and hardness. **S**: Up to 5 cm. **F**: Accepts all standard aquarium foods.

Dr. Stanley Weitzman of the U.S. National Museum and Lai Lee Chan of the Fisheries Research Station in Hong Kong, in the June 1966 issue of *Copeia,* showed that there were two distinct races of White Clouds and that (1) the fish in question was not a White Cloud of either race, (2) *Aphyocypris pooni* is an invalid name, and (3) the fish in question is correctly known as *Hemigrammocypris lini.*

HEMIGRAMMUS BELLOTTII

HEMIGRAMMOPETERSIUS CAUDALIS (Boulenger)/
Yellow-Tailed African Characin

R: Zaire River and its tributaries. **H**: Peaceful unless kept with smaller fishes that it could devour. **W**: Water should be soft, slightly acid, and well aerated. Aquarium should be kept covered to prevent jumping. Temperature 25°C. **S**: About 8 cm. **F**: Will take dried foods, but a preponderance of live foods should be given.

Should be kept in groups of half a dozen or more. It has been spawned in captivity. Ventral and anal fins of males have white edges. Spawns much like *Phenacogrammus interruptus.* A ripe, mature pair is very likely to attempt spawning even when circumstances do not permit them to do the same things that they do in their native waters.

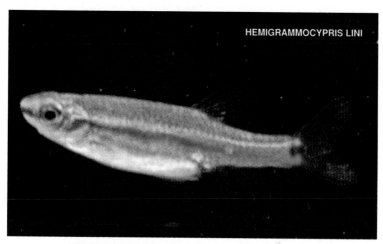

HEMIGRAMMOCYPRIS LINI

HEMIGRAMMUS BELLOTTII (Steindachner)/*Dash-Dot Tetra*

R: Upper Amazon tributaries. **H**: Peaceful and active; prefer to swim in a group of their own kind. **W**: Soft, acid water preferred. Temperature 24 to 27°C. **S**: To 2.5 cm. **F**: Because of their size, small foods of all kinds are recommended.

What a wealth of characoid species there is to be found in the Upper Amazon region! And the only reason we see them so seldom is because they share their home waters with the Neon Tetra, which outshines anything in that part of the river for beauty of colors. We can get some idea of what other characins there are in these waters by the ones that are included accidentally with these shipments, and *Hemigrammus bellottii* is one of these.

HEMIGRAMMOPETERSIUS CAUDALIS

HEMIGRAMMUS CAUDOVITTATUS Ahl/*Buenos Aires Tetra*

R: Region around Buenos Aires. **H**: Fairly peaceful with fishes its own size; should not be kept with thread-finned fishes, whose fins it nips. **W**: Neutral to slightly acid. Can withstand temperatures around 21°C for a time; should be kept about 25°C normally. **S**: To 10 cm. **F**: Seems to like dried foods as well as live foods; has a good appetite and should be fed generously.

Coming as they do from semi-tropical Buenos Aires, aquarium temperatures need not be very high. They will be quite comfortable in the low 20's (°C) and around 25°C they will usually exhibit a willingness to spawn. A bunch of bushy plants should be placed at one end of the tank and about one-fourth of the water drained off and replaced with fresh water. The pair is best separated for a day or two and well fed. When placed in the breeding tank they will soon begin to drive and scatter a large number of eggs all over.

HEMIGRAMMUS ERYTHROZONUS

HEMIGRAMMUS COERULEUS Durbin/*Coerulean Tetra*

R: Manacapuru, Brazil. **H**: Peaceful when kept with fishes of its own size. **W**: Neutral to slightly acid. Temperature 23 to 26°C. **S**: To about 7.5 cm. **F**: Will accept prepared foods, but should also get live and frozen foods.

This species was always thought to be deep red. In the interests of finding this fish and providing fish hobbyists with another beautiful species, perhaps one which could be bred more easily than the Neon or Cardinal Tetras, Dr. Axelrod decided early in 1964 to search for them once more. After much trouble, the proper stream was found by Drs. Axelrod and Terofal with the expert help of Harald Schultz, another member of the expedition. They netted tirelessly but could find no characins like the Coerulean Tetra. Finally they put poison in the water and began to put the fishes collected in this manner in formalin. Then came the big surprise: some of the characins in the formalin began to turn *red!* Taxonomic examination confirmed that this indeed was the described species, which only turned red after death.

HEMIGRAMMUS CAUDOVITTATUS

HEMIGRAMMUS ERYTHROZONUS (Durbin)/*Glowlight Tetra*
R: The Guianas and adjacent regions of the Amazon. **H**: One of the most peaceful of all tetras.
W: Should have a clean aquarium at all times, with slightly acid, soft water. Temperature 23 to
26°C. **S**: 4cm. **F**: Will eat dry food, but this should often be augmented with live and frozen
foods. **C**: Body greenish and very transparent, with a brilliant, glowing red or purple line running
from the upper edge of the eye to the caudal base.
To show off the Glowlight Tetra to its best advantage, some pains must be taken to provide it
with its proper setting. The bottom should be covered with black gravel and nicely planted. A
moderate light should come from above. All that needs to be done then is to place our little
jewels in their setting and wait for a few hours for them to get used to their surroundings.

HEMIGRAMMUS COERULEUS

HEMIGRAMMUS HYANUARY (Durbin)/*January Tetra*

R: Amazon tributaries near Leticia, Colombia. **H**: Very peaceful; prefers to be in a school with others of its own kind. **W**: Not critical; best is water that is neutral to slightly acid in character. Temperature 23 to 26°C. **S**: About 4 cm. **F**: Live or frozen foods are of course preferred, but dried foods are also accepted eagerly.

Males have a black adipose fin. The fact that they are hardy is fairly obvious to anyone who has ever kept them. Probably the reader is wondering why this fish is called the January Tetra. The original specimens were collected in a place called Lake January by the great ichthyologist Eigenmann in 1918.

HEMIGRAMMUS OCELLIFER

HEMIGRAMMUS MARGINATUS Ellis/*Bassam Tetra*

R: Venezuela to Argentina. **H**: Peaceful. **W**: Fairly soft and slightly acid. Temperature 24 to 26°C. **S**: To 7.5 cm. **F**: Live or frozen foods preferred; will also accept prepared foods.

Spawning is in the standard tetra manner, the fish laying eggs in bunches of bushy plants and then eating all they can find until they are taken out. In their home waters they probably spawn in schools, but in the comparatively narrow confines of an aquarium, using more than a pair results in two fish spawning and the rest following and gobbling up the eggs.

HEMIGRAMMUS HYANUARY

HEMIGRAMMUS OCELLIFER (Steindachner)/*Head and Tail Light*
R: Widely distributed throughout the Amazon region, especially in the southern part. **H**: Mostly peaceful, if kept with fishes their own size. **W**: Not critical, but warm temperatures are preferred. Temperature 25 to 26°C. **S**: About 4 cm. **F**: Will get along very well on dry foods.
A small school of at least six in a roomy aquarium that is lighted from above will show up best; here we are able to see the gleaming spots of gold in the upper half of the eye and at the base of the tail flashing as the fish move about in the open portions of the aquarium. Males are distinguished by their longer, more slender bodies and also a thin streak that runs horizontally across the anal fin. A breeding tank of about 30 liters, with a layer of glass marbles on the bottom, should be provided.

HEMIGRAMMUS MARGINATUS

HEMIGRAMMUS PULCHER Ladiges/*Garnet Tetra*

R: Peruvian Amazon, Loreto region. **H**: Peaceful; will not bother plants or other fishes. **W**: Prefers a roomy, well-planted tank. Most important requirement is warmth, 26 to 27°C. **S**: About 5 cm. **F**: Will not refuse dried foods, but should be given frequent changes to live or frozen foods. **C**: Greenish body with a small shoulder spot and indistinct horizontal line. Upper half of caudal base deep red, with black area below.

Given a good thermostatic heater that will keep the water at a constant 26 to 27°C, they will put on their most glowing colors. Males and females are equally beautiful, but the females can be distinguished by their stockier build and slightly deeper bellies. Not a ready spawner, but patience and good feeding will sometimes be rewarded.

HEMIGRAMMUS RODWAYI

HEMIGRAMMUS RHODOSTOMUS Ahl/*Rummy-Nose Tetra*

R: Lower Amazon region, around Aripiranga and Para. **H**: Peaceful; most at home with lively fishes of about its own size. **W**: Best kept in a well-planted, well established, well heated tank. Temperature about 26°C. **S**: 4 to 5 cm. **F**: Will get along fairly well on dried food, but should get an occasional meal of live or frozen food.

When kept in an aquarium that is well established and well planted, a small school of these fish flit around always active and alert, their noses glowing. Take the same group of fish and place them in a bare tank where the temperature is about 24°C or lower and the water is not to their liking, and immediately the fish become almost unrecognizable. The nose fades to the palest of pinks, and the black markings on the tail are so indistinct that they can scarcely be seen.

HEMIGRAMMUS PULCHER

HEMIGRAMMUS RODWAYI Durbin/*Gold Tetra*

R: Guianas and the Upper Amazon. **H**: Peaceful; prefers to be kept in a school. **W**: Not critical, but water should be somewhere near neutral. **S**: About 5 cm. **F**: Live foods preferred, but frozen and prepared foods are also readily accepted.

When the author (H.R.A.) visited Guyana, he was told that this fish was very common in the drainage ditches around the sugar fields and rice paddies just outside of Georgetown. There is a peculiar thing about this little beauty: they do not lose their color in captivity and they breed readily, but the offspring do not have the golden color! In their native waters, they are always golden. It was discovered that the gold color was not natural but due to a pathological condition.

HEMIGRAMMUS RHODOSTOMUS

HEMIGRAMMUS SCHMARDAE (Steindachner)/*Schmard Tetra*

R: Upper Rio Negro River, Brazil. **H**: Very peaceful. **W**: Soft, acid water preferred, but not essential. Temperature 24 to 27°C. **S**: Up to 5 cm. **F**: Dried as well as live foods.

Females can be distinguished from the males by their heavier bodies when gravid. Spawning is a stormy affair with the males and females diving into the plants and pressing their sides together. The eggs are laid and fertilized in the open water and then fall into the dense clumps of plants. The parents should be separated from the eggs after the spawning process concludes or they will most likely eat them.

HEMIGRAMMUS UNILINEATUS

HEMIGRAMMUS ULREYI (Boulenger)/*Tetra Ulreyi*

R: The upper reaches of the Paraguay River, where it enters Brazil. **H**: Peaceful; will not harm plants or other fishes. **W**: Most important thing is temperature, which should be kept from 25 to 27°C. **S**: Males about 5 cm.; females about 4.5. **F**: Will eat dried foods, but it should be varied with live or frozen foods.

The males are considerably smaller and more slender. Another way of sexing them is by looking at the silvery sac that contains the organs, easily discernible by placing a light behind them. The female's sac is blunt and the male's is pointed. Most of the tetra species can be sexed in this manner, and it is much more reliable than going by outward appearances. This species has not yet been imported in large numbers.

HEMIGRAMMUS SCHMARDAE

HEMIGRAMMUS UNILINEATUS (Gill)/*Featherfin Tetra*

R: Trinidad and northern South America from Venezuela to Brazil. **H**: Peaceful; a heavy eater that should have plenty of swimming room. **W**: Should have a sunny aquarium with fairly high temperatures, 26 to 27°C. **S**: Attains a length of 5 cm; most specimens smaller. **F**: Like all active fishes, a heavy eater. If possible, should be fed several times daily. Will take dried foods, but live foods should also be fed. **C**: Body silvery with a gold horizontal stripe. First rays of the dorsal and anal fins white, with a black streak behind. Brazilian variety has red fins.

Given a tank to themselves a pair, or better yet two males and one female, will soon begin driving about madly and depositing eggs all over the bushy plants. When the female begins to hide from the males and egg hunts are begun, the parents should be removed immediately or there will soon be very few eggs left. A successful spawning may number as many as 500 eggs, which hatch in about 60 hours. After two to four days the fry become free-swimming, at which time they may be fed very fine dried food or infusoria. Growth is very rapid under good conditions. Brazilian males have an anal hook.

HEMIGRAMMUS ULREYI

HEMIODOPSIS GOELDII (Steindachner)/*Goeldi's Hemiodus*

R: Guianas and the Rio Xingu, Brazil. **H**: Peaceful and highly active; likely to jump out if the tank is not covered. **W**: Neutral to slightly alkaline. Temperature 24 to 27°C. **S**: To about 15 cm. **F**: Prepared foods accepted, but likes to nibble on plants occasionally. Lettuce or spinach leaves should be provided for this reason.

Unless the few imported specimens breed prolifically, and it is not likely that they will, it is doubtful that we will ever see many of them in the aquaria of hobbyists. Then again, a collector may stumble on a large number of these in an out-of-the-way stream and get them on the market. This is a very active fish and should not be put in with quieter fishes that dislike being disturbed. Their tank should be kept covered.

HEMIODOPSIS GRACILIS (Günther)/*Slender Hemiodus*

R: Guyana and the middle Amazon River region. **H**: Peaceful toward other fishes. An active swimmer and skillful jumper. **W**: Soft and slightly acid. Temperature about 24°C. **S**: To about 15 cm; imported specimens about half this size. **F**: Greedy eaters that should get green (vegetable) foods in addition to prepared and freeze-dried foods.

There have been no reports of their ever spawning in captivity. Why? Perhaps, being such active swimmers, they require briskly flowing water in which to lay their eggs. Or they might spawn in deep water where they come from, deeper than we could give them in an aquarium.

HEMIODOPSIS GOELDII

HEMIODOPSIS QUADRIMACULATUS (Pellegrin)/*Barred Hemiodus*
R: Upper Amazon and Guianas. **H**: Peaceful and active; prefers to be kept in groups. A jumper; tank must be kept covered. **W**: Neutral to slightly alkaline, with good planting and a sunny location. **S**: To almost 13 cm. **F**: Should be given a good percentage of vegetable foods in addition to the usual live or frozen foods. **C**: Body brownish with a violet shimmer. Three black bands cross the body; caudal peduncle black. Caudal lobes have black edges.

The genus *Hemiodopsis* is represented by many species that are found in the Amazon Basin and northern South America. This species, like most others in the genus, is a peaceful but active fish. It is a good jumper and will find a way out of your aquarium if given a small opening through which to jump. Its tank should be well aerated to accommodate its high metabolism.

HEMIODOPSIS GRACILIS

HEMIODOPSIS STERNI Géry/*Stern's Hemiodus*

R: Upper Juruena River, Brazil. **H**: Peaceful but should be kept with other very active fish. **W**: Neutral to slightly alkaline. Temperature 23 to 26°C. **S**: To about 10 cm. **F**: Dried foods accepted, but live or frozen foods needed occasionally. Vegetable substitutes like lettuce leaves are recommended. **C**: Body yellowish tan with three large spots on the sides and a spot on the lower part of the caudal base, which ends in a black streak on the tail lobe.

Although there are no complete reports on their behavior as yet, a safe bet is that they are as active as the rest of the group and should not be kept with lazy species that would be made nervous by their constant activity.

HEPSETUS ODOE

HEMIRHAMPHODON POGONOGNATHUS (Bleeker)/*Long-finned Halfbeak*

R: Malayan Peninsula, Borneo, Sumatra, Banka. **H**: Strictly a surface fish. Not as aggressive as *Dermogenys* but do tend to squabble among themselves. **W**: Not critical. Medium hard water at temperatures of 24° to 26°C is recommended. **S**: Reaches a length of at least 19 cm. **F**: Live foods are best, but remember that these fish feed primarily at the surface so the food should remain in that region.

This is a livebearer, the long andropodium (the halfbeak version of the gonopodium) extending as far back as to the caudal fin base. Males court the females but do not display the large variety of movements as in *Dermogenys* and do not court for as long a period as species of that genus. Fry should not be left with the female (which should be isolated when she becomes gravid) but should be removed to a separate tank when seen. The fry are dropped in batches of one to three per day over a period of several weeks.

HEMIODOPSIS STERNI

HEPSETUS ODOE (Bloch)/*African Pike*

R: Widely distributed all over tropical Africa. **H**: Vicious, greedy, and predatory; can only be kept with their own kind or larger fishes. **W**: Not critical, but soft, slightly acid water is best. Temperature 24 to 27°C. **S**: To 30 cm. **F**: Living smaller fishes only; possibly they may be trained to eat strips of raw fish. **C**: Body olive green, belly golden. Young specimens have dark spotted fins. *Hepsetus odoe* has been known to science since 1794 and is very rarely imported. It would be no problem for a collector to find them; they occur all over tropical Africa. Although they might make interesting showpieces for public aquariums, only young ones would be of a size small enough for the average hobbyist's tanks, and very few hobbyists would find them interesting enough for theirs.

HEMIRHAMPHODON POGONOGNATHUS

HERICHTHYS ALFARI

HERICHTHYS ALFARI /*Pastel Cichlid*

R: Both slopes of Costa Rica as well as the Atlantic slope of western Panama. **H:** Territorial and therefore slightly aggressive (moreso when spawning or guarding young). Not recommended for a community tank with small fishes. **W:** Will do well in most waters as long as extremes are avoided. Does best in neutral water with a temperature between 22 ° and 28°C. **S:** Reaches a length of at least 20 cm. **F:** Not fussy about food; any typical aquarium foods are accepted.

The males apparently grow larger than the females (twice as large in one report). Females also develop a dark spot in the dorsal fin, and ripe females show an intensely barred pattern. A female sets up a territory from which conspecifics are excluded. Eventually a sexually active male in breeding color is let into her territory, and they both share its defense. Courtship follows, and so does the usual terrorizing of tankmates, uprooting of plants, and other sorts of mayhem well known to cichlid enthusiasts. Selected parts of the rock surfaces are cleaned and pits are dug in the gravel in preparation for the eventual spawning. The eggs are laid by the female, who is followed by the male in his fertilization run. The eggs, vigorously guarded by the female, are transparent, but dark eyes can be seen just before hatching on about the fourth day.

The fry are moved to one of the pits and then to another and so on as the parents tend their progeny. The male wards off any outside intruders quite successfully. In about a week the fry become free-swimming and the parents increase their protection. They even stir up the gravel so that the fry might be able to find some bits of food in the debris. Parental care in one instance was said to last eight weeks, at which time the young began to show a pair of dark spots.

For those who have spawned the commonly available species of *Herichthys* and want to add newer ones to their list, keep an eye out for the pastel cichlid —you'll be glad you did.

HERICHTHYS (*AMPHILOPHUS*) ATROMACULATUS

HERICHTHYS (*AMPHILOPHUS*) ATROMACULATUS (Regan)/*Three-Spot Cichlid*
R: Rio San Juan, Rio Atrato, and Rio Calima basins in Colombia, as well as San Blas Province in Panama. **H**: Somewhat aggressive and reported to be a digger. **W**: Not critical as long as there are no extremes. Temperature should average between 22 to 26°C, slightly higher when ready to spawn them. **S**: A rather large cichlid reaching a length of about 25 cm; probably smaller in aquaria. **F**: Will eat most of the prepared foods as well as live foods. Because of its size larger foods are necessary.

The care of this fish does not differ from that of other similar species of *Herichthys*. A large tank outfitted with plenty of rockwork is necessary. Plants are usually not recommended, as this fish is reported to be a digger and the plants will not survive. If you wish to try artificial plants they may work. Feeding is not a problem. With a hearty appetite this fish will accept just about any of the usual aquarium foods. As it grows, however, the portions must get larger to keep it satisfied.

HERICHTHYS (*THORICHTHYS*) AUREUS (Günther)/*Golden Cichlid*

R: Guatemala and southern Mexico. **H**: Like the large cichlids, they should not be trusted with smaller tankmates that they might bully. They are also apt to dig. **W**: Not critical. **S**: Wild specimens attain a length of 15 cm; tank-raised specimens considerably smaller. **F**: Any of the live foods, including some of the smaller water beetles. Some vegetable matter, such as lettuce or spinach leaves, is also taken.

An important characteristic of this fish is that they require a certain amount of vegetable matter in their diet. This is a warning to the aquarist that any soft-leaved plants, such as water sprite *(Ceratopteris)*, should be avoided and the tough-leaved ones, such as *Sagittaria* or the *Cryptocoryne* species, should be given preference. Spawning is accomplished in typical cichlid fashion with the male and female dividing the parental duties between them. Fry are easily raised. People who have raised them say that the parents should not be disturbed in any way while eggs are present or they will eat them.

HERICHTHYS (ARCHOCENTRUS) CENTRARCHUS

HERICHTHYS BIFASCIATUM (Steindachner)/Usumacinta Cichlid

R: The Usumacinta basin of Mexico and Guatemala. **H:** This species, like other cichlids, may be aggressive, especially when spawning. They are also plant eaters. **W:** Not critical as long as extremes are avoided. A temperature range of about 23° to 27°C is recommended. **S:** These cichlids attain a length of about 25 cm. **F:** A variety of foods both live and prepared are accepted. Some plant material should be offered.

Herichthys bifasciatum is an open spawner. It will spend some time excavating sand pits throughout the tank and cleaning potential spawning sites before actual spawning. One hobbyist reported this activity might last several weeks. When spawning becomes imminent, the spawners color up quite beautifully. At this time also the sexes can most easily be distinguished. The female exhibits a somewhat dark color on the lower part of her head and the ventral part of her body. Outside of this time the two are hard to distinguish although males may become slightly larger than females. About 500 eggs are deposited on a flat stone or flower pot. Once hatched they are moved to one of the open pits and guarded by the parents. The free-swimming fry are able to handle newly hatched brine shrimp.

HERICHTHYS (*THORICHTHYS*) AUREUS

HERICHTHYS (ARCHOCENTRUS) CENTRARCHUS (Gill & Bransford)/*Flier Cichlid*
R: Costa Rica and Nicaragua. **H**: Territorial but gets along well with other fishes of the same size if given plenty of room. **W**: Not critical as long as conditions are not extreme. Temperature 24 to 27°C. **S**: 20 to 22 cm in the aquarium; larger in nature. **F**: Not a fussy eater. Will take a variety of frozen and prepared dry foods.

Herichthys centrarchus, introduced into the aquarium hobby in 1967 by Dr. William Bussing, follows the typical breeding pattern adhered to by the majority of New World cichlids: that is, it is an open substrate spawner. The spawning site seems to be chosen by the male, but once a pair has spawned the female becomes the dominant fish. They are not particularly choosy about where they spawn and are as likely to lay their eggs on the aquarium glass or the slate bottom as on a rock. The eggs hatch in a few days, and the fry are free-swimming within a week.

HERICHTHYS BIFASCIATUM

HERICHTHYS (HERICHTHYS) CYANOGUTTATUS (Baird & Girard)/*Texas Cichlid*

R: Southern Texas and northern Mexico. **H**: All the bad cichlid habits: digs a great deal and uproots plants; usually quarrelsome if kept with other fishes. **W**: Not critical; not sensitive to temperature drops. Best breeding temperature about 24°C. **S**: In native waters up to 30 cm. In captivity seldom exceeds 15 cm. **F**: Large specimens require chunks of food, such as cut-up earthworms or pieces of beef heart or other lean meat.

Those who intend to keep *H. cyanoguttatus* should provide them with a Texas-size aquarium, 150-liters or better. Once they have made themselves at home, a pair may some day begin digging holes all over the place. They usually select a flat stone and begin to clean it carefully and meticulously. Then the female, after acting coy for awhile, will allow herself to be coaxed to the stone and will deposit 500 eggs or more on it, closely followed by the male who sprays them with his sperm. The fry hatch in 5 to 7 days.

HERICHTHYS FACETUS

HERICHTHYS DOVII (Gunther)/*Dow's Cichlid*

R: Great Lakes of Nicaragua and both slopes of Costa Rica. Habits: A very large and very aggressive cichlid. **W**: Not critical. A temperature of 20° to 26°C is acceptable. **S**: Attains a length of at least 35 cm in nature, but larger (to 50 cm) in aquaria. **F**: Will accept any type of aquarium food and then some. Remember that this is a large species that requires large items. Spawning is in the typical cichlid substrate spawning technique. A large size difference does not seem too important when these fish are ready to breed, although when things get rough (and they do) it is best to be ready to separate the pair if the weaker individual is getting torn up too badly. Apparently the female selects the spawning site and lays the eggs with the male following behind fertilizing them. The female stands guard and even drives the male out of the vicinity of the eggs as she guards and fans them. In about three days the eggs hatch; the fry are moved from pit to pit in typical cichlid fashion. At the end of a week the fry are free-swimming and can be fed newly hatched brine shrimp, microworms, and other small foods. The fry grow fairly rapidly on a varied diet and soon start to assume their characteristic color patterns. Be sure to segregate the young by size, as they are cannibalistic, the larger ones preying upon their smaller brothers and sisters.

342

HERICHTHYS (HERICHTHYS) CYANOGUTTATUS

HERICHTHYS FACETUS (Jenyns)/*Chanchito*

R: Southern Brazil (Rio Grande do Sul, Rio Parana, and tributaries). **H**: Likely to be quarrelsome and uproot plants. Should not be kept with smaller fishes. **W**: Not critical. Temperature should be between 24 to 27°C. **S**: In their habitat, up to 30 cm; in the aquarium, 20 cm. **F**: Greedy eaters; larger specimens may be fed canned dog or cat foods in addition to insects, garden worms, water beetles, tadpoles, and pieces of fish or lean beef. Will only eat dried foods if very hungry.

They lay their eggs on a flat stone, flowerpot, or one of the glass sides of the aquarium and then both parents take meticulous care of their spawn, mouthing them often to make sure that no dirt settles on them. In 3 to 4 days the young hatch and are immediately transferred to holes that the parents have been digging previously. The yolk-sacs are absorbed in about another week, and the youngsters then begin to swim out of the holes, to be herded back by the watchful parents.

HERICHTHYS DOVII

343

HERICHTHYS FESTAE (Boulenger)/*Festae Cichlid*

R: Guayas basin of Ecuador **H:** A large territorial cichlid that is best kept with similarly large fishes. **W:** Not critical. Temperature about 22 to 26°C. **S:** Reaches a maximum length of about 28.5 cm (average size 20 cm). **F:** Generalized feeder which will accept anything from live fishes to plants.

They are continuous spawners in the wild. That is to say that at any time of the year at least some segments of the population will be in spawning condition. But they do have a peak spawning time that coincides with the rainy season. At this time the rivers overfllow, forming flood plains. The spawners migrate to these flooded areas where there is more space, additional food sources and warm, shallow water where the eggs hatch more quickly and growth of the young is rapid. When the waters recede the fish are forced back to the main river.

Obvious sexual differences are not apparent, although the two sexes can easily be distinguished by examination of the breeding tubes (females' blunt and larger, males' more slender and smaller). The ovaries are said to be small, containing about 3,000 eggs one mm in diameter. Courtship is typical for cichlids, and spawning usually occurs in the flowerpot or caves (caves in nature). There is some parental care. The recognizable pattern appears in the young by the time they are about 3 cm and they are ready to spawn at about 13 cm when they are a year old.

HERICHTHYS (AMPHILOPHUS) LABIATUS

HERICHTHYS (NANDOPSIS) FRIEDRICHSTHALI (Heckel)/*Friedrichsthal's Cichlid*

R: Atlantic coast of southern Mexico (approximately Rio Coatzacoalas east) to Costa Rica. **H:** Aggressive, even with very large cichlids. Not so aggressive with members of its own species, however. **W:** Not critical. This species can withstand temperature extremes of near 10°C to almost 35°C for short periods of time. **S:** Up to about 20 cm. **F:** Will eat most aquarium foods. Live foods preferred.

Friedrichsthal's Cichlid is very aggressive and cannot safely be housed even with cichlids larger than itself. Spawning has been accomplished and the behavior is quite typical in many respects. There are the usual fin-spreading displays and jaw-locking behavior as well as the scouring of a flowerpot or rock surface in preparation for egg deposition. The male will usually dig a pit or two some distance from the selected spawning site in preparation for the moving of the fry. The female will deposit some 700 golden-orange eggs on the flowerpot or slate where they are continuously fanned by one parent while the other stands guard.

344

HERICHTHYS FESTAE

HERICHTHYS (AMPHILOPHUS) LABIATUS (Günther)/*Red Devil*
R: Nicaragua and Costa Rica. **H**: Very vicious; should be kept by themselves. **W**: About neutral and fairly soft. Temperature 24 to 26°C. **S**: To about 38 cm. **F**: Carnivorous; will eat small living fishes and can be trained to accept strips of fish fillets. Young specimens will take dry foods. There is a great deal of variability in the structure and coloration of this species: some are bright red; others are white or yellow; some have black-tipped fins and tail and black lips; and some have thick rubbery lips. All are scrappy and should have a large tank to themselves. There is a bit of a problem when it comes to providing food for them; they seem to like to eat living fishes, and while in many places it is not too difficult to get them live bait fish, they can probably be "trained" to eat clams, mussels, food shrimp, or pieces of fish fillet. In their home waters they can be caught on hook and line, using the same tactics as for bass.

HERICHTHYS (NANDOPSIS) FRIEDRICHSTHALI

345

HERICHTHYS MACULICAUDA (Regan)/*Blackbelt Cichlid*

R: Atlantic slope of Central America from Guatemala and southern Belize to the Rio Chagres in Panama. **H:** A large cichlid that is aggressive toward members of its own species. **W:** Does best in moderately hard, neutral to slightly alkaline water. Temperature range 22 to 30°C. **S:** Reaches a length of 30 cm. **F:** A heavy eater but not fussy about its diet. Will accept almost any type of aquarium foods. Vegetable matter should be included in its diet.

Males have a more extensive red area on the head and throat and are generally larger than the females. A large male's fins are slightly longer than the female's. Males are behaviorally more aggressive than similarly sized females. Spawning activity starts with pit digging (down to a hard surface); after a typical *Herichthys* spawning, the eggs are laid in one of the pits. Eggs and fry are tended by the female (sometimes both parents are involved), while the male guards the periphery of their territory. In some instances a sheltered area such as a cave will be used as the spawning site. Up to l,000 or more large (about 2 mm) grayish to pale brownish eggs may be deposited at a single spawning. At 26°C they hatch in three days and the fry are free-swimming in another four days. They can take newly hatched brine shrimp immediately and are fast growers. Parental care lasts about five or six weeks, when the fry are about 5 cm long. At this time the young get along together quite well, but as they grow they become more intolerant of one another and fights occur more frequently. The black band appears when they are about 8 cm long.

HERICHTHYS (THORICHTHYS) MEEKI

HERICHTHYS (NANDOPSIS) MANAGUENSIS (Günther)/*Jaguar Cichlid*

R: Nicaragua. **H:** A quarrelsome species that will kill smaller (and sometimes larger) fishes if given the chance. **W:** Not critical; does well in waters ranging from moderately soft and acid through hard and alkaline. **S:** Up to 35 cm. **F:** Eats all meaty foods. **C:** Pattern very variable in the placement of the vermiculations and blotching according to the mood of the fish.

Most *H. managuensis* specimens will want to rule the roost, and they'll take on anything in their way on the road to that objective. It's not odd that a fish that is territorial by nature will be aggressive, especially where it is kept in cramped quarters with other fishes that cannot help but intrude into its territory, but this species carries things a little too far, since the territory it stakes out for itself usually seems to include the entire tank. Its belligerence, however, is tempered by its intelligence, and grown *H. managuensis* exhibit well developed individual personalities, showing distinctive likes and dislikes of a type to endear them to some hobbyists.

HERICHTHYS MACULICAUDA

HERICHTHYS (THORICHTHYS) MEEKI (Brind)/*Firemouth*
R: Northern Yucatan. **H**: Peaceful for a cichlid; will get along with most fishes that do not harass it. **W**: Not critical; requires large tank with some open space and rocks for shelter. **S**: 12.5 cm; females about 10 cm. **F**: Predominately living foods, such as daphnia, tubifex worms, grown brine shrimp, etc.
One of the most beautiful and popular cichlids. Pairs usually get along fairly well together, but when spawning the male may forget his manners if the female is not ready for him and may kill her if she is not removed until her eggs have developed. They are usually good parents and the young are easily raised. This fish is recommended only if the hobbyist has a large aquarium that presents a good number of hiding places.

HERICHTHYS (NANDOPSIS) MANAGUENSIS

HERICHTHYS NICARAGUENSE (Guenther)/*Spilotum*

R: Great Lakes of Nicaragua and Atlantic coast of Costa Rica. **H:** Relatively peaceful but more aggressive and prone to digging when spawning time approaches. **W:** Not critical. Successful spawning has been achieved with hard and soft water, a neutral pH, and a temperature of about 80-82°F. **S:** Attains a length of up to 23 cm, the female usually somewhat smaller than the male. **F:** Not critical. Will accept most any types of aquarium foods.

With the approach of spawning the colors of both sexes intensify, the male becoming dark and appearing a bit more purple in color. The fish start digging around the selected cave, and a few hours prior to actual spawning the breeding tubes appear. Egg laying takes place in one of the holes dug in the sand, usually somewhat hidden from view—*C. nicaraguense* is normally a secretive spawner. Approximately 800 or so pinkish eggs are deposited in the pit, fertilized immediately by the male, and apparently picked up by the female, which mouths them and spits them out again. The eggs are reportedly non-adhesive, an unusual occurrence in the genus *Herichthys* .

The eggs hatch in about 72 hours and the fry become free-swimming in about another five days. The fry are large enough to accept newly hatched brine shrimp immediately. This food can be supplemented with a good grade of flake food crushed into smaller particles.

Eggs and young are guarded by both parents and can be left with them for several months, although occasional instances of egg-devouring have been reported for this species.

HERICHTHYS (ARCHOCENTRUS) OCTOFASCIATUS

HERICHTHYS (ARCHOCENTRUS) NIGROFASCIATUS (Günther)/*Convict Cichlid*

R: Guatemala, El Salvador, Costa Rica, and Panama. **H:** A typical cichlid not to be trusted with smaller fishes. **W:** Not particular about water. Moderately hard water suits it fine, with temperatures between 20 to 27°C. **S:** To 15 cm; breeds at 8 cm. **F:** Eats everything but does exceptionally well on frozen brine shrimp and frozen beef heart. The young thrive on microworms from their free-swimming stage on.

These fish are very simple to breed if they are given the barest of essentials. Set up a 60- to 80–liter aquarium. The bottom should be sand to a depth of about 5 cm. The pair will select a spawning site on a rock or inverted flower pot and spawn as soon as they have been conditioned for the reproductive act with copious feedings of frozen brine shrimp, beef heart, and tubifex worms. They exercise extreme parental care of the spawn and will probably dig holes in the sand after the young are free-swimming into which to herd the young. The fry do very well on microworms until they are old enough for larger forms of live foods.

HERICHTHYS NICARAGUENSE

HERICHTHYS (ARCHOCENTRUS) OCTOFASCIATUS (Regan)/*Jack Dempsey*
R: Veracruz, Mexico to Honduras. **H**: Very aggressive and loves to dig and uproot plants. Should be kept only with large fishes that can take care of themselves. **W**: Not critical; temperature should average about 25 °C, slightly higher when it is desired to spawn them. **S**: 20 cm. for males; females slightly smaller. **F**: Has a healthy appetite; chopped-up earthworms are a delicacy, as is chopped beef heart small enough to be swallowed easily. **C**: Mature males are deep brown to black, with a black round spot at the center of the body and another at the tail base. A pronounced roughneck, it is almost sure to harass smaller fishes put in with it, so make sure if it is going into a community tank that its tankmates are of a comparable size. For all its other bad habits, the Jack Dempsey is a very gentle parent and breeding a pair is not usually fraught with a great deal of difficulty. Both parents take excellent care of eggs and fry, and the youngsters are quite pretty when they are about 2.5 cm long. At this time the large spot on the side is very prominent and ringed with blue or greenish yellow. It is possible with a healthy, vigorous pair to raise as many as 1,000 youngsters in a single season.

HERICHTHYS (ARCHOCENTRUS) NIGROFASCIATUS

HERICHTHYS SAJICA (Bussin)/Sajica *T-bar Convict*

R: Pacific slope of southern Costa Rica from just south of Punta Mala to the Rio Esquinas basin. **H:** Relatively non-aggressive and generally not biters. A good candidate for some community aquaria. **W:** Not critical. pH 6-8. **S:** Males attain a length of about 9 to 10 cm, females about 7.5 cm. **F:** Will accept a wide variety of aquarium foods; some vegetable matter should be included.

Spawning is typical for the group, but it selects caves as the spawning site whenever possible. The eggs, however, are rather small, translucent, and relatively numerous (more than 200); that is to say, more characteristic of cichlids that spawn in the open. Preparations for spawning include the usual digging and nipping. The color darkens anteriorly (especially the head), the posterior portion of the body turning shining blue, violet, or greenish gray. The eyes are characteristically bright. The eggs are guarded by the female as the male guards the larger territory. T-bar Convicts are reliable parents. The eggs hatch in about three days at about 26°C, and the fry become free-swimming after another six or seven days. The young are relatively easy to raise although there may be a problem as they attain a length of just under 25 mm—at least some breeders report the fry die at this time from unknown causes.

HERICHTHYS (NANDOPSIS) SALVINI (Günther)/*Salvin's Cichlid, Yellow-Belly*

R: Central America, from Guatemala and Honduras into southern Mexico. **H:** Can be very rough toward other fishes and its own species, but in an appropriately large tank provided with rocks and caves it may be entirely peaceful. **W:** Not critical; the species is especially tolerant of cool water. **S:** To about 15 cm. **F:** Takes all meaty foods.

The eggs are laid on a firm base, usually a rock that forms part of a cave or shelter in which the fish will spawn, although they don't always spawn in a cave, sometimes laying the eggs on a rock surface in open water. The eggs hatch within three days at a temperature of around 26°C, and the fry are zealously guarded and herded. In some cases both parents care for the fry, but sometimes the female alone will undertake all parental supervision; in no case in which both parents are left with the eggs and fry will it be the male alone who cares for the babies.

HERICHTHYS SAJICA

HEROS SEVERUS (Heckel)/*Severum*

R: Northern South America to the Amazon River, except in the Magdalena River. **H**: Typical of the large cichlids, it will become quarrelsome when breeding time rolls around. Requires a large aquarium and will uproot plants and dig many holes in the gravel. **W**: Not critical; clean, slightly alkaline water seems to be best. **S**: Up to 20 cm. **F**: Small specimens may be fed with all the various live foods; when they become large chopped garden worms should be given on occasion.

Young specimens of this fish do not greatly resemble their parents and often create a problem when they grow up. Young fish are usually quite peaceful and their owner gets the mistaken impression that this attitude will continue. As they get bigger, they will "pair off" in the usual cichlid fashion and begin to prepare a site for spawning. Every other fish that dares to come near is driven away fiercely, and bloody fights may ensue. If given their own tank, spawning proceeds normally as a rule, and eggs and fry are seldom eaten. There is also an albino variety of this fish available today, with a light golden body and pink eyes.

HERICHTHYS (NANDOPSIS) SALVINI

HERICHTHYS (ARCHOCENTRUS) SPILURUS (Günther)/*Blue-Eyed Cichlid*
R: Central America. **H**: Relatively peaceful for a large cichlid. **W**: Not critical. **S**: Up to 18 cm; females smaller. **F**: Needs the addition of vegetable material such as spinach to its diet.
This is not an especially difficult species to breed, breeding in the familiar cichlid manner. Pairs are inclined to be somewhat secretive about spawning, but a sure sign is the change in the coloration of the female. The head and breast become dusky and the gold band on the side becomes more brilliant. The ventral fins become coal black. It was thought for a time that *H. spilurus* and *H. nigrofasciatus* were color variations of the same fish. Both species are known to occur in the same bodies of water, which is taken as evidence that the color patterns of the living fishes play an important part in preventing hybridizing in nature. These species, however, have been successfully crossed under aquarium conditions, producing hybrids that resembled *H. spilurus* more than *H. nigrofasciatus*. The hybrids were more pugnacious than either parent.

HERICHTHYS TETRACANTHUS

HERICHTHYS SYNSPILUM (Hubbs)/ *Redheaded Cichlid*
R: Atlantic slope of Central America from the Rio Usumacinta basin of Guatemala to the coastal rivers of Belize. **H:** Very aggressive toward conspecifics but seems to tolerate other large cichlids. **W:** Moderately hard water with a neutral or slightly alkaline pH. Temperature range from 22 to 30°C. **S:** Reaches a length of about 30 cm (standard length). **F:** A heavy eater that will accept almost any type of aquarium food. Vegetable matter should be included.
Spawning generally starts with the digging of several pits in the sand deep enough to expose the tank bottom. It has been reported that in some instances caves or flowerpots have been used, so apparently this species is quite flexible in its spawning behavior. The pale brown eggs, about 2 mm in diameter, are placed in the pits (or in the cave, etc.) after typical *Herichthys* spawning rituals. The female tends the eggs and fry and the male patrols the territory on guard for intruders for about five weeks, after which the young are forgotten and the parents are ready to spawn again. The 200-800 eggs hatch in about four days (at 25°C) and become free-swimming five days later. The newly hatched fry, about 5-6 mm long and with a narrow black midlateral stripe, are able to handle newly hatched brine shrimp. Growth is rapid (2-3 cm after a month).

HERICHTHYS (ARCHOCENTRUS) SPILURUS

HERICHTHYS TETRACANTHUS (Cuvier)/*Cuban Cichlid*

R: Cuba. **H:** Typical aggressive cichlid that establishes a territory when spawning. It cannot be trusted with very small fishes. **W:** Not important. A temperature range of 22-27° C and soft and slightly acid to neutral to slightly alkaline water is adequate. Will stand brackish conditions. **S:** Attains a length of about 25 cm. **F:** Accepts a wide variety of normal aquarium type foods. Live foods are preferred.

When not in breeding condition the sexes are quite similar, although the male may be a bit larger. While spawning the females exhibit a dark blackish ventral area and dark vertical bars crossing a silvery white ground color. After a lot of cleaning and preliminary sparring (this is where hiding places should come in if the female is not receptive) a flat rock or slate is selected as the spawning site. The area around it is cleared. Actual egg laying then proceeds normally and there may be as many as 600 eggs deposited. The female is responsible for the job of fanning the eggs and otherwise caring for them while the male patrols the periphery of the territory defending it against actual or supposed enemies. The fry are raised in the usual manner. The same pair may stay together to spawn several times or the male may seek out other females.

HERICHTHYS SYNSPILUM

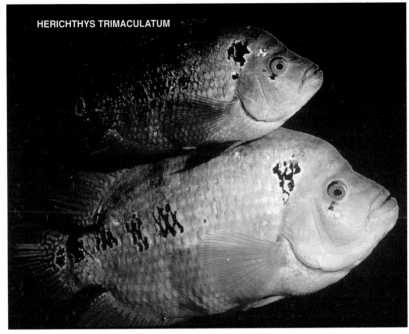

HERICHTHYS TRIMACULATUM (Gunther)/*Three-Spot Cichlid*

R: Pacific slope of Central America from Laguna Coyuca, Mexico, to Rio Lempa, El Salvador.
H: Typically aggressive toward its own kind and its tankmates, it can only be placed with other large "rough" fishes. **W:** Not critical. Has spawned in soft water with a pH of 6.8 and a temperature of about 27°C. **S:** Attains a length of 18 cm or more. **F:** Not a fussy eater, it will accept most good quality aquarium foods.

Although they grow to a pretty fair size (to 18 cm or more), a pair can be spawned in a tank as small as 80 liters. It should be provided with a sandy bottom, some hiding places in case the mating rituals get too rough, and a good substrate for the deposition of the eggs (although they will dig down to the tank bottom if nothing else is available). Pre-spawning activities include the appearance of the breeding tubes, a darkening of the color (to almost black), and the cleaning of the spawning site. Typical mating rituals such as jaw-locking occur until the pair is ready. Eggs are deposited in the cleaned area by the female, with the male following behind fertilizing them. When several hundred eggs have been laid and spawning ceases, the female will stay up above them fanning them with her fins. The male is at the periphery of the breeding site ready to do combat with any interlopers.

The eggs hatch in about two or three days and the fry may be moved by the parents to more sanitary quarters such as a pit in the sand in a relatively secluded part of the tank. In another four days or so the fry become free-swimming. The male and female can be left with the fry as they appear to be good parents. In fact, one aquarist saw the fry pecking at the sides of the parents' bodies in a fashion similar to discus fry. Whether this represents a similar nutritional behavior is not yet known.

HEROTILAPIA MULTISPINOSA

HEROTILAPIA MULTISPINOSA (Günther)/*Rainbow Cichlid*

R: Costa Rica and Nicaragua. **H**: A good community tank species for a cichlid its size; normally peaceful except when spawning. **W**: Not sensitive to hardness or pH. Prefers temperature between 21 to 27°C; avoid extremes. **S**: Reaches 10 cm, but may spawn at around half that size. **F**: Not choosy. Eats live, frozen, or dry foods. **C**: Usually golden brown with a black lateral stripe made of connected blotches; the eye is red. When guarding eggs or fry, the entire lower part of the body (including the fins) turns dark gray; some individuals turn completely black. Several hundred eggs are attached to a rock and fanned by the parents for three days, when hatching occurs. The nearly invisible fry are immediately removed by the parents to depressions dug by the male in the gravel. Until the fry are free-swimming (about one week), they are constantly fanned and moved around by the adults.

HETERANDRIA BIMACULATA

HETERANDRIA BIMACULATA (Heckel)/*Twin-Spot Livebearer*

R: Central Mexico to Guatemala and Honduras between latitudes 15°N and 20°N. **H:** Aggressive, especially the females, and not suitable for a community tank. **W:** Not critical. Originally came from mountain streams, but also inhabit slow-moving and even brackish water. **S:** Males attain a length of 4 to 5 cm, females 8 to 9 cm. **F:** A voracious feeder. Will take live foods of almost any kind.

The Twin-Spot Livebearer is an aggressive fish, especially the females, and is not a suitable addition to a community tank. Their own tank should be densely planted to provide respite from aggressive individuals, but sufficient swimming space must be left. The water should be clean, well-aerated, and kept at a temperature between 22 and 26°C. They are voracious feeders that prefer live foods of all kinds.

The males possess gonopodia, so there is no difficulty in telling the sexes apart. In addition, the females grow to a length almost twice that of the male. The breeding tank should be densely planted. The gestation period is four to six weeks duration, after which the female might give birth to well over 100 young. The young are 12 to 15 mm long at birth and grow rapidly. They soon are fighting among themselves just like their parents. The plants should provide the necessary shelter to avoid serious damage. In about a week or so they are fully pigmented, and in six months they are sexually mature.

Several subspecies have been described: *H. b. bimaculatus* from the lowlands of Vera Cruz; *H. b. jonesi* from central Vera Cruz above 2,300 meters; *H. b. peninsulae* from Campeche and Yucatan; and *H. b. taeniatus* from southern Vera Cruz, Guatemala, and Honduras.

HETERANDRIA FORMOSA Agassiz/*Mosquito Fish, Least Killifish*

R: U.S., North Carolina to eastern Texas, coastal. **H**: Peaceful; males are small enough to be eaten by bigger fishes, so this species is best kept by itself. **W**: Not critical, as long as the water is not too far from neutral. Temperature about 24°C. **S**: Males about 2 cm; females almost 3.5 cm. **F**: All small live foods, also frozen. Prepared foods also taken.

Two or three youngsters are born every day for about a week. The youngsters, if the parents are well fed, are seldom in any danger of being eaten and can be raised in the same tank with them. This makes for a tankful of varying sizes, and a small tank takes quite a while to become crowded. This livebearing species cannot be considered a community fish, because the tiny males would not be safe from the larger species who could swallow them.

HETEROPNEUSTES FOSSILIS (Bloch)/*Heteropneustes*

R: Southeast Asia from Sri Lanka and eastern India through Burma and Thailand to South Vietnam. **H:** Very aggressive and predatory on small fishes. Hunts at night. Best suited for single species tank. **W:** Not critical. Water chemistry within normal limits and good filtration plus a temperature between 21° and 25°C are acceptable. **S:** A fairly large species that reaches a length of about 70 cm in nature but only about half that in aquaria. **F:** A meaty diet is recommended including beef heart, various worms, and even small fishes. Remember they feed at night.

The tank should be large and provided with a soft substrate. It should be decorated with rockwork and driftwood that provide hiding places for this light sensitive species during the bright daylight hours. Plants may be added as long as they are large, hardy species. The water chemistry is not too important as long as it is within normal aquarium limits. A pH of 6.0-8.0 and hardness up to 30°GH are acceptable. Temperatures between 21° and 25°C are recommended. Good filtration is also necessary.

Spawning in captivity has been accomplished a number of times. Sexes are similar although the male may be a bit more slender than the female. Depressions in the sand are constructed by fanning them out with their fins and after some prespawning courtship (including the female nuzzling at the male's genital area) a ball of 2 mm eggs is laid in one of them. Both parents guard the eggs and fry. The fry can take newly hatched brine shrimp and other similar live foods.

H. fossilis has an accessory breathing apparatus and can survive out of water for several hours much like their cousins the clariid catfishes. One word of caution—the pectoral fin spines are poisonous so care must be exercised when they are handled.

HOMALOPTERA ORTHOGONIATA Vaillant/*Saddlespot Loach*

R: Indonesian region (Borneo, Sumatra, and Java) to Thailand. **H:** Peaceful fishes that usually can be kept in a community situation. They do squabble among themselves but no damage is done. **W:** Not critical. A temperature range of 20° to 24°C is adequate. **S:** Attains a length of about 12 cm. **F:** Will take a variety of foods and will also scour objects in the tank in typical loach fashion.

The Saddlespot Loach is a very prettily marked species that has attained a small following among aquarists. It is a peaceful species that can be kept in a community tank as it basically ignores its tankmates. Members of the same species, however, may get some attention and some squabbling may occur but without any harm being done.

Keeping this species is quite simple. It requires no special water conditions and is quite satisfied with a pH that is slightly acid or slightly alkaline. Slightly soft to moderately hard water and a temperature of 20° to 24°C also are acceptable. Regular partial water changes should be made. About 25-35% twice a month is sufficient. Plants included in the tank should be well rooted.

HOLOBRYCON PESU (Müller & Troschel)/*Mourning Tetra*

R: Amazon River system and the Guianas. **H**: A beautiful schooling fish that can grace every large community aquarium with its fast moving, darting action and its voracious appetite. **W**: Not very sensitive to the water in which it is kept as long as the temperature ranges between 24 and 29°C. It tolerates salt but does better in soft, acid water with a pH of 6.6. **S**: Under 10 cm. **F**: Though it does better on a weekly ration of live foods, it has been kept for a year on just frozen brine shrimp and dry food. **C**: As the fish gets older, the black edge on the tail gradually fades and the intense black on the adipose gradually covers the whole adipose.

If this fish came from Zaire or from Australia it would be a very popular fish because its sides are gleaming silver with a reddish blue cast and its adipose fin is stark black, contrasting beautifully with its black-edged tail. This black "outergarb" is what suggested the name "Mourning Tetra" to the author (HRA).

HOPLOSTERNUM THORACATUM

HOPLIAS MALABARICUS (Bloch)/*Tiger Fish; Trahira*

R: Central and northern South America. **H**: Predatory on fishes it can swallow. Not generally regarded as a good aquarium fish. **W**: Not critical; can exist in soft to medium-hard water and prefers dim light. Temperature 24 to 26°C. **S**: Attains a length of about 50 cm. **F**: Small fishes are eagerly hunted down. Chopped fish or brine shrimp and possibly earthworms might provide suitable substitutes.

The Tiger Fish or Trahira builds a nest similar to that of the bowfin, *Amia*. Spawning occurs above the nest, with the female cupping her anal fin to receive the eggs and at the same time enveloping the male's genital area. This apparently ensures fertilization of the eggs. The female then relaxes the anal fin and the eggs, which are adhesive and cling to one another, drop into the nest. As many as 2,500 to 3,000 eggs are deposited over a period of about two weeks. These egg masses are reported to be over 2 meters in diameter and somewhat resemble tapioca. The male guards the nest (even if the sggs are removed) as the female moves off after egg deposition. The eggs hatch in about 52 hours. Males are said to be more slender, with a longer and more pointed snout; their color is also darker and more mottled.

HOLOBRYCON PESU

HOPLOSTERNUM THORACATUM (Valenciennes)/*Port Hoplo, Atipa*

R: Found throughout northern and central South America. **H**: A bottom feeder that must come up to the surface for air at short intervals. **W**: Not critical. **S**: Up to 15 cm. **F**: Will eat what other fishes in tank will eat; frozen foods and tubifex worms bring it to peak condition.

There are usually two species of *Hoplosternum* imported from South America: *littorale* and *thoracatum.* Some authors claim that there are several subspecies of *H. thoracatum* based upon slight meristic characteristics and the fact that they occur over so wide a range. The present author takes the opinion that they are all one species. They freely interbreed and the individual differences that have been noted as subspecific characteristics are within the tolerances of individual variation.

HOPLIAS MALABARICUS

HORADANDIA ATUKORALI Deraniyagala/*Midget Minnow, Green Carplet*

R: Sri Lanka. **H**: Peaceful and active; timid in the presence of larger fishes. **W**: Can take both soft, acid water and hard, alkaline water, as long as extremes are avoided. Temperature 22 to 28°C. **S**: 3 cm. **F**: Accepts all foods that are small enough to be swallowed.

The Midget Minnow spawns by laying adhesive eggs in plant thickets; the eggs, as is to be expected from the size of the parents, are very small. The newly hatched fry are also very small, and they therefore require feedings of infusoria, as they are unable to swallow brine shrimp nauplii during the first days of their life. *Horadandia atukorali* eggs have a fairly short incubation period (about a day and a half to two days).

HYPHESSOBRYCON AXELRODI

HYPHESSOBRYCON AGULHA Fowler/*Red-Tailed Flag Tetra*

R: Upper Amazon region. **H**: Peaceful; likes to swim in schools. **W**: Soft, slightly acid water. Temperature 24 to 26°C. **S**: About 45 cm. **F**: Will accept dried foods, but live or frozen foods should be given frequently.

Like *Hemigrammus bellottii,* young specimens of *Hyphessobryon agulha* are frequently mixed in with Neon Tetras when shipments come in. Here we have a fish which, when it grows to its full size, is a very attractive proposition and an asset to any aquarium. It greatly resembles *Hyphessobrycon heterorhabdus,* the popular Flag Tetra. There is even an added touch of color: the tail of the male is bright red.

HORADANDIA ATUKORALI

HYPHESSOBRYCON AXELRODI (Travassos)/*Calypso Tetra, Ruby Pristella*
R: Trinidad. **H**: Peaceful; likes to swim in schools. **W**: Soft, slightly acid water. Temperature 24 to 26°C. **S**: About 3 cm. **F**: Takes all foods eagerly, including dried flakes, but should have an occasional meal of live or frozen foods.

Anyone who has had experience with other *Hyphessobrycon* species finds it very difficult to recognize this as one of them. Probably the only reason it had missed being "found" in all the biological surveys of the fishes of Trinidad is its close resemblance to *Pristella maxillaris*. When H.R.A. found these fish in a small pool at the edge of the Piarco Airport, the collecting party gasped at the sight of a hundred "drops of blood" in the net. No fish as red as this one had ever before been found in Trinidad, which had more fish collectors per square mile than any other country in the world.

HYPHESSOBRYCON AGULHA

HYPHESSOBRYCON BENTOSI Durbin/*Rosy Tetra*

R: Amazon Basin and Guianas. **H**: Peaceful; should be kept in groups of at least six. **W**: Soft, slightly acid water is best. Temperature 24 to 27°C. **S**: To 5 cm. **F**: Prepared foods accepted, but live and frozen foods preferred.

The Rosy Tetra is the largest member of the so-called *"callistus* group." A handsome fish such as this deserves a few extra pains to bring out its best colors. To do this, rule number one is to give it a dark background. If your tank has its back to a wall and gets its light from the front, that is good. If the front light is sunlight, that is even better. As for the background, paint the back glass with dark green paint, either the ordinary type or the crackle finish paint sold for this purpose by most petshops.

HYPHESSOBRYCON EQUES

HYPHESSOBRYCON BIFASCIATUS Ellis/*Yellow Tetra*

R: Southeastern Brazil, near the coast. **H**: Very peaceful; will not attack other fishes or plants. **W**: Neutral to slightly acid. Temperature 22 to 24°C. **S**: Up to 5 cm. **F**: All foods gratefully eaten, prepared as well as live or frozen.

This is an easy species to breed. Spawning takes place among the bushy plants, and the parents must be removed as soon as the spawning is completed. Eggs hatch the day after they are laid, after which the tiny young can be seen hanging from the glass sides and the plants. Once the yolk-sac is absorbed and they begin to swim, feeding may be begun with very fine foods, to be followed in a few days with newly hatched brine shrimp.

HYPHESSOBRYCON BENTOSI

HYPHESSOBRYCON EQUES (Steindachner)/*Callistus Tetra*

R: Southern Amazon and Paraguay basins. **H**: Peaceful and active; should have a well-planted tank and be kept in a school of not less than six individuals. **W**: Fish will show their best colors if the water is slightly acid and very soft. Temperature best around 24°C. **S**: About 4 cm. **F**: Prepared foods accepted, but to keep them in the best of condition they should get live or frozen foods frequently.

The Callistus Tetra is a peaceful and active fish that requires an aquarium 30 liters or larger. The tank should have a dark background and soft, slightly acid water. This species does best when it is in the company of its own kind and, although it makes a good community aquarium fish, should be kept in groups with a minimum of six individuals.

HYPHESSOBRYCON BIFASCIATUS

HYPHESSOBRYCON ERYTHROSTIGMA (Fowler)/
Bleeding Heart Tetra, Tetra Perez

R: Upper Amazon. **H**: Peaceful if kept with fishes of its own size. **W**: Slightly acid, soft water. Temperature 23 to 26°C. **S**: To 8 cm. **F**: Live or frozen foods preferred; prepared foods taken if hungry.

This is not a fish for the small aquarium; it is an active species that requires a good deal of "elbow room" and should get it. Given this, a well-conditioned pair will spawn readily and in a manner similar to that of the other *Hyphessobrycon* species.

HYPHESSOBRYCON GRIEMI

HYPHESSOBRYCON FLAMMEUS Myers/
Flame Tetra, Red Tetra, Tetra from Rio

R: Region near Rio de Janeiro. **H**: Peaceful; best kept with other small fishes and in a school of at least six. **W**: Not critical; water is best if slightly acid and soft, but this is not absolutely essential. Temperature of 24 to 26°C. **S**: To 4 cm. **F**: Prepared foods accepted, but live or frozen foods are preferred.

Spawning occurs among fine-leaved plants, and their owner is sometimes amazed at the amount of eggs that can be released by such a small female. Hatching occurs in two to three days, and once the fry begin to swim free they must be fed with very fine-grained prepared foods or infusoria. Growth proceeds rapidly; with good attention the fry are raised to maturity in about six months.

HYPHESSOBRYCON ERYTHROSTIGMA

HYPHESSOBRYCON GRIEMI Hoedeman/*Griem's Tetra*

R: Brazil, in the vicinity of Goias. **H**: Perfectly peaceful; like the other small members of the family, they also prefer to be kept in groups of at least six. **W**: Soft, slightly acid water is best but not necessarily essential. Temperature 24 to 26°C. **S**: About 4 cm. **F**: Prepared foods are accepted, but live or frozen foods are preferable.

The deep pink of the caudal and anal fins is only slightly indicated in most available specimens, but with good care and feeding it becomes increasingly evident. This color is also often lost when the fish is frightened by being placed in a too-bare aquarium or in an aquarium where it is being constantly pursued by larger fishes.

HYPHESSOBRYCON FLAMMEUS

HYPHESSOBRYCON HERBERTAXELRODI Géry/*Black Neon Tetra*

R: Rio Taquary, Brazil. **H**: Peaceful toward other fishes; prefers to be kept in a group of at least six. **W**: Soft, slightly acid water preferred but not essential. Temperature 25°C. **S**: About 3 cm. **F**: Hearty eaters; prepared foods as well as live or frozen foods are eaten with equal gusto.

In a well-planted aquarium, a number of them swimming around makes a pleasing sight with the broad, velvet-black area on the lower half of the sides and the startling, enamel-white stripe above it. When the light comes from above, this white stripe takes on a gleaming light blue color .

HYPHESSOBRYCON MEGALOPTERUS

HYPHESSOBRYCON HETERORHABDUS (Ulrey)/*Flag Tetra, False Ulreyi*

R: Lower and middle Amazon region. **H**: Peaceful and very active. **W**: A little sensitive if not given soft, slightly acid water. Temperature should be kept around 25°C. **F**: Will take dried food readily, but should also get frequent feedings of live or frozen foods.

This very attractive tetra masqueraded under a false name for many years. When it was first introduced into Germany in 1910, it was mistaken for *Hemigrammus ulreyi*. Call it what you may, it is a pretty little fish and an asset to any aquarium. Trouble is, we seldom get to see any numbers of tank-raised specimens, and we are still dependent upon imported specimens for our aquaria. They usually take very well to captivity, and the females seem to fill up with eggs, but the usual result is either nothing at all or only a few youngsters.

HYPHESSOBRYCON HERBERTAXELRODI

HYPHESSOBRYCON MEGALOPTERUS (Eigenmann)/*Black Phantom Tetra*
R: Brazil. **H**: Peaceful and active. **W**: Soft, acid water is best, especially for breeding. Temperature 23 to 26°C. **S**: 4 cm. **F**: Accepts live, frozen, and dried foods.
Hyphessobrycon megalopterus spawns in thick bundles of plants (nylon spawning mops may also be used), and for a small fish it is quite prolific, sometimes scattering up to 400 eggs at one spawning. The eggs hatch in a little over a day at a temperature of 25°C, but they are quite susceptible to fungus, especially if put into a tank with too much light.

HYPHESSOBRYCON HETERORHABDUS

HYPHESSOBRYCON METAE Eigenmann & Henn/*Purple Tetra*

R: Rio Meta, Colombia. **H**: Peaceful, but tends to be shy; should not be kept with large or aggressive fishes. **W**: Soft, slightly acid water is best, especially for breeding purposes. Temperature 24 to 28°C. **S**: To 5 cm. **F**: Although live foods are preferred, frozen foods will be accepted without trouble; will often accept flake foods as well.

For breeding purposes, bunches of fine-leaved plants such as *Myriophyllum* should be placed in the aquarium. The water should be soft and on the acid side of neutral. Water may be made acid by filtering it through peat moss or by adding tannic acid. Only females that appear gravid should be used. The spawning ritual may appear violent, with the fish pressing up against each other and diving into the plants.

HYPHESSOBRYCON PULCHRIPINNIS

HYPHESSOBRYCON PERUVIANUS Ladiges/*Loreto Tetra*

R: Peruvian Amazon. **H**: Peaceful and a bit shy; should not be kept with large or aggressive fishes. **W**: Soft, slightly acid water is best but is not absolutely essential. Temperature 24 to 28°C. **S**: 5 cm; most specimens smaller. **F**: Live foods preferred, but frozen or prepared foods are accepted without any trouble.

The Loreto Tetra is similar in shape to the Neon Tetra. Males of this species are slimmer than the females and their swim bladders are completely visible when the fish is seen against a strong light. The more robust females have only a partially visible swim bladder. The Loreto Tetra is a hardy and undemanding fish. Under optimum conditions these fish will develop a brilliant purple coloration.

HYPHESSOBRYCON METAE

HYPHESSOBRYCON PULCHRIPINNIS Ahl/*Lemon Tetra*
R: Rio Tapajos, Brazil. **H**: Peaceful; happier in a group of at least six. **W**: Soft, acid water is desirable but not essential. Temperature 24 to 27°C. **S**: To 5 cm. **F**: Live foods preferred, but frozen and prepared foods are accepted.
Spawning these little beauties is not always simple. Females frequently have a bit of trouble expelling eggs, and it may sometimes be necessary to combine a male with several females before a successful spawning is achieved. Eggs are laid in fine-leaved plants in the usual *Hyphessobrycon* manner.

HYPHESSOBRYCON PERUVIANUS

HYPHESSOBRYCON SCHOLZEI Ahl/*Black-Lined Tetra*

R: Vicinity of Pará, Brazil **H**: Peaceful; will not harm other fishes or plants. **W**: Soft and slightly acid water is preferable but not essential. Temperature 23 to 26°C. **S**: To 5 cm. **F**: Prepared foods accepted readily, but they should be supplemented with frozen and live foods.

When they are put in a tank where there are not enough plants and the lighting is not proper, the Black-Lined Tetra becomes just a silvery fish with a black stripe. This is one of the easiest members of the genus to breed. They spawn like many other *Hyphessobrycon* species, hanging their eggs among fine-leaved plants.

HYPHESSOBRYCON SWEGLESI

HYPHESSOBRYCON STEGEMANNI Géry/*Savannah Tetra*

R: The savannahs of northeastern Brazil, between the lower Rio Tocantins and the Rio Capim. **H**: Peaceful; likes to travel in schools. **W**: Soft, slightly acid water. Temperature should not drop lower than 24°C. **S**: To 5 cm. **F**: Does very well on dried foods, but should also get occasional feedings with live or frozen foods.

This fish comes from clear, swiftly-moving rivers that have a relatively stable temperature of 24°C. The pH of the water varies with the time of year. During the summer dry season, the pH of the river water varies from 5.2 to 5.8. During the heavy downpours of the rainy season, however, the pH will move toward the alkaline side of neutral.

HYPHESSOBRYCON SCHOLZEI

HYPHESSOBRYCON SWEGLESI (Géry)/*Swegles' Tetra*

R: Amazon region near Leticia, Colombia. **H**: Peaceful; like the other tetras, they prefer to be in schools. **W**: Soft, slightly acid water is preferred. Temperature 24 to 26°C. **S**: About 4 cm. **F**: Easily fed; prefers live foods, but frozen and prepared foods also accepted. **C**: Body reddish brown with a large lateral spot of black. Male's dorsal fin is high and pointed, the female's is smaller and round.

Hyphessobryon sweglesi, originally called *Megalamphodus sweglesi*, is a colorful and generaaly peaceful little tetra that makes a fine display in community aquaria when housed with other peaceful species roughly its own size. Spawns in typical *Hyphessobryon* fashon, but the tiny fry are not easy to raise.

HYPHESSOBRYCON STEGEMANNI

HYPHESSOBRYCON TAKASEI Géry/*Coffee Bean Tetra*

R: Amapa Territory in northern Brazil. **H**: Very peaceful; will not harm plants or other fishes. **W**: Soft, acid water is optimal. Temperature 24 to 26°C. **S**: About 3 cm. **F**: Prefers live foods, but will accept frozen, freeze-dried or dried foods as well.

The Coffee Bean Tetra is separable from all other tetras to date by the very large humeral or shoulder spot which is unique not only because of its size but also because of its coffee bean shape.

HYPOPOMUS ARTEDI

HYPHESSOBRYCON VILMAE Géry/*Vilma's Tetra*

R: Northern and central Brazil. **H**: A lively nature yet not aggressive, but can be a fin-nipper. **W**: Somewhat on the acid side; a small fluctuation of DH will be tolerated. Temperature 24°C. **S**: To 4 cm. **F**: Will accept freeze-dried foods and also dry foods; live foods are naturally relished.

This gorgeous fish is not readily available, but maybe some day, if there is a demand, *Hyphessobrycon vilmae* might become as popular as some of the other well-known aquarium tetras; some say that this species is even more appealing to the eye than *Hyphessobrycon stegemanni,* another species that Harald Schultz discovered.

HYPHESSOBRYCON TAKASEI

HYPOPOMUS ARTEDI (Kaup)/*Spotted Knife Fish*

R: Brazil and the Guianas. **H**: Peaceful toward other fishes that are not small enough to be swallowed; likely to be belligerent toward their own kind. **W**: Not critical, but the fish is sensitive to fresh water. The tank should be well planted and offer a number of places to hide. Temperature about 24°C. **S**: To 43 cm. **F**: Prefers large live foods or chopped lean beef. **C**: Yellowish to brownish with darker spots.

Tell a non-hobbyist that there is a fish that has no dorsal fin, no tail fin, and no ventral fins, and also has its anus just below its head, and he will doubt your sanity! Then tell him that this fish swims by rippling its anal fin and can swim as easily backward as forward by reversing this rippling motion, and your friend will begin to make excuses to get away as quickly as possible before you get violent. So you better have one of these fish around to show him.

HYPHESSOBRYCON VILMAE

HYPOSTOMUS BOLIVIANUS (Pearson)/*Bolivian Sucker Catfish*

R: Bolivia, in the Amazon tributaries. **H**: Seldom bothers other fishes. **W**: Neutral to slightly alkaline. Temperature 24 to 27°C. **S**: To 15 cm. **F**: All live and frozen foods eagerly accepted, especially worms; requires algae or a vegetable substitute like lettuce leaves.

The body is well protected by rows of sharp spines on the sides, and the stiff, sturdy first ray of the pectoral fins is similarly armed, making this fish not only a dangerous one to handle but also a difficult one to remove from the meshes of a net. All of the plecostomus-type catfishes are very difficult to capture in their native waters because they invariably seek out streams where there is a great deal of brushwood in the water where they can hide. Seining is impossible, and the fish cannot be driven out into clear spots. They merely dodge from one hiding place to another.

HYPSELECARA CORYPHAENOIDES

HYPOSTOMUS PLECOSTOMUS (Linnaeus)/*Sucker Catfish, Plecostomus*

R: Most of South America. **H**: Peaceful toward other unrelated fishes, but sometimes very scrappy among themselves. **W**: Slightly hard, alkaline water preferred. Temperature 24 to 27°C. **S**: To 60 cm in natural waters; most captive specimens get no bigger than 30 cm. **F**: Live worms or frozen foods are eaten greedily, also cut-up pieces of earthworms.

The Plecostomus is a fish that is most active at night and during the day generally remains hidden in the shade of some rocks. Do not let this preference for a shady spot convince you to put this fish into a tank where there is little sunlight, because our friend will always find a spot to its liking during the daylight hours and at night will come out and graze on the algae prone to proliferate in a tank that is sunny and has fairly alkaline water.

HYPOSTOMUS BOLIVIANUS

HYPSELECARA CORYPHAENOIDES (Heckel)/*Black Chuco, Chocolate Cichlid*
R: Amazon and Rio Negro Systems. **H**: At maturity aggressive towards other Chocolate Cichlids, but relatively tolerant of other fishes. **W**: Tolerant of a wide range of water conditions as long as extremes are avoided. **S**: Up to 20 cm. **F**: Accepts all meaty standard aquarium foods, showing more preference for frozen and live foods than for granulated and flake foods.

The first specimens of the fish originally called *Chuco axelrodi* were the products of the Axelrod-Yepez Ichthyological Expedition to Venezuela in May, 1971. The purpose of this expedition was to find new species of value from an aquarium standpoint. One of the most promising species caught was the Black Chuco. At the time this fish was described as "rich, velvety black, the black of a good Black Molly" and thought to be a very valuable find. For many years after its discovery, however, this species could not be found again. Then, in 1977, additional specimens were discovered on a subsequent expedition to Brazil. It was found that these specimens only turned black when dead and the living specimens were brown. It was eventually found to be a synonym of *Hypselecara coryphaenoides*.

HYPOSTOMUS PLECOSTOMUS

HYPSELECARA TEMPORALIS (Günther)/*F Cichlid*

R: Central Amazon. **H**: A typical cichlid with earth-moving habits when spawning. They also tear up plants when planning to spawn. Best kept with large plastic plants. They will eat fishes small enough to gulp down in one swallow. **W**: A very hardy fish. Tolerates water from 6.0 to 8.4 pH. Temperature from 21 to 29°C. Hard or soft water is agreeable. **S**: To 20 cm. **F**: They eat most fish foods.

They are easily recognized by the two vertical spots and the long lateral line marking which, when viewed with the fish's head down, looks like an "F"; this has given this cichlid its common name.

Spawning is quite simple, merely a matter of putting a male and female in the same aquarium with plenty of space and good feedings of dried and frozen foods. The young are free-swimming in about 4 to 5 days depending upon the temperature. Remove the parents after spawning.

HYPSELEOTRIS GUENTHERI

HYPSELEOTRIS COMPRESSUS/*Empire Goby*

R: Papua New Guinea to northern and eastern Australia. **H**: Cannot be kept with very small fishes. This is a predatory bottom-living species. **W**: Tolerant of most types of water conditions, but does best in harder, more alkaline water with a little salt added. Temperature 18 to 24°C. **S**: Grows to a length of about 10 cm. **F**: Will take a wide variety of aquarium foods. Prefers live mosquito larvae.

The aquarium need not be overly large, and the water conditions can vary somewhat without major harm to the fish. It is recommended that the water be on the hard and alkaline side with a little salt added for best results. Feeding is not a problem. This fish accepts most aquarium foods readily, including flake foods. In its natural habitat the Empire Goby is noted for its destruction of mosquito larvae, and this of course would be the best food to offer your fish whenever it is available. The Empire Goby should be treated as a predator and not kept with fishes small enough for it to swallow.

Spawning has not been reported, but close relatives deposit their eggs on a rock surface. The eggs hatch in approximately two weeks or less depending upon the temperature.

HYPSELEOTRIS GUENTHERI (Bleeker)/*Chameleon Sleeper*

R: Sumatra to New Guinea, the Solomons, and east to Fiji and Samoa. **H**: Peaceful; all foods readily accepted. **W**: Slightly alkaline, fairly hard water preferred; brackish water is tolerated. Temperature 23 to 26°C. **S**: About 6 cm. **F**: Will eat anything, but may also include plants in its menu; should get live foods occasionally. **C**: Usually a muddy brown with a darker horizontal stripe. The male's fins have a blue edge, the dorsal fin with blue dots.

This seldom-imported fish has a wide range in the western Pacific islands. It is a regular chameleon in the way it can undergo color changes with startling speed. Males can be distinguished by the blue edge on the fins and a number of large blue dots in the dorsal fin. The female's fins are transparent and the blue edge is missing.

HYPSELEOTRIS COMPRESSUS

HYPSELEOTRIS KLUNZINGERI (Ogilby)/*Australian Pink Sleeper*

R: The coastal waters of Australia. **H**: A fin-nipper that should only be kept with fishes its own size. **W**: Prefers slightly alkaline, hard water; brackish water is tolerated. **S**: It is rarely found to exceed 10 cm. **F**: Prefers live foods, but takes pelleted foods and frozen foods readily. **C**: Some specimens have red, brown, and blue edges on their fins.

When kept in a school of about a dozen fish in an 80-liter aquarium with hard water, the fish become very active and colorful, but they seem to be extremely short-lived. The longest that one has stayed alive (on record) is less than a year; perhaps this is due to the manhandling the fish gets before it is shipped.

IGUANODECTES SPILURUS

ICTALURUS PUNCTATUS (Rafinesque)/*Channel Catfish*

R: U.S.A., Great Lakes to Florida and Texas. **H**: Small ones are excellent scavengers and peaceful. **W**: Not critical as long as the water is clean and not too warm. Temperature about 18°C. **S**: Only babies are recommended for the aquarium; reaches 90 cm in length. **F**: Tubifex worms and frozen brine shrimp are eaten with gusto by juveniles, but adults have large mouths and large appetites.

If you should ever get one of these, don't expect to raise it to full size. Literature on this species tells us that it is one of the larger catfishes, attaining a weight of 12 kg or more! Kept in an aquarium, however, small specimens take a long time to grow to a size where they must be given to a public aquarium. We kept an 8 cm specimen for several months in the TFH main office, where it was well-behaved and did its cleaning-up duties very efficiently.

HYPSELEOTRIS KLUNZINGERI

IGUANODECTES SPILURUS (Günther)/*Slender Tetra*
R: Middle and lower Amazon region and the Guianas. **H**: Peaceful and active; very likely to jump. **W**: Not critical, but best suited to soft, slightly acid water. Temperature from 24 to 28°C. **S**: To 9 cm. **F**: Live foods preferred, but others accepted.

Once in a while a few specimens of this fish find their way into "mixed" shipments; most dealers have a hard time making an identification, in case their customers should ask. Note the long, gracefully streamlined body, which proclaims the fish as an active swimmer. No long, flowing, decorative fins here! Fish like this are also capable of prodigious leaps, and their aquarium should be covered at all times. The black upper caudal lobe and colorless lower one give one the feeling that the fish has suffered an injury or that something is wrong, but this is the normal coloration.

ICTALURUS PUNCTATUS

INDOSTOMUS PARADOXUS Prashad & Mukerji/*Paradox Fish*

R: Lake Indawgyi, northern Burma. **H**: Peaceful; given to resting on the bottom for long periods or drifting through the water slowly. **W**: Soft water; pH about 6.8. Temperature 20 to 24°C. **S**: About 2.5 cm. **F**: Live baby brine shrimp preferred, but it may be trained to accept substitutes. Because of its coloration, it blends in very easily with its background and may be difficult to locate at times. Although a sedentary species, the Paradox Fish is completely capable of light-ning-like bursts of speed that may carry it completely out of the water. The aquarium should be covered. Temperatures between 20 and 21°C are tolerated, although around 24°C seems best. Spawns on substrate, depositing about 20 1 mm diameter clear greenish eggs. Eggs and fry are guarded by the males..

IODOTROPHEUS SPRENGERAE

INPAICHTHYS KERRI Géry & Junk/*Blue Emperor*

R: Upper Rio Aripuana, Mata Grosso, Brazil. **H**: Similar to the Emperor Tetra, but perhaps more timid. **W**: Water should be soft to medium hard with a pH around neutral. Temperature about 26 to 28°C. **S**: Reaches a length of at least 5cm. **F**: Will accept frozen or dried foods but prefers live foods.

The male will display vigorously in front of the female before spawning and will try and entice her into the fine-leaved plants by swimming into them and back to the female, trying to press his body against hers. When she follows him they swim through the plants, where the female will stop over a chosen spot and the male will press his body against hers again in typical tetra fashion.

INDOSTOMUS PARADOXUS

IODOTROPHEUS SPRENGERAE Oliver & Loiselle/*Rusty Cichlid*
R: Lake Malawi, Africa. **H**: Pugnacious toward its own species and territorial, but much less destructive than some of the larger mbuna. **W**: Hard, alkaline water is best; a teaspoonful of non-iodized salt added per 4 liters of aquarium water may be beneficial. **S**: About 9 cm for females; 10 cm for males. **F**: Will take all standard aquarium foods, but the basic diet should include some vegetable matter as well as meaty items like frozen brine shrimp.

The female parent incubates the eggs in her mouth for about three weeks before releasing the fry. The female should be placed in a tank by herself as soon as it is certain that spawning has been completed and no more eggs will be laid and picked up after fertilization by the male, and she should be allowed to remain with the released fry until they no longer need her — which will be evident from the fact that she no longer pays them any attention.

INPAICHTHYS KERRI

IRIATHERINA WERNERI

IRIATHERINA WERNERI Meinken/*Featherfin Rainbow*

R: Northern Austrailia and New Guinea. **H**: Peaceful and active. **W**: pH and hardness are not critical, as long as extremes are avoided. Temperature 24 to 27°C. **S**: To about 4 cm. **F**: Accepts most standard aquarium foods, but only in small sizes.

Iriatherina werneri is a non-spectacular but interesting species of rainbowfish (family Atherinidae). Although it is not highly colorful, its small size and peaceful nature, coupled with the graceful good looks of the males in their long-finned elegance, make it a desirable fish. The water in which the original specimens were collected was turgid, slow-moving, and weed-choked, but they probably exist in clearer and more swiftly flowing waters as well.

JENYNSIA LINEATA

JENYNSIA LINEATA (Jenyns)/*One-sided Livebearer*

R: Southern Brazil, Uruguay, and Argentina about the mouth of the La Plata River, between 20° and 35°S. **H:** A livebearing species that is a ftn-nipper and therefore not suited for a community tank of delicate fishes. **W:** Not critical, but does best in slightly alkaline water with perhaps a little salt added. Temperatures may vary from about 17° to 25°C. **S:** Males grow to 30-40 mm; females 90-120 mm. **F:** Will accept a wide variety of living and prepared foods.

The common name One-sided Livebearer refers to a real or imagined idiosyncrasy of this fish. It has been reported that males are either right-sided or left-sided; that is, the gonopodium will swing either to the right or to the left, while movement in the opposite direction is restricted. The females have their sex-opening partially occluded by a large scale so that it accepts only a right-sided male or a left-sided male. If you can only afford one pair, be sure that they are compatible. Fertilization is intrafollicular, and development appears to occur in the ovarian lumen. Nourishment for the embryo occurs via folds of ovarian tissue extending into the gill chamber of the embryo and occupying the mouth and pharynx. (Thus this fish is truly vivipa- rous.) Additional nourishment in the later stages may also occur by some embryos cannibaliz- ing others in the ovarian cavity. After about a six-week gestation period (at 24 °C) anywhere from 10 to 80 young may be born. More normally about a dozen or two 12-20 mm-long fry emerge from a female that doesn't look as if she were ready to burst as many other livebearer females do. The young are ready for newly hatched brine shrimp and other assorted small foods.

It takes about three to four months for the young to reach sexual maturity. In females it seems that a bright yellowish to orange spot will develop in the same place as the gravid spot of other livebearers. It has been theorized that this might be a sign of a virgin female, as after the initial contact with a male it disappears. It is not known whether it will reappear if females are isolated for a long period of time. This would take a fairly long while, since females are able to store sperm and even when isolated from contact with any males will give birth to several broods of young.

JORDANELLA FLORIDAE Goode & Bean/*American Flagfish*

R: Florida, especially in the southern portion. **H**: Males are apt to be very quarrelsome, especially at spawning time; it is best to give pairs their own aquarium. **W**: Prefers a sunny aquarium with slightly alkaline water. Temperature should be around 21°C, slightly higher for spawning. **S**: About 5 cm. **F**: Will eat dried as well as live foods, but should get a good deal of vegetable matter in its diet.

Its breeding habits are unusual for a cyprinodont. Eggs are often hung among surface plants in the usual cyprinodont manner, but sometimes we also find them near the bottom or on the bottom, guarded by the male. It is not usually necessary to remove the female as she is rarely molested. Spawning may last over a period of a week. The male takes care of the young cichlid-fashion after they hatch. Incubation lasts five to six days.

JULIDOCHROMIS MARLIERI

JULIDOCHROMIS DICKFELDI Staeck/*Dickfeldi*

R: Lake Tanganyika, Africa. **H**: Territorial in nature and aggressive toward members of its own species. **W**: Hard, alkaline water. Temperature 24 to 27°C. **S**: Reaches a length of almost 10 cm. **F**: Not critical, so can be coaxed onto most of the standard aquarium foods.

This non-mouthbrooding African cichlid is territorial and will not tolerate members of its own species being too close. If the aquarium provided is too small, the territory guarded will encompass the entire tank and any additional individuals will be forcibly ejected of killed.

The cave and the area immediately surrounding it are cleaned and cleared by the female or both partners. The female is nudged by the male in the area of the vent and displays before her until she starts laying eggs on the roof of the cave. The male follows in the same upside down position and fertilizes the eggs. Both parents tend eggs and young.

JORDANELLA FLORIDAE

JULIDOCHROMIS MARLIERI Poll/*Marlier's Julie*

R: Lake Tanganyika, Africa. **H**: Adult males are apt to become very scrappy unless given a large aquarium. **W**: Hard, alkaline water. Temperature 24 to 27°C. **S**: About 10 cm. **F**: Living foods are preferred, but will take frozen foods if they are not available.

Although this species is probably the most scrappy of the *Julidochromis* species, it is also thought by many to be the most attractive. Because it is very territorial, this fish requires a large aquarium if it is to contain more than one male cichlid. *J. marlieri* is a substrate spawner that lays its eggs in rocky caves. There will be 100-200 fry in a typical spawn, and they are fairly large when they become free-swimming. It is not necessary to separate the parents from the fry, as they get along very well.

JULIDOCHROMIS DICKFELDI

JULIDOCHROMIS ORNATUS (Boulenger)/*Julie*

R: Lake Tanganyika, Africa. **H**: Because of their special water requirements, they should be kept by themselves. If more than one male is kept, each should have his own spot. **W**: Very hard and alkaline water made by treating it with sodium bicarbonate and calcium. Temperature 24 to 27°C. **S**: About 7.5. cm. **F**: Very finicky eaters that seem to prefer tubifex worms and glassworms. **C**: Lemon-yellow with three dark brown horizontal stripes in the upper half of the body and a large dark spot at the caudal base.

This species is omnivorous, eating both algae and insects. In the aquarium, however, *J. ornatus* is a very picky eater. This species seems to prefer live foods such as tubifex worms and glassworms, althouhg some hobbyists avoid live tubifex as a matter of course.

J. ornatus is a substrate-spawner that lays many eggs in comparison to the small number of large eggs laid by many mouthbrooders in the Rift Lakes. This species is among the most commonly offered for sale of the Tanganyika cichlids.

JULIDOCHROMIS TRANSCRIPTUS

JULIDOCHROMIS REGANI Poll/*Convict Julidochromis*

R: Lake Tanganyika, Africa. **H**: Territorial, but not overly aggressive; seldom bother unrelated species that don't intrude into their territories. **W**: Hard, alkaline water preferred. Some aquarists add a quarter teaspoon of salt per liter to aquaria housing all *Julidochromis* species and all other fishes from Lake Tanganyika; although most such saline additions do the fish no harm, they are not strictly necessary. Temperature 24 to 27°C. **S**: About 10 cm. **F**: Will take all standard meaty foods; young fish do well on foods incorporating vegetable matter, especially algae.

J. regani lays its eggs in dark recesses in or around the cave-like rocky structures in which it prefers to spend most of its time. Spawns are not large, but the parents usually leave the fry alone. Since *Julidochromis* fry are fairly large when they become free-swimming, they are easy to feed on brine shrimp nauplii and suitable substitutes, and therefore are fairly easy to raise. Juveniles get along well with their parents if they are maintained in the same tank, but they often fight among themselves.

JULIDOCHROMIS ORNATUS

JULIDOCHROMIS TRANSCRIPTUS Matthes/*Masked Julidochromis*
R: Lake Tanganyika, Africa. **H**: Territorial in nature; aggressive with fishes that do not respect their territorial boundaries. **W**: Hard, alkaline water preferred. Temperature 24 to 27°C. **S**: About 10 cm in average adult size. **F**: Not finicky; will take standard aquarium fare. Foods that include a high proportion of vegetable material should occasionally be offered.

J. transcriptus is no more of a bad actor than its cousins within the genus. Like them, it is an attractive, interesting fish that feels most at home weaving and darting its way among rocky labyrinths erected in its tank to simulate the conditions of the rocky crannies in which it lives in Lake Tanganyika. Provision of rocky shelters or a close substitute is absolutely necessary to the well-being of *J. transcriptus* and the other *Julidochromis* species.

JULIDOCHROMIS REGANI

KROBIA ITANYI (Puyo)/*Dolphin Cichlid*

R: Northeastern South America, especially French Guiana. **H**: Very peaceful for a middle-sized cichlid but destructive of plants. **W**: Prefers hard and alkaline waters, but will live and spawn in softer, more acid water. Temperature 23 to 28°C. **S**: Male to 14 cm; female slightly smaller. **F**: Not fussy; accepts all live, freeze-dried and frozen foods. **C**: Body greenish brown, with black blotchy line extending from just behind the eye to just below posterior portion of dorsal fin. Black spot at upper base of tail; black line from mouth through eye.

The first specimens of *Krobia itanyi* to make an appearance on the aquarium scene were collected in the Itanyi River in French Guiana and transported to Dresden, Germany. The fish was an immediate hit with European aquarists, who appreciated it as much for its peaceful temperament toward other species as for its subdued yet attractive coloration. *K. itanyi* spawns by laying strings of slightly elliptical eggs on a flat surface, usually a smooth rock, although other surfaces have been pressed into service on occasion. Up to 500 eggs may be laid and fertilized. This species formerly was in the genus *Aequidens*.

KRYPTOPTERUS MACROCEPHALUS

KRYPTOPTERUS BICIRRHIS (Valenciennes)/*Glass Catfish*

R: Thailand to Indonesia. **H**: Peaceful; should not be kept singly, and should also not be kept with very active fishes. **W**: Water should be slightly alkaline and have a hardness that does not surpass 10 DH. Temperature about 24°C. **S**: To 10 cm. **F**: Should be given living foods such as tubifex worms, white worms, daphnia, etc.

As with most of the transparent catfishes, the body organs are enclosed in a silvery sac that shows how compressed and far in front these organs are in some fishes. As they are nocturnal in their habits, they need a darkened aquarium. They are also happier when kept in a group and should not be combined with other fishes that are highly active. Their tanks should be well planted, and they seem to enjoy getting under a broad leaf and remaining there with their fins undulating.

KROBIA ITANYI

KRYPTOPTERUS MACROCEPHALUS (Bleeker)/*Poor Man's Glass Catfish*
R: East Indies. **H**: Harmless and very peaceful; should be kept in groups. **W**: Soft, neutral to slightly alkaline water best; slightly acid water is tolerated. Temperature about 24°C **S**: To 11 cm. **F**: Prefers small living foods, but will take freeze-dried, dried, and frozen foods, provided the pieces are not large.

K. macrocephalus has been referred to as the Poor Man's Glass Catfish primarily because its chief claim to prominence, its "transparency," is less pronounced than that of its more popular look-alike, the true Glass Catfish, *K. bicirrhis*. In many cases *K. macrocephalus* is accepted only as a second choice in the absence of *K. bicirrhis*. Like its relative, it is a completely inoffensive fish, even toward those much smaller than itself.

KRYPTOPTERUS BICIRRHIS

KURTUS GULLIVERI Castelnau/Nursery *Fish*

R: Northern Australia and New Guinea. **H:** The male incubates the eggs on a hook that develops on his head. **W:** Lives equally well in fresh and brackish waters. Probably hard, alkaline water is preferred. Can survive low oxygen conditions. **S:** Attains a length of 63 cm. **F:** Requires a well balanced diet, perhaps heavy on shrimp or other meaty foods such as live fishes.

The main claim to fame of this fish is its unusual method of incubating its eggs. With maturity the male (only) develops a hook on the supraoccipital bone that points downward and forward. It forms an almost closed ring when complete, and when spawning is imminent the skin covering it thickens. Unfortunately, the actual spawning has not been observed, but the female somehow attaches her egg mass to this hook (they are held in place by a filamentous network) and the male proceeds to carry them in this manner until they hatch. Not only does this provide protection from potential predators, but by carrying the eggs the male can take them to more suitable water conditions if the area becomes polluted or oxygen deficient.

LABEO FORSKALI

LABEO CHRYSOPHEKADION (Bleeker)/*Black Shark*

R: Thailand. **H:** Peaceful toward other fishes, but likely to be scrappy among themselves. **W:** Water should be slightly alkaline, about 10 DH. Temperature 24 to 27°C. **S:** To 60 cm. **F:** Will take practically any food, but exceptionally fond of algae and other vegetable matter.

This is a fish with an excellent appetite; it spends most of its waking hours in search of food. Vegetable matter is preferred, and they can always be counted on to do an excellent job of cleaning up an algae-infested aquarium. Lacking this, a leaf of lettuce or spinach is also appreciated. Probably because ordinary-sized aquaria inhibit their growth, chances are that very few Black Sharks attain sexual maturity, and both males and females look so much alike that they would have to be dissected to distinguish them.

KURTUS GULLIVERI

LABEO FORSKALI Rüppell/*Plain Shark*
R: Northeastern Africa. **H**: Peaceful with other species; quarrelsome with members of its own species. **W**: Not critical, provided extremes are avoided. Temperature 22 to 26°C. **S**: To about 50 cm in nature; usually seen much smaller. **F**: Takes all standard aquarium foods; should have vegetable matter included in diet.

Labeo forskali has not been bred in the aquarium and little is known of sex differentiations, so it is not known whether combativeness between individual *L. forskali* is related to the sex of the fish; males are probably more aggressive than females, especially toward other males. In common with a number of other *Labeo* species, *L. forskali* also has a peculiarly shaped mouth as an adaptation for grazing algae, and it should be provided with suitable vegetative fare. It is not, however, an active eater of plants.

LABEO CHRYSOPHEKADION

LABEO VARIEGATUS Pellegrin/*Harlequin Shark*

R: Upper Zaire River. **H**: Aggressive; should not be kept with fishes that cannot take care of themselves. **W**: Water quality is not critical, but avoid extremes. Temperature may vary from 21 to 27°C. **S**: To over 30 cm in nature; much smaller in the aquarium. **F**: Will take almost any live, frozen, or dried food used for aquarium fishes; a heavy eater.

For those aquarists who want a variety of "sharks" and want to get away from the usual blacks and red fins, *Labeo variegatus* is the answer. It is a hardy, quite attractive fish that will be around for a long time. The juveniles are yellowish, mottled with various shades of black and brown, with perhaps some red thrown in for good measure.

Caring for the Harlequin Shark is easy. All it needs is a large, well-planted aquarium with plenty of aeration.

LABEOTROPHEUS TREWAVASAE

LABEOTROPHEUS FUELLEBORNI Ahl/*Fuelleborn's Cichlid*

R: Lake Malawi, Africa. **H**: One of the most peaceful of the Malawi cichlids, but should be kept with large fishes. **W**: Should be fairly hard and alkaline. Temperature 24 to 27°C. **S**: Over 12 cm. **F**: Largely vegetarian, but animal foods are taken; will accept large dried foods with gusto. **C**: Very similar to *Pseudotropheus zebra*, with dark bars on a blue background and the posterior portions of anal and dorsal with large orange spots — many other color varieties.

Labeotropheus fuelleborni is a maternal mouthbrooder with an incubation period of three to four weeks. Broods range in size from 25 to 75 offspring, and the fry are fairly large upon release. Adults grow to over 13 cm, with the male being slightly larger and more colorful than the females.

LABEO VARIEGATUS

LABEOTROPHEUS TREWAVASAE Fryer/*Red-Top Trewavasae*
R: Lake Malawi, Africa. **H**: Should be kept in large aquaria with ample hiding places to prevent bullying. **W**: Should be fairly hard and alkaline. Temperature 24 to 27°C. **S**: About 10 cm. **F**: Largely vegetarian, but will accept animal foods. **C**: Males blue with about 12 darker bars, dorsal red; females gray or tan, mottled black and orange — many other color varieties.
The female is uniformly mottled black, yellow, and sometimes blue. There are, however, many different color forms. The species is a mouthbrooder. The female broods the offspring, and when they are molested they may return to the protection of her mouth. This may occur as late as three or four weeks after hatching. The young are all colored like their mother.

LABEOTROPHEUS FUELLEBORNI

LABIDOCHROMIS CAERULEUS Fryer/*Sky-Blue Labido*

R: Endemic to Lake Malawi. **H:** Well-mannered for a Lake Malawi cichlid, it does not seem to bother other fishes and is usually not bothered itself. **W:** Hard, alkaline water is necessary, with temperatures of about 23 to 26°C. **S:** Relatively small, attaining a maximum size of about 9 cm. **F:** Will readily accept most aquarium foods, including a good quality flake food. Brine shrimp and bloodworms are especially liked.

Spawning is accomplished very much as in the other mbunas, but with certain variations. Since the head of the brooding female is so narrow, fewer of the relatively large eggs will actually fit into the space available, so fewer offspring are produced at one spawning. If you obtain a dozen or more young you should consider yourself lucky. Occasionally more eggs are laid than the female can handle. In such cases the male *may* take them up himself. Whether he eats them or incubates them seems, however, to depend upon the individual. *Labidochromis caeruleus* does not normally bother the young, but for more safety the brooding female should be isolated in an incubation tank and the fry separated as soon after their release as convenient. The female should be given a short rest before being readmitted to the community tank.

LABIOBARBUS BURMANICUS

LABIDOCHROMIS VELLICANS Trewavas/*Vellicans*

R: Lake Malawi, Africa. **H:** Aggressive, but usually smaller than most other mbuna and less apt to do damage to tankmates. **W:** Hard and alkaline; the addition of some sea salt might prove beneficial. Temperature between 23 to 28°C. **S:** Usually does not exceed 10 cm. **F:** Not critical; will eat a variety of aquarium foods — in nature picks insects and small invertebrates.

Both sexes bear "egg spots" on their anal fins. Spawning takes place with the female picking up the eggs and brooding them. She can be removed and placed in a tank of her own where she will incubate the eggs and fry for about three weeks before releasing them. Typical of this narrow-jawed genus, the eggs are usually few in number, 10 to 15 being relatively good for a single spawning. The fry can be fed newly hatched brine shrimp along with a good flake food.

LABIDOCHROMIS CAERULEUS

LABIOBARBUS BURMANICUS (Day)/*Long-Finned Shark*
R: Southeast Asia. **H**: Usually peaceful, even tending to be shy; large specimens will be more aggressive. **W**: Slightly alkaline water of about 10° DH. Temperature 24 to 26°C. **S**: To 28 cm. **F**: All kinds of live foods are preferred but some vegetable matter, like lettuce or spinach leaves, should be added.
Although generally peaceful, this fish can turn nasty when fully grown. Large specimens, however, are not common, and this fish is not widely seen in the hobby.

LABIDOCHROMIS VELLICANS

LABIOBARBUS FESTIVUS

LABIOBARBUS FESTIVUS (Heckel)/*Signal Barb*

R: Probably restricted to the island of Borneo. **H:** Generally shy but active. Does best if more than one is kept to a tank. **W:** Not critical within normal limits. A temperature range of about 23-28°C is recommended. **S:** Attains a length of about 20 cm. **F:** Eats a variety of plant and animal foods. Small sized live foods are preferred.

This is a very attractive barb with its black and red dorsal and caudal fin markings contrasting with the silver and black body pattern. It is also a shy species, at least at first, and the tank should be set up with sufficient hiding places created from things like driftwood and rockwork. Heavy planting is also recommended. The lighting should be moderate.

Because of its eventual size (about 20 cm) and being an active species large tanks are needed. The water conditions are not critical as long as extremes are avoided. A temperature range of 23° to 28°C is sufficient. Clean water should be provided by means of adequate filtration and regular water changes.

The Signal Barb does best on live foods, including such items as bloodworms (chironomid larvae) and other aquatic insects, tubificid worms, and *Daphnia*. If they get very hungry they will also accept frozen and freeze-dried foods, as well as flake food, but may also be tempted to nibble at some of the more tender plants.

Spawning has not been recorded. It has been noted that the males are more slender and more colorful than the females, a common trait among the barbs.

LADIGESIA ROLOFFI

LADIGESIA ROLOFFI Géry/*Jelly Bean Tetra*

R: Sierra Leone, West Africa. **H**: Initially very shy; it will attempt to jump out of its tank, so a covered tank is a definite necessity; reasonably hardy and peaceful. **W**: Temperature should be from 24 to 26°C, and the pH should be on the acid side, 6.7. **S**: To 4 cm. **F**: Will accept dry foods after a certain amount of training; freeze-dried foods are accepted willingly and live foods are never refused.

The sexes in this fish follow a familiar pattern in aquarium fishes whereby the male is much more colorful and larger in size. Spawning, if attempted by the aquarist, should be patterned after the naturally existing conditions of the Jelly Bean Tetra's home in Africa: slowly running forest brook water, temperature 26°C, hardness 5.1 (German scale) and no aquatic plants except for ferns growing on protruding rocks.

399

LAETACARA CURVICEPS (Ahl) (incorrectly *Acara thayeri*) *Flag Cichlid, Thayer's Cichlid*
R: Amazon River and its tributaries. **H**: Peaceful except when spawning; does not dig and uproot plants as much as most cichlids. Can be safely kept in community aquaria. **W**: Water should be soft and about neutral to slightly acid. Temperature about 24°C; for breeding, 28°C. **S**: 7.5 cm; breeds at 6.5 cm. **F**: Live foods such as tubifex worms, enchytrae, daphnia, mosquito larvae, etc. If earthworms are fed, they should be chopped. **C**: Back brownish green, sides silvery gray shading to blue posteriorly. Anal and caudal fins have bright blue spots.
Because of their comparatively small size, they can be bred in aquaria as small as 40 liters, but of course a larger aquarium gives the fry a better start. The male, easily distinguished by his longer, more pointed dorsal and anal fins, will signify his intentions to spawn by taking possession of a particular spot and cleaning off a rock or section of the glass. He then half drives, half coaxes a female to the spot. Finally, after a few false starts she pastes row after row of eggs on the surface that was prepared, closely followed by the male who fertilizes them. They then guard the eggs and fan them with their tails.

LAMPRICHTHYS TANGANICANUS

LAETACARA DORSIGERA (Heckel)/*Red-Breasted Cichlid*
R: Paraguay and Amazon basins. **H**: Very peaceful and an ideal community tank species. **W**: Not critical. It has spawned in tap water of 7 DH and pH 7.0, but does as well in slightly acid, softer water. Temperature 23 to 27°C. **S**: Attains a length of about 8 cm. **F**: Not a fussy eater; will accept a variety of aquarium foods including flake foods.
Color changes with the approach of spawning include a darkening of the ventral area of the female and a reddening of the abdominal and pectoral areas of the male (hence the common name). The male in his finery displays before the female and even nudges her in the abdominal region if she is receptive. The ovipositor appears and the colors of both sexes intensify. The female cleans a flat area and swims over it in a few dry runs as the male patrols the tank. Eventually some eggs are laid and they are fertilized by the male. After about an hour, up to 1,000 small, clear eggs have been deposited on the stone. Hatching occurs between 40 and 48 hours later (depending upon temperature), and the fry may quickly be transferred to a pre-prepared pit in the sand. The red of the male intensifies even more at this time. The female devotes much of her time to caring for the brood, while the male is more concerned with protection of the nest area. In another four days the fry are free-swimming. They can be fed newly hatched brine shrimp or other similar sized food. Frequent water changes in the tank with the fry are highly desirable.

LAETACARA CURVICEPS

LAMPRICHTHYS TANGANICANUS (Boulenger)/*Tanganyika Pearl Killie*
R: Lake Tanganyika, Africa. **H**: Peaceful and quite shy; should be kept in a well-planted, covered tank. **W**: Slightly alkaline. Temperature about 24°C. **S**: Males about 15 cm; females slightly smaller. **F**: Living foods such as daphnia, tubifex worms, and adult brine shrimp.
Seeing a pair swimming around with the sun shining on them is a sight guaranteed to make any aquarist gasp. The rows of tiny dots gleam brightly with an incandescent blue. The fish must be seen in the proper light to be appreciated. They are peaceful, even timid. Other fishes kept with them, which are large enough not to be swallowed, are left alone. Being an active fish, a large tank is preferable and should be covered to prevent their loss by jumping.

LAETACARA DORSIGERA

LAMPROLOGUS BREVIS Boulenger/*Dwarf Shell-Dweller*

R: Endemic to Lake Tanganyika, Africa. **H:** Tends to be territorial, protecting a particular shell and a small region around it. **W:** Needs hard, alkaline water. The temperature should be in the range of 22 ° to 28°C. **S:** Reaches a length of usually no more than 5 cm. **F:** Will accept most aquarium foods, but especially likes live foods such as brine shrimp, *Daphnia*, and mosquito larvae.

As a shell-dweller, *L. brevis* spends most of its time in or around an empty shell, usually a species of the genus *Neothauma*. It is best to supply them with several shells, as these little cichlids will change residences as they grow or locate a shell more "desirable" than the one they currently occupy. If that shell is already occupied they may even try to evict the present owner. With a selection of shells to choose from and uncrowded conditions, serious arguments will not develop. Spawning takes place in the shell as well, with both potential spawners cleaning out any sand that may be inside. The female deposits up to about 40 eggs per spawning, although the average spawn consists of approximately 25 eggs. Yet even with these low numbers the tank can quickly become so overpopulated that the adults stop spawning. The female remains in the shell with the eggs while the male stands guard outside. In about a week or so the eggs hatch. The fry are easy to raise on an initial supply of newly hatched brine shrimp followed by a more varied diet of normal fish foods.

LAMPROLOGUS BUESCHERI

LAMPROLOGUS (NEOLAMPROLOGUS) BRICHARDI Poll/*Lyretail Lamprologus*

R: Lake Tanganyika, Africa. **H:** Scrappy among themselves, but usually not pugnacious toward other species. **W:** Hard, alkaline water preferred. Temperature 24 to 27°C. **S:** Up to about 9 cm. **F:** Live foods, especially live brine shrimp, are best, but frozen and flake foods are accepted; sometimes refuses to eat granulated dry foods. Diet should include vegetable substances.

When *Lamprologus brichardi* spawns it becomes a recluse; the eggs are deposited within the caves and crannies formed by the rock piles in the tank, and in most cases their owner doesn't even know the fish has spawned until he sees baby *Lamprologus*.

LAMPROLOGUS BREVIS

LAMPROLOGUS BUESCHERI Staeck/*Buescher's Lamprologus*

R: Lake Tanganyika. **H:** Generally shy and secretive. Should have subdued lighting and sufficient hiding places. **W:** Typical for Lake Tanganyika cichlids. The water should be hard and alkaline with a temperature between 22°C and 27°C. **S:** Attains a length of about 6-7 cm. **F:** Will eat a variety of foods but does better with a high-protein diet.

As it is rather light-shy, *Lamprologus buescheri* should be given subdued lighting along with the secluded shelters.

Spawning has been accomplished although the few reports are not sufficient to establish hard and fast rules yet. The egg production is said to be low, up to about 50 or so, but this might be due to many factors, including young, inexperienced fish. It is therefore still expensive and will probably remain that way for a while yet.

LAMPROLOGUS (NEOLAMPROLOGUS) BRICHARDI

LAMPROLOGUS CALLIURUS/*Shell-dweller*

R: From deep water off the northeastern coast of Burundi, near Magara, Lake Tanganyika. **H:** Shy and retiring; peaceful. One of the *Lamprologus* species that prefers shells for living and breeding. **W:** Hard and alkaline, typical of Lake Tanganyika tanks. **S:** Males about 6 cm or more; females somewhat smaller. **F:** Will accept any of the usual aquarium foods.

In Lake Tanganyika snail shells tend to collect in troughs or trenches and the shell-dwellers, lacking other shelter in open sandy areas, have adopted these shells as their homes and breeding sites.

Spawning apparently is relatively easy in this hardy fish. Unfortunately not much is seen as the female will disappear into the shell and the male will follow for a short period. The male then remains outside the shell and the female remains hidden inside it, coming out only to eat. Eventually the female will reappear with her progeny. The eggs and fry are large, the latter able to tackle baby brine shrimp immediately, although a more varied diet including worms, *Daphnia*, and crushed flake food is highly recommended. The young fish can be seen hopping about the bottom like little gobies chasing the shrimp. Hatching time is about a week to ten days.

LAMPROLOGUS (LEPIDIOLAMPROLOGUS) ELONGATUS

LAMPROLOGUS (ALTOLAMPROLOGUS) COMPRESSICEPS Boulenger/*Compressiceps*

R: Lake Tanganyika, Africa. **H:** Peaceful toward other fishes, but cannot be trusted with those it can swallow. **W:** Alkaline water, about pH 8.0. Temperature 24 to 27°C. **S:** 10 to 11 cm. **F:** Medium-sized living foods, such as adult brine shrimp, small fishes, or cut-up earthworms.

It does best on living foods such as tubifex worms, large adult brine shrimp, and small fishes. In the lake it feeds on small fishes and copepods.

This is a hidden substrate spawner that spawns among the rocks in the littoral region of the lake. It prefers privacy; mating takes place in narrow and enclosed caves. It is extremely difficult to spawn in the aquarium unless the conditions are ideal.

LAMPROLOGUS CALLIURUS

LAMPROLOGUS (LEPIDIOLAMPROLOGUS) ELONGATUS Boulenger/*Elongatus*
R: Lake Tanganyika, Africa. **H**: Decidedly predatory; not to be kept with any other fishes that it can swallow. **W**: Hard, alkaline water preferred. Temperature 24 to 27°C. **S**: Up to about 15 cm under aquarium conditions. **F**: Favorite food is smaller live fishes swallowed whole. It will also accept prepared meaty foods and is partial to frozen bloodworms.
This is not a mouthbrooding species; it lays its eggs in caves and is very variable in its choice of which part of the cave will be the site of attachment for the eggs. Sometimes it's the bottom of the cave. Very many small eggs are laid, and the parents guard them jealously. They are very brave in defending their young and will successfully chase away — kill, if they have to — fishes much larger than themselves.

LAMPROLOGUS (ALTOLAMPROLOGUS) COMPRESSICEPS

LAMPROLOGUS (NEOLAMPROLOGUS) FURCIFER Boulenger/*Sail-Fin Cichlid*

R: Lake Tanganyika, Africa. **H**: Aggressive; will not tolerate any other tankmates. **W**: Requires hard and alkaline water. Temperature not critical, but should be within the normal range for tropical fishes, 24 to 27°C. **S**: Normally about 15 cm. **F**: Live food preferred, but will readily take most aquarium foods.

After some pre-spawning displays by the male, the female *L. furcifer* deposits a number of eggs on one of the flat surfaces in a flowerpot or on the roof of a cave. The male follows behind fertilizing them. This continues until all the eggs are laid (reports of up 25 have been published), at which time the male is barred from the vicinity.

LAMPROLOGUS (NEOLAMPROLOGUS) LELEUPI

LAMPROLOGUS (LEPIDIOLAMPROLOGUS) KENDALLI/ (Poll & Stewart)/*Nkambae*

R: Nkambe Bay, Lake Tanganyika. **H**: A quarrelsome species, even when quite small. **W**: Coming from Lake Tanganyika this species requires hard, alkaline water. Normal aquarium temperatures are sufficient. **S**: Attains a length of at least 14 cm, possibly up to 20 cm. **F**: Accepts a variey of foods including small feeder fishes (guppies).

Nkambae is one of the more aggressive cichlids, at least toward members of its own kind. This antipathy seems to hold even to the smaller specimens of about 30 mm length, with actual losses being suffered. Considering the cost of some of these fish it may be best to give them plenty of room and numerous hiding places. For adults, suggestions of tanks of 55-gallon to 125-gallon capacity have been recommended. The water should be set up as for any Rift Lake cichlid tank—hard and alkaline. This fish is said to be much more sensitive to chemical buildup or variations in water quality than most other *Lamprologus* species. The temperature can be within the normal range for most tropical fishes. Feeding is easy as most food items are acceptable. Live foods in the form of feeder fishes, etc. should be given. Nkambae hunts small live fishes by slowly approaching the prey, then grabbing it with a lightning-like dash.

LAMPROLOGUS (NEOLAMPROLOGUS) FURCIFER

LAMPROLOGUS (NEOLAMPROLOGUS) LELEUPI Poll/*Lemon Cichlid*
R: Lake Tanganyika, Africa. **H**: Inoffensive; can be kept with other fishes that can tolerate their water conditions. **W**: Alkaline water, about pH 8.0. The tank should be well planted and other hiding places provided as well. Temperature 24 to 27° **S**: To 10 cm. **F**: Prefers living foods on the small side, such as daphnia.

The males are distinguished by a larger head and more robust body. Pairs should be slected and given tanks of their own, which besides plants contain flowerpots from which the bottoms were knocked out. The pair will spawn cichlid-fashion in the flowerpots, and the eggs will hatch in three days. The parents should then be left with the eggs, and the female will assume all of the parental responsibility. Of the approximately 150 eggs that each pair lay, most hatch. The fry are raised without difficulty.

LAMPROLOGUS (LEPIDIOLAMPROLOGUS) KENDALLI

LAMPROLOGUS MEELI Poll/*Meeli*

R: Endemic to Lake Tanganyika. **H:** A relatively aggressive but small fish that will use a shell as a home and a spawning place. **W:** Needs hard, alkaline water (pH 8-9). **S:** Attains a length of about 7 cm. **F:** Eats most types of aquarium foods. Beef heart is said to be a good conditioning food.

For spawning, a pair in a 40-liter tank or a male with three or four females in a larger tank (80 liters or more) is sufficient. After some courtship the pair will select a particular shell and spawn in it. Sometimes the eggs are hidden well back in the shell and the only indication of a spawning is the guarding parents, but other times eggs can be seen in the entrance of the shell. The creamy white eggs hatch in about four days, and in another three or four days the fry are moving about. The female guards the eggs and fry, herding the fry into the shell when danger threatens. The male usually guards the larger territory (the first line of defense). After about a week the female takes less care with the brood, allowing them in the shell but not herding them as before. The fry are fed newly hatched brine shrimp immediately along with other suitable foods. Some 20% to 30% of the water can be changed weekly in the fry tank.

LAMPROLOGUS MUSTAX

LAMPROLOGUS MOORII Boulenger/*Moore's Lamprologus*

R: Endemic to Lake Tanganyika. **H:** Not as aggressive as most other Rift Lake cichlids; it will fit into a community tank of suitable fishes. **W:** Needs hard, alkaline water. A temperature range of 21 to 26°C is adequate. **S:** Grows to a length of about 10-12.5 cm. **F:** Will accept a wide variety of aquarium foods. Some vegetable matter should be included in its diet.

Spawning occurs in one of the caves in a territory in the manner of typical substrate-spawners. At least one of the parents guards the eggs and fry. In about a week the guarding parent will probably be seen herding a school of the fry in the vicinity of the cave. Newly hatched brine shrimp will be taken by the fry along with a variety of other similar sized foods. Like other *Lamprologus* species, the fry grow rather slowly.

408

LAMPROLOGUS MEELI

LAMPROLOGUS MUSTAX Poll/*White-cheeked Lamprologus*

R: Southern shores of Lake Tanganyika. **H:** Substrate-spawning Rift Lake cichlid in which the conspecific aggression is relatively high. Tends to be territorial. **W:** Typical of Lake Tanganyika cichlids. Hard, alkaline water with a temperature kept in narrow limits, usually between 26 and 27°C. **S:** Attains a length of about 10 cm; breeds at about 6 or 7 cm. **F:** Will accept a variety of aquarium foods.

As the young fish grow they should start to "color up" at about 2.5 cm. At 5 cm they should be fully colored and will start squabbling among themselves. Breeding might be possible when they reach 6 or 7 cm in length. Sexual differences include a larger size for the male and the usual plumpness of the female as she fills with eggs. The male's colors also intensify. For more sure-fired sexing the genital openings can be examined. That of the female is round and flat and considerably larger than that of the male. In nature *L. mustax* spawns among the rubble, but in aquaria they will use whatever is available. The flowerpot is usually the choice. With the group of six, one or more pairs will usually take charge of the tank and keep the other fish at bay. It would be best to remove these other fish. The spawning pair will usually spend a lot of time in the flowerpot, and the actual time of spawning may be quite difficult to determine. At least at first it might be best to let them raise their young, which will eventually be seen outside the flowerpot. The initial spawns are low in number but should build up to 60 or more as the fish mature fully (the first spawn may occur when they are a year old). The fry can be left with their parents until they reach a size of about 2.5 cm, even though they decide to spawn again.

LAMPROLOGUS MOORII

LAMPROLOGUS OCELLATUS (Steindachner)/*Ocellated Shell-Dweller*

R: Endemic to Lake Tanganyika, Africa. **H:** The most aggressive of the shell-dwellers that have come to light so far. Does well as a single species in a moderately small tank. **W:** Prefers hard, alkaline water. A temperature in the range of 22 ° to 28 °C is recommended. **S:** Attains a length of about 6.5 cm. **F:** Will accept a wide variety of aquarium foods. A varied diet with some live foods is best.

L. ocellatus is reputed to be the most aggressive of the shell-dwellers being imported at the present time. If the intruder is large and potentially dangerous, the little *Lamprologus* will disappear into its shell for protection, leaving at most a little bit of its tail sticking out. The shell is also used as a spawning site. After some preliminary courtship the female is allowed into the male's territory and they take turns excavating any sand or debris from the shell they have selected. For the actual spawning, both male and female will disappear into the shell for a time. The male comes out and defends the territory as the female remains within, completely hidden from prying eyes. Approximately 40 eggs are laid that hatch in about a week to ten days.

LAMPROLOGUS TETRACANTHUS

LAMPROLOGUS PLEUROMACULATUS Trewavas & Poll/*Pleuromaculatus*

R: Endemic to Lake Tanganyika. **H:** Apparently not as aggressive or territorial as other sand dwellers (except when spawning) and can be kept with fishes its own size. **W:** Like other Rift Lake cichlids needs hard, alkaline water. A temperature range of 21° to 27°C is adequate. **S:** Grows to a length of 10-12 cm. **F:** Accepts a variety of foods both live and prepared.

Spawning *Lamprologus pleuromaculatus* is not difficult. Although some squabbling between the potential spawners occurs there are usually no fights that result in any great amount of damage. The flower pot or a smooth rock surface may be cleaned as well as several pits dug in the sand in preparation for spawning. Mutual side by side displays and some rotations about one another with fins spread may occur previous to the serious business of egg-laying. The "T" position is assumed as in many other similar cichlids. During these events the female turns a deep brown. Up to 100 snow-white eggs are deposited on one of the cleaned surfaces and are guarded vigorously by the female—even from the male. The observations noted that the female mouthed the eggs and guarded them but apparently did not fan them. Perhaps additional reports will indicate a fanning action. The eggs hatch in about three days at about 26°C. The female then takes the fry and moves them to one of the previously prepared pits. There they are guarded until they are free-swimming, about seven days hence.

LAMPROLOGUS OCELLATUS

LAMPROLOGUS TETRACANTHUS Boulenger/*Tetracanthus*

R: Known only from Lake Tanganyika. **H:** A generally aggressive and predatory cichlid that should not be kept with smaller fishes. **W:** Hard and alkaline as with most African Lake Cichlids. Temperature 23° to 28°C. **S:** Attains a length of about 8 inches. **F:** Not particular about type of food, will eat any good aquarium food including small live fishes.

Spawning is typical of a substrate spawner, the eggs being deposited on the rocks or flower pots. During the pre-spawning period (and sometimes when they are not even spawning) gravel may be shifted around their tank to suit their fancy, but usually blocking your view of the spawning site. A male may spawn with more than one female, with clutches of eggs in more than one location in the tank. The eggs are whitish, about 1/16th of an inch in diameter, and up to 500 or more in number. They hatch in about three days, and the fry are free-swimming in about seven days. The fry will accept newly hatched brine shrimp and crushed flake food at first, but their diet should be expanded as they grow. The parents protect the eggs and fry—at least until they start getting the spawning urge again. The fry should then be removed as they may be eaten by the parents as they "clean up" the tank for the new spawning.

LAMPROLOGUS PLEUROMACULATUS

411

LAMPROLOGUS (NEOLAMPROLOGUS) TRETOCEPHALUS Boulenger/*Five-Bar Cichlid*
R: Lake Tanganyika, Africa. **H**: Territorial; provide plenty of caves and hiding places, as each individual male will set up a territory and defend it. **W**: Moderately hard water with a pH of around 7.6-8.0. Temperature in the middle 20's (°C). **S**: To about 14 cm. **F**: Not critical; will eat most live and prepared aquarium foods.

Breeding tubes are evident at the approach of egg-laying, and a flat rock, slate, or flowerpot is cleaned for that purpose. The eggs are laid and fertilized and the female then takes up the chore of fanning them while the male returns to his territory and does not take part. The eggs are small, about 1.5 mm long, and white. Hatching takes some three to four days, whereupon the female moves them to the "security" of one of the pits she has prepared. In about another four days the fry have become free-swimming.

LEIARIUS MARMORATUS

LATES CALCARIFER (Bloch)/*Silver Barramundi; Giant Perch*
R: Semi-tropical and tropical regions of the Indo-West Pacific from southern China to Australia and west to the Persian Gulf. Inhabits pure fresh water as well as estuaries and near-shore waters. **H**: Predatory and should not be trusted with fishes much smaller than themselves. **W**: Very tolerant of different conditions, as would be expected. It's probably best to add a small amount of sea salt to the water. Temperatures in the normal range are sufficient. **S**: With good care it will normally outgrow most hobbyists' tanks. Attains a length of over 1 1/2 meters and up to 54 kilos (but most are much smaller). **F**: Will accept a wide variety of aquarium foods. Meaty foods are best, and small live fishes are avidly hunted down.

The Silver Barramundi spawns from the Australian spring to late summer. Large numbers of small (about 0.87 mm) eggs are released and in the salinity of 2-3% they float. At a temperature of 27° to 28 °C they hatch quickly. The larvae are about 1.5 mm long and still have a yolk sac that is absorbed by the fifth day. This fast-growing fish attains a length of approximately 45 cm at the end of the first year (already much too large for any but the largest tanks), 73 cm by the end of the second year, and 87 cm by the end of the third year.

LAMPROLOGUS (NEOLAMPROLOGUS) TRETOCEPHALUS

LEIARIUS MARMORATUS (Gill)/*Marbled Catfish*

R: Marañón River (Amazon system), Peru. **H**: Somewhat light-shy and retiring, so rock caves and other shelters should be available; peaceful with fishes that it cannot swallow. **W**: Not critical; adapts easily to most water conditions as long as extremes of pH and hardness are avoided. Temperature 21 to 27°C. **S**: Attains a length of 60 cm or more in aquaria; reaches a larger size in nature. **F**: Does best on live foods of suitable size and beef heart and other animal-based foods; freeze-dried, frozen, and pellet foods are readily taken by young fish; learns to accept oatmeal.

The young and adult Marbled Catfish are so different in color and pattern that one would hardly suspect them of being the same fish. As the fish grows older it darkens; the dark spots give way to a beautiful wavy marbled pattern. The caudal fin lobes, which are rounded in the young, become much prolonged and pointed (especially the upper lobe) in the adult.

LATES CALCARIFER

LEIARIUS PICTUS (Müller & Troschel) / *Painted Catfish*

R: Amazon basin. **H**: Retiring and peaceful for its size but should not be kept with fishes it can swallow; caves, driftwood, and other types of shelter should be provided. **W**: Not critical, although extremes of pH and hardness should be avoided. **S**: Reaches a length of 60 cm or more. **F**: Takes a wide variety of live, freeze-dried, or frozen foods; learns to accept cooked oatmeal.

The handsome catfish is one of the most attractive members of the family Pimelodidae and immediately attracts the attention of hobbyists. Even the long, graceful barbels are alternately ringed with black and white. In younger individuals these barbels reach backward beyond the caudal fin; in mature fish they are relatively shorter but still extend beyond the dorsal fin. *Leiarius pictus* is typical of the pimelodid catfishes in that it is naked; that is, it has no scales or other bony armor covering its skin.

LEIOPOTHERAPON UNICOLOR

LEIOCASSIS SIAMENSIS Regan/*Barred Siamese Catfish*

R: Thailand. **H**: Peaceful toward fishes it cannot swallow; mostly nocturnal in its habits. **W**: Soft, slightly acid water that has been aged for at least a week. Temperature 22 to 25°C. **S**: To 16 cm. **F**: All sorts of live or frozen foods.

There are no visible sex differences, and thus far there have been no accounts of their reproductive habits. A characteristic of this group is the large adipose fin, which is also seen in the *Synodontis* species from Africa. The large mouth indicates that it could swallow smaller fish in the same aquarium, so do not keep your fancy Guppies or Neon Tetras in its company or they might disappear.

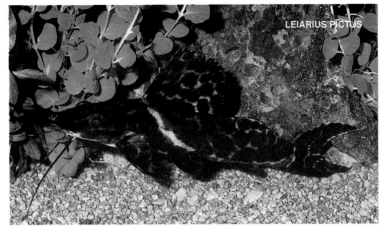

LEIOPOTHERAPON UNICOLOR (Guenther)/*Spangled Grunter*

R: Widely distributed in Australian river systems. **H:** Active and easy to maintain but is an aggressive species not only toward other fishes but to members of its own species. **W:** Tolerates a wide variety of conditions even to full seawater. pH and temperature ranges quite wide. **S:** Attains a length of 25cm but averages around l5cm. **F:** Omnivorous, feeding on aquatic insects, crustaceans, mollusks, and plant material.

Maturity is reached in males at about 5.8cm and in females at about 7.8cm. Sexes usually cannot be differentiated until near spawning time when the genital papillae are visible (in females it is thicker and heavier). The fish move upstream in flowing water or to shallow water of ponds to spawn. This occurs at night at a tmeperature of 20°-26°C. The bottom is soft. More than 20,000 eggs are scattered over the bottom (up to 100,000 or more in large, older females). These are demersal (sinking), non-adhesive, and less than one millimeter in diameter. They hatch in about 50 hours and become free-swimming after 93 hours. At this time the fry search for food. The young fish school as do some adults, but the tendency is greater in the juveniles.

LEPIDARCHUS ADONIS Roberts/*Adonis*

R: Restricted range in southern Ghana. **H**: Peaceful; prefers subdued light. **W**: Soft, clean, acid water is best for this species but not critical. Temperature 24 to 26°C. **S**: 4 cm for both males and females. **F**: Small live foods preferred, aquatic crustaceans being the preferred first foods; also accepts finely granulated or shredded dry foods.

Some pairs maintained by E. Roloff of Karlsruhe, Germany, spawned readily enough in small aquaria containing water at a pH of 6.0 and a hardness of about 2 DH. The temperature of the water in the spawning tanks was 25°C.

The eggs, which had been deposited in spawning mops, hatched in about 36 hours when maintained at the spawning temperature, but the fry didn't become free-swimming until a week passes. They are large enough to take brine shrimp nauplii immediately upon becoming free-swimming, and they grow quickly. One big drawback in the production of this species by commercial breeders is the small number of eggs produced at each spawning. An average of only 25 eggs or so per spawning does not make for wholesale production, but it is hoped that individuals that become adapted to aquarium life will be more prolific. This almost scaleless species prefers to keep out of bright light, so their aquarium should provide shady areas.

LEPIDOGALAXIAS SALAMANDROIDES

LEPIDOCEPHALUS THERMALIS (Valenciennes)/*Lesser Loach*

R: Sri Lanka and southern India. **H:** Generally peaceful, it prefers to stay partially buried in the bottom substrate with only the anterior third of the body exposed. **W:** Very tolerant of most water conditions. A pH of about 7.0 and a temperature between 25° and 28°C are adequate. **S:** Attains a length of about 5 to 7.5 cm. **F:** Mostly live foods are preferred, but it can be coaxed onto frozen foods if small particles are fed.

Spawning has not been recorded, but educated guesses have it spawning like its cousin the Coolie Loach. It is reported that it has blue-green eggs.

When handling this species, remember that it possesses an erectile suborbital spine that could become entangled in a net when moving it from one tank to another. If it does become entangled in a net, try to just let it free itself by inverting the net in water and letting it swim free.

LEPIDARCHUS ADONIS

LEPIDOGALAXIAS SALAMANDROIDES Mees/*Salamander Mud Minnow; Shannon Mud Minnow*

R: Endemic to the extreme southwestern corner of Australia. **H:** Generally peaceful; should not be housed with larger, more aggressive ftshes. Said to estivate when water dries up. **W:** Acid water (pH below 6) with a rather cool temperature range (preferably 12-15°C) necessary. **S:** Females generally grow to 4.5 cm, males to 3.54 cm; maximum length for the species 6.7 cm. **F:** Will only eat live foods, preferably small crustaceans (brine shrimp) and insect larvae (mosquito larvae, bloodworms, etc.).

The females are generally larger than the males. Males have a dark band extending from the tip of the snout to the tail base, as well as a modified anal fin. This appears when the male attains a length of about 2.5 cm (females become sexually mature at about 3.5 cm). Mating follows a brief courtship (which may be absent) and involves copulation and internal fertilization. The males pursue the females from behind, rolling them over slightly and then clasping the ventral keel. About a week after mating the ovipositor appears and about 100 to 140 small eggs are laid. These hatch quickly, and small juveniles can be found by the early spring. During the summer the young reach 2.5 cm. Larger individuals are scarce, for it is said that the parents die shortly after spawning, making them annual fishes like some of the killifishes.

LEPIDOCEPHALUS THERMALIS

LEPISOSTEUS OSSEUS

LEPISOSTEUS OSSEUS (Linnaeus)/*Longnose Gar*
R: North America: Gulf states, Mississippi Basin northward to Great Lakes, eastern seaboard.
H: Highly predatory and not to be trusted with fishes small enough to swallow; rather slow-moving most times, but capable of great burst of speed. **W**: Not at all critical; often found surviving where other fishes have succumbed. Tolerates a wide temperature range, so suitable for the coldwater or tropical aquarium. **S**: To 2 meters in nature, much less in aquaria; size can be reasonably controlled, although very large aquaria are eventually required. **F**: Live fishes preferred; acclimated fish can often be coaxed to accept strips of beef heart or other substitutes.

The gars of the family Lepisosteidae, of which the Longnose Gar is the most widespread and common, once flourished in Europe but are now extinct there although they are still represented in North America. Here they have prospered since the Eocene, still retaining certain features long since abandoned by the other modern fishes. One such feature is the hard, bony, diamond-shaped scales they possess. Locked each to the other by a peg-and-socket arrangement, they form excellent armor. Gars are capable of breathing air. The air is "swallowed" at the surface into the gas bladder, which serves as a respiratory organ.

This oddity and its close relatives are more popular as aquarium fishes outside the United States than their home country; Japanese aquarists are especially fond of them. *Lepisosteus osseus* is a tough fish in the sense that it is able to withstand poor living conditions, but it is not an especially vicious species. In fact, it is often picked on by fishes its own size. The long, pointy, tooth-studded snout is used adeptly to snatch living prey, and it is interesting to watch a Longnose Gar maneuver its victims down its throat headfirst after having captured them broadside. Small fishes must of necessity be the main food for small Longnose Gars (that is, those under 25 cm in length), but larger individuals are of course capable of eating larger prey—which is why they should be housed only with fishes too big for them to swallow.

LEPOMIS CYANELLUS

LEPOMIS CYANELLUS Rafinesque/*Green Sunfish*

R: United States from about South Dakota and Colorado eastward to New York and south to the northern part of Mexico. **H:** Very aggressive toward other sunfishes; males often will kill females of their own species. Reported able to swallow a fish half their own size. **W:** Very tolerant of water conditions. Temperature range anywhere from 5-29°C. **S:** Attains a length of up to 17 cm or more. **F:** Will accept a wide variety of foods including earthworms, brine shrimp, *Daphnia,* beef heart, small fishes, etc.

The Green Sunfish is one of the more aggressive of the sunfishes and cannot be safely kept with other species of *Lepomis.* The body is less deep than most other sunfishes and the colors are rather drab. Like the Bluegill there is a dark blotch at the base of the soft dorsal fin. In fact it has often been mistaken for the Bluegill and unknowingly introduced into many lakes where it normally did not occur.

In nature the food varies from aquatic insects to small fishes. In captivity it will accept most items generally available to aquarists such as earthworms, brine shrimp, *Daphnia,* beef heart, and small fishes.

The tank should be as large as possible and provided with a sandy bottom. Hiding places should be provided in the form of plants and rock decorations, but expect to have the plants uprooted from time to time. The water conditions are not critical as this species is very tolerant of overcrowding and poor tank conditions.

The Green Sunfish has been spawned in captivity and is said to breed in a manner similar to the other sunfishes. The male constructs a hollow in the sand with his tail and courts the females to attract them into the nest. The pair will circle the nest side by side as the female deposits her eggs and the male fertilizes them. If not removed promptly, the female will be killed. In nature the female will deposit eggs in several nests as they are attracted to one male and then another and they often will deposit eggs in the nests of other sunfishes, leading at times to hybridization. The male remains guarding the nest against other fishes until the eggs have hatched and the fry are large enough to go off by themselves. It is perhaps wise to separate the male from the young and raise them separately. The young Green Sunfish grow quickly but do not attain their full colors until maturity. This starts at about a size of two inches, and their best colors remain until they pass the four-inch size.

LEPOMIS GIBBOSUS (Linnaeus)/*Sunfish, Pumpkinseed*

R: Maine to Florida and west to the Mississippi. **H**: Should be kept by themselves or with others of the same genus. **W**: Tank should be roomy and the water clean. Room temperature suffice without any additional heat. **S**: Seldom larger than 15 cm. **F**: Hearty eaters that require frequent feedings with large live foods such as chopped earthworms or frozen foods like beef heart.

The male fans out a depression in an open space and then lures the female into it. Eggs are laid and guarded by the male, who drives away the female after she has finished. Eggs hatch in two to three days, and the fry are easily raised.

LEPOMIS MEGALOTIS

LEPOMIS MACROCHIRUS Rafinesque/*Bluegill*

R: United States from Minnesota to Texas (and south to northern Mexico) and eastward to the East Coast from New York to Florida. Introduced into areas as far west as California. **H**: Generally aggressive. Diggers and plant uprooters. **W**: Not critical. A cool-water species but can tolerate temperatures from 5-29C. **S**: Reaches maturity at about 9 cm, but a record Bluegill of 37.5 cm has been recorded. **F**: Easily fed on a variety of foods including earthworms, small live fishes, beef heart, etc.

The Bluegill is a nest-builder, the male constructing a hollow in the sand by movements of his caudal fin. He will assume an angle of about 45°, head up, during the nest building as his fin sweeps away the sand below it with powerful strokes. He then proceeds to attract a female to his nest, where she deposits anywhere from 15,000 to 70,000 eggs. During the actual spawning the pair take a side-by-side position, swimming in slow circles around the nest, the male taking the inner position. She is then driven away (and must be removed from the aquarium) but in nature may be courted by another male and spawn again if she has any eggs left. The male fertilizes the eggs and remains guarding them until they hatch and grow enough so that they can make it on their own. At this point the parents and young can be separated by the aquarist.

LEPOMIS GIBBOSUS

LEPOMIS MEGALOTIS (Rafinesque)/*Longeared Sunfish*

R: Eastern United States, Canada to the Mexican border. **H**: Best kept by themselves. **W**: Not critical, but water should be clean and well aerated. **S**: Wild specimens 20 cm; in the aquarium seldom over 13 cm. **F**: Hearty eaters whose live food diet can be supplemented with chopped beef heart, liver, etc.

In the aquarium medium-sized specimens that have recently reached maturity are the most brightly colored. The Longeared Sunfish prefers a little more sunlight than the others, so their tank should be in a position where it gets a few hours of direct sunlight daily. During the winter months these fish should get a "rest period" of lowered temperatures, about 4 to 7°C. This is essential to their well-being, and if they do not get this period the number and quality of the eggs laid the following spring may easily be a disappointment.

LEPOMIS MACROCHIRUS

LEPORINUS AGASSIZI Steindachner/*Half-Striped Leporinus*

R: Central Amazon region. **H**: Fairly peaceful and fond of nibbling algae from glass or plants. **W**: Neutral to slightly acid. Temperature 23 to 26°C. **S**: About 9 cm in the aquarium; likely to grow much bigger. **F**: Will take prepared foods, but live and frozen foods are preferred; fond of nibbling a lettuce leaf.

This species is very hardy and peaceful. The Half-Striped Leporinus appreciates a large aquarium that is not too densely planted. The aquarium should have a gravel bottom. Frequent water changes are suggested, but one must be careful not to let the temperature drop below 21°C. Although this fish is not particular about its food, it should be given a fair amount of vegetable matter. If *L. agassizi* does not get a sufficient amount of greens, it will tend to nibble at the aquarium plants. Specimens up to 9 cm are usually noted in the aquarium, but it is known that this fish will grow to a larger size.

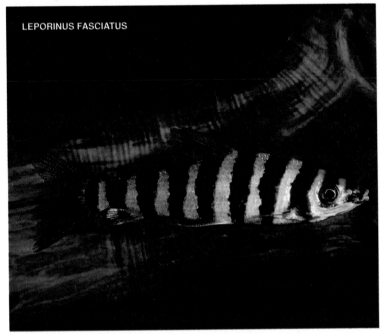

LEPORINUS FASCIATUS

LEPORINUS ARCUS Eigenmann/*Lipstick Leporinus*

R: Venezuela, the Guianas, and parts of Brazil. **H**: Peaceful; likely to jump out of an uncovered tank. **W**: Neutral to slightly acid. Temperature 23 to 26°C. **S**: Reaches 40 cm, but are only 5-10 cm when imported. **F**: Live and frozen foods preferred; should have an occasional lettuce leaf to nibble on.

Scientific works mention the similarity between this *Leporinus* species and another one, *L. striatus*. There may, however, be more differences as the fish fully mature or show their breeding colors. Perhaps some day someone with a very large tank will raise this beauty to a size where the female's eggs and the male's sperm ripen. Most of the *Leporinus* species are very skillful jumpers and for this reason are very difficult to capture in a seine.

LEPORINUS AGASSIZI

LEPORINUS FASCIATUS (Bloch)/*Banded Leporinus*

R: Widely distributed in South America from the Guianas to the La Plata. **H**: Active and peaceful toward other fishes, but inclined to be destructive to plants; keep their tank covered because they jump. **W**: Neutral to slightly alkaline water. Being active, they require a good-sized tank. Temperature 23 to 26°C. **S**: In their home waters to 33 cm; in captivity, seldom over 15 cm. **F**: Omnivorous, with a preference for vegetable matter; crushed lettuce leaves or spinach leaves should be frequently provided.

They swim in a head-down position and constantly graze on the algae that cover the plant surfaces. When all the algae have been cleared away they will switch their attentions to the soft shoots and leaves of higher plants. A good substitute is to give them frequently a supply of crushed lettuce leaves, but of course there is always the danger that they will pass up the lettuce and re-direct their attentions to the aquatic plants again. Another ruse is to use plastic plants.

LEPORINUS ARCUS

LEPORINUS FRIDERICI (Bloch)/*Friderici*

R: The Guianas to the Amazon River. **H**: Peaceful toward other fishes; a jumper, so the tank must be kept covered. **W**: Neutral to slightly alkaline. Temperature 24 to 27°C. **S**: In nature, up to 41cm; in captivity, seldom over 15 cm. **F**: Live or frozen foods, with frequent feedings of vegetable substances such as crushed lettuce leaves or chopped spinach.

This is a difficult fish to catch in their native waters, and many of them go sailing high over the top of the net in magnificent leaps when they feel confined. The native boys who handle the nets must duck with lightning-like reflexes when a fish comes flying at them or they could easily get a black eye. This jumping ability is shown to a lesser degree in the confines of an aquarium. The fish can attain a size of up to 41 cm, as it does when wild.

LEPORINUS PELLEGRINI

LEPORINUS MELANOPLEURA Günther/*Spot-Tailed Leporinus*

R: Eastern Brazil, between the Amazon River and Rio de Janeiro. **H**: Peaceful toward other fishes; a jumper that must be protected by keeping its tank covered. **W**: Neutral to slightly alkaline. Temperature 24 to 27°C. **S**: To 20 cm; usually sold at 8 to 10 cm. **F**: All live foods and frozen foods; prepared foods are also accepted, and an addition of vegetable matter is very beneficial.

The first ones to be sold to hobbyists reached the market as early as 1926, but to date there have been no accounts of any spawnings. One of the theories as to why some aquarium fishes have eluded all efforts to spawn them is that the larger species that have been stunted for some time in an aquarium (which does not allow them full development) never attain sexual maturity.

LEPORINUS FRIDERICI

LEPORINUS PELLEGRINI Steindachner/*Pellegrin's Leporinus*

R: Upper and lower Amazon, Peru, Espirito Santo, Rio de Janeiro, Sao Paulo, Rio Paraguay, the Guianas. **H**: Peaceful and active; should have a covered tank, as it is likely to jump. **W**: Neutral to slightly acid; water should be well aged. Temperature about 24°C. **S**: 7 to 10 cm in the aquarium. **F**: A good eater, will eat dried foods as well as all kinds of live foods.

Tank-raised specimens of *Leporinus pellegrini* should be much easier to spawn than their wild ancestors, having been in aquaria all of their lives and accustomed to the comparatively cramped quarters allotted them. Pellegrin's Leporinus is said to spawn very much like the barbs, scattering eggs all over the aquarium and then eating them if not taken out. This should be one fish that should be easy to raise, judging by the appetite the grown ones have. Like the other *Leporinus* species, a little green food should be given.

LEPORINUS MELANOPLEURA

LEPORINUS STRIATUS Kner/*Striped Leporinus*

R: Amazon River south to the Parana in Uruguay. **H**: Peaceful and very active; tank should be kept well covered. Temperature 23 to 26°C. **W**: Neutral to slightly alkaline. **S**: About 30 cm in nature; in captivity about half that. **F**: Omnivorous; likes to nibble on plants, so should be given an occasional lettuce or spinach leaf.

Although this species is not a particularly picky eater, it should be given a good amount of vegetable matter in its diet. The Striped Leporinus is both peaceful and active. *Leporinus* species are all confined to South America, where they inhabit gravel-bottomed, slow-moving streams. Juveniles are more strikingly colored than adults. This species, like the rest of the genus, tends to be a headstander. Sexual distinctions are not known. This fish has not yet been bred in captivity.

LEPTOLEBIAS MINIMUS

LEPTOBARBUS HOEVENI (Bleeker)/Pink-Tailed *Barb*

R: Sumatra, Borneo, and Thailand. **H**: Peaceful, possibly even shy. Should be treated like a rasbora. **W**: Not critical as long as extremes are avoided. Temperatures in a normal range of 22° to 27°C are recommended. **S**: Attains a length of up to half a meter. **F**: Omnivorous and accepts a wide range of foods, both animal and vegetable.

This fish seems to be omnivorous and will accept a wide variety of foods. In Thailand the Pink-Tailed Barb is caught on hook and line with a variety of baits including prawns, paste, and pieces of various succulent leaves. Smith, in his *Freshwater Fishes of Siam, or Thailand,* states that this is sometimes called a "mad" fish, for when large fruit capsules of the chaulmoogra tree (*Hydnocarpus*) become available (they may fall into the stream from the tree or may be washed in from the banks by rainwater) the fish gorge themselves. The result is that they become intoxicated or "mad," for they behave in an unusual manner. At this time the flesh is shunned by the local people for it is considered to be poisonous.

426

LEPORINUS STRIATUS

LEPTOLEBIAS MINIMUS/Gaucho

R: Northwest of Rio de Janeiro in pools that dry out seasonally. **H**: Must be kept by themselves. **W**: Soft, slightly acid water. Temperature 24 to 26°C. **S**: To 4 cm. **F**: Small live foods. **C**: Body green with bright red bars that extend into the vertical fins. Eyes are a beautiful green. Females plain greenish brown.

A small tank can be used, with a 3 cm layer of peat moss on the bottom. Eggs are deposited in the peat moss. The parents are removed and most of the water is drained off. The tank is then placed in a shaded location where the temperatures run from 20 to 24°C for a period of 15 to 20 days. The contents are then poured into a fine-meshed net and gently squeezed out. Then the peat moss is loosened again and placed in a jar. In two or three months the peat moss with the eggs is placed in a tank of soft, slightly acid water, where the eggs hatch very quickly, most of them within a few hours.

LEPTOBARBUS HOEVENI

LEPTOLUCANIA OMMATA (Jordan)/*Swamp Killie, Pygmy Killifish*

R: Southern Georgia to Florida, in swamps. **H**: Peaceful, but should not be kept with large fishes. **W**: Neutral to slightly acid water; tank should be well planted. Temperature 21 to 24°C. **S**: To about 4 cm. **F**: Small living foods are preferred, but dried foods are accepted.

A pair will soon spawn among fine-leaved plants. The eggs are very small and hatch in about ten days. At first they should be fed infusoria. Once they have graduated to larger live foods such as baby brine shrimp, growth is very rapid. It is interesting to speculate as to why an "eye-spot" occurs in some fishes.

LIOSOMADORAS ONCINUS

LIMNOCHROMIS AURITUS (Boulenger)/*Auritus*

R: Lake Tanganyika, Africa. **H**: Relatively shy and retiring; this fish will not display well unless it feels completely at home in its tank. **W**: Hard, alkaline water is best, but softer and more acidic water are accepted, especially by tank-raised fish. Best temperature range, 24 to 28°C. **S**: About 12 cm. **F**: Live foods are especially relished, but all standard prepared foods are taken; avoid a steady diet of tubifex if feeding live foods.

This species is a mouthbrooder, but instead of producing a very limited number of compara-tively very large eggs it produces instead many small eggs, enough to provide upward of 400 fry from a single spawning. Occasionally enough eggs are produced that even a large female can't cram them all into her mouth, and the male in such cases usually will then accommodate the leftover eggs in his.

428

LEPTOLUCANIA OMMATA

LIOSOMADORAS ONCINUS (Schomburgk)/*Jaguar Catfish*
R: So far known only from some sections of Brazil and Peru. **H:** Light-shy, cruising around the tank in subdued light or at night in search of food. Not known to be aggressive. **W:** Prefers slightly soft and acid (pH 6.5-6.9) water. Otherwise the water conditions are not critical. **S:** Attains a total length of a least 15 cm but may get substantially larger. **F:** Will accept a variety of foods, though live foods such as chopped earthworms are preferred.

The Jaguar Catfish is named for its spotted pattern that resembles the pattern of the jungle cat of that name. Younger specimens seem to have a more blotchy pattern, these blotches breaking up into smaller and smaller spots as the catfish matures. Throughout life there is a characteristic pale streak extending from the head to the base of the tail. This streak is of the same color as the background and may vary from almost orange to pale yellowish to white. The back is usually more brownish.

LIMNOCHROMIS AURITUS

429

LOPHIOBAGRUS CYCLURUS (Worth & Ricardo)|Poison/*Slime Catfish*

R: Endemic to Lake Tanganyika, Africa. **H:** A nocturnal species that should not be housed with aggressive fishes because of its ability to emit a poisonous slime when disturbed. **W:** Not critical as long as typical Rift Lake conditions (hard and alkline water) are met. **S:** Rather small, attaining a length of about 10 cm. **F:** Will eat a wide variety of foods, but some vegetable matter should be included in the diet.

What makes this small species different from most other catfishes is its ability to defend itself by means of a poison. Whenever it is threatened or alarmed, as when it is netted out of an aquarium, it is able to exude a sticky transparent mucus. This material will mix with water and poison any fishes in the vicinity. It is therefore essential to keep it in a fairly large tank and with non-aggressive fishes, for if it is attacked it will certainly cause a great deal of trouble—at least a major water change and perhaps the demise of the inhabitants of the tank.

This species is therefore not for the novice who might make some fatal mistake by upsetting it. It is otherwise not difficult to maintain, for it is not demanding as far as water conditions and food are concerned. It does need the hard, alkaline water of the Rift Lake species, however.

LUCIOCEPHALUS PULCHER

LUCANIA GOODEI Jordan /*Bluefin Killifish*

R: Southern Florida. **H:** An active species which will sometimes pursue other fishes, but seldom attacks. **W:** Should be kept in roomy aquaria, well planted and cool (15°C). **S:** 5 cm. **F:** Small live foods only; dried foods are accepted only if the fish is starving.

This is a common little fish in Florida, but in spite of this we seldom see it offered by dealers. Probably the reason they do not like to handle them is that many people who buy them try to crowd them into a tank with tropical species, a thing which this fish does not like at all. They should not be crowded, and they cannot stand the 24 to 27°C temperatures we give to most of our tropical species. Given a roomy tank which is well planted and temperatures which range from 15 to 18°C, the males will put on a nice display and spawnings will be observed among the fine-leaved plants. Only three to five eggs will be expelled by one female per day, but this is kept up for about five weeks. The eggs hatch in about 14 days at 18°C. Higher temperatures result in many infertile eggs. When they hatch, they can be brought to the surface by placing a light over the darkened tank. They are then lifted out with a spoon and transferred to a rearing tank with similar water. After a week of infusoria feedings they are able to take newly hatched brine shrimp.

LOPHIOBAGRUS CYCLURUS

LUCIOCEPHALUS PULCHER (Gray) *Pike-Head*
R: Malaysia, Sumatra, and Borneo. **H**: Predatory fish that should never be kept with smaller ones. **W**: Soft, slightly acid water. Temperature 26 to 29°C. **S**: To 18 cm. **F**: Small living fishes are preferred over anything else.

The Pike-Head is a predator that feeds on all sorts of smaller creatures such as small fishes and the larger aquatic insects and their larvae. Their method of catching food is very interesting: the mouth opens very quickly to a funnel shape, causing the water to flow into it and take the greatly surprised prey with it. Their appetites should never be underestimated, and the owner often wonders where all those Guppies go.

LUCANIA GOODEI

LUCIOSOMA BLEEKERI Steindachner/*Bleeker's Apollo Shark*

R: Thailand and Laos. **H:** Tends to be aggressive toward its own kind and possibly to other species. **W:** Not critical as long as extremes are avoided; treat like rasboras. **S:** Can attain a length of over 30 cm. **F:** Will eat almost anything reasonable, but its feeding activities are generaly restricted to the upper levels.

For spawning set a string of airstones along the length of the tank and attach spawning mops to each airline. These mops should be dark green in color and at least 30 cm long. Sexes can be determined by heaviness of the female and the fact that the males will be chasing the females. The female should be placed in the breeding tank and conditioned on nourishing foods (preferably live) for about two weeks or until she appears very swollen with eggs. The male is then introduced. Apollo sharks breed like rasboras. The male will start to court the female almost immediately, swimming parallel to her and wagging his tail back and forth (tailbeating). The male will arch his body and open his mouth wide. The spawning embrace is fairly typical, and as the fish quiver up to 100 eggs are released. These are not very adhesive, and care must be exercised when removing the spawning mops so as not to dislodge them. The spawning of the adults lasts about an hour. The fry hatch in a couple of days and become free-swimming in about five days. For about a week after they have become free-swimming, feed them with infusoria. After that time they should be able to handle newly hatched brine shrimp.

MACROGNATHUS SIAMENSIS

LUCIOSOMA SETIGERUM (Valenciennes)/*Long-Finned Apollo Shark*

R: Borneo, Sumatra, and Thailand. **H:** Aggressive with its own kind and with other active fishes that frequent the surface. **W:** Not critical, but extremes should be avoided **S:** To about 25 cm. **F:** Not particular; will take a high quality flake foods and other items that sink slowly, and *Drosophila* and small mealworms are excellent.

The Long-Finned Apollo Shark is aggressive toward members of its own kind and will also attack other active surface fishes. If more than one are kept in an aquarium, be sure to provide some hiding places (plants will do nicely) for the losers of any battles. Fortunately, the Long-Finned Apollo Shark usually ignores the more sluggish bottom fishes, but do not trust it with fishes too much smaller than itself.

LUCIOSOMA BLEEKERI

MACROGNATHUS SIAMENSIS (Günther)/*Spot-Finned Spiny Eel*
R: Thailand. **H**: Fairly peaceful with fishes its own size or not too much smaller, but it has been known to attack tiny species and half-grown individuals of large species. **W**: Soft, slightly acid water is best. Temperature 24 to 29°C. **S**: Up to 25 cm. **F**: Usually reluctant to accept dry foods, although will sometimes pick these up from the bottom; tubifex worms are eagerly accepted. The most interesting habit of spiny eels (both *Macrognathus* and *Mastacembelus* is their ability to dig into and remain buried in the aquarium gravel, where they sometimes remain for long periods of time with just the head sticking out, or even completely buried. Another characteristic, but one of more annoyance and less pleasure for their owner, is their propensity to escape from whatever tank they are kept in. This is accomplished more by a "climbing" maneuver than by jumping.

LUCIOSOMA SETIGERUM

MACROGNATHUS ZEBRINUS (Blyth)/*Zebra Spiny Eel*

R: Burma. **H**: A generally peaceful fish, but not above eating baby fishes. **W**: Not critical if extremes are avoided. Temperature 22 to 26°C. **S**: Up to 46 cm in the wild; usually seen at no more than 13 cm. **F**: Small moving live foods are preferred, but prepared foods are readily accepted, provided pieces are not too large.

The Zebra Spiny Eel should be maintained in a dimly lighted, well-planted tank that offers it many hiding places. Aquarists keeping the species will note that fish maintained under these conditions will show much less of a tendency to enter the gravel. Since constant movement through aquarium gravel, which is much harder and sharper than the silty bottoms underlying the fish's native waters, can be harmful to the species in the long run, providing proper hiding places will make the Zebra Spiny Eel much more comfortable. *M. zebrinus* definitely suffers if kept in a tank that is too brightly illuminated.

MACROPODUS OPERCULARIS OPERCULARIS

MACROPODUS OCELLATUS/*Round-tailed Paradise Fish*

R: Southern China and Korea. **H**: Tends to be aggressive (especially males) when spawning. A bubblenest builder. **W**: Not critical. **S**: Males grow to 8-10 cm, females to 7-9 cm. **F**: Will accept almost any aquarium food including dry flake food.

If a ripe female is available to a male he will probably immediately start building a bubblenest. If the female approaches him at this time he usually drives her away. In about two days the nest is complete and the advances of the female, in the form of proddings of his abdomen with her snout, are no longer rebuffed. The general aggressiveness of the male toward the female diminishes, and eventually there is an attempt at an embrace in typical betta or gourami fashion. Initial embraces produce no eggs, then only one or two, then more and more. The male comes out of the embrace first and starts picking up the eggs and placing them into the nest, adding more bubbles all the time. This goes on for about one or two hours until the female is depleted. The male tends the eggs and the female goes on about her business. If any other fish, including the female, attempts to approach the nest it is chased away quickly. In about 28 hours the eggs hatch; 3 1/2 days later the fry are free-swimming,. They can be fed brine shrimp, rotifers, and *Daphnia* nauplii. Water changes in the fry tank are beneficial.

MACROGNATHUS ZEBRINUS

MACROPODUS OPERCULARIS OPERCULARIS (Linnaeus)/*Paradise Fish*
R: China and Taiwan. **H**: Very quarrelsome, even toward their own kind. **W**: Very adaptable to any water conditions. An unheated aquarium suffices, and for breeding 21 to 24°C is high enough. **S**: About 8 cm. **F**: A greedy eater that should be fed often and generously; all kinds of foods are accepted.
The males build bubblenests frequently, and a female that is not yet ready for egg-laying should be kept away from him until she is or the nasty-tempered male may mutilate or even kill her. A great number of floating eggs are laid, which are gathered by the male and placed in the nest. The male's ferocity becomes most apparent when spawning is over and he guards the nest, so the female should be removed at that time. Young hatch in 30 to 50 hours and are very easy to raise.

MACROPODUS OCELLATUS

MACROPODUS OPERCULARIS CONCOLOR Ahl/*Black Paradise Fish*

R: Not specifically known. Said to come from the East Indies. **H:** Not as aggressive as *M. opercularis opercularis*. Two males will normally fight, and plants may be torn up. **W:** Prefers neutral to slightly acid water and a temperature between 20 and 25°C. **S:** Males attain a length of about 12 cm, females only 8 cm. **F:** Live foods are preferred (glass worms, *Daphnia*, tubifex worms, etc.).

The Black Paradise Fish is very close to the common Paradise Fish, *M.opercularis opercularis,* and is thought by some to be one and the same species. On the other hand, some consider the Black Paradise Fish to be a separate species. Perhaps it is best to follow Myers in his belief that it is a subspecies coming from somewhere in the East Indies. The Paradise Fish ranges from Korea to China and Vietnam. The two are distinguishable by color, the Black Paradise Fish being plain brownish and the Paradise Fish barred with blue and red. There are other differences as well. The Black Paradise Fish is less aggressive and can be added to a community tank without fear of the inhabitants being molested. However, two male Black Paradise Fish do not get along very well and immediately start fighting.

MALPULUTTA KRETSERI

MALAPTERURUS ELECTRICUS (Gmelin)/*Electric Catfish*

R: Tropical Africa, except for some lake and river systems. **H:** Decidedly predatory, so not safe with other species. **W:** Neutral water in the medium-soft range is best. Temperature 23 to 28°C. **S:** Over 60 cm in nature, but rarely seen at this size when offered for sale. **F:** Prefers small live fishes, which are usually swallowed whole; will also eat plants.

The most interesting point about *Malapterurus* is, of course, the fish's capacity for discharging an electric current. This current is much weaker than that generated by the South American Electric Eel, *Electrophorus electricus,* but much stronger than that of the African elephant-noses of the family Mormyridae.

MACROPODUS OPERCULARIS CONCOLOR

MALPULUTTA KRETSERI Deraniyagala/*Malpulutta*
R: Sri Lanka. **H**: Peaceful; should be kept only with small species. **W**: Soft, slightly acid water optional. Temperature 24 to 27°C. **S**: About 4 cm. **F**: Mosquito larvae eagerly taken; can be trained to take frozen and freeze-dried foods.
Males build a nest containing a few bubbles between floating plants. The embrace is typical of bubblenest-building anabantoids, and the amber eggs are lighter than water. The fry hatch in two days at 27°C and become free-swimming in three more. The entire mating procedure is gentle and the adults can be left with the fry if necessary.

MALAPTERURUS ELECTRICUS

MASTACEMBELUS ARMATUS (Lacépède)/*White-Spotted Eel*

R: India, Sri Lanka, Thailand, and Sumatra. **H**: Mostly nocturnal; should have places where it can hide. **W**: Not important as long as the water is clean. Temperature 24 to 27°C. **S**: To 76 cm in native waters. **F**: Living or frozen foods, especially worms.

Like many of the eel-like fishes, the spiny eels are nocturnal in their habits. Have no fear that tubifex worms will get into your bottom gravel and foul the water while they are there! The spiny eels are excellent diggers and will do a thorough job of getting every one out. Some even sleep under the gravel! Known to science since 1798, this species was first introduced to aquarium hobbyists around 1922. The unpaired fins are all connected in this species.

MELANOCHROMIS AURATUS

MASTACEMBELUS ERYTHROTAENIA Bleeker/*Spotted Fire Eel*

R: Java, Borneo, and Sumatra. **H**: Mostly nocturnal and a bit shy at first; hiding places should be provided. **W**: Not important as long as the water is clean. Temperature 24 to 26°C. **S**: To 46 cm. **F**: Very fond of worms and other live foods such as daphnia and brine shrimp.

Its unusual body shape, color pattern, and hooked, trunk–like snout make it a stand-out in any collection. Like so many species that can undulate the dorsal as well as the anal fin, it can swim backward as well as forward and is a mighty tricky proposition to get into a net. It is largely nocturnal in its habits and unfortunately does not come out often, except when it is hungry and smells food. It is most at ease when a number of hiding places such as rocks or plant thickets are provided. Often, too, it burrows into the gravel with only its eyes and snout protruding.

MASTACEMBELUS ARMATUS

MELANOCHROMIS AURATUS (Boulenger)/*Auratus, Malawi Golden Cichlid*
R: Lake Malawi, Africa. **H**: This fish should be kept in large aquaria with large fishes; males are particularly aggressive. **W**: Should be fairly hard and alkaline. Temperature 24 to 27°C. **S**: About 12 cm; aquarium-bred usually smaller. **F**: Accepts all standard aquarium foods.
This species is a maternal mouthbrooder with an incubation period of three to four weeks. The size of its brood ranges from 12 to 40, depending upon the conditions of the aquarium and the age of the fish. Fish carrying their first broods usually have fewer fry. It should be noted that this species is very aggressive when mating. Males always seem to be looking for a mate and will disrupt fish three times their size to prevent them from spawning in their territory.

MASTACEMBELUS ERYTHROTAENIA

MELANOCHROMIS CRABRO

MELANOCHROMIS CRABRO Ribbink & Lewis/*Chameleon Cichlid, Chameleo*
R: Endemic to Lake Malawi, Africa. **H:** Very territorial and aggressive, the aggressiveness directed not only toward other species but also among themselves. **W:** Typical hard, very alkaline water preferred. A temperature of about 22° to 27°C is sufficient. **S:** Attains a length of about 15 cm. **F:** Will accept most aquarium foods fed to other Lake Malawi cichlids.

This is the fish that has been going under the name of *Pseudotropheus "chameleo"* for such a long time. It has appeared in many articles in the aquarium literature, and it is highly possible that under the present rules of nomenclature one of these uses of the name might constitute a valid description. In such an event the name would have to be changed to *Melanochromis chameleo,* assuming that the fish is indeed a species of *Melanochromis.* Obviously the problem of the correct name for this species is still unsettled. The name "Chameleo" or Chameleon Cichlid apparently was given to this fish due to its ability to change patterns from a vertically barred pattern to almost a checkerboard design.

This is one of the more aggressive species of mbuna, and it is often difficult to find suitable tankmates even among the species of *Pseudotropheus* and *Melanochromis* available to hobbyists. Male Chameleo are very aggressive toward each other, making it necessary to house them in a large tank with a great many rockwork caves that they can defend or hide in. Several individuals in a tank will soon set up a hierarchy or peck order, and fighting should become reduced to a certain extent. With limited space a single male with several females usually works out well.

Like other mbuna, this species is a maternal mouthbrooder. It will spawn in a community tank, the male keeping all intruders out of his territory very efficiently. Spawning is normal for mbuna, occurring on a flat rock. The female picks up the eggs after each fertilization pass by the male. When she is finished she retires to a secluded spot to incubate her brood. It is risky to a certain extent to move the female to a separate tank while she broods the eggs because she will have lost her place in the pecking order during that time and will be in for a tough time when returned (perhaps she will even be killed). Instead, she can be moved just in time to drop the fry and then returned to the community tank before she is even missed. Some females will eat during the incubation time and are not in a weakened condition after delivery of the young. The brooding time is normal for mbuna; i.e., about 20 to 22 days. About 25 to 50 young are brooded. Upon release the young Chameleo can take newly hatched brine shrimp immediately.

MELANOCHROMIS JOHANNI (Eccles)/*Johanni*

R: Lake Malawi, Africa. **H**: Quarrelsome and aggressive; males are active bulliers of other males and active killers of uncooperative females. **W**: Hard, alkaline water preferred but not strictly necessary. Aquarium-raised individuals are especially tolerant of water quality deviations from the ideal. Temperature 24 to 27°C. **S**: Up to 12 cm. **F**: Accepts all standard aquarium foods. **C**: There are two major color variations among adult males of this species: a striped type in which the basic dark body color is overlaid with two blue stripes along the flanks and a type in which the dark body color is interrupted by a pattern of blue blotches. In both types the blue color is carried into the dorsal fins, and the dorsal is edged in blue in both types. Females and young fish are an overall golden to orange color.

This fish is a reliable spawner. It is very easy to differentiate the sexes, as adult males are dark-bodied with blue stripes or spots, whereas females are light-bodied, ranging from yellowish to orange in overall coloration. *M. johanni* is a mouthbrooder in which the female broods her eggs. There are comparatively few eggs laid, but the eggs are large and so are the fry; the fry are therefore easy to feed and to raise. Females that have finished brooding a group of young should be given a period of rest and recuperation.

441

MELANOCHROMIS VERMIVORUS Trewavas/*Purple Mbuna*

R: Lake Malawi, Africa. **H**: Quarrelsome; smaller fish of the species tend to be greatly bullied by larger individuals. **W**: Hard, alkaline water is best. Temperature should be maintained at 23 to 27°C. **S**: Up to about 11 cm. **F**: Takes all standard aquarium foods; should have vegetable matter added to the diet. **C**: Extremely variable according to age, mood, condition of the fish, and its status within it own community.

Melanochromis vermivorus is a mouthbrooding species. A female brooding eggs should be removed to the relative security of a small tank by herself in which she can release and tend her fry, and she should not be returned to the community from which she came until she has been allowed to regain her pre-brooding condition. If she is returned too soon, she is in great danger of attack and in her weakened condition probably would not be able to defend herself successfully.

MELANOTAENIA FLUVIATILIS

MELANOTAENIA BOESEMANI Allen & Cross/*Boeseman's Rainbowfish*

R: Vogelkop Peninsula of Irian Jaya, New Guinea. **H**: Generally peaceful and easy to breed. **W**: Not critical, although the fry are sensitive to small changes in water chemistry. **S**: Males to 9 cm, females to 7 cm. **F**: Will eat almost any aquarium foods available.

A fairly large well-planted tank will house a small community of these fish easily. Dr. Gerald R. Allen, one of the describers of this species, used a 100-liter tank for a half-dozen individuals that eventually spawned. water chemistry is no problem, although the fry and young are quite sensitive to even small changes. If the tank is well planted the fry can be raised with the parents. This is in contrast to most other species of rainbowfishes, which will usually feed on the youngsters. Make sure the parents are well fed, however. Feeding is no problem as Boeseman's Rainbowfish will accept almost any of the available aquarium foods.

Mature fish are relatively easy to sex. Males are quite colorful, being bluish gray anteriorly and bright red-orange posteriorly, with a narrow middle zone with alternating light and dark vertical bars. The females have the usual longitudinal dark stripe as well as a series of narrow longitudinal reddish or orange stripes following the scale rows. Males are also larger (about 9 cm) than the females (about 7 cm). The only requirements for successful breeding are a well planted tank, a balanced nutritious diet, and a suitable spawning medium such as Java moss. Courting is typical of the rainbowfishes, and the eggs are deposited on the Java moss. They can be harvested periodically or left with the parents. The various sizes of young from different spawnings can be seen living among the plants. They can be fed anything suitably small enough, including crushed flake food.

MELANOCHROMIS VERMIVORUS

MELANOTAENIA FLUVIATILIS (Castelnau)/*Pink-Ear Rainbowfish*

R: Northern Australia. **H:** Peaceful; can be kept in a community aquarium or in small groups. **W:** Not critical; a small amount of salt may he added. Temperature 18°-22°C. for maintenance, slightly higher for breeding. **S:** Grows to about 9 cm. **F:** Will accept a wide variety of dry or live foods.

Spawning the Pink-Ear Rainbowfish is relatively easy. They spawn in a manner similar to the top-spawning killifishes and can be provided with the same floating spawning mops or fine-leaved plants. The temperature should be raised to 22 to 25°C.

The sexes are relatively easy to distinguish. The males are more brightly colored and have more pointed dorsal and anal fins, while the females have rounded dorsal and anal fins which are smaller and lack the dark edges. The colors become brighter with the approach of the spawning season (summer in Australia). The eggs are usually laid in the morning, when the sun is on the tank, and can be seen hanging by tiny threads from the spawning mop or plants. Eggs are deposited for a period of several days and may amount to several hundred per spawning. The parents, if well-fed, will normally not bother eggs or fry. For those who do not wish to take chances, the eggs can be harvested from the mops and hatched artificially. Hatching takes a week to ten days at 25°C. The fry are small and require very fine food for the first few days. Some breeders say that powdered dry food is sufficient, but others set up an infusoria culture. After about a week newly hatched brine shrimp or microworms can be fed. Once these foods are accepted the rest is easy; growth is fairly rapid.

Some males tend to be aggressive toward other males, so it is best to keep just one per tank or enough so that the aggression is well scattered among the tank inhabitants.

MELANOTAENIA BOESEMANI

MELANOTAENIA HERBERTAXELRODI Allen/*Lake Tebera Rainbowfish*

R: Known only from Lake Tebera, Papua New Guinea. **H:** A very peaceful fish that can be kept in a community aquarium or in small groups. **W:** Prefers a pH of 7.0 to 7.8; hardness is not important. The ideal temperature range is about 20 to 26°C. **S:** Attains a length of 8.5 to 9.0 cm in standard length. **F:** Will accept a wide variety of foods, both live and prepared.

Keeping the Lake Tebera Rainbowfish is no problem. A moderate sized tank of about 80-liter capacity is recommended, although it will survive quite well in smaller tanks. Water hardness does not seem to be a factor, but pH seems to be important. A pH of 7.0 to 7.8 is acceptable, but the higher ranges are best (in the natural habitat it is recorded as 7.8). If the pH dips too low the fish become milky white, breathe very rapidly, and show other signs of stress. Water changes and a gradual change of pH toward the alkaline side will help alleviate this problem.

Spawning is accomplished in typical *Melanotaenia* fashion, with the female depositing about 30 or so eggs per day in the aquatic plants. They adhere to the plants by the sticky threads common to this group. The eggs are left alone by the parents and will hatch in about one week at 22 to 24°C. The fry are also ignored by the parents, but if the spawning is continuous those fry that have grown to 12 mm or more may eat the newly hatched fry, so it is best to separate them periodically. Fry are small and should be fed with egg yolk and green water for the first week. They then can take microworms and newly hatched brine shrimp.

MELANOTAENIA NIGRANS

MELANOTAENIA MACCULLOCHI (Ogilby)/*Dwarf Australian Rainbowfish*

R: Northeastern Australia in the region of Cairns. **H:** Peaceful; prefers being kept in small groups. **W:** Slightly alkaline water to which a little salt (about a quarter teaspoon per liter) has been added is best. Temperature 23 to 26°C. **S:** Up to 7 cm. **F:** Not a choosy eater; prepared foods accepted as readily as live or frozen foods.

When pursuing a female during spawning time the male's colors not only become intensified, but a wide lemon-yellow stripe appears on the sides, to disappear as quickly as it came. Eggs are laid in bushy plants; young hatch in seven to ten days and are very easily raised.

MELANOTAENIA HERBERTAXELRODI

MELANOTAENIA NIGRANS (Richardson)/*Dark Australian Rainbow*
R: Northern tip of Australia. **H**: Peaceful and very hardy; prefers to be kept in small groups. **W**: Neutral to slightly alkaline water to which a small amount of salt has been added. Temperature 19 to 24°C. **S**: To 8 cm. **F**: Easily fed; accepts prepared foods as readily as live or frozen foods. A well-conditioned pair is placed into a tank of at least 60 liters capacity which has been planted with *Myriophyllum, Cabomba,* or some other fine-leaved plant. It is not necessary to watch the fish and remove them the minute they have finished spawning. They seldom touch their eggs. When a good amount of eggs can be seen hanging by little strings from the plants and the fish have lost interest in each other, the parents can be removed. The incubation period is seven to ten days. The fry are hardy.

MELANOTAENIA MACCULLOCHI

MELANOTAENIA SPLENDIDA

MELANOTAENIA SPLENDIDA (Peters)/*Pink-Tailed Australian Rainbow*
R: Queensland, Australia. **H**: Peaceful; a good community fish. **W**: Soft, slightly acid water preferred. Temperature 24 to 26°C. **S**: To 12 cm. **F**: Not a choosy eater; will take prepared as well as live or frozen foods.
Spawning will often occur on several consecutive mornings among the fine-leaved plants. The eggs attach to the plants with fine filamentous threads. The eggs hatch in eight to ten days depending upon the temperature, which should be about 25°C. The parents may be left in the breeding tank until the young hatch. It should be noted that the parents place the eggs in an area of the aquarium that is sheltered from the light.

MELANOTAENIA TRIFASCIATA

MELANOTAENIA TRIFASCIATA (Rendahl)/*Banded Rainbowfish*
R: Northern Australia. **H:** Generally peaceful with other fishes; but they set up a pecking order among themselves. **W:** Not too critical. A hardness of near 0 to 16°GH and a pH of 5-7.4 are adequate. The temperature can be between 21° and 25° C. Water changes are a must.
S: Attains a length of 11cm in the wild but only 7.5 cm or so in captiviy.
F: Will accept a wide variey of foods but live foods are of course preferred.
Rainbowfishes are starting to make a strong showing in the aquarium world these days as new and more colorful species are being imported from Australia and New Guinea. They are relatively easy to keep and breed. A 25-gallon tank is just about right for two to three males and twice as many females. The hardness of the water can be from near 0 to 16 dGH and the pH between 5 and 7.4 The temperature range should be between 21° and 25° C. The tank can be decorated with driftwood and plants but leave an open area in front to allow them freedom in swimming. Java moss makes a good spawning medium. A slight current is also beneficial. Frequent partial water changes are highly recommended.
The males will quarrel among themselves until they establish a pecking order. The brightest male will be the dominant fish. Rainbowfish are continuous spawners if kept in top condition with a good diet of live foods (mosquito larvae, *Daphnia*, whiteworms, etc.) and even frozen and flake foods offered frequently. The male courts the female with jerky swimming motions and trembling, the latter especially evident when spawning is near. The male tries to lure the female into the spawning area by back and forth swimming as if to show her where the site is located. At the site he remains in an oblique position (head down) and vibrates. A ready female will swim to a site she prefers and remains there until the male swims to her side. They press together with violent trembling and eggs are extruded like a cluster of grapes. They separate quickly and violently, the swirling motion scattering the eggs. The eggs settle down on the plants or even reach the bottom. They are adhesive (many threads) and there may be up to 200 in number.

MESONAUTA FESTIVUS (Heckel)/*Flag Cichlid*

R: Widely spread all over the central Amazon region. **H**: Fairly peaceful for a cichlid; small specimens make good community tank fish, but when they grow larger they should have their own tank. **W**: Conditions are not as important as the fact that the water should be clean and have an exceptionally high oxygen content. For this reason they should be given plenty of room. **S**: Up to 15 cm. **F**: Varied diet of living foods; will reluctantly eat dried foods.

No danger of confusion here with any of the other cichlid genera. The line that runs upward diagonally from the mouth to the tip of the dorsal fin identifies *Mesonauta* species without question. Differentiating between the sexes is another story; males are a bit larger, with longer fins, but a not fully developed male and a fully developed one could easily be mistaken for a pair, and the only way to be really sure is by comparing the genital papillae, or breeding tubes, when they are ready to spawn. The female's tube is much thicker than the male's.

METYNNIS MACULATUS

METYNNIS HYPSAUCHEN (Müller & Troschel)/*Plain Metynnis*

R: Amazon region; widely distributed. **H**: Peaceful; fond of swimming in schools. **W**: Must be kept in a large aquarium. Water should be 10 to 15° DH and slightly acid (pH 6.8). Temperature 24 to 26°C. **S**: Up to 15 cm. **F**: Will take and should get live or frozen foods, but the most important item is vegetable nourishment, such as lettuce leaves, etc.

A pair will swim through the plant thicket and cuddle against each other tetra-fashion, releasing as many as 2,000 eggs. These hatch in 70 hours at about 26°C, and the fry do not begin to swim freely until about a week later. They are easily raised on brine shrimp and finely chopped spinach.

MESONAUTA FESTIVUS

METYNNIS MACULATUS (Kner)/*Spotted Metynnis*

R: Guianas down to Rio Paraguay. **H**: Peaceful toward other fishes of comparable size; are happiest when kept in groups. **W**: Soft, slightly alkaline water is best. The tank should be roomy and afford some shelter. Temperature 22 to 24°C. **S**: To 18 cm; usually collected and sold at about 5 cm. **F**: Special attention must be given to their vegetable diet requirements by giving them lettuce and spinach leaves plus live foods.

The *Metynnis* species are related to the vicious piranhas, which are known and feared throughout most of tropical South America. Although there is a superficial similarity in body form, to an ichthyologist there is an immense difference in skull structure and in the digestive organs. The piranhas are of course strictly carnivores, while the *Metynnis* species are almost as strictly vegetarians.

METYNNIS HYPSAUCHEN

MICRALESTES ACUTIDENS (Peters)/*Sharp-Toothed Tetra*

R: Nigeria to Angola and the Zambezi basin. **H**: Peaceful and active fish that require adequate swimming room. **W**: Soft, slightly acid water that is clean and well aerated is best. Prefers warmth, about 26°C, but a drop to 23°C or so is tolerated. **S**: 6 cm maximum. **F**: Not critical; may be maintained on dried foods with only occasional feedings of live foods.

What the Sharp-Toothed Tetra lacks in bright colors it makes up for in good activity and good behavior; it minds its own business and bustles around without bothering the others. Don't let the name "Sharp Toothed" scare you. These teeth do no damage to other fishes or plants. Because the collectors have so many highly colored and therefore better-selling species to offer, we do not often get to see these lesser-colored fish, and to the best of our knowledge they have not yet been spawned in captivity.

MICROCTENOPOMA CONGICUM

MICROCTENOPOMA ANSORGEI (Boulenger)/*Ornate Ctenopoma*

R: Tropical West Africa. **H**: Peaceful when given plenty of space and kept with fishes of the same size or larger. **W**: Not critical, but the water must be kept warm, 25 to 29°C. **S**: To 7 cm. **F**: Large live foods, preferably small living fishes. Cut-up earthworms or pieces of beef heart are also taken greedily. **C**: Body brownish, with 6 to 7 bluish to greenish bars on the sides, extending into the dorsal and anal fins.

This species has been spawned in captivity. The male, distinguished by its brighter colors, is said to build a firm bubblenest. The young are easy to raise. This fish is a greedy eater and very fond of the larger live foods, especially small fishes. Their tank should be a roomy, well-planted one. It is interesting to watch a *Ctenopoma* stalk its prey. An unbelievably quick lunge, and the little fish is gone!

MICRALESTES ACUTIDENS

MICROCTENOPOMA CONGICUM (Boulenger)/*Congo Ctenopoma*
R: Lower Congo River. **H**: Fairly peaceful with larger fishes. Likes a large, well-planted tank/ **W**: Not critical, but temperature should be kept high, about 25°C. **S**: To 8 cm. **F**: Large live foods, small living fishes preferred. They can be trained to accept pieces of fish, shrimp, etc.
Microctenopoma congicum is said to be quite easy to spawn, although the feat is seldom attempted because of the small demand for this fish. The male chooses a dark corner of the tank, often a spot under a floating leaf. Here he builds a bubblenest. When this is completed he concentrates on getting the female to cooperate by getting under the nest. He wraps his body around her like a *Betta* and everything proceeds accordingly. Eggs hatch in 24 to 30 hours and the fry become free-swimming in 2 to 3 days.

MICROCTENOPOMA ANSORGEI

MICROGEOPHAGUS ALTISPINOSA Haseman/*Bolivian Butterfly Cichlid*

R: Rio Idamore Basin in northern Bolivia. **H:** Aggressive toward other species mainly during fry care. Occasional intraspecific quarrels occur without injury. **W:** Not important. Conditions in natural habitat are hardness 4 dGH, pH 7.6, and temperature 27°C. Water changes are recommended. **S:** Males 70mm; females 65mm. **F:** Will accept a variey of aquarium foods but live foods should be provided as often as possible.

Males normally have more pointed fins and are a bit more aggressive. They will court the females with spread fins, some trembling of the body, and even some tail beating. The female when not ready for spawning will spurn these advances and depart. When she is ready, however, she will answer his advances with similar behavior. The male may excavate several hollows in the gravel with or without the help of the female, and both sexes will thoroughly clean one of the flat stones. At this time the genital papillae are visible, the female's being the larger of the two. Spawning progresses in a normal fashion as the female makes several dry runs over the selected site. Eventually the first eggs appear and the male follows her to fertilize them. This is repeated again and again until about 500 pale amber colored eggs are deposited. The female tends the eggs, fanning them and removing any infertile or funguses ones if necessary.

MICROGLANIS POECILUS

MICROGEOPHAGUS RAMIREZI (Myers & Harry)/*Ram, Ramirez's Dwarf Cichlid, Butterfly Cichlid*

R: Rio Orinoco basin, Venezuela and Colombia. **H:** Timid, very peaceful. Should have their own well-planted, well-heated (27°C) aquarium. **W:** Aged water, slightly acid. Tank should be placed so that some sunlight falls in every day for several hours. Temperature 27-29°C. **S:** 5 to 5.5 cm; females only slightly smaller. **F:** Live foods, preferably enchytrae or tubifex worms. Dried foods are taken with hesitation.

Breeding this fish is not an impossible job. A pair that eats eggs and fry consistently should be separated from their eggs and artificial hatching resorted to if offspring are desired. A number of small stones should be provided, of which the parents choose one upon which to spawn. When spawning is over, the stone is lifted out very carefully and placed into a jar that is hung under the outlet tube of an outside filter. That is to say, the tube that returns the clean water to the aquarium. The clean, flowing water running over the eggs keeps them free of sediment and provides the same action the female gives when she fans them with her fins. The fry will hatch in 60 to 72 hours.

MICROGEOPHAGUS ALTISPINOSA

MICROGLANIS POECILUS Eigenmann/*Dwarf Marbled Catfish*
R: Brazil, Surinam, Guyana, and Venezuela. **H**: Peaceful and nocturnal; the tank in which they are kept should have a number of retreats where the fish can hide when the light is bright. **W**: Soft, slightly alkaline water is best. Temperature 24 to 26°C. **S**: To 7 cm. **F**: Live foods are preferred, especially worms; frozen foods are second choice, then dry foods.

The catfishes are a tremendous group. They include fishes that are downright ugly, some that are not quite as ugly but are kept strictly for utilitarian reasons, and others that are quite pretty. Some have no objection to a brightly lighted tank, but others will come out into the light only when there is food available and they are hungry enough to subjugate their fear and distaste for the light to come out of hiding and quickly gobble up as much food as they can get into their mouths before rushing back to shelter again.

MICROGEOPHAGUS RAMIREZI

MICROPHIS BRACHYURUS Bleeker/*Indian Freshwater Pipefish*

R: Widely distributed in Indo-Pacific. **H**: Peaceful with any fish that cannot be swallowed. **W**: Should have brackish water, although the salt can vary in concentration from light to heavy; tank should not be too heavily aerated. Temperature 24 to 29°C. **S**: About 20 cm. **F**: In the home aquarium, this fish will accept only newborn livebearers.

The odd trumpet-like mouth is very small at its opening, and the fish has difficulty in eating anything that is not small enough to be ingested whole. This complicates matters for the hobbyist who wants to keep this fish, and it has been found that specimens kept in aquaria will accept nothing but newborn livebearers, which it is quite expert at stalking and catching, despite the lack of speed. In its reproductive methods the pipefish is very odd, for the female lays her eggs in a pouch formed by folds in the abdomen of the male. The eggs hatch in a day and a half to two days.

MISGURNUS ANGUILLICAUDATUS

MIMAGONIATES MICROLEPIS (Steinbachner)/*Croaking Tetra*

R: Southeastern Brazil, Rio Grande do Sul. **H**: Peaceful and active; does not disturb plants. **W**: Should be kept in a roomy aquarium at a temperature slightly lower than most tropical species, 21 to 24°C. **S**: Males about 5.5cm; females about 4.5cm. **F**: Not a fussy eater; besides live foods, will also eat dried foods.

As the name implies, this fish has the power to make tiny croaking noises. These noises are made by getting a gulp of air at the surface of the water, then swimming below and releasing it. This is likened to the chirp of an insect by some. Something that has not yet been fully explained goes on when this fish breeds. There is an active driving beforehand, but then the female leaves the male and lays the eggs without any further contact with the male. Internal fertilization takes place.

MICROPHIS BRACHYURUS

MISGURNUS ANGUILLICAUDATUS (Cantor)/*Weatherfish*

R: Japan and northern China. **H**: Peaceful with other species. **W**: Water conditions are not too important, as long as extremes are avoided. Temperature 21 to 26°C. **S**: Up to 20 cm. **F**: Takes all regular aquarium foods, but living worms are preferred.

The name "Weatherfish" is derived from the fact that the fish are known to be sensitive to changes in barometric pressure, and their changes in motion during periods in which the barometric pressure changes sharply have given the fish the reputation for being able to forecast the weather accurately. Changes in activity accompanying a drop in pressure, signifying a storm, are especially noteworthy. In the home aquarium the fish are interesting for their habit of diving headfirst under the gravel, sometimes keeping the whole body completely out of sight, at other times keeping the head or part of the head above the level of the sand.

MIMAGONIATES MICROLEPIS

MOENKHAUSIA DICHROURA (Kner)/*Spot-Tailed Moenkhausia*

R: Guianas to Paraguay. **H**: Peaceful and active; tank should be covered, as this fish can jump. **W**: Soft, acid water preferred. Temperature 20 to 24°C. **S**: To 8 cm. **F**: A good eater that is not fussy as to food; should get some live or frozen foods, however.

This is a good fish to show someone who considers himself an authority on aquarium fishes and ask him to identify. Nine times out of ten he will give a careless glance and say it is *Rasbora trilineata*, a fish from the East Indies that is very familiar to hobbyists and has an almost identical pattern in the tail. Then it will be your turn to ask him if he ever saw a *Rasbora* with an adipose fin, which is sure to cause the "expert" to look again, this time more carefully. The author (HRA) was almost fooled the same way, but first asked where the fish came from. The dealer, who had a tankful and did not know what they were either, admitted that they came from South America and gave me a pair to get identified for him. They lasted in my tanks for several years with no special attention.

MOENKHAUSIA PITTIERI

MOENKHAUSIA OLIGOLEPIS (Günther)/*Glass Tetra*

R: Guyana and the upper Amazon region. **H**: Quite peaceful, but must not be kept with smaller fishes. **W**: Soft, slightly acid water and a large tank are required. Temperature 22 to 25°C. **S**: 11 cm, usually smaller. **F**: Must be fed generously with mostly live or frozen foods; if hungry they may nip plants.

Most people who buy this fish get young ones without realizing how they grow and grow until they find themselves with bigger fish than they had bargained for. *Moenkhausia oligolepis* is a hardy fish and asks little more than a large aquarium and plenty of food. There has been an albino form on the market that has a white body, pink fins, and red eyes. The Glass Tetra has been accused of being a plant-eater, and rightly so. However, an examination of the intestines discloses the fact that they are short, which is not at all typical of a fish that normally lives on vegetable diet.

MOENKHAUSIA DICHROURA

MOENKHAUSIA PITTIERI Eigenmann/*Diamond Tetra*
R: Environs of Lake Valencia, Venezuela. **H**: Peaceful and very active. **W**: Large, well-planted tanks are best. Temperature 24 to 27°C. **S**: To 6 cm. **F**: A good eater that will take practically any kind of food but should have a supplement of vegetable matter, like lettuce leaves. **C**: Body color yellowish, darker above; upper half of body gleams golden, the lower part iridescent; unpaired fins milky violet.

This is an extremely hardy and long-lived fish, and once established in a tank that suits them they will live for a long time. They are also easy to spawn but are by no means an "easy" species. Eggs are laid among bushy plants in a manner similar to the large tetras. The young hatch in 48 to 60 hours. After the yolk-sac is absorbed they are very easy to raise.

MOENKHAUSIA OLIGOLEPIS

MOENKHAUSIA SANCTAEFILOMENAE (Steindachner)/*Yellow-Banded Moenkhausia*

R: Paraguay Basin. **H**: Peaceful toward other fishes and very active. **W**: Not critical, but slightly acid, soft water is preferred. Temperature 24 to 26°C. **S**: To 7 cm. **F**: Omnivorous, with a good appetite; if fed with a good amount of vegetable substances, it will not nibble plants to any great extent.

Spawning is quite simple: a pair, where the male is active and the female has become heavy with eggs, is placed in an aquarium that is clean and has several plant thickets. The temperature should be brought to 27°C, when the male will soon be observed chasing the female. Eggs are laid among plant thickets. The pair should be removed as soon as they lose interest in each other and begin searching for eggs. Hatching takes a day or two, depending on temperature and other conditions.

MONOCIRRHUS POLYACANTHUS

MOGURNDA MOGURNDA (Richardson)/*Purple-Striped Gudgeon*

R: Eastern and northern coastal Australia. **H**: Should be kept with its own kind or larger fishes that can take care of themselves, or it may bully its tankmates. **W**: Alkaline water with a slight addition of salt is best. Temperature 22 to 26°C. **S**: 10 cm. **F**: Should get a preponderance of live or frozen foods.

They spawn quite willingly on rocks and the glass sides of the aquarium. The male takes charge of the eggs and keeps fanning them thoroughly for about a week, at which time they begin to hatch. It is best to remove him at this time and leave the fry to fend for themselves.

MOENKHAUSIA SANCTAEFILOMENAE

MONOCIRRHUS POLYACANTHUS Heckel/*Leaf Fish*

R: Tropical South America; Amazon, Rio Negro, Guianas. **H**: Occurs in sluggish streams, where it feeds on smaller fishes and aquatic insects; peaceful in the aquarium toward anything it cannot swallow. **W**: Soft, slightly acid water. Temperature about 26°C. **S**: Up to 10 cm. **F**: Small ones may be fed with the usual live foods; larger ones must get living small fishes.

The Leaf Fish will consider it beneath its dignity to forage for food and prefers to stalk it. A supply of small expendable fishes must therefore always be on hand. Some hobbyists who are possessed of infinite patience and have a great deal of time at their disposal find that it is sometimes possible to tame Leaf Fish and get them to swallow a strip of cut fish by dangling it in front of them. They breed easily and lay sticky eggs under a leaf.

MOGURNDA MOGURNDA

459

MONODACTYLUS ARGENTEUS (Linnaeus)/*Mono*

R: Coastal waters from eastern Africa to Fiji. **H**: Shy and often gets panicky when frightened; best kept in a small group in a roomy tank. **W**: Slightly alkaline water with about a quarter teaspoon of salt to each liter is acceptable. Temperature 23 to 25°C. **S**: Wild specimens attain 23 cm; seldom exceed half of that in captivity. **F**: All sorts of live foods. **C**: Body silvery, with a golden sheen above; two black vertical bars, one through the eye and the other through the pectoral base.

Many fishes like this never attain sexual maturity in captivity under any conditions, even in a marine aquarium. We still have a great deal to learn about the spawning rhythms of many of our aquarium fishes and what triggers them. This is what adds zest to the aquarium hobby and makes it possible for an informed amateur to lend a hand to the ichthyological experts by making his findings known. The Mono is a good fish to keep with others that have the same requirements as to a slight salinity in the water, such as mollies.

MONODACTYLUS ARGENTEUS

MONODACTYLUS SEBAE (Cuvier)/*Fingerfish*

R: Tropical West Africa coast. **H**: Shy; should be kept in a very large, well-planted tank. **W**: Alkaline water with some salt added, about a quarter teaspoon for each liter. Temperature 24 to 27°C. **S**: Wild, fully grown specimens up to 20 cm. **F**: All sorts of live foods.

The overall length of grown specimens is given as 20 cm, and the body is one-third higher than it is long, resulting in a fish that is almost 28 cm high! A fairly active fish with these dimensions, it may be readily imagined, would require lots of "fin room." This rare beauty is a showpiece of public aquaria, which would be best equipped to handle them.

MORMYROPS ENGYSTOMA Boulenger/*Torpedo Mormyrid*

R: Lower Zaire River. **H**: Should not be kept with smaller fishes that it could swallow; usually peaceful with larger fishes. **W**: Neutral to slightly acid water. Temperature 24 to 26°C. Tank should be well planted and partly shaded. **S**: to 35 cm. **F**: Tubifex or small earthworms are the preferred foods.

Scientists are particularly interested in the mormyrid group. They have come to the amazing conclusion that the brain of these fishes, when weighed and compared to the weight of the rest of the body, is larger in proportion than that of a human being. Most of the mormyrids are night-feeders and are endowed with a keen sense of smell. The majority of them have tiny mouths with which they sift out worms, crustaceans, and molluscs from the bottom mud.

MYLOSSOMA DURIVENTRE

MYLEUS RUBRIPINNIS (Müller & Troschel)/*Redhook Metynnis*

R: Guyana and Surinam to Brazil. **H**: Peaceful and shy if kept by itself, but less so if kept in small groups; cannot be safely kept with vegetation because of their plant-eating tendencies. **W**: Clean, soft, and highly oxygenated water is necessary. Temperature (at least for breeding) should be about 25 to 27°C. **S**: Matures at about 9 to 12 cm; maximum size not known. **F**: Takes a variety of foods, but their diet must contain vegetable matter.

Actual spawning consists of the male coming close to the female, almost appearing to wrap his anal fin around her. The eggs are scattered over the bottom during a period of about three to six hours. After that time there may be as many as 300 to 500 pale yellowish eggs some 1.8-2.2 mm in diameter covering the floor of the tank. At this time the eggs should be removed as there is evidently no parental care whatsoever.

MORMYROPS ENGYSTOMA

MYLOSSOMA DURIVENTRE (Cuvier)/*Hard-Bellied Characin*

R: Southern Amazon region, Paraguay, Paraná, La Plata. **H**: Peaceful toward other fishes, but larger specimens are likely to damage plants. **W**: Soft, slightly acid water in a well-planted tank. Temperature 24 to 28° C. **S**: To 23 cm in their natural waters; imported specimens much smaller. **F**: All kinds of live and frozen foods, supplemented with some vegetagle substances like chopped spinach, etc.

Like the *Metynnis* species, the larger ones (8 cm and up) are likely to destroy plants, which is about the only thing that can be said against them. There are no recognizable sexual differences given in the reference works; probably if they ever show up we would see them only in grown specimens.

MYLEUS RUBRIPINNIS

463

MYSTUS MICRACANTHUS

MYSTUS MICRACANTHUS (Bleeker)/Two-Spot Catfish

R: Southeast Asia from Thailand to the islands of Sumatra, Java and Borneo. **H:** Generally peaceful, especially when young. Active swimmer although shy in the presence of bright light. **W:** Not critical as long as extremes are avoided, but seems to prefer slightly acid water. Temperature 24 to 28°C. **S:** Reaches a length of about 15 cm. **F:** Will eat a wide variety of aquarium foods that sink to the bottom.

Few species of the genus *Mystus* are generally available to aquarists. Until recently only two, *M. tengara* and *M. vittatus,* were seen on a regular basis. Now a third species, *M. micracanthus,* has made its debut. It is not striped like the other two, but has the characteristic black spot just behind the head at the start of the lateral line.

Keeping *Mystus micracanthus* is not difficult. The aquarium should be provided with a number of sheltered areas such as caves or bushy plants where this fish can retire when frightened. When first placed in the tank *Mystus micracanthus* will hide a lot (especially if the light is bright), but this will pass as it gets used to the new surroundings and new owner. The water conditions are not critical but extremes should be avoided. It is said to prefer slightly acid water that is not too hard and rather warm temperatures of 24 to 28°C. Feeding these catfishes does not present a problem as they will accept almost any foods suitable for aquarium fishes. Be sure that the foods sink to the bottom where they can be reached or that other fishes do not eat everything up before it can reach the bottom. The preferred morsels seem to be various types of worms.

Nothing is known about the breeding habits of this species. This species has been listed under other genera such as *Bagrus, Hypselobagrus* and *Macrones,* this last name being the only one still used in some literature.

MYSTUS VITTATUS

MYSTUS VITTATUS (Bloch)/*Striped Catfish*

R: India, Burma, Thailand and Sri Lanka. **H:** A peaceful, active catfish. Tends to be shy at first in bright light. **W:** Can be kept in a wide variety of water conditions but seems to prefer slightly acid, soft water. Temperatures 24 to 28°C. **S:** Reaches a length of 21 cm. **F:** Will take most aquarium foods offered if they sink to the bottom. Prefers worms.

Mystus vittatus and *M. tengara* are often confused because of the similar color pattern and, indeed, it is very difficult to distinguish them. The Striped Catfish grows to a larger size than *M. tengara* (21 cm as opposed to l0 cm), has a median groove on the skull that does not reach the occipital protrusion in *M. tengara* it does), and has a greater number of teeth along tne inner edge of the pectoral fin spines (16 in contrast to 8-l0 in *M. tengara)*. It is quite possible that the differences are not great enough to warrant keeping these fishes as separate species and that when further studies are made *M. tengara* would be considered a synonym or a subspecies of *M. vittatus*.

The Striped Catfish is not difficult to keep. It is quite tolerant of most aquarium conditions although it is said to prefer slightly acid (pH of about 6.5), soft water. The tank should be well planted and provided with sheltered areas such as rock caves, driftwood, etc. At first the Striped Catfish will be quite shy and stay in these caves, especially during the day or when there is bright light. However, with proper care and few disturbances your fish will eventually spend more time out in the open. It will actively search for food along the bottom as most catfishes do, stirring up the debris or mulm wherever it goes. It will feed on whatever food particles it finds there but prefers chironomid larvae (blood worms) and worms of different sorts. Because of the large size it eventually attains, a correspondingly large tank must be provided. Also, although the aquarium-sized individuals are peaceful, large adults may cause problems.

This species is expected to spawn in a manner in which the eggs are laid on the bottom among the debris or plants. The spawning involves a lively circling courtship during which audible "squeaks" are heard. The eggs are comparatively large and yellowish white in color. Rearing the fry has not been reported.

NANDUS NANDUS (Hamilton-Buchanan)/*Nandus*

R: India, Burma, and Thailand. **H**: A voracious species that will eat any fish up to three-fourths of its own size. **W**: Soft, acid water is optional. Temperature 22 to 26°C. **S**: Up to 20 cm. **F**: Live fishes; some can be trained to take worms and beef.

Nandus nandus is best kept in a dimly lighted aquarium with plenty of plants and rockwork. This will help to overcome the fish's great shyness. It is difficult to select tankmates that are neither so small that they will be eaten nor so large that they might take advantage of the ' retiring nature of *Nandus*.

NANNAETHIOPS UNITAENIATUS

NANNACARA ANOMALA Regan/*Golden Dwarf Cichlid*

R: Northern South America. **H**: Peaceful and shy except when guarding young. **W**: Neutral to slightly alkaline. Temperature 23 to 26°C. **S**: Males to 8 cm; females to 5 cm. **F**: Prefers live foods but can be trained to take ground beef heart.

Nannacara anomala is the perfect answer for the hobbyist who wants to observe the family life of cichlids and does not have the large tank which would be required to spawn one of the larger kinds. A 20-liter tank is ample for the purpose, and it does not tkae long to get a pair ready.

A week's feeding with a variety of live foods is generally all that is needed to get a healthy female almost bursting with eggs and an equally healthy male to put on his brightest colors. A flowerpot laid on its side is often a preferred spot, but the male may pick out a rock or clean off the glass in a corner of the tank. Fifty to seventy-five eggs is an average spawning, and it may happen that the pair will share the duties of caring for the eggs and young.

NANDUS NANDUS

NANNAETHIOPS UNITAENIATUS Günther/*One-Lined African Tetra*
R: Equatorial Africa. **H**: Peaceful; a good community fish that does not bother plants. **W**: Soft and slightly acid. Requires some warmth, about 24 to 26°C. **S**: Males 5 to 6 cm; females slightly smaller. **F**: Live foods preferred, but will take dry foods.

Females may be distinguished by their deeper body and duller colors, while males have a more pronounced horizontal stripe and a wider dark marking in the first dorsal fin rays. Eggs are scattered all over the plants and bottom. They hatch in 40 to 50 hours, and the tiny young begin to swim in about five days. An infusoria culture is a necessity for the first few days, but once they have survived this stage and are able to handle newly hatched brine shrimp the battle is won and the fish grow well from then on.

NANNACARA ANOMALA

NANNOSTOMUS BECKFORDI Günther/*Beckford's Pencilfish*

R: Guianas, Paraná, Rio Negro, middle and lower Amazon. **H**: Peaceful toward other fishes and plants; should be kept in a group of their own kind or other related species. **W**: Prefers soft, slightly acid water but is not intolerant to other types. Temperature 24 to 27°C. **S**: To 5 cm. **F**: Prefers smaller living foods, but can be accustomed to taking frozen or dried foods when the others are not available.

This species is fairly easy to breed, but the young in their first stages are difficult to feed because of the tiny mouths. For this reason most of the pencilfishes sold are still imported. In their native waters there are large schools to be found in the backwater streams, and collecting them is a very simple matter. As with most wild-caught fishes, the colors are unbelievably brilliant and lovely, and it is hard to believe that the comparatively pale fish one brings home and puts into the aquarium can recapture their natural finery, but they do under proper conditions.

NANNOSTOMUS EQUES

NANNOSTOMUS BIFASCIATUS Hoedeman/*Two-Striped Pencilfish*

R: Guyana, Surinam, French Guiana. **H**: Peaceful toward other fishes and plants. **W**: Soft, slightly acid water. Temperature 24 to 27°C. **S**: About 5 cm. **F**: Small live foods are preferred, but frozen and dried foods are also accepted. **C**: Body brown with two dark stripes, one from the top of the eye to the upper caudal base and another from the snout to the lower caudal base.

In Guyana thousands of pencilfishes are collected in the small, almost dried-out streams that meander across the savannahs in the Rupununi District. Many of the streams are shaded by palms, and the water is slightly brown from decaying vegetation. There must be multitudes of tiny infusoria in these waters when the egg hatch, and it would be very interesting and helpful to science in general and the hobby in particular to know just what these organisms are and the exact chemical composition of the water in which they thrive.

NANNOSTOMUS BECKFORDI

NANNOSTOMUS EQUES Steindachner/*Brown-Tailed Pencilfish*
R: Guyana and Orinoco to lower Amazon. **H**: Peaceful; swims with the head tilted upward, and prefers to swim in schools. **W**: Soft, neutral to slightly acid water. Temperature 24 to 27°C. **S**: To 5 cm. **F**: Most foods are taken from or near the surfaces; mosquito larvae are particularly relished by mature fishes.
This fish feeds on insects in the upper water layers or on the water's surface, but it will take most aquarium foods while in captivity. Males of this species are much slimmer than the females and are also more colorful. This fish prefers to breed on *Ludwigia* or *Hygrophila* leaves and is not difficult to spawn in an aquarium.

NANNOSTOMUS BIFASCIATUS

NANNOSTOMUS ESPEI (Meinken)/*Barred Pencilfish*

R: Guyana. **H**: Peaceful and active; a skilled jumper whose tank should be covered. **W**: Soft water, neutral to slightly acid. Temperature 24 to 27°C. **S**: To 5 cm. **F**: Not choosy as to foods, but very partial to live daphnia.

Barred Pencilfish are active and like to swim in small groups. Both sexes show a similarity of finnage, but the deeper body and more irregular markings of the female make it easily recognizable. They spawn in bushy plants like most of the other pencilfishes.

NANNOSTOMUS MARGINATUS

NANNOSTOMUS HARRISONI Eigenmann/*Harrison's Pencilfish*

R: Guyana and the upper Amazon. **H**: Peaceful, a good community tank fish. **W**: Aged water that is slightly acid, hardness less than 10°DH and a temperature of 24° to 27°C. are recommended. **S**: Attains a length of about 5 to 6.5 cm. **F**: Small live foods preferred but will eventually accept flake foods.

Several individuals are best kept together in the community tank. For spawning a separate small tank can be set up with well-aged water that has been filtered through peat for a short time. Bushy plants such as *Myriophyllum* should be added and the light reduced somewhat. The pairs are placed in the spawning tank in the evening, and with luck the spawning will take place the following morning. *N. harrisoni* spawns among the plants, depositing up to 100 eggs. If the plants are thick enough the eggs will be hidden from the parents, who just might be tempted to eat them. The eggs hatch in about a day and the fry drop to the bottom. In a day or two they may be seen hanging from the plants or side of the aquarium, and by the end of 4 or 5 days they are free-swimming. The parents should be removed immediately after spawning. The fry can be fed the small-sized newly hatched brine shrimp or infusoria at first, with items added as soon as they can be handled by the young fishes. Growth is relatively slow. The males are generally more slender than the females.

NANNOSTOMUS ESPEI

NANNOSTOMUS MARGINATUS Eigenmann/*Dwarf Pencilfish*

R: Guyana to Colombia and the lower Amazon. **H**: Very peaceful; an excellent community fish. **W**: Neutral to slightly acid; requires heat, about 26°C. **S**: Maximum about 3 cm. **F**: Prefers small live foods, but will take dry food if necessary.

Sexes are not easy to distinguish, except for the female's slightly heavier body and a little more red in the dorsal and anal fins of the male. Breeding them is made difficult because of the fact that the parent fish are very quick to eat their own eggs. These eggs have very little adhesive power and most of them fall to the bottom. A bed of glass rods, which lets the eggs through and holds back the parents, can be used with success here. The young are very small when they hatch, which makes them difficult to feed.

NANNOSTOMUS HARRISONI

NANNOSTOMUS TRIFASCIATUS Steindachner/*Three-Lined Pencilfish*

R: Upper Amazon region. **H**: Peaceful toward other fishes and plants; should not be kept with active fishes. **W**: Soft, slightly acid water that has been run through peat moss. Temperature 24 to 27°C. **S**: To 6 cm. **F**: Small live foods are best, with frozen or dried foods given only when living foods are not available.

Most hobbyists who keep pencilfishes consider *Nannostomus trifasciatus* the beauty of the group and are usually unanimous in expressing the opinion that this species is the most difficult to spawn. Strangely enough, in its habitat in Guyana this was the most common species everywhere we (HRA and the T.F.H. expedition) fished. The usual catch was about as many *Nannostomus trifasciatus* as all the rest of the *Nannostomus* species put together. Our best catch was made in a little stream in the vicinity of Lethem, near the Brazilian border. The stream was no more than hip-deep in most places, but the variety of characins caught there was no less than amazing. We even caught some piranhas in this little stream, which was seldom more than 30 m wide, scarcely enough to call it a creek. *Nannostomus trifasciatus* is one of the larger pencilfishes, attaining a length of 6 cm. It is happiest in a sunny tank with a number of its own kind.

NANOCHROMIS DIMIDIATUS

NANNOSTOMUS UNIFASCIATUS Steindachner/*One-Lined Pencilfish*

R: Middle and lower Amazon tributaries, Rio Negro, Guyana, Orinoco. **H**: Peaceful and somewhat timid; prefer to be kept in a small group. **W**: Soft, slightly acid water. Temperature 23 to 26°C. **S**: To 6 cm. **F**: Live and prepared foods of small size, preferably food that will remain at or near the surface.

The One-Lined Pencilfish has been known to science since being named by Steindachner in 1876, yet we see them so seldom that many works do not even list them. This species is an attractive aquarium fish that is easy to keep and not difficult to breed. Males have an anal fin that is rounded below and brilliantly colored, while the females have an anal fin that is straight. This species should be kept in a well-planted aquarium with soft, well-aged, acidic water.

NANNOSTOMUS TRIFASCIATUS

NANOCHROMIS DIMIDIATUS (Boulenger)/*Dimidiatus*

R: Zaire basin. **H**: Usually very peaceful in the community aquarium. **W**: Soft, slightly acid water. Temperature 24 to 26°C. **S**: Males 9 cm; females 6 cm. **F**: All sorts of live foods, preferably those which sink to the bottom; frozen foods also accepted. **C**: Body dusky with a purplish sheen; horizontal dark line may be present; back part of dorsal fin and top of caudal fin bright red.

This cichlid will breed readily if given the proper conditions and a tank of its own. *N. dimidiatus* prefers to spawn on the sloping face of a flowerpot. After spawning, the female cares for the eggs and later the brood. The eggs hatch in about three days and the fry are free-swimming in an additional three to four days.

NANNOSTOMUS UNIFASCIATUS

NANOCHROMIS PARILUS (Boulenger)/*Congo Dwarf Cichlid*
R: Zaire basin. **H**: Apt to be a bit quarrelsome at times; best kept by themselves. **W**: Soft, slightly acid water is best. Temperature 24 to 26°C. **S**: Up to 8 cm for males; females about 2 cm smaller. **F**: Live foods of all kinds; at times when none is available, frozen foods may be provided temporarily. **C**: Sides of body blue, belly bright green; dorsal fin is orange to white with a black edge and a white stripe; upper half of tail striped.

Females are a docile lot and submit meekly to the advances of the males when they are ready to spawn. When the male has finished his duties of fertilizing the eggs, the erstwhile meek little female turns into a tigress and gives the male a severe drubbing every time he gets anywhere near the eggs. For his safety he should be removed at this time and put into another tank while the female guards the eggs and fry.

NEMATOBRYCON LACORTEI

NEETROPLUS NEMATOPUS Günther/*Little Lake Cichlid*
R: Nicaragua (the Great Lakes) and Costa Rica. **H**: Generally peaceful except when spawning; a territorial species. **W**: Prefers hard alkaline water to which some salt has been added. Temperature not critical, but should have sufficient aeration. **S**: Reaches a standard length of just over 9 cm. **F**: Will take any normal aquarium foods.

Neetroplus nematopus is expected to be a very popular aquarium cichlid by virtue of its interesting habits and engaging personality. It is relatively hardy (although it needs adequate aeration), easily fed (will take any of the normal aquarium foods), and easily bred. Unfortunately, its dependence on adequate oxygen makes it difficult to ship so that its availability will be limited until better shipping methods or domestic breeding can supply the demand. About 50 to 250 or more reddish or wine-colored adhesive eggs are laid in a protected spot in the territory (often the roof of a cave) that can be readily defended. The small (under 2 mm) oval eggs hatch in about one to one and a half days at 26 to 29°C. In another four to five days the fry are free-swimming. Both eggs and fry are aggressively defended by both parents.

NANOCHROMIS PARILUS

NEMATOBRYCON LACORTEI Weitzman & Fink/*Rainbow Tetra*

R: San Juan basin, Colombia. **H**: Peaceful; inclined to be a bit shy. **W**: Soft, slightly acid water is best. Temperature 24 to 27°C. **S**: To 5 cm. **F**: Live foods are best, but the fish can be trained to accept frozen and dried foods.

There are two *Nematobrycon* species: *N. palmeri* and *N. lacortei*. *N. lacortei* was known for a time as *N. amphiloxus*. Weitzman and Fink found that the type specimens of *N. amphiloxus* were in fact a variety of *N. palmeri*. Regardless of how they're named, both fish are colorful and innoffensive additions to an aquarium.

N. lacortei and *N. palmeri* are geographically isolated in nature but will hybridize in the aquarium. They spawn like most tetras, laying their eggs in bushy plants.

NEETROPLUS NEMATOPUS

NEMATOBRYCON PALMERI Eigenmann/*Emperor Tetra*

R: San Juan basin and Atrato Rivers, Colombia. **H**: Peaceful and a bit shy; inclined to remain singly or in pairs rather than forming a school. **W**: Clean, soft, slightly acid water is best. Temperature 23 to 25°C. **S**: To 5 cm. **F**: Excellent appetite; will accept dried or frozen foods, but of course live foods are preferred.

They spawn like most tetras, laying their eggs in bushy plants. Some breeders prefer to use spawning mops or bundles of fine nylon filaments, both of which are readily accepted and more practical to use than the usual bundles of *Myriophyllum* or other bushy plants.

NEOLEBIAS ANSORGEI

NEOCERATODUS FORSTERI (Kreffty) *Australian or Queensland Lungfish*

R: Mary and Burnett Rivers, Queensland, Australia. Introduced into other freshwater streams in southern Queensland. **H:** A sluggish, peaceful fish. Only small individuals are suitable for aquaria as they soon outgrow all but the largest tanks. **W:** Not critical. Has the ability to utilize atmospheric air if conditions become too foul. **S:** Attains a length of 1.7 meters (5.6 feet) or more and a weight of 50-60 kilograms (to more than 130 pounds). **F:** Essentially carnivorous, but plant material is also a part of its diet.

Spawning is accomplished from about August to October (early spring in Australia) at night in shallow water (up to about a meter in depth). Yabba Creek, a tributary of the Mary River, has such shallow places that are ideal spawning sites where eggs can be found at the right time of the year. The bottom is sandy or gravelly and the water is reasonably clear. Spawning behavior initially involves the roaming about an area by a pair of fish apparently searching for a suitable spawning site. Then a "follow the leader" situation develops where the trailing individual nudges the flanks of the other. The leading fish, apparently the female, eventually dives through the surrounding plants, the male immediately following and fertilizing the eggs as they are shed. The eggs are said to resemble small, transparent grapes and are frequently found attached to floating stands of water hyacinth.

NEMATOBRYCON PALMERI

NEOLEBIAS ANSORGEI Boulenger/*Ansorge's Neolebias*
R: Cameroon to lower Zaire basin. **H**: Peaceful and very shy in a community tank; should be kept by themselves. **W**: Sensitive to hard, alkaline water; water must be well-aged and should never undergo great changes. Temperature 24 to 28°C. **S**: To 4 cm. **F**: Small live foods only. The unique square dorsal fin looks like nothing one would find on a tetra. The fish is sensitive to water changes and hard water. They breed readily, but the fry are difficult to raise. Eggs are laid in plant thickets and hatch in 20 to 24 hours. The tiny fry have small mouths and must at first be given very fine infusoria.

NEOCERATODUS FORSTERI

NEOLEBIAS TREWAVASAE Poll & Gosse/*Trewavas's Neolebias*

R: Nile to lower Zaire River. **H**: Peaceful and very shy in a community tank; should be kept by themselves. **W**: Sensitive to hard, alkaline water; water must be well aged and the aquarium should never undergo large percentage water changes. Temperature 22 to 28°C. **S**: To 5 cm. **F**: Small live foods only, of a size comparable to a newly hatched brine shrimp.

Neolebias trewavasae is a micropredator that lives on small animals found on the river bottom or among the plants. During breeding time, the temperature should be raised to 30°C. This species breeds among the plants, depositing batches of a dozen eggs at a time. Three hundred or more eggs can be laid. The fry hatch in about one day.

NEMACHEILUS FASCIATUS

NEOLEBIAS TRILINEATUS Boulenger/*Three-Lined Neolebias*

R: Congo basin. **H**: Peaceful and shy. **W**: Not very critical, but best is slightly acid and soft water. Temperature 23 to 26°C. **S**: To 4 cm. **F**: Live and frozen foods greatly preferred, but when not available dry foods can be given for a time. **C**: Back brown, sides silvery with three dark horizontal stripes, fins are reddish.

The African continent is notoriously stingy toward the aquarium hobbyist when it comes to producing tetras. Most of the characins from Africa have some drawback: they become too big for the average home aquarium, they gobble up the plants, they cannot get along with other fishes, they cannot be induced to spawn, etc., etc. The *Neolebias* species are a notable exception. *Neolebias trilineatus* is a small peaceful fish which usually will not bother plants and can easily gotton to spawn. *N. trilineatus* should be placed in a fairly large aquarium which gets a good amount of sunlight and is not very heavily planted. Best temperatures range from 23° to 26°C. The reason for the fairly large aquarium is that sometimes spawns are surprisingly large.

Eggs are scattered among plants and sometimes all over the bottom. At 25°C the fry hatch in 26 to 32 hours, and in five days they become free-swimming. This is a fish that seldom shows its best colors unless conditions are ideal. The lower half of the body should show a pink flush. Males are distinguished by their reddish fins and slightly higher dorsal fins.

NEOLEBIAS TREWAVASAE

NEMACHEILUS FASCIATUS (Valenciennes)/*Barred Loach*

R: Sumatra, Java, Borneo. **H**: Best given a tank of their own; chooses and defends its own territories. **W**: Soft, slightly acid water. Temperature 24 to 26°C. **S**: To 9 cm. **F**: Likes worms and other live foods, but not a fussy eater.

Although it has an elongated body and markings like our old friend the Kuhli Loach, plus a set of barbels, the similarity between the two fishes ends right there. *Nemacheilus fasciatus* does not have the snaky, eel-like motions of the Kuhli Loach and has a more useful-looking and more nicely shaped set of fins. It carries itself more like a fish than like a large worm or small snake.

NEOLEBIAS TRILINEATUS

NOMORHAMPHUS CELEBENSIS Weber & de Beaufort/*Celebes Halfbeak*

R: Celebes, Indonesia. **H**: Generally peaceful but will eat fishes small enough to swallow; should probably be kept by themselves. **W**: On the hard side with a pH of 7.0 or higher; regular water changes are recommended. Temperature should be around 23 to 28°C. **S**: May reach 10 cm. **F**: Must have live foods such as Guppies or brine shrimp.

In *Nomorhamphus* the eggs are fertilized in the ovary but only partially develop there. The still undeveloped young are released into a uterus where the egg capsules are resorbed. The developing young absorb a nutrient (secreted by the uterus walls) through their body surfaces at first but later only through the mouth opening. Six to eight young may develop in each uterus at one time (never more than sixteen total) and after they are born are replaced by more eggs, which were developing in the ovary during this time.

NOTHOBRANCHIUS FURZERI

NOTESTHES ROBUSTA (Gunther)/*Bullrout*

R: Queensland and New South Wales, Australia. **H**: A bottom-dwelling species that should not be kept with fishes it can swallow. **W**: Tolerant of a wide range of water conditions. Will even live in brackish water. **S**: Attains a length of about 30 cm, but more commonly is 15 to 20 cm long. **F**: Will accept many different foods, including small shrimp, worms, and fishes.

The Bullrout is a scorpionfish, and as such one would expect it to be strictly a marine fish. Yet this one is found in freshwater streams along the Australian eastern seaboard. Although they do not go much beyond the limits of brackish water, when there are spells of heavy rains they may extend downstream into estuaries.

Larger Bullrouts are said to be quite good eating and are caught by line fishermen as well as in commercial fishing nets. The fishermen have learned to be very careful when handling the Bullrout as the dorsal spines are just as poisonous as those of some of their marine relatives. In addition, there are spines on the head that one must be careful of. Even when the fish is dead the spines are still capable of inflicting a painful wound on the careless handler.

The Bullrout eats a fairly wide variety of meaty foods such as worms, small crayfishes, small fishes, and freshwater shrimp. Therefore, feeding them in an aquarium should pose no special problems. Remember that they have a fairly large mouth and can and will swallow small fishes that are placed in the same tank.

In nature the mottled or variegated color pattern of the Bullrout makes it very difficult to detect when an individual is sitting quietly on the bottom among the water plants in its habitat.

NOMORHAMPHUS CELEBENSIS

NOTHOBRANCHIUS FURZERI Jubb/*Furzer's Notho*

R: Guluene River, Zimbabwe (near the Zimbabwe-Mozambique border). **H:** An annual species that should be kept in a tank of its own. Active; sometimes males are aggressive toward their tankmates. **W:** Best results are obtained with hard, alkaline water. Temperature range 22°C to 26°C. **S:** Males attain a length of about 5 cm, females about 4 cm. **F:** Prefers live foods but will accept frozen foods with a little coaxing.

Spawning is accomplished over peat moss after much active chasing and driving. The peat moss should be removed periodically (every six or seven days), dried, and stored in the usual plastic bags for a period of five and a half to six months before the first wetting. Hatching may not occur at the first wetting, so the peat should be redried and wetting should be tried again in about a month. Even when hatching starts, you might have to give the fry a little assist with the egg shells. The fry are relatively large and can take newly hatched brine shrimp immediately. They grow very rapidly and may have one of the fastest growth rates of all of the killifishes. Sexes can be determined in about four weeks, and in another week or two they are ready to start spawning.

NOTESTHES ROBUSTA

NOTHOBRANCHIUS GUENTHERI (Pfeffer)/*Günther's Notho*

R: East Africa. **H**: Somewhat pugnacious; should be kept in pairs in their own tank. **W**: Water should be soft and slightly acid. Temperature 24 to 26°C. **S**: To 6 cm. **F**: Live foods only.

These fishes make their home in shallow pools that are well filled in the rainy months and then become gradually smaller and shallower as the dry season progresses, finally drying out altogether. In order to reproduce itself through this dry season a fish must either be equipped to breathe atmospheric air and to go into a period of estivation through the dry, hot months, or it must die and be survived by eggs that can live through the dry season. The former is done by several of the lungfishes and the latter is accomplished by several "annual" fishes, of which this is one.

NOTHOBRANCHIUS JUBBI Wildekamp & Berkenkamp/*Blue Notho*

R: Temporary pools along the coastal road from Malindi to Garsen, Kenya. **H:** Annual species. Should be kept in a tank of their own. Males are aggressive toward females, so shelter areas should be provided. **W:** Tolerates a wide variety of water conditions but does best in soft, slightly acid water to which some salt has been added. Temperature range 20-23°C. **S:** Males attain a length of about 7.5 cm, females only 5 cm. **F:** Prefers live foods but will accept frozen foods with some coaxing.

This fish was known under the incorrect name of *Nothobranchius neumanni* for a long time, but it was eventually recognized as being different from the true *N. neumanni* and was often referred to as *N.* sp. aff. *neumanni*. In 1979 it was finally described as *Nothobranchius jubbi* by Wildekamp & Berkenkamp. The common name Blue Notho has been used almost throughout its history and seems to be more stable than the scientific name.

The Blue Notho is one of the largest species in the genus, attaining a length of about 7.5 cm in males, though females are smaller, reaching a length of only 5 cm. It is relatively easy to keep and breed in a 20-liter tank that has been provided with a 5-cm bottom layer of peat moss or sand. The water conditions are not critical, but best results are obtained with soft, slightly acid water to which a teaspoon of salt per four liters (as a preventative against velvet) has been added. Be sure there is adequate aeration, and a 25% water change each week is recommended. Feeding is not difficult. Live foods such as brine shrimp, bloodworms, and whiteworms are preferred, but Blue Nothos will eventually accept frozen foods as well. Remember to feed enough, for the energy requirements of the annuals are quite high. Poorly fed individuals will decline very rapidly.

Males are generally rough on the females when spawning, so either arrange some hiding places for the females in the breeding tank or condition them separately, placing them together in the spawning tank only for a few hours. A close-fitting cover is also recommended to prevent the fish from jumping out. If the spawners are left together, the peat should be collected every two weeks and the eggs incubated in the dried peat for about three months. If the eggs are to be incubated in water, wait until they are well embryonated, then dry them for about two weeks before any attempts at hatching are made. The fry are fairly large and can handle newly hatched brine shrimp right away. Feed enough to ensure rapid growth, making sure that the tank is cleaned after feedings. In three weeks adult brine shrimp can be taken, and by six weeks of age the young fish are about 3 cm long and should be sexable. In another two weeks a pair could begin to start laying eggs, just a few at first but with the number increasing with age. The Blue Notho will probably live for a period of only about one year in captivity.

NOTHOBRANCHIUS GUENTHERI

NOTHOBRANCHIUS JUBBI

NOTHOBRANCHIUS KIRKI Jubb/*Redbelly Notho*

R: Environs of Lake Chilwa in southeastern Africa; more populous on the side of the lake bordering Malawi than on the side bordering Mozambique. **H**: Less pronouncedly aggressive than other *Nothobranchius* species. **W**: Variations in pH from 6.6 to 7.4 easily withstood; water can be slightly saline. Best temperature range is in the low 20's (°C). **S**: Mature males vary from about 4 to 5 cm; mature females from about 3 to 4 cm. **F**: Prefers living foods but accepts meaty prepared foods, especially frozen foods.

Both eggs and fry of *N. kirki* are larger than those of *N. rachovi,* making the Redbelly Notho fry easier to raise on newly hatched brine shrimp. Additionally, male *N. kirki* don't belabor the female of their species as much as male *N. rachovi* do, and this helps to simplify the breeding arrangements. Also, the eggs do not have to be stored as long as those of *N. rachovi* before being ready to hatch; the wet storage time for *N. kirki* eggs is only between two and three months.

NOTHOBRANCHIUS MELANOSPILUS

NOTHOBRANCHIUS KORTHAUSAE Meinken/*Korthaus's Notho*

R: Island of Mafia off the coast of Tanzania. **H**: A scrappy fish; plenty of cover should be provided if kept with conspecifics. **W**: Found in soft acidic water in the wild, but adapts well to neutral or slightly acid water. Temperature 20 to 23°C. **S**: To 5 cm; females slightly smaller. **F**: Prefers live foods such as brine shrimp or fruitflies, but can be adapted to fresh and prepared dry foods. **C**: Dark vertical crossbars covering the posterior body and the dorsal, anal, and caudal fins. Brassy yellow ground color with blue-green on each scale. Bright yellow-green inter-band color on the median fins. Females are a drab yellowish brown.

N. korthausae will spawn in a 1 cm layer of finely sifted peat moss or in a 0.5 cm layer of glass beads placed in a shallow dish and submerged in the aquarium. If the latter method is used, it is advisable to sprinkle a bit of fine peat moss over the beads. This will prevent the fish from having a washed-out appearance over the white bed of beads. The eggs require a minimum of three months in slightly damp peat moss.

NOTHOBRANCHIUS KIRKI

NOTHOBRANCHIUS MELANOSPILUS (Pfeffer)/*Beira Notho*
R: Vicinity of Beira, Mozambique. **H**: Should be kept in their own tank. **W**: Soft, slightly acid water with a layer of peat moss on the bottom **S**: Males to 5 cm; females slightly smaller. **F**: Live foods only, and there should be an almost constant supply.

This species is almost always ready, almost too ready, to spawn if kept in good condition. If there is only one female available, a male will soon have her quite battered and she should then be given a few days of rest. Like the other *Nothobranchius* species, eggs are buried in a layer of peat moss on the bottom. They may be removed, peat moss and all, when there is a let-up in the spawning. This is kept in a slightly moist stage for three to four months; the eggs hatch when they are put in water again.

NOTHOBRANCHIUS KORTHAUSAE

NOTHOBRANCHIUS PALMQVISTI Lönnberg/*Palmqvist's Notho*

R: East Africa. **H**: Somewhat pugnacious; should be kept in their own tank. **W**: Water should be soft and slightly acid. Temperature 24 to 27°C. **S**: To 6 cm. **F**: Live food only.

Palmqvist's Notho spawns in a fashion similar to that of other members of its genus. Its eggs have a four-month incubation period when stored in peat moss. Hatched fry should be given infusoria or prepared liquid fry food upon hatching. Egg hatching can be hastened by warm water of about 27°C.

NOTHOBRANCHIUS RACHOVI

NOTHOBRANCHIUS PATRIZII (Vinciguerra)/*Patrizi's Notho*

R: Coastal Kenya and Somalia, East Africa. **H**: Peaceful. Like other Nothos should probably be kept in a single species tank. **W**: Not critical as long as extremes are avoided. Frequent water changes are recommended. A temperature of 20° to 24°C is sufficient. **S**: Males grow to about 5.5 cm, females a bit smaller at 4 cm. **F**: A variety of live foods is preferred but prepared foods may be accepted.

The tank for keeping and breeding this fish can be approximately 40 litters. It should contain Java moss or similar plants for females and submissive males to take refuge in, and a 2-inch layer of peat as a substrate for spawning. A plentiful and varied supply of food should be offered, especially live foods such as mosquito larvae, *Daphnia*, and cyclops. The water conditions are not critical as long as extremes are avoided. A pH of neutral to slightly alkaline and moderately hard water are sufficient. A temperature range of 20° to 24° C is best. Frequent water changes (approximately 50% weekly) are recommended.

For spawning, two males and four females should be added to the spawning tank. The males may be a bit scrappy (spread fins displays and mouth wrestling) but with adequate cover no real damage is done. The dominant male swims about looking for a receptive female. Finding one, courtship follows with abrupt jerky moves, fins widely spread, and attempts to position his body next to hers. Unreceptive females head toward the surface where the male will probably ignore her. Receptive females move toward a suitable spawning site, usually the bottom peat. When she stops the male sidles up to her and places his dorsal fin over her back and his anal fin around her ventral region. The spawners remain still for a brief time then shudder or vibrate as the eggs and sperm are released. The fish separate, usually driving the eggs into the substrate by the water current thus produced. The spawning bouts are repeated several times per day.

NOTOBRANCHIUS PALMQVISTI

NOTHOBRANCHIUS RACHOVI (Ahl)/*Rachow's Notho*

R: East Africa, in the vicinity of Beira. **H**: Quarrelsome toward other fishes; should be given their own tank. **W**: Water should be soft and slightly acid. Temperature 24 to 27°C. **S**: To 5 cm. **F**: Living foods only.

A jewel such as this deserves its own setting, and it is best to give them a tank with only their own kind. Like the other *Nothobranchius* species, their life span is comparatively short and once they have attained maturity spawnings are frequent and feedings must be generous.

NOTOBRANCHIUS PATRIZII

OMPOK BIMACULATUS (Bloch)/*One-Spot Glass Catfish*

R: Sri Lanka, Indo-China, Thailand, Burma, Java, and Sumatra. **H**: Only small specimens are adaptable to aquaria, and they should not be kept singly; single fish are short-lived. **W**: Very adaptable to practically any clean water. Temperature 23 to 28°C. **S**: To 46 cm in native waters; about half that in the aquarium. **F**: Live or frozen foods preferred.

Ompok bimaculatus is found throughout a rather wide range which includes most of the Indian-Southeast Asia area. It is a very popular fish wherever it occurs, not as an aquarium fish but as an item on the menu. Being fairly common, it is easy to get under ordinary circumstances. The natives often have pools that they stock with this fish, feeding them all sorts of table refuse and eventually reaping a rich harvest.

OPHTHALMOTILAPIA VENTRALIS

OPSARIDIUM CHRISTYI (Boulenger)/*Copper-Nose Minnow*

R: Lower Congo River and its tributaries. **H**: An active fish that can only be trusted with others that are as large or larger. **W**: Slightly acid, clean, well aerated water. Temperature 22 to 25°C. **S**: Up to 15 cm. **F**: Has a healthy appetite and will take dried as well as living foods. It is particularly fond of insects that have been dropped on the surface.

Females can only be distinguished when fully grown. At this time they show a deeper belly while the males are more slender and also more highly colored. We have only one account of their spawning, and that a sketchy one. A tank of at least 60 liters is provided, and a layer of pebbles or glass marbles is placed on the bottom. A ripe pair or, better yet, several pairs are placed here. The water should not be more than 25 cm above the layer of pebbles or marbles. If all goes well, the fish will pursue each other in a lively manner, dropping eggs at intervals; these fall to safety between the pebbles.

OMPOK BIMACULATUS

OPHTHALMOTILAPIA VENTRALIS (Boulenger)/*Powder Blue Ventralis*
R: This species is endemic to Lake Tanganyika. **H:** A mouthbrooder that is territorial though not overly aggressive toward other fish. **W:** Typical for cichlids of Lake Tanganyika—hard and alkaline water with a temperature of about 23° to 28°C. **S:** Do not grow much greater than 12cm in length. **F:** Will accept a variety of foods including vegetable matter. Live foods that stay in the water column are preferred.

During the actual spawning the female enters the nest as the male lies flat, apparently releasing sperm. The male rises off the stone just above the female but leaving the bright yellow tips of his ventral fins resting on the stone. The female positions herself in the nest and the male leaves to chase unwanted visitors away. The female releases an egg and picks it up in her mouth and departs. In the wild some females may wander to nests of other breeding males and the process is repeated. The original male will start courting other females if present or keep his attention on the same female if she is the only one. Brooding time depends on temperature, being about three weeks at 28°C but four weeks if the temperature drops to 22°C. In the wild the females release the fry in shallow water where they form schools often mixed with several other species of cichlids.

OPSARIDIUM CHRISTYI

OREOCHROMIS MOSSAMBICUS (Peters)/*Mozambique Mouthbrooder*

R: East Africa. **H**: Suitable companions only for large fishes. **W**: Not important. **S**: Up to 38 cm; mature at 10 cm. **F**: Eats anything.

Males establish spawning territories that are guarded against all intruders including the female, unless she makes suitable responses to his hostile behavior. The nest, which is a hollow depression, is used only to receive the eggs. The female immediately takes them into her mouth, and the male ejects sperm near the spot where they were laid. The female circulates the sperm-laden water through her mouth, thus fertilizing the eggs. The fry hatch in about 11 days and periodically return to the female's mouth for about a week.

ORYZIAS LATIPES

ORYZIAS JAVANICUS (Bleeker)/*Javanese Rice Fish*

R: Java and Malaysia. **H**: Peaceful toward other fishes and will not harm plants. **W**: Water should be neutral to slightly alkaline, with a little salt added. Keep at 26 to 29°C. **S**: Males to 3 cm.; females to 4 cm. **F**: Live foods greatly preferred; other foods are not picked up once they fall to the bottom.

The male drives the female actively until they come to a quivering halt among the plants. Here the eggs are expelled and fertilized. The eggs hang in a bunch attached by a tough string to the female's vent and are sometimes carried about in this manner for hours. Finally the string snags against something solid, usually a plant leaf or twig, and the eggs come to rest. Hatching takes place in 10 to 12 days, and until they begin to grow the tiny youngsters must be provided with infusoria.

OREOCHROMIS MOSSAMBICUS

ORYZIAS LATIPES (Schlegel)/*Medaka*

R: Japan and nearby islands. **H**: Active and peaceful, although a male will occasionally rough up a female; a very good community fish. **W**: Slightly soft, acid water desirable. **S**: Females about 5 cm; males slightly smaller. **F**: Takes all foods.

Certainly not a flashy fish, it is still quietly pretty, with its golden body (the old wild strain is no longer seen) set off by iridescent blue-green flecks and the beautiful large, almost luminescent, eyes. The breeding habits of the fish offer a remarkable opportunity to view the life cycle from egg to free-swimming fry, for the eggs can be observed in bunches on the female, and they can later be observed attached to plants.

ORYZIAS JAVANICUS

OSPHRONEMUS GORAMY Lacépède/*Giant Gourami*

R: Great Sunda Islands; introduced in other places as a food fish. **H**: Peaceful; because of their size they should be kept only with large fishes. **W**: Not critical as long as the water is clean. Temperature 23 to 28°C. **S**: Up to 60 cm. in natural waters; about half that in the aquarium. **F**: Should get large amounts of shrimp, clams, mussels, etc., to which is also added vegetable matter such as boiled oatmeal.

They build a bubblenest and the male stands guard over the eggs and young. Sexes can be distinguished in mature specimens by a roundness in the dorsal and anal fins of the females. In males these fins are pointed. Mature fish 30 cm or more in length are said to be excellent show objects for large public aquarium. Their food should contain a good amount of vegetable matter, such as boiled oatmeal and the like.

OSTEOGLOSSUM BICIRRHOSUM

OSTEOCHILUS HASSELTI (Valenciennes)/*Hard-Lipped Barb*

R: Burma and Thailand to Java, Borneo, and Sumatra. **H**: Peaceful if kept with fishes of its own size. **W**: Neutral to slightly acid water; tank should be well planted and of a good size. Temperature 24 to 27°C. **S**: Grows to a little over 30 cm in length in nature; about half that in the aquarium. **F**: Live foods with an addition of vegetable substances.

Osteochilus hasselti is a well-known food fish in Thailand as well as Java, Borneo, and Sumatra. It is a large, handsome, well-formed fish that has two pairs of barbels on the upper lip and none on the lower. The mouth is well adapted for algae-nibbling and tearing at other soft plants. The upper and lower lips are lined with papillae, and there is a bony structure behind the lower lip. In central and southeastern Thailand it is called *pla soi khao* because of a fancied resemblance to a dove which is called *nok khao*.

OSPHRONEMUS GORAMY

OSTEOGLOSSUM BICIRRHOSUM Vandelli/*Arowana*

R: Guianas and most parts of the Amazon. **H**: Only small ones may be kept together; big ones are best kept alone. **W**: Should be moved as little as possible. Temperature 24 to 26°C. **S**: To about 60 cm, but usually much smaller. **F**: Greatly prefers fishes that can be swallowed whole, but can be trained to take pieces of raw fish, shrimp, etc., from the fingers.

The Arowana gives its viewer a look into an ancient prehistoric world, the Jurassic Age. The Arowana is one of the few remaining living examples of this group. They make very interesting aquarium fishes, but only the largest aquarium will hold a full-grown specimen. Their swimming movements are very lithe and fluid, reminding one of those of a snake. The scales are very large and opalescent, reflecting many colors when the light hits them. The large "landing barge" mouth betrays its predatory nature and healthy appetite.

OSTEOCHILUS HASSELTI

493

OSTEOGLOSSUM FERREIRAI Kanazawa/*Black Arowana*

R: Rio Branco, a tributary of the Rio Negro in Brazil. **H**: Large specimens won't hesitate to swallow anything they can cram into their very spacious mouths, but neither adults nor young specimens are quarrelsome with fishes not regarded as food; rather unpredictable in temperament, frequently showing disturbance when there is no visible cause for alarm. **W**: Soft, slightly acid water desirable. Temperature 25 to 28°C. **S**: Wild adult specimens run up to about 40cm; juveniles of about 8 cm are most often seen. **F**: Variable from individual to individual; some will take prepared aquarium foods, while others refuse all except small live fishes.

In nature, the Black Arowana is usually found in heavily vegetated areas that are shallow and often stagnant. Aquarium water should be soft and slightly acidic. Although this fish will often accept prepared aquarium foods, live foods should be included in their diet. Young Black Arowanas are usually the only specimens available for the average aquarist. Dealers are able to sell the young fish at a much lower price than the adults. Many of the juveniles, however, are offered for sale at such a young age that their yolk-sacs are still attached. These young fish demand greater care than the adults and are much less adaptable to aquarium life.

OXYELEOTRIS LINEOLATUS

OTOCINCLUS AFFINIS Steindachner/*Midget Sucker Catfish*

R: Southeastern Brazil. **H**: Peaceful. **W**: Soft, slightly acid water is best, with dense plant growth and good light. Temperature 21 to 29°C. **S**: 5 cm. **F**: Main staple is algae that are scraped off leaves, rocks, and the glass sides of the aquarium, but will accept other foods.

Otocinclus affinis busies itself by going around the aquarium using its sucker-like mouth to rasp algae off wherever it may have formed in the aquarium. The fish is particularly useful, because of its size, in removing algae from places which are beneath the notice of large sucker species, like the plecostomus catfishes. But there is a strange thing about this little catfish: there seems to be no middle ground in its adaptability to a given set of tank conditions.

Unfortunately, it often works out that this fish does poorly rather than well. This is attributable to a lack of sufficient algal growth in the tank to support the fish. Where not enough algae or only the wrong kinds of algae are available, *Otocinclus affinis* will linger for a while but eventually die off. Although the species is bred only infrequently, the feat is not impossible if the stock is given good care. Eggs are placed *Corydoras*-fashion against the glass sides of the tank; the small eggs hatch in two days.

OSTEOGLOSSUM FERREIRAI

OXYELEOTRIS LINEOLATUS (Steindachner)/*Lined Sleeper*
R: Queensland, Australia and New Guinea. **H**: Will eat anything that will fit into its mouth; a predator not suitable for the community aquarium. **W**: Hard, alkaline water. Temperature about 21°C. **S**: Over 48 cm when fully mature; smaller in aquaria. **F**: Live or frozen foods.
The Lined Sleeper has been reported to have spawned under aquarium conditions. The male is larger than the female and has longer fins and brighter colors. The male selects the nesting site, pursues the female, and later aerates the eggs. The eggs are adhesive and will attach to plants, gravel, or rocks.

OTOCINCLUS AFFINIS

OXYGASTER ANOMALURA

OXYGASTER ANOMALURA van Hasselt/*Knife Barb*

R: Thailand, Java, Borneo, Sumatra, and Malaysia. **H**: Peaceful and active; a jumper. **W**: Soft, slightly acid water is best. Temperature 21 to 30°C. **S**: Up to 13 cm. **F**: Will accept live, dry, and frozen foods; despite its size, this fish prefers small foods.

The Knife Barb, so named for its keeled or "sharp" belly, is a harmless cyprinid which is best suited to larger tanks because it gets big and because it does best in a tank in which it has plenty of room to swim freely. Rarely imported, *Oxygaster anomalura* is not in great demand: it is neither a pretty fish nor is it especially interesting, so no one seems to miss it, although it was offered some years ago on the aquarium market. All of the *Oxygaster* species are restless, nervous fishes. They swim back and forth from one side of the aquarium to the other almost continually, like the *Danio*, *Brachydanio* and some *Puntius* species. However, *Oxygaster anomalura* keeps more to the upper reaches; its mouth is definitely adapted to feeding at the surface.

The Knife Barb has not been bred in this country, but a spawning report on *Oxygaster atpar* states that the mating pair go through vigorous circular motions before the eggs are laid. The eggs are small and non-adhesive, and they hatch in about a day at a temperature of 26°C. The fry remain near the surface, where they can easily be fed on dust-fine dry foods.

OXYGASTER OXYGASTROIDES (Bleeker)/*Glass Barb*

R: Thailand and the Greater Sunda Islands. **H**: Harmless to other fishes and plants; likes to swim in schools. **W**: Soft, slightly acid water. Temperature 24 to 27°C. **S**: To 20 cm in native waters; in the aquarium about 13 cm. **F**: Prefers live foods that remain near the surface, like mosquito larvae; can be accustomed to dry foods.

The Glass barb loses most of its claim to the popular name as it becomes bigger. In their natural water this species attains 20 cm in length, but in the aquarium a fish half that size is considered large. Small fish have a very glassy transparency, much of which is lost later. The dark spots in the caudal lobe also tend to disappear in time and the fish become very plain, greenish silvery with a dark stripe running from behind the gill-plate to the caudal base and another much narrower stripe from behind the belly to the bottom of the caudal base.

The upturned mouth indicates that it gets most of its food at or near the surface. Another thing to remember is the size of the pectoral fins. This is the mark of the jumper, a fish that can easily "take off" from the surface and land on your living room rug. Never keep them in an uncovered aquarium.

PACHYPANCHAX HOMALONOTUS (Dumeril)/*Green Panchax*

R: Madagascar. **H**: Peaceful with fishes too large to be swallowed. **W**: Not critical; salt can be added. Temperature 22 to 26°C. **S**: Up to 10 cm; usually smaller. **F**: Live, frozen or freeze-dried foods accepted.

Spawning usually occurs in the morning in fine-leaved plants. The adults will eat the eggs if they find them. The male is a strong driver, and for this reason it is desirable to use a fairly large aquarium or several females. Two or three eggs are generally deposited at a time. Occasionally a female may extrude several eggs at one time that remain attached to her vent until they are brushed off on plants. Unfertilized eggs turn white within half an hour. Hatching takes from 14 to 16 days at 24°C. Fry are large enough to accept newly hatched brine shrimp upon becoming free-swimming.

PANAQUE NIGROLINEATUS

PACHYPANCHAX PLAYFAIRI (Günther)/*Playfair's Panchax*

R: East Africa, Seychelles, and Madagascar. **H**: Apt to be a bit "bossy" with smaller fishes; should be kept in a sunny, well-planted aquarium. **W**: Neutral to slightly alkaline water. Temperature 23 to 26°C. **S**: About 8 cm. **F**: Live foods of all kinds, but will take dried foods if hungry.

Eggs are hung in bushy plant leaves near the surface, where they can be seen hanging by fine threads. The shells are hard enough that they can be picked out carefully with the fingers and placed in a separate tank for hatching. This takes place in 10 to 14 days, and the youngsters can swallow newly hatched brine shrimp at once. Growth is rapid, and the young must be sorted frequently because of the disparity in size between the younger and the older ones. Once they have reached a size where they can no longer swallow each other, all is well. *Pachypanchax playfairi* has an unusual trait that is worth mentioning: the scales, especially along the back, stand out instead of lying close to the body. This is natural and must not be diagnosed as a disease symptom.

PACHYPANCHAX HOMALONOTUS

PANAQUE NIGROLINEATUS (Peters)/*Panaque*

R: North-central South America. **H**: Peaceful with other species but aggressive among themselves. **W**: Not critical. Temperature 21 to 27°C. **S**: Usually seen at 15 or 18 cm; much larger in nature. **F**: Accepts most aquarium fare but should be provided with vegetable substances as well.

Should be provided with a suitable resting place within the tank, because besides being averse to bright light it also is territorial and wants a place to call its own. *Panaque nigrolineatus* has not yet spawned under aquarium conditions; no doubt the species requires a very large tank to house the prospective spawners, which are very large at maturity.

PACHYPANCHAX PLAYFAIRI

PANAQUE SUTTONI Schultz/*Blue-eyed Panaque*

R: Below the mouth of the Rio Yasa, Venezuelan Rio Negro, western Maracaibo Basin, Venezuela. **H:** Territorial, and may engage in boundary fights with other species; also aggressive toward its own kind. **W:** Not critical as long as extremes are avoided. Regular partial water changes are recommended. **S:** Attains a length of at least 25 cm. **F:** Should be heavily supplied with algae or some substitutes. Other normal aquarium fare accepted.

The diet of the Blue-eyed Panaque should consist largely of vegetable material. Algae growing on the tank surfaces are soon depleted and substitutes must be provided. Although the usual substitutes are accepted, zucchini seems to be a favorite used by catfish fanciers.

Sexual dimorphism is manifested in the interopercular spines (longer in the male) and the smaller irregular spines on the pectoral fin spines (also longer in the male). The female tends to be more round-bodied when filling with eggs than the slimmer male. Initial pre-spawning reactions seem to be a change in color (the hint of gold iridescence becomes predominant) and initiation of a cichlid-like head-to-tail vibration that is broken off and repeated at intervals. Unfortunately, the courting procedure can become quite violent, leading in many cases to the death of the female if the two are not separated. Although this pre-spawning behavior has been observed by some aquarists in this country, further spawning activity has not yet been reported. One suggestion is to provide the aquarium with a separator, one that will allow visual contact as well as a flow-through system in case any stimuli from odors produced are needed.

PANGIO JAVANICUS

PANGASIUS SUTCHI Fowler/*Siamese Shark*

R: Malay Peninsula. **H:** Relatively peaceful, but will eat fishes small enough to swallow. **W:** Not critical, but soft acid water is preferred. Temperature 22 to 27°C. **S:** 18 cm, but usually smaller. **F:** Prefers live or frozen foods.

P. sutchi has a tendency toward hysteria. When frightened they dash madly around the aquarium, colliding with the sides, rocks, plants, and other fishes. These flights are generally terminated by the fish sinking to the bottom where they lie on their sides or backs until they recover. Normally this species is an extremely graceful swimmer, which comes to the top periodically for air. *Pangasius sutchi* is a schooling fish that is extremely uncomfortable without company.

PANAQUE SUTTONI

PANGIO JAVANICUS (Bleeker)/*Javanese Loach*

R: Java and Sumatra. **H**: Peaceful and able to slither into almost inaccessible places and pick up food other fishes cannot reach. **W**: Clean water. Temperature about 24 to 28°C. **S**: About 8 cm. **F**: They pick up most uneaten foods but are very fond of tubifex and white worms.

Their tank should not be only well planted but also have some flat rocks beneath which the fish can dig. Sexes can be told only when the females become heavy with eggs, but the problem there is whether the ones that do not fill up with eggs are males or not. The best way is to keep several pairs in the same tank, as this genus is not averse to "community spawning." The young frequently remain hidden for a week or more after hatching and are easily raised on chopped worms or the like. The parents should be removed when it is seen that they have spawned.

PANGASIUS SUTCHI

PANGIO KUHLII (Valenciennes) *Coolie Loach, Kuhli Loach*

R: Northeastern Bengal, Assam, Malaysia, Burma, Thailand, Java, Sumatra, Borneo, Singapore and Malacca. **H**: A peaceful little fish found on muddy bottoms in its native waters. Hides from bright light and becomes active at night. **W**: They prefer clean, clear water with a temperature of 24 to 28°C. The use of coarse gravel should be avoided. **S**: 10 cm; matures at 7 cm. **F**: A good scavenger that can be counted on to pick up much of the food other fishes leave uneaten. It has the ability to slither into almost inaccessible places and eat any food that would otherwise die there and foul the water. The trouble is that most aquarists think that it can subsist only on "leftovers." This is far from the truth, and enough living foods should be fed to insure a good supply for the "Coolies." These fish have a protective tough transparent skin over the eyes which enables them to dig into the sand without injuring themselves. If the sand is too coarse and has sharp edges, however, the nose and mouth can be injured.

PANGIO SEMICINCTUS

PANGIO MYERSI (Harry)/*Slimy Myersi*

R: Southeastern Thailand. **H**: A nocturnal swimmer; prefers hiding during the day, so wholesalers use inverted, split coconut shells in their aquaria. **W**: Prefers soft, acid water with a pH of 6.2. Temperature 26 to 28°C. **S**: Less than 7.5 cm. **F**: Worms, frozen brine shrimp and anything that will fall to the bottom and not require teeth to chew are acceptable.

The Slimy Myersi is so-called because it seems to have a slimier skin than the other loaches and is thinner. When a few hundred are kept together in a tank, they "ball up" and are very sensitive to light, preferring to remain hidden in the sand or in a dark corner. They are not recommended for the community aquarium, as you will never see them, except at night, and then the slightest shadow will send them darting back into hiding. Not much is known about its breeding habits.

PANGIO KUHLII

PANGIO SEMICINCTUS (Fraser-Brunner)/*Half-Banded Loach*

R: Sunda Islands. **H**: Peaceful, often remains hidden when the light is bright and comes out at night. **W**: Clean, clear water with a temperature of 24 to 27°C. Do not give them a bottom with coarse gravel. **S**: A little over 7.5 cm. **F**: An excellent scavenger that will pick up uneaten food, but should get its share of live food, too.

Their activities, which are largely nocturnal, include a very thorough cleaning of the bottom gravel, and much food is eaten which would have been out of reach of the other fishes. Coming as they do from streams with muddy bottoms, their mouths are quite soft and coarse gravel will easily cause severe injury.

PANGIO MYERSI

PANGIO SHELFORDI (Popta)/*Shelford's Loach*

R: Borneo. **H**: Peaceful. Usually remains hidden during the day and comes out at night. When feeding time arrives it may come out even though it is light. **W**: Although quite tolerant of varied conditions, optimum would be medium soft (about 5 DH) water with a slightly acid to neutral pH. Temperature should be 21 to 24°C. **S**: To about 8 cm. **F**: Not critical. Foods that sink to the bottom, like worms, can be used.

In view of their nocturnal habits, suitable hiding places must be furnished. Therefore, their aquarium must include rocks, slate or other material that creates caves or dark niches for the loaches. The water should be medium soft (about 5DH or less) and have a pH that is neutral to slightly acid although they are very tolerant and can exist with a pH as high as 7.6 or as low as 6.4. The temperature should not be too high as they seem to show discomfort at temperatures as high as 26°C; 21 to about 24°C will do.

PAPYROCRANUS AFER

PANTODON BUCHHOLZI Peters/*Butterfly Fish*

R: Tropical West Africa. **H**: Harmless to other fishes, but better kept by themselves to prevent damage to their filamentious ventral fin extensions. **W**: Soft, slightly acid water is preferable. The tank should not be too heavily planted; it must have a large surface and be covered. Temperature 23 to 27°C. **S**: To 10 cm. **F**: Prefers live insects but it can be trained to take bits of shrimp.

Pantodon buchholzi is the only species in the genus, and the genus *Pantodon* is the only one in the family Pantodontidae. The large pectoral fins, which when outspread resemble a butterfly's wings, can be used for gliding over short distances in much the same manner as the oceanic flying fishes. The Butterfly Fish inhabits weedy, slow-flowing pools where it lies almost motionless near the surface and waits for its prey to pass by.

PAPYROCRANUS AFER (Gunther)/*African Featherfin*

R: Gambia to the Congo. **H:** Very timid; peaceful when young. Larger individuals may be predatory. Usually active at twilight or in subdued light. **W:** Does best in soft water that has been filtered through peat. Temperature about 24 to 28°C. **S:** Reaches a length of up to 60 cm. **F:** Will take most live foods generally provided to aquarium fishes.

Most aquarists would know this fish under a different name, *Notopterus afer*. The change to *Papyrocranus* was made by Dr. P.H. Greenwood in 1963. *Papyrocranus afer* has a small flag-like dorsal fin like the species of *Notopterus* but lacks pelvic fins and has a serrated ventral keel. The anal fin is very long and confluent with the caudal fin. Locomotion is by means of undulations of this fin; the fish, by means of the direction of these undulations, can move either forward or backward with great facility. The coloration appears to be variable, with the young being light brownish with dark markings and older fish with a brownish body with light spots or dashes. Never bred in captivity.

PARACHEIRODON AXELRODI (Schultz)/*Cardinal Tetra*

R: Upper Rio Negro and Colombian waterways. **H**: Perfectly peaceful and active. Likes to swim in schools, and therefore it is best to keep at least 6 of them together. **W**: Water should be soft, clean, and on the acid side, about pH 6.5 or lower, in order to have the fish show its brightest colors. Temperature 21 to 24°C. **S**: to 5 cm. **F**: All foods, either live or prepared, should be given with their small size in mind. Not a fussy eater. **C**: Back is brown on top. Horizontal stripe a brilliant blue-green. Lower part of body bright red, belly white.

This living jewel is without a doubt the most gorgeous of all freshwater aquarium fishes. The Cardinal Tetra does best in aquaria that are not too bright and have soft, slightly acidic water. The tank should have a dark background and dark gravel. The species is very peaceful and should be kept with fishes of a similar nature. Furthermore, Cardinal Tetras should be kept in groups of six or more, as they like to school and are most appealing when they move together. This is not an easy fish to breed.

PARACHEIRODON SIMULANS

PARACHEIRODON INNESI (Myers)/*Long-finned Neon Tetra*

R: Upper course of the Rio Solimoes (= Amazon) and Rio Purus. **H**: Very peaceful; should be kept only with small fishes or in a tank of their own. **W**: Soft, clear, slightly acid water is preferred and brings out their best colors. Best temperature about 24°C. **S**: Maximum 4 cm; most specimens seen are about 2.5 cm or less. **F**: Medium or finely ground dried foods, with occasional feedings of small live foods.

The first ones to reach America were shipped from Germany on the ill-fated dirigible "Hindenburg," which crashed a short time later. Breeding this beautiful fish is not an impossibility, but many attempts result in failure. The most important ingredient is soft, acid water and a compatible pair. The eggs are very sensitive to light.

PARACHEIRODON AXELRODI

PARACHEIRODON SIMULANS (Géry)/*False Neon*

R: Rio Negro, Brazil. **H**: Peaceful; likes to travel in schools. **W**: Water should be acid and very soft. Temperature 24 to 26°C. **S**: About 2.5 cm. **F**: Small living foods preferred; probably would accept prepared or frozen foods readily. **C**: Bright blue iridescent streak from opercle to caudal base; with an area of red above the anal fin.

The new fish arrived in Switzerland as part of a shipment from the Aquario Rio Negro in Brazil and might have been sold unnoticed if it were not for the eagle eye of Chris R. Schmidt, Jr., a young scientist who spotted "something different" among the Cardinal Tetras. The Rio Negro and its tributary streams are far from being completely studied, and probably there are many more new and beautiful species to be found there for the fish hobbyist.

PARACHEIRODON INNESI

PARAMBASSIS BACULIS (Hamilton-Buchanan)/*Pla Kameo or Burmese Glassfish*
R: Burma, India, and Thailand in the Sikuk River, in the headwaters of the Menam Chao Phya, in the lower Menam Nam, and in the Bung Borapet. **H**: A dainty but beautiful small fish; peaceful. **W**: Strictly a freshwater species that prefers the higher temperatures of the upper 20's°C. **S**: Rarely larger than 5 cm. **F**: Prefers live foods, but accepts frozen brine shrimp and some dry foods in pellet form. Requires copious amounts of live food such as microworms and daphnia. This species does best in relatively warm aquarium water. The aquarium should be heavily planted with dark gravel and should be given plenty of sunlight. The Burmese Glassfish is very peaceful and should only be kept with fishes that have a similar nature. Spawning produces 150 or more eggs, which hatch in one to two days depending upon the temperature of the water. They fry are very small and should be fed infusoria.

PARAMBASSIS RANGA (Hamilton-Buchanan)/*Glassfish, Glass Perch*

R: Northern India, Bengal to Burma. **H**: Very numerous in rice paddies and other shallow bodies of water in their habitat; peaceful in the aquarium. **W**: Requires somewhat hard water with a light salt content. Once established in an aquarium, they should be moved as little as possible. Temperature about 26°C. **S**: 5 cm; in nature they become slightly larger. **F**: Some prepared foods are grudgingly accepted, but the bulk of foods given should be alive. **C**: Body light amber with a glassy transparency. In the males, the soft dorsal fin and the anal fin have a bright blue edge.

The fish breeds quite readily, but the fry are so small that they usually die of starvation before they become large enough to eat foods like newly hatched brine shrimp. An annoying trait the fry also have is that they do not hunt for food, but they will only snap at it when it swims near them. Males are distinguished by the bright blue edge on the soft dorsal and anal fins, of which there is only a trace on the female. A 20-liter aquarium is of sufficient size for spawning, and eggs are deposited in a clump of floating plants like *Riccia* or *Nitella*.

PARAPOCRYPTES SERPERASTER

PARAPOCRYPTES SERPERASTER (Richardson)/*Slim Mudskipper*

R: Southeast Asia from India to China, most numerous in Malay Archipelago. **H**: Aggressive. **W**: Warm, brackish water required. Temperature 24 to 27°C. **S**: To about 25 cm. **F**: Will accept only rich, meaty foods; in most cases only living foods; tubifex worms, earthworms, and small live fishes are accepted, and will gladly take soft-bodied insects.

The Slim Mudskipper is not in the same genus (*Periophthalmus*) as the mudskippers best known to aquarium hobbyists. But the similarity in looks, temperament and odd habits is striking enough to make this fish's common name quite appropriate. *Parapocryptes* is more directly tied to a watery existence than *Periophthalmus*, because whereas the latter often leaves the water and emerges onto completely dry land, sometimes even climbing up into mangrove branches, *Parapocryptes* never ventures onto completely dry terrain but strays from the water only as far as mud flats.

This is not an easy fish to keep. In the first place it demands live food, and even when it is provided with an adequately rich and varied diet it is susceptible to fungal infections of the fins. *Parapocryptes* also is a sluggish fish, remaining mostly in one place and showing liveliness only when offered food or when frightened. The species also is disturbed when maintained in tanks that are brightly lighted, even though it is not a strictly nocturnal species.

PARAUCHENIPTERUS GALEATUS

PARAUCHENIPTERUS GALEATUS (Linnaeus)/*Starry Cat*
R: Northern and eastern South America. **H**: Generally peaceful, but larger specimens will eat smaller fishes if given the chance. **W**: Slightly acid, soft water. Temperature 23 to 26°C. **S**: To 18 cm. **F**: Will accept most aquarium fish foods, but prefers tubifex worms or frozen foods.
The Starry Cat requires a medium to large tank. Although it will accept most prepared aquarium foods, live foods such as tubifex worms should be fed from time to time. *P. galeatus* should only be kept with fishes its own size or larger as it will eat smaller fishes.

Closeup of head of *P. galeatus*, showing three pairs of well developed but not very elongated barbels.

PARAUCHENIPTERUS INSIGNIS

PARAUCHENIPTERUS INSIGNIS (Steindachner)/ *Woodcat*

R: Northern South America. **H:** Nocturnal. Fairly peaceful but should not be trusted with small fishes. **W:** Not critical, but prefers a pH of neutral to slightly acid and a temperature in the range of 24° to 29°C. **S:** Attains a length of at least 13 cm. **F:** Not fussy about foods and will accept a wide variety of aquarium foods. Be sure vegetable matter is included in the diet.

The Woodcat is a very interesting species that one sees only rarely for sale, and even then it is usually seen only as a single individual. Thoughts of breeding such a fish may never enter the mind of the average aquarist, but it can be done. For those catfish enthusiasts or breeders of the "oddballs" who want something different, try this one!

A tank of about 220 liters or more should do the trick. It should be supplied with bottom gravel, plants (including floating plants such as water sprite), and perhaps some rocks or driftwood for hiding places as well as decoration. The water should be neutral to slightly acid (6.0-7.0) and the temperature in the upper range of 24° to 29°C. It accepts a wide variety of foods. As a nocturnal species it seeks shelter during the day, but come sunset it actively starts searching for food. It is best then to feed just before "lights out" to ensure that it eats properly.

Males and females are easily distinguished even at an early age. At about 4 to 6.5 cm the males are a mottled color, whereas the females are quite plain. But then some really different and interesting changes occur as they grow. At 8 to 9.5 cm in size the male's dorsal spine has become quite curved, so much so that anyone not "in the know" might think that it was deformed. The upper jaw barbels also change from the soft, small structure of the juvenile to the broader, stiffer, longer ones of the adult. The anterior part of the anal fin of the male becomes modified into an intromittent organ. The fish are ready to spawn at an age of about 18 months and a size of 10 to 13.5 cm. At the approach of the spawning season the males undergo some temporary sexual changes: the barbels of the upper lip become stiffer and these barbels, the upper part of the head, and the outer edge of the first dorsal spine become covered with many small tubercles. The female of course becomes more rounded and fuller looking as she fills with eggs.

PAREUTROPIUS DEBAUWI (Boulenger)/*Three-Striped Glass Catfish*
R: Kinshasa region of the Zaire River. **H**: Very active and peaceful; should be kept in groups rather than singly. **W**: soft, slightly acid water is preferable. Temperature 24 to 26°C. **S**: Maximum a little over 7.5 cm. **F**: Live foods such as daphnia, tubifex worms, and white worms.
If you are looking for a catfish that does not look or act like one, this little beauty is for you. A group of about a half-dozen of these makes for a picture of ceaseless nervous activity, and the fish looks as if it would sink to the bottom if it did not struggle constantly to stay afloat. This is definitely a schooling fish, and single specimens are generally short-lived. The dorsal fin is small and as is characteristic of the group it appears far in front, near the head. The pectoral and dorsal fins are each provided with a sturdy, sharp spine. These are held stiffly out and a netted fish is sometimes difficult to disentangle. The barbels are very short, but there are three pairs.

513

PARODON PONGOENSE (Allen)/*Pongo Pongo*

R: Peruvian Amazon, Ecuador, and Colombia. **H**: Peaceful, prefer to school. **W**: Soft acid water is preferred. Temperature from 23 to 30°C. **S**: About 5 cm. **F**: Prefers live foods but can readily take frozen brine shrimp and prepared dry foods.

One day while visiting a pet shop my (HRA) attention was called to this fish because of its unbelievable swimming habits. The fish never stopped swimming at a very rapid rate in a rather tight circle in schools. There were about twelve fish in the school, and they swam very quickly in a circle about 10 cm in diameter, making a complete circle about twice every three seconds. They always swam about 5 cm off the gravel in the aquarium, which was about 30 cm deep.

PARODON PONGOENSE

PAROSPHROMENUS DEISSNERI (Bleeker)/*Licorice Gourami*

R: Bangka. Sumatra, and Malay Peninsula. **H**: Peaceful, but unsuitable for the community tank because of its shy temperament; needs shelter of some sort for its well-being. **W**: Soft, acid water is recommended (some aquarists use a small peat filter so that the water turns an amber color but remains very clear and clean) at a temperature of about 24 to 25°C. **S**: One of the dwarf species reaching a length of only 4 cm. **F**: Live foods such as daphnia, cyclops, Grindal worms, and mosquito larvae are best.

The Licorice Gourami is not a bubblenest builder in the true sense, and the actual spawning is accomplished without the aid of bubbles at all. But they do come into play at a later time. The spawning site usually selected is the roof of a cave, the inside upper surface of a flowerpot or some other such surface. The male will court the female by displaying in front of her with fins spread and his body tilted at an angle.

The actual embrace and egg-laying are similar to most other gouramis, with the male's body wrapped in a "U"-shape around the female for about 10 to 12 seconds. The eggs are extruded at that time and fall to the bottom of the tank. The female recovers from this nuptial embrace first and goes in search of the eggs, the male soon following. The parents bring the eggs to the cave roof, to which they will adhere (in harder water the eggs may not become attached and will fall back to the bottom of the tank) until they hatch.

PAROSPHROMENUS DEISSNERI

PAROSPHROMENUS FILAMENTOSUS Vierke/*Spike-Tailed Licorice Gourami*

R: Endemic to southern Borneo near Kalimantan. **H:** A quiet and peaceful species. **W:** Not critical Soft water is better than hard. Temperatures from 24° to 30°:C are acceptable. **S:** Attains a maximum length of about 4 cm (only 2.5 cm without the tail). **F:** Not choosy about its food as long as it is live.

The Spike-Tailed Licorice Gourami is a quiet, peaceful species that reaches a length of only about 4 cm, and that includes the tail, which is about 1.2 cm by itself. The central filament in the tail helps distinguish this species from its close relative *P. deissneri*. It actually is the prolongation of the middle ray of the caudal fin, and it is almost always black in color and appears in both sexes. This is not a very demanding species; a pair can live quite comfortably in a 20-liter aquarium supplied with rock caves and a few plants for decoration. The water quality is not important, although soft water seems to be better than hard water. A temperature between 24° and 30°C suits them fine. They are not choosy about food as long as it is live. *P. filamentosus* is said to live for a period of about 30 months.

The males are a little longer, a little less robust, and have a longer caudal filament than females. In spawning condition the male's colors intensify. His back above the upper stripe is golden and the dorsal base and much of the caudal fin are red to red-brown. The ventral and anal fins exhibit a bright blue color, and the head in the right light will reflect a blue luster. The male constructs a bubblenest below the surface of the water, usually on the roof of a cave. The male comes to the surface for air with which to make the bubble and deposits it in the nest. The bubbles are very adhesive and normally will not be displaced even if the rock is turned upside down.

As spawning time approaches the male courts the female with intensified colors and spread fins, and when she is very close convulsively flicks the brilliant blue ventral fins. The female turns pale, losing the horizontal dark stripes, and the pair begins to circle with fins spread. The male may assume a head-down position at times. If the female does not respond, the male will position himself crosswise to her again. This courtship may last for hours, even continuing after the male succeeds in enticing the female to a point under his bubblenest. The activity increases until finally they embrace in normal gourami fashion. The pair may sink about 2-3 cm in the water before hanging suspended in midwater. The male relaxes slightly, and the female recovers to start collecting the milky white eggs that were accumulated on the male's anal fin. She places them in the nest. This spawning embrace is repeated about every ten minutes for a period of about three hours. The female then leaves the cave and the male takes up his duty of caring for and guarding the eggs.

At a temperature of about 26°C the eggs hatch in 48 hours. The milky white fry hang like little commas among the bubbles of the nest. When the fry become free-swimming they can first be fed infusoria, and after about three days newly hatched brine shrimp or the smallest natural foods are accepted. Frequent partial water changes are beneficial in raising the fry. With a good diet of live foods, the parents can be ready for spawning in about a week although they may take a rest period lasting several months. Parents may or may not decide to eat the fry, so for safety they should be removed.

The Spike-Tailed Licorice Gourami is an interesting labyrinth fish that is good for aquarists who have little space and who do not wish to go to a lot of fuss over their fishes.

PAROSPHROMENUS FILAMENTOSUS

PECKOLTIA VITTATA (Steindachner)/*Striped Sucker Catfish*

R: The Amazon and the Rio Paraguay. **H**: A typical bottom-feeder that spends most of its time loafing about the bottom of the aquarium or going over plant leaves, trying to get every bit of the algal growth from them. Shy and spends much time hiding. **W**: Prefers water a bit on the cool side, around 21°C. **S**: Up to 15 cm. **F**: Does very well on frozen brine shrimp and pellet foods; should be offered some tubifex worms now and then.

It is one of the more attractive catfishes, but there doesn't seem to be enough of them in any one place to warrant an all-out collecting trip for them. They will probably continually come into this country a few at a time, but as soon as helicopters are available in quantity to help fish collecting, this is one of those fish that will most benefit.

PELTEOBAGRUS FULVIDRACO

PELTEOBAGRUS BRASHNIKOWI Berg/*Russian Catfish*

R: Russia, in central reaches of Amur River. **H**: An active species, more crepuscular than nocturnal; peaceful, but not to be trusted with fishes small enough to be swallowed whole. **W**: Acidity/alkalinity factors are not critical, but the species will not tolerate prolonged maintenance under temperature conditions prevailing in tropical aquaria. Temperature 10 to 18°C. **S**: Up to almost 12 cm. **F**: Takes all live foods and most meaty prepared and frozen foods.

P. brashnikowi has two advantages over the bullheads when considering coldwater catfishes: it is smaller than any of them, growing to a maximum of about 12 cm, and it is less of a strictly nocturnal fish, which makes it much more visible in the tank, since it does not have the same tendency toward secretiveness as the bullheads. *P. brashnikowi* lays about 500-1,000 eggs, which are deposited among tangles of roots. They hatch in about 72 hours. Sex distinctions are unknown.

PECKOLTIA VITTATA

PELTEOBAGRUS FULVIDRACO (Richardson)/*Tawny Dragon Catfish*

R: China. **H**: Semi-retiring and generally peaceful with fishes of comparable size except for slow-moving or long-finned fishes; should not be trusted with fishes that might be swallowed. **W**: Wide tolerance for pH and hardness; extremes best avoided, as with most fishes. Since range extends well into cold water regions, probably withstands temperature as low as 4°C or less. **S**: 25 cm in nature; probably less than half that in the aquarium. **F**: Takes live foods such as small earthworms, frozen brine shrimp, beef heart, tablet and pellet foods, and probably most foods containing animal protein.

It is a handsome fish that has, in addition to the attributes of many of the other small and medium-sized catfishes belonging to its family, the ability to withstand cold water. Since interest in coldwater fishkeeping is increasing, a beautiful catfish should be a welcome addition to the non-tropical aquarium as well as the tropical. *P. fulvidraco* is suitable for both. Care is not difficult. As with its bagrid relatives such as the Barred Siamese Catfish hiding places such as rocks and caves are appreciated. Pieces of well-seasoned and properly conditioned driftwood also make good cover for bagrids and similar catfishes.

PELTEOBAGRUS BRASHNIKOWI

PELVICACHROMIS PULCHER (Boulenger)/*Kribensis*

R: Tropical West Africa, especially the Niger Delta. **H**: Peaceful; does some digging, but mostly under rocks, and plants are seldom uprooted. **W**: Not critical. Temperature 23 to 25°C. **S**: Males up to 8 cm; females to 6 cm. **F**: Live and frozen foods.

P. pulcher is not large enough to really put it in a class with the big cichlids, and at the same time it is rather large to be called a dwarf cichlid. Its behavior in mixed company is very mild, but for its most appealing feature, just look at the colors! It is best when first attempting to spawn a pair to keep them in separate tanks until the female becomes heavy with eggs.

The ideal spawning site is a flowerpot with a notch knocked out of the rim and set upside down on the bottom. There will be a great deal of activity, the male carrying out huge mouthfuls of gravel from inside the flowerpot, when suddenly one day both will disappear, to come out very rarely. Then a very comical situation develops. The little female will forcibly eject the male every time he tries to go in. Put him in another tank or he may get hurt. The female takes complete charge of the eggs and young but should be removed when the youngsters become free-swimming.

PELVICACHROMIS ROLOFFI

PELVICACHROMIS ROLOFFI (Thys van den Audenaerde)/ *Roloff's Kribensis*
R: Sierre Leone and eastern Guinea. **H:** Generally peaceful, even tending to be shy. **W:** Neutral to slightly acid (pH 6.5) water at a temperature of 24 to 26°C for keeping, slightly higher for breeding. **S:** Attains a maximum length of a little over 7.5 cm. **F:** Will accept a variety of aquarium fare but prefers live food.

One of the less common krib species is *Pelvicachromis roloffi*. It is a relatively small krib with the maximum length just over 7.5 cm. The color pattern includes in most individuals a row of spots along the base of the dorsal fin and some scattered spots in the caudal fin. However, these spots are quite variable and apparently not an indication of sex. Some females are said to have well developed spots, whereas some males have hardly any spots. It is not difficult to distinguish the sexes once you have seen a number of specimens. The males have the longer and more pointed fins, as is the case in so many other cichlid species. The breeding color of the female is quite distinct: the pelvic fins turn black, and the belly region becomes a beautiful violet color.

The tank housing Roloff's Kribensis should be fairly large and provided with a gravel bottom, some cover for battered mates, and caves or overturned flower pots with entry holes for possible spawning sites. The water should be neutral to slightly acid (it is about pH 6.5 in the natural habitat) with a temperature between 24 and 26°C. The hardness doesn't seem to be a problem, but between 6 and 8 DH seems to be suitable for this species. Periodic water changes are highly recommended.

Spawning can usually be precipitated with a slight rise in temperature (to about 27°C) and a water change. Courtship is similar to the other krib species. As mentioned above, the female's pelvic fins become black and her belly violet. Spawning is accomplished in privacy in the caves or inside the flower pot. The female apparently remains with the eggs and early fry, guarding them while the male forages for food and guards the perimeter of the territory against possible egg-snatchers. Rearing the young seems to pose no difficulty. The usual first foods such as newly hatched brine shrimp and powdered flake food seem to be adequate until they can handle larger fare.

521

PELVICACHROMIS SUBOCELLATUS *Gunther/Ocellated Krib*

R: Coastal regions of western Africa from Gabon to the Moanda region of Angola; this includes the lower Congo. **H:** Relatively peaceful, but will establish and defend a territory, especially when ready to spawn. **W:** Not critical. A temperature of 23 to 25°C is adequate. **S:** Attains a maximum size of about 12 cm. **F:** Will accept a variety of foods including *Daphnia*, tubifex, bloodworms, and even prepared foods.

Territories are generally set up by potential spawners. Both the male and female set them up, the female selecting a site immediately adjacent to that defended by the male. It is the female that adopts the more active role in courtship, maneuvering and twisting in front of the male so that her bright red belly is prominently displayed. The females also are aggressive toward one another and vie for the dominant position. It is the dominant female that usually winds up pairing with the male. The two spawners disappear into their preselected cave or flower pot, where the eggs are deposited. The actual laying of the eggs and the early stages in the development of eggs and fry are not often seen as they occur in the privacy of the cave or flower pot. After about ten days or so the young fish make their appearance. All this time the parents guard the eggs and fry, the female carrying a heavier burden of fanning than the male. The fry can be fed newly hatched brine shrimp, microworms, and other suitably small food items.

PERIOPHTHALMUS BARBARUS

PELVICACHROMIS TAENIATUS (Boulenger)/*Spriped Kribensis*

R: Lower Niger River, West Africa. **H:** Generally peaceful, even timid except when breeding. **W:** Soft, slightly acid water is best; the tank should be well planted and provide hiding places. Temperature 24 to 26°C. **S:** Male 8 cm; female slightly smaller. **F:** Live foods are preferred, but finely chopped beef heart is also accepted and even relished.

A flowerpot with a notch about one inch in diameter cut or broken out of the edge is partially filled with gravel, set upright in a dark corner and covered with a piece of slate. The male will soon be swimming in through the notch and returning with mouthfuls of gravel. Then one day it will be noticed that the female has taken possession and will not let him enter. A careful lifting of the slate will reveal that she is guarding eggs. In about ten days the young are free-swimming.

PELVICACHROMIS SUBOCELLATUS

PERIOPHTHALMUS BARBARUS (Linnaeus)/*Blotched Mudskipper*
R: East Africa to Australia. **H**: Cannot be combined with any other group of fishes; shy at first, but later can be tamed effectively. **W**: Water must have salt, ¹/₂ teaspoon to the liter, added; there should be an area where the fish can climb out of the water. Temperature 24 to 27°C. **S**: To 15 cm. **F**: Worms and living insects.

In the aquarium, mudskippers are not the easiest fishes in the world to keep. Their tank should be shallow and have a large surface. Their water, what there is of it, should have about a half teaspoon of salt added to it per liter. The sand should be sloped to come out of the water, and a few flat rocks may be placed at the water's edge. It is important that the air be warm and moist, so the tank must be kept tightly covered.

PELVICACHROMIS TAENIATUS

PERIOPHTHALMUS PAPILIO Bloch & Schenider/*Butterfly Mudskipper*

R: Western Africa from Senegal to the Zaire River. **H**: Cannot be maintained with any other class of fishes; they soon overcome their initial shyness. **W**: Water must have a salt content, about a half teaspoon to the liter; areas must be provided for the fish to climb out onto a dry perch. **S**: Attains a size of 16 cm. **F**: Living insects or small earthworms; tubifex worms are also welcome; can be trained to take other foods.

The expression "helpless as a fish out of water" does not apply to the mudskippers. They actually seem to prefer the land to the water and are awkward swimmers. Students of ecology can see in these fishes a remarkable adaptation of a creature to a highly individual biotope. Mudskippers inhabit muddy tidal flats where very little water is left at low tide.

PETENIA SPLENDIDA

PERRUNICHTHYS PERRUNO Schultz/*Leopard Catfish; Perruno*

R: Apparently known only from the Lake Maracaibo basin. **H**: An aggressive predator, this catfish should not be kept with fishes smaller than itself. **W**: Not critical. A temperature range of 21-25°C, a pH of 5.8-7.2, and a hardness below 15°dGH is sufficient. **S**: Attains a length of about 60 cm. **F**: A meaty diet is recommended with the accent on live foods, all kinds of which are accepted. Small individuals will accept frozen foods as well.

Among the features ascribed to this fish are the greatly depressed head, the very long banded maxillary barbels that reach to the caudal fin, the superior eyes, and especially the size and position of the patches of vomerine and palatine teeth. The dorsal spine has a flexible produced tip that extends beyond the branched rays (which number 7 or 8). The pectoral spine is broad and heavy, with spines on both edges. The tail is forked. The pattern is more or less reticulated in smaller specimens but evolves to a spotted one in adults.

Because of their feeding habits two things are recommended. First, their tankmates should be relatively large. Large cichlids and large tetras fit the bill very well. Secondly, because they eat so much a good filtration system must be used to help keep the tank reasonably clean. Finally, floating plants have been used with success to help keep the tank somewhat less brightly lit. Many catfishes, the Leopard Catfish included, do best in dimly lighted tanks.

PETENIA SPLENDIDA Guenther/*Red Snook*

R: Southeastern Mexico, northern Guatemala, and Belize; Atlantic slope from the Rio Grijalva basin to the Rio Usumacinta and the Belize River. **H:** A large predatory fish that should not be trusted with smaller fishes. **W:** Not critical. Has been found in clear waters in Belize. **S:** Attains a length of 38 cm or more. **F:** Does well on live foods such as goldfish, with the addition of balanced prepared foods.

Spawning has been accomplished in a 160-liter tank with a male and female that paired naturally. The tank was provided with a flat piece of slate. Gravel was often pushed around the tank until the pair was satisfied. The first spawning of the pair yielded 200 to 300 eggs, few of which hatched. During spawning and for about a week or two afterward the pair did not eat as much as they normally would.

PETITELLA GEORGIAE Géry and Boutiere/*False Rummy-Nose Tetra*
R: Upper Amazon basin. **H**: Peaceful; best kept in schools. **W**: Soft, acidic water is preferred, but not critical. Best temperature is 23 to 25°C. **S**: To 8 cm. **F**: Accepts all standard aquarium foods and especially relishes live freshwater crustaceans like daphnia.

Petitella georgiae, first described in 1964, happens to be involved in one of the most persistent cases of look-alike mix-ups that the aquarium hobby has known. The similarity to *Hemigrammus rhodostomus* (and others) in external distinguishing marks is indeed remarkable, and it is difficult for even a trained eye to distinguish between these fishes. The structure of the teeth is especially different, and tooth structure is a very important morphological character in the taxonomic placement of the tetras.

PETROCHROMIS TREWAVASAE Poll/*Filament-fin Petrochromis*
R: Lake Tanganyika, probably restricted to the shoreline of the west coast of the lake beween Moba and Sumbu. **H**: Tends toward aggression, especially when its own kind is involved. **W**: Typical for Lake Tanganyika fishes—hard and alkaline. **S**: Usually less than l5 cm. **F**: A vegetarian by nature but will accept a variety of aquarium foods. Must have a good proportion of vegetable matter in its diet for best results.

Spawning is not a very violent affair, although in confined quarters or without enough hiding places the females may suffer. Chases and displays occur until the pair move into a more secluded area between rocks or under an overhang to spawn. The female picks up the eggs and broods them for up to five weeks, the eggs hatching after about a week. About 15-20 fry are a good spawn. Telltale signs of mating are the courtship display, the descent of the female's ovipositor, and the female's reduction of her intake of food (indicating incubation, as the female will take food at this time but in reduced quantities). The fry will accept newly hatched brine shrimp and other similar foods but do better if they receive some vegetable material like their parents. Placing them in a tank where algal growth is luxuriant would help greatly.

PETITELLA GEORGIAE

PETROTILAPIA TRIDENTIGER Trewavas/*Blue Petroilapia*

R: Lake Malawi, Africa. **H**: Quarrelsome toward other fishes and therefore should be kept by themselves. **W**: Hard, alkaline water; the addition of salt is indicated, ¹/₄ tablespoon per liter. Temperature 24 to 27°C. **S**: Males 10 cm; females a little smaller. **F**: Live or freeze-dried foods; add some foods of vegetable origin.

Petrotilapia is a mouthbrooder. Males have large yellow spots on the anal fin. These spots have an interesting application: when the female has finished picking up the eggs she has laid, the male spreads out his anal fin before her. She sees the spots and tries to pick them up, thinking she has missed some eggs. Instead she gets a mouthful of sperm, which fertilizes the eggs she has already put in her mouth.

PETROCHROMIS TREWAVASAE

PHAGO MACULATUS Ahl/*African Pike Characin*

R: West Africa, in the Niger River. **H**: A decidedly nasty fish that will kill for the sheer pleasure of killing. **W**: Neutral, medium-soft water best. Temperature 23 to 24°C. **S**: Up to 20 cm, but usually seen much smaller. **F**: Needs plenty of meaty foods, preferably live fishes, although it will also accept dead ones.

This mean fish is seldom available because of the irregularity of West African fish shipments, but you can bet that *Phago* is not missed except by a few hobbyists who are willing to put up with its vicious nature for the sake of owning an oddity. In effect, the African Pike Characin is the piscatorial counterpart of the weasel, for *Phago,* like the weasel, kills more than it needs to satisfy its hunger. It almost seems that the fish takes pleasure in killing, and *Phago* even goes the weasel one better by torturing its victims before dispatching them.

PHALLOCEROS CAUDIMACULATUS

PHALLICHTHYS AMATES (Miller)/*Merry Widow*

R: Atlantic coastal regions from Guatemala to northern Panama. **H**: Peaceful toward other fishes, but very fond of eating its own young. **W**: Slightly alkaline water is best. Temperature 22 to 24°C. **S**: Males 3 cm; females 7 cm. **F**: Should have some algae on which to nibble, as well as prepared, frozen, and live foods.

The Merry Widow once was a very popular livebearer. An usual feature of the male of this species is an exceptionally long gonopodium. Although this species is relatively easy to breed, live foods should be fed as a conditioner. Plant food should also be included in their diet. The brood number in a large female is about 45.

PHAGO MACULATUS

PHALLOCEROS CAUDIMACULATUS (Hensel)/*Caudo*

R: From Rio de Janeiro to Paraguay and Uruguay. **H**: Peaceful at all times; not greatly inclined to eat their young if well fed. **W**: Slightly alkaline water that is well filtered and clean; the tank should stand in a sunny location. Temperature 23 to 26°C. **S**: Males up to 3 cm; females to 6 cm. **F**: Small sizes of live and prepared foods, supplemented with algae, which is nibbled from plants and glass sides. **C**: Yellowish to golden with black irregular markings.

Females are not very productive. The fry are a little delicate at first, but once they begin growing the battle is over.

PHALLICHTHYS AMATES

PHENACOGASTER PECTINATUS (Cope)/*Pectinatus*

R: Middle and upper Amazon basin. **H**: Generally peaceful at all times. **W**: Soft, slightly acid water. Temperature 22 to 27°C. **S**: About 5 cm. **F**: This species is omnivorous and should be given a mixed diet of plant and animal matter; it will accept prepared flake food but prefers small live or frozen foods.

This species is a lively and very peaceful shoaling fish. In nature it feeds upon aquatic plants, drifting insects, and, to a certain extent, the water's surface film. *P. pectinatus* will thrive on small foods such as brine shrimp or daphnia. Tufts of fine-leaved plants should be placed in the aquarium if spawning is to be tried. The spawning ritual is often violent, with fish diving at each other around the aquarium and finally into the plants. If there is a successful breeding, remove the parents before they eat their eggs.

PHOXINUS ERYTHROGASTER

PHENACOGRAMMUS INTERRUPTUS (Boulenger)/*Congo Tetra*

R: Zaire River region. **H**: Peaceful toward fishes of comparable size; a school fish that prefers to swim in groups. **W**: Soft, slightly acid water that has been treated with the addition of an acid peat moss. Temperature about 24°C. **S**: Males to 8 cm; females to 6 cm. **F**: Large live and frozen foods, supplemented by coarse prepared foods. **C**: Large opalescent scales; fins grayish violet with white edges; indistinct yellowish horizontal stripe.

The eggs are laid among plants near the bottom. When they are finished the parents should be removed. Hatching takes place in six days and in 24 to 36 hours the young are free-swimming. Being quite large, they will take newly hatched brine shrimp at once; growth progresses at a rapid rate.

PHOXINUS ERYTHROGASTER (Rafinesque)/*Southern Redbelly Dace*

R: Eastern United States west of the Alleghenies and in the Mississippi River tributaries. **H:** A cool-water species tending to be predaceous. Not recommended for the community tank. **W:** Requires cooler conditions than the "tropical" fishes; generally 15-21°C is sufficient. **S:** Attains a length of 8 to 9 cm. **F:** Not fussy; will eat a wide variety of aquarium foods from flake foods to live brine shrimp.

Spawning in nature occurs in late spring (May to June) when schools of Southern Redbelly Dace congregate in pools. Several males chase a single female. Spawning occurs when, while swimming up a riffle, the males press on either side of the female. The fish maintain their position with the help of the tubercles and by wedging between stones. Facing upstream, the female is squeezed and there is rapid vibration when the eggs are released and fertilized. Examination of some females 6-8 cm in length revealed between 6,000 and almost 19,000 eggs. The eggs are adhesive and become attached to the bottom pebbles.

PHRACTOCEPHALUS HEMIOLIOPTERUS (Schneider)/*Redtailed Catfish*

R: Amazon River and many of its tributaries. **H**: Should not be kept with fishes they can swallow; otherwise they are fairly peaceful. **W**: Not at all critical; best water is soft and about neutral. Temperature 22 to 26°C. **S**: At least 90 cm in nature, probably larger. **F**: Omnivorous and has an excellent appetite.

Being quite attractive with their red tails, the dark upper parts, and white underparts of their bodies, some baby specimens occasionally find their way into the American market, and they grow and grow until their owners wonder where they will put the fish next. Native fishermen often catch these, but they will not eat the flesh because it is dark and they want fishes with white flesh. Eating a fish with dark flesh seems to violate one of the native superstitions, of which there are very many.

A pair of these handsome catfish has been exhibited by the Cleveland Aquarium, where they have grown to a much greater size than that of the 444 mm (about 18 inches) given by Fowler in his book "Os Peixes de Agua Doce do Brasil". The fish is no newcomer to the scientific world, the genus having been established by Agassiz as early as 1829. These fish are said to be excellent eating by those who do not object to the dark meat, and some day the fish may be introduced to tropical streams in other parts of the world for the purpose of providing a source of food.

PHRACTOLAEMUS ANSORGEI Boulenger/*African Mudfish*

R: Mouth of the Ethiope River, Niger Delta and the Upper Congo. **H**: Apparently not very aggressive. Can be kept with smaller fishes. **W**: Soft, slightly acid water best, with a temperature acrout 24 tO 26°C. **S**: Attains a length of about 16 cm. **F**: Bottom-feeder with a preference for worms.

Phractolaemus ansorgei is a very interesting and unusual fish. It is the sole member of the family Phractolaemidae, which for quite some time was bounced around from group to group as supposedly related to the Clupeidae (herrings), Osteoglossidae (arowanas) or Cyprinidae (barbs). Presently the family Phractolaemidae is placed in the order Gonorynchiformes along with the families Chanidae (with the milkfish, *Chanos chanos)* and Kneriidae *(Kneria)*.

The African Mudfish is elongate, mostly tubular, but with the posterior part somewhat flattened. The mouth is small, almost toothless, proboscis-like and capable of being extended forward. The small dorsal fin is located on the back just behind the middle of the body.

It was aquarists who apparently led to discovery of another oddity about this fish. They noticed it coming to the surface for air, much as a betta or gourami might do. When examined in detail it was found that there was a duct from the gut that led to the swim bladder, allowing this latter organ to act as an accessory breathing organ. This may tie in with the African Mudfish's normal habitat of muddy, weedy waters. It is reported to plow into the mud with the mouth, searching for its favorite food-worms of all types. In an aquarium, however, it accepts such items as tubifex worms, brine shrimp and even flake foods. These are taken only from the bottom (as far as known).

Breeding habits are not known although the sexes can be readily distinguished when adults. The male develops spawning tubercles on the head and some short spines, one per scale, on the middle and upper portions of the caudal peduncle. The females lack both these structures.

PHRACTOCEPHALUS HEMIOLIOPTERUS

PHRACTOLAEMUS ANSORGEI

PHRACTURA ANSORGEI Boulenger/*African Whiptailed Catfish*

R: Nigeria, Cameroon, Zaire. **H**: Very shy and should be given many places to hide; avoid moving them frequently. **W**: Clear and considerably acid water. Temperature 22 to 23°C. **S**: About 13 cm. **F**: Eats live daphnia and tubifex greedily, but should get vegetable substances in addition.

Phractura ansorgei spawns quite readily, but the young must have generous feedings of foods that are predominantly vegetable matter. The fish are inclined toward shyness, so their tank should be well planted and have a number of retreats where they can hide.

PIMELODUS CLARIAS

PIMELODELLA GRACILIS (Valenciennes)/*Slender Pimelodella*

R: Northern Amazon region into Venezuela. **H**: Peaceful with any fish it cannot swallow; nocturnal. **W**: Not sensitive; best is neutral to slightly alkaline water. Temperature 24 to 27°C. **S**: Usually to about 18 cm, but has been recorded to twice that size. **F**: A very greedy eater with strictly carnivorous habits; tubifex worms are consumed very eagerly.

The Slender Pimelodella gets rather large in the aquarium but it is otherwise a peaceful fish when kept with others it cannot swallow. It becomes very numerous in its native waters. Scientists who have studied this species in its natural habitat mention running into hordes of a very similar Pimelodella species in the Takatu River in Guyana.

During the latter part of the dry season when the river is very low, thousands of squirming, long-whiskered pimelodellas can easily be caught in the collector's seines. Most collectors find this species so numerous that they are thrown back and the collectors concentrate on rarer species. Prolific as they are in their native waters, there is no record of their breeding in the aquarium. They are greedy eaters and feedings must be generous.

PHRACTURA ANSORGEI

PIMELODUS CLARIAS (Bloch)/*Spotted Pimelodus*

R: Central America south to central South America. **H**: Peaceful with fishes too large to swallow; nocturnal. **W**: Any clean water suits this hardy fish. Temperature 20 to 26°C. **S**: To 30 cm; only young specimens are suitable for the average tank. **F**: Larger live foods like cut-up earthworms are preferred, but other foods like chunks of lean beef are also relished.

As with most nocturnal fishes, they are seen most frequently in a well-planted tank that does not receive a great deal of sunlight. In such a tank they feel secure and make themselves quite at home. This is not an algae-eating fish. Generous feedings of such foods as cut-up earthworms or other animal fodders should be provided. Chopped beef heart or other beef is excellent, but care must be taken that the fish receive enough during the dark hours and at the same time that there is nothing left to foul the tank in the morning.

PIMELODELLA GRACILIS

PIMELODUS ORNATUS Kner/Ornate *Pimelodus*

R: A wide-spread catfish from Surinam, Guyana, Brazil, Peru, Bolivia, Paraguay, Colombia, and Venezuela. **H:** A diurnal species that is quite active, requiring room to swim. Although not very aggressive it can take care of itself. **W:** Not critical. Does well in neutral water of moderate hardness. A temperature of 24° to 26° is adequate. **S:** Attains a length of about 28 cm. **F:** Feed a lot of meaty foods, including live fishes, earthworms, and adult brine shrimp.

Juveniles differ slightly from adults in the following manner. There is a third dark horizontal band extending from the ventral fins to the caudal. This disappears with growth. There is also a dark band the width of the fin in the dorsal which becomes reduced to a blotch with growth.

Keeping this species poses no major problems. A large aquarium is recommended as this species is a constant and powerful swimmer. Perhaps a 40-gallon tank or even larger should be used. Since it is a peaceful species it can be accommodated in a community tank with other fishes. These should preferably be middle and upper region fishes and of a size that the Ornate Pimelodus cannot swallow. Angelfish should not be included. If other bottom fishes are added they should be nocturnal to avoid conflicts.

The tank can be decorated in the normal manner with hiding places (caves from rocks, driftwood, etc.) provided. Plants are not bothered but because of the activity of this catfish they should be well rooted. A cover is recommended as this fish can jump. Sand or gravel for the bottom should not contain sharp edges.

The water itself is not critical. A neutral pH (6.5-7.2) and moderate hardness (15-18° dGH) are quite acceptable. Water changes are highly recommended as the barbels of this catfish seem to deteriorate as ammonia and nitrites build up. Under proper water conditions the barbels will usually regenerate in a few weeks. Some current provided by a power filter should also be added.

PIMELODUS PICTUS Steindachner/*Angelicus Pimelodus*

R: Colombia, in the region of Mitu. **H**: Peaceful; may be kept with much smaller fishes. **W**: Adapts to most water conditions that are not too far from neutral. Temperature 22 to 25°C. **S**: About 11 cm in the aquarium; in nature probably much larger. **F**: Accepts dried as well as frozen or freeze-dried foods.

In the March, 1965 issue of *Tropical Fish Hobbyist* magazine, Dr. Herbert R. Axelrod describes an expedition that he undertook with Bill Riese. Among the many species they found was one catfish that they immediately dubbed "Pimelodella angelicus" after the African species *Synodontis angelicus,* which it resembles. The resemblance, however, is in reverse: where *S. angelicus* has white spots on a black background, this fellow has black spots on a white background. *Pimelodus pictus* is nocturnal in its habits as so many of the other *Pimelodus* species are. *P. pictus* are not all averse to swimming in the lighted section of the aquarium, and they readily adjust to normal aquarium conditions. They are not predatory.

PIMELODUS ORNATUS

PIMELODUS PICTUS

PINIRAMPUS PIRINAMPU (Spix)/*Long-finned Catfish*

R: Guyana, Brazil, Venezuela, and Paraguay. **H**: Predatory, so should be kept with fishes too large to swallow; larger specimens do well with other similar-sized catfishes and large cichlids. Needs a large aquarium with plants, driftwood, or other retiring places. **W**: Adapts well to most water conditions that are not extreme in pH or hardness. Temperature 22 to 27°C. Small fish should not be allowed to become chilled. **S**: Probably a meter or more in nature; perhaps half this in a very large aquarium. **F**: For small fish, live or frozen brine shrimp, small worms, ground-beef heart, and other live or frozen foods; once feeding is established, almost any animal-based food is acceptable.

Pinirampus pirinampu has an extremely long adipose fin (which may be a third the length of the fish), and its barbels or "whiskers" are also exceptionally long and are flattened toward the base. Like other pimelodids of a similar nature, *Pinirampus* has a large mouth and it is capable of swallowing sizable fishes, so caution should be used in selecting tankmates.

PLATYSTACUS COTYLEPHORUS

PLATYDORAS COSTATUS (Linnaeus)/*Chocolate Catfish*

R: Middle Amazon region. **H**: Nocturnal; it digs into the soft mud during the daytime. **W**: Not critical; in Brazil it lives in small, hot, dirty pools. Temperature in the upper 20's (°C). **S**: 10 cm. in length. **F**: Prefers worms, frozen brine shrimp and beef heart; accepts the bulkier dry foods as a substitute.

The Rio Urubu, near the small town of Itacoatiara, contains some beautiful fishes, from the famous discus to the vicious piranha. In some of the tiny intermittent feeder streams that carry water to the Rio Urubu during the rainy season are to be found some very interesting fishes. By poking our nets into the mud and straining out whatever the mud contains, we sometimes come up with interesting surprises. When Harald Schultz and I (HRA) caught this beautiful Chocolate Catfish, the same net also had a few snakes in it!

PINIRAMPUS PIRINAMPU

PLATYSTACUS COTYLEPHORUS Bloch/*Mottled Whiptailed Banjo Catfish*

R: Northeastern South America from the Guianas to Brazil. **H:** A rather shy and retiring species that should be kept only with non-aggressive fishes. **W:** Not important as long as extremes are avoided. May tolerate a reasonable amount of salt in the water. Temperature range about 23° to 27°C. **S:** Attains a length of a bit over 30 cm. **F:** At first will accept only living tubificid worms and earthworms, but most specimens may be coaxed into eating frozen foods eventually.

The family Aspredinidae (banjo catfishes) is divided into two subfamilies, the Bunocephalinae, which are basically freshwater catfishes, and the Aspredininae, which inhabit mostly coastal regions of the Guianas and northern Brazil. They occur in the sea, in brackish water, and in estuaries and tidal portions of rivers. *Platystacus cotylephorus* belongs to the subfamily Aspredininae. This subfamily is characterized by a long-based anal fin. One of the most interesting aspects of the biology of this species is the fact that the female carries her eggs firmly attached to the underside of her body, which is modified into a spongy area just for that purpose. Females bearing eggs occasionally are imported. Mating habits are virtually unknown.

PLATYDORAS COSTATUS

PLATYSTOMATICHTHYS STURIO (Kner)/*Sturgeon Catfish*

R: Throughout the Amazon Basin. **H**: Fairly peaceful, but grows to a considerable size and is a predator on smaller fishes. **W**: Not critical. Temperature 22 to 26°C. **S**: May reach a size of up to 60 cm. in length. **F**: Will eat a variety of foods.

When young *Platystomatichthys sturio* arrive at the dealers they are usually rather emaciated. It is best then to give them some peace and quiet in a subdued light tank without very active fishes that would find sport in nipping at the long worm-like filaments. The young catfish should be fed in semi-darkness and, until they have gained some weight and have acclimated to the tank conditions, live food in the form of tubifex, baby Guppies, small earthworms, etc., is recommended.

POECILIA CHICA

POECILIA CAUCANA (Steindachner)/*Cauca Molly*

R: Southern Panama to eastern Colombia. **H**: Peaceful. **W**: Neutral to slightly alkaline. Temperature about 25 to 28°C. **S**: Males about 3 cm; females about 6 cm. **F**: Will take prepared foods, but should get occasional feeding of live or frozen foods. **C**: Body blue and belly silver; dorsal fin yellow to orange with a black edge; males have about a dozen light vertical bars.

Young are born in relatively small batches, 10 to 25 depending on the age and size of the female. Like all mollies, they should be kept in uncrowded tanks that are well aerated. Unlike most of our mollies, the parents are very quick to eat their young unless they are well protected by plant thickets in which to hide.

PLATYSTOMATICHTHYS STURIO

POECILIA CHICA Miller/*Chica*

R: Mexico, from the Rio Cuetzmala, Rio Purificacion, and Rio Cihuatlan. **H:** A lively fish that should get plenty of room. This livebearer does not bother its young. **W:** A pH of 6.6-6.8, dGH of 12-14°, and temperatures between 21-32°C are recommended. **S:** Attains a length of about 20-25mm. **F:** Will accept a variety of aquarium foods but the main diet should be algae or vegetable-based flake food.

Every 30-35 days between 30 and 40 7mm long young can be expected from a mature female. The adults do not molest these young so that several generations can exist in one tank at the same time. It is best to provide some dense plants for the young and even for the adults to serve as shelter from real or imagined dangers. The young males possess a dark longitudinal band along most of the body side that, with growth, breaks up into individual spots. The color of adults varies with mood and the position of the fish in a hierarchical scheme. The dominant male generally has a yellowish gonopodium and a pitch black body and black dorsal and caudal fins—very striking coloration indeed.

In the female there is a very interesting phenomenon. The gravid spot is normally dark but becomes lighter with increasing gravidness, the opposite of what occurs in many other livebearers. Sexual activity in the males is also stimulated by means of the release of pheromones by the females.

Poecilia chica has been crossed with the Lyretail Black Molly, producing some very colorful and interesting progeny.

POECILIA CAUCANA

A male of one of the xanthistic varieties of *Poecilia latipinna*.
Albino and black varieties also exist.

POECILIA LATIPINNA (Le Sueur)/*Sailfin Molly*

R: Southeastern coastal United States south to Yucatan. **H**: Peaceful toward other fishes, but best kept by themselves. **W**: Slightly alkaline water with a light addition of salt, a quarter teaspoon to the liter. Temperature 25 to 29°C. **S**: Males to 10 cm; females to 13 cm. **F**: A hearty eater that should be fed frequently with a preponderance of foods that have a vegetable content.

One of the most abused of all aquarium fishes is the Sailfin Molly. Very seldom does one see them kept with a perfect understanding of their requirements and habits, and consequently the specimens one sees are of a very poor quality. In the first place, the fish in its natural waters usually seeks a place where the water is shallow and becomes quite warm during the day. For this reason fish kept in captivity should be kept at higher temperatures than one generally gives to tropical species. Pursuing the topic still further, the warmer water holds less oxygen than the cooler water and in order to give them the oxygen they require, mollies should have a large, uncrowded tank. A study of their internal organs as well as observation of their habits tells us that they are largely vegetarians, and their food should contain a good percentage of vegetable matter.

Coming as they do from mostly brackish water, the addition of salt to their aquarium water is important. Females about to have young should not be moved, if possible, and breeding traps should not be used. Given a well-planted aquarium of her own, a molly will seldom eat her young.

POECILIA MELANOGASTER

POECILIA MELANOGASTER Günther /*Black-Bellied Limia; Blue Limia*

R: Jamaica and Haiti. **H**: Peaceful toward all but newly born young (including its own). **W**: Neutral to slightly alkaline. Temperature 22 to 25°C, slightly higher for breeding. **S**: Reaches a length of 6.5 cm for females; 4 cm for males. **F**: Needs a varied diet and frequent changes of food.

With sufficient plants in the aquarium and the fish well fed, the Blue Limia can be left to breed in the tank. The babies are rather quick and will use the plants as protection until they are large enough to prevent predation by the parents. For more precise breeding the sexes can be separated until young are wanted. Then the female is placed in the breeding tank first to be followed by the male once she has become acclimated. The gestation period is about 28 days, and broods of 10 to 80 may appear depending upon the size and health of the female.

POECILIA LATIPINNA

POECILIA MELANOGASTER

With dorsal unfurled to almost the maximum and its orange chest contrasting with the blue spangling of the fins and body, this male *Poecilia velifera* shows why the Saifin Mollies are as popular as they are.

The female (lower fish) of this pair of *Poecilia latipinna* is much less full in the belly area than a heavily pregnant female of this livebearing species would be.

POECILIA MEXICANA (Steindachner)/*Mexicana Molly, Shortfin Molly*

R: Atlantic slope from Rio San Juan, Mexico, southward to Colombia and to the Colombian West Indies. **H**: The behavior of this species is not consistent; individual specimens vary from completely peaceful to nasty. **W**: Hard, alkaline water is preferred; the tank should have a good amount of vegetation and be well lighted. Temperature 23 to 26°C. **S**: Up to 11 cm; males 1 cm to 2 cm smaller than the females. **F**: Should be given a diet with a good amount of vegetable matter, and live foods are taken readily; dry prepared foods are also accepted, although not preferred. **C**: There are many color forms; the principal colors are gray or black on the body with orange markings.

Poecilia mexicana has been a taxonomic problem for many years. In the past, it has been put in and out of synonymy with *P. sphenops* several times. There are several color varieties of *P. mexicana* and two subpecies, *P. m. mexicana* and *P. m. limantouri*. In the wild, this species feeds by removing accumulated algae from rock surfaces, eating both plant matter and also the small insects and crustaceans that live in the algal mat. In the aquarium, this species should be given a good amount of vegetable matter in its diet. This fish is a livebearer and is not difficult to breed in captivity.

POECILIA NIGROFASCIATA (Regan)/*Humpbacked Limia*

R: Haiti and Dominican Republic. **H**: Peaceful toward other fishes, but is very much apt to eat its own young. **W**: Slightly alkaline water required. Temperature should not be lower than 25°C. **S**: Males up to 5 cm; females slightly larger. **F**: Not critical; will take dried foods as well as live or frozen foods.

One of the most interesting features of this fish is the transformation in shape of the males as they get older. The back and lower posterior region accumulate fatty tissue, and they have a deformed appearance which makes them look like a fish with spinal curvature, in spite of the fact that the spine remains perfectly normal. An unusual bit of coloration which also appears in the males is the relatively long black gonopodium.

Rather than the normal four weeks of "gestation," the females may take as long as six weeks before they release their young. Broods are small in number but make up for it by their size.

POECILIA RETICULATA

POECILIA PARAE Eigenmann/*Two-Spot Livebearer*

R: Northeastern South America. **H**: Inclined to be nasty; a fin-nipper. **W**: Slightly alkaline, medium-hard water. Temperature 26 to 30°C. **S**: 4 to 5 cm. **F**: Accepts all regular aquarium foods.

The Two-Spot Livebearer is not a very colorful fish and will always be in the shadow of its very popular cousin the Guppy. In the wild this fish inhabits standing water found in ditches and small ponds as well as larger bodies of brackish water found near the coast. In the aquarium, the water should be on the alkaline side of neutral, and it is often a good idea to make a water mixture of 5% sea water.

This is a difficult fish to breed for several reasons. Broods are small, 10 to 20 fry, and the young are very delicate, most expiring in a matter of days. The males mature at 1 cm. Newborn young should be fed infusoria. Adults should be fed small live foods and should have a good amount of vegetable matter in their diet.

POECILIA NIGROFASCIATA

POECILIA RETICULATA Peters/*Guppy*

R: Trinidad, Venezuela, Barbados, and parts of northern Brazil and the Guianas. **H**: Peaceful, very active and prolific. **W**: Soft, slightly alkaline water is best; clean, well-filtered water is important for healthy conditions. Temperature 23 to 26°C. **S**: Males to about 4 cm., usually less; females to about 6 cm. **F**: Good eaters that should be fed a variety of foods, live, frozen, or prepared; frequent small feedings are preferable. **C**: Wild males have gray bodies with black and varicolored markings; fancy specimens are bred in all imaginable colors and fin shapes.

Wild specimens are not particularly pretty; short fins, a gray body, and some black markings with a few spots of red, yellow, or green would describe the males, and a plain gray body the females. From these the breeders have developed many strains in a rainbow of colors and with long, flowing fins in a variety of shapes. Many countries in the tropics have taken advantage of the prolific nature and wide adaptability of the wild fish and have introduced them into mosquito-infested areas, where they could be counted upon to do an excellent job of eating the mosquito larvae almost as quickly as they hatched.

A newly born batch of Guppies is, of course, of mixed sex, but this cannot be told until the age of about four weeks is attained. Whether the young Guppies are separated from their mother is in part a matter of choice and in part a question of her tendency to eat them. A variety of Guppy traps are used, and about the only advice that can be given at this stage is that a large one be used so that the female is not unduly confined, if one be used at all. If the mother is well fed she will not eat her young, but if there is any danger of this occurring then it is most important that the young and the mother be separated.

POECILIA PARAE

POECILIA RETICULATA

The young males and females can be separated from one another at about a month and prior to this stage will not have mated, although a more mature male in the same tank is believed to be capable of fertilizing even very young females. This should, therefore, be avoided. The separated male and female fry should then be raised in groups to the age of three or four months to get as much size on them as possible and to prevent too early breeding.

If one is breeding for fancy fish this procedure involves two most important principles. First, early breeding of females tends to slow down their growth undesirably and thus reduce not only the size of the mother herself, but also to reduce the size and batch size of the young she may produce. Big mothers throw big babies. Secondly, even if it is desirable to mate small batches of Guppies together rather than to try and raise them in pairs, it is not desirable to raise all of a batch of fry together because some degree of selection must be exerted. Even further, if a batch of males of variable development is left together with females, the smaller and smaller-finned males are the quickest to mature and are liable to fertilize the females much more frequently than their larger and slower-moving counterparts. This again will result in the reverse type of selection to that which is desired. Nevertheless, it is not desirable to try to raise individual pairs. These are hard to feed properly without water pollution and they do not seem to get on so well as when in the presence of several other pairs, which embodies a degree of competition in feeding and mating and also prevents too great a degree of inbreeding.

POECILIA RETICULATA

POECILIA RETICULATA

POECILIA RETICULATA

POECILIA RETICULATA

POECILIA RETICULATA

POECILIA RETICULATA

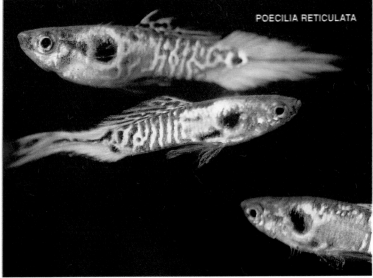

POECILIA RETICULATA

POECILIA SPHENOPS Valenciennes/*Sphenops Molly*

R: Mexico and Central America, also parts of northern South America. **H**: Individual specimens show marked differences in behavior; some are completely peaceful and others are nasty. **W**: Hard, alkaline water best; tank should have plenty of plants and be well lighted. Temperature 23 to 26°C. **S**: Up to 10 cm; usually seen about half this size. **F**: Doesn't like dry food unless it contains a high percentage of vegetable matter; small crustaceans form a good meaty portion of the diet.

The Sphenops Molly, although not as tough as some other livebearers, like the Platy and Guppy, is generally more robust than *Poecilia latipinna* and *P. velifera*. First of all, it requires less space for proper growth, but it has advantages besides this. It is easier to feed, as it accepts dry and frozen foods more readily, and it is easier to keep with other species, because it is not so dependent on the special water conditions needed for other mollies. A pretty fish, *Poecilia sphenops* is usually seen as one of three varieties: plain black, mottled black with orange tail, or gray-green with orange tail. The male fish has the orange tail.

POECILIA SPHENOPS

POECILIA SPHENOPS

POECILIA SPHENOPS

POECILIA VELIFERA (Regan)/*Yucatan Sail-Fin Molly*

R: Yucatan. **H**: Individuals vary; some are peaceful and some, especially large males, are bullies. **W**: Hard, alkaline water with salt added is best. Temperature 23 to 26°C. **S**: Up to 13 cm. **F**: Needs plenty of vegetable matter, especially algae, in diet, but also takes meaty foods. *Poecilia velifera* is not often seen today, mostly because *P. latipinna* can be found wild in the southern states along the Gulf Coast, where it is sometimes caught and shipped as a pool-raised fish. When in good condition, *Poecilia velifera* is tough to beat for looks, for it is truly a beautiful fish, especially with the majestic dorsal fin at full spread.

POECILIA VELIFERA

POECILIA VITTATA

POECILIA VITTATA Guichenot/*Banded Limia*

R: Cuba. **H**: Peaceful; likes to nibble algae, but will seldom damage plants. **W**: Slightly alkaline water with about one quarter teaspoon of salt per liter added. Recommended temperature 25°C with a sunny aquarium. **S**: About 6 cm; females about 10 cm. **F**: Not critical; will take dried foods as well as live and frozen foods, but should also get some vegetable nourishment.

A sunny tank with a high temperature is the prime requirement for this *Poecilia* species. The fact that a tank of this sort will produce some algae is grist for the mill, for this species loves to graze on algae. As a rule they confine their appetites to this and do not nip at the plants in the aquarium. As a precaution it is well, however, to avoid using the softer-bodied plants like water sprite. In the absence of algae a leaf of spinach or lettuce will give the necessary vegetable nutrition.

This fish is inclined to be a bit shy in a sparsely planted aquarium and will not be at ease unless the planting is heavy. This will also afford protection to the fry when they are born and give them a place to hide from their ever-hungry parents. As with other *Poecilia* species, broods are not very large numerically, but they make up for their small number by being unusually big when they are born, which makes them easier to raise.

POECILIOPSIS GRACILIS

POECILIOPSIS GRACILIS (Heckel)/*Porthole Livebearer*

R: Atlantic and Pacific watersheds from southern Mexico to Nicaragua. **H**: Peaceful toward other fishes and does not harm plants; seldom even harm their own fry. **W**: Neutral to slightly alkaline; avoid chilling and keep the temperature at 24 to 27°C. **S**: Males to 3 cm; females to 5 cm. **F**: Not fussy eaters; will consume all foods they can swallow, but of course should get some occasional live foods.

Breeders who could be producing these lesser-known fish are so busy supplying the demand for platies, swordtails and mollies for which there is a ready market that they do not take up their time and space with slow-selling species. Forty years ago this little livebearer was in fairly good supply, as were many others which the younger hobbyists of today have never seen and in all probability will never see. *Poeciliopsis gracilis* is a model citizen in the community aquarium. They do not uproot or bite chunks out of plants and if fed properly will seldom attack their young. A very desirable fish, the Porthole Livebearer would be an asset to any livebearer collection.

POLYCENTROPSIS ABBREVIATA Boulenger/*African Leaf Fish*

R: Tropical West Africa. **H**: Greedy eaters that can swallow a fish almost as large as themselves; not to be kept in a community tank. **W**: Soft, acid water is best. Temperature 26 to 28°C. **S**: To 8 cm. **F**: Earthworms and smaller unwanted living fishes preferred, but can be trained to take chunks of beef heart.

The African Leaf Fish, unlike its South American counterpart, does not go around imitating a dead leaf all day, but the markings are similar and permit it to blend unnoticed into the background. Another point of similarity is the huge mouth which can engulf a good-sized fish with no trouble at all. The tail is so transparent that it looks as if it had been chopped off; this and the huge head and mouth give the appearance of a fish which has been cut in half and allowed to swm around. The African Leaf Fish has a surprising manner of spawning. It builds a bubblenest of large proportions, preferably under a floating leaf. The parents then circle underneath the bubbles in an upside down position, releasing and fertilizing the eggs. For her safety the female should be removed when this is finished. The male guards the eggs and fry when they hatch after 48 hours. After they become free-swimming the male's job may be considered at an end and it is best to remove him.

POLYPTERUS ORNATIPINNIS

POLYCENTRUS PUNCTATUS (Linnaeus)/*Spotted Leaf Fish*

R: Northeastern South America and Trinidad. **H**: Aggressive and capable of swallowing fishes almost as large as themselves; should not be kept in a community tank. **W**: Neutral to slightly acid and soft. Temperature 24 to 26°C. **S**: To 10 cm. **F**: Smaller fishes and pieces of earthworm preferred, but can be trained to take pieces of beef heart or other lean meat, shrimp or fish.

Polycentrus punctatus is an aggressive, nasty, greedy, and vicious fish that is capable of overcoming and devouring prey close to its own size in total length. Spawning occurs in craters in the aquarium gravel. The fry are known to be cannibalistic and, since they often grow at different rates, should be sized and separated from each other. The parents will usually not eat the young unless scared or underfed.

POLYCENTROPSIS ABBREVIATA

POLYPTERUS ORNATIPINNIS Boulenger/*Prettyfin Bichir*

R: Upper and Middle Congo (Zaire). **H:** A nocturnal predator that cannot be trusted with smaller fishes. **W:** Not critical as long as extremes are avoided. Soft, slightly acid water best at temperatures between 21° and 29° C. **S:** Attains a length of at least 40 cm total length. **F:** Accepts a variety of aquarium type foods. Small feeder fishes are also welcome.

When spawning occurs the male swims parallel to the female and curls over her while folding his fin over her back. He curves his body to fit hers and pushes her toward the rocks and plants. In this "S" or "J" shape they quiver as a number of eggs are released and fertilized. Spawning lasts over a period of three to four days with at least 20-30 eggs released per day or as many as 200-300 per spawning. The parents should be removed as soon as spawning is completed. The eggs are brownish in color and about 2 mm in diameter. They hatch in 2-4 days and are ready for newly hatched brine shrimp in about a week. After two weeks the fry are 18-19 mm in total length and can receive chopped tubificid worms.

POLYCENTRUS PUNCTATUS

POPTELLA ORBICULARIS

POPTELLA ORBICULARIS (Valenciennes)/*Silver Disc Tetra*

R: Amazon Basin as well as from Guyana, Colombia, and Peru to Paraguay. **H:** A generally peaceful fish which does best in schools or small groups of its own kind. **W:** Prefers soft and slightly acid water. The temperature should range from 23 to 27°C. Water changes are recommended. **S:** Attains a length of about 11 to 12 cm. **F:** An omnivorous species that will accept a variety of aquarium foods.

Poptella orbicularis is one of those tetras which are basically silvery and compressed. It has commonly been called a silver dollar tetra, but that name is usually reserved for the Myleinae. It has also been confused with *Gymnocorymbus thayeri* (which had been called *Moenkhausia bondi*), but differs from that species by its deeper body and the presence of the saddle-shaped predorsal "spine" hidden under the skin. *Poptella* was formerly known as *Ephippicharax*, and the name *Ephippicharax orbicularis* might be seen in the older literature.

Since this fish grows to a length of 11 to 12 cm and is best kept in schools or small groups, large tanks are highly recommended. The water should be soft and slightly acidic, with temperatures in the range of 23 to 27°C. Frequent water changes are usually beneficial and are also recommended. Plants are useful in providing shelter when the fish are frightened and may even provide some sustenance for these omnivorous fish. Most other aquarium foods are acceptable as well.

Poptella orbicularis is a prolific breeder under the correct conditions. Sexes are distinguished by the more rounded body of the female and the dark anterior rays of the anal fin of the male. This latter distinction has not been confirmed, however. Spawning takes place in the open water (similar to other free-spawning characins) and near the surface, where there is a great deal of lively splashing in the process. A cover for the tank might be useful. The numerous fry are not difficult to raise using standard methods for egglayers.

POTAMOTRYGON LATICEPS Garman/*Freshwater Stingray*

R: Amazon basin. **H**: Spends all of its time on the bottom, sometimes almost covered; small specimens are bottom-feeders and will seldom attack other fishes. **W**: Slightly alkaline water with fine gravel on the bottom. Temperature 24 to 27°C. **S**: Up to 122 cm. **F**: Worms, bits of shrimp, clam, etc.

What is the most feared fish in South American waters? Before you jump to the wrong conclusions and say that it is the piranha, let me hasten to tell you that it is the stingray. There are many more instances of natives being injured painfully by its whipping tail than there are cases of piranha bites. A stingray will lie on the bottom in the sand and change colors to blend exactly with its surroundings. Here it is the master of any situation. Other fishes cannot (and will not) attack it, and its only danger is that of being trampled upon. This is where its very effective weapon comes into play. The "stinger" does not make much of a wound going in, but it has many barbs on its surface that rip the flesh when it is withdrawn. There is no injection of poison as with a snake, but the slimy coating causes an agonizingly painful swelling and infection. Freshwater Stingrays often bury themselves in the gravel, sometimes covering themselves almost completely, with only the eyes and the top of the head showing, and sometimes covering only the far edges of the body disk. Because of their semi-burrowing habit the gravel in their tank should not be coarse or large. Stingrays often position themselves vertically along the sides or front of the tank, rippling the outer fin edges to maintain position. There are at least 8 species in the genus *Potamotrygon*.

PRIAPELLA INTERMEDIA

PRIAPELLA INTERMEDIA Alvarez/*Blue-Eyed Livebearer*

R: Eastern Mexico north of the Yucatan Peninsula to Vera Cruz. **H**: Peaceful. **W**: Hardness and acidity factors are of no great importance as long as extremes are avoided. Temperature in the mid 20's (°C) are best. This species is especially susceptible to abrupt chills. **S**: Up to 5 cm.; usually seen a bit smaller; males and females both reach the same approximate size. **F**: Not at all choosy as to types of food accepted, taking all standard live, prepared, and frozen foods eagerly. The method of feeding, however, is important, as this species has a tendency to ignore all foods that are not available to it at the top level of the water; once they hit the bottom, the fish lose interest unless they are very hungry.

One big difference between *Priapella* and more common aquarium livebearers is the size of the broods delivered: *Priapella* is a much less fecund fish, producing an average of only about 12 babies per brood at intervals of five weeks. Another difference is that in female *Priapella* the dark marking near the vent that indicates gravidity is either absent or so faint as to be indistinguishable.

PRIONOBRAMA FILIGERA (Cope)/*Glass Bloodfin*

R: Tributaries of the Rio Madeira. **H**: Peaceful, very active fish that prefer to be in groups. **W**: Soft, slightly acid water is best; the tank should afford a good amount of swimming room. Temperature 23 to 26°C. **S**: To 6 cm. **F**: Prepared foods accepted, but live foods should be given at least several times a week. **C**: Body transparent with a light blue tint and dark blue shoulder-spot; anal and caudal fins red at the base; anal with a white edge.

The Glass Bloodfin is an active, attractive fish when kept in a group. They are skilled jumpers, so the tank in which they are kept should be kept covered at all times. They spawn in a helter-skelter fashion, the males pursuing the females like danios and scattering eggs all over the tank, where most of them fall to the bottom. As soon as the driving is finished the breeders should be removed or the eggs will be eaten. Fry hatch in a day at 26°C and grow rapidly.

PROBARBUS JULLIENI

PROBARBUS JULLIENI Sauvage/*Seven-Striped Barb*

R: Thailand and the Malay Peninsula. **H:** Peaceful; should not be kept with aggressive fishes.
W: Not critical as long as extremes are avoided. Normal aquarium temperatures are adequate.
S: Attains a length of up to 1 meter, but usually far less in aquaria. **F:** Not fussy, but because it
only takes food from the bottom, foods that sink are essential.

The Seven-Striped Barb occurs in freshwater streams with mostly sandy or muddy bottoms,
usually in deep, clear water. It is highly esteemed as a food fish and is caught by fishermen with
set-lines and various nets. Individuals are caught on hook-and-line with a worm bait or even on
hooks baited with rice balls.

Although this species attains a length of about a meter, aquarists would rarely see one even
half that large. More likely small ones would be imported and grow in large aquaria to more
than 30 or 40 cm. In spite of its large size, this is not an aggressive species and may even be
said to be peaceful, if not docile. If it is to be kept in a community tank its tankmates should not
be aggressive. Definitely no aggressive feeders should be in the tank, as this species cannot
compete with them and may waste away without proper nourishment. In the wild the
Seven-Striped Barb feeds chiefly on water plants, so vegetable matter should make up a large
part of its diet in an aquarium. It is said to enjoy munching on lettuce and makes quick work of
some live aquarium plants. The food supplied should be of a type that sinks or at least should
be weighed down so that this fish, which is a bottom-feeder, will be able to make use of it. Water
conditions are not important as long as extremes are avoided. Temperatures in a range of
about 22° to 27°C are acceptable. Breeding has not been reported and probably will not be
seen in aquaria under normal conditions given the size this species attains. However, in a
rather large tank (500 liters or better) and with early maturing fishes, it just might be possible. *P.
jullieni* grubs through the substrate in its efforts to find food, so it has a tendency to stir up small
swirls of detrius; in this regard it serves much the same purpose as *Corydoras* catfish and other
bottom-grubbers.

PROCATOPUS NOTOTAENIA

PROCATOPUS NOTOTAENIA Boulenger/*Blue Lady Killie*

R: Southern Cameroon to southwestern Nigeria. **H**: Non-aggressive; moderately active. **W**: Soft, slightly acid water optimal. Temperature 19 to 24°C. **S**: Males 3 cm; females slightly smaller. **F**: Live, frozen or dried foods accepted.

There are two anatomical peculiarities in the fish. First, the male has a spine-like projection behind the gill covers; second, the ventral fins are placed extremely far forward for a killifish. This dwarf species does not require a lerge aquarium. The temperature should be between 19 and 24°C. This dwarf species does not appreciate warmer temperatures. *P. nototaenia* seems more comfortable in a heavily planted aquarium.

This species spawns readily in nylon mops placed near the bottom. The eggs hatch in 14 to 21 days at 21°C. Resting eggs are common, but they may be stimulated to hatch by placement in a small container with a small amount of dried food. This creates an oxygen deficiency that will sometimes stimulate hatching. Infusoria is required as a first food. The fry are difficult to raise and are sensitive to water changes.

PROCATOPUS SIMILIS

PROCATOPUS SIMILIS Ahl/*Nigerian Lampeye*

R: Western Cameroon and southern Nigeria; Fernando Po **H:** Peaceful, but usually kept in small tanks by themselves. **W:** Soft, neutral to slightly acid water preferred. Temperature 20 to 26°C. **S:** Males 7 cm, females 5 cm in total length. **F:** Frozen and flake foods accepted but live foods (especially fruit flies and brine shrimp) are preferred.

The tank housing the Nigerian Lampeye need not be large; successful spawnings occur regularly in 10- to 20-liter aquaria. Since they come from fast-moving streams, it is advisable to provide a current in their tank. This can usually be accomplished by means of a small power filter or high aeration.

The water should be soft, the carbonate hardness not exceeding about 5 DH, and around neutral or even slightly acid. Some aquarists add about a tablespoon of salt to a 20-liter tank. For general keeping, a small group makes a nice display in a tank; for breeding you may want to use a couple of pairs or a trio of one male per two females. (The males are the more colorful of the pair). Although *P. nototaenia* has been successfully spawned using spawning mops, *P. similis* spawned in porous rocks. It may be that these fish are flexible enough to use different substrates, so it might be best to provide both the spawning mop and porous rocks. One aquarist observed the spawning behavior, which included a display by the male to attract the female. The pair would approach one of the rocks side by side and move around it wiggling from time to time in the current. After about 15 to 20 seconds the female would break off but return as the male started to display again. The rock(s) with eggs may be removed to the hatching aquarium after about a week to ten days. The fry usually are seen a few days later (total time 12 to 14 days) and should be able to take small newly hatched brine shrimp. The rock spawning habit is probably an adaptation to spawning in running water. The eggs are deposited in clefts or crevices in the rocks where they immediately expand and become wedged more tightly in place so that the current doesn't carry them off. Growth is relatively slow at first, but maturity should be reached in about nine months or so.

PROTOPTERUS ANNECTENS

PROTOPTERUS ANNECTENS Owen/*African Lungfish*

R: Widespread from central to southeastern Africa, mostly in low-lying swampy areas. **H**: Strictly a predator; will ignore small fast-moving fishes but will eat anything slow enough to be caught. **W**: Not critical. **S**: To well over 60 cm. **F**: Younger specimens will accept most standard aquarium foods.

The order Dipneusti is a very ancient order of primitive fishes that once, according to fossil records, were widely distributed over the major land masses but are now confined to central South America, central Africa and eastern central Australia. There are two families of these little fishes: the Lepidosirenidae and the Ceratodontidae. The family Lepidosirenidae contains the living genera *Lepidosiren* (South America) and *Protopterus* (Africa); the family Ceratodontidae contains only one living genus, the Australian *Neoceratodus*. All of these fishes are called lungfishes because of their capacity for extracting oxygen from the atmosphere as well as from water. The organs by which the lungfishes are enabled to do this are about as close to true lungs as any fish possesses, and they are definitely distinct from the types of auxiliary breathing apparatus possessed by anabantoids and certain other fishes. Their possession of these "lungs" allows the fishes to survive in waters that dry out completely or almost completely in the dry season that occurs annually in their home areas. With the onset of the dry season, *Protopterus annectens* excavates a burrow in the still-moist ground or pond-bed surrounding its home waters and envelops itself in a cocoon of mucus; the cocoon covers every portion of the fish except its mouth, through which aperture it must breathe while enveloped in the mud. When the rainy season begins, the fish awakens from its state of estivation and begins its slow-moving predatory existence in its ephemerally watery world.

571

PSEUDACANTHICUS LEOPARDUS (Fowler)/*Orange-Trim Sucker Catfish*
R: Guyana. **H**: Peaceful with other species, but sometimes quarrelsome with other plecostomus-type catfishes. **W**: Soft, slightly acid water should be used if possible, but the fish can take variations from this if not too great. Temperature 22 to 27°C. **S**: Up to 15 cm. **F**: Will take prepared foods from the bottom, but the biggest part of the diet consists of algae scraped from rocks, leaves, and the sides of the aquarium.

One of the main features of the appearance of this fish, besides the touches of color that are such a welcome relief in a type of fish that usually has no color at all, is the magnificent high dorsal fin. This fin is made even more atractive by the large, irregularly scattered spots. *P. leopardus* has been spawned at least once in this country, but the spawning was accidental. The breeding was not observed, but young fish were raised. It would indeed be a lucky thing for hobbyists if *P. leopardus,* which is among the prettiest of the sucker cats, is also among the easiest to breed.

PSEUDOCORYNOPOMA DORIAE

PSEUDOCHALCEUS KYBURZI Schultz/*Kyburz Tetra*
R: Colombia. **H**: Active and aggressive, even with their own kind. **W**: Soft, slightly acid water. Temperature 24 to 26°C. **S**: To 8 cm. **F**: Various live foods including insects.
In 1965, Dr. Herbert R. Axelrod asked Dr. Leonard P. Schultz, Curator of Fishes at the Smithsonian Institution, to identify a characid fish that he had collected in the Rio Calima, Cauca Valley, Colombia, South America. Dr. Schultz determined that the specimen represented a new species referable to the genus *Pseudochalceus* Kner. The color of this new fish is quite interesting: its back is yellowish brown, with its mid-side a light purple. Its lower side and belly are grayish white tinged with pink, while its dorsal and adipose fins are a light yellowish hue. The upper and lower rays of the caudal fin are tinged with a most attractive rosy gray that is dotted with purplish brown spots. Even with this pleasant coloring, this fish looks a little on the mean side, because of the very menacing structure of its teeth, although that in itself would not constitute grounds for labeling this fish as predatory.

PSEUDACANTHICUS LEOPARDUS

PSEUDOCORYNOPOMA DORIAE Perugia/*Dragonfin Tetra*

R: Southern Brazil and the La Plata region. **H**: Will not annoy other fishes or chew plants. **W**: Soft, slightly acid water. Temperature 21 to 25°C. **S**: To 8 cm. **F**: Will take any foods, but live foods are of course preferred.

There are never more than a very few Dragonfin Tetras available at any time. It is not the easiest fish in the world to keep and breed, and it does not ship very well. In its native waters it sometimes has to withstand some very cool temperatures, at times as low as 16°C. This of course is not a recommendation to keep it as cool as that, but it is a warning that high temperatures should be avoided. Another thing the fish is sensitive to is drastic changes in water.

PSEUDOCHALCEUS KYBURZI

PSEUDOCRENILABRUS MULTICOLOR (Hilgendorf)/*Dwarf Egyptian Mouthbrooder*

R: All over eastern Africa south to the lower Nile. **H**: Fairly safe in the community aquarium. **W**: Not critical. Temperature between 24 and 27°C. **S**: Males to 8 cm; females slightly smaller. **F**: Live and frozen foods preferred; dry foods are taken.

One of the most unusual and intriguing methods of reproduction is that id the mouthbrooding cichlid species. *Pseudocrenilabrus multicolor* is the smallest of the group and also the most generally available, and it is with this species that the hobbyist usually makes his first acquaintance. the actual egg-laying is frequently missed, and their owner is unaware that there was spawning until he observes the bulging throat of one of the females. Here is what happens: the male digs a shallow hole, usually in an out-of-the-way corner. This done, he coaxes and almost forces the female to join him in the hole, and eventually 30 to 80 eggs are laid. The female then picks up the eggs in her mouth. Here the eggs remain for ten days until they begin to hatch, constantly provided with circulating water by the breathing motion of the mother and constantly moved around by a sort of chewing motion. When the fry hatch, they are faithfully guarded by the mother. If danger threatens, she opens her mouth and lets the little ones swim inside, where they are packed in like a sardine can.

This attractive lille fish, usually in good supply and available at very reasonable prices, is a very good species for hobbyists who want to breed and raise cichlids. They lack the size of the mouthbroofing *Tilapia* species and the nasty temperament of some of the mouthbrooding Lake Malawi cichlids.

PSEUDODORAS NIGER

PSEUDOCRENILABRUS PHILANDER (Weber) /*South African Mouthbrooder*

R: Throughout southern Africa. **H**: Aggressive; should be kept with species of similar size and temperament. **W**: Not critical. **S**: 8 to 11 cm. **F**: All foods accepted eagerly.

P. philander is a wide-ranging species and has a number of geographical variations, not only in color but also in size. The most attractive form is from Beira and resembles a large Egyptian Mouthbrooder. The back and belly of the male are iridescent blue. Fins are brilliant red with blue tips. The anal fin is cobalt blue on the anterior portion. The lower lip is blue, and the throat and belly are reddish when the fish is excited. Other forms tend to lack red coloration.

PSEUDOCRENILABRUS MULTICOLOR

PSEUDODORAS NIGER (Valenciennes)/*Black Doradid*
R: Guyana through much of Amazon from sea level to 900 meters. **H**: Very peaceful, even with small fishes; light-shy. **W**: Not critical. Water should be clean, well filtered, and aerated. **S**: To nearly a meter in length and over 7 kg in weight. **F**: Will take a wide variety of foods but should get some vegetable matter; make sure foods are sinking types as this fish is a bottom-feeder. The decor of the tank should be such that caves or other sheltered areas are formed. Rocks, driftwood, etc. may be used in their construction, but the main idea is to provide a place where *Pseudodoras niger* can get in out of the light. Particularly light-shy, the Black Doradid will stay in its cave much of the time that the tank is brightly lit. When the lights are dimmed it will start cruising around the tank in search of food. Once at home in a tank the Black Doradid will often dash out into the light for some morsel(s) of food but retreats quickly back to its home.

PSEUDOCRENILABRUS PHILANDER

PSEUDOGASTROMYZON MYERSI Herre/*Myers's Hillstream Loach; Hong Kong Plecostomus*

R: Hong Kong Island. **H:** Peaceful and suitable for a community tank. Generally useful as an algae eater. **W:** Not critical, but sufftcient aeration and regular water changes are recommended. **S:** A rather small species attaining a length of only about 5 cm. **F:** This is an algae-eater and should have sufftcient quantities of vegetable matter.

Pseudogastromyzon myersi is a hillstream loach (family Homalopteridae), not a catfish. The common name that has been given to this fish in the trade, Hong Kong Plecostomus, refers to the general shape and habits of this species, not to any relationship to a catfish. In fact, suckermouth catfishes like the Plecostomus have the mouth modified into a sucking disc by which they adhere to surfaces in order to maintain themselves in position in streams with a strong current. Myers's Hillstream Loach has the same problem with the fast-flowing waters but handles it in a different manner. The attachment device is developed from modifications of the pelvic and pectoral fins and skin folds along the ventral surface. This creates a suction so the fish does not have to expend a great deal of energy just to stay in one spot. It has the added advantage of leaving the mouth free so the fish is able to feed more easily in the current. Feeding is usually accomplished by scraping algae from the surface of rocks, plants, etc.

The keeping of this and other hillstream loaches does not seem to pose too many problems. Since they are fishes of fast-flowing water, it would be expected that they do best in clean, clear water with plenty of aeration and regular water changes. They are quite peaceful and small and can be added to most small-fish community tanks. Larger predatory fishes might just make a meal of the loaches. In addition, Myers's Hillstream Loach has a utilitarian function in a home aquarium: it is an algae-eater. Its small size, peaceful nature, and algae-eating trait make it an excellent aquarium fish.

PSEUDOMUGIL GERTRUDAE

PSEUDOMUGIL GERTRUDAE Weber/*Gertrude's Blue-Eye*

R: New Guinea and Aru Islands to Queensland, Australia. **H:** A peaceful, active species. **W:** Not critical, but prefers hard alkaline water, perhaps with some salt added. The best temperature range is 20 to 26°C. **S:** A small species rarely exceeding 2.5 cm in length. **F:** Does well on live foods such as mosquito larvae, tubificid worms, etc.

Gertrude's Blue-Eye is a small but beautiful fish from New Guinea, the Aru Islands, and northern Queensland in Australia. Collecting sites in New Guinea included waters which were turbid and brownish or turbid and grayish and in one instance what was referred to as a swampy lagoon. Their main diet consisted of a variety of small aquatic insect larvae.

The aquarium need not be too large, especially if they are kept alone. This species can be kept in a community tank of relatively non-aggressive fishes, but it is not at its best under such conditions. Bunches of fine-leaved plants should be added if any thoughts of spawning your fish are entertained. The water should be on the hard, alkaline side, with the addition of some salt beneficial. Aquarium specimens prefer good feedings of live foods, especially mosquito larvae, but will adapt to other frozen, freeze-dried, or dried foods in a short time.

Males and females are easily distinguished. The male's first dorsal, pelvic, and sometimes anal fins have long filamentous extensions; the pectoral fins have short filamentous extensions; and the caudal fin has extensions from the upper and lower edges giving it somewhat of a lyretail shape. The pelvic fin extensions are the most noticeable, reaching in some instances to the posterior tip of the anal fin. The female lays large eggs among the fine-leaved plants where they adhere and can be removed periodically for hatching in a separate tank. This hatching time varies with temperature but averages about two weeks. The fry are ready for newly hatched brine shrimp almost immediately.

PSEUDOMUGIL SIGNIFER Kner/*Southern Blue-Eye*

R: Australian states of Queensland and New South Wales. **H**: A peaceful, active fish. **W**: Prefers alkaline, slightly hard water but is adaptable to life in water of different composition. Best temperature range 22 to 26°C. **S**: To about 6 cm for males. **F**: Accepts all standard aquarium foods except large, chunky prepared foods.

Ripe males and females should be maintained in a tank that contains either real or artificial bushy fine-leaved plants; the parents will chase through the tank, entering the plants from time to time to expel and fertilize the eggs, usually one at a time. The eggs will adhere to the spawning medium by sticky threads and can be harvested individually by removing each egg from the medium or by putting the egg-bearing medium into a separate tank for hatching.

PSEUDOPIMELODUS RANINUS TRANSMONTANUS

PSEUDOPIMELODUS RANINUS TRANSMONTANUS (Regan)/*Peruvian Mottled Catfish*
R: Peruvian Amazon, near Iquitos. **H**: Peaceful, but should not be trusted with fishes that are small enough for it to swallow. **W**: Soft, slightly acid water. Temperature 24 to 27°C. **S**: To 13 cm., possibly bigger. **F**: Will eat almost any kind of food, but should get some live food, especially worms, when available.

Most catfishes are not exactly God's noblest creatures where color is concerned, but this one is something pretty special. That it has nice colors is fairly obvious, and we are told that they are peaceful as well. Just the same, it is best to avoid tempting fate too much by remembering that the big mouth is capable of swallowing quite a morsel and might not hesitate to gulp down a smaller fish. Most of the *Pseudopimelodus* species come from waters near the Amazon River basin but this one comes from a point far upstream, the streams near Iquitos, Peru, where the Neon Tertras and many other beautiful fishes come from. The Indians in this picturesque country have found it profitable to collect fishes and bring them to the shippers who export them from this thriving little city. The aquarium hobby has even taken a foothold here; William Vorderwinkler, former editor of *Tropoical Fish Hobbyist* magazine, reported that he was agreeably surprised when he saw a large, beautifully set-up aquarium in a hotel lobby. It was crowded with many Pencilfishes and there were also a great many Blue Tetras (*Microbryon cochui*) *P.R. transmontanus* is not a very active species and will stay well hidden in an aquarium if provided with suitable hiding places.

PSEUDOPLATYSTOMA FASCIATUM (Linnaeus)/*Tiger Catfish, Shovelmouth*

R: Northern South American. **H**: A strictly predaceous species that will swallow anything it can catch and engulf; a twilight and nighttime prowler. **W**: Soft, slightly acid water optimal, but the species can take a fairly wide variation in pH and hardness factors. Temperature 23 to 28°C. **S**: Up to 90 cm, but usually seen much smaller. **F**: Prefers small living fishes.

Pseudoplatystoma fasciatum is a good-looking, interesting, hardy pimelodid catfish, a very fine species for stocking a large display aquarium, where it is sure to get a lot of attention even from people who ordinarily pay no mind to fishes. In order for a fish to have a chance to live peacefully with a Tiger Catfish, it has to be too big to swallow or too fast to catch; with especially large *Pseudoplatystoma,* a fish has a chance if it's too small to be noticed. Medium-size fishes, especially those that like to stay in a certain area in the tank, will be eaten.

PSEUDOSPHROMENUS DAYI

PSEUDOSPHROMENUS CUPANUS (Cuvier)/*Spike-Tail Paradise Fish*

R: Southern India and Sri Lanka. **H**: Generally peaceful. **W**: Water should be fairly soft and acidic. 23 to 26°C is the best temperature range; slightly higher for breeding. **S**: To about 8 cm. **F**: Accepts all standard aquarium foods.

The male usually chooses the underside of a broad leaf that has outer margins that curl down, providing a cupped hollow, and he places bubbles into the hollow. After that the parents embrace under the bubblenest and the female expels the eggs; the male retrieves the sinking eggs and places them into the nest. The female often attempts to help with the egg-retrieval chore, but after spawning is over the male becomes much more of a bully than he has been previously, and at this point it is best to remove the female. The male tends the eggs carefully, and many times he will move the nest from the spawning area to the water surface.

PSEUDOPLATYSTOMA FASCIATUM

PSEUDOSPHROMENUS DAYI (Stansch)/*Day's Paradise Fish*
R: Southeast Asia. **H**: Peaceful and easy to keep. **W**: Not critical as long as it is clean and warm. Temperature 24 to 28°C. **S**: Up to 8 cm. **F**: Not at all choosy; will thrive on most foods (prepared, frozen, etc.).
The fins of the female are less developed and have less color than those of the male. The best colors are shown when higher temperatures are provided. Spawning begins with the construction of a bubblenest by the male. A lively chase follows, the eggs falling to the bottom, where they are retrieved by both parents and spit into the bubblenest (which is often quite small). At 28°C the eggs hatch in about a day. The fry are guarded by the male.

PSEUDOSPHROMENUS CUPANUS

PSEUDOTROPHEUS ELONGATUS Fryer/*Slender Mbuna*

R: Lake Malawi, Africa. **H**: Quarrelsome; should be kept in a well-planted tank by themselves. **W**: Alkaline and very hard; add one tablespoon of non-iodized table salt for every four liters. Temperature 24 to 27°C. **S**: In the aquarium about 10 cm, but probably larger in nature; females are slightly smaller than males. **F**: Frozen, freeze-dried, or live foods are best.

Pseudotropheus elongatus can easily be distinguished from its mbuna look-a-likes by being a little longer and more slender, which is the reason for the name *elongatus*. Both sexes are blue with broad vertical dark bands, but males are much brighter blue with a dark head. This species is not difficult to spawn if adequate conditions are maintained. This fish is a maternal mouthbrooder with an incubation period of two to three weeks. A usual spawning will consist of between 30 to 40 fry.

PSEUDOTROPHEUS LIVINGSTONI

PSEUDOTROPHEUS LANISTICOLA Burgess/*Snail-Shell Mbuna*

R: Lake Malawi, Africa. **H**: Quarrelsome; many rock caves or holes should be provided if kept with other cichlids. **W**: Alkaline and very hard. The optimum temperature range is about 24 to 27°C. **S**: Reaches a size of about 9 cm. **F**: Not fussy; will take almost any food. **C**: Not one of the species known to have color morphs.

Pseudotropheus lanisticola is one of the more intersting of the Lake Malawi cichlids. It does not live among the rocks like the rest of them. It lives instead in the empty shells of a snail, *Lanistes*. Spawning is similar to that of the other *Pseudotropheus*. Fortunately, *P. lanisticola* is able to live in a regular mbuna aquarium without shells.

The female incubates the eggs in her mouth. She should be removed from the community tank when holding eggs and isolated until the fry are well able to care for themselves. There are generally few eggs, about 20 or so, but the parental care ensures that most of them will have an excellent chance for survival. The sexes are generally similar in appearance and no indication of how to sex them outside the breeding period (aside from examination of the genital papillae) has been recorded. There are bluish individuals and yellowish individuals, the bluish ones typically being breeding males.

PSEUDOTROPHEUS ELONGATUS

PSEUDOTROPHEUS LIVINGSTONI (Boulenger) */Livingstone's Mbuna*
R: Lake Malawi, Africa. **H**: Quarrelsome and aggressive; a large number of rock caves and holes should be provided. **W**: Alkaline and very hard. Temperature between 23 and 26°C. **S**: To 16 cm. **F**: Omnivorous; does well on a variety of foods but prefers live or frozen foods.
This species is not often seen in the aquarium, and it is often confused with *Pseudotropheus lanisticola*.

PSEUDOTROPHEUS LANISTICOLA

PSEUDOTROPHEUS LOMBARDOI Burgess/*Kennyi*

R: Lake Malawi, Africa. **H**: Aggressive; tank should be provided with many caves or other shelters. **W**: Typical of Lake Malawi cichlids, hard and alkaline with a pH of 7.6 or higher. Temperature 22 to 28°C, with an optimum nearer the upper range. **S**: Can attain a length of 13 cm or more. **F**: Omnivorous; will accept most types of fish food including frozen brine shrimp and flake foods.

The female broods the eggs and fry in her mouth for about ten days to three weeks depending upon temperature, after which she releases them more and more often and for longer periods of time until they are no longer allowed back into the mother's buccal cavity. The spawning is rarely witnessed, but the female will show up with an extended buccal area indicating that she is tending eggs or fry.

PSEUDOTROPHEUS TROPHEOPS

PSEUDOTROPHEUS MICROSTOMA Trewavas /*Small-Mouthed Tropheops*

R: Lake Malawi, Africa. **H**: Quarrelsome; a large number of rock caves and holes should be provided. **W**: Alkaline and very hard. Optimum temperature between 24 to 27°C. **S**: Reaches a length of about 15 cm. **F**: Omnivorous; will take almost any prepared food offered. **C**: Few if any variations from the basic color and pattern are known.

Pseudotropheus microstoma may be known under several names or combinations of names due to its close affinities to *Pseudotropheus tropheops*. Its habits are similar to the well-known *P. zebra* or *P. tropheops*, but since it is recognizable mostly by its color pattern other morphs might be simply regarded as *P. tropheops* varieties. The males and females are distinguishable by color, the females being more drably colored compared with the bluish males that exhibit very dark bars.

PSEUDOTROPHEUS LOMBARDOI

PSEUDOTROPHEUS TROPHEOPS Regan/*Tropheops*

R: Lake Malawi, Africa. **H**: One of the more peaceful of the mbuna, but still retains the quarrelsome habits of these cichlids. **W**: As with most species of *Pseudotropheus,* this one can stand a wide variety of water conditions but does best (and will probably only breed) in hard alkaline water. **S**: About 10 cm. **F**: Omnivorous; does well on a variety of foods including flake foods. **C**: A complex species with many color morphs.

The actual spawning takes place among the rocks, apparently safely away from the other cichlids in the tank, and is not commonly observed. Many aquarists know that spawning has occurred only by the appearance of the female. Once spawning has occurred and she has a batch of eggs in her mouth, the lowered gular area is quite obvious. She is generally removed to more isolated quarters where emergence of the fry occurs some weeks later The fry may be left in with her for the early stages of development and while the female regains her strength.

PSEUDOTROPHEUS MICROSTOMA

PSEUDOTROPHEUS ZEBRA

PSEUDOTROPHEUS ZEBRA (Boulenger)/*Zebra, Malawi Blue Cichlid*

R: Lake Malawi, Africa. **H**: Very quarrelsome. **W**: Should be fairly hard and alkaline. Temperature 24 to 26°C. **S**: About 10 cm. **F**: Omnivorous, and for this reason should get both plant and vegetable foods; does well on a balanced dry food diet. **C**: Body various shades of blue with six to eight bluish black bars and blue fins; anal has some round orange spots and forehead a black bar.

Pseuotropheus zebra, commonly called the Zebra or the Malawi Blue Cichlid, is an mbuna from Lake Malawi and has been reported to have over a dozen color varieties. Among these forms are: a solid red morph, called the red zebra; a solid blue morph, called the cobalt blue; a solid green morph, called the green zebra (this morph also is often called a cobalt, as the cobalts can vary in color from blue to greenish blue); an orange-blotched morph called the OB; a mottled form called the marmalade cat; a white morph; a yellow morph; a white form covered with black freckles, called the peppered zebra; a solid orange form called the tangerine form; and an albino form. It has been found that a number of these "forms" are actually valid species (one red zebra is now *estherae*, a cobalt zebra is now *callainos*, etc.).

This species is a maternal mouthbrooder with an incubation period of between three to four weeks. Normal brood sizes are between 30 to 40 fry. Good aeration and filtration are particularly important after the eggs have been laid and collected by the female. The eggs are extremely susceptible to fungus, and the developing eggs, with their high metabolism, need a good supply of oxygen.

With mouthbrooders, the fry seek refuge in a parent's mouth. Most Rift Lake cichlids are surprisingly gentle with their own fry and seldom need to be separated from the brood (whereas separation is always essential with many other cichlids). Baby brine shrimp (or other similar fine live foods) should be given to the fry. The fry will remain close to their parents for an additional one to two weeks. During this time the parents will herd the stray fry. The fry grow quickly and should double in size within one month.

PTEROLEBIAS LONGIPINNIS Garman/*Common Longfin*

R: Northern Argentina northward into southeastern Brazil. **H**: Peaceful with other species, but males fight among themselves. **W**: Acidity and hardness factors are not very important, provided the water is clean. Temperature 17 to 22°C; higher temperatures are to be avoided. **S**: Males about 8 cm; females 6 cm. **F**: Does best on live foods; will accept meaty prepared foods but will quickly go off its feed if maintained on monotonous diet of dry foods.

Pterolebias longipinnis is a prolific, reliable spawner that can easily be spawned in small aquaria. Male and female completely submerge themselves in the bed of peat moss used as the spawning medium, so the layer of peat moss at the bottom of the tank (or in the spawning pot, if larger breeding quarters are used) should be about 7 cm deep. The damp peat moss containing the eggs should be stored for about seven months; most of the fry will hatch out when the peat moss is covered by 2 cm or so of aged soft water.

PTEROLEBIAS PERUENSIS

PTEROLEBIAS PERUENSIS Myers/*Peruvian Longfin*

R: Upper Amazon region. **H**: Usually peaceful, but should be kept by themselves. **W**: Soft, considerably acid water; for spawning, a layer about 2 cm deep of peat moss should be provided on the bottom. Temperature 18 to 23°C. **S**: About 7 cm for males; females about 5 cm. **F**: Live foods of all kinds.

At the little city of Leticia, Colombia, the author (HRA) was privileged to travel a short distance up the Amazon River to a point where Peru could be seen across the immense river. Here we went up a small tributary stream to the fish collector's trading post. Most of the smaller, brightly colored fishes in the area were to be found in the storage troughs, and the author recalls being asked for a scientific identification of two species. One was *Colomesus asellus,* and the other was called "Africano" by the natives. This turned out to be our friend *Pterolebias peruensis.* It would have been highly interesting to see where the Indians were catching these fish, but time did not permit. This is one of the "annual" fishes that lays its eggs in the mud on the bottom of small bodies of water that dry out in the dry season. The fry hatch when the rains begin and the dried-out ponds fill up once more. In the aquarium they spawn in a layer of peat-moss on the bottom. In addition to being larger than the females, the male *P. peruensis* also are more colorful and more elaborated in their finnage, especially the caudal fin.

PTEROLEBIAS WISCHMANNI

PTEROLEBIAS WISCHMANNI Seegers/*Wischmann's Pterolebias*

R: Ucayali River, Peru. **H:** A peaceful, quiet species usually staying near the surface or in the vegetation. **W:** Not critical. Neutral water of average hardness is recommended. A temperature range of 24-27.5° C is proper. **S:** Males reach a length of 6 inches, females only 5 inches. **F:** Live foods preferred, especially insect larvae.

Wischmann's Pterolebias is an attractive fish that was collected in a small bog not far from the Amaquirir River (Ucayali system) in Peru. The water averaged only 8 inches deep and the bottom was covered with a thick layer of leaves. The pH was neutral to slightly alkaline (7-7.5). This species, which attains a length of about 12.5 cm (females) to 15 cm (males), is generally sluggish, resting most of the time near the surface or in vegetation or where it can quickly dart for cover. A 20-gallon tank is recommended. The water chemistry is not critical and neutral water of average hardness and temperatures of 24° to 27.5° C are adequate. Live foods should be offered as often as possible, especially chironomid and mosquito larvae. Other foods are accepted. As the temperature is increased the amount of food required also increases.

Sexual dichromatism is evident in this species. The caudal fin of the male has yellow and/or yellow-orange stripes on the ventral edge while in the female there is a narrow orange-yellow stripe bordering the entire posterior edge caudal fin. This is evident at about an age of 3 to 4 months when the fish are 5 cm to 6 cm long. The male also has fewer anal fin rays than the female (15 and 17 respectively). Spawning is accomplished by burying the eggs in a peat substrate. The peat is removed and dried and stored for a period of six to ten months at a temperature of about 19° to 22° C. At that time neutral water of average hardness is added and the eggs should hatch in 20 to 30 hours. For the first 5 to 8 hours the fry remain on or very near the bottom. After this they begin to swim about and look for food. The fry are fairly large (about 6 mm long) and are dark and slender. They are ready for newly hatched brine shrimp or other suitable food immediately. With proper care growth is rapid. In a month they are 16 mm long and are light in color. The fins are still transparent. After two months they are 25 mm or more long and begin to attain a darker color. By fourteen weeks they are sexually mature.

PTEROLEBIAS ZONATUS Myers/*Lace-Finned Killie, Banded Longfin*

R: Venezuelan drainage of the Orinoco River. **H**: Males not overly aggressive, but in close quarters they may nip at each other's fin ray extensions. **W**: Does well in soft acid water but will readily adapt to neutral or slightly alkaline water. Best maintained between 20 to 24°C. **S**: Males grow to 15 cm in the wild and females reach half that size; aquarium-raised individuals are not quite this long. **F**: Feeds heavily on mosquito larvae and other surface-dwelling insects, but will adapt well to frozen or prepared foods.

P. zonatus breeds in the typical fashion of the annual "peat divers," but because of their relatively peaceful nature they can be spawned in drum bowls of four liters or so. The female initiates the spawning activity, and both parents dive down into an 8 to 10 cm layer of peat moss to lay their large (2 mm) adhesive eggs. The eggs must be incubated in this peat moss, which has been dried to the consistency of fresh pipe tobacco, and require a minimum dry period of eight months.

PTERONOTROPIS WELAKA

PTERONOTROPIS HYPSELOPTERUS (Günther)/*Sailfin Shiner*

R: South Carolina, Georgia, Florida, and Alabama. **H**: A peaceful, active fish that will not molest its tankmates. **W**: Clean, soft, slightly acid water and a large, well-planted tank are preferred. **S**: 8 cm. **F**: Will take dried as well as live or frozen foods.

Pteronotropis hypselopterus is one of our most beautiful native fishes; it occurs in good numbers in Georgia's Okefenokee Swamp region. In spite of its obvious good looks, the usual antipathy toward any fish which does not come from some far-away place exists, and dealers will seldom stock them. The author once saw a tankful of beautiful specimens in a dealer's store, all males. When asked if there were any females available, the dealer said that the collectors had thrown away all of the females and kept only the more colorful males, thinking that the females were something else.

It is an active but peaceful fish that is usually swimming where it can be seen. For their complete well-being, they should get a period of two to three months each year in an unheated aquarium at room temperatures. At the end of this period their temperature can again be increased gradually.

PTEROLEBIAS ZONATUS

PTERONOTROPIS WELAKA (Evermann & Kendall)/ Bluenose Shiner

R: Restricted to the area from eastern Florida (St. Johns River) to the Pearl River which forms part of the boundary between Louisiana and Mississippi. **H:** Peaceful. Can be kept with other fishes of similar size and temperament. **W:** Not critical. Tolerates a wide range of pH and hardness, but for best results should be kept in soft, slightly acid water. Temperature range from about 6 to 26°C, but prefers it cool. **S:** Reaches a maximum length of about 65 mm (average 50 mm). **F:** Will accept a wide range of aquarium foods.

The sexes are easily distinguished. The males have a large black dorsal fin and a large anal fin that is yellow with a black band; silvery scales are found on the sides of the body. At breeding time the males develop a bright blue area from the snout to behind the eyes on the upper part of the head. The breeding females at most will have a blue tip to the snout. They have smaller, less colorful fins and lack the silvery lateral spots. Young *N. welaka* are difficult to distinguish from several other species of *Notropis*. Spawning has occurred in captivity but apparently only accidentally—a pair spawned among some fine-leaved plants soon after their introduction to the tank.

PTERONOTROPIS HYPSELOPTERUS

591

PTEROPHYLLUM LEOPOLDI

PTEROPHYLLUM LEOPOLDI (Gosse)/*Long-Nosed Angelfish*

R: Essequibo River to lower Amazon region. **H**: Peaceful with fishes of its own size. **W**: Water should be soft and slightly acid. Temperature 24 to 26°C. **S**: To about 10 cm. **F**: Prefers live or frozen foods, but accepts prepared foods when hungry.

The Long-Nosed Angelfish is not as common or popular as its close relative the Scalare. Because it is a third smaller than the Scalare, the Long-Nosed Angelfish is more suitable for smaller aquaria.

PTEROPHYLLUM LEOPOLDI

PTEROPHYLLUM SCALARE

PTEROPHYLLUM SCALARE (Lichtenstein)/*Angelfish, Scalare*

R: The Amazon basin, the Rupununi and Essequibo Rivers of Guyana, with specimens also found in French Guiana and Surinam. **H**: **W**: Clean, neutral water. Temperature 23°C. **S**: 13 cm in length; 15 cm in depth. **F**: Most prepared or live foods. **C**: This species is found in "ghost" forms without bars, in solid black, in "lace" forms with some black markings, and with long fins; these are all mutant forms that have been fixed by inbreeding.

Lichtenstein first described this fish in 1823 as *Zeus scalaris* from Brazil. The name was subsequently changed to *Platax scalaris* in 1831 by Cuvier and Valenciennes and finally to *Pterophyllum scalaris* by Heckel in 1840. Günther changed the *scalaris* to *scalare* in 1862, and so it has been ever since. *P. scalare* is the Angelfish every aquarist is familiar with. Since 1928, when Ahl described *P. eimekei* from the mouth of the Rio Negro in Brazil, there has been considerable confusion as to which species was which. Dr. L.P. Schultz carefully studied specimens of both "species" and found that the counts for the syntype of *P. eimekei* coincide with the median counts of *scalare* and thus concluded that *eimekei* is a synonym of *scalare*.

The Scalare is easy to breed and millions of tank-raised specimens are sold every year all over the world. Many color and finnage varieties have been developed. This species prefers to spawn on broad-leaved water plants. Both parents care for the eggs and fan them with their fins to ensure adequate oxygenation. The fry hatch after 24 to 40 hours at 27 to 31°C. The young are collected by the parents after they hatch and placed in depressions in the bottom gravel for several days until they can swim. A successful brood can have as many as 1,000 fry.

Pterophyllun scalare hybrids spawning.

Golden hybrid of *Pterophyllum scalare*.

Black, long-finned hybrid of *Pterophyllum scalare*.

PTERYGOPLICHTHYS GIBBICEPS (Kner)/*Clown Sucker Catfish*

R: Upper Rio Negro at Marabitanos. **H**: A typical sucker catfish of the "plecostomus" type. It likes to loaf about the bottom or attach itself to the glass front of the aquarium. **W**: Not sensitive to water conditions as long as the water is warm (over 24°C) and not too hard or alkaline. Tolerates a pH of 6.0 to 7.0 and water less than 15 DH. **S**: Up to 35 cm. **F**: As a scavenger, it doesn't require too much in the way of live foods. But it does like plenty of frozen brine shrimp and pelleted dry food.

One of the sailfin catfishes of the family Loricariidae. Becomes very large so a suitably large aquarium is necessary. Relatively peaceful and can be kept in community tanks with large fishes. It is active at night searching for food and will feed on algae.

PUNTIUS BIMACULATUS

PUNTIUS ARULIUS (Jerdon)/*Longfin Barb*

R: India. **H**: Peaceful, especially when kept with barbs of equal size. Very lively. **W**: Soft, slightly acid water; tank should be placed so as to receive occasional sunshine. Temperature 24 to 26°C. **S**: Up to 12 cm. **F**: Live foods of all types; frozen foods of small size, such as frozen daphnia, should not be fed often. Accepts dry food.

The Longfin Barb is peaceful; about the only time the fish evidences animosity to others is during spawning time, when one male may threaten other males to keep them away from the females. Spawning takes place in thick bundles of floating plants after much energetic driving by the male. The eggs, which are adhesive and stick to the plants, are eaten eagerly by the parents.

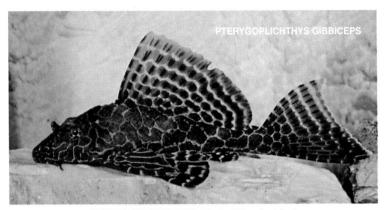

PTERYGOPLICHTHYS GIBBICEPS

PUNTIUS BIMACULATUS (Bleaker)/*Two-Spot Barb*

R: Apparently endemic to Sri Lanka. **H:** Generally peaceful and rather shy, even when kept in a community tank. **W:** Not critical, but prefers slightly acid water. A temperature of 22° to 26° C suits them fine. **S:** In the wild to about 7 cm; in captivity usually less than 6 cm. **F:** Omnivorous, but shows a distinct preference for live foods.

The male apparently takes the initiative in spawning, parading tirelessly in front of a plump female and attempting to drive or entice her into the plants. Spawning apparently can take place at any time of the day and at almost any level of the tank; some are shy spawners that will hide when disturbed, others continue unabated regardless of distractions. Once spawning is completed the parents should be removed or they will quickly devour whatever eggs they may find.

The fry hatch out in 22 to 24 hours and are free-swimming in about 108 hours. In about two and a half to three weeks the characteristic black spots will appear. Free-swimming fry are ready for newly hatched brine shrimp and small cyclops, but they will also accept very fine flake food or other small commercially prepared fry foods. Growth is rapid, and in eight to ten days chopped tubifex and other comparable foods can be fed. If properly conditioned with a balanced diet of nutritious foods, the female will be ready to spawn again in a little over two weeks. A typical spawn will yield about 250 fry.

PUNTIUS ARULIUS

PUNTIUS CONCHONIUS (Hamilton-Buchanan)/*Rosy Barb*

R: India. **H**: Very active, continually swimming from one end of the tank to the other; generally well-behaved. **W**: Water can vary a little from neutral in either direction; likes a well-planted tank, but must have swimming room. Temperature 22 to 24°C. **S**: Up to almost 15 cm, but usually seen much smaller, about half this size. **F**: Takes all foods.

They spawn by scattering eggs into bunches of plants. Properly conditioned, the species is eager to spawn and requires no special preparations, except that for best results they require big tanks for both spawning and rearing the fry. Rosy Barbs are very active swimmers and very heavy eaters, often rooting around in the gravel much like Goldfish. They should be kept in long, low tanks, preferably by themselves; kept in a school, the males will swim around each other with fins fully spread and colors at their gleaming best in an effort to outshine their brothers.

PUNTIUS GELIUS

PUNTIUS FILAMENTOSUS (Valenciennes)/*Black-Spot Barb*

R: Sri Lanka, India, Burma. **H**: Peaceful with fishes its own size; a good jumper. **W**: Slightly acid to neutral; not too hard. Temperature 23 to 26°C. **S**: Up to 13 cm. **F**: Takes all foods.

Spawning pairs of this species will chase back and forth over the length of the tank a few times before settling down to the actual spawning act; the eggs are laid in bunches of plants, which should cover at least one-fourth of the bottom area of the tank. Once driving by the males has begun, the fish should not be interrupted, as this often results in a complete cessation of breeding activity for a period of weeks. Eggs hatch in about two days, and the newly emerged fry are soon able to take newly hatched brine shrimp.

PUNTIUS CONCHONIUS

PUNTIUS GELIUS (Hamilton-Buchanan)/*Dwarf Barb*

R: Central India, Bengal and Assam. **H**: One of the most peaceful of all the barb species; in their native land they occupy quiet waters, usually in small schools near the shore. **W**: Not critical, but avoid too high temperatures; 22 to 24°C is ample. **S**: Females 4 cm; males 3.5 cm. **F**: Good eaters, but food should be small.

The spawning act usually takes place in the morning, with the female beginning by chasing and annoying the male until he turns the tables on her and drives her vigorously all over the tank. Unlike most of the other barbs, these do not usually strew their eggs among the bushy plants but prefer to stick them on the underside of broad-leaved plants, which should be provided instead of the usual *Nitella* or *Myriophyllum*. The parents do not indulge in the usual "egg-hunt" after breeding is completed, but leaving them in the breeding tank serves no further purpose. Fry hatch in about 24 hours.

PUNTIUS FILAMENTOSUS

PUNTIUS HAASIANUS (David)/*Sickle Barb*

R: Mozambique. **H**: Peaceful, timid, and inclined to hide. **W**: Soft, slightly acid water. Temperature 22 to 28°C. **S**: 3 cm. **F**: Prefers small live foods, but will accept dry and frozen foods.

There is a very definite physical characteristic that enables the hobbyist to tell the sexes apart. This is unusual in a barb, because with most barbs the aquarist must rely on such changeable evidence as comparative color brilliance, fullness of the body, etc. Not so with the Sickle Barb! The anal fin of the male of this species is shaped very differently from that of the female. The Sickle Barb breeds in normal barb fashion.

PUNTIUS NIGROFASCIATUS

PUNTIUS LINEATUS (Duncker)/*Striped Barb*

R: Singapore and Malay Peninsula. **H**: Peaceful and active; harmless to plants. **W**: Soft, slightly acid water. Temperature 24 to 27°C. **S**: Up to 10 cm; usually smaller. **F**: All sorts of food accepted, but occasional meals of live foods are necessary for the best condition. **C**: Body olive-green with four horizontal lines on the sides; dorsal and anal fins show a pink flush at times.

The females do not seem to fill up with eggs as they should, and when one of the rare spawnings takes place only a few hatch. Once we get a few generations that have spent their entire lives in the aquarium, the story will be different. A school of half-grown Striped Barbs and Tiger Barbs in a large, well-planted aquarium should make a breathtaking exhibit at a fish show, sure to put the exhibitor in the running for a trophy.

PUNTIUS HAASIANUS

PUNTIUS NIGROFASCIATUS (Günther)/*Black Ruby Barb*

R: Sri Lanka. **H**: An active swimmer, but inclined to nip fins. **W**: Soft, slightly acid water. Temperature 24 to 28°C. **S**: 6 cm. **F**: Accepts all foods, but small living foods are preferred. **C**: Male purplish red with broad black bars and purple-black fins; female lacks male's red color and black fins.

Sexes are not difficult to distinguish, because the black bars on the male and the black in his fins are always more crisp and distinct than in the female, even when he is not showing his best colors. The Black Ruby Barb spawns in typical *Puntius* fashion, but the fish requires a larger tank than its size would indicate. The fry hatch more quickly if the temperature of the water is kept a degree or two below that used for spawning.

PUNTIUS LINEATUS

PUNTIUS SACHSI (Ahl)/*Golden Barb*

R: Malay Peninsula. **H**: Peaceful and active. **W**: Soft, slightly acid water. Temperature 21 to 28°C. **S**: 6 cm. **F**: Accepts both live and dry foods.

For spawning, fine-leaved bunch plants or their artificial substitutes, such as nylon mops, are required. The parent fish chase wildly back and forth over the length of the tank until the female is ready to enter the spawning area. Once there, the male and female quiver side by side and the female releases the eggs, which are immediately fertilized by the male. During the first entrances into the plants there may be no eggs expelled, but there are only a few such dry runs before the female is able to produce eggs. The eggs hatch in 24 hours at a temperature of 27°C.

PUNTIUS TICTO STOLICZKANUS

PUNTIUS SOMPHONGSI (Benl & Klausewitz)/*Somphongs's Barb*

R: Thailand. **H**: Peaceful and active, but sometimes nips plant leaves. **W**: Soft, slightly acid water. Temperature 24 to 27°C. **S**: 10 cm. **F**: Has a good appetite and is not a fussy eater; will accept dried as well as live or frozen foods.

If there is ever to be a good supply of this handsome barb available to hobbyists it looks as if they will have to be bred somewhere unless a better source of supply is found in Thailand. Somphongs Lek-Aree, who was probably the best-known and most active collector in Thailand, declared that it was the rarest of all rare Thailand fishes and that in all of his collecting expeditions he had found only six. Two died on the return trip and another died in his aquarium. The other three were sent as a Christmas present to Dr. Gerhard Benl in Munich, Germany.

PUNTIUS SACHSI

PUNTIUS TICTO STOLICZKANUS (Day)/*Stoliczka's Barb*

R: Eastern Burma, near Rangoon. **H**: Active and peaceful in the community aquarium. **W**: Like other barbs, not critical. Temperature 24 to 26°C. **S**: A little over 5 cm. **F**: Frozen or live foods preferred, dried foods accepted.

For spawning, a tank of at least 60 liters should be richly planted, or a great many eggs will be eaten. The eggs do not have any great adhesive power, and a great many fall to the bottom instead of adhering to the plants. Fry hatch in 30 to 36 hours and begin swimming two days later. Finely powdered dry food is fed.

PUNTIUS SOMPHONGSI

PUNTIUS TITTEYA (Deraniyagala)/*Cherry Barb*

R: Sri Lanka. **H**: Peaceful; a good community fish. **W**: Soft, slightly acid water; well planted tank. Temperature 22 to 28°C. **S**: 5 cm. **F**: Accepts both live and prepared foods; particularly likes small living crustaceans.

During the actual spawning act the color is intensified to an oxblood hue, and although the deepness of the color at this time is not of long duration (it loses much of its dark, rich quality after spawning), the fish is still nicely colored if maintained under proper conditions. Inducing the species to spawn is not too difficult if they have been well treated during their period of acclimatization. Eggs are scattered into plant thickets, where they are eagerly sought out and eaten by the parents, who should be removed as soon as possible.

PUNTIUS SP.

PUNTIUS VITTATUS (Day)/*Banded Barb*

R: Found mostly in rice paddies throughout India. **H**: Peaceful and active; prefers to move in schools. **W**: Not critical; will adapt to almost any kind of water. Fairly soft water with a temperature of about 24°C. **S**: 5 to 6 cm. **F**: Will eat dried as well as live foods; easily kept.

The female's body is much deeper, and she is usually somewhat bigger than her mate. *Puntius vittatus* seem to be happier when they are swimming in a school; in their native waters they are seldom found singly, but usually in large schools. This fish has been compared to *P. conchonius* in ease of keeping. They seldom get sick and make little demands of their owner. They spawn readily, scattering their eggs among plant thickets. The fry hatch in about 36 hours and become free-swimming a day or two later.

PUNTIUS sp./*Odessa Barb*

R: Unknown, possibly Sri Lanka or India. **H:** An active, constantly moving species that tends to be slighty aggressive toward members of its own kind. Not the best barb for a communiy tank. **W:** Normal water chemistry acceptable. A temperature of about 27°C and a neutral to slightly alkaline pH have been used in successful spawnings. Dark gravel and low light conditions are recommended. **S:** Attains a length of about 6 cm. **F:** Not fussy about food. Will accept all kinds of aquarium foods including flakes.

The Odessa Barb has been around for many years now and still its specific identity has not yet been determined. It was said to have been discovered in a bazaar in Odessa, and it still retains that city's name as part of its common name. Attempts to find out where it actually came from have failed although best guesses are Sri Lanka or nearby India as several species with similar coloration are known from these areas. It has also been proposed that the Odessa Barb is a hybrid involving at least *Puntius conchonius*. This has not been confirmed but still remains a possibility.

PYGOCENTRUS NATTERERI (Kner)/*Natterer's Piranha; Red-Bellied Piranha*

R: Widely distributed throughout the Amazon and Orinoco basins. **H**: Vicious; must be kept alone in the average tank. **W**: Soft, slightly acid water. Temperature 24 to 27°C. **S**: Up to 30 cm in natural waters; shipped specimens usually much smaller. **F**: Smaller living fishes or strips of raw fish or beef heart. **C**: Back steel gray with many tiny shining scales; large black spot on sides; throat, belly, and anal fin bright red.

This is the most widely distributed and most commonly found of the piranha group, and it is also probably the most handsome of the lot. There has been a good deal of controversy as to how dangerous the piranha really is. Many believe that a piranha is not really dangerous until it feels it is trapped and confined, and then it attacks in self-defense. Most piranha bites are sustained when the fish are being handled. This is not to say that a hungry piranha is never a dangerous proposition.

PYRRHULINA LAETA

PYRRHULINA BREVIS Steindachner/*Short-Lined Pyrrhulina*

R: Widespread in South America. **H**: Very peaceful in the community aquarium. **W**: Soft, slightly acid water. Temperature 24 to 27°C. **S**: To 6 cm. **F**: Small live foods preferred, but will take frozen and prepared foods.

The Short-Lined Pyrrhulina, although not as attractive as many of its close relatives, is a very peaceful fish that will not disrupt a well-organized community aquarium. The species has not been seen very often in the aquarium hobby. This is partly due to the confusion concerning this group of fishes; species often appear under the wrong name.

PYRRHULINA LAETA (Cope)/*Long-Lined Pyrrhulina*

R: Guyana and the central Amazon region. **H:** Very peaceful; can be kept in a community aquarium with non-aggressive fishes. **W:** Slightly soft, acid water is best. Temperature should be about 20°C but higher (to 24°C) for breeding. **S:** Attains a length of about 8 cm. **F:** Will accept dry foods but has a strong preference for live or at least frozen foods.

The female may approach the male and may be chased away until the male is ready. As the female continuously returns to the leaf, the male eventually accepts her and refrains from aggression against her as she excitedly swims all around him and the leaf. Sometimes the male nudges the female if she remains quiet for a while near the leaf. The pair finally get together with side by side egg-laying with the usual "S"-shaped body twists, trembling, etc. The eggs are said to drop onto the leaf, to which they adhere. This is repeated until as many as 500 or more eggs cover the leaf. Once spawning is completed the male drives the female away and stands guard over the eggs until they hatch about 24 to 30 hours later. The male can then be removed for safety. In three to four days the fry become free-swimming and are ready for tiny live foods such as rotifers. After a few more days they should start to accept newly hatched brine shrimp.

PYRRHULINA SPILOTA Weitzman/*Blotched Pyrrhulina*

R: South America, specific origin unknown. **H**: Very peaceful in the community aquarium. **W**: Soft, slightly acid water. Temperature 24 to 27°C. **S**: 6 cm. **F**: Small live foods are preferred, but it will also accept frozen and some prepared flake foods.

The attractive dwarf fishes of the genus *Pyrrhulina* are relatively unknown as aquarium fishes compared to many of the other characoids. In general *Pyrrhulina* species are surface fishes with upturned mouths and flat heads. *P. spilota* was described in 1960 by Dr. Stanley H. Weitzman. The specimens that were available to him were imported for distribution in the aquarium hobby; their exact origin is unknown.

QUINTANA ATRIZONA

PYRRHULINA VITTATA Regan/*Banded Pyrrhulina*

R: Amazon in the Santarem region, Rio Tapajoz. **H**: Very peaceful in the community tank. **W**: Soft, slightly acid water. Temperature 24 to 27°C. **S**: To 7 cm. **F**: Small live foods preferred, but will also take frozen and prepared foods.

This species is a ready spawner, but sometimes a bit of patience and a number of fish are required for results. A pair will choose a broad submerged leaf and clean it thoroughly, then lay eggs on the clean surface. The male guards and fans them, and the fry hatch in 24 to 28 hours. Once they are swimming there is no point in keeping the parents with them any longer. The youngsters should get infusoria for at least a week, after which fine dried foods and then newly hatched brine shrimp are fed.

PYRRHULINA SPILOTA

QUINTANA ATRIZONA Hubbs/*Black-Barred Livebearer*

R: Cuba. **H**: Because of their size, they should be kept only with small fishes; otherwise they may tend to be shy. **W**: Not critical. Prefers a sunny tank that is well heated, 24 to 26°C. **S**: Males about 2 cm.; females about 3 cm. **F**: Not choosy, but the food particles should be small in size.

As with most livebearers, there is no question which are the males. Broods are quite small even with fully grown fish, and more than thirty young is unusual. The fry are tiny and must be carefully fed with very fine foods at first, almost like the fry of egg-layers. With proper feeding, however, they grow rapidly and in three to four months are ready to have young of their own. These fish do a little picking on algae from the plants but never extend their appetites to the plants themselves.

PYRRHULINA VITTATA

RACHOVIA HUMMELINCKI de Beaufort/*Coastal Spot-finned Killie*

R: Colombia and western Venezuela, in the coastal deserts and plains. **H:** Not very aggressive although some hiding places should be provided for the females. Sluggish. Some males unpredictable.**W:** Not critical. Neutral to slightly acid water, preferably soft, is sufficient. Temperature range about 22-26°C, but tolerates warmer (to 32°C) water well. **S:** Males about 75 mm, females about 65 mm. **F:** Can generally be persuaded to eat all kinds of foods suitable for aquarium species but prefers live foods.

Rachovia hummelincki is an annual killifish from Colombia and western Venezuela that sometimes occurs only a few kilometers from the sea. There are three known types of *R. hummelincki* differing in the color of the band at the lower edge of the caudal fin: orange, yellow, or white. The body is brownish and covered with bluish to whitish spots. Another form that is very similar but differs in having red spots on the body was known for some time as the red-spotted *R. hummelincki* (as opposed to the blue-spotted *R. hummelincki);* the red-spotted form was eventually described as a different species, *R. pyropunctata.* This latter species has similar variability in color of the caudal fin band.

Rachovia hummelincki does well in captivity. For spawning them a small container (drum bowls are often used) of 2-21/2 gallons (8-10 liters) capacity is sufficient for a pair or trio. The water should be neutral to slightly acid and of moderate hardness. A temperature of 22 to 26°C is adequate. There should be about 2.5 cm of peat moss on the bottom or a suitable spawning mop and a few plants that can serve as refuges for harassed females. Otherwise these fish are not very aggressive. All kinds of aquarium foods are acceptable, especially live foods. The eggs are deposited in the peat at the bottom of the aquarium (although these are annual fish they are not divers like *Cynolebias* or *Nothobranchius).* The peat containing the eggs should be taken out of the bowl at intervals and replaced with new peat. The egg-laden peat can be partially dried and stored in plastic bags for about three to six months. At the end of this time the material can be re-immersed in water so that the fry can hatch out. The newly hatched fry can be started on microworms for a week or so then graduated to newly hatched brine shrimp.

The young of *Rachovia hummelincki* do not grow as rapidly as do many other species of annuals, but they seem to live a bit longer, two to three years being a normal lifespan.

RACHOVIA MACULIPINNIS

RACHOVIA MACULIPINNIS (Radda)/ *Venezuelan Spot-Finned Killie*

R: Venezuela. **H:** Peaceful, but like other killifishes should be kept in a tank by themselves. **W:** Not critical, but does best in soft, slightly acid water that is clear and clean. The best temperature range is 18°24°C. **S:** Attains a length of up to 10 cm in their natural habitat but only about 7.5 cm in captivity. **F:** Live foods are preferred, but it will accept frozen foods.

This attractive killifish was apparently first discovered by Mr. Leo Hoigne in 1961. Specimens were made available to Dr. Franz Weibezahn, who proceeded to write up the scientific description. He selected the name *Pterolebias maculipinnis,* in reference to the spotted fins. Mr. Hoigne distributed some of the fish to people in the hobby under that name but cautioned them not to use it in print until Dr. Weibezahn's paper was published. Unfortunatly, an article by Radda did appear in a German magazine prior to Weibezahn's publication of the scientific description. It used the name *Pterolebias maculipinnis* Weibezahn and included a short color description, a key to the species, and an illustration (albeit rather poor), criteria that established Radda as the author of the name. More recently, Taphorn and Thomerson (1978) removed *maculipinnis* from the genus *Pterolebias* and placed it in *Rachovia* along with *brevis, hummelincki* and *pyropunctata.* *Rachovia maculipinnis* is an annual species, the eggs normally being incubated in peat moss for periods from four to eight months. It does not appear to be a strict annual as the eggs have been hatched after a water-incubation of only two months. It is a soil-breeder, so 5-8 cm of peat moss should carpet the bottom of its spawning tank. The water type is not critical, although soft, acid water that is clear and clean goes far in keeping the fish at their best. Live foods are preferred, although frozen foods such as brine shrimp and beef heart are accepted.

Rachovia maculipinnis is a diver, hence the necessity of the peat moss bottom layer for spawning. Two to three females should be supplied for each male for better egg production. The fairly large, amber-colored eggs can be water-incubated for about two months or peat-incubated for up to eight months (with six or seven months being optimum). Eggs that do not hatch on the first try can be dried and tried again in a few days. The newly hatched fry can take small brine shrimp nauplii, making feeding at this early stage relatively easy. Take care, however, not to overfeed since the fry are sensitive to dirty water. For best results provide plenty of room, clean water, and live foods. Males should be recognizable in about five weeks and may be ready to spawn by the time they reach ten weeks of age. They live an average of about nine months.

RACHOVISCUS CRASSICEPS Myers/*Golden Tetra*

R: Coastal blackwater streams of southeastern Brazil, from Parana perhaps to Rio de Janeiro. **H:** Relatively peaceful community tank species. **W:** Not critical; widely adaptable to various kinds of water, but for breeding may require a pH of about 5.0 to 5.5 and a DH of 2 to 3. Temperature 18 to 28°C; courtship occurs at the middle to upper range of these temperatures. **S:** Attains a length of about 4.5 cm. **F:** Will accept a variety of aquarium foods, including flake food. Live foods are recommended for breeding.

The fish is not shy and is a good community tank fish although courting males can be rather aggressive. Both sexes have a brassy golden color on the sides of the body, and in some lights this color may take on a purple metallic sheen. The adipose fin is a deep red in both the male and female. All colors are more intense in the males. In some lights the male shows golden metallic scales scattered over the sides.

So far the fish has been taken only from soft, acid, blackwater streams very near the Atlantic Ocean, where it occurs together with *Corydoras macropterus, Mimagoniates barberi,* a species of *Otocinclus*-like catfish, and a species of *Rivulus.*

Courtship (but no breeding) has been observed in aquaria. The courtship was similar to that of other small characids, the male vigorously chasing and displaying to the female.

Another species, *Rachoviscus graciliceps* Weitzman and da Cruz, was discovered in 1977 by Brazilian ichthyologists in small coastal streams of Bahia, Brazil. This new fish is similar in color to *Rachoviscus crassiceps* but has a more slender head and body as well as several technical differences. *Rachoviscus gracillceps* has been bred in aquaria, spawning in the usual characin manner by laying slightly adhesive eggs on finely branched aquatic plants. The young are easy to raise by using standard procedures for rearing aquarium fishes. (Contributed by Dr. Stanley H. Weitzman.)

RASBORA AGILIS Ahl/*Black-Striped Rasbora*

R: Sumatra. **H:** Peaceful, active swimmers; will mix with other active species in a community aquarium. **W:** Water should be clean, very soft, and with a pH of about 6.6. Temperature 24 to 28°C. **S:** About 8 cm. **F:** Will take dried foods, but live or frozen foods preferred.

Females have deeper bodies. For spawning, a tank of not less than 40 liters should be provided with several bunches of bushy plants. Spawning is sometimes extended over several days, and the usual practice is to leave the breeders in until the first fry are seen. The youngsters grow slowly in the first few days and should be given infusoria as well as finely powdered dry food. After two to three weeks the rate of growth increases, and in a half-year the youngsters attain a size of 4 cm and more.

RACHOVISCUS CRASSICEPS

RASBORA AGILIS

RASBORA ARGYROTAENIA (Bleeker)/*Silver Rasbora*

R: Japan, China, Thailand, Malacca, Malaysia, Java, Bali, and Borneo. **H**: Peaceful toward other fishes, but likely to be shy if kept alone. **W**: Soft water, about 5 to 8 DH. Should be kept about 23°C, but drops in temperature down to 18°C are tolerated. **S**: Attains a size of 15 cm in natural waters and about 10 cm in captivity. **F**: Being an active fish, it requires generous feeding; will accept dried foods, but these should be supplemented with live foods.

Even though it lacks much of the color that we associate with the rasbora species, *Rasbora argyrotaenia* lends a great deal of life to the community aquarium with its ceaseless activity, its gleaming silvery body, and the black edging of its tail. Sexes can only be determined with certainty when mature. At this time the male retains his slim outline, but the female becomes heavier in the belly.

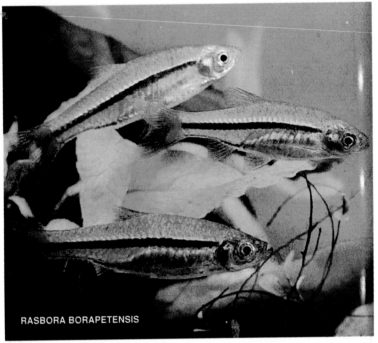

RASBORA BORAPETENSIS

RASBORA BANKANENSIS (Bleeker)/*Banka Rasbora*

R: Island of Banka and the neighboring region of Sumatra. **H**: Peaceful; likes to swim in schools. **W**: Soft and slightly acid. Temperature 24 to 27°C. **S**: To about 8 cm. **F**: Prepared foods accepted, but live or frozen foods should form at least a part of the diet.

The island of Banka, from which this rasbora comes, is frequently spelled "Bangka" and lies off the northern coast of Sumatra. This little fish looks almost completely colorless, but scientific descriptions tell us that it has a blackish stripe which begins faintly at the opercle and gets a little plainer toward the tail. The anal fin on some specimens is said to have a black tip. Dr. Martin Brittan says there are about 45 known species in the genus *Rasbora*, and H.M. Smith says that rasbora species are among the commonest freshwater species found in Thailand.

RASBORA ARGYROTAENIA

RASBORA BORAPETENSIS Smith/*Retailed Rasbora*
R: Thailand (Bung Borapet). **H**: Peaceful; likes to swim in small schools and does not nibble at plants. **W**: Soft, acid water. Temperature 24 to 27°C. **S**: To 6 cm. **F**: Eats anything, but should get live foods occasionally.
For breeding they should be given a tank of at least 40 liters capacity with some bushy plants. The water should be soft, about 2 to 3 DH, and the pH acid, 6.5 or 6.6. A ripe pair, where the female is heavy with eggs and the male active and in good color, is put into this tank and the water temperature raised to 27°C. Eggs are laid in the plants and hatch in 36 hours.

RASBORA BANKANENSIS

RASBORA CAUDIMACULATA Volz/*Greater Scissortailed Rasbora*

R: Malaysia and Sumatra. **H**: Peaceful and active, but should not be combined with small fishes. **W**: Soft, slightly acid water. Temperature 24 to 27°C. **S**: To 20 cm. **F**: Eat just about anything, but should get live foods occasionally.

This handsome Rasbora has great resemblance to its smaller cousin *R. trilineata*, the Scissortail, because of the usual pattern in the tail. Closer examination also shows that the first impression is not so accurate, because the three stripes which are prominent are missing here, and there is only one faint stripe.

There are as yet few reports of any spawnings, and the probability is that this will require a large tank. In their home waters this fish is said to attain a length of 20 cm. Their aquarium should be firmly covered at all times; the author once lost a good pair because the cover glass was not replaced well enough and both jumped out. It is a pity that we do not see this graceful, beautiful fish more often.

RASBORA DANICONIUS

RASBORA CEPHALOTAENIA (Bleeker)/*Porthole Rasbora*

R: Malaysia, Sumatra, and Borneo. **H**: Peaceful at all times. **W**: Prefers soft, slightly acid water. Temperature 24 to 26°C. **S**: To 13 cm in natural waters; captive specimens somewhat smaller. **F**: Takes all foods, but should get live or frozen foods occasionally.

As its popular name indicates, the sides are adorned by two rows of dots. The dots meet at the operculum and at a point just short of the caudal base. As with other *Rasbora* species, these are perfectly peaceful toward their tankmates, as long as they do not have to suppress the near-irresistible temptation resulting from being with fishes that are small enough to swallow. The fish has a violet flush, as is commonly found among many of the *R. cephalotaenia*. It has long been known to science, but hobbyists see it all too seldom. Few books list it and, to the best of our knowledge, it has so far not been spawned.

RASBORA CAUDIMACULATA

RASBORA DANICONIUS (Hamilton-Buchanan)/*Golden-Striped Rasbora*

R: Southeast Asia from Thailand through Burma and the Andaman Islands to western India and Sri Lanka. **H**: Peaceful and hardy; prefers to be in company with others of its own species. **W**: Medium hard (about 10 DH), neutral to slightly acid (pH 6-7) water kept at a temperature between 22 to 25°C is best for this species. **S**: Reaches a length of 20 cm in nature, but rarely gets to be more than 8 to 9 cm in captivity. **F**: Not critical; normal aquarium foods, including dried foods, will be accepted. They should be conditioned on live foods for spawning.

The courtship consists of displays and chases by the male as the female hides among the plants until she is ready to spawn. Then they assume a side by side position and the male attempts to curl his body around hers. This site has apparently been selected by the female, and the eggs are shed among the leaves of the plants. The process is repeated, with the female choosing other spawning sites. Once spawning has ceased the adult fish should be removed as they often will eat the eggs.

RASBORA CEPHALOTAENIA

RASBORA DORSIOCELLATA Duncker/*Hi-Spot Rasbora*

R: Southern Malaysia and adjacent Sumatra. **H**: An active fish, usually forming schools near the surface. **W**: Prefers soft, neutral to slightly acid water and warm temperatures. **S**: To 6 cm. **F**: This is an active fish that requires frequent feedings; it does well on dried foods, but live foods help bring out the colors.

A prolific breeder, the Hi-Spot Rasbora can be successfully bred by using fine-leaved plants such as *Nitella* or *Myriophyllum,* or a spawning mop made of nylon yarn. Many eggs are attached to the plant tufts and hatch in one or two days. The fry can be fed infusoria or other fine foods. Spawning is best at 25 to 27°C and can be initiated by feeding live food. Sexes are hard to distinguish, but if kept in a school the fish will find their own mates.

RASBORA EINTHOVENI

RASBORA DUSONENSIS (Bleeker)/*Yellowtail Rasbora*

R: Thailand, Malaysia, Sumatra, and Borneo. **H**: Peaceful and active; should have a large tank with a tight cover. **W**: Soft, somewhat acid water. Temperature 24 to 28°C. **S**: 15 cm. **F**: Not choosy; will eat dried as well as live foods.

This rasbora, and for that matter most other rasboras, is an active jumper and must be protected from its own exuberance by a tight-fitting cover. *R. dusonensis* is frequently confused with *R. argyrotaenia,* which is much more common in the Asiatic collecting areas. The only difference is that the dark stripe is wider and not as pronounced in *R. dusonensis.* Both are beautiful and well worth the trouble of keeping them, but it is necessary to let them have a roomy aquarium, which their active nature requires.

RASBORA DORSIOCELLATA

RASBORA EINTHOVENI (Bleeker)/*Brilliant Rasbora, Einthoven's Rasbora*
R: Malacca, Malaysia, Thailand, Sumatra, and Borneo. **H**: In its native waters it travels in schools; an active swimmer, so it should be given adequate quarters with a good amount of swimming space. **W**: Not critical, but prefers soft, acid water and temperatures between 24 to 26°C; for spawning, about 27°C is best. **S**: Up to 8 cm. **F**: Being an active fish, they should be fed frequently; dried foods are accepted but should be supplemented with frozen foods.

Sexes are difficult to distinguish; the only difference is the heavier body of the females. One might have what is thought to be a pair and find that it is a ripe and an unripe female. The species is easily spawned; the non-adhesive eggs fall to the bottom, which should be covered with pebbles to prevent the parents from eating them.

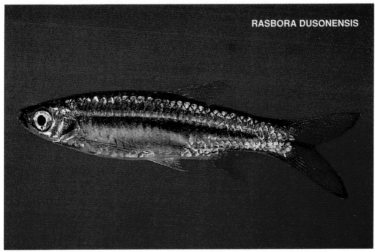

RASBORA DUSONENSIS

RASBORA ELEGANS Volz/*Two-Spot Rasbora, Elegant Rasbora*

R: Malaysia and the Sunda Islands. **H**: Peaceful and active; good community tank fish. **W**: Soft, slightly acid water. Temperature 24 to 28°C. **S**: To 13 cm. **F**: Easily fed with live, frozen, or dry foods.

Males are usually a bit smaller than the females and have deeper colors. A ripe pair will spawn readily in the same manner as the barbs, with a great deal of driving and hide-and-seek among the bushy plants, coming to a frequent quivering halt among the plants and scattering adhesive eggs. Like the barbs, the breeders will eat their eggs if they are not removed as soon as spawning is completed. Hatching takes place on the following day; fry are easily fed with hard-boiled egg yolk squeezed through a cloth until they are able to handle newly hatched brine shrimp.

RASBORA KALOCHROMA

RASBORA HETEROMORPHA Duncker/*Rasbora, Harlequin Fish*

R: Malaysia, southern Thailand, Sumatra, and Java. **H**: Peaceful and harmless to even the smallest fishes; they are active swimmers that prefer to travel in schools. **W**: Comes from very soft and acid water, and this is what they should get. Temperature 24 to 27°C. **S**: 5 cm; usually a little smaller. **F**: Will accept dried foods, but should get frequent feedings with live and frozen foods.

Almost every picture that depicts a group of tropical aquarium fishes will include Angelfish, Discus, and our little friend *Rasbora heteromorpha*. The little red fish with the black triangle is almost as well known as the ubiquitous Guppy. Sexes can usually be distinguished by a fine gold line along the upper part of the triangle in the males and the heavier, deeper body of the females. Eggs are usually laid on the underside of a wide plant leaf and afterward ignored by both parents. Fry hatch in 24 to 26 hours and should be given infusoria at first.

RASBORA ELEGANS

RASBORA KALOCHROMA (Bleeker)/*Big-Spot Rasbora*

R: Malaysia, Sumatra, and Borneo. **H**: Peaceful and a continuous swimmer. **W**: Warm (24 to 27°C), soft, acid water. **S**: Reaches a total length of 10 cm. **F**: Takes dry, frozen, and live foods equally well.

A remarkable similarity between the Big-Spot Rasbora and the Two-spot Rasbora is easily seen. Both fish are of similar size, shape, and color and both may be found in the same parts of Malaysia and Sumatra. Yet technical differences such as scale counts and number of fin rays prove that the two species are not so closely related to each other as might be thought from superficial observation. In both the Big-Spot and the Two-Spot, the larger blotch is at midside. In *Rasbora kalochroma,* the small spot is behind the head; in *R. elegans,* it is at the base of the caudal fin.

RASBORA HETEROMORPHA

Rasbora heteromopha spawning on the underside of a *Cryptocoryne* leaf.
On the facing page, the pair lay their eggs on top of the leaf.

RASBORA MYERSI Brittan/*Myers's Rasbora*

R: Malaysia, Sumatra, Borneo, and Thailand. **H**: Peaceful toward any other fishes that it cannot swallow. **W**: Soft, neutral to slightly acid water. Temperature 24 to 27°C. **S**: 15 cm. **F**: Live, frozen or dried foods taken equally well.

One look at this *Rasbora* species should serve to convince anyone as to why it is so seldom seen in the collections of fish hobbyists. It just simply does not have any outstanding colors, unless you could call attention to that slight tinge of black in the tail. Doubtless collectors in Asiatic waters have the same problems as do the South American collectors: a netful of fish is brought up, and 95 out of 100 are of no value for several reasons: they are or get to be too big for the aquarium, they are undesirable because they are vicious toward other fishes, or, most of all, they have no colors to make them decorative and desirable in the aquarium.

RASBORA SOMPHONGSI

RASBORA PAUCIPERFORATA Weber & de Beaufort/*Red-Line Rasbora*

R: Sumatra. **H**: Peaceful and well-behaved in mixed company. **W**: Water should be somewhat acid, pH 6.2, and soft, DH 2 or 3. Temperature 24 to 27°C. **S**: About 6 cm. **F**: Live foods preferred, but all kinds are accepted.

Spawning is similar to the other long-bodied rasboras: bushy plants should be provided and also a generous amount of swimming space. Males drive actively , coming frequently to a stop alongside a female among the plants; the pair scatter eggs all over, many of them falling to the bottom. Fry hatch in 24 to 36 hours.

RASBORA MYERSI

RASBORA SOMPHONGSI Meinken/*Somphongs's Rasbora*

R: Thailand. **H**: Peaceful; a good community fish. **W**: Soft, acid water desirable. Temperature 23 to 28°C. **S**: About 3 cm. **F**: All types of food accepted, provided that it is small enough to be swallowed.

For spawning, which is accomplished through the laying of eggs in bunches of plants or synthetic plant fibers, soft and acid water is a necessity. The fry are very tiny, as is to be expected from the size of the parents, and they require plenty of infusoria for the first few days of their free-swimming life. *Rasbora somphongsi* is not a brilliantly colored fish, but its quiet beauty can be shown off better if it is kept in a well-planted tank having a dark background and bottom.

RASBORA PAUCIPERFORATA

RASBORA STEINERI Nichols & Pope/*Chinese Rasbora*

R: Southern China, Hainan Province. **H**: Peaceful and well-behaved with other fishes. **W**: Soft and considerably acid water. Temperature 23 to 26°C. **S**: Up to 8 cm. **F**: Live foods preferred, but all kinds are accepted.

Most of China is in the Temperate Zone, and there are very few fishes of interest to the fish hobbyist available today from waters that are warm enough to be considered "tropical." *Rasbora steineri*, from Hainan Province, is one of the exceptions. In appearance it resembles the much better-known *R. borapetensis*, the main difference being that *R. borapetensis* has a shade brighter red in the tail toward the base. There is as yet no record of any spawning of *R. steineri*. Probably it spawns like the other long-bodied *rasbora* species, but any guess may be far off base.

RASBORA TRILINEATA

RASBORA SUMATRANA (Bleeker)/*Sumatran Rasbora*

R: Thailand, Malaysia, Sumatra, Borneo, and Southeast Asia. **H**: Peaceful toward other fishes that are too large to be swallowed. **W**: Soft, slightly acid water preferred. Temperature 23 to 26°C. **S**: 15 cm in captivity. **F**: Not choosy as to foods, but should have live or frozen foods frequently.

The Sumatran Rasbora is a species that requires an expert to identify it positively because of the extreme variability of its colors. Here is how Dr. Martin R. Brittan describes them: "May have dark stripe, a stripe posteriorly only, or none at all; if present, stripe may or may not end in a spot at the base of the tail; spot may be present without stripe. Streak above anal may be variable in shape, and is often absent. Tail may or may not have dark margin or dark tip to lobe." Care and spawning for this species are similar to that of *Rasbora somphongsi*.

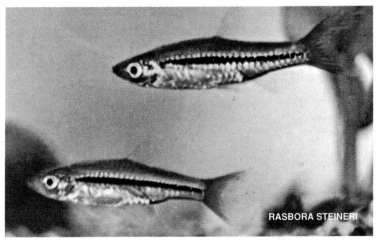

RASBORA STEINERI

RASBORA TRILINEATA Steindachner/*Three-Lined or Scissortailed Rasbora*

R: Sumatra and Borneo, where it is common. **H**: Peaceful, active swimmers who should have plenty of swimming space in their aquarium. **W**: Soft, acid water with a pH of about 6.5. Temperature 24 to 26°C. **S**: Up to 10 cm. **F**: Will accept dried foods as well as live foods.

Females are a trifle longer than the males and considerably bigger around. After considerable driving, the male gets the female into some bushy plants, where he wraps his body about hers and 15 to 25 eggs are expelled and fertilized. The eggs have very little adhesive power and many fall to the bottom. The first of the fry hatch after 24 hours. In five days the youngsters begin to swim, at which time they may be fed with very fine dry foods, followed in a week or so by newly hatched brine shrimp.

RASBORA SUMATRANA

RASBOROIDES VATERIFLORIS (Deraniyagala)/*Singhalese Fire Barb*

R: Sri Lanka. **H**: Very peaceful active fish that should be given adequate swimming space. **W**: Soft, acid water like the other species. Temperature should not sink below 25°C. **S**: Maximum length 3.5 cm. **F**: Will accept dried foods as well as live or frozen foods.

Females are easily recognizable by their lighter colors and heavier dimensions. Males are active drivers and pursue the females into plant thickets, where a very rapid spawning act takes place. The eggs have little adhesive power, and most of them fall to the bottom. The pair should come out as soon as the eggs have been laid or most of them will be eaten. The water level should then be reduced to 15 cm. The young will hatch in 36 to 40 hours.

RHADINOCENTRUS ORNATUS

RASBORICHTHYS ALTIOR Regan/*Green False Rasbora*

R: Singapore. **H**: A peaceful, schooling species. **W**: Not critical; soft, slightly acid water is preferred. Temperature 15 to 26°C. **S**: 9 cm. **F**: Standard foods are accepted readily.

Breeding can be accomplished in a 40-liter aquarium heavily planted with bunch-plants such as *Cabomba*. A pair or a trio of two males and one female can be used for breeding. The female should be conditioned separately and introduced into the aquarium at least 24 hours before the males. Water in the breeding aquarium should be soft and slightly acid; spawning is apparently stimulated by sunlight. The eggs are adhesive and hatch in about two days at 24° C. Fry should be fed infusoria for about a week and then converted to newly hatched brine shrimp.

RASBOROIDES VATERIFLORIS

RHADINOCENTRUS ORNATUS Regan/*Southern Soft-Spined Rainbowfish*

R: Southern Queensland and northern New South Wales, Australia. **H**: Active mid-water swimmers; peaceful. **W**: Neutral to slightly alkaline water to which a little bit of salt has been added. Temperature should range from about 22 to 26°C. **S**: Attains a length of about 8 cm. **F**: Will readily accept most common aquarium foods, but for best conditioning should have some live foods.

Spawning is not too difficult and can be accomplished in a manner similar to that of the other rainbowfishes. The tank is set up with some fine-leaved plants and the spawners introduced after about a week of conditioning. Once spawning is completed the parents can be removed, although they are said to leave the eggs alone if well fed. The eggs can be seen hanging by small threads from the plants. Hatching occurs in about one week, and the fry are hardy and rather easy to raise. The first food should be infusoria, but baby brine shrimp can be added before too long.

RASBORICHTHYS ALTIOR

RHINICHTHYS ATRATULUS (Hermann)/*Blacknose Dace*

R: United States and Canada from Manitoba and Nova Scotia through the Great Lakes and eastern U.S. to the northern parts of Georgia, Alabama, and Mississippi. **H:** A non-aggressive species but busy. **W:** A cool-water fish, but tolerant of a variety of water conditions. It comes from clear, swift-flowing streams, so it prefers some currents or eddies in the aquarium. **S:** The largest fish are up to 10 cm, but the average size is nearer 6.5 cm. **F:** Takes a wide variety of foods and readily adapts to aquarium fare, including flake foods.

Rhinichthys atratulus, as can be deduced from its distribution, is a coolwater fish, the maintenance temperature generally being less than 20°C. It prefers a tank with plenty of room and some gravel on the bottom and it will swim in currents or eddies (formed by power filters) which resemble the water motions of its home streams. Food is no problem. Blacknose Dace will accept almost any aquarium foods, including flake foods, although their natural diet consists of aquatic crustaceans, worms, or insects (bloodworms or chironomid larvae constitute a large part of their diet in some areas), as well as large algae and other plant material.

When the stream temperatures rise to about 21°C in the springtime, the Blacknose Dace generally start to spawn. The males are easily distinguished from the females because they have longer pectoral, pelvic, and anal fins. When spawning approaches, males develop nuptial tubercles over the head, fins, and much of the body surface and also develop a rust-red coloration laterally with some orange or red on the pectoral fins. Spawning occurs in shallow riffle areas over rubble or gravel bottoms where the water is only a few inches deep. There are four subspecies of *Rhinichthys atratulus,* each with its own spawning peculiarities. In some a nest of small pebbles is constructed by the pair, into which the female deposits her small (0.8 mm) amber eggs. The males court the females as they enter the area, and actual egg deposition occurs when the male and female orient side by side over the nest. The eggs are extruded during violent vibrations which last only a few seconds. One reference contends that no further care is given the eggs, whereas another maintains the nest is vigorously guarded by the male from egg-snatching dace in the vicinity. The spawners are even said to at times dine on their own eggs during spawning.

RHODEUS SERICEUS

RHODEUS SERICEUS (Pallas)/*Bitterling*

R: Middle Europe. **H**: Peaceful, but not a good community fish, as it is not a tropical species and cannot take normal aquarium temperatures. **W**: Water composition is not of great importance as long as extremes are avoided. Temperature 14 to 21°C. **S**: Up to 8 cm. **F**: Accepts most commercial foods; paste foods are especially good.

Very few American hobbyists have had any experience with this fish, but it is popular in Europe, where there is less stress placed on tropical species and more attention is paid to native fishes. Perhaps the Bitterling is more favored in Europe because of its interesting habits; European hobbyists pay more attention to behavioral characteristics than Americans do. In any event, the Bitterling is fascinating in its breeding pattern. Many fishes go to great lengths to protect their young, but the Bitterling really confounds its enemies: the female uses her extremely long ovipositor to place her eggs within living molluscs, where they are safe from all harm. The hatched fry remain in their living refuge until they become free-swimming. The mollusc, usually a mussel, is not to be considered as a victim, because the young *Rhodeus* are not parasites and take nothing from the bivalve. As a matter of fact, the protection afforded by the young fish only serves to even up the score between mollusc and fish, for many young bivalves spend their larval stages attached to the skin of fishes, who thus transport them to new homes.

RIVULUS AGILAE Hoedeman/*Agila Rivulus*

R: Coastal Guianas. **H**: Best kept with its own kind or similar fishes. **W**: Soft, slightly acid water is best. A temperature around 22°C is best, but gradual drops in temperature are tolerated. **S**: To 5.5 cm. **F**: Living foods preferred; frozen or prepared foods only accepted when very hungry. The species was described by J.J. Hoedeman in 1954 and was found in a small rocky stream. It is a small fish that reaches adulthood at five to six months of age and usually reproduces at eight months, when it will have reached only a little more than 5 cm. in body length. The Agila Rivulus is most closely related to *Rivulus breviceps* from Guyana and Surinam and to *Rivulus geayi* from French Guiana. *Rivulus agilae* does best when kept at temperatures between 18 to 23°C.

RIVULUS HARTI

RIVULUS CYLINDRACEUS Poey/*Cuban Rivulus*

R: Cuba. **H**: Fairly peaceful in the community aquarium. **W**: Soft, slightly acid water preferred. Temperature 24 to 26°C. **S**: Males slightly under 5 cm.; females slightly larger. **F**: Should get live foods only, but will accept dried foods if hungry.

Eggs are laid in bushy plants near the surface, a few each day, and take from 12 to 14 days to hatch. There are several ways to separate the eggs from the breeders. One is to pick out the eggs every few days. A simpler method is to leave the breeders in with the eggs, which they seldom eat, for about 10 days and then fish out the parents. Still another is to remove the plants with the eggs every 10 days and place them in similar water to hatch. The fry are free-swimming upon hatching.

RIVULUS AGILAE

RIVULUS HARTI (Boulenger)/*Hart's Rivulus; Giant Rivulus*
R: Trinidad, Venezuela, and eastern Colombia. **H**: Peaceful and likely to remain hidden; will not harm any fish it cannot swallow. **W**: Not at all critical, but slightly sensitive to lower temperatures. The temperature should never be allowed to drop below 24°C. **S**: 10 cm. **F**: Should get live foods, but will take dry food when very hungry.

Some of the *Rivulus* species, of which this is one, have a strange habit that is not mentioned in most of the books; they will often jump out of the water and cling to the glass sides of the aquarium above the surface or to the cover glass for considerable periods of time. When they feel themselves beginning to become dry, they drop back, sometimes to repeat the procedure soon afterward.

RIVULUS CYLINDRACEUS

RIVULUS HOLMIAE Eigenmann/*Golden-Tailed Rivulus*

R: Guyana. **H**: Adept at jumping through the smallest opening; peaceful, but will eat small fishes. **W**: Soft, slightly acid water optimal, but not necessary. Temperature 22 to 25°C. **S**: About 10 cm. **F**: Will accept living, frozen, or freeze-dried foods.

After the pair has gotten used to the aquarium, the male will start courting the female. As he becomes more persistent in his courtship, he presses his body against the female's, forcing her against a plant leaf or against the bottom. At this time the eggs are laid either singly or in groups of two. A single female may lay up to 100 eggs in a twenty-four-hour period if she has been well conditioned. The eggs hatch in 10 to 14 days, and the fry gather near the top. The fry are large enough to accept newly hatched brine shrimp at once.

RIVULUS MAGDALENAE Eigenmann/*Magdalena Rivulus*

R: Magdalena basin, Colombia. **H**: Colorful, peaceful killifish suitable for community tanks of non-aggressive fishes. Best kept in single-species tank, though. **W**: Not critical, but does best in slightly soft water. Temperatures between 23°and 26°C are adequate. **S**: Males attain a length of about 40-45 mm, females about 50 mm or so. **F**: Will accept a variety of aquarium foods. Tubificid worms and live brine shrimp are recommended for conditioning.

This is one of those fishes that have all the attributes of a good beginner's aquarium fish. It is colorful, undemanding and easy to keep, and breeds easily. The parents can be left with the fry (they leave *most* of them alone), and the fry are easy to raise. What more could one ask?

A 10-gallon (about 40 liters) aquarium is sufficient for several pairs. It should have slightly soft water, not too hard, at a temperature of about 25° or 26°C. A few centimeters of gravel can be added and plants selected with the idea of giving protection to harassed females or newly hatched fry. The addition of a spawning mop that extends from surface to gravel is suggested. Normal aeration and filtration are recommended. Feeding is no problem as most aquarium foods are accepted. Live foods such as tubificid worms and brine shrimp should be offered as conditioning foods.

The sexes are easily distinguished. The males are smaller but more colorful. The characteristic bright red-orange caudal fin edge sets off the darker bluish gray body and caudal peduncle color of a spawning individual. Bluish green iridescent reflections and spots of bright red add to the pleasing coloration. The female is rather drab by comparison. She is grayish to tanish with a multitude of darker spots or blotches. These spots are a bit more numerous and darker posteriorly. At the upper edge of the caudal base is a dark spot surrounded by a clear area. Some reddish spots may be present on the body. The male will chase the female around the tank (not viciously as in many fishes) and they will stop occasionally to spawn. The pair line up side by side, embracing, the male's dorsal fin draped over the back of the female, and they tremble. As they move off it can be seen that a single relatively large egg is left behind. They will spawn in the mop but also in the plants and even in the gravel. Eggs can be collected at intervals and hatched in slightly soft, clean water. The fry that hatch out in the parents' tank from missed eggs have a good chance to survive. Hatching occurs in about ten days to two weeks. The large fry are able to eat newly hatched brine shrirr.p and other suitable fry foods. In about three months the largest may reach a length of about 25 mm (none should be less than 20 mm). In about four weeks the sexes can be distinguished as the females start to develop the caudal spot. At four months both sexes are in full color and the males are in their breeding colors.

RIVULUS HOLMIAE

RIVULUS MAGDALENAE

RIVULUS PUNCTATUS (Boulenger)/*Spotted Rivulus*

R: Paraguay, Bolivia, and western Brazil. **H**: Generally peaceful, but shy with other fishes. **W**: Soft, slightly acid water. Temperature 24 to 27°C. **S**: To 8 cm. **F**: All sorts of live foods; dry foods taken only when very hungry.

The Spotted Rivulus is a real rarity, and is seldom seen in hobbyist collections today. Another fish, *Rivulus dorni,* has been mistakenly offered as this species by dealers from time to time. The fish pictured here was caught by Harald Schultz in the Mato Grosso region of Brazil. The V-shaped arrangement of dots in the after part of the body is highly reminiscent of the bars in *R. strigatus,* another very attractive member of the genus. All *Rivulus* species are excellent jumpers and can leap surprisingly high out of the water. A covered tank is therefore a necessity if you do not want to find your precious fish on the floor some morning.

RIVULUS TENUIS (Meek)/Mexican *Rivulus*

R: This species occurs in southern Mexico, Guatemala, and Honduras. **H:** Peaceful fish that are best kept in a species tank. Excellent jumpers so tank should be properly covered. **W:** Can be kept under typical aquarium conditions but prefer very soft water (6°dGH) for breeding. **S:** Attains a length of about 7 cm. **F:** A good selection of live foods necessary for best results.

The Mexican Rivulus belongs to the elegans-complex and has no longitudinal stripes although the female has the rivulin spot. They are normally surface fish that are good jumpers, and the tank in which they are kept must be properly covered.

The tank need not be very large, and a 10-gallon tank is sufficient if only the single trio is kept. The substrate is not important other than to hold in place the fine-leaved plants necessary for breeding. The water is not important for general maintenance as long as extremes are avoided. For spawning this fish, however, very soft (6°dGH) water is recommended. Sexes are easily separated by their color differences, the male being the more colorful. A single male with a couple of females per tank is ideal. If the sexes are separated and conditioned with a variety of live foods they should spawn rather quickly when placed together. The male will court the female by swimming around her and nudging her, trying to guide her to a chosen spawning site. If the female is ready, she will comply and examine the area for a suitable site. The male remains in the vicinity until she has selected the site, then rubs up against her. Both fish bend into an "S" shape and vibrate, releasing eggs and sperm simultaneously. This is repeated several times until the eggs are depleted. The relatively large (about 2mm) adhesive eggs can be transferred to separate hatching quarters (a container that holds 10 cm or more of water) for about two weeks. At this time the fry usually swim to the surface of the water where they can be collected and moved to a larger tank. An alternative method is to move the spawners every two weeks, leaving the fry to be reared where they were spawned. The initial foods for the fry are the usual newly hatched brine shrimp or other suitable sized fare.

RIVULUS PUNCTATUS

RIVULUS TENUIS

RIVULUS UROPHTHALMUS Günther/*Golden Rivulus*

R: Guianas to the lower Amazon region. **H**: Prefer to be kept by themselves, but a large tank is not essential; they like to hide in plant thickets and are very active jumpers. **W**: Soft, slightly acid water is best. A temperature around 24°C is best, but it is not sensitive to gradual drops. **S**: 6 cm. **F**: Live foods are essential, preferably those that remain near the surface, like mosquito larvae.

The genus *Rivulus* is one which is not generally noted for its brilliance of colors. Most of the species have a coloration which blends in with their native background, making them a drab lot. *Rivulus urophthalmus* is one of the exceptions, even in the green form which we seldom see. The upper two-thirds of the body is covered with horizontal rows of red dots. This species often has a xanthic variation, which is the one which most hobbyists are offered. Here the entire body is a golden yellow instead of green, and the red dots are exceptionally brilliant. Probably these yellow fish occur quite frequently in their native waters, but such a fish would seldom attain full growth. Its color would be equivalent to a death warrant, because such a fish would find many enemies. However, in aquarium the golden ones can be separated from the green ones in a batch of fry and raised to maturity without being attacked by enemies, and the results are beautiful.

This fish is easily spawned. A few eggs are laid daily among floating vegetation. These are picked out and allowed to hatch separately, which they do in 12 days. The fry are easily raised.

SANDELIA CAPENSIS

ROEBOIDES SP./*Glass Characin*

R: Central and South America. **H**: Although often said to be peaceful, this fish should not be trusted with smaller fishes. **W**: Neutral water of medium hardness. Temperature 23 to 26°C. **S**: To about 15 cm. **F**: Prefers live or frozen foods of all kinds, but will sometimes accept prepared flake foods.

Glass Characins swim in a slightly inclined head-down position rather than the normal horizontal position. The lower lobe of the caudal fin in many mature specimens is often stronger than the upper lobe due to its swimming pattern. These fish are very active and should be given adequate room to swim and some sunlight. The fish generally spawn among water plants after active courtship rituals.

RIVULUS UROPHTHALMUS

SANDELIA CAPENSIS (Cuvier & Valenciennes)/*Cape Bushfish*
R: South coastal drainage basin of South Africa. **H:** Predatory on small fishes but can be kept in a community situation with sturdy cichlids and catfishes. **W:** Not critical. A pH of 6.7-7.8 and a hardness of 10-30° dGH is acceptable. Temperature range should be about 18-22°C. **S:** Attains a length of just over 21 cm. **F:** Omnivorous, feeding on aquatic insects, crustaceans, and even small fishes. Some vegetable matter should be included in the diet.

A relatively large tank with a strong filter flow is suggested. The Cape Bushfish can be kept in single species tanks or in a community tank with sturdy cichlids and/or catfishes. In this latter situation a single specimen or a single pair only should be included. *Sandelia capensis* preys on small fishes so they should not be placed in the same tank unless they are meant as food. Gravel can cover the bottom and strongly rooted or bunch plants can be added. Rocks and driftwood are not needed but can be added for esthetic reasons.

Sexes are similar but the male tends to be slimmer and the female more robust, especially when she is filled with eggs.

ROEBOIDES SP.

SATANOPERCA JURUPARI (Heckel)/*Eartheater, Demon Fish*

R: Northern South America. **H**: Generally peaceful; fond of digging in the sand and searching for edible bits, but seldom uproots plants if they are well rooted. Mouthbrooder. **W**: Temperatures should be kept high, about 26°C. Water should be neutral to slightly acid. **S**: Up to 23 cm in the wild state; not over 15 cm in captivity. **F**: Will eat dried foods, but should be given an occasional feeding with live foods; white worms and tubifex preferred.

The large, flat, pointed head of this cichlid, with its big eyes, is what usually attracts the hobbyist to this fish. It is constantly digging for food particles in the bottom. Their real claim to being something unusual is their manner of breeding. They will lay their eggs in typical cichlid fashion, then guard and fan them for a day or so. The eggs are then picked up by the male or female or both and incubated in the mouth. After they hatch, the babies will seek refuge in the parents' mouths until their size no longer permits them to be accommodated. Breedings of this beautiful fish are rarely reported, and we are dependent mostly on importations for the stock which is offered for sale. Although the males may be recognized by their more pointed anal and ventral fins, this difference is not highly pronounced, and the only sure way to sex them is to look for the breeding tubes when the fish are ready for spawning. The male's will be slender, and the female's much heavier. A well-mated pair will generally spawn with regularity once they have become accustomed to their surroundings. A tank of at least 20 gallons is recommended.

SCARDINEUS ERYTHROPHTHALMUS (Linnaeus)/*Rudd; Red Feather*

R: Europe and Asia at least to the Aral Sea. **H**: A peaceful, schooling species that does well in a communiy tank of similar type fishes. **W**: Not critical. This is a coldwater species that does best at temperatures between 10° and 20°C. High oxygen content attained by good filtration, good aeration, and regular partial water changes is necessary. **S**: Up to about 40 cm. **F**: Eats a variety of live and prepared foods. Some vegetable matter should be included.

The Rudd is common in standing and slow-flowing waters of Europe to western Asia around the Aral Sea. It is a peaceful schooling species that does best in a single species tank or with other cold-water cyprinids. It is a fish of the middle to upper layers, feeding less near the bottom than the Roach *(Rutilus rutilus)*. The tank should be relatively large as this species attains a length of up to 40 cm. Plants that can withstand the cooler temperatures (temperature range recommended for this species is 10° to 20°C) should be added, leaving sufficient room for swimming, and the substrate should be of soft sand. A high oxygen content (which the fish requires) can be obtained by good filtration, good aeration, and regular partial water changes. Most foods are accepted but a good portion of the diet should be vegetable matter.

Because of its size the Rudd can only be spawned in captivity in very large tanks—if at all. In the spring (about April to June) more than 100,000 eggs are laid on aquatic plants in shallow water. The males develop breeding tubercles and brilliant coloration and can easily be spotted at this time. The eggs are 1-1.5 mm in diameter and hatch in one to two weeks depending on temperature. Hatched fry are about 4.5 mm long and for the first few days hang on the vegetation. They can grow to as much as 9.8 cm in one good year but under poor ecological conditions some may barely reach 7.5 cm in three years. The young feed on diatoms, algae, and copepods in nature; the larger fish eat aquatic insects, crustaceans,and even small fishes.

SATANOPERCA JURUPARI

SCARDINEUS ERYTHROPHTHALMUS

SCATOPHAGUS ARGUS (Gmelin)/*Spotted Scat*

R: Tropical Indo-Pacific region along the coasts. **H**: Peaceful toward other fishes, but will graze on aquatic plants right down to the roots. **W**: Fairly hard, alkaline water with a teaspoon of salt per four liters of water added. Temperature 23 to 26°C. **S**: To 33 cm in their home waters; about half that in captivity. **F**: Live foods of all kinds, with the addition of vegetable substances like lettuce or spinach leaves; will also eat frozen foods.

Actually the Spotted Scat is an estuarine fish that spends its time in coastal waters. We do not know much of its spawning habits, but it is thought that spawning takes place in marine water around coral reefs. The young ascend the streams and grow through their juvenile stages in fresh or only slightly brackish water. It is at this stage that most of them are collected, and for this reason they can be kept in fairly fresh water with only a little salt added to make them feel at home. A translation of the generic name is "offal-eater," which is given to the fish because it is frequently found near the sewer outlets of coastal cities. The reason may be that they are after what comes out of the pipes, or that they are attracted to the smaller life which feeds on this. Scats are very hardy, long-lived fish if given conditions they like and live for a long time in captivity. Captive specimens of course never attain the size they would reach in their home waters where they could make their migrations into salt water.

SCATOPHAGUS TETRACANTHUS (Lacepede)/*African Banded Scat*

R: Coastal waters of East Africa. **H:** Generally peaceful and active. May nibble at aquarium plants if available. **W:** Prefers hard, alkaline water with 3-4 teaspoons of sea salt per 10 liters should be added. Temperature 23-28°C. **S:** Attains a length of approximately 40cm. **F:** Eats a wide variety of foods. Live foods and some vegetable matter are recommended.

The African Banded Scat is the scat least seen in imports. It comes only from East African waters regardless of reports of it from Australia and the East Indies. These latter records are probably referable to *Selenotoca multifasciata*. It inhabits marine, brackish, and fresh waters although the adults may be more marine oriented while the juveniles prefer fresh or brackish waters.

The tank selected should be at least 20 gallons capacity, although larger sizes are better. Decorations can include rockwork and driftwood and plants that are tolerant to salt. The area in the front of the tank should be left relatively clear for these open water swimming fish. The water should be hard and alkaline with approximately 3 to 4 teaspoons of sea salt per 10 liters of water added. The temperature should be in the range of 23-28°C.

The African Banded Scat eats almost all types of aquarium food. Live foods are preferred and some vegetable matter in the form of algae, spinach, "green" flake food, or even aquatic plants (which they like to nibble on).

These are peaceful, active schooling fish that do not bother other fishes and so are suited for community aquaria housing fishes that require similar conditions.

Although this species has not been reported as having been spawned in captivity, some aspects of its life history are known. The eggs are pelagic, probably spawned in bays fed by rivers. The larvae pass through a "tholichthys" stage like that of the marine butterflyfishes wherein the head is encased in bone and bony plates extend posteriorly from it. At some time in its early life history the juveniles move up into the rivers into slightly brackish or even fresh water.

SCATOPHAGUS ARGUS

SCATOPHAGUS TETRACANTHUS

SCHILBE MARMORATUS Boulenger/*African Shoulder-Spot Catfish*

R: Zaire River and its tributaries. **H**: Peaceful; inclined to be shy, so hiding places should be provided. **W**: Soft, neutral to slightly acid water. Temperature 24 to 27°C. **S**: To 16 cm. **F**: Prefers live foods, but may possibly be trained to accept frozen foods.

There are a great many catfishes which come from African waters. Some are highly interesting in color and habits, and others have a great similartiy to our North American bullheads. *Schilbe marmoratus* has only one feature which makes it a little different: on a drab body there is a large round black spot. One thing which can be said in their favor is that they are not particularly nocturnal in their habits. If kept in a tank which gets too much light, however, they tend to be shy and inclined to hide.

As with so many other timid species, the more hiding places that are provided, the more often they are seen. Having a place where they can retreat gives them confidence in the safety of their surroundings and gives them the courage to venture forth, which otherwise they would not have. Boulenger named this fish in 1911, and it has been known to the hobby since about 1956.

SCLEROPAGES FORMOSUS

SCHISTURA NOTOSTIGMA (Bleeker)/*Fighting Loach*

R: Sri Lanka. **H**: Best kept by themselves in pairs or several pairs in a large tank with a number of hiding places. **W**: Not critical, but the water should be clean. Temperature 24 to 27°C. **S**: To 8 cm. **F**: Any kind of food accepted, but there should be live foods given at times.

Here is one loach where the males are easy to distinguish: in the male the upper lobe of the tail is considerably longer, looking like that of a rooster. Both sexes attain a length of 8 cm. Fighting consists mostly of maneuvers in which one fish attempts to grasp the other's pectoral fin. Although they have no teeth in their jaws, they can manage to tear away pieces of the fin membrane.

SCLEROPAGES FORMOSUS (Müller & Schegel)/*Barramundi; Asiatic Arowana*
R: Southeastern Thailand, Sumatra, Borneo, and Bangka. **H**: Will eat small fishes; excellent jumper. **W**: Not critical. A temperature between 22 to 28°C should suffice. **S**: To 90 cm and a weight of over 7 kilograms. **F**: Surface feeder in nature on insects but will also take small fishes and crustaceans (shrimp, etc.); smaller individuals will take daphnia, brine shrimp, etc.
Scleropages formosus is a maternal mouthbrooder, the eggs being taken into the mother's mouth immediately after they are laid. The incubation period is not known specifically for *S. formosus,* but in another species it is estimated to be about 10 to 14 days. The eggs themselves are large, about 10 mm in diameter on the average, and vary in number from 50 to 200.

SELENOTOCA MULTIFASCIATA (Richardson)/*False Scat; Silver Scat*

R: New Guinea to New Caledonia; warm Australian coastal waters. **H**: Peaceful toward other fishes but cannot be trusted with plants. **W**: Fairly hard, alkaline water with a teaspoon of salt added per four liters of water. Temperature 23 to 26°C. **S**: To 10 cm. **F**: Live foods, with the addition of vegetable substances like lettuce or spinach leaves; will also eat frozen foods.

Only a highly trained eye can spot the difference between this attractive fish and one of an entirely different genus, *Scatophagus tetracanthus,* the Striped Scat, with which and as which it is frequently shipped. *Selenotoca multifasciata* has a slightly more elongated body and the soft parts of the dorsal and anal fins are smaller than in the Striped Scat. Otherwise they are practically identical, both in appearance and habits. The Silver Scat has a highly variable number of black bars on the sides which give way to vertical rows of spots.

As with many other fishes which have barred markings, the bars in young specimens probably split now and then to become two. Exactly the same attention should be given the *Selenotoca* species as was specified for the Scat, and they are very likely to be just as hardy and long-lived as their better-known cousins.

SEMAPROCHILODUS THERAPONURA

SEMAPROCHILODUS TAENIURUS (Valenciennes)/*Silver Prochilodus*

R: Amazon basin. **H**: Peaceful, but very likely to nibble at plants; tanks should be kept covered at all times, as the fish jumps. **W**: Soft, slightly alkaline water. These are active swimmers, and they like a roomy tank. Temperature 23 to 26°C. **S**: To 30 cm. **F**: Mostly vegetable foods should be offered, such as lettuce or spinach.

Not as often imported as *Semaprochilodus theraponura* but even more beautiful is *Semaprochilodus taeniurus*. The body, which in *S. theraponura* is a slightly golden color and without markings, is silvery white and is covered with horizontal rows of black dashes. In the middle from a point below the dorsal fin to the caudal base is a thin black line which looks as if the pigment in a row of dashes flowed together. The same characteristic stripes seen in *S. theraponura* adorn the caudal and to a lesser extent the anal fin of *S. taeniurus*, but the intervening areas are white. The thick, rough lips proclaim both *S. taeniurus* and *S. theraponura* as algae-nibblers, and vegetable matter is an important item in their menu. Lacking this, the fish will become listless, sluggish, and prone to disease. A large, well-lighted tank is a necessity with this fish, and another is a tight-fitting cover.

SELENOTOCA MULTIFASCIATA

SEMAPROCHILODUS THERAPONURA (Fowler)/*Flag-Tailed Prochilodus*

R: Guyana and the central Amazon region. **H**: Peaceful, but its vegetarian habits may lead it to nibble on plants; a skilled jumper, so tank must be kept covered. **W**: Soft, slightly alkaline water. Temperature 23 to 26°C. **S**: To 35 cm; imported specimens seldom exceed 13 cm. **F**: Mostly vegetable food should be offered, such as lettuce leaves, spinach, or boiled oatmeal; live foods also accepted.

In their native Guyana they attain a size of 35 cm, at which size the natives catch them for food. Netting them is difficult; they leap nimbly over the net, often even over the collector's head, as soon as they feel the confines of the seine. A young specimen in full color is certainly a thing of beauty with its reddish fins and large striped tail. As the fish gets older the colors fade and finally it is scarcely recognizable as the same species. As is the case with many of these large fishes, no external sex differences have yet been observed.

SEMAPROCHILODUS TAENIURUS

SERRASALMUS HOLLANDI Eigenmann/*Holland's Piranha*

R: South of Amazon basin. **H**: Vicious; cannot even be kept with another of its own kind. **W**: Soft, slightly acid water. Temperature 24 to 27°C. **S**: About 13 cm. **F**: Smaller living fishes preferred; can be trained to take strips of raw fish.

The hobbyist who keeps a fish with dental equipment sharp and strong enough to amputate a finger or at the very least inflict a serious wound should not do so unless he takes some very important precautions: 1) Keep the tank where children cannot get at it; 2) Be very careful when netting the fish; 3) Don't ever put your hand close to it!

SICYOPTERUS HALEI

SERRASALMUS RHOMBEUS (Linnaeus)/*White Piranha; Spotted Piranha*

R: Amazon river system and northeastern South America. **H**: Dangerous to most other fishes; perhaps smaller ones can be kept with larger fishes in a community tank. **W**: Soft, slightly acid water. Temperature 24 to 27°C. **S**: to about 32 cm. **F**: Does well on fishes and raw meat.

Piranhas have often been divided into the very dangerous ones and the less dangerous ones. The White Piranha falls into the latter category, but this does not mean that it cannot inflict a bad wound on a person while being handled. This also does not mean it is not dangerous to other fishes — it is. Any fish placed in a tank with this piranha runs the risk of being killed and eaten, even members of its own kind. It is therefore recommended that only one White Piranha be kept and that one in a tank by itself.

Like other piranha species *S. rhombeus* shuns brightly lighted areas in its tank and prefers more shaded areas; one way to provide shade, or at least a less bright illumination, is to have a good cover of floating plants. Oddly enough, as the White Piranha ages it becomes very dark, almost black, in color.

SERRASALMUS HOLLANDI

SICYOPTERUS HALEI Day/*Mountain Goby*

R: Sri Lanka. **H**: Peaceful; clings to glass or rocks with sucker-like pelvic fins. **W**: Requires cool (21°C), well-aerated, clear water. **S**: Average 10 cm; females larger than males. **F**: Prefers a lush growth of algae on rocks and aquarium glass; will also eat prepared foods containing a large amount of vegetable matter.

Cool temperatures are required if the Mountain Goby is to do well in the aquarium. At temperatures above 24°C, it turns pale and begins to act confused and nervous. The water must be kept clean and be well aerated in order to simulate its stream habitat. Be sure to keep the tank covered tightly, as the Mountain Goby is able to climb up the sides of the tank by using its pelvic sucker, and it is able to squeeze through cracks less than 1 cm wide!

SERRASALMUS RHOMBEUS

SIMOCHROMIS DIAGRAMMA Günther/*Diagramma; Diagonal Bar Simochromis*
R: Endemic to Lake Tanganyika. **H**: Generally aggressive but suitable for an African lake cichlid community tank; prone to chasing each other about the tank, but with little damage done. **W**: Hard and alkaline water desirable. Temperature should be about 26°C (24 to 29°C). **S**: Reaches a length of about 18 cm or more, but will breed at about 10 cm. **F**: Will eat almost any type of normal aquarium foods, but will usually do better if algae and some vegetable matter are available.

The Diagramma is typically a rock-dweller and can be found in most rocky areas of the lake. It is more tolerant of murky water than the other species. They can inhabit the surf-churned waters near the shoreline and can often be seen darting in and out of the rock crevices, the males usually chasing the females. This chasing carries over into the aquarium, and one report indicated the male chased the female for hours on end over a period of several weeks.

SORUBIMICHTHYS PLANICEPS

SORUBIM LIMA (Bloch & Schnieder)/*Shovelnose Catfish*
R: Magdalena and La Plata river systems in South America. **H**: A lazy, fairly slow-moving fish, but one that is capable of eating smaller fishes. **W**: Soft, slightly acid water is best but is not of prime importance. Temperature 22 to 28°C. **S**: Up to 45 cm, although imported specimens are rarely anywhere near this size. **F**: Body olive to gray, lighter on the belly; a dark stripe runs over the back, and another runs along the sides and into the tail.

The Shovelnose Catfish does not seem to take part in an active chase of small fishes, but it manages to get its share nevertheless, usually at night. For proper growth, the fish should be located in a large tank; in a big tank, also, it has less chance of eating smaller fishes, especially fast-moving species. As with other fishes of the family Pimelodidae, the adipose fin is comparatively large and the barbels are long.

SIMOCHROMIS DIAGRAMMA

SORUBIMICHTHYS PLANICEPS (Agassiz)/*Spotted Shovelnose Catfish*
R: Amazon basin and Orinoco River, South America. **H**: Nocturnal; will eat any small fishes, but otherwise peaceful. **W**: Soft, slightly acid water; temperature 22 to 28°C. **S**: Up to 45 cm, although smaller in an aquarium. **F**: Live or frozen foods suitably large for the fish's size.

The fish is nocturnal and should not be given too much light. A large hiding place should be provided. It will be most active at night and will eat almost any food available, including smaller fishes that happen to be asleep at the time. This species is usually kept as an oddity.

SORUBIM LIMA

SPATHODUS ERYTHRODON Boulenger/*Blue-Spotted Goby Cichlid*

R: Lake Tanganyika, Africa. **H**: Not aggressive; care must be taken to choose tankmates that will not bother them. **W**: Hard, alkaline water with normal temperatures (23 to 27°C). **S**: About 8 cm. **F**: Not fussy; will accept most types of aquarium foods.

Sexing *Spathodus erythrodon* is a problem. It has been reported that the male has the brighter colors, but this has not been confirmed. You will have to buy a guaranteed pair or several smaller ones and hope that they will pair up naturally. The female incubates the dozen or more eggs much like the Malawi mbuna. In three to four weeks the fry are released and are then more than 6-8 mm long.

SPHAERICHTHYS OSPHROMENOIDES

SPHAERICHTHYS ACROSTOMA Vierke/*Sharp-nosed Chocolate Gourami*

R: Apparently restricted to the island of Borneo. **H**: A peaceful species very similar in temperament to the Chocolate Gourami (but perhaps a bit less shy). A single species tank is recommended. **W**: Soft, acid water is recommended in a well planted tank. A temperature in a range of 24° to 26° C is sufficient. **S**: This fish attains a length of just under 10 cm. **F**: Live foods of all kinds should be offered. Like its cousin it may not take to prepared foods readily.

Perhaps not as colorful as the Chocolate Gourami, the Sharp-nosed Chocolate Gourami is still quite an interesting fish. It comes from southern Borneo, about 250 kilometers northwest of Banjarmasin where it can be found in low reeds of the border area of the flooded forest rivers. *Sphaerichthys acrostoma* is quite peaceful but perhaps a little livelier and not so shy as *S. osphromenoides*. It can be kept in a community tank with equally peaceful and shy fishes but it is best to give them a tank all their own. The tank should be fairly well planted but with some swimming spaces left free. A dark substrate is better than a natural gravel or lighter one. The water should be soft (4-7° dGH) and on the acid side (pH 5.0). The pH can best be arrived at through use of a peat filter. The tank should be covered and the water level lowered slightly to allow them to come to the surface like other labyrinthfishes. A temperature of about 24° to 26°C is recommended. Live foods of all kinds should be offered. Spawning follows a similar pattern as other labyrinthfishes that spawn on the bottom. The eggs are white and sink to the bottom. The male picks up the eggs in his mouth where he broods them.

SPATHODUS ERYTHRODON

SPHAERICHTHYS OSPHROMENOIDES Canestrini/*Chocolate Gourami*

R: Malay Penninsula to Borneo and Sumatra. **H**: Peaceful and very shy; better kept by themselves. **W**: Very soft, slightly acid water. Temperature should never drop below 24°C, and should be around 28°C. **S**: 5 cm; usually a bit smaller. **F**: Live foods should be fed at all times; this fish shows little interest in dried or frozen foods.

This little beauty has always had the reputation of being delicate, but it will do very well if the proper conditions are provided. A prime requisite for this species is an adequate supply of heat. They come from a hot climate where they inhabit slowly flowing streams and ponds where they do not stray far from the surface, which makes this requirement fairly obvious.

SPHAERICHTHYS ACROSTOMA

STEATOCRANUS CASUARIUS Poll/*Lionhead Cichlid*

R: Malebo Pool, Zaire. **H**: Fairly peaceful for a cichlid. **W**: Should have hard, alkaline water. Temperature 24 to 28°C. **S**: About 10 cm. **F**: Will rarely accept dry foods, although some frozen foods, particularly frozen adult brine shrimp, are taken.

The Lionhead Cichlid breeds by laying its adhesive eggs in cave-like structures, and the male stands guard and takes care of them while they are hatching. After the eggs hatch both parents assume responsibility for their offspring. When the young venture from their cave to depressions, which are dug in the gravel by the male, the female hovers over them in an attitude of vigilance and attacks anything that may venture near. This species grows quickly.

STEATOGENYS ELEGANS

STEATOCRANUS TINANTI (Boulenger)/*Slender Lionhead Cichlid*

R: Central Africa, especially the Zaire River area. **H**: A bottom-dweller that spends most of its time in hiding. **W**: Prefers water that is warm (27°C) and neutral, the closer to pH 7.0 and a hardness of 3 degrees the better. **S**: A maximum size of 15 cm is rare. **F**: Usually will only eat live foods, though some pelleted dried foods and frozen brine shrimp serve well.

This is an undemanding and very peaceful species when not breeding. It is not an avid digger and will spawn in an inverted flowerpot with a narrow entrance. Both the male and female prepare the spawning site by carrying away gravel from inside the inverted flowerpot. The male guards the eggs and fans them with his fins. Several weeks after hatching, the young are collected by the parents from inside the artificial spawning cave and placed in a prepared depression in the gravel outside the cave.

STEATOCRANUS CASUARIUS

STEATOGENYS ELEGANS (Steindachner)/*Mottled Knife Fish*
R: Northeastern South America, Barra do Rio Negro, Guyana, lower Amazon River, and northern tributaries of the middle Amazon. **H**: Nocturnal; rarely seen during the daytime. **W**: Not critical; neutral, slightly soft water with a temperature between 24 to 29°C is good. **S**: Grows to a length of 18 to 20 cm. **F**: Readily accepts live brine shrimp as well as other live foods; will also eat prepared foods, chopped fish and shrimp, etc., with a little coaxing.

One unusual aspect of *Steatogenys elegans* is the possession of barbel-like organs in the mental region. Resting in deep groves under the chin that are open anteriorly but covered posteriorly, these barbel-like organs extend to the back of the head, under the base of the pectoral fins, and appear again in open grooves in the shoulder region above the pectoral fins. The construction of these organs is similar to that of some of the electric organs.

STEATOCRANUS TINANTI

STIGMATOGOBIUS SADANUNDIO (Hamilton-Buchanan)/*Knight Goby*

R: Indonesia, Burma, India, and the Philippines. **H**: A bottom-dwelling fish that requires live food. **W**: Originally from brackish water areas, this fish is not at home in soft water conditions. Add salt to the water, about one tablespoon for 8 liters. **S**: Up to about 9 cm. **F**: Must have copious feedings of live foods, preferably worms; frozen brine shrimp is eagerly taken once the fish has become accustomed to it.

Knight Gobies are hard to keep in good health without proper feedings of worms, and they require at least 10% of their water to be sea water or a fair substitute thereof. When all is said and done, they will probably jump out of the tank and dry out on your living room rug, but people still buy them. Perhaps you can find a reason for this fish being a member of your community tank, where, if you don't feed him, he'll start chewing on fishes about half his own size.

STURISOMA PANAMENSE (Eigenmann & Eigenmann)/*Royal Whiptailed Catfish*

R: Pacific slope of Panama to western Ecuador. **H**: Peaceful, although tends to be aggressive when guarding eggs. **W**: Prefers slightly acid water with a temperature about 22° to 26°C. **S**: Attains a length of at least 25 cm. **F**: Accepts a wide variety of foods, but a large proportion should be green vegetables or similar fare.

Sturisoma panamense is a very interesting species of loricariid catfish that (in spite of its scientific name) has a range that includes the Pacific slope of central to eastern Panama *and* both slopes of Colombia as well as ranging south to western Ecuador. It does well in the aquarium, and several spawning reports are available both in this country and in Europe. Since the Royal Whiptail attains a size of 25 cm or more, an 80-liter tank should be the smallest used to house the fish. Slightly acid water (pH 6.0-6.5) seems to be preferred, and a temperature in the range of 22° to 26°C is adequate. The tank should contain caves formed of rocks or slate (even flowerpots are used), and algae should be encouraged to grow for both adults and fry to feed on. A variety of foods are accepted, but a large proportion should be vegetable matter. A combination of *Daphnia*, chopped earthworms, and tubifex worms, along with spinach, lettuce, peas, and even string beans is excellent.

The sexes are easily distinguished. The sides of the posterior portion of the snout and cheeks of the male are covered with a thick coat of bristles, sometimes referred to as "whiskers," that are virtually absent in the female. The female when filled with eggs also is obviously "fatter" than the male. The female cleans a selected spawning site when spawning is imminent, "cheered on" of course by the male, who may nudge her from time to time. The female then begins to lay fairly large (3-4 mm in diameter) eggs in fairly straight lines on a firm surface (slate or rock), with the male following shortly behind her cichlid-fashion to fertilize them. Occasionally the male nudges the female again to induce her to continue if she pauses for too long a time. Upon completion of spawning the female no longer takes part in the action. The male Royal Whiptail takes up a position above the eggs where he constantly fans fresh water over them and defends them against any intruders.

The eggs darken with time until they start to hatch on about the eighth day, depending upon temperature. The completion of hatching may be swift but may also last another 48 hours. At this time the male no longer takes an active interest in the spawn. It is best if the fry now can be moved to a rearing tank that has a heavy growth of algae, but the fry also can be started on infusoria quickly followed by a vegetable food such as crushed lettuce, spinach, or even garden peas. Another reason to move the fry is that with proper conditioning the adults can be ready to spawn again in about three weeks.

STIGMATOGOBIUS SADANUNDIO

STURISOMA PANAMENSE

SYMPHYSODON AEQUIFASCIATUS AEQUIFASCIATUS

SYMPHYSODON AEQUIFASCIATUS AEQUIFASCIATUS (Pellegrin)/*Green Discus*
R: Brazil (Lago Teffe). **H**: Peaceful for a cichlid. **W**: Should have soft, slightly acid water; in extremely hard alkaline water, this species will waste away. Temperature 24 to 28°C. **S**: 30 cm. **F**: Dry foods not relished; frozen beef heart willingly accepted, as are live foods, but this fish should not be fed on any one food exclusively, as it needs variety. **C**: Body color a dark brownish green with nine vertical bars that vary in intensity; irregular blue streaks on body.

Discus of any species have always been held in high regard by aquarists because they are beautiful. Also, these fish have an attraction for another reason: discus specimens always sell for a good price, and many hobbyists have attempted to set up prospective pairs in hopes of getting them to spawn, thus providing themselves with a steady source of income. The trouble is that few people have succeeded in spawning the fish and raising young in great numbers on a regular basis. It is important to leave the parents with the fry, as the babies feed off the slime on the adults' bodies.

SYMPHYSODON AEQUIFASCIATUS AXELRODI

SYMPHYSODON AEQUIFASCIATUS AXELRODI Schultz /*Brown Discus*
R: Brazil. **H**: Peaceful for a cichlid. **W**: Soft, acid water best. Temperature 24 to 28°C. **S**: About 13 cm. **F**: Takes all live foods and some frozen foods (beef heart, liver, bloodworms); does not accept dried food with great enthusiasm. **C**: Body color varies from light to dark brown; nine vertical bars cross body and head; fins yellowish.

The Brown Discus, although less colorful than *Symphysodon aequifasciatus aequifasciatus* and *Symphysodon aequifasciatus haraldi,* is still a pretty fish and one much in demand. Like its relatives, *S. a. axelrodi* feeds its young from a thick coating of slime that forms on the body at spawning time.

661

Red hybrid *Symphysodon*.

SYMPHYSODON AEQUIFASCIATUS HARALDI

SYMPHYSODON AEQUIFASCIATUS HARALDI Schultz/*Blue Discus*

R: Rio Negro and its tributaries. **H**: Very peaceful; requires a large and well-planted aquarium. **W**: Soft, slightly acid water preferred. Temperature 24 to 29°C. **S**: Up to 20 cm; matures at about half that size. **F**: White worms, mature brine shrimp, and chopped beef heart.

Considered by many to be the most beautiful of the *Symphysodon* group, the Blue Discus possesses the additional advantage of being the hardiest fish in this specialized group. It breeds in the same way as its relatives, and the parents get along very well together. One of the many things that must be done to maintain any discus species in good health is to make many partial changes of water.

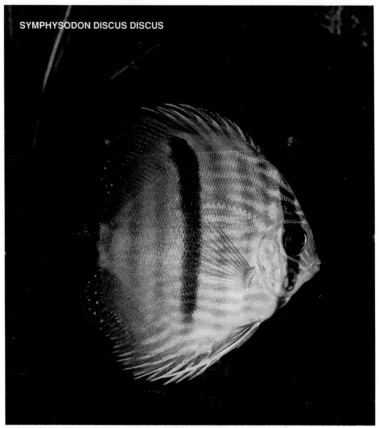

SYMPHYSODON DISCUS DISCUS (Heckel)/*Red Discus;*
Pompadour Discus; Heckel's Discus

R: Brazil. **H**: Peaceful for a cichlid. **W**: Soft, very acid water desirable; this species is especially susceptible to abrupt changes in water composition. Temperature 24 to 27°C. **S**: About 15 cm. **F**: Does best on live foods, but worms should not be fed too often.

When Angelfish were first introduced, hobbyists were quick to dub them "King of the Aquarium Fishes." This was quickly forgotten when the discus first made their appearance around 1932, and the title went to these regal newcomers. Their proud bearing, their wonderful colors, and their high price made them seem worthy of the title, and they still are. Although they are not exactly a rarity in their native waters, shipping them was quite a problem in the old days. Small ones were not easily found or caught, and the big ones had to have a shipping can all to themselves. Breeders had difficulty in getting them to spawn, and the fish remained very scarce and high-priced. Nowadays air transport has made their shipping faster, and new methods of packing them have cut down the weight problem.

Baby Discus feeding on parent's slime.

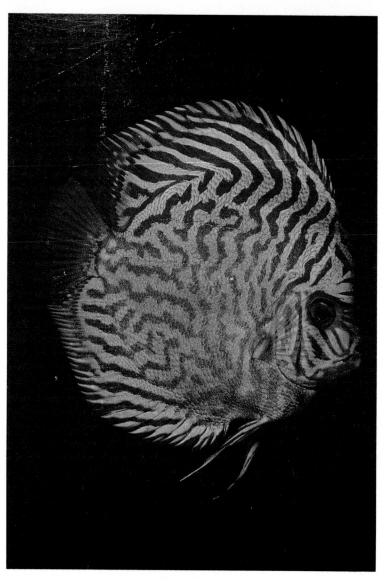

Discus hybrid.

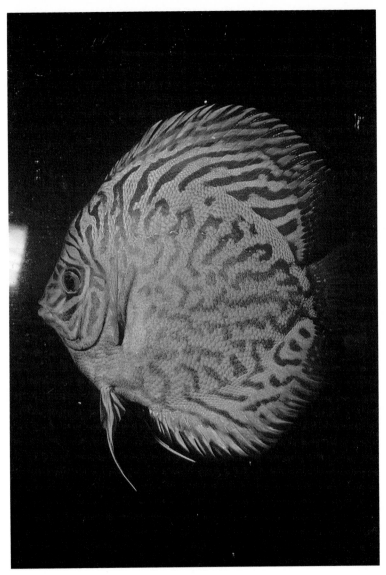

Discus hybrid.

Discus hybrid.

Discus hybrids.

SYMPHYSODON DISCUS WILLISCHWARTZI

SYMPHYSODON DISCUS WILLISCHWARTZI *Burgess/Pineapple Discus*

In late 1980 Dr. Axelrod made a startling discovery. Fishing south of the Amazon River in the huge Rio Madeira, Brazil, Axelrod took an eastern tributary known by the local people as the Rio Abacaxis. In the local language this means "Pineapple River." This was a blackwater river whereas the Madeira and Amazon are muddy white water. Traveling upriver a few hours, Axelrod discovered lovely terrain and huge rocky outcrops. Rocks are rare in the Amazon! Stopping to dive into the clear black water, Axelrod was amazed at the clarity of the water and as he swam close to the stones about 15 feet down he noticed movement typical of discus. Sure enough there were discus there. When he caught one, he was greatly surprised that it was very similar to *Symphysodon discus* since up to that moment every other *Symphysodon discus* had been found to the north of the Amazon in the Rio Negro.

Bringing the specimen to his boat, he photographed it and preserved the specimen. It was described by Dr. Warren E. Burgess as a new subspecies. Dr. Burgess named it in honor of Hans Willi Schwartz, who died shortly after the fish was discovered.

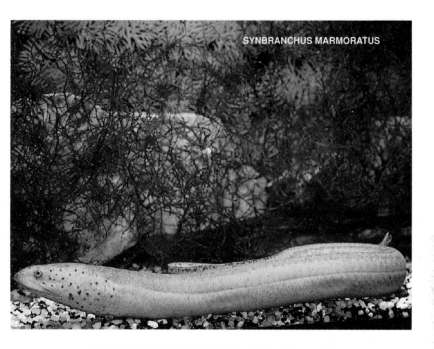
SYNBRANCHUS MARMORATUS

SYNBRANCHUS MARMORATUS Bloch/*Marbled Swamp Eel*

R: Both slopes of tropical Central and South America from southern Mexico to Brazil and Peru. **H:** Predatory fish that are best kept separately. **W:** Not critical. Temperatures of around 75-80°F. are recommended. **S:** May reach a length of up to 5 feet. **F:** Will accept most any food and is an avid eater.

Among the unusual fishes that make their way into the aquarium trade may be found the Marbled Swamp Eel. Almost every call for identification of an "eel" from South America can be answered by reference to this fish. This is not a true eel but an air-breathing fish that, along with other members of the order Synbranchiformes, has lost the paired fins (pectorals and pelvics) and has the dorsal and anal fins reduced to mere ridges. What is also very unusual and interesting is the fact that the right and left gill openings have fused to form a single slit-like gill opening across the middle of the throat. The eyes are small and located far forward.

These adaptations allow the Marbled Swamp Eel to pursue a nocturnal burrowing existence. It hunts at night for small fishes or other aquatic animals and remains holed up in its burrow during the day. In case the mudhole, pond, or ditch becomes uninhabitable, the Marbled Swamp Eel is capable of wriggling considerable distances overland to new and better living quarters.

The nest is constructed in the mud about one to four feet below the surface of the water. The eggs are spherical, about 3.4 mm in diameter, and are placed in the burrow where the male remains to guard them. They are translucent and gray in color and often in several stages of development. It has been suggested that the breeding season is toward the latter part of the rainy season. The young are commonly a uniform gray-brown in color.

671

SYNODONTIS ANGELICUS Schilthuis/*Angelicus; Polka-Dot Upside-Down Catfish*

R: Tropical West Africa. **H**: Peaceful with other fishes and will not uproot plants. **W**: Medium-soft, slightly acid to neutral water; tank should be heavily planted and provided with rock grottoes in which the fish may hide. Temperature 22 to 29°C. **S**: 20 cm. **F**: Will take prepared and frozen foods; likes algae and worms.

This is a nocturnal fish that hides in the mud during the day and comes out to feed only at night, the way many other mochokid (upside-down) catfishes do. But *Synodontis angelicus* seems to have a very distinct choice as to the area in which it will do its feeding; for some reason, the fish is attracted to places in which there is a lot of iron. They will congregate around rusty metal submerged in the water, and it almost seems as if they acutally graze on the surface of the metal!

SYNODONTIS CONTRACTUS

SYNODONTIS BRICHARDI Poll/*Brichard's Synodontis*

R: Zaire (Congo) River in the area of Kinshasa and the Malebo (Stanley) Pool; Regina Falls. **H:** Nocturnal in nature but may appear in the open more often in captivity. **W:** Not critical, a temperature of about 70-80°F. (22-27°C.) and neutral or slightly acid water are about right. **S:** Attains a length of about 6 inches. **F:** Will accept most aquarium foods such as brine shrimp, tubificid worms, beef heart, various dry foods, etc.

The tank housing the synodontids should be fairly large and roomy but with plenty of spots where they can hide. Although basically nocturnal fish in the wild and therefore in need of such hiding places, they do appear in the open areas of the aquarium quite often in captivity. It is best to keep the light at a relatively low level. If the newly purchased *Synodontis brichardi* suddenly starts darting around the tank banging into the sides, check for parasites that may be irritating the fish, a different type of water, or some form of shock. In the latter instance recommendations have been made to darken the tank and leave the fish as undisturbed as possible for about a week.

SYNODONTIS ANGELICUS

SYNODONTIS CONTRACTUS Vinciguerra/*David's Upside-Down Catfish*
R: Zaire; localized in and around Stanley Pool near Kinshasha. **H**: Peaceful and semi-noctur-nal; likes to rest in sheltered areas in a tank, especially grottoes formed by rocks. **W**: Soft or medium-soft water slightly on the acid side is best. Temperature shouldn't go below 24°C un-less fish is maintained in a very large aquarium. **S**: Up to 8 cm. **F**: Will accept all meat-based aquarium foods, but should have dried or freeze-dried foods that include substantial portions of vegetable materials.

Synodontis contractus, introduced to commercial aquarium channels some 25 years ago as the result of one of Dr. Herbert R. Axelrod's collecting/exploration trips to Africa, has one dis-tinct advantage over *Synodontis nigriventris,* which is still the most common of the upside-down catfishes: it's smaller and can be more comfortably accommodated in smaller tanks. *S. contractus* is also much chunkier in build and a trifle more colorful and attractive, although neither species can lay any claim to being "pretty." Their main attraction is their oddness, which lies primarily in the fact that they normally swim on their backs.

SYNODONTIS BRICHARDI

SYNODONTIS DECORUS

SYNODONTIS DECORUS Boulenger/*Decorated Upside-down Catfish*

R: Congo (Congo Basin including Lower Congo) **H:** Generally peaceful. **W:** Not critical. Temperature should range around 21° to 26°F. **S:** Grows to a length of over 25 cm. **F:** Will eat almost any foods that sink.

Synodontis decorus is one of the more popular upside-down catfishes imported from the Congo. The striped fins, spotted body, and elongate dorsal filament make it a very attractive species. It grows quite large and appears to undergo some color pattern changes as it grows. These are not totally understood, but it appears that in the smaller individuals there are fewer bars in the fins and the body spots extend ventrally to the belly. In larger individuals the fins stripes are narrower and more numerous and the body spots have faded out ventrally.

The dorsal filament, which seems to attract some of the nibblers in the community tank, will grow back if these annoying fishes are removed from the tank. *Synodontis decorus* is itself peaceful but may get into an occasional scuffle with another member of the genus. If your tank is well supplied with caves or other hiding places there should be no problem.

The tank itself should be large enough to allow this fish to grow—remember that although most aquarium specimens are in the size range of 4 to 6 inches, this species does grow to more than twice that size.

Feeding is no problem, for any food that reaches the bottom will normally be accepted by the Decorated Upside-down Catfish. Be sure that some food does reach the bottom in community tanks for often other more active fishes swimming in the middle or upper layers of the tank gobble up all the food before the catfishes can get at it.

When they are first introduced into your tank you will find that they remain hidden much of the time. Their shyness will eventually be overcome with patience. It has been suggested that placing several *Syndontis* in a tank with few caves causes them to be out more because they keep chasing each other out of the caves. It is much better to provide caves placed so the openings afford you a view of the interior so you can observe them. Of course, much of the shyness disappears at feeding time if they are hungry enough. No information on the breeeding habits of this species has been received.

SYNODONTIS MULTIPUNCTATUS

SYNODONTIS MULTIPUNCTATUS Boulenger/*Many-spotted Synodontis*
R: Endemic to Lake Tanganyika. **H:** Relatively peaceful. Does well in community tanks of cichlids from both Lake Malawi and Lake Tanganyika. **W:** Should have hard, alkaline water (pH 8-9) similar to that of the Rift Lake cichlids. **S:** Attains a length of about 28 cm. **F:** Will accept a variety of aquarium foods. Does best if provided with live snails from time to time.

The Many-spotted Synodontis is one of the most popular species of the genus *Synodontis*. It is a relatively common fish in Lake Tanganyika, occurring in schools of 300-400 individuals in the dim light of depths greater than 30 meters but also in shallow near-shore water where scattered individuals may be found hidden from the light in caves. It seems to have a definite preference for muddy bottoms. The natural food appears to be snails, which it removes from the shell before eating. Supplementing this diet may be small shrimp and insect larvae.

The aquarium that houses this species should be set up with hard alkaline water and rockwork forming caves, similar to that arranged for Malawi and Tanganyika cichlids. In fact, this catfish is commonly used as a tankmate for the Rift Lake cichlids.

Pierre Brichard was the first to discover some *S. multipunctatus* fry in the mouths of some recently captured Tanganyika cichlids. He assumed that this was more or less accidental or fortuitous. However, aquarists keeping community tanks of this catfish plus Rift Lake cichlids also found mouthbrooding cichlids with *Synodontis multipunctatus* fry in their mouths. It was eventually proved that the catfish was using the cichlids to brood their fry. In the excitement of the cichlid's spawning the catfish would make passes through the spawning area either to make a meal of the cichlid eggs or to drop their eggs when the female cichlids were apt to pick up and brood anything (there are reported cases where such cichlids would be trying to brood gravel)-or both. This "foster parent" activity seems to work with most mouthbrooding cichlids from both lakes.

The fry are relatively easy to raise on baby brine shrimp and other similar foods. The fry are patterned differently from the adults. There is a banded pattern, the bands breaking up into spots by the time the young are some 4-5 cm in length.

SYNODONTIS NIGRIVENTRIS

SYNODONTIS NIGRIVENTRIS David/*Blackbellied Upside-Down Catfish*
R: Central West Africa, the Zaire basin and tributaries. **H**: Peaceful; prefers to remain hidden in the darker regions of the aquarium and come out for food after dark. **W**: Soft, slightly acid water with little or no salt content. Temperature should range between 24 and 27°C. **S**: Females up to 8 cm; males a little smaller. **F**: Enjoys just about all kinds of foods; will come to the surface for dried food and grub in the bottom for worms.

Most fish are darker on the back and lighter on the belly. This makes their color blend in with the dark bottom when viewed from above (usually by a bird), and, when a larger fish or other enemy looks up at them, the light belly blends in with the glare from the surface. This fish has lighter back and a dark belly, which would give him the benefits of this camouflage when swimming upside-down.

676

SYNODONTIS NIGROMACULATUS

SYNODONTIS NIGROMACULATUS Boulenger/*Black-Dotted Upside-Down Catfish*
R: Luapula system, Mweru, Bangwelu, Lake Tanganyika, Upper Kasai, Upper Zambezi, Okovango, Cunene, and Limpopo. **H**: Retiring; active around twilight, so needs hiding places such as caves, rocks, etc; peaceful. Swims upside-down less than most *Synodontis*. **W**: Easily adapted to many conditions; most local water supplies are suitable after dechlorinization. The temperature range is about 18 to 29°C, with 23 to 25°C optimum. **S**: About 30 cm in nature, but only 20 cm in the aquarium. **F**: Omnivorous; live foods, freeze-dried, and fresh or frozen foods. Among the interesting or amusing habits of *Synodontis nigromaculatus* are its noise-making and upside-down swimming. The sound is produced in a manner similar to that employed by other catfishes, the rotating of fin spines in the sockets, the sound being carried to and amplified by the swim bladder. The upside-down swimming is less prevalent in this species than in some of the other upside-down catfishes.

SYNODONTIS NOTATUS Vaillant/*Spotted Synodontis*

R: Zaire basin. **H**: Reasonably peaceful, crepuscular catfish that does well in large aquaria. **W**: Not critical. Temperature 20 to 29°C. **S**: 25 cm. **F**: Omnivorous; prefers beef heart and brine shrimp.

Synodontis notatus, while a member of the "upside-down" catfishes (family Mochokidae) of Africa, does not frequently swim upside-down. Its oddity lies more in its capacity to produce loud growling noises that can be easily heard outside the aquarium. The noise is produced by grinding pectoral and dorsal spines in their sockets; through linkage with the gas bladder by modified bones known as the Weberian apparatus, the vibrations are amplified and broadcast into the water by means of the enlarged surface area of the gas bladder.

SYNODONTIS PLEUROPS

SYNODONTIS ORNATIPINNIS Boulenger/*Bar-Finned Upside-Down Catfish*

R: Congo. **H**: Generally peaceful and retiring. Prefers subdued light. **W**: Medium soft, slightly acid to neutral water. The tank should be well-planted and have enough rocks to provide a number of hiding places. The temperature range should be about 22 to 29°C. **S**: Attains a total length of about 22 cm, although one over 50 cm was reported from Lake Tumba, Congo. **F**: Will accept just about any type of good aquarium food. Be sure to feed some foods with vegetable matter as well.

One of the first fish to be snapped up when a shipment of Congo fishes arrives is most certainly the Bar-Finned Upside-Down Catfish, which often comes mixed in with *Synodontis brichardi*, another very popular species. It is strikingly patterned with bars on the body, a complicated pattern of lines on its head, and stripes or bars on the dorsal, anal, caudal, and pelvic fins. This pattern is not permanent, for as *Synodontis ornatipinnis* grows it changes considerably. The head loses the lines and becomes a plain dusky color; the body bars break up into two rows of spots; and the fin bars become more numerous but less well defined. Finally, older individuals have a very obscure pattern except for the fins, which seem to keep their barred pattern.

SYNODONTIS PLEUROPS Boulenger/*Big-Eyed Upside-Down Catfish*
R: Widespread throughout most of the Congo basin. **H:** Peaceful. Tends to be nocturnal at first but eventually appears more and more in the open. **W:** Not critical. Temperature between 22 and 26°C. **S:** Reaches a length of about 32 cm. **F:** Will take a wide variety of aquarium foods. Some vegetable material should be added.

Synodontis pleurops is relatively common in the Congo basin and regularly shows up in imports from that region. Its large, bulging eyes provided the basis for the common name. This large-eyed character makes one tend to believe that it is a more nocturnal species than some of the other *Synodontis* species. It would be best, then, to maintain a relatively low light level in their aquarium.

TANDANUS TANDANUS

TANDANUS TANDANUS (Mitchell)/Tandan; *Dewfish*

R: Eastern and southeastern Australia. **H:** Typical bottom-dwelling catfish that grubs in the sediment for its food. Relatively peaceful but not to he trusted with small fishes. **W:** Not critical as long as extremes are avoided. A temperature of about 22° to 26°C is sufftcient. **S:** Grows fairly large for an aquarium fish, attaining a length of about 70 cm. **F:** Will accept a variety of meaty foods.

The Tandan or Dewfish is one of the freshwater members of the family Plotosidae. It is restricted to the fresh waters of eastern and southeastern Australia and is said to provide good sport for anglers. Although some people consider it good eating, others do not care for it at all. Like most catfishes, the Tandan is essentially a bottom-feeder. In nature they dine on such things as shellfish and shrimps. When kept in ponds they will stir up the bottom almost continuously, causing a constant muddiness to the water. This of course also occurs in aquaria, so strong filtration and avoidance of light-weight bottom substrates are necessary.

The tank housing this species should be as large as possible considering the fish's potential large size of up to 70 cm. Rockwork and driftwood would be best for decorations, but plants may be added as well for some color. Leave an area in front of the tank where the Tandan can find and pick up its food easily and, if it is in a community situation, where you can observe the fish to see that it is able to get enough food before the other fishes finish it off. The water conditions are not critical as long as extremes are avoided. Normal aquarium temperatures will suffice.

The Tandan will accept a variety of foods, so feeding is not difficult. Chopped shrimp, chopped clams, and other meaty foods are recommended.

Spawning occurs in the Australian spring and early summer months when the water temperatures heat up. A saucer-shaped depression is excavated by the potential spawners in the sand and/or gravel. This can be as much as 200 cm in diameter. The sexes can be easily distinguished by examining the urogenital papillae; that of the male is cylindrical, that of the female is more triangular in shape. The non-adhesive eggs are about 3.2 mm in diameter and are demersal. The male is said to guard the eggs and young fry. In about a week (depending upon water temperature) the fry (about 7 mm long) hatch out. In the next two weeks these fry double in size and resemble more closely the adult fish.

TANGANICODUS IRSACAE

TANGANICODUS IRSACAE Poll/*Spotfin Goby Cichlid*
R: Endemic to Lake Tanganyika. **H:** A bottom-hopper like the other goby cichlids; quite aggressive toward members of its own species. **W:** Hard, alkaline water with a temperature in the range of 22° to 28°C A little salt added to the water should prove beneficial. **S:** Attains a length of only about 9 cm. **F:** Will accept a variety of items normally fed to Lake Tanganyika cichlids. Some vegetable matter should be included.

The tank housing these goby cichlids need not be extra large, although they are territorial and require more room than their small size might indicate. Regardless of the size of the tank, lots of hiding places, preferably at different positions in the tank, should be provided. Rocks are usually the building materials of choice. The water should be hard and alkaline as for the normal Rift Lake setup. Being fish that live in the difficult area of the surf-pounded shoreline, heavy aeration and perhaps a current should be provided for them.

Spawning is relatively easy once a compatible pair is found. However, because of the aggressiveness shown to conspecifics, finding such a pair may not be that easy. They may be compatible for a while, but with the onset of the breeding season the weaker individuals may succumb to the battering of the more aggressive ones. There is no obvious sexual dimorphism reported. Breeding tubes are different, but by the time they appear, the pair has already formed and may be ready to spawn. Spawning action involves the two members of the pair circling each other over the selected spawning site. There is also a great deal of fin-flaring and lateral displays visible. Eventually the female will lay some eggs on the substrate, the male following in the circling movement and fertilizing them. One of the parents picks up the eggs. Normally this would be the female, although one report said that in successive spawns of the same pair different fish incubated the eggs. In three to four weeks the fry are ready to emerge and will accept newly hatched brine shrimp. Small numbers of fry are the rule, with between 7 and 15 the limits so far recorded. They are 10-12 mm long and quite active, hopping about the bottom of the tank attacking the brine shrimp. They also seem to be aggressive at this stage as they dart from hiding place to hiding place taking swipes at the other fry that they meet. The parents seem to be no longer interested in the fry. The fry grow slowly but are easy to raise. They may attain a length of 9 cm in one and a half to two years.

TATEURNDINA OCELLICAUDA

TANICHTHYS ALBONUBES Lin/*White Cloud Mountain Minnow*
R: Small streams in the vicinity of White Cloud Mountain in Canton, China. **H**: Peaceful in the community tank; very active and prefers to swim in schools. **W**: Not critical. Best kept at a relatively low temperature, 18 to 21°C. **S**: 4 cm. **F**: Will eat dried as well as live foods; when it is desired to spawn them, live foods should be given.

This little fish has the distinction of being one of the easiest aquarium fishes to spawn. A pair placed together in a well-planted aquarium and fed well with live foods, preferably daphnia, will soon produce fry that they show little tendency to eat. When young, the green stripe glows so bright that they are often mistaken for small Neon Tetras. It must be remembered that this is not exactly a tropical species. It comes from comparatively cool mountain streams that are fairly well oxygenated; as a result, they would be very uncomfortable in a warm, crowded community tank.

TELEOGRAMMA BRICHARDI

TATEURNDINA OCELLICAUDA Nichols/*Peacock Gudgeon*

R: Papua New Guinea. **H:** May be territorial and therefore aggressive. It is best to separate the males or only maintain them in relatively large aquaria. **W:** Not critical. A pH of between 7.0 and 7.6 and a temperature of 22° to 25° seem to be best. **S:** Attains a length of 5.7 cm (female) to 6.5 cm (male). **F:** Not fussy about foods. Will eat dried foods but prefers live foods.

In one successful spawning, several pairs were added to the tank and settled in within a period of about 48 hours. The males set up territories that they defended from intruders. The fish were conditioned on a variety of live foods including *Daphnia*, whiteworms, cyclops, and mosquito larvae. After a short courtship (circling, flaring of fins, etc.) a spawning site was cleaned by one of the pair. The eggs were laid cichlid-style, the male following the female as he fertilized the eggs. Anywhere up to 200 eggs were deposited and were tended by one or both parents.

TANICHTHYS ALBONUBES

TELEOGRAMMA BRICHARDI Poll/*Brichard's Slender Cichlid*

R: Zaire basin. **H:** Playful, but sometimes quarrelsome with members of its own species. **W:** Medium-soft, slightly acid water best; tank should have plenty of rocks and caves to make the fish at home. Temperature 21 to 27°C. **S:** About 10 cm. **F:** Live foods much preferred, although some frozen foods are accepted.

Teleogramma species are bottom-dwelling cichlids. These fishes generally live under stones and rocks in rapidly moving streams. This species is a substrate-spawner where the female is more active than the male. The female, which is also more colorful than the male, develops a red girdle during breeding time. She sets up a territory in a rocky area, courts the male, and eventually guards the eggs once they are laid. The eggs are large, few in number, and are stuck with an adhesive to the rocks or walls of the nesting site. After spawning, the male is driven off. Hatching occurs in 72 hours.

TELMATHERINA LADIGESI Ahl/*Celebes Rainbow Fish*

R: Celebes. **H**: Peaceful; may be combined with other fishes with similar requirements. **W**: Water should have a slight addition of salt, a teaspoonful per 4 liters; tank should be sunny. Temperature 24 to 27°C. **S**: 8 cm. **F**: Will take dried foods, but should have frequent supplements of living foods.

When fully grown, there can be no doubt as to which are the males. One look at the gorgeous yellow dorsal and anal fins with the long filaments and black first rays is sufficient. One other thing this beauty is particularly sensitive to is a great deal of moving around. Once they have become adapted to the conditions in a tank, they should then be left alone. They are by nature a bit timid, and a tank where they are kept should have a sufficiency of plant life in which they can hide if any real or imagined danger is present. Eggs are laid in bushy plants and hatch in two days.

TELMATOCHROMIS DHONTI

TELMATOCHROMIS BIFRENATUS Myers/*Striped Telmat*

R: Lake Tanganyika, Africa. **H**: A relatively inactive, non-aggressive, retiring species compared to the vast majority of Rift Lake cichlids; sexes fight among themselves, however, and this species will tend to be more belligerent and territorial during spawning periods. **W**: Hard, alkaline water; pH between 8.0 and 9.0 is preferred. Temperature between 22 and 26°C. **S**: To 13 cm for males; smaller for females. **F**: Most aquarium foods are accepted, including live, frozen freeze-dried and flake foods; vegetable matter should be added to the diet.

Telmatochromis bifrenatus is a Lake Tanganyikan omnivore that is relatively peaceful compared to most Rift Lake cichlids. This species is a substrate-spawner that is not difficult to breed.

TELMATHERINA LADIGESI

TELMATOCHROMIS DHONTI (Boulenger)/*Caninus*

R: Lake Tanganyika, Africa. **H**: This is a fairly inactive, retiring species that usually causes no great problem because of aggressiveness, but the sexes quarrel among themselves, especially preceding spawning. **W**: Hard, alkaline water preferred but not strictly necessary. Best temperature range is 23 to 26°C. **S**: To 15 cm for males; smaller for females. **F**: Most live, frozen, and prepared (especially flake) foods accepted; vegetable matter should be added to the diet.

Spawning is almost always preceded by a roughing-up of the female, although sometimes the tables are turned, with the male on the receiving end. This is not a mouthbrooding species. Eggs are laid in cave-like structures; the female does most of the tending of the eggs, with the male usually staying outside the cave. It is best to leave the parents with their fry, as they take good care of them if left undisturbed. The fry are large enough to easily take newly hatched brine shrimp.

TELMATOCHROMIS BIFRENATUS

TELMATOCHROMIS TEMPORALIS Boulenger/*Temporalis*

R: Endemic to Lake Tanganyika. **H:** Aggressive toward other fishes, including members of its own species. **W:** Like other Rift Lake cichlids, it prefers hard, alkaline water and temperatures of 22-27°C. **S:** Attains a length of up to about 12.5 cm. **F:** Will accept almost any type of aquarium fish food.

The sexes differ slightly when mature, the male being more brightly colored with blue tones (the female is a drab olive-brown) and his dorsal and anal fins being more pointed than the female's; the male develops a cranial hump.

The tank they are housed in should be fairly large (at least 120-liter capacity if not more) and well provided with rocky caves and other hiding places. Flower pots have been used successfully as substitute caves. The water should be hard and alkaline as with other Rift Lake cichlids, and the temperature range can be about 22-27°C. After the usual preliminary courtship, spawning occurs in their home cave, usually on the ceiling but sometimes along the walls as well. The eggs are pale tan, oval, and up to 300 or so in number. They hang attached to the surface of the rock or flower pot and are guarded by the parents for about five days before they hatch. The fry are then kept in small depressions until they become free-swimming a few days later. Newly hatched brine shrimp and other small foods as well as leavings from the parents' food will be sufficient.

TERRANATOS DOLICHOPTERUS

TELMATOCHROMIS VITTATUS Boulenger/*Blunt-Headed Telmat*

R: Lake Tanganyika, Africa. **H:** Relatively docile for a cichlid. **W:** Fares best in hard alkaline water but can adapt to less stringent conditions. Temperature 23 to 28°C. **S:** To about 8 cm. **F:** Takes most standard aquarium foods but especially likes brine shrimp and daphnia.

T. vittatus is a substrate-spawner that enters rocky refuges to deposit its spawn, usually on the roof of the chosen cave. If maintained in good condition, *T. vittatus* readily spawns and the parents take excellent care of the young until they are able to fend for themselves. They even leave the fry alone after their parental obligations have been fulfilled, so it is possible to leave the fry and their parents in the same tank. The fry are free-swimming when they leave the spawning cave but remain at the bottom of the tank for between one and two months.

TELMATOCHROMIS TEMPORALIS

TERRANATOS DOLICHOPTERUS (Weitzman and Wourms) *Sicklefin Killie, Saberfin*
R: Venezuela. **H**: Timid, easily spooked. **W**: Soft, acid water best for breeding, but neutral to slightly alkaline water suitable. Temperature 20 to 23°C. **S**: 4-6 cm. **F**: Live foods preferred. **C**: Females much less spotted than males, especially on fins. Bluish sheen that overlies belly area (and sometimes fins) of male entirely lacking in female.

Like other annual species, *T. dolichopterus* doesn't need a large tank for spawning purposes; a 10-liter tank or large drum bowl is sufficient. The eggs, kept in peat moss, should be stored from four to six months before an attempt to hatch them out is made. Considering the small size of the adults, the fry are relatively large and are able to eat newly hatched brine shrimp immediately. It is important that all leftover food be removed from the tanks of both growing fry and adults as soon as it is noticed. This is a fairly timid species that does best if provided with a refuge from bright light; the fish should not be kept in a glare. If they are maintained in small aquaria, their quarters should be covered to prevent jumping caused by fright.

TELMATOCHROMIS VITTATUS

TETRAGONOPTERUS ARGENTEUS Cuvier/*Silver Tetra*

R: Amazon and La Plata Basins. **H:** Generally peaceful, but larger individuals may become unsociable. **W:** Prefers mature, slightly acid water with a hardness about 10°DH. Temperature should be about 24° to 27°C. **S:** About 10 cm. **F:** Will accept a wide variety of foods including brine shrimp, *Daphnia, Tubifex,* mosquito larvae, chironomid larvae, and flake foods.

Like many of the tetras, *T. argenteus* is an active fish better suited to being kept in schools. The young ones are better marked, as the shoulder bars fade with growth. The older individuals tend to be more aggressive and unsociable. Their tank should be fairly large if a small school is to be kept and well planted with less delicate plants. An open area for swimming should be provided. They make good community tank fishes. The water should be well aged and slightly acid. The hardness is best kept around 10°DH and a temperature of 24° to 27°C. will suffice. Most foods are accepted, but a varied diet including such items as brine shrimp, *Daphnia, Tubifex,* chironomid larvae, mosquito larvae, and some greens along with the flake food is recommended. Spawning has not been reported for this species.

TETRAODON CUTCUTIA

TETRAODON BIOCELLATUS Tirant/*Figure-Eight Puffer*

R: Southeastern Asia and Malay Peninsula. **H:** A fin-nipper; tends to be pugnacious. **W:** Does best in water to which a teaspoon of salt per 4 liters has been added. **S:** Up to 18 cm. **F:** Prefers large live foods like fishes or shrimp.

Puffers of all kinds continue to be popular in the aquarium hobby despite the several drawbacks that they present, and the reason lies mostly in the fact that buyers of these odd aquarium fishes buy them usually for their quaintness and what they take to be a nice oddity without realizing that puffers in general can be very bad actors. They look harmless enough, and they usually move at a very slow and deliberate pace, which gives people the idea that they couldn't do any harm even if they wanted to; such is not the case at all, because they often are decidedly pugnacious.

TETRAGONOPTERUS ARGENTEUS

TETRAODON CUTCUTIA Hamilton-Buchanan/*Malayan Puffer*

R: Malaysia and parts of India, in fresh and brackish waters. **H**: Quarrelsome toward other fishes and even among themselves. **W**: Hard, alkaline water with salt added, one teaspoon per 4 liters. Temperature 24 to 27°C. **S**: To 15 cm. **F**: Live foods in larger sizes or chopped-up pieces of table shrimp; crushed snails are a delicacy.

Unfortunately the Malayan Puffers are very quarrelsome even among themselves and should never be kept with other fishes. They are useful in the aquarium because of their love for snails and will depopulate a snail-ridden tank in short order. Their rabbit-like teeth are useful in crushing the shells and biting the tough flesh. The puffers soon lose their shyness and come begging for food at the surface whenever the tank is approached. Spawning the puffer is not the easiest thing in the world, but it has been done repeatedly. The females are easily distinguished by their larger size and lighter colors.

TETRAODON BIOCELLATUS

TETRAODON MIURUS Boulenger/*Congo Puffer*

R: Middle and lower Zaire River; found in fresh water only. **H**: A dangerous fish in the community aquarium; should be given a tank by itself or placed with others of its own kind. **W**: Soft, slightly acid water. Temperature 24 to 27°C. **S**: To 10 cm. **F**: Living small fishes, fully grown brine shrimp, or pieces of earthworms; they enjoy snails.

The Congo Puffer is a strange little fish. Its body colors are capable of considerable change, and it can match its surroundings quite easily as long as they are some shade of brown, red, or gray. Its eyes are set atop the head like those of a frog, and it frequently digs into the bottom to lie completely hidden from its prey, with only the eyes showing. When seen resting on the bottom, the shapeless blob of a body looks like nothing more than a rock lying there.

THAYERIA OBLIQUA

THAYERIA BOEHLKEI Weitzman/*Böhlke's Penguin*

R: Amazon region of Brazil (especially near Obidos). **H**: Peaceful, active fish that do well in a small group or school. **W**: Not critical but do better in neutral to slightly acid water; lights should not be too bright. Temperature 22 to 24°C. **S**: Maximum size is about 8 cm. **F**: Not critical; will eat most of the usual aquarium foods.

Thayeria generally spawn near the surface, and bright lights are said to cause damage to the eggs and young, so be sure the lights are dim. Male and female will eventually swim side by side with their vents quite close. At this time 30-50 eggs will be ejected into the water by the female as the male fertilizes them.

TETRAODON MIURUS

THAYERIA OBLIQUA Eigenmann/*Short-Striped Penguin*

R: Middle Amazon region. **H**: Active swimmers and peaceful; may be kept in a community aquarium. **W**: Water should be soft and slightly acid. Best temperature 24 to 26°C. **S**: 8 cm. **F**: Will take dried foods, but these should be alternated frequently with live foods.

Sexes are difficult to distinguish, practically impossible in immature fish. When maturity is reached, the heavier bodies of the egg-laden females identify them easily. Spawning takes place in bushy plants, and the eggs are brown in color. A prolific species, there may be as many as 1,000 eggs laid at a single spawning. It has been found advisable, when spawning is over, to draw off part of the water and replace it with fresh water. Hatching takes place in as little as 12 hours. When they begin to swim, the fry should get very fine foods.

THAYERIA BOEHLKEI

THORACOCHARAX STELLATUS (Kner)/*Silver Hatchetfish*

R: Amazon, Paraguay, Orinoco basins. **H**: An extremely peaceful fish; a good jumper, so its tank should be covered. **W**: Soft, slightly acid water a necessity; this fish dies easily if maintained in hard, alkaline water. Temperature 23 to 26°C. **S**: 8 cm. **F**: Floating foods of all kinds taken, provided they can be swallowed.

None of the hatchetfishes should be considered as really hardy fishes, and they are especially susceptible to some of the more common aquarium diseases, such as ich. Perhaps this is because they are often neglected when kept in a community tank. Unless precautions are taken to see to it that the hatchetfishes are fed in accordance with their specific requirements, that is, that food is made available to them at the top of the water, they will soon decline.

TILAPIA BUTTIKOFERI

THYSOCHROMIS ANSORGII (Boulenger)/*Five-Spot African Cichlid*

R: Liberia to Nigeria, in fresh and brackish waters. **H**: Peaceful for a cichlid; does some digging, usually around rocks, but plants are seldom uprooted. **W**: Slightly alkaline, with an addition of about a teaspoonful of salt per 4 liters of water; tank should be well planted. Temperature 24 to 26°C. **S**: Males to about 10 cm; females a little smaller. **F**: Live foods preferred, but they will also take frozen foods.

Females of this species have an unusual marking when sexually mature: they have a gleaming white spot on the sides near the anal opening. They can be distinguished from the males in other ways as well: they are a little smaller in size and the fins are smaller and more rounded. A well-mated pair will usually get along well and spawn regularly, preferring the privacy of an overturned flowerpot with a notch broken out of the rim to allow the pair to enter.

THORACOCHARAX STELLATUS

TILAPIA BUTTIKOFERI (Hubrecht)/*Hornet Tilapia*
R: Central West Africa. **H**: Peaceful when young, but decidedly aggressive when adult. **W**: Soft, acid water preferred. Temperature 24 to 28°C. **S**: Up to 26 cm. **F**: Live foods best although most standard aquarium foods are taken; especially likes live snails.

T. buttikoferi behaved themselves well in a 250-liter tank that also housed some African characins, but when the larger of the two fishes reached a length of about 10 cm, the deportment of both fish changed entirely. They became very aggressive and constantly chased the characins and uprooted and destroyed the plants in the tank; they soon started fighting between themselves as well.

THYSOCHROMIS ANSORGII

TILAPIA GUINEENSIS (Bleeker)/*Guinea Tilapia*

R: Coast of the Gulf of Guinea, West Africa. **H**: Not normally belligerent with other species unless their presence would deprive it of appropriate territory, but very aggressive among members of its own species, especially near spawning time; young fish of about the same size normally will not fight among themselves. **W**: Not critical as regards composition, but the temperature should remain above 22°C. **S**: To about 30 cm in nature; usually seen much smaller in the aquarium. **F**: A greedy eater that accepts all standard aquarium foods; should have vegetable matter in its diet.

Tilapia guineensis is not a truly pugnacious species that seems to be always looking for a fight, but it can take very good care of itself if attacked by other fishes, even much larger fishes. It is a highly territorial fish that will stake out an area in a tank and defend it against all comers almost regardless of size, and at spawning time it of course becomes even more defensive of its territory. *T. guineensis* is a substrate spawner, not a mouthbrooder, and is a very dedicated and jealous guarder of its eggs and fry. Well-conditioned adults will spawn at a wide range of temperatures, but 24 to 27°C is best.

TILAPIA THOLLONI

TILAPIA MARIAE Boulenger/*Tiger Tilapia, Mariae*

R: West Africa. **H**: Usually peaceful except when spawning. **W**: Not important as long as extremes are avoided. Temperature 22 to 28°C. **S**: Up to 18 cm in nature; 13 cm in aquaria. **F**: Will accept almost all standard aquarium fare; should have plant matter included in diet.

This is not a mouthbrooding species, instead spawning in the fashion of the pit-spawning New World cichlids like the *Laetacara* and *Herichthys* species. Although both parents occasionally are devoted to caring for the eggs, in many cases the male is a bad parent and avid eater of the spawn, and it is best to remove him from the tank right after spawning has been completed. At a temperature of around 26°C the eggs hatch in four days and the fry will become free-swimming in another two days or so.

TILAPIA GUINEENSIS

TILAPIA THOLLONI (Sauvage)/*Thollon's Tilapia*

R: Tropical West Africa from Zaire to Cameroon. **H**: Mature pairs should be kept by themselves; even young males are apt to battle fiercely. **W**: The tank should be provided with many possibilities for the female to hide; plants are eaten. Temperature 24 to 27°C. **S**: To 18 cm; usually smaller. **F**: In addition to the usual live foods, lettuce leaves are also relished and should be fed frequently.

Spawning them is simplicity itself; a well-fed pair is placed in a good-sized tank (80-liters or more). The male chooses a spawning site where he digs a hole in the bottom gravel. When things are prepared to his satisfaction, he begins to try luring and coaxing his mate to the pit. She soon gets the idea, and a large number of eggs are laid in the gravel pit. Both parents take care of the eggs and fry, which hatch in three to five days. A good first food for the fry is newly hatched brine shrimp.

TILAPIA MARIAE

TOXOTES CHATAREUS (Hamilton-Buchanan)/*Seven-Spotted Archer Fish*
R: India to the New Hebrides (including the Indo-Australian Archipelago, Thailand, Vietnam, Philippines, New Guinea, and northern and northeastern Australia). **H**: Peaceful to slightly aggressive; best kept with other brackish water fishes. **W**: Although pure fresh or pure salt water can be tolerated, brackish water is best. Temperature 22 to 28°C. **S**: A maximum size of about 20 cm is attained; usually smaller in aquaria. **F**: Live foods, especially insects, are best; other foods, even hamburger meat, are also accepted.

Not all of the food is obtained by shooting water droplets, but much is obtained by quick darts along the surface or even jumping. It was noted that when food was placed a distance above the archer tank to exhibit the shooting abilities, the first fishes tried, sometimes successfully, to leap out of the water and grab it. In nature young fish generally remain near the banks where logs, overhanging branches, etc. afford some sort of protection.

TRICHOGASTER LEERI

TOXOTES JACULATOR (Pallas)/*Archer Fish*
R: India, Burma, Malaysia, Philippines, East Indies, and Thailand. **H**: Usually peaceful, but individual specimens can be aggressive; not a good community fish unless kept with other fishes liking slightly brackish water. **W**: Water should be slightly salty; tank should be large. Temperature 23 to 29°C. **S**: Over 15 cm, but always sold at a much smaller size. **F**: Best food is live insects that the fish captures for itself, but it will accept meaty substitutes; some hobbyists claim that it will accept dry food, but this depends on the individual fish.

The Archer Fish is always in demand, for the fish's peculiar method of catching food evokes wonder in everyone who is privileged to watch it. *Toxotes* is equipped with a strange mouth structure that enables the fish to expel pellets of water at resting insects that come within range; it sometimes even shoots at flying insects, and it can occasionally be coaxed into shooting at pieces of meat suspended within its range of vision. To do this with any degree of accuracy, of course, the Archer Fish must be able to allow for the refractive property of the water itself, and this it has learned to do.

TOXOTES CHATAREUS

TRICHOGASTER LEERI (Bleeker)/*Pearl Gourami, Leeri, Mosaic Gourami*
R: Thailand, Malay Peninsula, Penang, Sumatra, and Borneo. **H**: Peaceful and inclined to be a bit shy; may be kept in any community aquarium. **W**: Not critical, but water should be rather warm, about 26°C. A full-grown pair should be kept in a good-sized tank, at least 60 liters. **S**: 10 cm. **F**: Will eat any kind of dried foods, but should also get live foods occasionally.
Their tank should be roomy and well planted, and away from slamming doors and street noises. A healthy pair can easily be induced to spawn in such a tank. The driving that takes place before spawning is not as wild as in the other gouramis; they always seem to maintain themselves with a great deal of dignity. The bubblenest is apt to be large, and the number of eggs may be very high. At this time especially it is important to avoid frightening them. Usually the female may be left with the male while the eggs are being guarded.

TOXOTES JACULATOR

TRICHOGASTER MICROLEPIS (Günther)/*Moonbeam Gourami*

R: Thailand. **H**: A fairly peaceful fish, but large specimens tend to be bullies, at least with others of their species. **W**: Soft, slightly acid water best, but this is not of great importance. Temperature 24 to 29°C. **S**: Up to 15 cm. **F**: Takes prepared, frozen, and live foods.

The male builds a large bubblenest that is not very high; not much vegetable matter is woven into this nest, and the bubbles are allowed to float rather freely. During spawning, the color of the thread-like ventral fins becomes intensified, changing for a short time from orange to red. For best results in breeding, the water depth in the breeding tank should be low and floating plants should be present to give the fish a feeling of security.

TRICHOGASTER TRICHOPTERUS

TRICHOGASTER PECTORALIS (Regan)/*Snakeskin Gourami*

R: Southeastern Asia. **H**: Peaceful and entirely harmless to other fishes, even young ones. **W**: Soft, slightly acid water. Temperature 24 to 27°C. **S**: To 26 cm in their home waters; mature at 10 cm. **F**: Not choosy as to food; dry food accepted as well as frozen and live foods.

The male builds a large bubblenest and, if she is of good size, the female will be found to be extraordinarily productive. Another thing in their favor is that the parent fish will never eat their young. They also cannot be coaxed to eat the young of other fishes or even snails. This gives the hobbyist the opportunity of raising a family of Snakeskins without ever having to remove the parents, as long as the tank is large enough to accommodate all of them. The youngsters can be raised easily by feeding progressively larger sizes of dried foods, beginning with the finest sizes and as the fish grow giving them coarser sizes. Naturally, an occasional feeding with live foods such as newly hatched brine shrimp is a welcome change in the diet.

TRICHOGASTER MICROLEPIS

TRICHOGASTER TRICHOPTERUS (Pallas)/*Three-Spot Gourami, Blue Gourami*
R: Southeast Asia and the Indo-Malayan Archipelago. **H**: Peaceful in a community tank with
fishes that are not too small. **W**: Not critical, but slightly acid, soft water is best. Temperature 24
to 28°C. **S**: To 15 cm. **F**: Takes any food, dried as well as live or frozen.
The Blue Gourami, a cultivated color pattern, has become so popular that it has backed the
plainer wild Three-Spot Gourami right out of the picture, so much so that only real "old timers"
still know what a Three-Spot looks like. The Blue Gourami is a very attractive fish and by far the
most available color form. A pair can almost always be counted on to spawn in a tank that is to
their liking; that is to say, one that has a fair amount of plants, a good-sized surface, and
enough heat. About 26°C is a good spawning temperature, and one does not need to worry
about there being too much depth as one does with the Siamese Fighting Fish. A large bubblenest
is built, usually in a corner. Here the males coaxes the female until she gets the idea and lets
him wrap his body around hers. If she is well filled, a spawning may be huge, 700 to 800 eggs.
Although she is seldom damaged by the male, it is still advisable to remove the female after
she has finished with her egg-laying chores. The male takes good care of his babies.

TRICHOGASTER PECTORALIS

699

TRICHOPSIS PUMILUS (Arnold)/*Pygmy Gourami*

R: Vietnam, Thailand, Malaysia, and Sumatra. **H**: Peaceful, but because it is shy it is best to keep them only with their own kind. **W**: A large aquarium is not required. 26°C is good; for spawning 29°C. **S**: Males about 3 cm.; females slightly smaller. **F**: Will take prepared as well as the smaller live foods.

Sexes are not always easy to distinguish, but the males usually have a bit of light edging on their dorsal and anal fins, and these fins are a bit larger and come to more of a point. These fish love a warm temperature and are apt to be "touchy" to keep if it is not given to them. Spawning them is very much dependent upon the compatibility of the pair. We have seen the rankest amateurs get spawning after spawning, while some of the so-called "experts" are unable to get them to breed at all. There is a small bubblenest, usually hidden under a floating leaf, into which about 50 eggs are laid. They hatch in about 30 hours, and the male takes care of the brood.

TRICHOPSIS VITTATUS

TRICHOPSIS SCHALLERI (Ladiges)/*Three-Striped Croaking Gourami*

R: Thailand. **H**: Peaceful, emits a faint croaking sound, especially during spawning activity. **W**: Soft, slightly acid water. Temperature 23 to 25°c. **S**: About 6 cm. **F**: Live or frozen foods of all kinds; dry foods would probably be accepted.

Place a pair in a small tank with a single *Cryptocoryne* plant. The male will build a small bubblenest under one of the leaves. They embrace in typical labyrinth fish fashion, and after each embrace three to six eggs are produced. The male guards the eggs, which hatch on the third day. He is a good father and guards the more than 200 fry very closely. They become free-swimming on the seventh day.

TRICHOPSIS PUMILUS

TRICHOPSIS VITTATUS (Cuvier)/*Croaking Gourami*

R: Vietnam, Thailand, Malaysia, Sumatra, Java, and Borneo. **H**: Peaceful and shy; should be kept by themselves because of their high temperature requirements. **W**: A well-covered, well-heated aquarium is necessary or this fish may prove to be sensitive. A temperature of 27 to 29°C should be maintained. **S**: Males a little over 6 cm; females slightly smaller. **F**: Will take dried foods if hungry, but prefers live foods, especially white worms.

If given a sunny aquarium that is shallow and well covered, pairs will begin to spawn in the spring months. A few broad-leaved plants should be present with the leaves floating, for the preferred spot will be under these leaves. Fry hatch in 24 to 35 hours and are tiny at first.

TRICHOPSIS SCHALLERI

TRIGONECTES STRIGABUNDUS Myers/*Brazilian False Panchax*

R: Rio Tocantins, Brazil. **H**: Peaceful with fishes it cannot swallow. **W**: Soft, slightly acid water. Temperature 24 to 26°C. **S**: To 6 cm. **F**: Live foods of all kinds; can be trained to take frozen foods.

The sexes are unmistakable: the female lacks the black chin sported by the male and has shorter, more rounded fins. When we had several pairs of these fish in our office we were fortunate to have them spawn for us. The female expelled about a dozen eggs, which were fertilized by the male and hung from her vent for quite a time by a thread until they were brushed off and hung from a plant.

TROPHEUS DUBOISI

TRIPORTHEUS ANGULATUS (Spix)/*Narrow Hatchetfish*

R: Middle and Lower Amazon, Rio Madeira, Rio Negro, Orinoco, and the Guianas. **H**: Active and peaceful with other fishes of its own size. **W**: Not critical; tank should be in a sunny location and permit ample swimming space. Temperature about 25°C. **S**: Wild specimens attain a size of about 20 cm. **F**: Not very fond of dried foods, so should be richly fed with living foods such as daphnia or adult brine shrimp.

Its long pectoral fins and keeled belly identify it as a jumper, and a tank with these fish in it should always be kept covered or they are very likely to be found on the floor. There is an interesting peculiarity of structure that this species shares with some of the African characins: the middle rays of the caudal fin are elongated and black in color, waving like a pennant far behind the tips of the caudal lobes. If the fish were not such an active swimmer, this elongation would make an irresistible target for other fishes and would often get nipped off. So far there have been no recorded spawnings and there are no known external sex differences.

TRIGONECTES STRIGABUNDUS

TROPHEUS DUBOISI Marlier/*Duboisi*

R: Lake Tanganyika, Africa. **H**: Peaceful for a cichlid. **W**: Hard, alkaline water preferred. Temperature 24 to 26°C. **S**: About 9 cm. **F**: Live foods, preferably tubifex and white worms.
Tropheus duboisi is a very popular cichlid from Lake Tanganyika. In its natural environment, it lives among algae-covered rocks in the littoral region of the lake. Several color morphs are known, the most common being the narrow olive-banded, the white-banded, and the rainbow. Sexes are difficult to tell apart. *Tropheus duboisi* is a difficult fish to breed under the best conditions. The species is a maternal mouthbrooder that lays few (6 to 12) comparatively large eggs.

TRIPORTHEUS ANGULATUS

TROPHEUS MOORII Boulenger/*Moorii*

R: Lake Tanganyika, Africa. **H**: Inhabits rocky bottoms in Lake Tanganyika and should be provided with some rocks in the aquarium. **W**: Slightly alkaline. Temperature 24 to 28°C. **S**: Up to 10 cm; sometimes slightly smaller. **F**: Live foods, but will also eat grated beef heart; should have vegetable matter as well. **C**: Many color variations.

Over 30 color varieties of this species have been found around the lake, possibly more color morphs than have been found in any other Rift Lake cichlid. These color varieties include an olive form, a yellow-bellied form, a brown form, a green form, a red-striped form, an orange-striped form, a rainbow form, a black form, a solid orange form, a yellow form, a blue-black form, a red and a yellow form, and a tangerine form.

This species grows up to 10 cm. It is peaceful with other fishes but can be rough with its own kind if crowded into too small an area or when breeding. *T. moorii* is a maternal mouthbreeder that lays few (6 to 12) comparatively large eggs. Incubation periods range from four to five weeks. It is important not to disturb this species when brooding, as it is temperamental and will eat or spit out its eggs.

UARU AMPHIACANTHOIDES

TYTTOCHARAX MADEIRAE Fowler/*Bristly-Mouthed Tetra*

R: Middle and upper Amazon basin. **H**: Peaceful, but because of their small size they should have a tank of their own; prefer to swim in schools. **W**: Soft, slightly acid water. Temperature 24 to 27°C. **S**: Up to 2 cm. **F**: Smallest live foods like newly hatched brine shrimp.

Tyttocharax madeirae is a highly interesting fish for several reasons. Most interesting is a pocket at the caudal base of the males that may be a gland. Its function is yet to be determined. Another interesting feature is the fact that the numerous tiny teeth are not confined to the mouth but bristle all over the lips and snout.

TROPHEUS MOORII

UARU AMPHIACANTHOIDES Heckel/*Uaru, Triangle Cichlid*

R: Amazon basin and the Guianas. **H**: Should be as undisturbed as possible in a large shaded tank; may be kept with Angelfish or discus. **W**: Clean water and a number of hiding places should be provided. High temperature, about 26°C. **S**: 26 cm. **F**: Larger live foods, such as full-grown brine shrimp, cut-up earthworms.

This large cichlid is seldom available and is only to be recommended for the aquarist who has a special interest in cichlids and has large facilities for keeping them. As is often the case, young specimens are so different in color that they are sometimes shipped as a "new species." According to the records of their breeding, they spawn like most other cichlids. The young are said to be very delicate, and pulling them through the first stages of development is supposed to be very difficult.

TYTTOCHARAX MADEIRAE

XENENTODON CANCILA (Hamilton-Buchanan)/*Silver Needlefish*

R: Southeast Asia. **H**: Surface swimmer and will jump out of tank if it is not covered; at times it appears to be motionless, as if hanging in air. **W**: An addition of some sea-salt would be beneficial. Temperature range from 22 to 26°C. **S**: Up to 30 cm. **F**: Prefers live foods including all kinds of smaller fishes.

Because of the size *X. cancila* attains and its tremendous food requirements when mature, it is probably only suitable for large public aquaria. Even though the younger specimens are not as choosy about their eating habits, they nevertheless grow quite rapidly, and before you know it you will have to face the great task of providing it with all kinds of live fishes. Another bad characteristic of this species is its ability to jump in such an extraordinary fashion.

XENOOPHORUS CAPTIVUS

XENOMYSTUS NIGRI Günther/*African Knife Fish*

R: Broad east-to-west range in tropical Africa. **H**: Soft, acid water is best. Temperature range 24 to 28°C. **W**: A nocturnal prowler; should be provided with good cover within the tank. Young, small fish are peaceful, but older fish are quarrelsome among themselves and definitely predatory upon small tankmates. **S**: Up to 20 cm; usually seen much smaller. **F**: Accepts all standard aquarium foods, but especially prefers live and frozen foods; floating dry foods are usually not accepted.

This rather colorless but highly interesting fish has been popular in the hobby for a long time, popular in the sense that whenever a dealer has them for sale they are usually sold out very quickly, for their novelty appeals to many hobbyists who are looking for something different. Unfortunately, once they get the fish home and into a tank they wonder why it seems to be uncomfortable, always seeking a place to hide. The reason, of course, is that *Xenomystus nigri,* like the other African knife fishes, is primarily a nocturnal species.

XENENTODON CANCILA

XENOOPHORUS CAPTIVUS (Hubbs)/*Green Goodeid*

R: Rio Panuco near Jesus Maria, Mexico. **H:** Peaceful. Can be kept in a community tank with other peaceful fishes. **W:** Not critical, but be sure not to let it get too acid or too soft. Temperature range about 20 to 25°C. **S:** Attains a length of about 4.5 cm. **F:** Will accept a wide variety of aquarium foods. A supplement of spinach or other greens is recommended.

The male will chase females around the tank and through the plants when courting. He will stand almost on his head, trembling in front of a female to gain attention, and if she moves away will start his pursuit all over again. Eventually the female will succumb to his advances and he will press against her side as fertilization takes place. In about six weeks the 20 to 25 young are born (10 to 20 if the first brood of the female). Four weeks after that the sexes can be distinguished as the anal fin of the male starts to become modified into the gonopodium. At eight weeks of age they reach puberty, and another six weeks after that their first young can be seen.

XENOMYSTUS NIGRI

XENOPTERUS NARITUS (Richardson)/*Bronze Puffer, Naritus*

R: Southeast Asia, primarily Burma, the Malay Peninsula, and Thailand. **H**: A fin-nipper and not to be trusted, even with fishes much larger than itself. **W**: Softness and acidity factors not critical as long as extremes are avoided, but the addition of non-iodized salt at the rate of about one teaspoonful for every 8 liters of tank capacity will help the fish. This is a warmth-loving species, and the temperature should not be allowed to fall below 21°C for more than a day at a time. **S**: Up to 30 cm in nature. **F**: Live foods, especially tubificid worms, are best, but meaty prepared foods are accepted.

Xenopterus naritus differs from the fishes of the more popular puffer genus *Tetraodon* most obviously in its markings (or lack of markings, actually), because although all of the *Tetraodon* species that are seen with any degree of regularity in the aquarium trade are highly patterned species with stripes, bars, vermiculations, and spots over their bodies, *X. naritus* is of an over-all uniform color. Other physical differences are much less immediately obvious. One thing that *X. naritus* shares with other puffers is that nice set of powerful teeth that all use to good effect in crushing snails and nipping fins. All of the puffers have the dentition to inflict wounds.

XIPHOPHORUS EVELYNAE

XENOTOCA EISENI (Rutter)/*Red-Tailed Goodeid*

R: Mexico, Rios Tepic and Compostela south into Jalisco, at least to Magdalena; Rios Tamazula and Tuxpan in southern Jalisco south to Atenquigue. **H**: Peaceful; does well with others of the same species of all sizes, except possibly for equal sized males, which may tend to be scrappy over females. **W**: Not critical as far as pH is concerned (pH 6-8 presents no problem), but hard water (DH 8-10 is sufficient) is necessary. Temperature 20 to 29°C. **S**: Reaches a length of 8 cm. **F**: Omnivorous; accepts a wide variety of live or prepared fish foods, and vegetable-based flake food is recommended to balance the diet.

Young females may drop up to a dozen young, but older and more mature females can have broods of 50 to 75 young every six weeks. The embryos are nourished in a uterus through a cord and placental arrangement apparently equivalent to that found in mammals. The young are born with the cord and placenta still attached (but dropped within the first 24 hours), upside-down, and tail first. They are relatively large at birth, averaging about 12 mm.

XENOPTERUS NARITUS

XIPHOPHORUS EVELYNAE Rosen/*Puebla Platy*

R: The entire Rio Tecolutla system in Puebla, Mexico. **H:** As peaceful as other species of platy and relatively active. **W:** Clean, clear water that is slightly alkaline and somewhat hard. A temperature of 20° to 24°C is sufficient. **S:** Males attain a length of about 35-40 mm, females 45-50 mm. **F:** Small live foods are best. Some vegetable matter should be available.

Maintenance of this species is very much like that for the popular platies seen in every pet shop. The tank need not be very large but the water should be very clean and clear. It should be well aerated. The bottom can be covered with aquarium gravel and plants added according to the decorating ability of the aquarist as long as sufficient open spaces are left in which the fish can swim. The water itself should be slightly alkaline and somewhat hard. The water temperature is best kept at the lower end of the scale for tropical fishes, about 20 to 24°C.

XENOTOCA EISENI

XIPHOPHORUS HELLERI

XIPHOPHORUS HELLERI Heckel/*Swordtail*

R: Southern Mexico to Guatemala. **H**: This fish is very variable in temperament; some individuals show very little aggression toward other fishes, while others, especially large males, are out and out bullies. **W**: Slightly alkaline, medium hard water; an addition of salt is sometimes of benefit, but this is not necessary. Temperature 21 to 27°C. **S**: Wild specimens up to 13 cm; almost always seen much smaller than this. **F**: Accepts all regular aquarium foods, but there should be variety. **C**: Swordtails come in many different colors, with many different patterns. Red, green, black, albino, and other forms are available.

The Swordtail is an extremely popular fish and one of the prettiest. Easy to keep, easy to breed, colorful, fast-growing, always available… the list of the fish's good points could stretch on and on. The male Swordtail is a beautiful fish, and his "sword," which is an extension of the caudal fin, is one of the most striking physical characteristics possessed by any aquarium fish. Unfortunately, many Swordtails today do not have the same majestic tail of the original Swordtail, but they do have color, and this makes up somewhat for their lack of tail development. One of the prime factors that has served to popularize the Swordtail is the fact that the fish is a livebearer and thus can be bred with extreme ease. Even beginners in the aquarium hobby have no great difficulty in sexing and breeding this species, although they do often run into the problem of raising good-size young, something that the beginner is not able to do until he has mastered at least the fundamentals of aquarium management. Large females can give birth to more than 150 young at one time at intervals of about a month, so it is easy to see why this is considered a prolific fish.

Xiphophorus helleri pair, male in foreground.

XIPHOPHORUS MACULATUS

XIPHOPHORUS MACULATUS (Günther)/*Platy*

R: Mexico to Guatemala. **H**: Peaceful and active; a very good community fish if not kept with soft-water species. **W**: Water should be slightly alkaline and medium-hard; tank should be well planted and lighted. Temperature 21 to 27°C. **S**: Females up to 8 cm; males smaller. **F**: Takes all aquarium foods; also like to pick algae from plants and aquarium ornaments. **C**: An extreme variety of solid colors and combinations.

The Platy possesses every good point that is enjoyed by other livebearing species, and it is an improvement over many of the others in that it is a peaceful fish which never goes out of its way to make trouble. The Platy is an old scientific standby, for it was used in many experiments valuable in the fields of genetics and medicine. Like the Swordtail, it is a popular fish for beginners, and it is better suited to the beginner than the Swordtail because it is hardier, more peaceful, and smaller. This last factor is important, for it makes it possible to grow large, healthy Platies in less space than is required for Swordtails and in much less space than is required to grow a good Molly. The dependably prolific Platy produces broods of young on an average of once a month, but this time can be shorter or longer, depending mainly on temperature. Many advanced hobbyists look askance at the Platy, considering it as nothing more than a beginner's fish, but other advanced hobbyists specialize in them after they have mastered many of the rarer and more expensive egg-laying species. For sheer bright color, a good Platy can beat most other fishes.

It seems that there is no end to the beautiful possibilities in breeding fancy Platies. The discriminating aquarist can find an individual Platy possessing especially attractive and unique markings, and with a great deal of work he can fix a strain of Platies possessing these same characteristics.

Xiphophrus maculatus pair; the male is the upper fish.

XIPHOPHORUS MONTEZUMAE

XIPHOPHORUS MONTEZUMAE Jordan & Snyder/*Mexican Swordtail*
R: Rio Panuco, Mexico. **H**: Peaceful with other species. **W**: Neutral to slightly alkaline medium-hard water is best; salt may be added but is unnecessary. Temperature 20 to 26°C. **S**: Female 6 cm; males 5 cm. **F**: Accepts all usual aquarium foods; also browses on algae.
The Mexican Swordtail is not as readily bred as its relatives, and it also has smaller broods, although the gestation period is about the same as in Platies and other Swordtails.

XIPHOPHORUS MONTEZUMAE

XIPHOPHORUS PYGMAEUS Hubbs & Gordon/*Pygmy Swordtail*
R: Rio Axtla and Rio Choy, Mexico. **H**: Peaceful toward other fishes and plants. **W**: Not critical as long as the water is clear and clean. Temperature 23 to 27°C. **S**: Males 4 cm; females slightly larger. **F**: All foods accepted.

X. pygmaeus has been found in a restricted area of the Rio Axtla in the deeper waters near the banks. It lives within the shelter of the rocky substrate and dense vegetation. The water in this area is fast-flowing. The males are 2.5 to 3 cm. long, while the females are up to 4 cm long. *X. nigrensis,* once-considered a subspecies of *X. pygmaeus,* is found in the warm source areas of the Rio Choy and also lives in deep, heavily vegetated areas among the rocks. This species is one of the rarest swordtails. The males grow to 3 or 4 cm, and the females grow to 4 cm. While *X. pygmaeus* shows only a minimal extension of the lower caudal fin rays, *X. nigrensis* develops a short sword comparable in size with that of *X. montezumae. X. nigrensis* has a black lower border on its short sword whereas *X. pygmaeus* has no pigmentation in that area.

ZACCO PLATYPUS

ZACCO PLATYPUS (Temminck & Schlegel)/*Featherfin Minnow*

R: Japan, Taiwan, China, and Korea. **H:** Not to be trusted with fishes it can swallow. Fairly active. **W:** Not critical. This is a cool-water fish that cannot stand high temperatures for long periods of time. **S:** Attains a length of up to 20 cm. **F:** Accepts most foods but prefers live or frozen foods. Small live fishes are beneficial.

This colorful cyprinid is rather closely related to the more familiar species of the genus *Barilius*. It is a cooler water species inhabiting Japan, Taiwan, China (as far north as Manchuria), and Korea. It is a food and game fish although the taste of its flesh is not considered to be too good. It reaches a length of 20 cm or more.

This is an active fish with a relatively large mouth. It will dispose of any fishes in the aquarium that are small enough to swallow, but when placed with comparably sized species it will behave itself. A large tank should be provided to allow sufficient freedom of movement. Plants and driftwood may be used for decoration. The water chemistry is not critical as long as extremes are avoided. Since this fish comes from temperate to even cold climates, the water temperatures should be correspondingly low. It should do well in a native fish tank kept at room temperatures. Feeding is no problem. A basic diet of live feeder fishes augmented with a variety of frozen foods will be sufficient.

Nuptial males are quite beautiful, with a bluish green back (the color extending across the body as tan bands that narrow and/or disappear ventrally) and pinkish sides and ventral area. Add to this the enlarged anal fin formed by the prolongation of some of the middle and anterior fin rays, and you have a very satisfying aquarium fish. Breeding males, much like many carps and other cyprinids, have numerous tubercles on the head. Spawning in the wild (at least in Japan) is said to occur in the spring and summer as the water is warmed by the sun.

ZOOGONETICUS QUITZEOENSIS

ZOOGONETICUS QUITZEOENSIS (Bean)/*Picotee Goodeid*

R: Basin of the Rio Lerma, Mexico. **H:** A peaceful, retiring species. **W:** Prefers water that is a bit on the hard, alkaline side. The addition of a teaspoon of salt per 4 liters has been suggested. **S:** Females attain a length of about 45-50 mm; the males are somewhat smaller. **F:** Accepts a variety of different aquarium foods. Tends to be a sluggish eater.

The Picotee Goodeid is an interesting little fish from the Rio Lerma basin in Mexico. It tends to be a bit shy and retiring, rarely showing aggression. The body is tan to grayish with a number of dark blotches, especially along a line from the snout to halfway back on the sides. These dark blotches are evident even in newly born fry. The male has thin yellow-orange edges to the dorsal and anal fins.

The tank should be relatively large for the size of the fish, an 80-liter aquarium housing four to five pairs of breeders. The water should be clean and clear, with regular water changes of about 25% or more each week.

Slightly hard, alkaline water suits them best, with a temperature of about 25° to 27°C adequate. Gravel is usually not required (except for anchoring plants), but plants such as Java moss, *Riccia*, or water sprite must be added. The plants help the fish to overcome any shyness they might have as well as protect the fry from renegade parents that decide to turn on them. Actually these fish are not aggressive although males might chase each other about from time to time. Slightly darkened conditions (such as a dark bottom) usually aid in bringing out the best colors of the fish.

A single-species tank is best for any goodeid, and a small "family" group is recommended for this species. The parents normally do not bother the young. Feeding is not difficult as far as type of food is concerned. The problem is to get them to eat enough, as they are not very eager eaters.

These small fish (females about 45-50 mm, males 35-40 mm) produce a small number of young at a time, with 8-12 being on the high side. Fry size is about 12 mm total length. Whereas the parents should get a couple of meals a day, the fry should get up to four feedings. Brood intervals seem to average about 45 days. Unfortunately the females do not store sperm as do many poeciliids so they must be impregnated by the male each time. Although a lot of chasing may be going on in the tank all the time, impregnation normally occurs only about twice a month.

An aquarium without plants cannot truly be called an aquarium. Takashi Amano designed and photographed this cubic aquarium. He has written three major books on aquarium plants and aquarium layouts. The series is entitled NATURE AQUARIUM WORLD volumes 1, 2, and 3. These books and his outstanding photography have set a new standard in aquarium management.

Aquarium Plants and Their Cultivation

The interest in aquatic plants has undoubtedly increased over the last fifty years to the extent that aquarists not only regard them as necessary adjuncts to the decorative aquarium but also cultivate them for their own attraction and biological peculiarities. The reason for this growing interest is two-fold; firstly, the importation of exotic marsh and water plants has, as a result of more frequent collecting trips throughout every continent, brought desirable new and often very rare species into commercial supply in America and western Europe and hence into the hands of aquarium plant connoisseurs. Secondly, since Dr. James W. Atz first pointed out the balanced aquarium myth, most aquarists have abandoned the naive assumption that the purpose of a few specimens of *Elodea* and *Vallisneria* in an aquarium is to establish the gaseous exchanges which complement those of the fishes' respiration. Consequently plants have been regarded more as objects with which to decorate the aquarium, creating not only a pleasant visual effect but also a more natural habitat for the fishes. Of course the basic principle of the complementary respiratory exchanges of fishes and plants within a container is sound, but it was long ago grossly exaggerated in the idea of the balanced aquarium.

Despite the new enthusiasm shown in aquarium plant culture, there are still many aquarists who make little attempt to lay out rockwork and plants in imaginative designs or to cultivate and propagate their plants. These two aspects of plant culture are quite distinct. The layout of an aquarium is largely determined by the aquarist's imagination, patience and concepts of pleasing visual effects. In creating an attractive design the important theme is one of contrast between high and low, light and shade, erect and horizontal, entire leaves and dissected leaves, smooth leaves and ruffled leaves and so on. In an aquascape created by the imaginative aquarist the illusion of depth, the interest at all levels of the water and the apparently natural growth of the plants will be conspicuous features. Though improvements in aquarium layout usually accrue from practice and experience, aquascaping is an individual ability and no hard and fast rules exist to discipline the beginner. The other aspect of aquarium plant culture, the actual propagation and manipulation of the plants, deserves a more comprehensive discussion. Two natural methods of reproduction, sexual and vegetative, occur among plants. Sexual reproduction may involve the formation, dispersal and germination of seeds, as in the flowering plants, or the union of sex cells formed by a separate plant body derived from minute spores, as in the ferns and other flowerless plants. The first type of sexual reproduction is mentioned later in relation to the propagation of the rarer flowering aquatic plants. The second type is referred to in the section devoted to the interesting aquarium plants which belong to the lower groups of the plant kingdom. Natural methods of vegetative propagation are discussed throughout wherever they are relevant to the needs of the aquarist. Let us now discuss the manipulation of some familiar aquarium species.

Manipulation is usually understood as gardening. Pruning, for example, is employed to improve the appearance of underwater foliage. Of the gardening methods, we may first distinguish the cutting back of premature floating leaves which tend to replace the submerged leaves on vigorous specimens of *Aponogeton, Echinodorus, Nymphaea* and other large heterophyllous plants. This is usually progressive pruning designed solely to impair the vigor of the plant, thus delaying the climax of its cycle.

Manipulative pruning of species of aquarium plants often yields the finest bushes of foliage in the underwater scene. The principle of this pruning is that removal of the stem apex eliminates the inhibition of the dormant axillary buds by hormones from the apical bud. This principle is an important feature of the growth habit of many terrestrial plants, though the precise details of the physico-chemical mechanism whereby the inhibition is maintained or removed are unknown. Some species, such as *Hygrophila*

Echinodorus latifolius   *Cardamine lyrata*

Hygrophila siamensis   **Lysimachia numularia**

polysperma, have a branching habit without removal of the apical bud, and lateral shoots develop freely once the plant is established. Extremely accommodating as regards compost, temperature and pH value of the water, this post-war introduction from India was the first truly aquatic species of its genus to become popular in the aquarium hobby. Its bushy habit renders it useful for masking the sides and corners of tanks, and its bright pale green leaves in pairs along the stems contrast with the fine-leaved bushy species of *Cabomba, Limnophila* and *Myriophyllum.* The beautiful rich green sprays of the related giant species *Hygrophila corymbosa* are, with their bold lanceolate leaves, more strikingly handsome but less easy to trim to the desired shape.

A popular species equally decorative and equally accommodating as *Hygrophila polysperma* is *Cardamine lyrata,* whose stems branch freely if the apical buds are nipped from time to time. Its fast-growing but delicate stems bear rounded lobed leaves of a brilliant fresh green; these leaves adjust themselves so that they are exposed to the maximum light intensity and the plant thus forms a fine bush which looks admirable in front of tall dark rock formations. Another round-leaved species superficially similar to *Cardamine lyrata* is *Lysimachia nummularia,* a plant frequently inhabiting moist garden soil but easily acclimated to submerged life in coldwater or tropical aquaria. Like *Hygrophila* and *Cardamine,* it readily forms adventitious roots from the lower nodes and after removal of the apical buds soon forms a dense bush of rich green foliage. *Bacopa caroliniana* is a familiar round- to oval-leaved aquarium plant which was known in England for a while, due to a dealer's error, as *Macuillamia rotundifolia.* Its stout, fleshy, ridged stem is extremely buoyant, and roots develop slowly from the nodes; despite these disadvantages this unusual species is often seen in aquaria. It is a difficult plant to model, for it is easily twisted out of shape and does not branch as freely as other species planted as cuttings. Its stems and leaves are unusually hairy, and out of water the plant has a pronounced fragrance. A fourth, and rare, roundleaved species is *Micranthemum orbiculatum,* whose thin, frail-looking stems bear tiny round, slightly folded leaves which quickly respond to the direction of light.

Production of bushes of foliage is also possible with fine-leaved species by nipping out apical buds. The three main genera of aquarium plants with dissected leaves, *Myriophyllum, Cabomba* and *Limnophila,* all respond to this treatment by growing many lateral shoots. There are many species of *Myriophyllum* native to the United States and to the countries of western Europe; a less common species suitable for tropical aquaria is *M. elatinoides,* with whorls of delicate shining green leaves divided into hair-like segments. All the species of *Cabomba* commonly available to aquarists are suited to water at all temperatures from 10°C to about 27°C. The two most frequent species are *Cabomba caroliniana* and C. *aquatica,* the former being distinguished by the formation of narrow floating leaves prior to the flowering phase. Its pretty white flowers are insect-pollinated and develop into small fruits borne downward in the water within the dying remains of the petals. A rosy-hued variety of C. *caroliniana* is sometimes available, as is C. *furcata,* a species which has the leaves set closely

Myriophyllum spicatum **Cabomba caroliniana**

Limnophila sessiliflora

Sagittaria graminea

together on the stems. The leaves of *Limnophila sessiliflora* are more finely divided than those of *Cabomba* and are whorled, not paired.

The water wisteria, *Hygrophila difformis,* introduced to aquarists in 1954, is a splendid fast-growing species with a wide range of leaf shapes from entire, smooth-margined, oval leaves to deeply divided toothed leaves superficially resembling those of the Indian fern, *Ceratopteris thalictroides.* The leaves are borne close together on the stout erect stem and from their axils arise lateral shoots; these are encouraged by removal of the apical bud and the plant very quickly forms a luxuriant bush of bright green foliage. The species tolerates a wide range of water conditions and will thrive in a compost of barren gravel, sand or any of the sand/soil mixtures.

Of course, there are a few species used by aquarists which grow naturally in a habit which displays their foliage to remarkable advantage. Well-known examples are species of *Sagittaria,* such as *S. latifolia* and *S. subulata,* both of which spread their long fleshy leaves from the crown in a conspicuous manner quite unlike the habit of species of *Vallisneria,* with which they are often confused by novices. *Acorus gramineus* var. *pusillus,* the dwarf rush, and *Acorus gramineus* and its variegated form are even better examples. Their narrow flattened tapering leaves spread out in the form of a fan as they mature and are replaced by younger ones. The fan arises from the almost horizontal rhizome and the dwarf habit, unusual appearance and shallow root run all contribute toward the value of these species in the foreground of an aquarium, where they require nothing of the manipulation necessary to control the more rampant species of aquarium plants.

Takashi Amano calls this design THE COL-ORS OF THE FOOTHILLS. It features Car-dinal Tetras, Paracheirodon axelrodi, *with the plants* Echinodorus tenellus, Cryptocoryne pontederifolia, Microsorium pteropus, Cyperus helferi *and* Vallisneria.

Flowerless Aquatic Plants

Most aquarium plants are prevented from flowering by the culture methods used to maintain their decorative submerged foliage. Even so, they have the ability to flower and set seed. A few of the most interesting and attractive plants used by aquarists never produce flowers, and they belong to groups lower in the plant kingdom which reproduce not by flowers but by inconspicuous spores. The methods the plant uses to produce and disperse these spores are often complicated and only visible under the microscope; since spores are seldom seen they need not concern us here, for these plants rarely reproduce themselves sexually, even in nature. Instead, as is characteristic of almost all water plants, they multiply vegetatively, either by baby plants produced viviparously on the parent or by fragmentation, which in floating species often occurs at a prodigious rate.

Ceratopteris thalictroides (from *keras* and *pteris,* the Greek words meaning *horn* and *fern),* the Indian fern or water sprite, is a popular aquarium plant which may be grown floating or submerged. Indigenous to tropical America, Asia, the East Indies and China, it grows in stagnant pools, rooted in the mud, and is often collected as fresh food. A French botanist distinguishes two varieties, one from Sumatra with finely dissected fronds, the other from tropical America as far north as Florida with broad, only slightly

Ceratopteris thalictroides

indented fronds. This distinction is not really justified, as the shape of frond produced depends on the age of the plant and the depth of water in which it is growing. Fronds which are mature or from deep water are twice divided, while fronds which are juvenile or from shallower water are usually smaller, broader and less divided, with oblong pinnae. Fronds of all sizes and shapes may often occur on one good plant. Only sterile fronds are produced by rooted submerged plants, the pinnae unfolding as the fleshy quadrangular stem grows from the crown, at first horizontally and then

Cryptocoryne affinis

Cryptocoryne beckettii

straightening up to the light. Floating specimens have profuse branching roots with dense root-hairs, while the sterile fronds recline on the surface, forming a rosette of up to 75 cm in diameter. Erect fertile fronds may be produced from the crown to a height of 70 cm; they are finely divided with linear segments bearing longitudinal lines of sporangia which contain the spores. In aquaria, fertile fronds are uncommon, but the plants readily produce viviparous youngsters at the notches of the fronds. These are best detached and floated at the surface until they have strong enough roots to be planted. The bright yellowish green fronds of *Ceratopteris thalictroides* are unlike any other aquarium plant and contrast excellently with the dark green foliage of many species of *Cryptocoryne*.

The rapid spread of *Ceratopteris* is characteristic of two other genera of water ferns, *Salvinia* and *Azolla*. The first of these, which was dedicated to Antonio Mario Salvini, a Florentine professor of the seventeenth century, is a cosmopolitan genus inhabiting lakes, pools and stagnant ditches. From the horizontal stem of the large form of *Salvinia auriculata* arise two rows of rounded pea-green surface leaves, clothed beneath with brownish hairs, the upper surfaces glistening with a dense covering of curious looped white hairs which repel any drops of water falling on the plant. Beneath each pair of leaves hangs a cluster of finely branched, rust-colored submerged leaflets; these are not roots as is often thought. The small form of *S. auriculata* has leaves 6 mm long but is otherwise very similar.

Salvinia auriculata

Once introduced to an aquarium, these plants soon cover the surface by rapid vegetative multiplication and they need rigorous control. They thrive under the bright lights of an aquarium hood or the diffuse light of a tropical pool and, though preferring warm water, may be acclimated to cold water.

Species of *Azolla* (from the Greek *a*-without, and *zoe*-life, alluding to the rapidity with which the plant dries up) are just as adapted to the floating habit as *Salvinia,* their covering of short hairs imprisoning air and preventing them from being submerged. *Azolla nilotica,* a much-branched species, grows to 15 cm long and, with *Salvinia* and *Ceratopteris,* is important as a constituent of the sudd, the dense floating masses of vegetation which block slow-moving rivers in flat open country, for example the Nile and the Ganges. *Azolla mexicana* is a smaller purplish species from

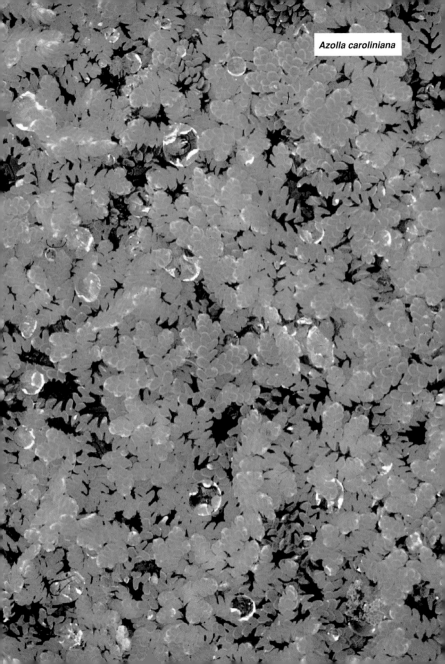

Azolla caroliniana

Azolla nilotica

Azolla filiculoides

the irrigation ditches of Mexico and the southern United States. The two most widely distributed species are the smallest and the two most well known to aquarists. These are *Azolla caroliniana* and *Azolla filiculoides,* which have in the last ninety years demonstrated the efficiency of their vegetative reproduction and dispersal by spreading all over Europe from their origin in western North America, Central and South America. Both seem to have been introduced into Europe via botanic gardens. *A. caroliniana* reached Europe in 1872, spreading through France by 1879, to England in 1883 and to Italy in 1886. It is rare in England, *A. filiculoides* being confused with it.

Azolla filiculoides was introduced to France by a Bordeaux botanist in 1879 and 1880. In England in 1888, a teacher is said to have procured some from Glasgow and put it in a ditch at a village on the Norfolk Broads. Heavy floods in August, 1912 carried it up the main rivers and spread it all over the Broads. Now locally common in England, particularly in the warmer humid counties of the southeast and southwest, it is prevented from spreading to the northwest by hard winter frosts.

Identical to the naked eye, both species have a branched stem with thin pendulous roots and overlapping leaves above in two rows alternating right and left. Each leaf has two lobes; the upper floats and possesses chlorophyll and a symbiotic blue-green alga, while the lower is submerged and colorless. The hairs on the upper surface of the leaves of *A. fliculoides* are unicellular, while those of *A. caroliniana* are bicellular. The overall bluish green tint of the two species becomes purplish red in strong sunlight, particularly in late summer.

The plants reproduce by fragmentation and spread rapidly until the whole aquarium or pool surface is covered by the tufted mass.

While the fern *Azolla* appears more like a leafy liverwort, another flowerless aquarium plant, *Riccia,* actually is a liverwort. The plant is a simple flat thallus which branches dichotomously. *Riccia fluitans,* a cosmopolitan species dedicated to Ricci, an Italian botanist, is common in aquaria, bright green tangled masses floating just beneath the surface. It is just as attractive when pegged to the gravel and allowed to grow into a dense carpet.

Ricciocarpus natans is a related floating species which is much rarer, but like *Riccia* species, it is found in ponds and ditches rich in mineral and organic matter. It is quite similar to the common duckweed, having lobed thalli about 5 mm in diameter, each lobe being bright green and bearing shaggy purple scales beneath.

Riccia fluitans

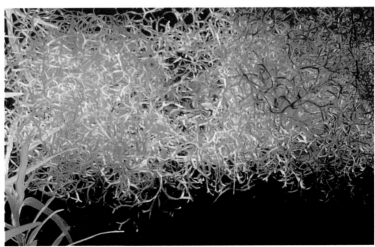

The freshwater moss *Fontinalis antipyretica* is an attractive aquarium plant growing naturally in rapid hill streams. Its specific name alludes to its waterholding capacity and its supposed use in bandaging burns; its common name is willow moss. In general appearance it is very similar to its terrestrial relatives with its thin, wiry, brownish stems clothed with alternate triangular leaves of a deep translucent green. Underwater it forms thickets and is useful as a spawning and decorative plant, but it is only suitable for coldwater aquaria. A finer-leaved variety, light green in color, *Fontinalis antipyretica* var. *gracilis* is suitable for warm water.

Among the dwarf plants so popular nowadays in front of rocks in an aquarium waterscape are species of the genus *Marsilea.* These ferns from shallow waters and mud flats in temperate and tropical regions of the world are named in honor of an eighteenth century Italian botanist, Fernando Conte Marsigli. In growth habit *Marsilea* has rhizomes creeping in the mud or sand, sending up erect stalks alternately on each side which bear four pinnae rather like a four-leaf clover. The pinnae unfold from the coiled bud when the stalk reaches its prescribed height, which varies from 2 to 12 cm. Many species are available to the aquarist: *M. quadrifolia,* from central Europe and Japan; *M. drummondii* from Australia; *M. vestita,* from the Pacific coast of America; and *M. mucronata,* from the high plains, Rocky Mountains and southwestern states, are probably the most common. Be-

Fontinalis antipyretica

OVERLEAF:
Takashi Amano entitled this aquarium GREEN PARADISE. It features the fishes *Nematobrycon palmeri, Hemigrammus erythrozonus, Aplocheilichthys normani* and *Microgeophagus ramirezi.* The plants are *Glossostigma elatinoides, Riccia fluitans, Eleocharis acicularis, Sagittaria subulata (pusilla), Microsorium sp., Micranthemum unbrosum, Anubias barteri (nana), Bolbitis heudeloti, Mayaca fluviatilis, Rotala macandra, Didiplis diandra, Cardamine lyrata, Ludwigia arcuata, Hydrocotyle leucocephala* and *Echinodorus amazonicus.* Photo and design by Takashi Amano from his book NATURE AQUARIUM WORLD.

ing amphibious plants, they all show a distressing tendency to form floating and aerial leaves; these may be prevented by judicious pruning and planting in water of more than 15 cm.

Very closely related to *Marsilea* is the peculiarly named tropical fern *Regnellidium,* of similar habit but usually larger and with leaves of only two light green pinnae. It may be rooted or left floating with the rhizome just beneath the surface, the roots hanging below. When *Marsilea* and *Regnellidium* are grown as marsh plants they form spores within stony beanshaped sporocarps borne singly near the base of the leaf stalks.

Marsilea quadrifolia

Regnellidium diphyllum

Mature sporocarps germinate readily in water if they are first cracked. They imbibe water and after a few minutes a strange worm-like structure emerges and slowly swells until it disintegrates, releasing the spores.

Another relative of *Marsilea* is similar to hair grass; this is *Pilularia globulifera,* the pillwort, from temperate regions of Europe. A plant of shallow pond margins, its slender creeping rhizome may be rooted or free-floating. Narrow cylindrical leaves grow alternately from each side of the rhizome to 8 to 10 cm tall. They are fresh green and circinately coiled like those of *Marsilea.* A common but easily overlooked plant of Great Britain and the U.S.A., it is more frequent in the west than in the east. It may be gathered wild and used as a dwarf carpet plant in the coldwater aquarium.

The last flowerless aquarium plants of interest are not true ferns; they are the strange plants of the genus *Isoetes* (from the Greek, *isos*-equal, and *etos*-year, referring to the evergreen nature of the plants). Known popularly as the quillworts, most species inhabit the stony beds of bleak barren mountain lakes in the cold and temperate regions of the world. *Isoetes lacustris,* native to northern Europe, has a tuft of spiky green leaves with transverse white markings and profuse roots growing from a stout rootstock. The leaves usually bear spores in cavities on the inside of the wide leaf base. When planted in small groups, this handsome species has a striking appearance in a coldwater aquarium. Other species, such as *I. garnierii,* introduced into France from the Sudan in 1947, and *I. bolanderi,* native to the western United States, are suitable for warm water.

None of the species of aquatic ferns, mosses and liverworts just described are demanding in their culture requirements. All thrive under a wide range of light intensities, though the floating species enjoy the higher intensities more than submerged species. Gravel, coarse sand or a sand/soil mixture suits all the rooted species, sand giving a closer root hold to *Marsilea* and *Pilularia,* which sometimes tend to be disturbed by bottom-feeding fishes. *Isoetes, Pilularia* and to a certain extent *Fontinalis,* coming from lakes and streams poor in dissolved salts, are lime-hating and must be given non-calcareous gravel or sand and rather acid water.

Isoetes malinverniana   **Isoetes lacustris**

Large Tropical Aquatic Plants

Gone are the days when Amazon swordplants were rarities in aquaria. Many of the thirty or so species of *Echinodorus* from the American continent, such as the Amazon swordplant, *E. paniculatus,* and the chain swordplant, *E. grisebachii,* have variable growth forms. All species of *Echinodorus,* however, produce bushes of bold foliage and are therefore eminently suitable as centerpieces and specimen plants. Their leaf stalks are short and they will not produce floating and aerial leaves unless the light intensity is too high. Most species are now commercially plentiful, including the unusual *E. berteroi,* the cellophane plant, which grows through a series of leaf forms, and *E. tenellus,* the pygmy chain swordplant.

A few species are still rare and have not been introduced to some European countries. *Echinodorus major,* the ruffled swordplant from Brazil, with its spectacular furled strap-shaped leaves up to half a meter tall, and *E. grandiflorus,* the Amazon spearplant from tropical America, with its large spearshaped leaves, are examples of such plants.

The water orchid is a rare specimen plant; it is often erroneously named *Spiranthes odorata,* a species which will not survive under water. The form usually grown in aquaria is probably a variety of *Spiranthes latifolia,* a bog species readily adaptable to continued submerged growth. From the fleshy

Echinodorus berteroi

Overleaf:
The Red Crypto aquarium, so named by Takashi Amano, is decorated with *Cryptocoryne parva, Cryptocoryne cordata, Cryptocoryne affinis, Cryptocoryne lucens, Cryptocoryne blassii* and *Fontinalis antipyretica.* The fish are *Rasbora heteromorpha.* Photo and tank design by Takashi Amano from his book *NATURE AQUARIUM WORLD*

Barclaya longifolia

tuberous roots, essential for the plant's survival, grow spreading emerald green lanceolate leaves. Growth is slow, but if the plant is in shallow water under bright light it will produce an aerial stem bearing pale yellow flowers.

Two very rare species of *Barclaya* were introduced in 1958 by Dr. Herbert R. Axelrod; both come from Thailand and belong to the same family as *Cabomba* and the water lilies, the Nymphaeaceae. *Barclaya longifolia* forms a bush of tapering wavy leaves which are prettily veined and olive to midbrown in color. *B. motleyi,* the other species, produces spreading leathery leaves about 7.5 cm wide, whose young pinkish red color matures to a shade of coppery brown.

The genus *Aponogeton* has been much exploited by aquarists, and most of the available species have erect undulating and twisting foliage arising from a tuberous rootstock. Contrary to popular opinion, *A. crispus* is not synonymous with *A. undulatus;* it is a distinct and uncommon species originating in Sri Lanka and India. *A. cordatus* is also uncommon, coming from Southeast Asia and therefore, with *A. undulatus,* producing the undivided flower spike of Asian species which contrasts with the U-shaped double flower spike of African species such as *A. ulvaceus. A. crispus* may be recognized when young by its short petioles which bear the narrow lanceolate leaves in an erect attitude; when mature the species has narrower leaves than either *A. undulatus* or *A. cordatus*. The leaves of *A. undulatus* are smoothly undulating and of a conspicuous bronze-green tint whereas those of *A. cordatus,* the loveliest species of the three, are very closely crinkled at the margins, deep rich green in color and though not fully translucent, show the longitudinal and transverse veins as a molded lattice. *A. natans* quickly forms floating leaves, though its submerged foliage of broad, bright yellowish green, slightly wavy leaves may be maintained by ruthless cutting of the leaves which push toward the surface.

The species of *Aponogeton* about which most has been written is of course *A. madagascariensis,* the Madagascar lace plant. The leaves, which may attain a length of 20 to 25 cm, are borne on slender brittle petioles arising from a tuberous rootstock and are at first reddish bronze, later assuming a deep green hue. The blade of each leaf consists of seven parallel veins joined transversely by short minor veins, forming a regular lace-like network with almost no cellular tissue. Though of fragile appearance, these skeletal blades are comparatively tough and strong. The species produces an aerial inflorescence which consists of a twin spike bearing the white flowers. On numerous occasions *A. madagascariensis* has

Inflorescences of *Aponogeton* species at different stages of development

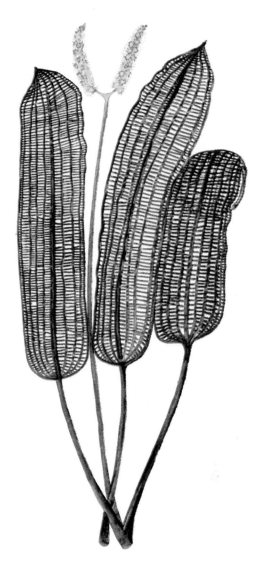

Aponogeton fenestralis

been found to produce submerged inflorescences, as frequently happens in the hardy pool species *A. distachyus,* the Cape water hawthorn. Self-fertilization occurs before the inflorescence opens and seedlings slowly develop while still attached to the bud. The lace plant occurs in Madagascar between 100 and 900 meters above sea level, rooted in non-calcareous sand in the crevices between stones in semi-shaded slowmoving water.

The submerged leaves of species of *Aponogeton* show an interesting structural series. Those of *A. natans* and *A. distachyus* are the least translucent and have the least conspicuous veins; those of *A. crispus, A. undulatus* and *A. cordatus* are more translucent with the veins in relief, while *A. ulvaceus* has fully translucent foliage. In the rare Madagascan species *A. bernierianus,* the cellular interstices of the leaf partially degenerate, but the lace network is not as fully apparent as in the related *A. madagascariensis.*

There is considerable confusion over names in the genus *Cryptocoryne,* too. That usually offered for sale as *C. cordata,* with elongated, tapering, olive to bronze leaves, is really *C. beckettii;* the commercial species of that name, with pointed smooth bright green leaves, is the small growth form of *C. nevillii. C. haerteliana* was a temporary name derived from the surname of the German who imported the then unknown plants at the end of the 1930s. Later they were identified as plants of *C. affinis,* the correct name which dates from 1893. The plant offered as *C. axelrodii* very closely resembles the species *C. undulata.* The true *C. cordata* is a rare and only occasionally imported plant. It is a dark green species growing to about 30 cm tall, with rounded, mottled leaves resembling those of *C. griffithii.* A distinctive species of comparatively recent introduction from Thailand is *C. balansae,* whose spreading leaves are bright shining green with a deeply crinkled surface. Of an equally bright shade of green are the leaves of *C. johorensis;* they are broad and pointed and have recurved basal lobes.

A delightful Sinhalese species, *C. thwaitesii,* is little known to aquarists; it is a most desirable plant for the connoisseur. Discovered by Kendrick Thwaites, a director of the Peradeniya botanic garden from 1857 to 1880, it is a slowgrowing species with finely serrated, delicately marked leaves up to 6 cm long and dark green in color. In deep water its leaves tend to lengthen and become tinted with yellow and brown. This rare species produces very few stolons, and its lilac and blue aroid inflorescence has been seen by only one or two people.

Cryptocoryne retrospiralis

Cryptocoryne griffithii

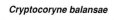
Cryptocoryne balansae

Cryptocoryne sp.

Cryptocoryne cordata

Cryptocoryne axelrodi

Cryptocoryne lutea

Cryptocoryne lucens

During the second half of the nineteenth century the Italian explorer Odoardo Beccari brought to Europe many extensive collections of tropical Asiatic plants, among which was *Cryptocoryne ferruginea,* from Borneo. This is a large handsome species growing to a height of 40 cm, with broad rich green leaves borne on sturdy stalks. The shape of the leaf varies, a feature common to most species of *Cryptocoryne,* but the surface is nearly always deeply crinkled and the margin is waved. Specimens grow well in dim electric light and should not be exposed to direct sunlight; they must be given ample space in which to spread their foliage.

C. versteegii is one of the only two species of *Cryptocoryne* at present known to occur in New Guinea, where G. M. Versteeg discovered it in 1907 on the Lorentz River. It is a dwarf plant suitable for the aquarium foreground, where its rigid triangular green leaves make a conspicuous display. The upper surface is glossy and is never mottled with areas of anthocyanin pigmentation. The rate of growth of this species is variable; there are numerous reports of its never producing a new leaf for many months. When conditions suit it, however, subterranean stolons are formed in abundance and its inflorescence is not uncommonly produced.

Introduced to European aquarists in 1954 by an Amsterdam importer, *Cryptocoryne walkeri* resembles *C. beckettii,* though it does not usually reach a comparable size. It also differs in having shorter and broader leaves which do not usually curl back and which may be slightly ribbed at their margins. It lacks the distinctive olive-green hue of *C. beckettii. C. ciliata is* one of the large and fairly common species which grow consistently when submerged in tropical aquaria. The tapering pale green leaves are usually gently furled and borne erect on stout stalks to an overall height of 40 to 50 cm.

The beautifully colored inflorescences of species of *Cryptocoryne* are seldom formed when the plants are growing submerged; for some species to bloom is rare indeed, whatever the growth conditions. Plants seem to bloom more readily if they are rooted in a rich compost of about three parts leaf mold, two parts peat and one part coarse sand contained in closed tanks or glass jars and kept at a temperature of 24°C. At first the plants should be just submerged, the water level being gradually reduced until the foliage is growing in humid air at a temperature of 20 to 21 °C. Some species such as *C. ferruginea* and *C. retrospiralis* are unfortunately less amenable to this treatment and must be kept partially submerged.

C. retrospiralis is an unusually slender species with wavy mid-green leaves only 3 to 6 mm wide. Other *Cryptocoryne* have been introduced but most of them are unidentified and not in supply. One species, probably from Indonesia, has attractive tapering and undulating leaves about 2.5 cm across at their widest point. When young they are a bright yellowish green, but within a couple of weeks the color has passed through olive to rich brown. The newest introduction is a very beautiful species with oval to spade-shaped leaves, reddish with dark brown markings above and mahogany red underneath. This superb specimen plant, which grows to a height of 38 cm or more, has been described as *Cryptocoryne siamensis.*

Stenospermation popayanense var. *aquatica,* an unusual aroid introduced to Europe in 1950 by a Frenchman, is native to Colombia and thrives in an aquarium temperature of 15 to 27°C. When transplanted it does not lose any leaves as *Cryptocoryne* often does, and during the course of a year it forms many clusters of leaves. The plant slightly resembles *Cryptocoryne ciliata,* and its firm lanceolate pointed leaves have conspicuous veins. The flowers are surrounded by a typically aroid spathe that is pure white in color.

Even more exploited than the Aponogetonaceae, the Araceae have yielded all the species of *Cryptocoryne, Anubias, Acorus, Stenospermation* and *Pistia* which may be used in aquaria. Quite a few years ago, two species of another aroid genus, *Lagenandra,* appeared in commercial supply in England. One of them, *Lagenandra ovata,* had been previously cultivated in aquaria as *Aglaonema simplex* until it was correctly identified. Both the species of *Lagenandra* are indigenous to the coastal regions of southern India and Sri Lanka, where they grow in brackish water as well as in fresh water. Leaves are continuously produced along the creeping rootstock and there is consequently a fine display of young and mature foliage in all levels of water. Each leaf emerges from the sheath of the preceding one and the unrolling blade is borne on a stout petiole. Mature leaves have blades of about 25 cm in length and an approximate overall length of 40 to 45 cm. *Lagenandra ovata* has dark green petioles which bear lighter green blades with rather wavy margins. *L. lancifolia* is one of the half dozen or so species of aquatic plants which have variegated foliage; its dark green blades have a marginal silver band and are borne on reddish petioles.

All the plants discussed make superb specimens in decorative aquaria, but as most of them are bog species, they must be given a rich non-calcareous soil. They are most conveniently grown in a compost of garden soil, peat moss and sand confined within a small plant-pot and covered with gravel to prevent clouding of the water. Species of *Aponogeton* appreciate more sand and less humus. Plants

Barbs, tetras and Rasboras disport over a field of *Lagenandra lancifolia*.

Lagenandra thwaitesi   *Cryptocoryne nevillii*

may be propagated by division of the rootstock or by germination of fertile seed. Young seedlings of *Lagenandra* and young plants from the stolons of *Cryptocoryne* and *Stenospermation* should be grown as bog plants in a peaty soil at a temperature of 18 to 22°C. With some of the less vigorous species of *Cryptocoryne,* such as *C. thwaitesii,* care is needed to avoid removing stoloniferous young plants from the parent plant before they are sufficiently robust. Some aroids such as the *Lagenandra* and *Cryptocoryne* species prefer the more shaded sites in the aquarium and so contrast with species of *Aponogeton,* which must be bathed in bright overhead light and must be given ample room if they are to display their undulating foliage. The tendency of species of *Echinodorus* and *Aponogeton* to produce floating leaves is discouraged by pruning, a process which sets back the life cycle and at the same time discourages the formation of flowers. Of course, some species such as *Aponogeton cordatus* retain their submerged foliage more easily than others and still flower even when drastically pruned. Some species mentioned may lose a few leaves after transplanting, but when once established they produce leaves throughout the year, rarely showing any annual rest period and indeed often flowering out of their natural season.

Lagenandra lancifolia

Cryptocoryne affinis

Cryptocoryne bullosa

Flowering Plants With a Floating Habit

Floating plants are put to various uses by aquarists: when distributed evenly over the surface of the water, they reduce the intensity of light reaching the submerged plants; in masses they are of use to many spawning fishes, and they provide a sheltered habitat for fry; they have a decorative value; and for such fishes as *Leporinus* they are food. Their use results primarily from their habits of growth; some species are small and much-branched, forming a dense network of vegetation, while others have conspicuous aerial foliage and profuse submerged roots. An earlier section I discussed species of the genera *Ceratopteris, Salvinia, Azolla, Riccia* and *Ricciocarpus,* all of which had floating habits; now some genera of flowering plants shall be considered.

Bladderworts, of the genus *Utricularia,* when not in flower live completely submerged just below the surface of the water; the plants are rootless and have branched axes bearing finely divided segments from which arise small utricles or bladders. The usual botanical concepts of stem, root and leaf are of little value in describing species of *Utricularia;* some authors have regarded the whole plant body as a root system, while others have tried to differentiate between stems and leaves, interpreting the bladders as modified leaflets. Whichever interpretation is accepted, the

Utricularia sp.

Utricularia sp.

structure is certainly anomalous and shows the plasticity so characteristic of aquatic plants. The family Lentibulariaceae, to which the bladderworts belong, contains mainly marsh plants, and Goebel suggested in 1891 that the aquatic *Utricularia* are descendants of marsh forms which have become more and more involved in aquatic life. Species such as *U. minor* and *U. intermedia* are capable of producing terrestrial forms, though these do not flower.

Each bladder has a thin translucent wall usually two cells thick and is filled with water and bubbles of air; several long multicellular bristles surround the truncated entrance from which a colorless flexible valve slopes into the cavity of the bladder. There is no doubt that minute animals, particularly crustaceans such as *Daphnia* spp., *Cypris* spp. and *Cyclops* spp., are trapped within the bladders where they die slowly, possibly by asphyxiation; bacterial decay reduces the bodies to a soluble form appearing as a murky fluid which is probably absorbed by the hair-like glands in the lining wall of the bladders. Their ability to trap newly hatched fry is unquestionable.

Utricularia vulgaris

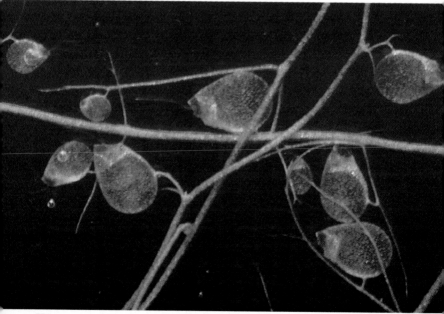

Eichhornia crassipes

In shallow water some species of *Utricularia* form "earth-shoots" which have sparse segments; these anchor the plant very firmly in the mud or sand. Another modification, known as an "air-shoot," is produced by *U. vulgaris* and *U. neglecta;* it seems to be a reduced inflorescence, thread-like, white and bearing stomata through which gaseous exchange occurs between the atmosphere and the internal tissue.

The yellow flowers of most species of *Utricularia* are borne on an aerial shoot which is maintained erect by a whorl of much-divided segments just beneath the water surface. Bladderworts reproduce vegetatively by fragmentation and, in species inhabiting temperate regions, by turions or "winter buds." In *Utricularia vulgaris,* for example, the apical region of each shoot forms, between August and November, a tight cluster of sturdy reduced leaves which is covered by a layer of mucilage. Such turions may remain attached to the parent plant throughout the winter, or they may break off and rise to the surface where the foliage opens and growth recommences in the early spring. In natural conditions turions are only formed in the fall, but they can be induced at any other time of the year by conditions of poor nutrition.

Few aquatic plants have caused serious economic problems; three which do possess this singular distinction are well-known floating species, *Pistia stratiotes,* the water lettuce, *Eichhornia crassipes,* the water hya-

Pistia stratiotes

cinth or devil's lilac, and *Salvinia auriculata*. *Salvinia auriculata* has been stimulated into an explosive phase of reproduction by conditions associated with the rising flood waters of the Zambesi. *Pistia stratiotes* forms rosettes of pale green spatulate leaves whose upper and lower surfaces are covered with minute water-repellent hairs. Over seventy per cent of the volume of each leaf is occupied by air, and when the plant is free-floating, a spongy air-filled tissue develops near the base of the leaf;

Salvinia minima

Salvinia natans

this tissue, which seems to give the plant extra buoyancy, is not formed when the rosettes are stranded on mud. In the bottom of a groove at the tip of each leaf is a small pore through which drops of water are actively extruded, usually in the early morning. Such water pores are also to be found at the apices of the leaves of most species of *Eichhornia*. During periods of bright illumination the leaves of *Pistia* spread out almost horizontally, from which position they move vertically, closing together during the night.

Pistia stratiotes reproduces itself vegetatively by proliferating young rosettes, each of which is borne away from the parent by a cylindrical fleshy stolon just beneath the water surface. When such reproduction occurs rapidly, the rosettes, stolons and profuse white roots become entangled and form a surface network which rapidly colonizes creeks, backwaters and shallow river margins. As a result *Pistia* often constitutes a great hindrance on the rivers of equatorial Africa, such as the Ogowe and the tributaries of the Congo. In her book *Travels in West Africa,* published in 1897, M. H. Kingsley wrote, "It is very like a nicely grown cabbage lettuce, and it is very charming when you look down a creek full of it, for the beautiful tender green makes a perfect picture against the dark forest that rises from the banks of the creek. If you are in a canoe, it gives you little apprehension to know you have got to go through it, but if you are in a small steam launch, every atom of pleasure in its beauty goes, the moment you lay eye on the thing. You dash into it as fast as you can go, with a sort of geyser of lettuce flying up from the screw; but not for long, for this interesting vegetable grows after the manner of couch-grass…and winds those roots round your propeller."

The vegetative reproduction of species of *Eichhornia* is very similar to that of *Pistia stratiotes;* young rosettes arise from the leaf axils of the parent and are borne out along the water surface by stout stolons. The two most frequent species, *Eichhornia crassipes* and *E. azurea,* are native to the swamps and water meadows of Brazil but have been introduced to many other countries during the last hundred and fifty years. First introduced to the Old World about 1829, *E. crassipes* had become a serious hindrance on the waterways of Java and Singapore sixty years later. In 1896, after high winds and storms had swept Florida, it blocked the St. John's River for twenty-five miles, although it was only six years before that that it had been accidentally introduced there. It also flourished in Australia and Cambodia, causing similar problems for local industries which used the inland waterways for transport. It has now spread over the African continent, colonizing the headwaters and upper reaches of the Nile River.

The size and shape of the leaves of *Eichhornia crassipes* vary at different stages of development and in different external conditions; this feature of the plant habit is known as heterophylly. Young leaves are very slender and have small circular blades; in succeeding leaves the relative proportions of the blade and stalk change, until the mature form with its ragged transparent sheath, swollen air-filled stalk and thin orbicular blade is attained. The anatomy of the leaves suggests that the blade and stalk are not equivalent to the lamina and petiole of the leaves of other aquatic plants such as *Nymphaea* spp. and *Nuphar* spp.; they probably correspond only to the petiole, the tip of which becomes flattened and widened to produce the blade. Bright light and a low temperature seem to induce more prominently swollen air-filled tissue in the stalk than do high temperatures and poor illumination. The swelling is considerably reduced in leaves formed while a plant is stranded on mud or on marshy ground.

Masses of flowering *Eichhornia*

As aquarium plants, both *Eichhornia crassipes* and *Pistia stratiotes* flourish in a humid atmosphere and with natural illumination, but they do not grow very satisfactorily in artificial light. Their range of temperature tolerance is from about 18 to 29 or 32°C, though these are not absolute limits. *Eichhornia crassipes* produces a short-lived aerial spike of large clawed flowers, violet-blue in color and often speckled with yellow. *E. azurea is* distinguished by its erect oval leaves and sessile pale blue flowers. After its introduction to Singapore, *E. crassipes* was cultivated by the Chinese, who sold its flowers in the streets. *Pistia stratiotes* produces insignificant flowers from which develop berries containing large numbers of minute seeds. It is also cultivated in China for hog food, though it must first be chopped and boiled.

The roots of both *Eichhornia* and *Pistia* form convenient natural spawning mops; those of *Pistia stratiotes* are usually white or brown, while mature roots of *Eichhornia crassipes* bear dense rows of lateral roots, in all of which there develops a purplish magenta pigment.

The family Hydrocharitaceae, whose members are all aquatic, contains three genera of floating plants known to aquarists: *Hydrocharis, Limnobium* and *Stratiotes.* The frog-bit, *Hydrocharis morsus-ranae,* forms a rosette of bronzed pale green leaves, from the base of which hang long unbranched roots densely clothed with root-hairs. From the nodes of long slender stolons which grow horizontally, just below the surface of the water, from each parent rosette, young rosettes arise throughout the summer. In autumn, or during adverse conditions, these stolons form terminal turions, each of which is enclosed by two scale leaves. When these turions break off, they usually sink to the substratum where they remain dormant until the following spring; the center of gravity of each turion is in the basal stalked end and so they remain morphologically upright. A minimum limiting intensity of light, especially at the yellow and red end of the spectrum, is required for germination to occur; then the bud scales open, the young leaves develop air-filled lacunae and the growing plant rises to the surface.

The aerial male and female flowers of the frog-bit are borne on the same plant though at different nodes; the female flowers are solitary whereas the male flowers arise in groups of two or three enclosed within a spathe. Whether male or female, each flower has three obovate white petals which are marked with yellow at their base and which usually appear ragged and crumpled. Flowers only appear if the plants are brightly illuminated almost daily throughout late spring and early summer.

Hydrocharis morsus-ranae is a widespread inhabitant of pools, small lakes and stagnant water; though it grows more successfully in cold water, it can be acclimated to a tropical aquarium. A more suitable species for warm water is the American frog-bit, *Limnobium stoloniferum*-also known as *Trianea bogotensis*-which differs from *Hydrocharis* in the structure of its leaves, which are thick, fleshy and cordate in shape.

Stratiotes aloides, the water soldier or water aloe, is a curious semi-floating species whose affinities with *Hydrocharis morsus-ranae* are revealed by the similar structure and arrangement of its flowers. The petals are larger and, in England at least, the fruit is rarely, if ever, produced. The species occurs all over Europe and northwestern Asia;

Hydrocotyle vulgaris

Limnobium stoloniferum

in the northern region the plants are female while in the south they are nearly all male. A few hermaphrodite plants have been recorded from time to time. The flowers of most members of the family Hydrocharitaceae have rudimentary male and female organs.

The stiff but brittle leaves of the water soldier sometimes grow as long as 50 cm and are usually covered with small spines, particularly at their margins. The young leaves of the offsets which are produced in the autumn are a bright rich green in color, though this becomes dark and brown as the plant matures. Each plant forms only a few roots, but these are fast-growing, increasing at an average rate of 6 to 8 cm per twenty-four hours, short-lived and quickly replaced by new ones. That plants are often unbalanced when any of these roots are experimentally destroyed suggests that their function is primarily to maintain the equilibrium of the surface rosette.

The famous rising and sinking of *Stratiotes aloides* was thought by the first observers to occur twice within each year; it is now known that the plant rises in the spring, flowers during the early summer and in late summer sinks back to the bottom of the water, where it forms offsets. The mechanism of these movements is probably a chemical one; during the summer an incrustation of crystalline calcium carbonate is deposited on the aerial leaves by the evaporation of a very dilute solution of that compound which seems to be secreted on the leaf surface by certain cells. This process, together with the waterlogging of old decaying leaves in late summer, increases the specific gravity of the plant, and it sinks. While the plant is submerged, the calcium carbonate is slowly redissolved in the water, and in spring the rapid growth of young succulent leaves probably decreases the specific gravity of the plant, which then floats up to the surface.

Though rather a large species for a coldwater aquarium, the water soldier is a fascinating plant for the outdoor pool, and there is commercially

Stratiotes aloides, showing both emersed and submersed leaves as well as flower.

Stratiotes aloides, artist's conception.

available a smaller variety, growing to about 15 cm in diameter, which flourishes in a tropical aquarium, though it does not show the same regular cycle of movements.

Trapa natans, the water chestnut, is an equally curious species with a floating habit. It occurs in many European localities and in Siberia, the Caucasus and the Far East, but it is rarely in commercial supply. It is now extinct in many places where fossil deposits have shown that it once occurred, for example Belgium, Holland, Sweden, Scotland and the lowlands of Switzerland. It is an annual species, developing from a dark brown sculptured nut, the horns of which seem to anchor the young seedling in the substratum. When the nut germinates, the first structure to emerge is the hypocotyl, which bears the two rudimentary shoots and the root. One of the two shoots is dormant while the other grows upward, producing small narrow leaves which quickly die and are replaced by adventitious roots. At the surface this shoot forms a symmetrical rosette of triangular serrated green leaves; these have glossy waxed upper surfaces and dilated petioles. The root does not respond to the force of gravity and grows upward at an angle of about 45 degrees to the vertical; it later produces many lateral roots which soon grow downward to the substratum. Though occurring naturally in temperate as well as tropical regions of the world, this species thrives in tropical aquaria.

Riccia fluitans

Trapa natans

Dwarf Aquarium Plants

There is a considerable demand from aquarists for low-growing and dwarf species suitable for the foreground of an aquarium. Aquatic ferns of the genera *Marsilea* and *Pilularia* and fern allies such as *Isoetes,* together with dwarf aroids of the genus *Cryptocoryne* and miscellaneous plants such as *Spiranthes latifolia,* have growth habits which render them useful to the aquarist. There are a number of other genera containing species

Cryptocoryne siamensis var. schneideri

with a striking appearance and a rosette or branching form of growth, all of which are admirable plants for cultivating in front of strata rockwork.

Hair grass, *Eleocharis acicularis,* forms thickets of very narrow cylindrical leaves and grows to a height of about 14 to 20 cm. New plants are produced at the nodes of slender stolons which creep along or just below the surface of the substratum; the species spreads very rapidly in clear water and a fine compost. When first planted in an aquarium, it should be given a sandy compost in which the sparse frail roots can easily anchor themselves, for in a coarse gravel medium it is apt to be uprooted by bottom-feeding fishes. The predominantly vertical growth of the plant gives it great value in relieving the horizontal lines of rock strata.

Spiranthes cernua

Elodea occidentalis

Elodea nuttallii and *E. minor* are both temperate plants which thrive in tropical aquaria under a wide range of light intensities. *E. nuttallii* will grow to a height of 30 or more centimeters, but if the apical bud of each stem is removed lateral branches readily develop and the plant can be induced to form a dense bush. Native to North America, *E. nuttallii is* distinguished from the equally widespread species of temperate regions, *E. canadensis,* the Canadian water weed or water thyme, by its paler green, twisted leaves, each of which has a bright red or brownish base. It may also be distinguished during the flowering phase; both *E. canadensis* and *E. nuttallii* have inconspicuous male and female flowers on separate plants, but whereas the male flowers of *E. canadensis* break away from the tubular spathes borne in the leaf axils and rise to the surface, those of *E. nuttallii* are carried up to the surface solitarily on thread-like stalks. The female

Eleocharis minima

Pilularia americana

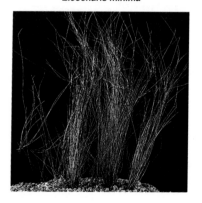

Elodea canadensis

Elodea minor

flowers of both species are borne up to the surface solitarily by an elongated floral tube; at the surface the flower opens and exposes its three receptive stigmas. Pollination is effected by the buoyant pollen grains liberated by the explosive rupture of the male flowers floating by chance onto these stigmas.

Elodea minor is a much smaller variant, though it has a similar growth habit to that of *E. nuttallii;* the pale green fragile stems bear tiny narrow yellowish green leaves which are recurved, similar to those of *Lagarosiphon major,* a species also known, erroneously, as *Elodea crispa.* Unlike those of other species of *Elodea,* the leaves of *E. minor* are not arranged in whorls on the stem. Both *E. minor* and *E. nuttallii* grow very quickly in any compost of sand or gravel, producing adventitious roots from the lower nodes of the stems once they have become established.

A foreground plant of unusual appearance which, though it grows naturally in peat bogs and acidic soils in the cooler regions of Europe and Africa, is adaptable to water at a temperature of 13 to 24°C is *Hydrocotyle vulgaris,* the pennywort. A creeping rhizome produces from each node one simple leaf consisting of a horizontal slightly lobed lamina borne on a slender petiole. The length of the petiole is extremely variable; when the plant is only partially submerged the petiole may be as short as 2 cm; but in an aquarium the petioles tend to elongate, and unless this tendency is controlled by judicious pruning the plant loses its attraction. Flowers are formed in the leaf axils when the species is growing out of water or only partially submerged; these are inconspicuous and develop into bilobed fruits which are about two millimeters in diameter. Another pennywort,

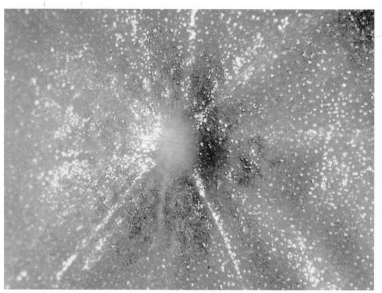

Closeup of leaf structure of *Hydrocotyle verticillata*

Hydrocotyle verticillata

Nymphoides aquatica

Hydrocotyle verticillata, occurring in the Atlantic Coast regions of North America, is very similar in structure to *H. vulgaris* and is equally useful in aquaria.

Most species of the genera *Nymphaea, Nymphoides* and *Nuphar,* all usually known as water lilies, are too large for either coldwater or tropical aquaria, but the species *Nuphar pumilum,* also known as *N. minimum,* is sufficiently small to be useful in the foreground of an aquarium. Growing from a stout rootstock, the leaves spread out so that their blades are exposed to the maximum illumination; the edges of the leaves are often furled, and the color is a rich translucent green. This plant has a wide temperature range and often grows only slowly, reaching a height of 10 to 15 cm after about a year.

Samolus floribundus, known as the water rose, is another dwarf plant which withstands a similarly wide range of temperatures. It produces compact rosettes of oval pale green leaves which are prominently veined; flowers are only formed when the plants are growing in boggy soil with most of their foliage out of the water. They grow profusely in a compost of sand or gravel and reproduce themselves under water by offsets arising close to the crown of the parent rosettes.

Lobelia dortmanna, the water lobelia, is a curious plant of Europe and parts of America; it inhabits the shallow margins of lakes with soft, rather acid water. From the short vertical stem there arise stout linear dark green leaves which bend horizontally at the tip; each leaf contains two large longitudinal air canals which give the plant buoyancy. The profuse simple white roots are frequently spirally coiled. Under natural illumination the species flowers in early summer, producing from each rosette a single scaly aerial stem bearing several bell-shaped flowers which vary in color from a very pale pink to a rich lilac. A related plant, known by the botanical name of *Lobelia cardinalis* var. *cardinalis* and originating in South Carolina, is more suitable for tropical aquaria, *L. dortmanna* being acclimated to water temperatures above 18°C only with difficulty. This plant has stout stems bearing oblong to lanceolate leaves and readily forms axillary branches after the removal of the apical buds. When grown in aquaria these two water lobelias should be rooted in a sandy medium. They thrive in any intensity of artificial light—which, however, does not encourage the formation of flowers.

Lobelia splendens

Subtropical and Temperate Plants

Several plants cultivated in tropical aquaria occur naturally not in the tropics but in subtropical and temperate regions, and their ability to grow in water at temperatures from 10 to 27°C seems to be due to the fact that they have a much more extensive range of temperature tolerance than do genuine tropical species. The aquarist is able to acclimate them to almost any desired range of water temperature; such species are exemplified by some of the most well-known aquarium plants, *Vallisneria spiralis*, *Egeria densa*, *Lagarosiphon major* and a few species of the genus *Myriophyllum*.

Vallisneria americana var. *biwaensis*

The genus *Vallisneria*, which belongs to Hydrocharitaceae, contains many plants of use to the aquarist. *Vallisneria gigantea* is native to the Philippines and New Guinea and has linear leaves growing to over a yard in length, brilliant translucent green in color and sometimes gently undulated. Its size restricts its use to large aquaria and tropical pools, but it has a wide temperature range, from about 12 to 27°C. *Vallisneria spiralis* is a smaller plant from temperate waters in every continent, and it thrives equally well in coldwater and tropical aquaria. It has linear tapering leaves produced from the short vertical stem, or crown, and reproduces vegetatively by runners above the surface of the substratum which form young plants at the nodes. The leaves of *V. americana* are spirally twisted while those of *V. spiralis* forma *rubriformis* are suffused with a reddish anthocyanin pigment which sometimes slowly disappears under artificial light and is

Vallisneria portugalensis

Vallisneria spiralis

more successfully maintained when the plants are grown in natural illumination and in water at a temperature lower than 21°C.

The pollination mechanism of *Vallisnceria spiralis* is an elaboration of that of *Elodea canadensis.* Male and female flowers are borne on separate plants; the solitary female flowers grow up to the surface on the elongated stalks of their spathes. Hundreds of male flowers, each containing two stamens and a small bubble of air, are formed within a spathe near the crown of the plant. When the spathe breaks open, the flowers are released to the surface where each one is ruptured. A man named Scott, the Director of the Calcutta Botanic Gardens, in 1869 reported "seeing under a noonday sun the innumerable florets freed from their spathes and ascending like tiny air-globules till they reach the surface of the water, where the calyx quickly bursts-the two larger and opposite sepals reflex, forming tiny rudders, with the third and smaller recurved as a miniature sail, conjointly facilitating in an admirable manner the florets' mission to those of the emerging females." The heavy female flowers depress the surface film and the males are blown to them, sliding down the slope and rubbing the sticky pollen from the dehiscing stamens onto the stigmas. The developing fruit then sinks through the water, partly due to its own weight and partly to the spiral contraction of the stalk.

A garden of *Vallisneria* makes a charming sight and, if thick enough, provides refuge for pursued small fishes.

The members of Hydrocharitaceae thus show an interesting range of floral structure. Most of the genera have unisexual flowers, but it is only in *Hydrocharis* and *Limnobium* that both sexes occur on the same plant. These two genera, together with *Stratiotes*, have conspicuous aerial flowers pollinated by insects. Other genera such as *Elodea* and *Vallisneria* have male and female flowers on separate plants and effect pollination at the water surface; in a related marine genus, *Halophila*, pollination takes place under water. Only in *Ottelia* do hermaphroditic flowers occur regularly; one species of this genus, *Ottelia ulvaefolia*, is occasionally available to aquarists. It comes from Madagascar and tropical areas of Africa and has translucent furled leaves similar to those of *Aponogeton ulvaceus* but with conspicuous carmine-tinted veins. It is a fragile plant though it has a temperature range of 18 to 32°C and will grow in fine sand or gravel.

Egeria densa.
The inset shows
flowers of this plant.

Egeria densa, also referred to as *Elodea densa,* is an American species which adapts itself to tropical or coldwater aquaria and to ornamental pools. Luxuriance of foliage is encouraged by natural illumination; in a tropical aquarium under artificial light the stems grow very rapidly and the leaves are smaller and paler green. Whereas the leaves of *Egeria densa* are arranged on the stem in whorls of four, those of *Lagarosiphon major,* previously known as *Elodea crispa,* are not whorled and usually bear short stiff hairs. Although it grows in North Africa in water at a temperature of 24 to 29°C, *Lagarosiphon major* is not as easily acclimated to warm water as is *Egeria densa.*

Egeria densa

Ludwigia repens X arcuata

A large number of species and varieties of *Ludwigia* are known to aquarists. *Ludwigia natans,* originating from the temperate regions of Europe, Asia and North America, is a fast-growing species with a temperature range of 15 to 27°C. Its stout stems bear oval bright green leaves in pairs and it forms branched adventitious roots from the lower nodes. The solitary greenish flowers are formed in the leaf axils only when the plant is growing out of water in damp soil. This species, and the related *L. arcuata,* are easily propagated by cuttings. *L. arcuata* is a less common species with slender stems bearing very narrow tapering leaves of a bronze-green color and with a more restricted temperature range.

Ludwigia repens

There are three genera of aquatic plants with a bushy growth habit and divided leaves occurring naturally in the cool waters of Europe and North America, yet possessing the ability to grow in water at higher temperatures. The genus *Hottonia* contains two species, *H. palustris*, the water violet, and *H. inflata*, a North American plant, which resemble each other in structure, culture requirements and tolerance of temperatures from about 10 to 21 °C. The whorled pale green leaves of *H. palustris* are divided into narrower linear flattened segments, and from the apex of the shoot axillary inflorescences grow up into the air under natural illumination in early summer. Each inflorescence bears whitish pink or lilac flowers and is kept erect by a symmetrical whorl of large leaves just below the water surface. The species does not produce any perennating organs; young branches arise from the base of the inflorescence and develop into new plants in the following spring. Both species of *Hottonia* will grow as floating plants or rooted in a sandy, loamy compost.

The hornwort, *Ceratophyllum demersum*, is an interesting pool or aquarium plant of unusual appearance, though the plumes of foliage are rarely as luxuriant in an aquarium as they are out-of-doors when the plant receives sunlight. The species does not form roots and, unless it is desired as a floating plant, should just be anchored in the aquarium gravel. Although the plant is brittle, young bright green leaves are hardened by a covering of cutin. In natural habitats, flowering and pollination frequently occur, but fruits rarely develop, as they require a water temperature of 27 to 32°C to attain maturity, and the plant reproduces mainly by fragmentation and by the production in late summer of dense shoot apices which remain dormant throughout the winter.

Two species of water milfoil, *Myriophyllum verticillatum* and *M. spicatum*, are widely distributed throughout Europe and North America and will thrive in aquaria at temperatures of less than 21°C. From the rhizomes of both species there arise erect branching stems bearing whorls of finely divided leaves, each with about fifteen to thirty segments, and in the summer months aerial spikes carrying male and female flowers which are wind-pollinated. The leaves of *M. verticillatum* are a deep rich green in

Hottonia sp.

Hottonia sp.

Myriophyllum spp.

color and are arranged in whorls of four whereas those of *M. spicatum* are bronze-green and are arranged in whorls of three or five. Toward the end of summer *M. verticillatum* forms club-shaped dark green turions at the apices of axillary branches. The leaves which constitute these turions are small and contain a high concentration of starch and other food reserves; in the spring the turions germinate, forming young plants anchored in the substratum by adventitious spirally coiled roots. Although naturally perennating organs, turions are formed by the plant in conditions of reduced light intensity, lowered temperature and reduced supplies of soluble nutrients.

A Brazilian species of *Myriophyllum*, *M. proserpinacoides*-the parrot's feather-has become naturalized in parts of North America and is one of the most beautiful aquatic plants. Its growth habit is really semi-aquatic as even when it is rooted its stems grow upward to produce whorls of finely divided bluish green leaves above the water. The leaves show diurnal movements, opening out in bright light and then closing up tightly round the shoot apex as the light fades; this habit is also shown by *Hygrophila corymbosa, Hygrophila difformis, Limnophila sessiliflora* and young plants of *Myriophyllum verticillatum.* As a result of its producing aerial foliage the parrot's feather is more suitable for the tropical or warm pool than for aquaria.

A common feature of aquatic plants is the tendency to produce pigmented foliage under certain conditions. The pigment is usually red or purple and, except in numerous horticultural varieties of water lilies of the genera *Nymphaea* and *Nuphar,* seems to be formed only in the superficial tissues of the leaves and stems. Species which often develop such pigment include *Bacopa caroliniana, Cabomba caroliniana, Azolla caroliniana* and *A. filiculoides,* several species of *Cryptocoryne* and *Echinodorus, Hydrocharis morsus-ranae, Vallisneria spiralis,* several species of *Ludwigia* and *Myriophyllum spicatum.* There is evidence, though it is sparse, that pigment formation is more conspicuous in plants grown in water at a temperature lower than is normal and subject to intense illumination, but a systematic investigation of the chemistry of these particular pigments and their distribution in aquatic plants is needed.

Myriophyllum aquaticum

Myriophyllum proserpinacoides

The Japanese Garden, so named by Takashi Amano, is decorated with *Micranthemum micranthemoides* as the centerpiece—with the smaller plants being *Marsilea angustilfolia,* the four-leafed clover. Photography and aquarium design by Takashi Amano from his book **NATURE AQUARIUM WORLD.**

How to Grow Aquarium Plants

The difficulties experienced by many aquarists in cultivating plants are worsened by there being few clear-cut rules or techniques. This is partly because of inadequate experimental data on the influence of physical and chemical factors on the growth of different species and partly because the cultivation of aquatic plants is still based, to some extent, on the myths and misconceptions of the early aquarists. It may be useful to discuss techniques of cultivation more fully. This survey is neither free from imperfections nor does it present any basically new techniques or ideas, but it does attempt to dispel some of the uncritical and often fantastic notions which, if their prevalence in the aquarium literature is any criterion, still influence aquarists.

The structure of a species determines the method of planting. Species which are obtained as cuttings, e.g., species of *Hygrophila, Cabomba, Limnophila, Ludwigia, Hottonia, Myriophyllum, Ceratophyllum, Cardamine, Lysimachia, Bacopa, Elodea, Egeria* and *Lagarosiphon,* should be planted in the following way:

(i) The leaves should be stripped from the lowermost nodes.

(ii) The shoots should be loosely tied in groups.

(iii) Each group should be pressed into the gravel or anchored on the surface of the gravel by attaching inert material.

Species of *Fontinalis* may be gathered from their natural habitats with the wiry stems attached to water-worn stones.

Species which are obtained as intact plants should be established as follows:

(i) Species of *Marsilea, Regnellidium, Pilularia, Acorus* and *Hydrocotyle* should have all their roots covered and their creeping rhizomes just beneath the surface of the gravel.

(ii) Species of *Microsorium* should also have their roots buried but their rhizomes creeping over the gravel.

(iii) Species of *Sagittaria, Vallisneria, Ceratopteris* and *Lagenandra* should have their roots buried and their short swollen stems, or "crowns," just above the surface of the gravel.

(iv) Species of *Isoetes, Aponogeton, Nymphaea* and *Nuphar* should have their stout tuberous or corm-like rootstocks just covered by the gravel.

Hygrophila corymbosa

(v) Species of *Echinodorus, Spiranthes, Barclaya, Cryptocoryne, Lobelia* and *Samolus* should have all their roots buried and the leaf bases at or just above the surface of the gravel.

Most aquarium plants have fragile organs, especially genuine aguatic species, the stems and leaves of which possess few strengthening elements and much spongy air-filled tissue, and care is needed in using wooden or metal planting sticks. Planting by hand, being less severe, is to be preferred. The texture of the rooting medium and the nature of the root system affect the efficiency of the planting method. For a species to become speedily established it is essential that it should have the most suitable rooting medium, particularly if the aquarium contains disturbing bottom-feeding fishes.

(i) Many species have deep vigorous root systems and grow well in fine or coarse gravel or very coarse sand.

(ii) Cuttings which have no adventitious roots require a fine gravel, which packs round and weighs down the plant better and facilitates the anchorage of young roots more than does coarse gravel.

(iii) A fine densely packing gravel is also useful for very buoyant species, such as *Lobelia dortmanna.*

Samolus floribundus in foreground.   **Samolus valerandii**

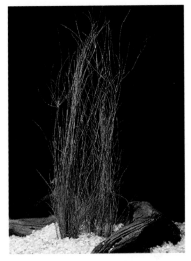

Eleocharis acicularis　　　　　　*Ceratophyllum demersum*

(iv) Species which have shallow root systems, e.g., *Eleocharis acicularis,* require a medium to coarse sand.

Roots are never formed by a few species, such as *Ceratophyllum demersum,* and are not induced to form by administering to the plant hormones of the beta-indolyl carboxylic acid series.

The possible advantages and disadvantages of mixing peat or soil with sand or gravel in the rooting medium have been debated at unnecessary length in the literature and I mention only these points:

(i) It is not fully known which substances different species absorb from the substratum in which they are rooted and which substances they absorb from the surrounding water. From observations of the thin permeable epidermis of the stems and leaves and the poorly developed roots, several pioneer plant physiologists assumed that aquatic plants absorbed all the necessary inorganic and organic substances directly from the surrounding water. There is no reason to suppose that all species require the same proportions of the different substances or that they all absorb similar relative amounts from the water and the substratum. It is reasonable to assume that aquarium plants which are bog species, growing naturally in rich organic soils, will benefit from the addition of loam to their rooting medium.

789

A properly balanced home aquarium scene using plant heights to great advantage.

(ii) To sterilize loam before using it in an aquarium destroys its value by killing most, if not all, of the microscopic bacteria, protozoa and fungi which convert the organic debris in the soil into a form which can be absorbed by the plants' root-hairs.

(iii) Peat alone is a useless addition since it contains no substances of great value to the plants. It will reduce the pH value of the water and if mixed with soil it will create a more open and less dense compost.

(iv) Sterilized gravel is not completely devoid of inorganic salts useful to the plants.

(v) The decaying leaves and feces which accumulate in the gravel probably supply many of the substances required by the plants.

(vi) An extensive layer of loam beneath the gravel of a large aquarium creates more problems than benefits. Since an undergravel filter cannot then be used, water does not circulate through the rooting medium, which therefore becomes foul and soon needs cleaning out. An undergravel filter normally causes water to circulate through the interstices of the gravel, removing noxious gases such as hydrogen sulphide which are by-products of bacterial action, and it incidentally draws the organic debris down to the roots of the plants.

(vii) Loam may be given to specimen plants grown in pots or to plants which are cultivated in separate aquaria without causing serious problems.

Of the many other factors affecting the growth of aquatic plants, the pH value of the water, light intensity and water movement are often discussed. As many species which are cultivated in nurseries and dealers' aquaria thrive in waters of a wide pH range it may be concluded that the hydrogen ion concentration of the water is not, for them, of prime importance. But the aquarist must not expect plants from temperate waters of extreme pH value either to acclimate themselves to or reach the climax of their life cycle in aquarium water of opposite pH value. For example, specimens of *Lobelia dortmanna* obtained from lakes in which the water may be pH 4 to pH 5 rarely thrive in aquarium water of pH greater than 7.

With an aquarium containing a variety of species of plants the aquarist attempts to provide an intensity of light which will be conducive to the growth of all the species but which, in fact, may not be the optimum for any one of them. In providing his plants with natural or artificial illumination the aquarist is involved in a conflict between:

(i) the different optimum intensities of light for different species,

(ii) the unknown intensity of light which will ensure healthy growth of the majority of species,

Planting (right) a cutting of *Hygrophila difformis* that
has just been snipped off the plant at left.

As plants grow (and die), reorganization is a must! Before you put your hands into the
tank, be sure they are free of soaps and chemical residues. Constant pruning and
removal of dead matter is a necessity for your aquarium garden.

(iii) the rampant growth of filamentous and free-swimming green algae, colonial blue-green algae and diatoms which occurs in intense illumination, and

(iv) the etiolation of fast-growing species, such as *Egeria densa* and *Lagarosiphon major*, which occurs in poor illumination.

It is important to remember that the intensity of light decreases with increasing depth of water because of reflection from the water surface and absorption by particles in suspension. Floating plants and vigorous submerged plants usually require the brightest illumination. Few species reach the climax of their life cycle, the flowering phase, without some natural illumination.

Bacopa monnieri

The proper way to hold a rooted plant prior to sticking it into a small pocket you've already dug into the sand.

When plants are of equal heights, they should be separated by color, with the brightest colors in the center of the aquarium.

It has been said that circulation of the water in aquaria is beneficial to plants which occur naturally in flowing waters. Examples of such plants are species of the genera *Myriophyllum, Ceratophyllum, Hottonia, Cabomba, Limnophila* and *Ceratopteris,* all of which have dissected leaves, and *Aponogeton.* Since the character of their foliage does not change in still water, movement of the aquarium water should not be considered essential for their successful cultivation.

Many aquatic plants, especially species of *Cryptocoryne,* lose some or all of their leaves soon after they have been introduced to an aquarium. The cause of this frequently reported phenomenon is not really known, but it has been vaguely suggested that the mechanical shock of transplantation, a difference in water temperature or pH value, or chilling prior to planting could be responsible.

Techniques used for the maintenance of aquarium plants are of three types:

(i) The trimming of plants.

(ii) Methods for vegetative propagation.

(iii) Methods for propagation by seed.

Trimming the foliage of aquatic plants is desirable for:

(i) Tidiness, but it should not be indiscriminate cutting; rather it should be a systematic removal of old or deformed leaves and shoots.

(ii) The stimulation of branching, by removing the apical bud of a shoot, thus partially eliminating the inhibition of growth of the axillary buds.

(iii) The prevention of the floating habit in species which are desired for the decorative value of their juvenile submerged foliage.

Vegetative propagation may be accomplished by two principal methods:

(i) By taking cuttings from established plants and by dividing rootstocks.

(ii) By cultivating natural reproductive structures produced by the plants.

Turions and dormant apices of species such as *Myriophyllum verticillatum, Ceratophyllum demersum, Utricularia vulgaris* and *Hydrocharis morsus-ranae* may be collected from wild habitats, ornamental pools or coldwater aquaria later in the year and induced to germinate in water at a temperature of 10 to 12°C. Offsets produced by rosette plants, e.g., *Samolus floribundus,* may be detached from their parents and grown in a sandy compost in shallow water. Young plants produced by stoloniferous species, e.g., *Cryptocoryne* spp. and *Vallisneria* spp., may similarly be detached from their parents and grown in the recommended compost. Plants produced viviparously by *Ceratopteris thalictroides* should be carefully removed from the parent and allowed to float until they have devel-

Microsorium pteropus

oped strong root systems. Fronds of *Microsorium* spp. which are bearing young plants should be left intact and pegged down horizontally on the surface of the gravel so that the offspring may take root without being disturbed. It is important in cultivating rare and slow-growing species, such as *Cryptocoryne thwaitesii,* that stolons and offsets should not be detached from the parent until the young plants are sturdy and almost independent.

Propagation by seed is often a long and tedious procedure. The difficulties of obtaining seeds from flowering aquatic plants are several:

(i) Sexual reproduction is remarkably uncommon in truly aquatic species, particularly those living in deep water, although they are capable of developing the necessary organs.

(ii) With dioecious species, there may not be available in the aquarium both male and female plants.

(iii) Natural methods of pollination, by insects, wind, etc., will probably not occur in aquaria, though they probably will occur in outdoor pools.

(iv) Artificial pollination is not easily accomplished with the small delicate flowers of many species and with the heterostylic condition of a species such as *Hottonia palustris.*

(v) Even if pollination and fertilization are successful the seeds may not mature.

An example of a splendidly planted aquarium which is tall and narrow.

Echinodorus uruguayensis

Aquarium plants are encouraged to flower by raising the temperature of the water, by allowing them sunlight during the later stages of growth and by refraining from pruning those species which naturally form mature floating or aerial leaves. Flowers may not be formed even after the aquarist has made all these three adjustments, or they may arise without his making any of them. Seeds are often formed by self-fertilizing species of *Echinodorus* and by species of *Lagenandra, Aponogeton* and *Ottelia.* If the aquarist is lucky enough to have male and female flowers produced simultaneously by a species which has hydrophilous pollination, e.g., *Vallisneria spiralis,* he may also get seeds produced.

Few hybrid aquarium plants have ever been obtained, though over three dozen natural hybrids occur in the pondweed genus *Potamogeton.* The rarity of inter-specific hybrids among aquatic plants is mainly due to:

(i) The practical difficulties of effecting pollination and fertilization which were mentioned above.

(ii) The species' having different flowering seasons or structurally different flowers which hinder or prevent cross-pollination.

(iii) The species' possessing some physiological incompatibility mechanism which prevents cross-fertilization.

(iv) The hybrid embryo's being inviable or later infertile.

Since those species in which sexual reproduction is rare usually propagate themselves rapidly by vegetative reproduction, the need for the aquarist to attempt to propagate them by seed is questionable.

Further Notes on Aquatic Plants

The following section gives additional information on the genera and species of a number of popular and/or interesting aquatic plants.

ANUBIAS SPECIES/*Water Aspidistras*

The water aspidistras are undoubtedly connoisseurs' plants; they are highly decorative in larger tropical aquaria, but their very slow rate of growth and propagation ensures that commercial supplies are limited and never cheap. The species known to aquarists are few and belong to the small genus *Anubias,* an aroid group related to *Cryptocoryne* and *Lagenandra,* which includes seven species in all. They are perennial rhizomatous plants from the bogs, marshes and shaded river banks of rainforests in tropical Africa. For most of the year in their natural habitats they grow above the surface of the water, being submerged for short periods during the rainy season. Yet despite this normal aerial habit they all survive for long periods when submerged in aquaria, though their growth is considerably retarded. This slow growth may be an advantage in large community aquaria, since it obviates the need for frequent pruning, assuring the aquarist of a splendid display of foliage.

The rhizome of *Anubias* is stout and branching, and since fertile seeds are difficult to obtain on the rare occasions of flowering, division of the rhizome provides the principal method of propagation. The rhizome creeps slowly along at or just below the surface of the compost, and care must be taken not to bury it too deeply when specimens are planted in the aquarium. The leaf bases should be just level with the surface of the compost. From the nodes of the rhizome there develop strong adventitious roots which branch profusely within the compost. Specimens rooted only in the shallow barren gravel of the aquarium bed show poor growth; for such sturdy plants a deep root run and an abundant supply of nutrients are essential. It is therefore recommended that specimens should be planted in pots at least 10 cm in diameter and in depth, containing a mixture of equal parts coarse sand, peat and old clay or garden soil, this compost being covered with gravel. In planting, the tough roots should be spread out in the compost, not bunched together, and the specimen should be firmly pressed down, a lighter layer of compost, then gravel, being sprinkled over the rhizome and around the leaf bases.

Anubias uruguayensis

Species of *Anubias* thrive in soft water of a slightly acid or neutral reaction. The temperature of the water should be above 21°C for most of the year; indeed, these plants will tolerate temperatures as high as 30 to 32°C. For a short period of relative dormancy it is preferable, though not essential, to reduce the temperature to within the range of 18 to 19°C. Intensity of illumination appears not to be an important factor in the cultivation of these plants, and they will thrive under artificial lights, even if they are on for only a few hours per day. Strong lighting seems to have no intrinsically harmful effects, though it does lead to the formation of thick "skins" of colonial blue-green algae on the foliage.

If sufficient tank space is available, cultivation of species of *Anubias* under bog conditions is strongly recommended, especially if the specimens purchased from dealers are comparatively young. Under such conditions, mature size and dense foliage are more rapidly achieved, and the resulting specimens may then be submerged in decorative aquaria. Sudden immersion after a prolonged period of aerial growth very rarely causes the disconcerting loss of foliage characteristic of many species of *Cryptocoryne*. Bog conditions may be simulated by keeping the plants potted in a rich compost of the type described above in a fairly deep tank in which the water is approximately level with the tops of the pots. In this culture technique humidity is probably the most important physical factor;

Anubias lanceolata

Anubias heterophylla

Anubias barteri

the tank must be covered and the atmosphere within as nearly saturated with water vapor as possible, a condition which is readily achieved by passing a vigorous air stream through the water for a few hours each day. Though some authorities state that both air and water temperatures should be as high as 25 to 30°C, It has been found that these plants thrive in such tanks if the water is about 23 to 26°C, with the air temperature varying between 20 and 23°C. Under such bog conditions mature plants may reach the climax of the life cycle and produce their inflorescences. Each inflorescence has the characteristic aroid structure, with a spadix bearing the actual flowers surrounded by a fleshy sheath-like spathe. Successful fertilization is followed by the development of small fruits which have a succulent wall and resemble berries.

Only four species are usually available to aquarists, and of these *Anubias lanceolata* is most frequently in commercial supply. It is a handsome plant reaching a height of 38 to 45 cm in cultivation, though wild plants often exceed this size. The lanceolate leaves are rich dark green in color, and each has a prominent midrib and many visible lateral veins. The leaf stalk is often tinted with reddish brown and the leaf blade sometimes curls back slightly along the margins.

Anubias barteri

Two rare small species, *A. nana* and *A. afzelii,* are admirable specimen plants for smaller aquaria or as foreground plants in larger tanks. Both bear considerable similarities in appearance to species of *Lagenandra.* They vary in height from 10 cm to 20 cm and have strikingly dark green leaves, the blades of which are often borne in a conspicuous horizontal attitude in *A. nana.*

Unlike many other amphibious plants, species of *Anubias* show little variation in vegetative structure between aerial and submerged forms; the aerial leaves are slightly thicker, tougher and larger, and their surface has a more conspicuous waxy gloss.

APONOGETON SPECIES/*The Madagascan Aponogetons*

The species of *Aponogeton* which are strictly endemic to the island of Madagascar and a few neighboring smaller islands constitute a remarkable group of aquatic plants. Some of them, such as *A. madagascariensis* and *A. ulvaceus,* have been known to aquarists for many years; others, such as *A. bernierianus, A. henkelianus* and *A. guilotti,* are less familiar. Why these plants should occur only in such a confined range is a question which has intrigued plant geographers for considerable time.

These species all resemble others of the genus in that they produce their foliage and inflorescences from a tuberous rootstock growing in the substratum. They are suitable only for tropical aquaria and should be cultivated for most of the year in water at a temperature within the range of 18 to 29°C; when the foliage begins to die down the temperature should preferably be reduced to about 13 to 16°C. Available reports suggest that in their natural ranges all the species occur in a wide variety of substrata, from thick organic mud to sand and pebbles. In the aquarium, each specimen should be planted in a flowerpot of 8 to 10 cm diameter which contains a compost of equal parts of coarse sand or gravel and loam or clay. The tuberous rootstock should be firmly buried with its growing point at, and the leaf bases just above, the surface of the compost. There are no reliable data on the influence of the pH value and the hardness of the water upon the growth of these species. The foliage is exclusively submerged, and growth is strong even if the illumination is of low intensity.

Adequate space must be afforded, because the large leaves spread outward from the rootstock and soon become tangled and damaged if they are unduly restricted. Given ample space, these and other species of *Aponogeton* provide some of the most magnificent plants available to aquarists.

There appear to be at least two forms of the lace plant, *A. madagascariensis*. The leaves of the most common form seen in aquaria rarely exceed a total length of 30 to 38 cm, the skeletal lamina being from 25 to 30 cm long and the slender petiole from 10 to 12 cm. A less common form has rather longer and much wider leaves with 8 to 12 principal veins, and the midrib of each leaf is sometimes inconspicuous. A third form bears leaves which may attain a length of 30 to 35 cm but a width of only 4 to 5 cm; these leaves are sometimes bluish green in contrast to the more usual olive-green or reddish green color. These different plants, which may be no more than growth forms developed in different prevailing physical conditions, all have the characteristic fenestration of the mature leaves; juvenile leaves, however, often show laminas in which only parts of the inter-

Closeup of a leaf of *Aponogeton madagascariensis*

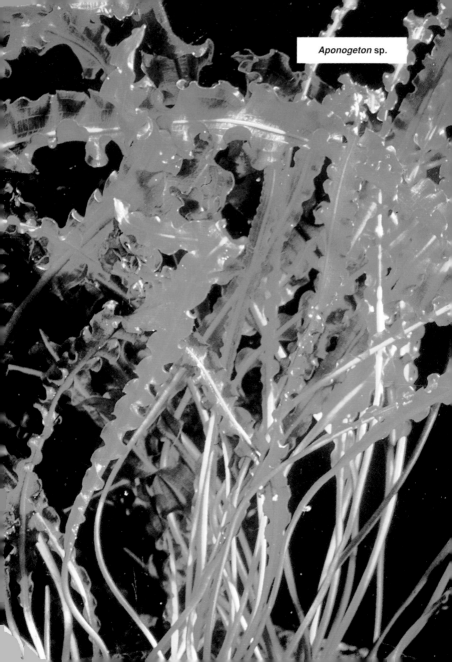

Aponogeton sp.

stitial tissue have been lost, giving an irregular "lace" effect. *Aponogeton madagascariensis* occurs principally in Madagascar, but it also occurs in the smaller islands of Sainte Marie and Nossi-Be.

Aponogeton henkelianus, found in the vicinity of the rivers Betsiboka and Ikopa in the regions of Ankasobe and Antsatrana on Madagascar itself, and *A. guilotti* both resemble *A. madagascariensis* in having skeletal leaves at maturity. *A. bernierianus,* however, resembles the juvenile specimens of *A. madagascariensis* because the leaves show an irregular "lace" effect, much of the interstitial tissue remaining even at maturity. The apex of each leaf is conspicuously pointed.

The fenestration of the leaves of these four species of *Aponogeton* has been the subject of much conjecture and is still not adequately explained. It has been suggested that this structural feature increases the surface area of the leaf available for gaseous exchange in photosynthesis and respiration and that it decreases the resistance of the leaf to the current of flowing water.

The fifth species, *Aponogeton ulvaceus,* occurs as a ricefield weed in central Madagascar; it is nevertheless one of the most beautiful of the genus. The leaves show no fenestration but are membranous and fully translucent. When the plant is mature, each leaf may reach a length of 45 cm or more and a width of up to 15 cm. Its shape is oblong-elliptical and its margins are deeply undulate; indeed, the whole leaf may be spirally twisted. Although the laminas are fragile and easily torn, the petioles on which they are borne are sturdy and fleshy, and the plant as a whole provides a strong and handsome specimen ideal as a centerpiece in a large tropical aquarium.

If allowed to develop to maturity, species of *Aponogeton* bloom quite readily under artificial illumination. The inflorescence of all species is typically aerial and first appears as a greenish elongated cone-shaped structure on a short stalk near the leaf bases. This stalk grows rapidly upward and on reaching the surface of the water it grows horizontally for a short distance before breaking through the surface; the horizontal part of the stalk is wider and more spongy and its buoyancy probably helps to maintain the aerial inflorescence erect. Above the water, the cone-shaped protective hood is shed and the inflorescence itself elongates, the flowers maturing in succession from base to apex. The African (including Madagascan) species of *Aponogeton* differ from others in having an inflorescence which is forked, the two arms diverging like the arms of a lyre. The flowers are often densely crowded on all sides of each arm, each flower usually possessing three petal-like segments, three pistils and six
810

Aponogeton madagascariensis

stamens. Among the various species, the flowers are most frequently white, those of *A. madagascarensis* having a pale yellowish tint and those of *A. henkelianus* being pale pinkish violet.

When the aerial inflorescence is produced, as in normal growth, natural pollination does not occur in aquaria and viable seeds are not formed. Occasionally some species, such as *A. madagascariensis,* produce inflorescences whose growth is apparently retarded, so that the stalk remains submerged. Self-fertilization takes place while the flowers are still enclosed in the protective hood. The resulting development of seeds is usually manifest as a swelling of the inflorescence, and the hood is thereby ruptured and shed. The seeds germinate rapidly, even while still attached to the remains of the inflorescence; sooner or later they fall to the substratum and there become rooted. Indeed, the appearance of several dozen tiny seedlings beneath the parent may be the first sign of this whole process that the unsuspecting aquarist notices.

The seedlings are very fragile and sensitive and often die at an age of four to five weeks unless they are carefully transplanted to a more suitable rooting medium. A mixture of equal parts of medium-grain sand and fine loam is recommended; a proprietary brand of good seed compost may also be used. The compost should be spread to a depth of 2 cm in a glass jar or small aquarium and covered with water from the aquarium in which the seedlings have developed. The water should be shallow at first, about 2 to 4 cm deep, and the depth should be increased gradually as the seedlings develop. The seedlings must be transferred to this container as rapidly as possible; they should be spaced about 2 to 5 cm apart, and the roots of each one should be lightly compressed into the compost. The temperature of the water should be varied as little as possible and should be within the range of 18 to 24°C. When the young plants have reached a height of about 6 to 8 cm they may be transplanted to 5 cm diameter pots.

Although considerable care and patience are essential, the cultivation of such seedlings provides a relatively easy method of propagating these valuable plants. Propagation is otherwise possible only on the rare occasions that a secondary growing point arises on the rootstock, which may be divided when the younger plant has reached a height of from 8 to 13 cm and become vigorous and sturdy.

APONOGETON SPECIES/*The Sinhalese Species*

The genus *Aponogeton* is distributed throughout tropical and subtropical Africa, Asia and Australia, and species from each of these areas have been introduced to aquaria and ornamental pools. Just as one group of species occurs only in Madagascar and its associated islands, so another group appears to be restricted in its natural distribution to Sri Lanka. Three of these species, *A. crispus, A. undulatus* and *A. natans,* are familiar to most aquarists. The cultivation of these and other species is in all respects similar to that of the Madagascan species.

The mature foliage of *Aponogeton crispus* consists of a thick rosette of narrow leaves arising from the terminal growing point of the

Aponogeton ulvaceus

stout tuberous rootstock. It is, however, one of the smaller species of the genus, and the leaves do not normally exceed a height of 30 cm; hence, the species is of great value in small and medium tropical aquaria. A group of three or four of these plants, spaced about 5 to 8 cm apart, provides a bold and striking feature. The elongated lanceolate leaves are usually bright green and have tightly crinkled margins and finely tapering apices.

Aponogeton undulatus is rather more variable in habit and generally taller at maturity, reaching a height of 50 to 60 cm. The foliage varies in color from pale green to dark green, olive or even bronze.

Each leaf is lanceolate, the lamina tapering at its apex and narrowing gradually to the petiole at its base. In contrast to *A. crispus,* the margin of the lamina is gently furrowed, so that the leaf appears to be smoothly undulate rather than crinkled. The lamina is usually between 20 and 40 cm long and from 1 to 5 cm wide at its widest point. In texture it is often more or less translucent. At maturity, and usually prior to flowering, *A. undulatus* produces long-petioled floating leaves which are pale green in color and narrowly lanceolate in shape, reaching a length of 5 to 13 cm and a width of 1 to 3 cm. The inflorescence arises in a manner similar to that of the Madagascan species: when the stalk emerges from the water, the inflorescence itself, which is then about I to 2 cm long and hooded, begins to grow, the lowermost flowers opening first. Within three to four days the inflorescence is mature and from 8 to 13 cm long. It resembles the inflorescence of other non-African species of *Aponogeton* in that it includes but a single spike of flowers, which, in *A. undulatus,* are white.

In the early stages of growth, *Aponogeton natans* closely resembles the less common Madagascan *A. ulvaceus* and is, indeed, sold as such by Sinhalese shippers and many aquarium dealers. The earliest leaves are broadly lanceolate to elliptical in shape and quite flat. Later they become more nearly oblong with deeply undulate margins. At the approach of maturity, the submerged leaves are from 20 to 25 cm long and 5 to 8 cm wide. These leaves are borne on stout petioles that are up to 20 cm long. Throughout growth the submerged foliage is pale green and membranous, though rather less translucent than that of *A. ulvaceus.* A fully mature plant also possesses long-petioled floating leaves which are oblong-elliptical in shape and have a rounded tip and abrupt base. They are from 5 to 15 cm long.

The Dutch authority H. W. E. van Bruggen has described a species of *Aponogeton* found in a consignment of plants imported to Amsterdam from the Atweltota in southern Sri Lanka. The species possesses a dark creeping rhizome thickly clothed with fibrous roots. The laminas are borne on angular petioles from 20 to 35 cm long. The lamina, the most notable character of which is its rigidity, which suggested the name *Aponogeton rigidifolius,* is from 25 to 50 cm long, 2 to 2.5 cm wide, narrowly lanceolate in shape and tapering very gradually to the petiole at the base. The texture of the leaves is nontranslucent, the color is dark green, and the margins may be flat or shallowly undulate. The inflorescence consists of a single spike about 15 cm long and densely clothed with white flowers.

Most of the species of *Aponogeton* that are admired and used by aquarists are strictly tropical and are of no value in cooler aquaria or ornamental pools out-of-doors, unless these are in warm humid localities. There are, however, several species of the genus with a natural distribution extending through subtropical and temperate regions of Africa and Australia, and these show greater tolerance of temperature fluctuations.

The Australian species *Aponogeton loriae* is suitable for cultivation in water at temperatures from 10 to 27°C and may, therefore, be grown in either tropical or cool aquaria. Its tuberous corm-like rootstock should be firmly anchored in a compost (of equal parts of coarse sand and loam) contained within a flowerpot 8 cm in diameter. It will also grow satisfactorily if it is merely rooted in the bottom gravel of the aquarium, provided that this is no shallower than 6 cm in order not to restrict the profuse adventitious roots which develop from among the leaf bases and grow to a considerable length. The bright yellowish green foliage is almost entirely submerged and arises as a rosette from the growing point of the rootstock. At maturity the overall height of the leaves is from 45 to 55 cm. Each lamina is from 24 to 40 cm long and is borne more or less erect on a sturdy petiole. Apart from their color and rougher texture, the leaves bear a marked resemblance to those of *Aponogeton undulatus,* being lanceolate in shape and having undulating margins. At the time of flowering a few floating leaves may arise. These leaves are borne on long thin petioles and are from 5 to 8 cm long and oblong-elliptical in shape. The aerial inflorescence is from 5 to 10 cm tall and consists of a solitary spike of yellow flowers. As has previously been noted for other species of *Aponogeton,* the inflorescence is produced in aquaria even if the illumination is only artificial. *A. loriae* also resembles other species in requiring adequate space to spread its submerged foliage and in becoming depauperate or incompletely developed if cramped.

One species which is eminently suited to cultivation in heated pools or in pools out-of-doors in temperate countries in summer is *Aponogeton desertorum,* the dog-with-two-tails, which was formerly known as *A. kraussianus* and is distributed in Africa northward from Cape Province to Angola, Ethiopia and Eritrea. Its tuberous rootstock grows in mud and produces long-petioled leathery floating leaves, each of which is from 8 to 15 cm long, 5 to 8 cm wide, oblong in shape and rounded at both base and apex. In common with other African species, *A. desertorum* produces a twin-spiked inflorescence. The inflorescence stands about 15 cm above

Aponogeton rigidifloris

the surface of the water, and each arm bears many sweetly scented sulphur-yellow flowers. In southern Africa, together with species of *Nymphaea, Aponogeton desertorum* is important as a rampant weed of irrigation dams. It is occasionally imported with other aquatics into the western world and there cultivated in horticultural nurseries. Its cultivation is relatively easy. It should be rooted in an ample volume of a compost of equal parts of loam and clay, to which a little sand and organic manure has been added, contained within a large pot or wire basket and submerged at a depth of not more than about 60 cm. Frost and ice usually kill the rootstock, so it is recommended that the plant be lifted before the winter if it is out-of-doors and stored in damp moss or soil until the following April.

The Cape water hawthorn, *Aponogeton distachyus,* which is native to South Africa, has been used as an ornamental aquatic for many years and, probably by periodic escape, has become more or less naturalized in numerous localities in western Europe and the U.S.A. Except in very harsh winters, because it is a hardy plant, it need not be removed from an outdoor pool. Its tuberous rootstock is edible, and each spring it produces many floating leaves which quickly spread over the available water surface if conditions are good. Each leaf is about 15 cm long by 4.5 cm wide, oblong-elliptical in shape and rounded at both base and apex. The two arms of the inflorescence sometimes float on the water or stand about 5 cm above it. On each arm there are usually about ten fragrant white flowers, each of which possesses just one petal-like segment and from 6 to 18 jet-black anthers. The petal-like segments are unusually large and stand out laterally from the spike so that each arm of the inflorescence appears much wider in proportion to its length than is typical for other species of *Aponogeton.*

The Cape water hawthorn should be cultivated in a manner similar to that described for *A. desertorum,* and it thrives equally well if it is rooted merely in clay. Its tolerance of different rooting media and of a wide range of temperatures renders it one of the most versatile plants for pools. Another related plant, the blue water hawthorn, *Aponogeton leptostachyus lilacinus,* resembles *A. distachyus* in general structure, differing only in its bluish violet flowers and in not being completely hardy. It may be grown out-of-doors in summer but must be lifted inside with the approach of cooler water. Aquarists possessing large cool or heated tanks may cultivate both water hawthorns as aquarium plants, but some natural illumination is usually necessary to induce flowering, and the specimens must be pruned annually to prevent growth from becoming too rampant.

818

Bacopa amplexicaulis   *Bacopa monnieri*

BACOPA AMPLEXICAULIS

This plant of the family Scrophulariaceae comes from the southeastern United States and from Central America. In its natural habitat it is found as both an emerged and amphibious plant.

The emerged form has a stem with a diameter of 2 to 4 mm. It grows creepingly, is weakly fuzzy and reaches lengths up to 1 meter in nature. The upper surface of the oval leaves is shiny green, while the underside shows a slight fuzz. The flowers are dark blue. On submerged specimens dark veins stand out on the leaves. The leaves are slightly wavy. The stems may be partly recumbent, so that under good conditions they soon cover a large part of the surface of the tank. Otherwise the plant also reproduces by means of cuttings from parts of the stalks.

Bacopa amplexicaulis is a good aquarium plant, but it needs acid water. Temperatures are of little importance. Direct sunlight is unfavorable, and the species thrives best in shadowy locations. Artificial lighting usually makes it grow up vertically. In order to give it the correct lighting conditions it is advisable to place some floating plants *(Ceratopteris, Salvinia)* on the surface. Growth is not especially quick, but even older leaves keep fresh for long periods. *Bacopa* should be protected against algae infestations; leaves covered with algae quickly rot and drop off. This is one reason why the plant should not be subjected to continuous bright light.

A close relative of the described plant is *Bacopa monnieri.* But even a quick glance shows us the difference between the two species. *Bacopa monnieri* has very small leaves without clear veins. In tall tanks the stalk may reach the same length as that of *B. amplexicaulis,* but then it loses its lower leaves. Also, it is richly branched out.

Lush stands of *B. amplexicaulis* are very ornamental and impressive. It is good advice not to meddle too much with the plant by moving it from place to place. The species is advisable for hobbyists with some experience.

CABOMBA SPECIES/*Fanworts*

The genus *Cabomba* comprises several species of beautiful submerged aquarium plants, some familiar to hobbyists, some new. All the species possess finely divided submerged leaves arranged in opposite pairs or in whorls, and prior to flowering they produce small floating leaves which are undivided and resemble, in miniature, those of water lilies of the genus *Nymphaea,* to which plants the *Cabomba* species are in fact related. Although they are perennial plants tolerating a wide range of temperatures, they are sensitive to harsh changes of conditions and must be cultivated with considerable care.

One of the most frequently grown species, *Cabomba caroliniana,* exists in several varieties, each differing in details of vegetative structure. The submerged foliage of all the varieties varies in color from a purplish brown to a bright green, the purple tints being developed more conspicuously in cooler water under good sunlight. The submerged leaves are paired and divided into segments which have spatulate tips. The most common form in aquaria is *C. caroliniana* var. *paucipartita,* which has comparatively few segments in each leaf, whereas var. *multipartita* when mature has huge leaves divided into many dense segments, each leaf reaching a diameter of 5 to 6 cm. The floating leaves of *C. caroliniana* are narrowly lanceolate; the flowers are white, with a yellowish center.

The submerged leaves of *C. aquatica* are finely divided and paired; the floating leaves differ from those of *C. caroliniana* in being rounded, and the flowers are rich yellow.

In addition to the above *Cabomba* species, three other species have become available to aquarists. *C. australis,* from the Argentine, Chile and Uruguay, has submerged leaves which are very finely divided into many hair-like segments which are bright green, sometimes tinted red on the underside at their tips. The basal segments usually grow at right angles to the petiole, giving the leaf as a whole a semi-circular shape. The floating leaves of this species are ovate to elliptical, and the flowers are white.

Cabomba caroliniana

From the Caribbean region and South America comes *C. piaubyensis,* which is a more slender and graceful plant than the other species. The submerged leaves are sparsely divided into numerous fine segments which are pale green in color at most temperatures but often suffused with reddish brown in cool water. The flowers are a striking deep mauve, and the floating leaves formed during the flowering phase are linear-lanceolate and acutely pointed.

Whereas most species of *Cabomba* have paired submerged leaves, *C. warmingii* commonly has whorls of three leaves at each node of the stem. The leaves are comparatively small and irregularly divided into many

Cabomba furcata

short segments; the color is commonly brownish green, and young growing shoots are brilliant mahogany red.

It is scarcely possible to give details of the overall size of species of *Cabomba,* because they readily adapt themselves to a particular depth of water and may grow to enormous lengths just under the surface. As a result of their habit of growth they are all easily propagated by cuttings taken from the long stems; the formation of adventitious roots from the lower nodes is quite rapid but may be further hastened by stripping off the lowermost leaves before planting the specimen. Once established, the plants may be induced to form bushes of foliage useful for background or side decoration in the aquarium by carefully removing the apical bud of each of the more vigorous shoots.

All the species appreciate a rich compost of equal amounts of coarse sand and clay or loamy garden soil; they do not tolerate very acid water, and they should be left to establish themselves and disturbed as little as possible. Frequent transplanting ruins their growth. In their natural geographical range most of the species extend into subtropical and warm temperate regions and tolerate quite low temperatures, at least during the winter months. Their growth is substantially improved if they are maintained in water at 18 to 25 °C for about eight months of the year and at lower temperatures of 10 to 15°C for the remaining time. The more tropical species, such as *C. aquatica,* will of course stand higher temperatures and should not be grown in water at less than about 15 to 17°C. Artificial illumination should be bright; growth becomes more luxuriant if the plants are exposed to some sunlight, at least during the summer months. The finely divided foliage is unfortunately liable to infestation with algae and fine sediment, and care must be taken to prevent this from spreading as soon as it appears. If the water is soft, not above 6 DH, the growth of algae is less troublesome.

Under natural illumination, and occasionally under intense artificial lights, the floating leaves and aerial flowers are produced, even in quite small tanks. The flower stalks show conspicuous post-floral movements, bending over, becoming submerged and eventually pointing vertically downward; this is a common adaptation for dispersal of the fruits, though it frequently occurs even when the flowers have not been pollinated.

CRYPTOCORYNE SPECIES

Many species of *Cryptocoryne* are not easy to cultivate, but the three to be described here, *C. affinis, C. becketti* and *C. axelrodi* have long been known to aquarists, and their sturdy growth in a relatively wide variety of conditions recommends them as suitable for novices. All species of *Cryptocoryne* must be handled with care. They should be potted in a compost containing soil or clay, peat and sand with the growing point of the rhizome at the surface of the compost. Their foliage must not be harshly cut back, and the plants must be left undisturbed, as they are rather slow in establishing themselves. The temperature of the water should normally be between 20 and 27°C; the illumination should be of low to medium intensity.

Cryptocoryne beckettii

Cryptocoryne affinis is one of the few species particularly suited to submerged growth; indeed, it usually deteriorates if its foliage is exposed above the water. From the creeping rhizome arise handsome lanceolate leaves to a height of 25 to 30 cm. The petiole is approximately equal in length to the lamina and is usually brownish red. The lamina, the margin of which is often slightly undulated, has a rich bluish green upper surface which frequently shows a silken sheen; the midrib and principal lateral veins are conspicuously pale, sometimes almost white. The leaves of mature specimens display a dark reddish purple lower surface, but this pigmentation is incomplete or is absent from young plants. The inflorescence of this species is usually produced on specimens growing in shallow water; its spathe normally opens just above the water surface, rarely while still submerged. The flag of the spathe is dark red and has a long tapering tip. The growth of *C. affinis* tends to be suppressed by intense illumination and is most

Cryptocoryne axelrodi

luxuriant in shade; the species is therefore particularly suitable for the foreground, where it is likely to be overshadowed by taller specimens. In such positions it rapidly covers all the available area by forming many stolons which grow horizontally through the bottom gravel, rooting and forming young rosettes of foliage at their nodes.

The Sinhalese species *C. beckettii* reaches a mature height of 10 to 12 cm when growing submerged. The robust rhizome, which may grow more or less erect, produces a dense cluster of leaves which seem to attain greater size and better color in slightly acid water and diffuse illumination. The petiole of each leaf is brownish and bears an elongated lanceolate to elliptical lamina, the upper surface of which is always olive-green to greenish brown, whereas the lower surface is often brownish purple. As was noted for *C. affinis,* these purplish and brownish tints become deeper with increasing age. The margin of the lamina is usually widely furrowed and partly folded back, and the principal veins are sometimes purplish on the upper surface. *C. beckettii* is also one of the easiest species to grow in bog conditions. Its aerial leaves are notably shorter and broader than the submerged ones. The species very rarely blooms when it is growing submerged; inflorescences may, however, appear on emergent plants growing in natural light or good artificial light for several hours each day. The flag of the spathe is greenish to ochre yellow, whereas its throat is at first dark chocolate brown and after two to three days more reddish brown. When the spathe opens, the flag, the left margin of which has irregular indentations, stands erect, but toward the end of the blooming period it bends over backward.

Cryptocoryne axelrodi is one of the most freely available and least expensive species of the genus. In coloring and habit its foliage is somewhat variable, and it is possible that there are several different growth forms. It resembles *C. becketti* in its overall size, attaining a maximum height of 10 to 12 cm, and since its foliage is most frequently borne erect it is seen at its best when numerous specimens are planted together in a group. To allow for subsequent growth, however, they should not be too closely planted; a space of 5 to 8 cm between specimens is adequate. The petiole of each leaf is usually reddish brown; the lamina varies in color from pale green to deep green and brown with the veins tinted purple or brown on both the upper and lower surfaces. On mature leaves the whole of the lower surface may be suffused with reddish purple. The lamina may reach a length of 15 to 20 cm and a width of 2 to 2.5 cm; it is narrowly lanceolate in shape, tapering to a fine tip, and its margin is usually furrowed.

Cryptocoryne axelrodi has a relatively slow rate of growth, but once it has become established it reproduces vegetatively by means of stolons bearing young plants at the nodes. When exposed above water its leaves are shorter and broader, and if it is so grown under diffuse light of medium to high intensity it may flower. The inflorescence is characterized by the spirally twisted upright flag of the spathe; the flag is bright brownish green, whereas the throat is of a similar shade but bears a faint yellow marking. The flag differs from that of *C. beckettii* in having an entirely smooth margin.

Cryptocoryne nevillii

This plant comes from Sri Lanka, where it grows in swamps and at damp spots. Often it is even found among grass coverings.

The white rootstock branches out very richly, which is why plants that have been kept under good aquarium conditions for a long time eventually form a real lawn. Maintained in aquaria, C. *nevillii* reaches a maximum size of only 10 cm. The leaf surface, lanceolate-oval in shape, has a length of 4.5 to 7 cm and a width of 1 to 2 cm. It is olive-green, with the underside a little lighter in color. The color of the leaves is constant under all conditions and never changes into any other tonality. The plant does not bloom below the surface. The flower spathe is cylindrical in its lower part and funnel-shaped at its upper part. The tip of the spathe has a thin pointed shape and measures about 3 cm in length. The throat of the flower

Cryptocoryne spiralis   *Cryptocoryne nevillii*

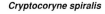

is dark red. The plant propagates easily by means of small shoots from the richly ramified rootstock as well as from independent rootstocks.

C. nevillii grows quite well, even if the water is on the hard side. Despite the fact that a temperature of 25°C is ideal, turning the warmth down to 18°C temporarily has no permanently damaging consequences. Although the plant takes its nourishment mainly from the soil, no special bottom stratum is demanded. Unwashed gravel will do perfectly well, especially if you place a fertilizer pill into it from time to time. Slow growth and slow reproduction have not posed any obstacles to the plant's becoming popular with hobbyists.

Cryptocoryne crispatula

C. nevillii groups into layers that form a green carpet in the foreground of the tank. The species grows satisfactorily even in rather deep tanks (up to 60 cm). If you want to get your plant to reproduce in a quicker way, choose a shallow tank (15 to 30 cm). Since the new leaves are of rather slow growth, be careful to protect them against algae infestations. This is the reason why it is advisable to keep many small algae-eating fishes in the same tank.

There are two forms of C. *nevillii,* a broad-leaved form and a narrow-leaved form. Both forms, unfortunately, are subject to leaf decay. But even plants attacked by leaf decay do not die quickly, because the rich root system of the plant provides the plant with a reserve of strength to fall back on.

Cryptocoryne pontederifolia

Cryprocoryne pontederifolia comes from Sumatra and northern Borneo. There it grows in the jungles as an amphibious plant, underwater during part of the year and emergedly after the floodings recede. In this latter form it also blooms. This plant is one of the attractive novelties which, although not often seen, soon becomes appreciated.

Emerged plants show leaves and stalks that are 10 to 15 cm long and usually are placed in a slanted position around the middle. The lower leaves touch the bottom and grow horizontally. The leaf stems are strong, green and generally as long as the leaves, these latter being tough and leathery, 6 to 7 cm long, 3 cm wide and oval. The surface of the leaves is light to brownish green, often with a golden tint. Along the veins the leaves sometimes are reddish brown, so that in certain cases only the veins show colors, while on other occasions the coloration spreads over large areas around the main veins.

The leaves of the submerged form turn upward at a slant and are not disposed horizontally like those of emerged plants. The green color of the surface is of a lighter shade, and with aquarium-grown plants it never becomes as colorful as that of plants kept in terraria. Plants that are kept always submerged reach larger dimensions, and the leaves with their stems measure up to 20 cm. The stems are longer than the leaves, so that underwater and emerged leaves are of about the same size.

The inflorescences of the plants bred in hothouses open fully. The complete inflorescence measures 7 to 15 cm. The petioles are very short (only a few millimeters); the kettle (thermophore) usually is 1.5 cm long, being narrowest in the lower part and flaring open upward. Viewed from above it is nearly colorless, rarely presenting little red dashes, while the inner walls turn an intense velvety purple. This coloration goes down to the widest point of the kettle, from whence it proceeds downward in the form of thin long stripes consisting of light red to purple dots disposed in regular rows. The tube of the inflorescence has the same width as the upper part of the

Cryptocoryne affinis

kettle, which makes *C. pontederiifolia* an exception within its genus. The spathe is opened vertically, very short, and shows a striking warty wine-red. The mouth of the tube is dark purple, also warty. The sheath is extended into a long erect little tail-like appendage which grows ever longer when the other parts of the flower are together. The walls of the kettle as well as of the tube are fleshy, very thick and brittle. The inflorescence is very attractive and interesting due to its huge size, and its many-colored hues reinforce this impression.

Cryptocoryne wendtii

Reproduction is mostly achieved from emergedly cultivated plants. *C. pontederiifolia* is one of the species in which the young do not grow directly out of the rootstock but come from offshoots. Out of its roots one parent plant generally puts forth two or three shoots, on each of which originates a new plant at a distance of 8 to 12 cm. Sometimes such offshoots continue growing further on, so that one single branching-out gives origin to two or three plants which in turn are able to grow independently and to divide into new specimens. Considering the fact that the species is sensitive and relatively rare, it is not advisable to cultivate it emergedly in the terrarium but rather to propagate it in special tanks in its emerged form. This is the only way of getting it to reproduce quickly.

When cultivated in the aquarium, *C. pontederiifolia* should be kept in very clear soft water at temperatures of 20 to 25°C, with a pH of 5 to 6.5 and under diffused lighting. The plant makes a very decorative centerpiece if planted in groups of three to five specimens. In winter it is advisable to adjust the supplementary lighting in a manner that the plants receive twelve hours of light each day. Otherwise during these shortened days it tends to lose its leaves, stops growing and only revives in spring if the relatively little branched rootstock has not died in a tank with insufficient lighting.

Cryptocoryne spiralis

Usually considered a slow grower and not much of a plant to look at, even though it is a member of the popular plant genus *Cryptocoryne, Cryptocoryne spiralis* is not a truly popular aquarium plant, although it finds its way into the tanks of specialists from time to time. In some ways the long tapering leaves make the plant look more like a *Vallisneria* species than a *Cryptocoryne* species; the flower and spathe form, of course, make it unquestionably a *Cryptocoryne* despite its superficial resemblance to plants of other genera; the flowering apparatus of *C. spiralis* is, as a matter of fact, among the most eye pleasing of all *Cryptocoryne* species, providing the small bit of distinction that the plant has. It is native to India, where it grows mostly in swamps that are only occasionally flooded.

The rootstock of *C. spiralis is* very strong and richly equipped with branches that bear five to 10 relatively long leaves. The leaves and stems are up to 35 cm long; the green leaves are elongatedly elliptical, often nearly in the shape of ribbons, measuring 10 to 20 cm in length by 1 cm to 2.5 cm in width. Both sides of the leaves show a fresh green, the lower side being of a slightly lighter hue, and the leaves have a strikingly protruding central vein, while the lateral veins are nearly indistinguishable.

**Flowering apparatus of a typical
Cryptocoryne species.**

Cryptocoryne lucens

The leaves taper at both ends, gradually melding into the leaf stalk at the basal end.

In fish tanks *C. spiralis* grows very slowly. It demands good illumination, preferably locations that receive direct sunlight during part of the day at least. If placed at darker or shaded spots it develops thin leaves and does not resemble the other species of the genus at all. It needs slightly acid to neutral water and temperatures above 20°C.

Specimens that are chosen to preserve and reproduce the species are best kept in an aquarium that is covered with a glass pane or a sheet of clear plastic. A fit substratum is peat moss fertilized with the usual plant foods, which should not contain any calcium derivatives. The plant is fertilized by means of an admixture of mineral solutions to the water according to the manufacturer's instructions. Under such conditions *C. spiralis* develops quite well; within a year a single parent plant may produce five to 10 offspring, which always grow from offshoots of the roots. These descendants only come directly from the rootstock. The offshoots often grow to a distance of up to 40 cm from the parent plant, and each of them puts forth one or (rarely) two new offshoots and plants.

If cultivated in this way, *C. spiralis* blooms easily and the plant gives origin to new inflorescences at intervals of three to six weeks. The flowers contain aromatic bodies that smell like roses.

ECHINODORUS SPECIES/*Amazon Swordplants*

The species of *Echinodorus* whose habit of growth and leaf shape place them within the popular designation of Amazon swordplants may be divided on the basis of overall size into two groups: the larger specimen types and the dwarf types. The larger species, including *E. paniculatus, E. amazonicus* and *E. berteroi,* reach a mature height of 25 cm or more and so are suited only to larger aquaria. The dwarf types, including *E. grisebachii, E. tenellus* and the newest introduction, *E. andrieuxii,* are suitable for all tropical aquaria and are particularly useful in the foreground, where they quickly form a carpet-like thicket of foliage.

Many species of *Echinodorus* are heterophyllous; this habit is notably illustrated by *E. berteroi,* which is sometimes known as the cellophane plant in allusion to its translucent foliage. This species occurs as a perennial swamp plant in the central and southern United States, the West Indies and Central America. It has a compact rootstock which may be split quite easily, and when submerged it first produces linear then lanceolate leaves, each with a short petiole and growing to a length of 20 to 30 cm. With increasing age the petiole becomes comparatively longer and the lamina shorter and broader until the mature cordate shape is attained in floating and aerial leaves. At maturity the inflorescence, composed of small white flowers, may be produced in good illumination; if this is kept submerged young plants often develop on it. The species produces no runners and should be rooted in a rich compost of coarse sand, soil and some peat: it tolerates temperatures above about 19 to 20°C and thrives in light of high intensity.

E. paniculatus is the species to which the popular name of Amazon swordplant was probably originally applied. The pale green lanceolate leaves have pointed tips, and the tissue of the lamina runs along part of the petiole at the base. The leaves are usually arched so that the plant forms a striking large rosette of foliage. Submerged specimens very rarely produce an inflorescence; if this does form, the flowers usually fail to mature, and young plants arise at intervals along the stalk, which may therefore be anchored to the aquarium gravel until the plants have become established. The species is widely distributed as an amphibious plant throughout much of the tropics and subtropics of South America. Two varieties of the normal species are commonly available to aquarists: *E. paniculatus* var. *rangeri* and *E. paniculatus* var. *gracilis. E. paniculatus* var. *rangeri* has noticeably broader leaves, whereas var. *gracilis* has linear to linear-lanceolate leaves. Specimens of all three attain a mature height of 40 to 50 cm and should be planted in 10 cm pots containing a compost of sand, clay or loam, and a little peat. In correspondence with their normal geographical range, these plants tolerate a wide range of temperatures, from about 18 to 32°C. Illumination need not be of high intensity.

Echinodorus parviflorus

The Amazon swordplant *E. amazonicus,* occurring in Brazil, is a smaller species which reaches a height of 25 to 38 cm. It is otherwise structurally similar to *E. paniculatus,* with pointed lanceolate leaves when it is growing in water. The aerial leaves have longer petioles and shorter, broader laminas with the venation in conspicuous relief on the lower surface. When the plant is partly or wholly above the water it produces a sturdy inflorescence as much as 60 cm in height. Submerged, its habit resembles that of *E. paniculatus,* since young plants are frequently formed on the flower stalks; its culture is also similar.

The three dwarf species of swordplant reproduce vegetatively by forming young rosettes at the nodes of fast-growing runners, several of which

836

Echindorus grisebachi

may be produced from the compact rootstock of a single parent. Indeed, once they are established these species often spread with embarrassing profusion, even if they are rooted only in gravel or coarse sand. Because of this tolerance of a less rich rooting medium it is unnecessary to pot specimens. However, they grow to greater size if the rooting medium is enriched by some soil or clay. All three species thrive as foreground plants even if they are overshadowed by taller plants and the light they receive is of very low intensity. They appear to be equally tolerant of different degrees of hardness in the water.

E. grisebachii is a perennial bog species from Central America; growing above water in natural habitats, it reaches a height of 15 to 20 cm, the leaves being dark green, pointed and elliptical to lanceolate. Submerged in aquaria, it rarely attains this size and its leaves are more commonly narrower; the shape is nevertheless variable, and broad-leaved and narrow-leaved forms are frequent. The temperature of the water should be between 21 and 29°C.

E. andrieuxii is also a vigorous grower, quickly forming numerous runners. The bright green sessile leaves are linear and spiky in young specimens, broader and arched in more mature ones. Young plants arising at the nodes of runners form many adventitious roots and soon establish themselves.

Often referred to as the pygmy chain swordplant, *E. tenellus* has been known to aquarists for many years; it has a vast geographical range, being distributed throughout much of North, Central and South America. In natural habitats the species rarely grows taller than 10 cm, and in tropical aquaria its height is most commonly 2.5 to 5 cm. The pale green narrow pointed leaves grow densely in arched rosettes, and by vegetative reproduction the species rapidly weaves a thick carpet over the compost. In the different regions of its natural range annual coldwater and perennial tropical forms probably occur; as a consequence of the extension of its distribution through temperate as well as tropical habitats, it tolerates a wide range of temperatures in aquaria and will grow well in water as cool as 7 to 10°C.

Although numerous species of *Echinodorus* have been cultivated extensively, *E. muricatus,* the Amazon spearplant, and *E. major,* the ruffled swordplant, are still comparatively rare in commercial supplies, especially in European countries. Both species are large and produce superb rosettes of foliage, and they are consequently highly prized specimen plants for tropical aquaria. In both habit and general structure they differ markedly from other members of the genus; they do, however, resemble other

Echinodorus bolivianus var. *magdalensis*

species in being perennial and in producing their foliage from a stout rootstock. They both adapt themselves readily to submerged growth and usually thrive in aquaria if they are given a rich deep rooting medium and illumination of medium to high intensity.

The popular name of *Echinodorus muricatus* indicates the shape of its mature leaves, each of which may attain a height of 35 to 40 cm. The petiole, which is stout and fleshy, varies in length from 15 to 25 cm and the lamina from 12 to 20 cm, the petiole normally being more or less erect and bearing the lamina at an inclined angle or even in a horizontal position. The vivid green lamina is shaped like the blade of a spear, with a finely tapering apex and an abrupt slightly rounded base; the only variation is in its width, juvenile leaves being relatively narrower than mature ones. There are from five to eleven principal lateral veins departing from the midrib at the base of each lamina. When fully established, the plant spreads its leaves to receive the maximum light and so forms a bold and handsome specimen ideal for central siting in the aquarium.

Echinodorus sp.

Echinodorus muricatus

Echinodorus major

The ruffled swordplant, *Echinodorus major,* bears a certain superficial resemblance to *Aponogeton undulatus,* from which its foliage may easily be distinguished by the blunter tips and the venation of the leaves. Each leaf is narrowly lanceolate, almost strap-like, and may attain a height in mature specimens of 40 to 50 cm and a width of from 3 to 5.5 cm. The lamina is usually eight to ten times longer than the petiole, which rarely exceeds 8 cm. The leaf tissue is somewhat translucent, especially in newly formed leaves, but this appearance is likely to be misleading, because both the lamina and petiole are characteristically tough and not easily broken. Other than the shape of the mature leaves, the feature which most clearly distinguishes this species from others of the genus is the beautifully furled margin of the lamina, to which the popular name of the plant alludes.

Both *E. muricatus,* which is native to northern regions of South America, and *E. major,* which is indigenous to Brazil, tolerate a relatively wide range of temperatures in aquaria, provided these vary toward greater rather than less heat, i.e., from about 21-22°C to 30-32°C. Probably the most important aspect of their cultivation is the nature of the compost, which must be

841

rich in organic and inorganic nutrients because a dearth of these results in depauperate specimens. A compost of two parts weathered clay or good garden soil, one part coarse sand and one part peat moss, well mixed to give a good crumb structure, is recommended for both species. The compost should be contained within a pot, the size of which depends largely on the age of the specimen when it is obtained. Young plants 5 to 13 cm tall may be planted in 5 to 6 cm diameter pots, but they will need transplanting to larger pots after about three months. Older and mature specimens must be in pots 5 cm or more in diameter, and the depth of the compost must not be less than 5 cm, because both species produce many strong adventitious roots which grow to a considerable length and soon become pot-bound. Propagation of both *E. muricatus* and *E. major* is extremely difficult because flowers are produced only very rarely, even in good conditions in aquaria receiving natural light. Young plants will develop adventively on the stalk of the inflorescence if this is kept submerged; even if flowers develop, viable seeds are rarely formed, and although they germinate very quickly the seedlings themselves grow slowly and take over eighteen months to reach a height of 4 to 5 cm. Occasionally the rootstock branches and a young rosette is formed at the side of the parent; should this occur, the young plant must not be removed until it has reached a height of 5 cm or more. If the rootstock is divided before this time, the young plant would be insufficiently vigorous to establish itself, and the health of the parent would also possibly be impaired. Since these two species are rare and valuable, the aquarist attempting to propagate them should exercise great patience and care.

THREE LARGE SPECIES OF ECHINODORUS

Upon seeing in their natural habitats mature specimens of the species of *Echinodorus* they cultivate in their tropical tanks, most aquarists would express considerable amazement at the remarkable differences of size and sometimes vegetative structure. Most species of this genus are perennial swamp plants growing with most of their foliage above the waterline. When they are cultivated as entirely submerged specimens, their leaves often become more slender and their maximum height often as little as one-half to two-thirds that which they attain in natural habitats. Nowhere is this overall difference in size between submerged and bog specimens more clearly seen than in three uncommon species,

Echinodorus cordifolius

Echinodorus macrophyllus, E. grandiflorus and *E. argentinensis,* which are occasionally available to aquarists and are ideal for either the larger aquaria of the connoisseur or aquaterraria and garden pools.

The general technique for the cultivation of these three species is identical to that recommended for *Echinodorus major* and *E. muricatus.* The need for both adequate space in which the foliage may spread and adequate depth for the unrestricted development of the root system cannot be over-emphasized. When submerged, all three species reach a height of 40 to 50 cm and to attempt to stunt specimens to a smaller size in order to keep them in aquaria of small and average dimensions often leads to a serious deterioration of the plants and, therefore, is not recommended. Illumination should be of high intensity and should preferably be supplemented with some sunlight, at least during the season of active vegetative growth. In garden pools in warm districts all three species may flower, producing aerial stalks bearing small blooms which may give rise to viable seed. The inflorescence of *E. grandiflorus* is particularly notable. It grows to a height of 1.5 m or more. In aquaria flowering is very rare, and even if an inflorescence is produced, seeds only occasionally develop. Plantlets are frequently produced, however, if the stalk of the inflorescence is sub-

Echinodorus cordifolius

Echinodorus osiris

Echinodorus horizontalis

merged; these plantlets should either be allowed to develop to about 4 to 5 cm tall and then separated and planted, or they should be pegged down to the aquarium gravel from the time that they appear. Very infrequently, the rootstock of these species forms a short lateral branch at the growing point of which a young rosette of foliage arises. The temperature of the water in which these three species are grown should be within the range 21 to 29°C, and it is baneficial, though not essential, for the natural rhythm of growth of the plant if this is reduced to 18 to 21°C for about three months annually.

The South American *Echinodorus grandiflorus* reaches a height of about 45 cm under water, though considerably more when it is emerged. It has a very stout rootstock from which arises a rosette of tough, handsome leaves of a rich mid-green color. There is little variation of leaf shape, the juvenile leaves being slightly narrower. The petiole is usually rather longer than the lamina, which is flat, oval to elliptical, and bears nine to fifteen prominent veins in relief on the lower surface.

Young specimens of the Brazilian *Echinodorus macrophyllus* bear a superficial resemblance to *E. muricatus* by virtue of the elongated elliptical or spear-shaped leaves. As the plant matures, however, the basal half of each leaf becomes proportionately wider so that the shape becomes more nearly cordate or even sagittate. The margin of the lamina is sometimes slightly furled and the basal part of each side of the lamina frequently stands out at an angle from the rest of the leaf. In addition to the midrib there are from eight to twelve principal lateral veins on each lamina and these are very conspicuous on the lower surface. The color of the leaves varies from pale to vivid green.

Echinodorus argentinensis, also native to Brazil, differs from other species in having very long petioles, a habit which may be of advantage in aquaria possessing a thick carpet of vegetation. Above water the petiole may attain a length of 50 cm, bearing a lamina some 18 to 23 cm long, but when the plant is submerged the overall length of the leaf rarely exceeds 38 to 45 cm. Juvenile leaves usually possess narrowly elliptical laminas,

Echinodorus tenellus

A well planted aquarium must be designed with open spaces in which the fishes can swim and be seen.

tapering very gradually at both base and apex; at maturity, the lamina is relatively wider, being broadly elliptical or roughly melon-shaped.

ECHINODORUS LATIFOLIUS

This plant, native to Central and South America, is a member of the family Alismataceae. Europeans have known this species for a long time under the erroneous name of *Echinodorus magdalensis*. *Echinodorus latifolius* is numbered among the smaller species of its genus, and certain stages of its development are very similar to those of other related species, such as *E. tenellus, E. austroamericanus* and *E. quadricostatus*. In its emerged form it is very suitable for stocking the larger and more compact parts of aquaterraria. Each plant develops 10 to 15 leaves which are disposed as rosettes. These leaves reach lengths of 10 to 15 cm and widths of 5 to 10 mm. Sometimes they are nearly stalkless, while on other occasions they change over slowly into shorter or longer leaf stalks.

Echinodorus latifolius is one of the ornamental plants which is most easily kept in our tanks. It will grow in very poor soil; that is, in pure washed sand, where it thrives reasonably well but reproduces very slowly. On the other hand, it is not affected by excesses of organic matter, which means that you can cultivate it in tanks with abundant nutrients and a large detritus content. It is not a typically tropical plant either, adapting quite well to the shorter days of the temperate zone. This also includes it in the group of those plants whose submerged forms develop quite well in winter without receiving additional lighting, meaning at spots where the duration of daylight is not extended artificially. *E. latifolius* is even more ornamental in winter than in summer, when it generally shows shorter leaves and reproduces abundantly.

Like that of all the smaller species of the genus, the reproduction of *E. latifolius* takes place by means of offshoots of the roots in the same manner as the reproduction of *Vallisneria*. Each of these shoots gives rise to from 10 to 20 new plants which may be cut off so that they grow a root system of their own.

Echinodorus latifolius is very suitable for stocking the front and central parts of fish tanks. It is advisable, though, to fence off its location with rocks in order to avoid excessive proliferation with the consequent spreading out to other spots in the aquarium intended to be occupied by other plants. If such spots are not fenced off, *E. latifolius* can be counted on to spread over the whole tank, especially in summer time, and you will only be able to hold it in bounds by means of the systematic elimination of its offspring.

Echinodorus latifolius
Inset: closeup of flower of
Echinodorus latifolius

This swordplant multiplies most quickly at temperatures that range from 25 to 30°C, but it also withstands lowerings of the thermometer down to 15°C without being harmed. Water chemistry is an absolutely secondary matter, and the intensity of the lighting is not important either. But under extensive lighting or at locations which receive direct sunlight, the submerged forms remain shorter than those growing at shadowy places. Contrarily, plants that are cultivated in emerged form in aquaterraria do quite well with plenty of light.

EGERIA DENSA

This widely distributed aquatic plant belongs to the family Hydrocharitaceae, which includes among others the genus *Vallisneria,* despite the fact that the external disposition of the plant body differs considerably from that of *Vallisneria. Egeria densa,* the best-known plant in the genus, ranges from the southeastern United States to Argentina. It is found over almost all the subtropical and tropical areas of the New World.

This plant often is confused with various of the *Elodea* species. The stalk with its fork-like branchings generally is richly and densely covered with leaves and reaches lengths up to 3 m. From the spots where it branches out, the stalk sends out unbranched white roots which serve either to attach it to the bottom or to absorb nutritional substances directly from its aquatic surroundings.

The deep green leaves generally are disposed in whorls of five. They are narrow-lanceolate and, depending on the conditions under which they grow, reach lengths of 16 to 35 mm, with widths of 3 to 5 cm. At first glance the edges seem apparently smooth, and only if you examine them under a magnifier or hold them up against the light will you see that they are slightly serrated.

Egeria densa shows the rare capacity to absorb nutrition through its whole surface, but especially through the leaves. The real function of the roots is only that of anchoring the plant to the bottom. This means that you can keep the plant in your tanks as a floating plant or as one that is rooted down. Both free-floating and rooted specimens send the most densely leaf-covered parts of their shoots upward, where they stay just below the surface. There they form a dense thicket which serves as a hiding place

Elodea nuttallii, less luxuriant in its foliage than *Elodea canadensis* and therefore less of a look-alike to *Egeria densa*.

for newly born fry of livebearers, while at the same time it represents a very convenient spawning medium for many species of fishes. Even anabantoids like to seek out these dense entanglements in order to build their bubblenests there.

Egeria densa rarely blooms in a tank, and it is quite probable that very few aquarists ever come to see its flowers. In larger tanks in hothouses, the plant blooms from May to August. The 23 to 35 mm flower stems grow out of the leaf insertions and end in a single male flower with three white petals, in the center of which one notices yellow stamens. The flowers have an average diameter of 10 to 23 mm and float on the surface of the water, out of which they grow occasionally to heights of 10 to 23 mm above the water. According to present experience, female flowers have never grown under artificial cultivation in tanks.

Egeria densa is able to withstand extremely hard water and has a reputation for being able to soften hard water in which it is kept, supposedly because of the plant's capacity to extract calcium salts from the water. The closely related *Elodea canadensis,* incidentally, was long used in Europe as a water purlfier, especially a decalcifier, and planted in pools formed by run-off from paper mills and distilleries. Both *E. densa* and *E. canadensis* therefore are well suited as decorative plants in hard-water tanks.

Elodea nuttallii

Egeria densa

There is a considerable difference in leaf coloration between *E. densa* specimens grown in soft water and those grown in hard water, the hard-water plants being a much deeper green. Soft-water plants are more yellowish green than deep green. The texture of the plant varies according to its water also, soft-water plants (both leaves and stems) being much more brittle.

Egeria densa is much less tolerant of bad lighting conditions than it is of widely fluctuating temperatures. It will take cold water very well, but it will not take poor lighting. For good growth, it must have sufficient illumination.

HETERANTHERA SPECIES

Fast-growing plants which may be manipulated to produce thickets of foliage and propagated rapidly by cuttings are of great value in aquaria. Starting from relatively few and inexpensive specimens, the aquarist may soon obtain a vast stock of plants which may be arranged in groves to conceal the background and sides of the aquarium and to provide a decorative curtain against which other large solitary plants may be seen to better advantage. Among the more common examples of such versatile aquarium plants are species of *Hygrophila, Ludwigia, Bacopa, Myriophyllum* and *Limnophila,* but there are two less well-known species of *Heteranthera* which may be used to similar effect.

The genus *Heteranthera,* which belongs to the same family as the water hyacinths and pickerel weeds, the Pontederiaceae, comprises some twelve tropical and subtropical amphibious plants inhabiting swamps and temporarily flooded areas in parts of the American and African continents. Just two of these twelve species, *Heteranthera zosterifolia* and *H. dubia,* are in frequent supply. Both have a wide range of temperature tolerance and may be grown in temperate as well as tropical aquaria i.e., in water at temperatures from about 17 to 32°C. They are able to withstand lower temperatures for short periods, but in general their growth is more consistent in warmer water so that they are popularly regarded as tropical species.

Naturally rhizomatous plants, they are normally obtained in the form of cuttings taken from the vigorous erect shoots. To accelerate the formation of adventitious roots, the lowermost five or six leaves should be carefully removed from each cutting. Groups of three or four cuttings should then be pressed gently but firmly into a compost of equal parts of coarse sand and loamy soil contained within 5 cm diameter pots and covered with a thin layer of aquarium gravel or coarse sand. Establishment of the plants is fairly rapid under most conditions, but it is preferable that this early cultivation be in water at a temperature of from 21 to 24°C and in bright illumination. The origin of lateral shoots from the nodes near the surface of the compost soon follows, and it may be induced elsewhere along the active ascending stems by nipping the apical bud. Once the plants have begun to thrive, they may be transplanted to their permanent positions or, alternatively, used as a source of further cuttings.

For the long-term cultivation of both species in established aquaria, the compost of sand and soil is recommended as a rooting medium. Both species will, however, grow well when they are rooted in coarse sand or gravel, particularly if this contains organic detritus, as indeed it would on the bed of an aquarium which has not been overhauled for some time. Illumination should be bright to intense; some sunlight encourages more luxuriant growth, but flowering often occurs under artificial light alone. If the species are to be used in cool water, the temperature of the water must be lowered gradually, for although both species are fairly hardy and less sensitive than many aquatic plants, a sudden drop in temperature has an adverse effect on the photosynthesis, respiration and other metabolic processes of the plant.

Heteranthera zosterifolia, the water stargrass indigenous to Bolivia and Brazil, is the slower growing of the two species. Submerged, its stems are rather brittle and the internodes are short, so that the opposite or alternate leaves are closely arranged. Each leaf is sessile, linear to narrowly lanceolate, and pale yellowish green in color. It attains a length of 5 to 8 cm and a width of up to 6 mm. Unless arrested the stems continue to strive upward through the water, eventually growing horizontally beneath the surface and producing small stalked orbicular leaves which float on the surface and help to maintain the rather inconspicuous pale blue flowers in the air above. When the plant is grown with its foliage above the water-line, the leaves are glossy, shorter and darker green, and their tips are rounded instead of pointed. The popular name "stargrass" alludes to the appearance of the apex of the shoot viewed from above.

Heteranthera dubia is more nearly a genuine aquatic. It may be grown above the water line only with difficulty. Its stems are stouter than those of *H. zosterifolia,* and the internodes are relatively longer so that numerous cuttings must be planted together to avoid a straggly appearance. The

Heteranthera zosterifolia

Heteranthera zosterifolia

leaves are linear, sessile, often reflexed, from 5 to 13 cm long and up to 6 mm wide. Both leaves and stems vary in color from a pale, almost translucent green through olive green to coppery bronze. Whereas the adventitious roots from the nodes of *H. zosterifolia* are branched and usually in tufts, those of *H. dubia* are solitary and unbranched. The shoots of *H. dubia* reach tremendous lengths, hugging the surface of the water and producing golden yellow aerial star-shaped flowers. This species thrives even when it is densely planted, and it is particularly recommended for the back and corners of the aquarium.

Closeup of *Heteranthera zosterifolia,* showing the sessile leaves.

Stones and wood can be used to enhance the value of plants. They can also keep conflicting (or similar) plants from growing into each other.

A very unnatural color combination is green and red, yet that combination is not highly unusual in an aquarium.

HYDROCLEIS NYMPHOIDES/*Water Poppy*

Most of the submerged aquatic plants cultivated by aquarists produce flowers only rarely under artificial illumination, and even these rare occasions are liable to be anticlimactic because the flowers are often inconspicuous and uninteresting. With the exception of several dwarf species of *Nuphar, Nymphaea* and *Nymphoides,* nearly all the aquatic plants which do produce splendid blooms are too large to be cultivated in aquaria. The water poppy, *Hydrocleis nymphoides,* is one of the very few plants whose size, habit of growth and readiness to bloom are all amenable to cultivation in tropical aquaria, and it is a great pity that the species is uncommon in the stocks of many commercial suppliers. The requirements for its growth are more straightforward than for numerous popular aquarium species, and any aquarist who encounters it will be amply repaid by its beauty and propagation, even if the initial cost of the specimen is high.

The water poppy is indigenous to standing and slow-flowing waters in Central and tropical South America, where it often forms dominant colonies in shallow flood pools and littoral regions. Closely resembling the water lilies in its habit of growth, it is a glabrous herbaceous plant which roots in the muddy substratum and produces floating leaves. The stems are long, creeping horizontally through the mud and rooting at the nodes. The leaves occur in clusters, each being borne on a slender petiole varying in length from 8 to 25 cm or even more, depending upon the depth of the water. The lamina reaches a length of 5 cm and a width of 2 to 4.5 cm; in shape it is broadly oval to orbicular, with an obtuse apex and slightly cordate base. The margin is entire, and on each side of the thickened spongy midrib are three principal lateral veins. The upper surface of the floating lamina is shining green and sometimes bears faint brownish markings, while the lower surface is of a paler color. Prior to flowering, the plant forms a long shoot which is often branched and ascends to the surface. From this shoot arise the aerial flowers which may be solitary or in clusters of two or three. Each flower may be as large as 5 cm in diameter and has three petals which are bright yellow with a rusty tint on the inner surface. The flower's several anthers are purplish.

Perhaps the most important point to be remembered in cultivating *Hydrocleis nymphoides* is that its growth soon becomes rampant if its rooting medium is very rich in nutrients and if it has no competitors at the surface of the water. The best technique is to establish the original specimen in a small pot containing a compost of two parts coarse sand to one

Hydrocleis nymphoides

part loam. Be sure that the roots are well spread and firmly anchored. Subsequently formed shoots may then be allowed to root in the gravel of the aquarium bed, where the concentration of nutrients is unlikely to be very high. There is some evidence that growth is more luxurious in soft water, but the species appears generally to be tolerant of a wide range of water conditions. The temperature of the water should be maintained, for most of the year, between 15 and 29°C. After flowering, the rate of growth slows down, and during this period the water may be cooled to a temperature between 10 and 15°C. Blooming is induced more effectively if the plant receives some sunlight, but flowers have developed on several specimens of mine which have received only bright artificial light. Propagation of the species is very easy since strong lateral shoots arise frequently at the nodes of the main creeping shoots, and these develop rapidly if they are carefully detached, complete with roots, and planted in the compost mentioned above. Should the increase of the plant in the aquarium be too profuse, one or two of the shoots should be cut back. It is recommended that this technique be followed as a normal part of the cultivation of the plant, rather than let the growth become rampant and then drastically cut back most of the shoots, a practice which usually results in the loss of the specimen.

HYGROPHILA CORYMBOSA

This well-liked plant, which is well known to aquarists as the temple plant, belongs to the family Acanthaceae. Representatives of this family are quite rare in temperate areas, the plants being mainly tropical ones, with a total of about 2650 species in about 520 genera.

Only a comparatively few acanthacid plants grow under water, and of these fewer yet are seen in our tanks. This makes it most likely that the future will bring further importations of plants of the family Acanthaceae, which are sure to become precious additions to the hobby. The genus which is best known to hobbyists up to now is *Hygrophila.*

Plants of the genus *Hygrophila* are found in Southeast Asia, in tropical Africa and on Madagascar. Many species are known, of which generally only *Hygrophila corymbosa* is grown commercially. Another species, which has not yet been completely identified, was introduced a few years ago and is slowly making headway among hobbyists. *H. corymbosa* was known as *Nomaphila stricta* and comes from Malaysia. In its natural habitat it is found as a robust swamp plant which grows up to 80 cm in length and has submerged and emerged leaves of differing shapes. Above the water surface it

Hygrophila corymbosa cuttings growing in a tank that has had its water level lowered.

Hygrophila polysperma

develops stalks measuring up to l cm in diameter, with leaves 10 cm long and 5 cm wide. The shape is broadly lanceolate, often even heart-shaped, with elongated tips and a remarkable saw-toothed edge. The whole plant, but especially the stalk, is covered with a delicate brownish green or reddish green down.

In its emerged form the species grows very quickly, with weekly increases of up to 15 cm. This is why commercial growers generally reproduce it in shallow water over fertile soil that has been enriched with admixtures of peat moss and humus. The vegetative tips, reaped from emerged specimens, are cut off in lengths of 15 to 20 cm and then stuck into soil below water at well illuminated spots until they grow roots. During this transplanting period the plants are very sensitive to poor lighting. When kept in shadowy locations they tend to lose their lower leaves. After 10 to 20 days, the coloration of the leaves changes from brownish green to light green. The submerged leaves are thinner than the emerged ones, being rather filmy. Later on there is a clear change of shape, with the leaves growing longer, becoming narrow-lanceolate and reaching lengths up to 15 cm with widths of 3 cm. At this stage the edges of the leaves are only vaguely saw-toothed. The stalks become bright green, and at the spots where the oppositely paired leaves insert, one sees a swelling on the stalks reminiscent of the nodes of a bamboo pole.

Sometimes the tips of the leaves show a reddish tint. Lately pet shops have been offering selectively bred plants with brownish to vividly red leaves. These plants do not represent an independent species but only an artificially bred form, despite the fact that at times it is designated as *Hygrophila* "*rubra.*"

H. corymbosa requires a tank with medium-rich bottom soil which is well supplied with detritus. The species is quite undemanding with regard to the water chemistry and does equally as well in slightly acid as in slightly alkaline water which is from soft to medium-hard. After having been placed under water, the plant demands ample lighting, which also favors it after it has rooted down. For this reason you can keep it together with species of the genera *Echinodorus, Myriophyllum, Cabomba* and similar ones, to which, considering their green coloration, the red variety will cause a striking contrast.

Hygrophila siamensis

Hygrophila difformis

Well-rooted specimens that have grown under water for longer periods are less exacting with regard to light, which means that you can cultivate them in more shadowed locations.

Temple plants are very adaptable. If you want to reproduce them, the best way to do it is in an aquaterrarium. The plant grows well as an indoor plant in flowerpots, but these have to be placed at well illuminated spots in the room or, in summer, in front of a window; daily watering is unavoidable. If you want to save time and work, simply place the flowerpot in a shallow dish which is kept filled up with water. If kept in this manner, the plant will bloom during nearly the whole summer season. The violet flowers develop at the leaf insertions.

LUDWIGIA PALUSTRIS

The genus *Ludwigia* is a member of the family Onagraceae, being practically the only genus of the family whose many species may be cultivated under water. Hobbyist literature mentions quite a series of species which, allegedly, are fit for growing in fish tanks. One of the names thus mentioned, for example, is that of *Ludwigia alternifolia,* a plant that in its natural habitat is subjected to only short floodings and therefore cannot be cultivated under water permanently by any means. One species, though,

Ludwigia palustris

which is well adapted for aquaristic purposes is *Ludwigia palustris,* especially the American variety.

Ludwigia palustris grows in Europe, Asia and the northern part of Africa. It has a creeping stalk which roots down at any spot where it grows leaves. The leaves are nearly without petioles, measuring 2 to 2.5 cm and showing a striking pattern of veins. The upper face of the leaves is a vivid green with a velvety luster, while the lower face may be bright green, olive or, if cultivated in dimly lit locations, sometimes a reddish brown. This plant is by far less colorful and ornamental than the American variety. It comes from temperate and subtropical zones of the Old World and generally dies off in winter when kept in an aquarium. This does not make it very fit for keeping in fish tanks, its use being restricted mainly to the terrarium, where it conquers its place in damp but cool and unheated installations.

In the southern states of the United States, *Ludwigia palustris* var. *americana* grows in shallow waters. The hobby generally knows it under the widespread but erroneous name of *Ludwigia natans.* This kind also develops a creeping stalk, and in its emerged form it is fit for both cold and warm terraria. It develops a dense low growth with shiny dark green leaves which differ from those of the European form because they do not possess the protruding veins and are considerably wider.

The stalks of the submerged form sometimes creep along the bottom, while at other times they grow vertically from the roots toward the surface of the water. The leaves on the stems are inserted in pairs on opposite sides of the stalk. They are broadly lanceolate or oval, the upper face a dark and shiny green, and with the lower face only rarely greenish, generally reddish brown to purple-red. They measure 2 to 3 cm in length and 2 cm in width.

The most beautiful form of this species is *Ludwigia palustris* var. *americana* forma *elongata.* The hobby has long known this form under the commercial name *Ludwigia mullerti.* Its leaves reach lengths up to 4 cm. The edges are slightly undulated, and the lower face of the leaves is always red or purple.

Ludwigia palustris blossoms only in its emerged form. The flowers develop in the leaf insertions and have long green cups that are grown together and drawn out into tips. Between these tips grow only a few minute yellow petals. The flowers are self-pollinating and easily develop minute seeds which germinate immediately. However, reproducing *Ludwigia palustris* by means of seeds does not pay, as it is much easier and quicker to reproduce the plant by sticking cut-off tips into the soil. If you want to

A nice planted aquarium but lacking in low plants and bottom covers to hide the gravel.

get a really beautiful *Ludwigia,* the thing to do is to plant three to five specimens together, cutting off their tips regularly whenever they grow longer than 10 to 20 cm. This causes the stems to branch out in forks, which in turn makes the plant develop into a large, densely leaved and branched bush which shows a lively pageant of shiny green and vivid purplish red colors, with the upper and lower faces of the leaves alternating as you look at them.

This is the reason why one should cultivate only plants of American origin which winter easily in well-illuminated tanks and are undemanding as to temperatures and also as to the chemical composition of the water. The plant does quite well when standing in pure sand and hard water. The best surroundings for the species are found in water with a neutral to slightly alkaline reaction.

Ludwigia demands abundant light and prospers if afforded direct sunlight during at least part of the day. Temperatures from 15°C up are sufficient, which makes our plant better for coldwater tanks than for heated ones.

Ludwigia palustris **Ludwigia** sp.

NAJAS SPECIES/*The Nymphworts*

The genus *Najas* comprises some 35 species, all of which are slender submerged fresh or brackish water plants inhabiting temperate and tropical regions. Many members of the genus resemble *Ceratophyllum demersum,* the hornwort, in having extremely brittle foliage and in succeeding equally well as floating submerged plants or as plants anchored in the substratum. The stem of most species is much branched and roots at the lower nodes while the narrow leaves are oppositely arranged or in whorls. The base of each leaf forms a tiny sheath around the stem and within each sheath are two minute scales. The inconspicuous unisexual flowers are usually hidden in the leaf axils. Each male flower is enclosed in a spathe and possesses just a single stamen; each female flower is naked and gives rise, after pollination and fertilization, to a single oval or elliptical fruit.

By virtue of their dense clusters of attractive translucent foliage, a few species of *Najas* may be recommended for use in aquaria, where they may prove of additional value for fishes that deposit their eggs in plant thickets and also as food for some species. Indeed, the introduction of the vegetarian *Sarotherodon melanopleura* is employed as a control measure in some areas of Africa where species of *Najas* occasionally infest dams and irrigation channels. However, aquarists growing these plants must remember their fragility and cultivate them in tanks containing no very active or vegetarian fishes.

The cultivation of species of *Najas* presents no serious problems. If it is desired that they should be rooted, cuttings should have the few lowermost leaves carefully removed and then be pressed gently into a compost of four parts coarse sand and one part garden soil covered by a thin layer of sand or gravel. The enrichment of the rooting medium with soil is not absolutely necessary, and some species will grow almost as luxuriantly when they are anchored in gravel alone. All the species branch profusely, so pruning to stimulate the formation of axillary shoots is unnecessary. A wide range of intensities of illumination is tolerated, but a very high intensity is not recommended as it frequently results in infestation of the dense foliage by filamentous and gelatinous colonies of green and blue-green algae.

Three species, *Najas horrida, N. indica* and *N. microdon,* are commonly available to aquarists. Others, some of which are difficult to identify with certainty, are less frequently seen in commercial supplies. *Najas horrida,* which is indigenous to most regions of the African continent and Madagascar, and *N. indica,* which is a native of Malaysia and Indonesia, are both tropical and subtropical species which may be cultivated in aquaria at temperatures of 17 to 29°C. The translucent bright green leaves of *N. indica* are arranged in close whorls along the slender but not too brittle stem. Each leaf is sessile, linear to narrowly lanceolate and reaches a length of 2.5 to 5.5 cm and a width of up to 6 mm. The margin of the leaf is deeply serrated. The leaves of *N. horrida* are relatively longer and narrower and are frequently reflexed; toward the base of established plants they are often whorled, whereas they are arranged in an opposite manner on younger growing stems. The leaf has an extremely coarsely toothed margin and varies in color from pale green to olive-green and even brown. The species resembles *N. indica* in being stronger and more wiry than most other species of the genus.

Najas microdon is a slender brittle plant of annual habit. Its smooth stems reach a length of about 30 cm and bear whorls of three leaves in the older parts, pairs of opposite leaves in the young regions. Each leaf reaches a length of 2.0 to 2.5 cm, is a pale translucent green and has a margin which is sparsely and minutely toothed. The natural distribution of this species has interested plant geographers for many years because of

Najas marina

Najas microdon

Najas minor

Najas sp.

its asymmetrical range on either side of the Atlantic Ocean; in North America the species is distributed throughout both the Atlantic and Pacific regions from about 30°N to about 50 °N, whereas its European range is much less extensive and more northerly (from about 51°N to about 62°N). In Europe the species occurs only in scattered localities on the northwest seaboards of the British Isles and Scandinavia. Fossil discoveries of the plant suggest that its range has become very restricted in post-glacial time, and a further interesting feature is that although the species has withdrawn from eastern and central Ireland to its present northern and western localities, the retreat in Scandinavia was southeasterly, toward the shores of the Baltic.

In aquaria, *Najas microdon* appreciates rather lower temperatures than the two species described above, from about 10 to 22°C. It may be of interest to note here that another aquatic plant, *Elodea nuttallii,* shows a similar native distribution and marked structural resemblances to *Najas microdon.* The linear-lanceolate pale green leaves occur in whorls of three to five on slender branching stems. Each leaf is translucent and its margin has tiny projecting teeth. *E. nuttallii* resembles other species of *Elodea* in temperate countries in forming winter buds. In aquaria it requires a temperature similar to that recommended for *Najas microdon* and its rooting medium should be composed of equal parts of clay and coarse sand.

NUPHAR AND NYMPHAEA SPECIES/*Water Lilies*

Water lilies are normally regarded as pool plants, yet there are a few species of *Nuphar* and *Nymphaea* which are naturally dwarf plants and are eminently suitable for cultivation in tropical aquaria. Some of these are natural forms, whereas others are plants which have been developed and cultivated in horticultural nurseries. All have the same general habit of growth and accordingly demand similar conditions. From the stout creeping rootstock there develop submerged juvenile leaves, followed sooner or later by floating leaves and aerial or floating flowers. Species of *Nuphar* are cultivated particularly for their submerged foliage, which is usually translucent and attractively furled. Water lilies must be planted in pots, which are much more convenient for subsequent handling of the specimens and for containing the necessary rooting medium. The compost should be a rich heavy fibrous loam; these plants will not grow successfully for long periods in barren gravel or sand. Some dealers offer rootstock cuttings of lilies all too frequently; such specimens must be avoided, as bacterial decay quickly starts at the cut end. Young thriving seedlings or established rootstocks should be obtained wherever possible. Most lilies are fast-growing plants, and care is needed to prevent them from becoming pot-bound; initially 5 cm or 8 cm diameter pots are adequate for species of *Nuphar* and 8 cm or 10 cm ones for species of *Nymphaea,* but after about twelve months specimens usually need transplanting to larger pots. Apart from this treatment, however, the plants should not be disturbed, and excessive pruning is not recommended, as it frequently leads to a deterioration of the stock.

The commonest aquarium species of *Nuphar* is the spatterdock, *N. pumilum,* a small plant with rich green translucent leaves and bright yellow flowers, which in its submerged phase provides a good foreground plant.

The wild European species, *Nuphar luteum,* is naturally a cool temperate plant; young specimens may be used in tropical aquaria for a limited period, though their rapid growth in the warmer water often produces ungainly plants. The leaves are pale green and reach a width of 20 to 25 cm.

The Cape Fear spatterdock, *Nuphar sagittifolia,* is probably the most useful and decorative species, useful by virtue of its producing only submerged leaves and decorative on account of the shape and translucence of these leaves. A mature specimen may attain a height of 30 cm or more, the leaves spreading out in a dense bush from the rootstock. Each leaf is

Nymphaea sp.

Nymphaea lotus

Nymphaea 'Attraction'

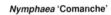
Nymphaea 'Comanche'

Nymphaea 'Paul Stetson'   *Nymphaea* sp.

sagittate, bright green in color and borne on a short petiole; the undivided margins of the leaf are usually curled back at intervals, giving a wavy outline. The species will thrive within the temperature range 15 to 27°C.

Two wild species of *Nymphaea* are suited to life in tropical aquaria. These are *N. tetragona,* from Asia and North America, and *N. maculata,* a common aquatic weed of tropical Africa. The former is well known as the pygmy water lily; its leaves reach a diameter of 5 to 8 cm, its white flowers 2.5 to 4 cm. Its growth in aquaria at temperatures of 21 to 26°C tends to be rapid, and it will tolerate much cooler water, down to 7 to 10°C. The floating leaves of *N. maculata* are even smaller, reaching a diameter of 3 to 4.5 cm. Cordate in shape, they have a glossy dark green surface attractively mottled with bluish red tints. The submerged leaves arising from the stout rounded rootstock are olive and sometimes bear similar mottled patterns. Under sustained good light this species forms white surface flowers about 4.5 to 5.5 cm in diameter with acutely pointed petals.

Nearly all species of *Nuphar* and *Nymphaea* require a high light intensity, preferably with some daily sunlight, at least during the growing season, though exceptions are afforded by *N. daubenyana,* which flowers freely in artificial light, and by *Nuphar sagittifolia,* which, in being exclusively submerged, tolerates lower intensities. If species with floating leaves are grown in aquaria under artificial lights, a sheet of glass should be placed between the lamps and the water surface to minimize the effects of heat on the leaves, thereby preventing scorching.

Bolbitis heudeloti here is used very effectively by using the plant's capacity to attach itself to rocks and driftwood, thereby providing shelter where none would otherwise exist.

NYMPHOIDES SPECIES/*Banana Plants* and relatives

The banana plant, which has attracted the interest of aquarists for many years, and its lesser-known relatives are all species of *Nymphoides,* a genus of some twenty tropical and subtropical plants. Despite their similarities of structure and growth habit, these plants belong not to the Nymphaeaceae, or water lily family, but to an unrelated family, the Menyanthaceae. Their vegetative resemblances to the water lilies provide a fine example of convergent evolution, the organs of these unrelated plants having become similarly adapted to a particular set of environmental factors, those prevailing in and at the surface of stationary or slow-moving water which fluctuates in depth.

The banana plant itself, *Nymphoides aquatica,* is native to southern North America and is an interesting specimen for aquaria within the temperature range 18 to 27°C. It will grow equally well as a floating or as a submerged rooted plant. The rootstock is short and compact, and below it hangs a cluster of curved tuberous roots closely resembling a stalk of bananas. Exposed to light, these roots develop photosynthetic pigments and appear green; buried in the compost, they are usually brownish white. When the specimen is planted, unmodified adventitious roots develop from the rootstock, anchoring the plant. If it is desired as a submerged specimen, the plant should be potted in a compost of equal parts sand and garden soil covered with gravel, and it should be so anchored that most of the tuberous roots are just above the surface of the compost, though these will have to be buried initially if the specimen has no other roots. Pots 5 to 8 cm in diameter are quite adequate for this species, and it is not absolutely essential to have a compost of soil, as the plants will thrive for long periods in ordinary gravel or coarse sand. Growth is more luxuriant, however, in the presence of additional inorganic and organic nutrients. When established, the species produces submerged leaves quite rapidly. These are usually few in number unless the water is deeper than 38 cm; they are roughly cordate, rather irregular in outline, somewhat crinkled, mid-green in color and borne on petioles varying from 2 to 15 cm in length, the leaves themselves reaching a diameter of 6 cm or more. Sooner or later, long petioles grow rapidly upward bearing cordate floating leaves which do not open until they reach the surface. The petioles continue to elongate for some time, so the leaves are carried away from the plant to some distance. This may be interpreted as an adaptation to possible sudden increases in water depth, the extra length of the petiole enabling the leaf to remain floating. These floating leaves reach a diameter of 5 cm.

Nymphoides peltata   *Nymphoides aquatica*

The best known relative of the banana plant is the fringed water lily, *Nymphoides peltata,* native to central and southern Europe, northern and western Asia and now naturalized in parts of the United States. It does especially well in water at temperatures from about 10 to 21°C but will grow quite successfully at higher temperatures. Reported failures with this species in tropical aquaria are almost certainly due not to the warmth of the water but to the restricted surface area available to the plant. It has an extensively creeping rhizome which forms adventitious roots profusely at the nodes and from which develop long-petioled floating leaves. These leaves are orbicular, deeply cordate at the base, up to 10 cm in diameter, sinuate in outline, purplish below and mottled with purple on the glossy green upper surface. Long floating stems with opposite leaves are eventually produced, and from the axils of some of these leaves aerial stalks bear clusters of four or five flowers to a height of 5 to 8 cm above the water. The flowers open in succession and last only for two or three days; each is about 4 cm in diameter and has five bright yellow petals which are lobed and have shaggy margins. This species is well worth cultivating, though its habit of growth demands a large aquarium, 90 cm or more long, or a heated pool. It will also grow well in outside pools but is likely to suffer in hard winters. When first obtained it should be rooted in a rich loam;

883

roots produced subsequently from the creeping rhizome will anchor themselves in the aquarium gravel or pool bed. In aquaria or indoor pools intense illumination is required, preferably with some sunlight if flowering is to be induced.

A similar habit of growth is shown by *Nymphoides indica,* which is indigenous to Southeast Asia and parts of Australia and is sometimes available to aquarists. It differs from the previous species in only one aspect of cultivation: it is suitable only for warm water at temperatures of 21 to 30°C, though it may be cooled for a rest period each year at 15 to 18°C.

Nymphoides aquatica growing in the wild in very shallow water.

RORIPPA NASTURTIUM-AQUATICUM/*The Water Nasturtium*

Easily propagated plants with finely divided foliage are understandably popular with aquarists. One species which possesses these attributes and yet is somewhat uncommon in either tropical or coldwater aquaria is the water nasturtium, *Rorippa nasturtium-aquaticum.* That it has not achieved the popularity enjoyed by, for example, the water wisteria, *Hygrophila difformis,* or the Indian fern, *Ceratopteris thalictroides,* is surprising, the more so because it is a common native or introduced member of the flora of lowland ditches, streams and rivers throughout many parts of Europe and the U.S.A. Aquarists wishing to procure it with minimum labor may do so by visiting the nearest retailer of fresh salad vegetables, for *Rorippa nasturtium-aquaticum* is known to most people as the familiar watercress!

The water nasturtium is a perennial herbaceous plant with smooth hollow shoots varying in length from 10 to 60 cm. In the shallow water of their

Rorippa nasturtium-aquaticum

natural habitat their stems are often procumbent (trailing along the ground) near their bases, where they develop tufts of fine adventitious roots from the lowermost nodes. The free portions of the stem either float near the surface of the water or grow erect under the water and above it. The leaves and stems are an even mid-green in color while those of a related and very similar species, *Rorippa microphylla,* are green for most of the year, becoming tinted strongly with purplish brown in late summer or whenever the water becomes unusually cool.

The water nasturtium is hardy, tolerating temperatures from about 4 to 27°C, and is therefore suitable for coldwater aquaria and garden pools in addition to tropical aquaria. In warm water, under light of a low intensity, the foliage sometimes becomes spindly and yellowish green; to prevent this etiolation, it is recommended that the illumination be as bright as possible. Once established, the plant grows rapidly and will form numerous lateral shoots of its own accord. Branching may be further stimulated by carefully pruning the apical bud of the main shoot. With remarkably little attention the water nasturtium soon develops into a magnificent bush of fine crisp foliage which looks exceptionally good in front of red or brown sandstone rocks.

SAGITTARIA SUBULATA

The home range of this plant is the eastern states of the U.S.A., where it grows in shallow waters and swamps. Emerged specimens have a lanceolate leaf surface on a stem that is about four times as long as the leaf. The leaf shows an oval, cylindrical shape. The submerged leaves change into a kind of phyllode, meaning a flattened, widened leaf stem. There are three subspecies of *Sagittaria subulata,* all cultivated by hobbyists under erroneous names.

One subspecies is *Sagittaria subulata subulata,* often mistakenly called *Sagittaria pusilla.* This is the smallest form, the submerged leaves of which reach lengths of 5 to 10 cm with a width smaller than 6 mm. The leaves are light green, and the plant does not bloom in depths over 15 cm. The only flowers it produces come forth in shallow water or from emerged forms.

Another subspecies is *S. subulata gracillima,* the submerged leaves of which grow to lengths of 20 to 40 cm; this plant is sometimes erroneously called *S. subulata* f. *natans.* Sometimes the leaves of this plant grow so long that they twist and fold below the surface of the water. This is dependent upon the conditions the plant is given. The inflorescence grows to lengths of 90 cm, the female and male flowers being white with sizes of 10 cm to 12 mm.

Sagittaria graminea   *Sagittaria platyphylla*

Sagittaria subulata

The most beautiful but least known of the three subspecies is S. *subulata kurciana,* the phyllodia of which reach lengths of 30 to 40 cm, sometimes strikingly spread out at the top. In tanks it blooms only rarely and resembles the *Vallisneria* species. All three subspecies often form lawns in the aquarium, the short forms of which are hard to differentiate.

The species as such thrives in neutral to slightly alkaline water. The temperature in the tank may vary between 17 and 24°C. The plant is very undemanding and presents no problems with regard to the composition of the soil. Lighting should be fairly heavy; best results are achieved when illumination corresponds to the duration of daylight under natural conditions. Floating plants placed above the *Sagittaria* species make them tend to develop rich roots.

S. *subulata* propagates very quickly and is not sensitive to algae. Since it often grows on the front side of the tank, very heavy growths often have to be torn out and replanted, because a dense growth would obscure the view into the tank. Under optimal conditions all three subspecies will form dense lawns in the aquarium.

Partial changes of water have a beneficial effect on the growth pattern of *Sagittaria subulata.* It has been noticed that plants that had reached a plateau in growth suddenly put on a spurt of new growth after part of their water was changed.

Sagittaria subulata

VALLISNERIA GIGANTEA

Vallisneria gigantea, of the family Hydrocharitaceae, is the largest representative of its genus. In its native range (Philippines and New Guinea) it is found in permanent waters one to two meters deep, where it covers large areas of the bottom with dense thickets.

The plant has a bulbous rootstock, out of which grow short but numerous bunches of roots. From the stalks originate ten to fifteen ribbon-like leaves that are 2 to 3.5 cm wide and 1 to 2 m long. These are vivid to pale green and usually show fifteen elongated veins which are mutually interconnected in slanted irregular lines. In shallower waters, with depths around 50 cm, the huge leaves reach the surface, winding in spirals that form a dense thicket. These spots are sought out by fishes that need hiding places in the upper reaches of the water.

Like many other *Vallisneria* species, *Vallisneria gigantea is* dioecious, meaning that there are male and female specimens, but sexes cannot be differentiated except during the blooming period. The female flowers grow on long and thin, often spirally twisted, stems on the surface of the water. On the tip of the stem sits an about 1 cm-long calyx, out of which grow three tongueshaped stigmas, from which in turn grows a tough, wart-like, yellow-white tissue. The male flowers form an inverted inflorescence near the bottom. At first this inflorescence is hidden with a filmy covering. Later on the covering opens, and the pollen sacs come loose and float up to the surface. There the pollen meets the female flowers, fertilizing them.

In aquaria female plants are the most prevalent, recognized by the very long thread-like stalks and the female blooms which float on the surface. The relatively rare male plants' flowers, which are hidden within the thicket of leaves near the bottom, are likely to escape notice. Their presence is detected only when the pollen comes free and floats on the surface, forming green circles of light green grains which are about 1 millimeter in size. So far it has not been possible to observe pollination and development of fruits under artificial conditions.

V. gigantea demands a roomy tank but above all a sufficiently high column of water. Practically, it is only suitable for tanks that are at least 50 cm deep, so that it has sufficient space for development. Planted in bunches of two or three individual plants, it will soon fill out the tank with its solid and extraordinarily long leaves.

The plant is undemanding as to soil conditions and the composition of the water. It grows to sufficient size in clean gravel. Its best development is reached in slightly acid water, a fact that makes it especially fit for larger and deeper aquaria which are stocked with *Cryptocoryne*. *Vallisneria gigantea* is sufficiently adaptable, however, to be kept in neutral or lightly alkaline waters too, together with larger or smaller species of *Echinodorus, Cabomba, Myriophyllum* and the like. Angelfish love to spawn on the solid leaves. With regard to temperature, the plant demands a minimum of 20°C but tolerates up to 30°C. Reproduction takes place vegetatively but nowhere nearly so quickly as that of the smaller *Vallisneria* species. The young plants originate from offshoots out of the rootstock, but each rootstock comes to the end of its growth with the development of a new plant. Each parent plant sends forth only two or three offshoots, which give rise to two to five descendants, after which reproduction stops. If you want a large number of young plants, separate them as soon as their leaves have reached a length of about 20 cm, transplanting them at this point. Two or three weeks after being moved, the new specimens put forth new offshoots.

Vallisneria gigantea

Flower of *Vallisneria gigantea*   *Vallisneria gigantea*

Commercial reproduction of *V. gigantea* consists of setting the plants into 15 to 20 cm deep dishes. Half of each dish is filled with peat moss, while the remaining space is filled up with clean gravel. The dishes with the plants are placed on the bottom of a garden pond with soft water, where they are left during the whole summer at a temperature of 14 to 20°C. Under such conditions V. *gigantea* reaches lengths of only 15 to 30 cm, but in compensation it reproduces vegetatively in large numbers, and from May to August each parent plant in a dish gives birth to quite a number of new plants, often with leaves that measure only 5 cm. The harvest that is reaped in this manner is transferred to hothouses, where it is kept at temperatures between 20 and 23°C. During daytime the plants receive twelve hours of supplementary lighting. Under such conditions the short, stunted young that were developed in the pond during the summer reach lengths of around 40 to 62 cm and are then completely fit for transfer into fish tanks.

This is a high-low planting design which doesn't look like much without middle-swimming fishes like most *Rasbora* and tetras.

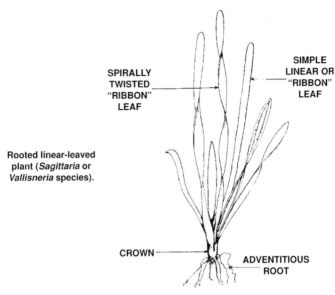

Rooted linear-leaved plant (*Sagittaria* or *Vallisneria* species).

SPIRALLY TWISTED "RIBBON" LEAF

SIMPLE LINEAR OR "RIBBON" LEAF

CROWN

ADVENTITIOUS ROOT

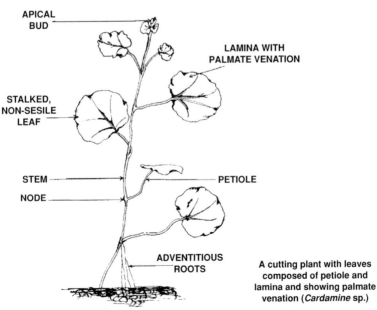

APICAL BUD

LAMINA WITH PALMATE VENATION

STALKED, NON-SESILE LEAF

STEM

NODE

PETIOLE

ADVENTITIOUS ROOTS

A cutting plant with leaves composed of petiole and lamina and showing palmate venation (*Cardamine* sp.)

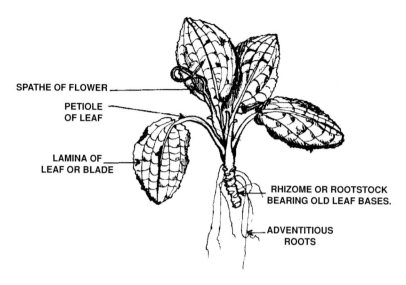

SPATHE OF FLOWER

PETIOLE OF LEAF

LAMINA OF LEAF OR BLADE

RHIZOME OR ROOTSTOCK BEARING OLD LEAF BASES.

ADVENTITIOUS ROOTS

Diagram of an aroid species.

GLOSSARY

Adventitious root: a root which develops from the node of a stem or similar organ, such as rhizome, stolon or runner.

Apical bud: the principal growing point of the stem.

Axillary bud: a bud, capable of developing into a lateral shoot, present in the angle between a leaf and the stem on which it is borne.

Dichotomous: dividing into two equal branches.

Dioecious: having male or female flowers on separate plants.

Etiolation: the formation of weak, spindly foliage deficient in chlorophyll; usually occurs in light of too low an intensity.

Heterophyllous: having leaves of different forms on the one plant.

Heterostylic: having flowers which differ in the relative length of their styles and stamens, such that any one flower is very rarely, if ever, selfpollinated.

Hydrophilous pollination: the transference of pollen from the anthers of the stamens to the stigmas on the surface of the water or under water.

Hypocotyl: that part of the stem of a seedling below the cotyledons.

Lamina: that part of a leaf which is flattened, to a greater or lesser degree, as the "leaf-blade."

Node: that part of the stem from which one or more leaves arise.

Petiole: the stalk of a leaf.

Physiological incompatibility: the existence of some chemical or physical factor in the reproductive organs of a plant which prevents fertilization.

Pinna: a part of the leaf of a fern, corresponding to a leaflet in some flowering plants.

Rachis: the continuation of the stipe in a fern leaf which is divided.

Rhizome: a stem growing more or less horizontally near the surface of the soil or gravel and sometimes appearing above it.

Rootstock: a very short, but often thick, stem growing vertically at or just above the surface of the soil or gravel; often referred to as the 'crown' of the plant.

Runner: a horizontal stem growing just above the surface of the soil or gravel and rooting at its nodes.

Sessile: a term used to describe a leaf which has no petiole.

Stipe: the stalk of a fern leaf; corresponding to the petiole in flowering plants.

Stolon: a horizontal stem growing just beneath the surface of the soil or gravel, as in numerous species of *Cryptocoryne.*

Stomata: minute pores in the surface of leaves and herbaceous stems through which exchange of gases with the atmosphere occurs.

Thallus: the body of a plant which is not differentiated into stem, root and leaf.

Turion: a modified bud, the leaves of which contain abundant storage reserves, by means of which the plant survives winter and renews its growth in spring.

Venation: the arrangement of veins in a leaf.

Vernation: the manner in which a leaf, or the parts of a leaf, are rolled up in the bud; also applied to the manner in which the frond of a fern unrolls.

Viviparous: bearing young plants on vegetative organs, such as leaves.

Whorl: a group of more than two organs of the same kind, for example leaves, arising at the same level.

Keeping Tropical Fish

Setting up an aquarium and maintaining it in good order so that beautiful scenes like the one shown here above of long-finned angelfish sedately gliding through their crystal-clear surroundings can be enjoyed in the home year in and year out is not difficult, but new aquarists must pay attention to the basics of aquarium technology.

WHY FISH?

People get into the aquarium hobby for a variety of reasons. Some are attracted by the ornamental value of aquaria. The relaxing, even therapeutic nature of a beautiful aquascape complete with glittering, brightly colored fish is undeniable. Recent technological advancements have also broadened the possibilities for planted tanks, many of which are underwater gardens in their own right, with few or even no fish.

An offshoot of this aspect of the hobby is the theme or biotope aquarium. Some people want a tank that houses one particular type of fish—perhaps all schooling fish, or all red fish. Others want to recreate a microcosm of a particular natural habitat, say an Asian stream or an African lake. Sometimes they take great pains to be exact and accurate, choosing only those plants and fish which would be found together in such an environment in nature.

Still another reason for keeping fish is the desire for a pet. Many people find appealing the idea of a friendly, attractive companion animal which

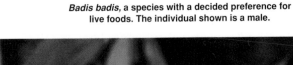

Badis badis, a species with a decided preference for live foods. The individual shown is a male.

Metynnis argenteus, much more herbivorous in its eating habits than its highly carnivorous cousins the piranhas. *Metynnis* and other fishes popularly called "silver dollars" can quickly denude an aquarium of its live plants.

does not need to be taken out for walks, doesn't disturb the neighbors, doesn't climb the draperies or shed hair all over the apartment, and won't get in a fight with somebody else's pet. But, you may protest, fish aren't *friendly*! Not all of them, true, but many of the larger cichlids and cyprinids do get to know their owners and learn to beg for food when they see them. Many aquarists are convinced of the intelligence and even affection shown them by their pet fish.

The tremendous diversity of behaviors and habits is a draw for many hobbyists. It seems that no matter what someone's preference is, there will be some fish species to satisfy it. Some fish are solitary, even to the point of killing any tankmates, while others will not thrive unless in a group of six or more of their species. Some fish are peaceful and get along with almost any other fish, but others are tyrannical bullies. Many fish are happy with any type of food, while others require specialized foods. Some fish will not eat vegetation even if starving, but others will finish off every plant in the tank. There are even fish whose fry actually feed off their parents' body slime. And breeding behavior ranges from the bitterling that lays its eggs inside a live shellfish to the tetra that lays its eggs on leaves above the water line, then splashes them to keep them wet until they hatch; from cichlids that carry their eggs and their fry around in their mouth to danios that eat their own eggs as fast as they lay them; and from fish that lay eggs in ponds which dry up and hatch later when the rains return to fish that give birth to fully-formed live young. Some species are so easy to spawn that many beginners have unintended breedings, while others frustrate even aquarists who have years of experience.

Yet other aquarists prefer piscine oddities. There are amphibious fish which spend as much time on land as they do in the water. Certain fish zap bugs by spitting at them, then eating them when they hit the water. Some burrow in the sand, some swim upside down, and some make noises audible from across the room. There are venomous fish, electricity-

Fishes of the genus *Periophthalmus* are very much at home skipping around on the mudflats in their home waters, and an aquarium housing them should include a non-aquatic area.

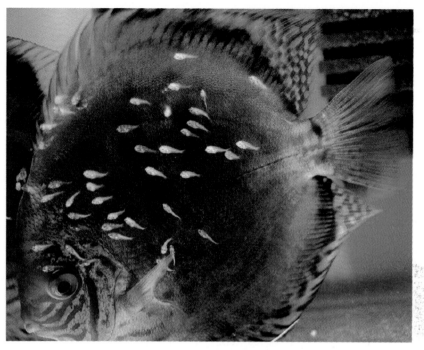

Discus fry feeding off the sides of an adult Discus.

producing fish, and blind, eyeless fish. Some fish can change color almost instantly, and others are so well camouflaged that they appear to be leaves floating by. While some have tiny mouths which they stick into cracks and crevices to find prey, others can swallow another fish half their size or larger. All this diversity and more attract many hobbyists with an eye for the unusual.

A small number of people start off breeding fish. Having a breeding tank as a first aquarium is a bit unusual, but it is a valid option. Usually aquarists have more success spawning their fish if they get a little general experience first, but there are many fish which can be bred by novice aquarists. This is underscored by the fact that many a beginner has been amazed to find his or her Zebra Danios, Cherry Barbs, White Clouds, or Convict Cichlids spawning unexpectedly in their first community aquarium, and anyone who follows the advice here should have no problem getting young from livebearers like Guppies and Mollies the first time around.

Closeup of the head of a *Mastacembelus species,* one of the spiny eels, completely submerged within the gravel in an aquarium.

Our purpose here is to present the basics of aquarium keeping so that the reader will be able to have a successful initial attempt with the ever more popular hobby of raising tropical fishes. While there is a lot of science behind these aquarium basics, very little direct knowledge of that science is necessary to be a successful aquarist. The focus, therefore, will be on keeping things simple, taking the easiest route possible. There are many possible refinements and alternatives to the basic procedures outlined in this chapter; they are not the only procedures which will work for the new aquarist. They are, however, procedures which will, in fact, work, and they will also provide a useful foundation for those people who go on to become more accomplished aquarists. For the beginner, minimizing choices can prevent a lot of confusion and frustration.

Malapterurus electricus, the Electric Catfis—not the only electricity-producing fish in the aquarium hobby, but one that's relatively powerful for its size.

Closeup of the head area of *Gnathonemus rhynchophorus,* one of the so-called "elephant-nose" fishes, showing the mouth adapted for extracting small prey from the substrate and crevices.

Getting Set Up

THE TANK

The choice of tanks can be a bit confusing. Most tanks today are made of glass panels held together with a silicone sealant, but acrylic tanks have a dedicated following. Price alone usually dictates that one start with a glass tank, though each type has advantages and disadvantages. The differences are summed up in the following table.

FEATURE	*GLASS*	*ACRYLIC*
WEIGHT	heavier	lighter
PRICE	less expensive	more expensive
FRAGILITY	more breakable	less breakable
OPTICAL CLARITY	slightly less clear	slightly more clear
SCRATCHABILITY	harder to scratch	easy to scratch
STRENGTH	thinner, stronger	must be thicker than glass
INSULATING ABILITY	not good	fairly good

Stock aquarium sizes range from 2 gallons to 180 gallons. Besides the regular rectangular shape, there are hexagons, flat back hexagons, pentagons, squares, bow-fronts, and, of course, custom tanks in just about any shape imaginable. There are very wide low tanks called "breeders" and narrow, extra-tall show tanks. The moldings come in black and various wood grains. So which is best?

Any rule of thumb is of only limited usefulness, but the appropriate one here is: Start out with a tank of 20 or more gallons that is not disproportionately tall. The reasons are simple. Lower rectangular aquaria have the greatest surface area to gallonage ratio, which means that they can support the most fish, and, importantly for the beginner, they have a greater margin of safety. Although it may seem counterintuitive, the larger the tank, the greater the chances of success. Successfully maintaining an aquarium requires an understanding and a regulation of a complex of parameters. It is easier to maintain a stable environment in a larger aquarium, which has more buffers against sudden changes, and it is more difficult to stay on top of water conditions sufficiently to maintain a smaller tank. While experienced aquarists can and do maintain even tiny one-gallon tanks, it is much more difficult than keeping a significantly larger one.

If plants are going to be part of the aquarium, beginners are well advised to stay with low tanks, regardless of the number of gallons. Plants will thrive under standard lighting in aquaria 12 to 16 inches deep, but deeper tanks often require specialized, very expensive lighting.

Is there an upper limit to size? Not exactly, though it is not recommended to start with a 180-gallon tank. The reason, however, is not the size, since a 180-gallon tank is much easier to maintain than a 20-gallon tank. The two drawbacks to such a large starter aquarium are the expense, which is much greater than for more reasonably sized tanks, and the physical difficulties in transporting, positioning, and equipping such a large tank. The only other problem would be the greater sum of money unwisely invested in the event tropical fish are not to your liking. You will, of course, be ahead, with that money being wisely invested, if you instead go on to a lifelong interest in the hobby.

Another factor to consider in choosing the aquarium size is weight. Tanks are heavy, but the water they hold is much heavier still. The weight

Tanks in pentagonal and other non-traditional shapes are available to hobbyists who have specific design ideas and needs; hoods and stands designed for use with such tanks are available also. Photo courtesy Perfecto Pentagon Aquarium Systems.

of a filled and decorated aquarium can be approximated by multiplying the number of gallons by ten and reading the answer in pounds. Thus a 20-gallon tank will weigh about 200 pounds, and that 180 gallon giant will strain a floor to the tune of almost a ton!

This consideration dictates that aquarium stands be designed for the job. Odd pieces of furniture or home-made supports can be fatally inadequate and are hardly worth any potential savings.

COVERS AND LIGHTS

It is best to purchase a tank and full hood or glass canopy combination. These consist of the aquarium, a glass canopy or plastic hood, and a strip reflector to light the aquarium. These "combos" are often available at a substantial saving over buying the components separately.

The hood or canopy provides a secure covering for the tank. This is necessary for several reasons. It prevents the fish from jumping out to a desiccated death (and almost any fish will jump, with many species regular

Full hoods and strip reflectors should be made of a non-corrosive material and should have their electrical parts well protected from the accumulation of moisture that's bound to occur under aquarium conditions. Photo courtesy Perfecto Pentagon Aquarium Systems.

escape artists). It keeps dust, dirt, little fingers, cats, and other foreign objects from getting into the tank. It protects the aquarium light from exposure to condensation and spray, which can cause electrical failure and dangerous shock risks (the plastic hoods have a clear glass section onto which the reflector fits). Finally, the aquarium cover cuts down considerably on evaporation, which preserves water stability and conserves heat.

These covers have one or more hinged sections to provide access to the tank, as well as knock-outs or cuttable strips which permit the use of heaters, filters, and other hanging accessories without allowing the egress of the tank inhabitants.

The light should be a fluorescent fixture with a bulb specifically designed for aquarium use. The determining factor for lighting is the type of plants, if any, that are desired. For no plants or only plastic plants, any bulb that shows off the fish's colors to advantage is fine.

For living plants, at least twice the normal amount of light is needed, and more if the tank is fairly deep and/or the plants are species which require high light intensities. There are special high-intensity, full-spectrum fluorescent bulbs designed for aquatic plants, and double-bulb reflectors are available which will fit in the place of the single-bulb ones. There are even more sophisticated lighting systems such as metal halide lights, but they are quite expensive and usually used only by advanced aquarists.

Sunlight, by the way, is generally not a good choice for lighting an aquarium, and a tank should not be located where the sun can beam onto it. Aside from a proliferation of algae, which is a likely result, when the sun is shining the tank will likely overheat, and even if not, when the sun is gone, the temperature of the tank will drop considerably, which is a sure invitation to disease for the fish. (For the same reason an aquarium should not be placed near a heat source or an air conditioning register.)

HEATING

Tropical fish, of course, require warm water, normally in the 74° to 80°F. range for most species, and an aquarium heater is necessary to maintain a constant temperature. There are two basic types, hanging and submersible. The hanging heater is suspended by a bracket from the rim of the tank, with most of the glass tube submerged in the water. Submersible units can be attached to the back glass with suction cups and are sealed so that the entire heater goes under water, with the electric cord running out over the top rim. Although submersibles are generally more accurate and more expensive, there is so much variation in quality and dependability within both types that this will not always hold true. Ask your dealer for a recommendation and for advice on size. Although heaters do differ in their lengths, the "size" of a heater that matters is the wattage. This ranges from 25 watts all the way up to 300 watts for most brands.

The penthouse of aquarium heaters is the substrate heater, either an undergravel heating unit or an undertank heater. These are used almost exclusively by very serious water gardeners, since it is plants, not fish, which benefit most from them, and since their price tag (as much as 50 times as much as regular aquarium heaters) sets them quite apart.

A word or two about heater wattages: obviously, the more water to heat, the more power the heater should have. But it is *not* true that twice as much water needs twice as many watts. Like any solid body, an aquarium full of water loses heat through its surface, and the volume-to-surface-area ratio determines how quickly heat will dissipate from the tank, so larger tanks can be heated more efficiently than smaller ones. This is because doubling of a tank's dimensions quadruples its surface area but octuples its volume. It is not necessary to worry about the math, however. Just think about it intuitively—which will cool off faster, a bathtub full of hot water, or a teacup full of hot water? That's the same principle we're talking about here.

Recommendations range from 2 watts per gallon all the way up to 10 watts per gallon, with 3 watts per gallon a good starting estimate. The lower figures are for large tanks and for small temperature increases; the higher ones are for smaller tanks and greater temperature increases. Of course, an aquarium kept in a chilly room will require a more powerful heater than the same one kept in a cozy, warm room. Normally a 75-or 100-watt heater will serve for a 20-gallon tank, and a 150-watt for a 55-gallon tank. Very large tanks may require two or more heaters. The manufacturer's directions will indicate how to correctly set the thermostat to maintain the desired temperature. On most heaters, any degree settings are approximations at best, and in any case an aquarium thermometer is absolutely necessary so that the water temperature can be monitored daily.

Floating and hanging thermometers are available, but the easiest to use are strip thermometers which attach to the outside of the glass and indicate the temperature with colored numbers. Every time the aquarist looks at the tank the temperature can be read at a glance.

FILTRATION

Nowhere has the aquarium hobby seen more technological advancement in recent years than in water filtering systems. There are three types of filtration to be aware of, and a multitude of technologies for accomplishing them.

Mechanical filtration is simply the removal of suspended solids from the aquarium water. This is normally accomplished by passing the dirty water through a fiber or sponge medium, though gravel and other media can be used. It keeps the water clean-looking, and, whenever the medium is cleaned or replaced, it removes the wastes from the aquarium.

There are many variations on this theme, from plastic boxes which sit on the aquarium bottom and contain filter medium and an airstone and lift tube to create the flow, to huge power filters, which hang on the tank or sit as canisters on the floor, and which use electrical water pumps to direct the water through various filter media. A reliable dealer can demonstrate the different filters and make recommendations.

Chemical filtration involves having the water flow through a reactive medium which removes impurities by binding them to the medium. Usually a section or chamber of the mechanical filter is used to hold chemical media. The most common medium for chemical filtration is activated carbon, which can absorb a wide variety of dissolved gases and other

Some canister filters combine mechanical, chemical and biological filtration activity in one powerful unit. Photo courtesy Eheim North America.

impurities. Rather than just make the water look cleaner, such filtration actually purifies it.

There are also specific chemical media for absorbing or adsorbing various substances, such as phosphates, nitrates, or ammonia. While these can be especially important in certain marine setups, where precise water chemistry is more of an issue, their use in freshwater aquaria is of less critical value. In any event, their use should never be intended as an alternative to proper management.

Biological filtration, or biofiltration, is often misunderstood and often made more complicated than necessary. Understanding it requires a knowledge of the nitrogen cycle. The most prevalent waste product in an aquarium (except perhaps for carbon dioxide) is ammonia. Fish give off ammonia in their excreta and through their gills. Decaying plant and animal material also produces ammonia. And ammonia is extremely toxic, moreso in a basic environment. It burns the gills of fish and can cause suffocation. Ammonia is also an excellent fertilizer, so healthy live plants can remove quite a bit, but except with extremely light fish stocking rates, not enough.

There are, however, bacteria which feed on ammonia, turning it into nitrites. These nitrites are still quite toxic to fish, but less so, and they serve as food for yet another set of bacteria, which convert them into nitrates, which fish can tolerate in much greater concentrations. It is apparent, then, that culturing these bacteria in an aquarium setup will serve to minimize toxins in the water. To do this requires four things: a culture medium, oxygen, food for the bacteria, and time.

These beneficial bacteria do not live freely in the water but grow only on solid surfaces. They do, of course, colonize plants, gravel, and the aquarium glass, but in nowhere near the necessary numbers. A biological filter, or biofilter, consists of a medium which maximizes surface area. Common examples are sponge, synthetic fibers, porous ceramic pieces, and plastic shapes.

Since these bacteria are all aerobic, they require oxygen, and the more oxygen they have, the better the job they do. This has led to the concept of the wet-dry filter, part of which is designed to expose a biofilter medium to the air, which contains many thousands of times the oxygen saturation of water. The two most common means of doing this are to spray or trickle the prefiltered water over the biomedium, through which it percolates in very thin sheets, maximizing its exposure to the air, or to spray prefiltered water onto spinning wheels of pleated medium, any part of which is exposed to the air except when it is directly under the spray. Thus, while the medium is always wet (since these are aquatic bacteria), it is also extremely well oxygenated (since these are aerobic bacteria). The bacteria colonize these systems in great numbers.

The original biofilter was the UGF—the undergravel filter. This dependable old standby has become the focus of a lot of controversy, and you will hear very emotional praise and very emotional condemnation of it. In the UGF water is drawn down through the aquarium gravel into a slotted plate, then lifted either by air or by mechanical pumps up through tubes to the surface. This, in effect, utilizes the gravel bed as a large biofilter, with the surface area of each grain of gravel serving as a colonizing site for the bacteria. The constant flow of oxygenated water prevents the growth of anaerobic bacteria (as long as no "dead zones" develop), which can produce deadly waste products of their own in unaerated gravel beds.

The major drawback of the UGF is that detritus is drawn down into the gravel, where it continues to decay, producing toxins, or worse, where it can impede the flow of water, creating anaerobic zones. These problems can be minimized by frequent vacuuming of the gravel and by slipping a siphon tube down an airlift and vacuuming under the plate. Also, a reverse flow

The diagram shows the basic operation of an undergravel filter of the regular (that is, non-reverse flow) type. Air is pumped down to the filter's return tube. Then air bubbles rising through the return tube draw water with them, creating a partial vacuum under the filter plate. Aquarium water therefore is drawn down through the gravel, bringing oxygen to the aerobic bacteria living in the gravel.

UGF can be utilized. With these, reverse flow powerheads are fitted with a sponge prefilter and attached to the lift tubes. Water is drawn through the sponge and sent down the tubes, then it percolates up through the gravel bed. This keeps the gravel much cleaner.

There is no definite answer to the UGF controversy. Aquarists have varying results with them, compared to other biofilters. Some people will advise tearing down a system just to get the UGF out, while others will just as adamantly advocate tearing down a system just to put one in, and both groups will claim their advice will save your fish. These filters do work and have been standby biofilters for decades. There is no doubt that many other biofilters are available today which have eliminated some of the problems associated with the UGF, but they are invariably more expensive and more complicated to run.

The sum of the controversies is this:

1. An undergravel filter is by no means necessary, but many aquarists find them extremely useful.

2. General (but far from unanimous) feeling is that a planted tank should not have one.

3. Fish which excavate gravel can expose the plate, which allows most of the water to flow through that exposed area, making much of the filter plate a dead zone. This can be prevented by having two layers of gravel, separated by a barrier such as plastic eggcrate, to prevent fish from digging all the way down to the plate.

4. It is still a simple, inexpensive, low-maintenance, fairly efficient biofilter, and many aquarists use them, sometimes as the *only* filter in their tanks. Others wouldn't be caught dead with one in their tanks.

You should talk to your dealer and ask to see some of the filters out of their boxes, or, if possible, in use. Ask about maintenance, cleaning, and other operating requirements. Then make your decision and don't be afraid to try something different later on if you aren't completely satisfied. Whatever biofilter you choose, however, it does not come out of the box fully functional, since it needs those bacterial colonies.

CYCLING AN AQUARIUM

This topic has been treated in a variety of ways, from extremely scientific, complete with graphs and charts of parts per million concentrations against time, to almost mystical, with arcane rules, absolute pronouncements, and fervent testimonials to the necessity of certain commercial products. But the basics are, as stated before—to cycle an aquarium, which means to culture the beneficial bacteria for biofiltration, requires four things: a culture medium, oxygen, food for the bacteria, and time. Clearly, a functional biofilter provides the first two. And there is no reliable substitute for the last. One thing about these "bugs" is that they live in the bacterial slow lane. You are probably familiar with the notion that bacteria multiply at extraordinary rates, able to colonize millions from a single original cell in a matter of hours. These nitrifying bacteria, however, are slow growers and need weeks to fully colonize the biofilter. The food to encourage the growth of bacteria is first ammonia, then nitrites.

These can be provided by setting up an aquarium with a very few, very hardy fish. After the tank cycles, more fish can be added, up to a normal stocking density. A tank can also be cycled chemically; usually ammonium chloride is used to simulate fish wastes. Some aquarists simply feed an empty tank fish food, which then decomposes and produces ammonia. But whatever the source of ammonia, the cycling is based on the fact that after enough ammonia-eating bacteria have colonized the biofilter, they will begin converting all that ammonia to nitrites, and the nitrite-eating bacteria can grow.

Filter media that have been "pre-colonized" with *Nitosomonas* and *Nitrobacter* bacteria shorten the amount of time needed to complete the nitrogen cycle and simultanously provide biological filration.Photo courtesy of Tropical Science.

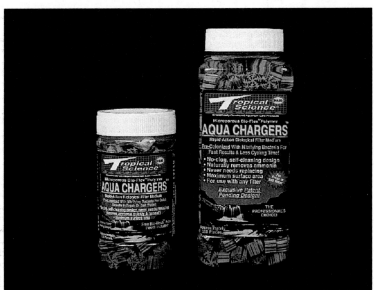

Monitoring the Cycling Process

This is a dangerous time for any inhabitants of the tank. It is necessary to have high ammonia levels to feed the fledgling bacterial colonies, so massive water changes are not recommended at this time, as they will remove too much of the ammonia. On the other hand, any fish will be stressed by the ammonia concentrations. Then, as the ammonia begins to subside and the nitrites begin to rise, the stress will lessen a bit, but, of course, by then the fish's resistance is also lowered.

The phenomenon known as "New Tank Syndrome" probably serves to frustrate more would-be aquarists than anything else. It is very hard to get a new tank, ornaments, plants, and other equipment, then set it up with only one or two fish. The toxic ammonia and nitrites which plague fish in a newly set up tank are invisible to the hobbyist, and the aquarium looks so *empty!* Patience is vital, as is diligent monitoring with ammonia and nitrite test kits. These kits are available in many different styles, from chem-lab liquid reagent types to tablet reagent kits to dipsticks. The concentrations of the chemicals being tested for are shown as color changes, which you can match against the chart provided.

Over a period of up to six weeks, the bacteria will establish themselves—first the ammonia-eating ones, then, once they have built up a sufficient concentration of nitrite wastes, the nitrite-eating bacteria will colonize. Test kits will let you "watch" the cycling. At first there will be a surge of ammonia production, which will begin to taper as nitrite production picks up. Finally both ammonia and nitrite should go to zero as nitrates accumulate.

Cheating on Cycling

There is a method for getting around a long cycling period. This is not really a method for getting around the amount of time it takes to build a biofilter, however. An established biofilter, or part of one, can be moved from its aquarium into a freshly set up one. Ironically, if this is done, it is important to stock the new tank immediately, lest the bacterial colonies begin to die off from starvation and the advantage be lost. Of course, the original tank cannot be left without a biofilter, so only part of the biofilter material can be transferred. Some aquarists keep several "extra" sponge filters going at all times in their tanks so that if they want to start a new tank, or if they need a hospital or quarantine tank, they can simply move one or more of these mature biofilters into it.

It is important to remember that cycling a tank is not a mystical ritual. Cycling can be adequately defined as "waiting for the bacterial colonies to stabilize optimally." While such a shortcut can greatly reduce cycling times, perhaps creating instant cycling, both the original aquarium from which the biofilter is taken and the new aquarium must be monitored, since problems can arise. Daily ammonia and nitrite tests will alert you to any dangerous rise in these poisons, while nitrate tests will indicate the degree of maturity of the biofiltration, since the end of cycling is signaled by an accumulation of only nitrates in the aquarium.

Nitrate Removal

What about these nitrates? They *are* much less harmful than ammonia or nitrites. But they are *not* beneficial. As they accumulate, they put stress on the tank residents. There are two methods to remove nitrates from the aquarium.

The first is with a denitrator. There are two types—electrical and bacterial. (As stated above, chemical media exist to extract nitrates, but they should not be used for routine nitrate maintenance.) Electrical denitrators use electric current to break the nitrates down. Nitrogen gas (the most abundant gas in our atmosphere) is released. They are expensive and not widely used at all. Bacterial, or coil denitrators, use an anaerobic chamber, colonized with denitrifying bacteria, to break the nitrates down to nitrogen gas. This sounds like an ideal solution—aerobic bacteria to take ammonia to nitrates, anaerobic ones to take nitrates to nitrogen gas. In practice, however, there is a much simpler method of dealing with nitrates than culturing finicky bacteria (oxygen kills them, so too great a water flow through the coil is devastating) which can also produce toxins themselves, such as the extremely dangerous hydrogen sulfide. This method is to dilute the nitrates by removing some of the water and replacing it with fresh.

Partial Water Changes

Frequent partial water changes are the most practical method of keeping nitrate levels low, but they have many other benefits. They remove pollutants not removed or poorly removed by any other filtration, such as pheromones and other complex organic substances. They replace trace elements. And they stimulate fish growth, health, and reproduction better than any tonic, supplement, or exotic diet ever could.

A multitude of factors will determine an appropriate water change regimen—tank stocking, type of fish (big sloppy ones versus dainty little ones), and personal factors such as number of tanks cared for or individual lifestyle and schedule. And, certainly, the availability of suitable water, and its expense, and the local need for conservation of water are all significant factors. The operating principle, however, is: the more the better, the more often the better.

There is no such thing as too much water change. Some of the most successful fish breeders swear by massive daily changes. Many even use

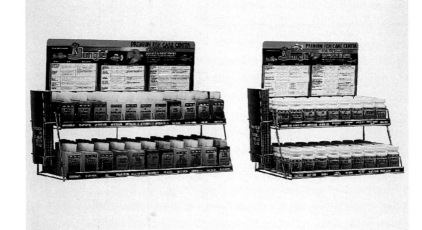

Water conditioners, treatments and clarifiers are available to aquarists seeking to make their water supply more hospitable to the species they want to keep. Photo courtesy of Jungle Laboratories Corporation.

a drip overflow system, in which the water in their tanks is *always* being changed. Almost every discus breeder relies on daily changes of 50 percent or more in every aquarium.

Like opening a window in a stuffy, crowded room, water changes perk fish up and make a visible immediate improvement in their well-being. The benefits are very quickly apparent to aquarists who commit to a significant water change schedule.

Some have opposing views on this matter, and they often cite cases where fish died right after a water change. Such apparent contradiction of the merits of changing water is, in fact, exact corroboration of the importance of water changes. How? Aquarists not committed to this procedure often allow long intervals between partial water changes. During that time the water of the aquarium can undergo extreme changes in chemistry, most notably a massive buildup of nitrates and a reduction in pH as the acids of metabolism accumulate. These changes, however, take place gradually, and as the weeks pass, the aquarium inhabitants slowly acclimate to them. A large water change at this point presents an extreme chemical shock to the fish, as the pH jumps up and the nitrates drop. Any change in water chemistry needs to be gradual, even if the change is for the better. Aquarists who regularly perform substantial water changes not only keep their water chemistry at favorable readings, they keep the water chemistry *stable.*

WATER CHEMISTRY–THE THREE H'S

No, an aquarist does not need a degree in chemistry to keep fish. The only requirement in this regard is a little knowledge about how different various water sources can be. While aquarists can become very involved in monitoring and managing a great many chemical parameters of their tanks' water, and some do, there are only three parameters that are vital for a beginning aquarist to know about–pH, GH, and KH.

It is most important to avoid extremes and to keep things as consistent as possible. If the tapwater has a pH of 7.2, it is better for a fish which prefers a pH of 6.7 to have a constant pH of 7.2 than to have the aquarist bounce the pH up and down with the addition of various chemicals. A source pH of 8.9 might require intervention on a regular basis, but it must be constantly monitored to prevent large swings in pH.

pH

Most aquarium fish will do fine in water with a pH between 6.5 and 7.5. There are species which thrive in a pH below 6.0, and other species want a pH of 9.0 or even higher, but as a general rule, roughly neutral water is best.

The measurement of the pH of water quantifies the potential of hydronium ion ($H+$), which is simply scientific jargon to say that the pH indicates whether the water is acidic, basic (alkaline), or neutral. Neutral is defined as 7.0, with lower values indicating acid conditions and higher values indicating basic conditions. The scale is logarithmic and inverse, which simply means that a reading of 3.0 is ten times more acid than 4.0, 2.0 is one hundred times more acid than 4.0, 1.0 is one thousand times more acid than 4.0, etc. This means that what look like small differences can be, in fact, much greater. While the vast majority of aquarium species are quite tolerant of a reasonable range of pH, none can handle a very rapid or very drastic change in pH. In fact, it is best to avoid any change of more than 0.2 pH units. Larger changes should be made in 0.2 increments over several days.

Such changes are made by adding various acids, to lower pH, or bases, to raise pH. Proprietary formulas are available which are buffered to maintain a specific pH as well. Since fish are more easily damaged by pH fluctuations than by less-than-ideal pH, the beginning aquarist is well advised to leave pH modifications for later, unless the pH of the available water source is extreme. Gaining experience with species which are less fussy about the pH will enable the aquarist to master the basics of fishkeeping before tackling any fine-tuning of the pH of the water.

GH

GH is general hardness, and it indicates how much dissolved minerals there are in the water. This is sometimes called total hardness, and it can be quantified in various ways, but it is commonly measured in parts per million, a reading of "120 ppm" indicating that there are 120 parts per million of dissolved mineral in the water. It is important to know and monitor the hardness of aquarium water, but since it can change only by adding minerals (as when soluble rocks or gravel are used in the aquarium) or by removing minerals (something that rarely happens unintentionally), hardness fluctuations are not the concern that pH fluctuations are.

Aquarists whose fish favor very hard water conditions use dolomite or crushed oyster shell as a substrate or as part of the filter medium. These leach minerals into the water which will raise both hardness and pH. Such materials, along with coral or limestone rocks, should not be used in the average aquarium for precisely this reason–they alter the water chemistry. There is really only one material which might be used as an ornament in the aquarium which will lower hardness, and that is driftwood. It does this by leaching organic substances into the water, including organic acids and buffers, some of which bind with the minerals in the water, taking them literally out of circulation. This rules driftwood out as an ornament in aquaria which house species that prefer hard, alkaline water.

As with pH, most fish are tolerant of any water which is not extremely hard or soft, as long as any changes are made gradually, and many species will do fine in water that is not their natural hardness, even if they might not breed successfully in these conditions.

A word about home water softeners–these devices remove the "hard" minerals, calcium and magnesium, and replace them with "soft" sodium. This results in a water in which soap is much more efficient, since calcium binds with soap molecules, causing both a lack of suds and the infamous ring around the bathtub. This is, however, a bizarre situation relative to natural aquatic habitats. Some fish come from waters full of calcium and magnesium, and others come from waters practically devoid of any minerals. Few if any, however, will ever meet water which is full of sodium but not calcium and magnesium. (Sea water, for example, has plenty of all three.) The effect of softened water (as opposed to soft water) on fish is not what you would expect, and while some aquarists have success using softened water, it must be realized that as far as the fish are concerned, this

Even some species that will adapt quite well to living in water very different chemically from their home waters might have very specific water requirement for breeding. The Cardinal Tetras shown here, for example, will live quite happily in aquariums having slightly alkaline water, but they'll normally spawn only in soft, acidic water.

is strange "hard" water, not the mineral-free water in natural soft water environments. Most softeners have a bypass switch which enables the owner to temporarily shunt water so it does not go through the machine; this is the best option for aquarists with water softeners to use when filling their tanks.

KH

KH is carbonate hardness, also known as alkalinity or buffering capacity. This is a measure of the amount of carbonates (usually calcium and magnesium carbonate) in the water. These particular minerals act as alkaline buffers. When acid is produced, as in decomposition, these minerals react with the acid, neutralizing it, so the pH remains stable and does not drop.

Carbonate hardness is very important, since it serves to keep the pH stable despite the natural production of acids in the aquarium. In very soft water, with little buffering capacity, there can be drastic pH drops in a very

An African cichlid, *Melanochromis johanni,* squaring off against a *Haplochomis,* another Lake Malawi dweller. Lake Malawi and Lake Tanganyika, the prime sources for African cichlids, both contain hard alkaline water.

short time. In many ways, the KH, or buffering capacity of aquarium water, is more of a concern than the general or total hardness, or GH.

Buffers

The topic of buffers deserves separate attention, since the buffering capacity of aquarium water is more important than its particular pH. Since fish are healthier at a constant pH, and since the normal metabolic processes in an aquarium tend to alter the pH, buffers help keep fish healthy. The buffering capacity of water can be defined as its resistance to change pH when acids or bases are added.

As mentioned, carbonate hardness serves to buffer the water against pH drops due to organic processes. In extremely soft water, with little or no KH, acid drops are a constant threat. The KH of the water can be increased by adding carbonate minerals, either in a proprietary formula or as small amounts of sodium bicarbonate (baking soda). As with all changes in water chemistry, these should be done gradually and over an extended period.

There are also acid buffers, usually organic substances, which can buffer the water against increases in alkalinity. This becomes a factor when softwater species are being kept in water that is modified (usually with peat) to be softer and more acidic. If the aquarist's water supply is naturally basic, without acid buffers being present in the aquarium water the regular water changes necessary for the fish's health would cause the pH to rise drastically every time a change was carried out. The buffering effect of these organic substances absorbs the alkalinity of the added water and prevents pH spikes.

TANK CAPACITY

Perhaps nowhere do beginning aquarists err more often than in overestimating the capacity of their aquarium to hold fish. They often see it as a matter of "room" or "space." In the same way that they might look at a birdcage to decide how many budgies it could hold without crowding, they visualize how much elbow room their fish will have within the walls of their tank. This, of course, ignores many things, most notably that unlike the birdcage open to the room's atmosphere, the fish are trapped in the volume of water in the aquarium, along with all their wastes and the wastes of the other inhabitants of the tank.

The actual stocking rate of an aquarium should be considerably below the number of fish that can "fit" into the tank without bumping into each other too much, and it should take into account a multitude of factors, with elbow room entering the equation only in that a fish must have enough room to turn around and swim freely. While this is normally a minor consideration, there are unfortunately too many large fish cramped in unsuitably small tanks, and there is a particularly false and malicious fallacy which surfaces regularly that a fish can be stunted to any particular size by keeping it in too small a tank.

So how should the stocking rate for an aquarium be determined? The carrying capacity of a given aquarium is based on several factors, some having to do with the tank itself and the water in it, and some having to do with the fish which will be placed into it.

Volume. The actual water volume of a fish tank is actually of almost no consideration when figuring how many fish can go into it. At what are considered even minimal stocking rates, the unnaturally high population densities severely limit the capacity of the volume of water to sustain the fishes' respiration. Instead, surface area is of much more importance.

Surface area. Gas exchange, notably oxygen (O_2) in and carbon dioxide (CO_2) out, takes place at an interface between the water and the air. This means that two tanks with the same surface area have approximately the same carrying capacity. It also means that a 50-gallon aquarium with a surface area of 4.5 square ft (length 3 ft x width 1.5 ft) has a *greater* carrying capacity than a 55-gallon tank with an area of 4 square ft area (length 4 ft x width 1 ft).

That popular shape of the 55-gallon aquarium comes in several heights. You can get 33,-40,-55,-and 60-gallon tanks that have a surface area of 4 square ft, and they all have approximately the same carrying capacity. Likewise for a 75-and a 90-gallon, which differ only in height.

Aeration. Aquarium aeration is often misunderstood. The sight of an airstone or diffuser profusely producing air bubbles which rise in a reverse cascade to the surface often leads people to think that all that air is being "pumped into" the water. Actually, very little gas exchange can take place on the surface of a bubble as it speeds toward the surface. These short-lived pockets of air actually serve principally to *move* the water. An absolutely still tank with a surface area of 3 square ft always has 3 square ft of water exposed to the air. Put that water in motion, however, and it is constantly turning over, effectively increasing the area as each "surface" is rotated under, raising a new "surface." Filter returns, powerheads, and other water movers also serve to aerate, even if they don't look as airy as a column of bubbles. In addition, many fish enjoy the currents produced, especially rheophilic species, which come from rapidly-moving waters.

Another function of aeration is to keep the surface agitated, preventing a film from forming. Such a film can come from oils in the food you use, from airborne pollutants, or from organic sources within the tank. Whatever its source, it can block a considerable amount of gas exchange. Of course, a hermetically sealed tank of fish would soon have all its oxygen depleted, and a seal of film on the surface can be almost as bad.

The safest way to view aeration is that it helps keep your fish healthy but does not appreciably affect the tank's carrying capacity. Relying on mechanical aeration to counteract overcrowding is an invitation to catastrophe from either a hot summer day, a temporary power loss, or an air pump malfunction.

Temperature. The warmer water is, the less oxygen it can hold at saturation. To make things worse, since fish are cold-blooded, the warmer the water, the faster their metabolism. In fact, a livebearer which gives birth about every 28 days at 72º will drop a litter about every 21 days at 80º. She will also live a shorter life, but the crucial factor here is that in warmer water the same fish will respire more than it does in cooler water, and the water has less oxygen in it to begin with. So, within your fishes' acceptable temperature range, you can keep fewer of them in a tank at the warmer end than you could in the same tank if you kept the temperature at the lower end of the range. This can become a significant factor in the summer, and air conditioning will help your fish as well as your family to stay comfortable.

Salinity. This is not normally a consideration in freshwater aquaria, but sometimes a significant amount of salt is added either for brackish water species or as a medication, and in a tank already pushed to capacity, this can be the fatal last straw. The higher the salinity of the water, the less oxygen it can hold. It is certainly something to keep in mind, especially if you take the step to marine tropical fish, which should be stocked at a rate at least three times less heavily than freshwater species.

Type of fish. Two factors come into play here. Obviously, fish which can breathe atmospheric air, such as the belontids and many catfish, can survive in tanks with lower oxygen saturations than most other fish could tolerate. This is why a single male *Betta splendens* can be kept in a small glass jar; it breathes air to supplement the oxygen it removes from the water with its gills. This factor is mentioned, however, only in the negative, since it is very dangerous to stock your tank thinking that overcrowded anabantoids will do just fine. These fish are still injured by waste products like ammonia, and it is all too common, for example, to see male Bettas with horrible ammonia burns on their fins because they were kept in the same stagnant, rotten water all the time. A total change once a day would be the minimum for a single betta in a small glass globe.

The second factor, which *must* be taken into account when stocking an aquarium, is the body and activity type of the fish you are planning to keep. Sedentary ambush predators obviously use less oxygen per unit of body weight than always-on-the-move schooling fishes. But that is assuming similar body masses, which might be true of a large toadfish and a small pacu, but is hardly the case when comparing a tetra with a cichlid of the same length, and is definitely not the case when six one-inch fish are compared to one 6-inch fish.

Remember the discussion of heat loss? Well, a similar principle applies here. The metabolism (and the respiration) of an animal depends on its mass—its volume, if you will. But volume octuples when length and height and width are doubled. So a two-inch fish has roughly eight times the mass of a one-inch fish of the same species. That does not mean it needs eight times as much surface area, since the rate of metabolism decreases as size increases (due to surface area and heat loss, among other things). A one-ounce rodent might eat its own weight several times a day, but a one-ton cow gets by on a mere 100 pounds or so of food per day. How does this translate into fish-per-gallon?

A 10-inch oscar might mass 1,000 times as much as a one-inch danio, or 100 times as much as 10 one-inch danios. The school of danios would not be crowded in a 20-gallon tank, and, in fact, could tolerate some tankmates. The oscar would be stretching the limit in that same 20-gallon tank. No, it wouldn't need a 200-gallon tank, but 30 gallons or more would suit it much better. So the use of the one-inch-of-fish-per-gallon rule should be used sparingly, taking into account that fewer fish is better and that you should at least double it for larger fish, and treble it or better for the largest fish.

This works to advantage going the other way, however. While a pair of 10-inch oscars would not be lost in a 6-foot, 100-gallon tank, considerably more than 20 one-inch fishes could be put into the same tank (minus the oscars, of course!) In fact, some spectacular setups feature a very large planted aquarium with several dozens of small schooling fish in it.

Compatibility. The compatibility of the fishes you choose to house together is important for many reasons, one of which is stocking rate. Small, peaceful, non-territorial fish can be stocked at a much higher rate than nasty, aggressive fish. Two pairs of 2-inch *Julidochromis ornatus*, for example, could commandeer the entire bottom area of a 4-foot long tank, making it "too crowded" to add a third pair. The same aquarium might comfortably house twenty or thirty similarly sized but non-territorial fish, like schooling tetras.

This concept can perhaps best be illustrated in the extreme. A 72-inch 135-gallon aquarium with one 20-inch male wolf cichlid (*Herichthys dovii*) would probably be completely stocked in terms of compatibility, but it could

Herichthys managuense is a chunky fish that grows to a relatively large size, and adults require large aquaria—especially considering that this species also is very combative.

carry a school of seven *Distichodus* of exactly the same size as the wolf cichlid. The same aquarium could probably house 25 or 30 mature angelfish, still cichlids but much more social, at least until they started spawning, or even 200-250 neon tetras, for whom compatibility is not an issue at all.

OUTFITTING THE TANK

In this section we will consider tanks which the aquarist intends to be a display object in the home. Tanks as stark as a bare aquarium with a sponge filter bubbling in it are often used for breeding or rearing or quarantining fish, and artificial objects such as pieces of plastic pipe and flowerpots are often used for general hiding places or for spawning caves. The needs and preferences of the aquarist dictate how a tank is decorated, if it even *is* decorated. A bare tank with a hunk of pipe in it is, however, rather self-explanatory, and it is rarely what a beginning aquarist wants.

There is considerable friction among some aquarists concerning appropriate decor. There are some who scoff at anything which is not "natural" and turn up their noses at dayglo plastic plants, sunken pirate ships, plastic "driftwood," and rainbow gravel. Others use their tanks as modern art pieces, filling them with air-operated divers, bubbling volcanoes, Roman ruins, and hot pink gravel. The friction really mounts with plastic plants, which green thumb aquatic gardeners scorn as feeble imitations, many aquarists view as useful within certain boundaries, and others feel are the only way to go.

The truth is that a "natural" aquarium would probably have a mud bottom, leeches, predatory insects, dangerous reptiles, and a beer can or two. On the other hand, a collection of animated ornaments can provide fish with the types of hiding places they naturally crave. So accept that beauty is in the eye of the beholder, and decorate your aquarium as you wish. Your fish will not give it a second look.

Bottom Substrate

The common substrate in aquaria is gravel. Sand and crushed coral are often used in marine tanks, or in African rift lake cichlid tanks, but sand is generally unsuitable for a freshwater aquarium.

There are many types of gravel available for the aquarium, from various natural mixes to epoxy-coated gravel in natural or decorator colors to dyed gravel in a full range of neon hues. If the tank will be planted, the smaller-particled gravels are generally best. With a UGF, medium-sized grains are best, and coarse gravels are useful for some large fish which like to excavate, like many cichlids. A few aquarium gravels are sharp rather than rounded, and colored glass chips are sometimes offered. Such substrates tend to become impacted, which can lead to dangerous anaerobic zones, but they must definitely be avoided if the aquarium will have bottom-rooting fishes like *Corydoras* catfish or *Botia* loaches, whose tender mouths and barbels will be injured by the sharp edges.

Rocks, Driftwood, etc.

Objects such as rocks, driftwood, and ornaments serve at least three functions. The first, obviously, is aesthetic. The aquarist can create practically any type of look with the objects available through local dealers. It is safer, at least at first, to purchase objects for decorating the aquarium rather than collecting them outside, so that their safety can be assured.

The second function is to provide a natural, safe, and reassuring environment for the fish so that they will feel comfortable and unthreatened and so that they will behave normally. Many ornamental structures sold for aquaria contain numerous nooks and crannies and hidden cavities where cave-dwelling fish can set up housekeeping or where flighty species can retreat when frightened. Timid fish will be more visible if they know there are

Closeup of the head area of a *Corydoras* species; the barbels of this species and others that continually grub in the substrate for food can be injured through the use of a bottom covering that is too sharp or coarse.

numerous hiding places into which they can retreat. Fish which normally hide completely all day, like mastacembelid spiny eels and many catfish, will probably follow their natural pattern and stay out of sight. They may, however, learn to come out and feed. In any event, denying them hiding places will certainly leave them visible, but they will also be stressed and will not thrive. In addition, a lack of hiding spaces may precipitate their departure from the tank, something such fish are notorious for anyway.

Another way in which decorative objects serve a natural purpose is in providing territorial boundaries. Fish which set up and defend territories often use such objects to define the borders. In fact, a sure way to give a newcomer to such a tank a reasonable chance of integrating into the pecking order is to rearrange all the objects in the tank when the new fish is added. Breaking up all the territories forces the residents to redefine their status, and the newcomer has the opportunity to take part in the hierarchy from the start.

The last function of ornamental objects is to alter the water chemistry. Driftwood leaches tannins and other organic substances into the water. These soften and acidify the water and tint it amber. This would rule out driftwood for an aquarium housing fish which require hard, alkaline conditions, such as many African cichlids. But driftwood is especially useful in an aquarium containing blackwater fishes such as many tetras and South American cichlids. Stones normally should be inert for aquarium use. Certain rocks, such as coral rock or limestone, leach carbonates into the water, creating hard and alkaline conditions. Typically reserved for marine tanks, such rocks are also ideal for fish such as rift lake cichlids or Central American cichlids and livebearers.

PLANTS

The topic of aquarium plants has already been discussed in a preceding section, primarily as regards the different types available. Here we'll talk strictly about plants' effects on the fish.

Underwater gardening is a rapidly growing facet of the aquarium hobby, and it is possible to cultivate magnificent aquatic gardens with the astonishing variety of plant species available to the aquarist. Even just a few plants in an aquarium provide a realistic, natural beauty that prompts many people to use them solely for their decorative value. Many aquarists, however, use plants more functionally than aesthetically.

All plants improve water conditions, since they take up waste products, notably carbon dioxide and nitrogenous wastes (ammonia, nitrites, and nitrates), and give off oxygen. This last trait of plants is often misunderstood, and the role of plants as "oxygenators" is usually grossly overemphasized. It is safest to assume that plants have no effect on the oxygen content of the water, especially in terms of potentially minimizing the need for mechanical aeration. This is because in all but the most lightly stocked aquaria, plants do not supply a significant amount of the required oxygen, and because plants produce oxygen only during lighted periods. Day and night, plants, like almost all living creatures, consume oxygen and give off carbon dioxide. The process of photosynthesis offsets this fact during the day, when oxygen production exceeds consumption and carbon dioxide consumption exceeds production, but at night the plants are merely competitors with the fish for the oxygen in the tank. In other words, if plants are numerous enough to significantly increase oxygen levels during the day, they will also be significant consumers of oxygen at night. It is best to consider only the role plants play in consuming nitrogenous wastes, which improves the water for the fish and makes it easier on the aquarist by competing with unwanted algae for these nutrients. Improperly cared-for plants can, on the other hand, add to the bioload with decaying vegetation.

Floating plants serve to provide shade for fish which prefer a darker aquarium. They also serve as a refuge for baby fish being pursued by hungry adults, for smaller fish being harassed by tankmates, or for unwilling females being chased by males ready to breed. Fish which build bubblenests often use floating plants as an anchor for their nests.

Some fish, such as the popular angelfish *Pterophyllum scalare*, prefer to lay their eggs on broad-leaved plants such as swordplants (*Echinodorus* sp.). Substitutes such as pieces of slate or plastic pipe are commonly used alternatives, but if the aquarist wishes to observe spawning behavior in as natural a setting as possible, live plants provide this opportunity.

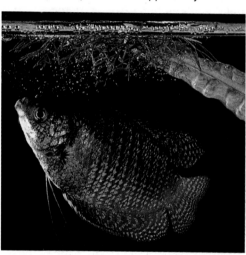

A male Dwarf Gourami, *Colisa lalia*, under his bubble nest, constructed around the floating plant *Riccia*.

Bunch plants, especially fine-leaved ones, are the natural spawning site for many fishes, and although there are artificial substitutes, many aquarists use live plants for this purpose. In addition, plants are a natural and beautiful way to provide fish with the hiding places they need to feel secure and to show their natural colors and behaviors.

Many fish are partially or largely vegetarian as well, and they view plants as a tasty snack. This, of course, can be a reason *not* to use plants in a tank, but many aquarists provide inexpensive and fast-growing plants as a supplement to their fish's diet. Duckweed, which can quickly overrun an aquarium, is eaten by many fish, and aquarists often cultivate tubs of duckweed just for this purpose.

Feeding

Traditionally, aquarium literature devotes a great deal of space to the topic of fish nutrition, including on the culture of live foods, which were once required for breeding success with most species. The truth today, however, is that very, very few species require live foods, even for breeding, even though live foods are still an excellent food for all fish. The last few decades have seen so much progress in research into the nutritional needs of fishes, and so much innovation in the preparation of commercial foodstuffs, that most prepared fish foods today are at least equal to live foods in quality, and in many cases superior to them.

Commercially prepared foods of all types in both dry and frozen forms incorporate such a diversity of animal-based and vegetable-based foodstuffs that by obtaining a number of them aquarists can be assured of providing a nutritionally balanced diet to their fish. Photo courtesy Hikari USA.

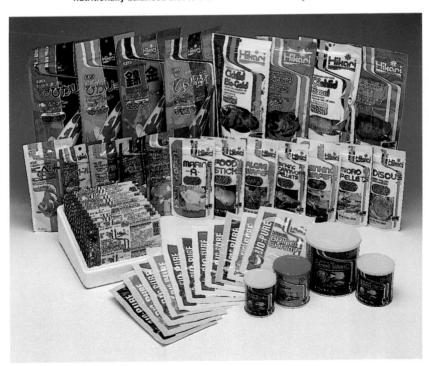

Some freeze-dried foods combine vitamins with insect larvae and worms to make especially tempting offerings. Such foods often contain crustaceans and algae as well. Photo courtesy of Blue Ribbon Pet Products.

Whether it's vitamins, correct protein proportions, natural color enhancers, or even taste/smell appeal to the fish, modern flake, extruded (pellets and sticks), and frozen foods provide a complete, balanced, and highly palatable diet for aquarium fish. Specialty foods abound as well, ranging from foods especially formulated for stomach-less koi–with variations depending on the water temperature–to vegetarian foods for herbivorous fishes, or even sponge-based foods for certain marine species. Many species which once required the movement of live foods to stimulate feeding now ravenously attack various prepared foods which have natural scent and flavor enhancers–the overwhelming olfactory stimulus overrides the lack of motion.

There is nothing wrong with culturing your own live foods, and it is a rare fish that doesn't get excited when fed them, but they are unnecessary except for a handful of finicky species. Live foods are extremely beneficial if you wish to breed your fish, in which case nothing conditions breeders faster, and almost without exception, the fry will do much better with initial live foods. There are numerous references in the literature which provide step-by-step instructions for growing brine shrimp, *Daphnia*, white worms, microworms, *Drosophila*, and other live fish foods. In the section on breeding fishes we will explain the basics of live food culture for fish fry.

ALTERNATIVE FOODS

Although frozen foods such as brine shrimp and bloodworms are very serviceable, appeal to fish almost the same as live foods, and are even available in discrete, one-feeding portions, freeze-dried foods provide all of the convenience of keep-on-the-shelf dry foods while retaining most of the appeal of live foods. In fact, with many fish, freeze-dried brine shrimp elicits a strong feeding response, and freeze-dried krill evokes a regular feeding frenzy!

Besides frozen and freeze-dried foods, there are dozens of different prepared foods on the market. There are different formulations for different dietary needs (carnivorous, omnivorous, herbivorous, breeding, growing, conditioning, etc.), different shapes (pellets, flakes, sticks, wafers, etc.), and different sizes (micro, mini, regular, maxi, jumbo, etc.).

There are foods specially formulated for Bettas, for Discus, for vegetarian catfish, for cichlids, for vegetarian cichlids, for marine fish, for fry, for

Many tropical fish are popular enough for food manufacturers to offer foods formulated specifically for them, and other foods are formulated for specific uses such as enhancing colors and inducing spawning. These foods often are based on high-quality marine fish proteins. Photo courtesy of OSI Marine Lab., Inc.

Goldfish, for Koi, for small fish, for large predators, not to mention the regular, "all-purpose" foods! Add to this the fact that most companies produce similar products and the choice multiplies. Your dealer can show you some of the choices and make recommendations. The important thing to keep in mind is the type of feeders you have in your tank—surface, midwater, or bottom. Even here the commercial foods help out, since most of them are formulated so that some of the food stays afloat, some sinks slowly though the middle regions of the aquarium, and some sinks right to the bottom. Of course, fish are quite inventive; catfish will sometimes swim upside down at the surface to get floating food, and a choice morsel on the gravel will attract the attentions of almost any fish.

There are three important rules about feeding fish, whatever you choose to feed them:

1. Do not overfeed.
2. Feed a great variety of foods.
3. Do not overfeed.

That's right, not overfeeding is the beginning *and* the end of feeding fish. The importance of moderation in feeding fish cannot be overemphasized. In nature, fish are constantly on the prowl for food, and periods of involuntary fasting are common. They are programmed to gorge themselves when food is available—against the times when it is not. Many aquarium fish become ill or die from overfeeding and overeating; it is a rare aquarium fish which dies of malnutrition. But fatty liver disease and intestinal blockages are not the only danger from overfeeding, nor by any means the most immediate.

Overfeeding means a greatly increased bioload, both from uneaten food which begins to decompose and from the increased waste output from fish who have overeaten. The commonly touted rule of thumb to feed only as much as the fish will clean up in five minutes is grossly liberal—your fish should consume all the food you give virtually *immediately*. Table manners are not fish's strong suit. They push, shove, inhale, steal, hog, and bully at dinnertime. In no time at all their bellies are tight, and in some cases their bellies are stretched almost to bursting. No matter how aggressively the fish feed, however, some food will escape their attentions and drift into the gravel, the decorations and plants, or even into the filter, where it will rot and contribute to the bioload on the tank the same as if it were still in the tank proper. In fact, fish, especially bottom feeders like *Corydoras* catfish or *Botia* loaches, will seek out leftover food from crevices in the substrate, but once it is sucked into the filter, there is no chance of that.

A common mistake leading to overfeeding is to mix very active, aggressive fish with meek, retiring species. If you increase the amount of food given, generally the bullies just overeat even more, and the shy fish still get almost nothing to eat. Food still gets lost in nooks and crannies, since it will get by the stuffed aggressors, but the timid fish will be afraid to go out and find it.

As for the rule to vary the fish's diet, this solves two problems. First, fish, like other animals, get bored with the same old thing for dinner every day. Varying the foods given to fish increases their appetite and conditions them. An assortment of different foodstuffs also covers any possible nutritional deficiencies in any one of them. The dietary requirements of different fish are not the same, and the nutritional content of different foods is not the same, so feeding assorted dry, freeze-dried, frozen, and flake foods provides a full complement of amino acids, lipids, carbohydrates, minerals, vitamins, trace elements, and natural color enhancers, and it avoids having anything left out. In addition, although many people will claim that fish do not have emotions, it is hard to think of better words than "happy" and "excited" to describe the behavior of fish when they are fed a lot of different flavorful, wholesome foods.

Breeding Fish

For many aquarists, breeding their fish is the ultimate goal. Unfortunately, many neophyte aquarists also have the goal of making a fortune breeding their fish. While many hobbyists make enough selling or trading their surplus fish to stores and to other aquarists to cover expenses, the most profit they ever see is a little spare cash to buy a few new fish. This is not a conspiracy on the part of pet shops to buy low and sell high. The profit realized from in live fish is extremely small, because the expenses involved are very high, so most people are amazed at the difference between the purchase price of their fish and the price stores will give them for their offspring—if they want them at all. The commercial operations can make a profit on fish at much lower prices than an aquarist with a dozen tanks or so could ever do. Add to this the fact that any fish an inexperienced aquarist is likely to breed is probably also being bred by lots of other aquarists, so the supply often outruns the demand.

Most hobbyists, however, do not have financial goals in mind when they try to breed their fish. Fish which are improperly cared for rarely breed, so breeding a particular species means that their owner is providing for their needs. Thus breeding is a signal of successful aquarium management. In addition, there is a thrill associated with spawning your fish and raising the young to adulthood which is a reward in itself. And, for many aquarists, spawning their fish enables them to expand their hobby and their experience by trading or selling the fry in order to obtain still other species. Even at a substantial loss over expenses, most fish spawns produce enough young to enable the breeder to purchase a pair or two of some new fish.

Perhaps most important to many aquarists considering breeding their fish is the fascination that comes from watching these (usually) small creatures in their variety of behaviors. Two of the most popular groups of fish are the cichlids and the catfish; both these groups have many different reproductive behaviors, most involving some sort of extended parental care. Not only are there mouthbrooding catfish and mouthbrooding cichlids, there are even catfish that trick the cichlids into mouthbrooding the catfish eggs and fry! Not all species are suitable for the beginning aquarist to keep, let alone breed, and some species have never been bred in captivity. In this section we will examine the breeding habits and requirements of the major groups of aquarium fishes.

The first requirement, of course, is a healthy pair of fish, conditioned for spawning. With some species, the sexes are immediately apparent, being

The killifishes are among the most sexually dimorphic of aquarium fishes, with the male usually much more colorful than the female, as in this pair of spawning *Nothobranchius rachovii*.

dimorphic in size and/or color and/or shape. With others, only the fish are able to tell each other apart. For some species, any male and any female will spawn, while others only spawn in groups of several males and several females, and yet others form pairs and are often quite fussy about choosing their mates.

Some species need very specific water chemistries to breed and may also require raising or lowering the water temperature or other "tricks" to induce spawning. A few fish will not consider reproducing unless heavily fed on a variety of live foods. And then there are fish like the Zebra Danio, *Brachydanio rerio*, which has been known to spawn in the plastic bag as they are being transported home from the pet shop.

The aquarium setup needed to breed fish also varies considerably. Some species can breed successfully in a community aquarium. Some will breed regularly in that environment, but in order to save any fry you would have to isolate the parents in a special breeding tank. Yet other species need particular breeding setups just to get them to spawn. The first group to consider for the beginning aquarist is one of the least demanding and ideal for the beginner—the livebearers.

No matter what fish are bred, however, success is much more certain when live brine shrimp are fed as soon as the fry are large enough to eat them, which ranges from immediately with livebearers and most cichlids to two or more weeks for the smallest fry, which need to be started on infusoria or microworms. Most fry grow very quickly, and as large a tank as possible should be used for rearing them. Since they must be fed continuously with live foods or many times a day with prepared foods, pollution of the tank is a constant threat. Daily water changes are the best way of dealing with this problem, though with the tiniest fry, these can often be put off for a short while due to the extremely small biomass in a tank full of minuscule fish and microscopic live foods.

INFUSORIA

Infusoria is a catch-all term for microscopic organisms. One of the best sources of them is a mature sponge filter. If this is what you have in the tank, you will see the fry pecking away at invisible goodies. Even fry large enough not to need such small food will graze contentedly. Another source is to take the dirty filter medium from a power filter, dump it into a container of tank water, let the debris settle, and siphon off the clear water, which will be loaded with microorganisms.

Paramecium, one of the ciliated protozoans found in many infusoria cultures.

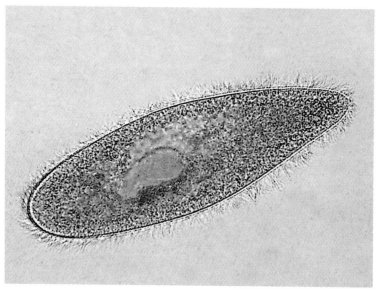

These infusorians can also be cultured in containers of tank water fed with some sort of decaying vegetation–anything from crushed lettuce leaves to banana peels to sheep manure can be used. These cultures can get quite rank, though aeration will help, and new ones should be started every few days, seeding them from an established culture. As soon as the fry are large enough, the aquarist who wishes to raise the maximum number of young will provide live brine shrimp nauplii. Frozen baby brine shrimp is a possible alternative, if there is enough water motion to keep the shrimp moving and stimulate the feeding response. If powdered flake food is fed in increasing amounts with live brine shrimp, the fry will soon learn to go after this immobile food.

MICROWORMS

Microworms, tiny livebearing nematodes, make an excellent fry food because while the tiny worms are great for large fry, their offspring, also present in the culture, are fine for the smallest fry, and the culture medium

Individual microworms, separated and greatly enlarged.
Microworms normally congregate in large groups.

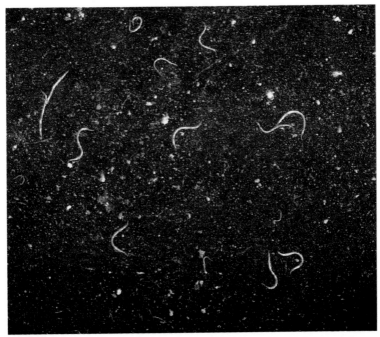

and microorganisms clinging to the worms provide even tinier food. These worms are available commercially in a dried state—water is added, and a few days later the culture is ready.

If you wish to grow your own cultures, use a paste made of powdered cereal such as baby cereal and water. Add a few grains of yeast and some microworms. Start new cultures every week or two, and don't try to keep cultures going very long or they will sour and spoil.

HATCHING BRINE SHRIMP

These should be hatched in jars of seawater (or 6 tablespoons of non-iodized salt per gallon) aerated with an airstone and with the addition of a pinch to a teaspoon of brine shrimp eggs. At 80 degrees they will hatch in under 24 hours. Remove the airstone and wait about five minutes for the egg shells to sink. There will be shells on the surface, shells on the bottom, and the orange nauplii swimming jerkily in between. If you put a light on one side, the phototropic shrimp will congregate there. Siphon them off with a piece of airline tubing draining into a piece of tightly woven cloth, such as a handkerchief. The cloth is then dipped into the aquarium, rinsing off the shrimp, which will quickly be snapped up by the fry, whose bellies will be pink and swollen if they are successfully feeding. The amount of salt added by feeding the shrimp this way is infinitesimal, and the fry will not survive long without partial water changes, so any salt will quickly be diluted anyway.

LIVEBEARERS

Most aquarists start their breeding experience with livebearers—Guppies, Mollies, Platies, and Swordtails. Although there are other fish which give birth to fully-formed young, some of them very difficult to keep and breed, the livebearers common in the trade are all members of the family Poecilidae, a family of fish widespread in Central America. The ubiquitous guppy originated in Trinidad, the Platy and Swordtail hail from Mexico, and one species of Molly, and the Mosquitofish, *Heterandria formosa*, are even found wild in the southern United States.

The male has a modified anal fin, known as the gonopodium, which is used to place sperm in the female's vent. The eggs are fertilized internally and retained inside the female until the fry are fully formed and ready to be born. This passive parental care enables the fish to produce relatively small broods of relatively large fry and still be reproductively successful. A newborn Guppy (*Poecilia reticulata*), whose adult size will be between one and two inches, and a newly free-swimming Oscar fry (*Astronotus ocellatus*), which will grow up to a foot in length, are remarkably similar. This large offspring size also means that feeding the babies is rarely a problem, in marked contrast to many species which produce extremely tiny fry.

The reason that almost all aquarists' first success with breeding fishes is with the livebearers is that for the most part, "breeding" these fish consists merely of providing some means by which the fry can escape predation by their parents. Healthy females of the common livebearer species will drop a brood of fry about every month. They breed quite indiscriminately, so any aquarium housing livebearers will normally have young present on a regular basis, though few will survive without some preparations on the part of the aquarist.

The ease of breeding these fish, plus the wide variety of naturally occurring colorations in these species, have made it possible for breeders to develop an astonishing variety of strains, which vary in size, shape, finnage, and coloration. Some of the strains are popular for a while and then fade into extinction, while others, like the red velvet swordtail, have been constant favorites since they were first produced.

There is, of course, a significant distinction between truly breeding livebearers and simply saving livebearer fry, at least there is once the initial thrill of getting the baby fish passes. The critical factor in propagating pure strains of Guppies, Mollies, Platies, and Swordtails is that once impregnated, the female can continue to produce young for many months without further insemination by a male. While extremely convenient for the fish, this trait makes it crucial for the livebearer breeder to obtain virgin females in order to control the pairings.

Thus early sex identification is the basis for a sound livebearer propagation program. In many species, the young females develop a gravid spot (a dark spot directly above the anal fin) very early. Males begin to develop the reproductive organ, the gonopodium, which distinguishes them from their sisters. Although males have to mature at least to this point to impregnate females, adult males can fertilize broods in females as young as one week of age! It is important, then, if virgin females are wanted for controlled matings, to raise the fry in a tank of their own.

Most people, however, start at the other end, with an already pregnant female. As her litter develops, her abdomen becomes visibly swollen. In varieties which show one, the gravid spot enlarges. It is even often possible to see the eyes of the fry through the maternal body wall in light-colored livebearers. Litter size varies, mostly according to the size of the mother. The smallest livebearer, *Heterandria formosa*, delivers a couple of fry per

A heavily pregnant female Guppy of a fancy strain. Female livebearers often become full of unborn young almost to the point of bursting.

day for a week or so. Jumbo Swordtails might drop several hundred fry at once. Without some intervention, however, few if any will survive, since all fish, including mother livebearers, relish baby livebearers as a tasty snack.

There are various ways of handling these pisciverously infanticidal tendencies. More popular in the past than now, breeding traps can be used. One such device isolates the female in a chamber with a slotted V-shaped floor. When the fry are born, they drop down through the slot and then instinctively swim up the sides of the V to the surface, secure from their hungry mother on the other side of the plastic wall.

This method, of course, requires identifying late-gestation females, catching them, and moving them into the traps. Unfortunately, this can cause premature births and the loss of the fry. On the other hand, moving the females too early results in serious pollution problems, as the small amount of water the female is entrapped in is easily fouled.

Therefore, a better method is one which mimics nature–with a human assist. A female is placed into a small tank of her own when first visibly pregnant and kept well fed. The tank is provided with floating plants or an artificial equivalent. When the fry are born, they swim up into the plants, and most of them avoid getting eaten. The female is removed as soon after the birth as possible, and the young are reared in the tank. Some breeders simply keep their tanks heavily planted, leaving the parents in all the time and relying on a number of fry to escape predation. This can be minimally successful even when an aquarium contains predators like cichlids, provided the cover is very dense and the tank is quite large. Plastic plants have a definite advantage here over live ones; being stiffer, plastic plants are harder to push aside, so when fry bury themselves into the foliage, larger fish have a tough time following. Covering the surface with a dense mat of floating plastic plants (the kinds designed to be anchored in the gravel) will result in a high survival rate.

Feeding livebearer fry offers no problem, for they are big enough to accept the smallest regular foods and do not require special feeding with microscopic organisms. While they will survive on a diet of powdered flake foods and proprietary liquid foods, to get real growth they should receive live newly-hatched brine shrimp as part of the diet. Livebearers also consume a considerable amount of vegetation, and algae or an algae-based food should be part of the feeding regimen.

EGGLAYERS

Fish whose eggs do *not* develop within the female are obviously egg-layers. This negative definition, however, covers a multitude of species (almost all fish) with a wide variety of breeding habits. Nevertheless, they can be broken down into a few large groups, with the fish in each group sharing many behaviors, making them similar in requirements for breeding.

An obvious consideration in breeding fish is the ability to distinguish the sexes. Sexual dimorphism in fish ranges all the way from absolute lack of any external sex difference to fish in which the male and female might well be mistaken for different species. Most of the egg scatterers show only minor differences, with males slimmer and slightly more colorful, but conditioned breeders are usually easily identified, since the females fill considerably with roe. Often females are larger, since it requires much more for them to produce eggs than it does for the males to produce sperm.

The killifish are generally an exception and exhibit a pronounced dimorphism to the point that the nondescript females of many species are

ABOVE: Spawning Zebra Danios, *Brachydanio rerio*. This egg-scattering species is among the easiest of all egglayers to get to spawn and to raise in quantity; its eggs are non-adhesive. BELOW: It is difficult to differentiate the sexes in many of the tetra species unless the fish are in condition to spawn, in which case the female fills with eggs and is then easily distinguishable from the more slender male. A pair of *Hemigrammus nanus* is shown here.

difficult to tell apart, while the males have marked differences in their spectacular coloration.

Many of the fish which show extended parental care have marked sexual dimorphism, with males often much more flamboyant. The common Betta, *Betta splendens*, probably is the best example. With the cichlids, in which both sexes provide brood care, the male's ability to defend the young is of equal importance with the female's ability to produce the eggs, so the male is often larger and more robust than the female. Males are sometimes more colorful and often have enlarged fins. They also often develop a nucchal hump—a fleshy bump on their forehead, which in some species can become grotesquely large. There are also many cichlids which are not sexually dimorphic at all.

A broad overview of spawning different types of fish will serve to acquaint the new aquarist with the range of reproductive behaviors shown by aquarium fish.

DIFFICULT SPECIES

The first group to consider is not a taxonomic group, but crosses genus and family lines and is defined simply by the relative breeding difficulty of the fish in it. Many tetras are included. There is tremendous variability in the willingness of *Hemigrammus, Hyphessobrycon,* and similar species to spawn. Some, like the ever-popular neon tetra, *Paracheirodon innesi*, can foil even many experts' attempts, while others will reproduce regularly in a community aquarium.

Many of the fish in this group are species which will adapt to many different water chemistries but will spawn only when conditions imitate their natural environment quite closely. For many, but not all, this means soft, acid water—known as "blackwater" due to the tannins and other organics leached into it. This is duplicated in the aquarium with the use of distilled or reverse osmosis (R.O.) water conditioned by using peat moss, either in the filter or as a substrate, or both. It is best for a beginner to choose a species which does not require such preparations.

EGG SCATTERERS

A great many fishes spawn by releasing quantities of eggs and milt, usually in plants. With many species the eggs stick to the plants until they hatch. Most tetras and barbs breed this way, many of them being group spawners which will spawn as pairs but spawn more readily when several fish can breed at the same time. Not only do they not have any parental care, they are typically voracious egg eaters, so the parents must be removed as soon as spawning is over if there are to be any fry.

A pair of Rosy Barbs, *Puntius conchonius,* spawning in a thicket of plants. The male of the pair is a much brighter red.

TETRAS

Many popular community tank species are usually small, often flattened fish, typically with an adipose fin–a small extra fin behind the dorsal. These fish are best represented in South America, with several species in Africa as well. This group includes a number of different families that contain the African and South American tetras, pencil fish, headstanders, and hatchetfish. Normally these fish are either netted by the tens of thousands in the wild and exported around the world, or they are bred commercially in huge outdoor pools in Asia and in Florida. Nevertheless, several species can be spawned in the aquarium, though many should be left until the aquarist has some experience breeding easier species.

Water requirements for a given species should be checked in the description of that species in the fish catalog section, but the basic tank setup is the same for all. The spawning medium should be bushy live plants or their equivalent. Whether this is realistic looking plastic plants or just a mop made of nylon or acrylic wool does not matter to the fish. Spawning is usually some variation of a wild chase punctuated by momentary pairings in the bushes, where male and female quiver side by side and produce eggs and milt. Some species tip upside down and attach the eggs to the undersides of broad leaves. The spawning sequence is repeated until the female is spent. The eggs normally adhere to the plants, and, if the parents are removed right after spawning and before they start dining on the eggs, they will hatch in a day or so and be visible as tiny transparent slivers hanging to the plants, the glass, or the bottom of the tank.

A few days later they will swim up into the water, having absorbed all their yolk sacs, and they must now be fed. These tiny fish need extremely tiny live foods, though there are substitutes (such as a hard-boiled egg yolk sieved through a piece of cloth and fed very sparingly), which can save some of them. The best food for them is infusoria or microworms.

CYPRINIDS

The cyprinid fishes are one major group of aquarium fish not supplied by the gigantic South American aquarium fish exportation industry. These carp-family fish are found in Africa, Asia, Europe, and North America and include barbs, danios, "sharks," rasboras, and minnows.

What is probably the easiest egglayer to spawn is in this group, the White Cloud, *Tanichthys albonubes*. This minnow thrives in cooler water and is best kept in an unheated aquarium. It generally does not bother eggs or fry, and a breeding colony can be established in a small planted tank. Many aquarists have been introduced to the thrill of spawning and raising their own fish with this peaceful, colorful little fish.

Spawning Glowlight Tetras, *Hemigrammus erythryzonus.*

A male White Cloud Mountain Minnow, *Tanichthys albonubes,* displaying before the female (background) in a pre-spawning maneuver.

Many barbs and danios are free breeders and suitable subjects for aquarists wishing to gain breeding experience. These are spawned like the characins, except that since most danios produce non-adhesive eggs, for them plants are usually omitted, and a bottom layer of peat, marbles, or coarse gravel is provided so that the eggs can sink out of sight and reach of the hungry parents. The young are usually easy to raise, with infusoria or microworms as the first food.

KILLIFISH

The Killifish, which include a huge variety of species in the family Aplocheilidae, are found worldwide, with most of the common aquarium species coming from South America or Africa. Among them are the so-called annuals, which have adapted to a habitat consisting of temporary pools that exist only during the rainy season. These species have an extremely rapid growth and maturation rate; they hatch when the rains arrive, mature, spawn, and then die when the dry season eliminates their home, while their eggs, safe in the mud, await the rain and a new cycle of life.

Killifish are among the most beautiful freshwater fish and have a dedicated following in the hobby, but they are not widely kept, since they have very specific requirements, typically require live foods, and are rarely suitable community aquarium subjects. Their naturally short lives mean that the aquarist must breed them pretty much constantly in order not to have a line die out.

Spawning is typically in one of two ways. Surface spawners place their eggs among hanging vegetation, and aquarists normally use nylon "mops" suspended from a float (cork or Styrofoam). When full of eggs, the mop is removed. Bottom spawners are kept in an aquarium with a bowl of boiled peat, into which the pair plunges to lay their eggs. After a time, the peat is removed and dried, and the eggs are stored in plastic bags until they are ready to hatch, at which time they are placed back into water.

Since the most common means of acquiring killifish is from a specialized hobbyist (often eggs are traded by mail), the aquarist desiring to try these fish can get specific care and breeding instructions from the supplying breeder, but should be warned that there are many controversies among breeders, and many of them have equal success with quite different techniques.

PARENTAL CAREGIVERS

This broad category covers a very wide range of behaviors, from fish which just are careful about where they place their eggs to fish which tend

RIGHT: This pair of dive-spawning killifish, *Cynolebias affinis,* has kicked up a cloud of peat moss during its spawning act. BELOW: In this pair of mop-spawning killifish, *Aplocheilus lineatus,* the female is in the foreground showing the vertical bar typical of females of this species.

their eggs until they hatch to fish which care for the young to various extents. Within each group there is considerable variation, but certain generalities can be made.

ANABANTOIDS

The fish in this group, which includes the popular species of the family Belontiidae as well as some closely related families, are adapted to oxygen-poor, stagnant water; they have an accessory labyrinth organ which enables them to breathe atmospheric air. In fact, these fish can "drown" if they are prevented from getting to the surface and the oxygen saturation of the water is low. This adaptation has influenced the manner in which they spawn. In most of these species, the male builds a bubblenest. He takes a gulp of air, then spits out several bubbles. He continues until a substantial nest has formed. It is normally anchored in some floating vegetation, and some species incorporate bits of plants into the nest.

Although some male gouramis are fairly gentle with their mates, with most anabantoids it is better to keep the pair separated by a glass divider. This way the male can see the female, which will encourage him to build a nest, but she will be protected from his vicious temper if she is not ready to spawn. Heavy feedings of choice foods will quickly fill a female with roe, and besides her increased girth, the aquarist can tell she is ready when she begins to show interest in getting to the male through the glass. Some females will even blow a few bubbles, and a rare one will actually build a nest.

Spawning should take place shortly after they are placed together. In any case, it is important to keep an eye on things so that the female can be removed if the male becomes too violent, and some cover, such as a clump of plants, should be provided. A bit of chasing and posturing is normal, but a willing female will respond to the male's courtship, and this will prevent him from attacking her, since he instinctively tries to drive away any fish, including females of his species, from his nesting area. A receptive female, however, causes him to switch from defense to courtship, and she is typically safe until spawning is over. In most species the female should be removed, and even in those species where the male tolerates the female's presence, she serves no purpose except to distract him from his paternal duties and perhaps invoke a defensive attack.

Spawning itself takes place close to the nest, with the male wrapping his body around the female's, at right angles to each other. Both fish often seem to go into a trance, and some eggs are expelled and fertilized. The male normally "wakes up" first and dives after the eggs, picking them up in

A male Pearl Gourami, *Trichogaster leeri,* constructing his nest.
Like most of the other gourami species, the Pearl Gourami
normally makes good use of plants in constructing the nest. The
Siamese Fighting Fish, *Betta splendens,* usually does not.

Betta splendens fry are easily visible in this bubblenest being tended by their father. Some of the fry have almost completely absorbed their yolk sacs, but they have not yet become free-swimming.

his mouth and blowing them into the nest. This is repeated until the female is empty and the nest is full.

His paternal duties consist of guarding the nest and of tending the eggs and fry. If an egg or newly hatched baby drop from the nest, he will scoop it up in his mouth and blow it back into the nest. When the fry become free-swimming, the male should be removed, and the fry need the tiniest of foods. It is important to maintain a cover on the tank as the fry develop so that the temperature of the air above the water remains the same as that of the water. When the labyrinth organ is developing, the fry are particularly sensitive to temperature fluctuations.

Variations on this basic pattern include anabantoids with floating eggs, and the bubblenest in these species is often neglected and perfunctory. There are also anabantoids which have taken parental care one more step and mouthbrood the eggs, but none of these are among the common gouramis and bettas available in the hobby.

Catfish

In recent years, catfish have risen in popularity. Many of the popular newcomers have yet to be bred in captivity, though it is usually assumed their spawning behavior will parallel that of similar species which have already been bred. Such assumptions in the aquarium hobby are sometimes proved drastically wrong, but they serve as a general guideline. Of all the families of catfish, two contain species which are commonly bred by aquarists.

CALLICHTHYIDS

The callichthyid catfish, or armored catfish, are represented in the hobby by numerous *Corydoras* species and a handful of *Callichthys, Dianema,* and *Hoplosternum* species. Both groups have very interesting peculiarities in their spawning behavior.

Corydoras are ubiquitous community tank members, and though, fortunately, the idea of keeping them as living vacuum cleaners has fallen out of favor, their peaceful, comical nature guarantees their continued popularity. These fish are typically group spawners, and it is only recently that the mystery of egg fertilization among them has been solved, though the basic spawning pattern has been known for a long time. Courtship concludes with the female mouthing the male's vent, after which she goes to a flat surface, often the tank glass, and "cleans" an area with her mouth.

Eggs of a *Corydoras* species attached to the glass side of the spawning tank. The opaque white eggs showing radiating strands have fungused and will produce no fry.

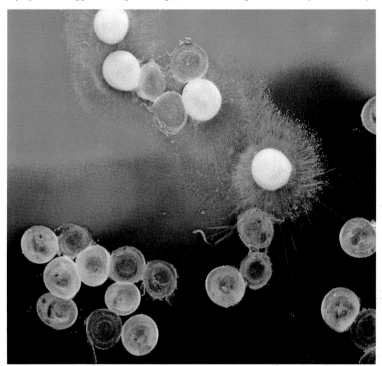

She typically has one or more eggs clasped tightly in her ventral fins. The eggs are then pasted to the surface, and the process is repeated. Observations concluded that the presence of the male at egglaying or attachment is not necessary for fertilization, and for quite a while it was thought that the female stored the milt in her mouth and applied it at the attachment site.

It is now known from laboratory observations, however, that the female actually ingests the sperm. It passes rapidly through her gut, and the eggs are fertilized ventrally as they are laid. Already fertilized when the female carries them in her fins, they are attached and left without further attention. Usually the parents will not bother the eggs or the fry, but most aquarists remove the adults after spawning is over. The "kittens" are generally easy to raise. While *Corydoras* do not actually exhibit parental care, they are included in this section both because of their extremely deliberate placement of the eggs (as opposed to the "shotgun" approach of most egg scatterers), and due to their close relationship to the "hoplo" cats, which show even more parental care, and the loricariids, which provide extended care.

Although very similar to the cory cats, the hoplos are bubblenest builders. The male usually chooses a large floating leaf, and sometimes he

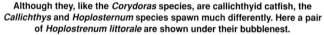

Although they, like the *Corydoras* species, are callichthyid catfish, the *Callichthys* and *Hoplosternum* species spawn much differently. Here a pair of *Hoplostrenum littorale* are shown under their bubblenest.

The loricarid catfish *Rineloricaria parva* guarding eggs laid on a plant leaf.

cuts a suitable leaf off a plant with a sharp edge on his pectoral fin and allows it to float to the surface. He builds a bubblenest under the leaf and entices the female below the nest, where spawning takes place. Many breeders substitute a plastic lid, as from a coffee can, for the leaf, and the nest is built on the underside of the lid. The eggs adhere to the surface, so the bubblenest does not serve to keep the eggs buoyant, as with some anabantoids. Perhaps it serves instead to insure that the leaf will not lose its buoyancy and sink as it floats along, taking the eggs down with it. In nature, the leaf normally drifts away, but in the aquarium the male may continue to guard the nest.

LORICARIIDS

Many species of the ever more popular suckermouth or "pleco" catfishes have been bred in the aquarium. The preferred spawning site is a cave, and a PVC pipe section of appropriate diameter is often supplied for this purpose. The eggs are deposited inside, and the male remains with them, guarding them jealously. After the fry hatch, he continues to provide defense. His paternal instincts are so intense that if the fry are removed and suspended in a net in the same aquarium, he will often make his way into the net to be with his offspring.

The fry are usually easy to raise, but many breeders insist on the importance of including wood in the diet of vegetarian species such as *Ancistrus* sp. The adults scrape off wood fibers as they clean driftwood of algae, and even small fry are seen grazing off wood in their aquarium.

These catfish are not considered free breeders, but many of them are within the grasp of any aquarist willing to provide optimal conditions and to exercise patience.

Cichlids

Probably no group of fish is more diverse in the parental care they demonstrate than the cichlids. Whole books have been written on the topic of cichlid spawning behavior, but we can cover a few highlights and generalizations here in this section.

Both parents are usually involved, though with some dwarf cichlid harem spawners the male's role is merely defense of his territory, within which his females care for their broods in their smaller subterritories. Mouthbrooding has evolved several times among the cichlids, with examples of species in which both parents brood the eggs, in which they take turns having the clutch in their mouths, and species in which the female does all of the mouthbrooding. There are also species which spawn on the substrate, guard the eggs, and then take them into the mouth, which continues to be a sanctuary for the young after they hatch if danger threatens.

The extended brood care by cichlids can extend to the offspring as well. A few species, such as *Lamprologus brichardi* from Lake Tanganyika, raise a few young from the first spawning or two. Then, with the added assist of the older offspring defending the territory, subsequent spawnings result in many more offspring surviving.

Cichlids are either open substrate spawners, which choose a large flat rock as a spawning site, or cave spawners, which excavate a spawning site. In the aquarium, sections of PVC pipe, clay flowerpots, or arrangements of driftwood and/or rocks will provide appropriate "caves."

Courtship among most cichlids can be quite a violent affair, and many aquarists suffer the loss of one of the fish–usually but not always the female–to mating-related aggression. Although there are species, like the angelfish, *Pterophyllum scalare*, which form fairly stable pairs that continue to spawn with each other, many cichlids form temporary pair-bonds just for the duration of one clutch of eggs. In an effort to choose only the fittest mates, these fish engage in active wrestling, jaw-locking, and other
956

ABOVE: A pair of *Apistogramma agassizi* preparing to spawn by laying its eggs on a rock in the open. This species and other dwarf cichlid species also will spawn in cavelike structures. RIGHT: A male *Satanoperca jurupari*, one of the cichlid species that lays its eggs on the substrate and later takes them into the mouth for incubation.

aggressive actions. In nature this ensures that only the strongest fish breed, but in the aquarium, should one fish be ready to breed and the other one not, the latter fish is trapped and unable to escape attack, often with fatal results.

The time-honored and still the best method for getting a compatible pair is to buy six or more juveniles and raise them together in a large aquarium. As they mature, they will pair off and often spawn in the same tank. Typically they will commandeer one-half or more of the aquarium, leaving the other fish cowering in a back corner—breeding cichlids are fearless in the defense of their brood.

The only group of cichlids which have promiscuous polygamy as a typical breeding behavior are the mouthbrooding cichlids of the African rift lakes. Most of these species pair only for the actual spawning act, which is immediately followed by the female taking the eggs into her mouth, where, safe in her buccal cavity, they hatch and absorb their yolk sacs. In some species the young are simply released at this point and ignored from then on. Other species continue to provide care, releasing the young to feed but signaling them at the first sign of danger, when they stream *en masse* back into their mother's mouth.

All but the smallest species of cichlids produce fry which can take brine shrimp nauplii from the start, and they grow quickly on a diet heavy in these crustaceans. Spawns range in size from about 100 to over 1,000 for the largest neotropical cichlids.

Typically the parents care for the young for a long time, herding them around as they search for food and protecting them from any real or imagined danger (such as the aquarist's hand). The fry of some neotropical cichlids, most notably the Discus (*Symphysodon* sp.), feed on the body slime of the parents, and they can be seen hanging on the adults' sides, grazing away. Such fish can be raised away from their parents, but usually fry kept with the adults for at least a week or so grow much better.

The brood care shown by most cichlid pairs is truly touching, and it accounts for much of the overwhelming popularity of this group of fish. Some of them are such ready breeders that they can almost be considered fool-proof. An aquarist interested in breeding cichlids has several such species to choose from—the hands-down favorite as the easiest being the convict cichlid, *Herichthys nigrofasciatus*.

Not the least bit cowed by being completely overmatched in size against its human opponent, this *Herichthys nigrofasciatus* parent bravely defends its eggs from the intruding finger.

Health Concerns

Keeping fish healthy is considerably easier than diagnosing and curing diseases. And keeping fish healthy is mostly a matter of following basic husbandry procedures—avoid overcrowding, avoid temperature or pH shocks, feed well but in moderation, and keep changing the water regularly. Such maintenance is worth a basketful of medications and accounts for the fact that many advanced hobbyists who naturally follow these procedures rarely have any problem with disease.

DISEASE PREVENTION

There are two sources of infection with disease organisms in fish. The first is if a fish is exposed to high levels of pathogens, and this happens when healthy fish are placed in confinement with diseased ones. The sheer number of pathogens overwhelms the heathy fish's immune system. The second way is if a fish is placed under stress and the stress compromises its immune system, so the pathogens in its environment, which normally cannot take hold, are therefore able to infect the fish. Thus preventing fish disease is virtually a matter of preventing fish stress.

PREVENTING STRESS

Just as with people, there are two types of stress fish can experience. They can be stressed physically. Such stresses include temperature and pH shocks, physical injuries, temporary starvation, and exposure to disease organisms.

They can also suffer "emotional" stresses. Fear is a powerful force in the lives of most fish, which must be constantly alert to predators. The fright response saves their lives daily, and nothing panics a fish more than being trapped and unable to flee. Of course, from the moment a fish is captured until it arrives in a properly set up aquarium in someone's home, it is subjected to many frightening things, but all the while it is confined in transport or holding containers without anywhere to hide. This type of stress can lead to a weakening of the fish's immune response and an increased susceptibility to disease.

QUARANTINE

If one considers the stresses a fish undergoes being trapped or netted, packed, shipped to a wholesaler, unpacked, thrown in with many other fish from many other places, then packed again and shipped to a dealer, unpacked, thrown in with many other fish from many other places again, and finally netted, packed, and taken home by an aquarist, if one thinks of all the temperature shocks, pH shocks, physical traumas, and frightening

Glowing with good health, this tankful of livebearers provides
witness to the good care that they've been given.

experiences a fish accumulates in this process, one would begin to wonder how any fish make it to the stores alive. It should be obvious that such a fish is subjected to both types of infection-causing scenarios repeatedly in its journey to the aquarist's tank.

Many dealers will routinely quarantine new arrivals, keeping them under observation to make sure that they are healthy before releasing them for sale. This is an excellent practice, and it greatly reduces the risk for an aquarist in adding new fish to his or her collection. There is still, however, reason to quarantine new fish at home, and, of course, this is absolutely mandatory if the fish are not quarantined by the dealer.

The reason quarantine at home is advisable in any case is that this is the final in the series of shocks and traumas for the fish. From this time on, hopefully, the fish will not be subjected to temperature, pH, or other fluctuations, nor will it be roughly handled or subjected to the stresses fish experience in bare tanks with no hiding places. Quarantining the fish gives it an opportunity to make this last set of adjustments, to get used to the water, the food, and the routine which the aquarist will supply. It also allows it to heal its bruises and abrasions, regrow its protective body slime, and become accustomed to the pathogens common to this new environment.

Of course, the aquarist's collection is simultaneously being protected from any pathogens this new fish carries which they have not had a chance to get used to. If they manifest themselves as disease during the quarantine period, only the new fish will be infected, and it can be treated in the quarantine tank.

At the end of the quarantine period, which should be a minimum of two weeks, with four or more preferable, the new fish still has to face an established community. To ease this transition, the aquarist should rearrange the tank decor if the fish in question are territorial. This forces all of the fish to set up new territories, giving the newcomer a much better chance than if it had to eke out a territory among all the established ones. It is also easier for a new fish to slip into a community unnoticed if the tank is fed just before the newcomer is added.

DIAGNOSIS

Sometimes, despite the aquarist's best efforts to prevent stress and eliminate infection, fish will become ill. The cause may be known, such as a power failure which caused a temperature drop and compromised the biofilter. Other times, some unobservable trigger makes one or more fish susceptible to the pathogens found in any non-sterile aquatic environment.

Fish which are ill may exhibit increased breathing rates, they may gasp at the surface, their bodies might have spots or lesions on them, they may lie listless on the bottom, with clamped fins, or they may show swellings of the eye or of the abdomen. If they have internal parasites, they may pass white feces, and they may lose their appetite or waste away even if still feeding normally.

The problem is that an ichthyological pathologist with microscope and lab is usually required to make a positive identification of many diseases and parasites, and this is sometimes only possible upon dissection after death. Fortunately, most medications available to the aquarist have rather broad targets, and all of the ailments an aquarist is most likely to encounter are usually treatable with one or two products.

This does not mean that medications should be administered willy-nilly. An experienced dealer can ask you specific questions, or even observe one of your sick fish, and make a knowledgeable recommendation. In addition, a number of books include photos and descriptions which assist in recognizing particular diseases and deciding which medication is best suited for the problem at hand. It is, however, important to realize that fish diseases are not particularly easy to diagnose, and often by the time the disease has made itself apparent, many if not all of the infected fish are beyond help. This is why disease prevention is much more important in the long run than disease treatment.

TREATMENT

Whenever possible, fish should be treated in a bare hospital tank (the quarantine tank can double as a hospital tank when needed). First, it isolates the sick fish so that it does not continue to expose its tankmates to the disease and so that it is safe from being picked on by healthy tankmates. Second, since it can be a much smaller aquarium, less medication is needed to successfully treat the disease. It also prevents the delicate biofilter in the main aquarium from being injured or killed by the medication. Although most aquarium remedies claim they are safe for the bacteria in the biofilter, almost all have some deleterious effect. In the case of antibiotics, it is almost certain that a dosage sufficient to knock out the disease organism will also be high enough to kill off the filter bacteria. Plants are also harmed by many medications.

Perhaps the best all-around cure and tonic is salt. Any non-iodized, chemical-free salt can be used. Salt promotes healing, kills or weakens many fungi and parasites, and is generally well-tolerated. Doses as high as two tablespoons per gallon, added gradually and then diluted back gradually, can be quite effective. Certain fish, notably scaleless fish, are extremely sensitive to any medication, including salt, while many other popular aquarium species can tolerate much higher doses. Some, like certain livebearers and cichlids, can even survive short periods in full-strength marine water.

ICH

The common white-spot disease. Many aquarists feel the name is pronounced "itch" and refers to the attempts fish make to scrape the parasitic spots off their body. Others consider it "ick" in reference to the yucky way it makes fish look and feel. Actually it is a shortened form of the name of the disease organism, the parasite *Ichthyophthirius*. This disease is quite prevalent, common when fish are chilled, extremely contagious, and potentially fatal. It is, however, also easily treated. The temperature should be raised a few degrees to speed up the parasite's life cycle, since it is most easily killed in its free-swimming stage, before it attaches to the fish. There are many commercial preparations to treat ich, most based on organic dyes such as methylene blue or malachite green, which are also useful in treating other ailments.

Obviously the telltale white spots that signal the outbreak of ich in a tank would be more easily discernible on a starkly black fish like this black Molly, but the spots are not the only symptoms of the disease; continual scratching against objects in the aquarium is another.

Fungus has attacked the wounds on the sides of this hapless cichlid.

OTHER PARASITIC INFECTIONS

Various other organisms can cause colored spots, rashes, or sliminess. One implicated organism is *Oodinium*, sometimes called velvet disease because of the way it manifests on the fish's skin. Many of these are treatable with the same preparations used for ich, or by medications specifically designed for external parasites.

FUNGUS AND ROT

Injuries and bad water conditions can lead to infections which appear as white cottony growths or as a wasting away of the fins. The first line of defense is to correct the bad conditions. Various antibiotics and other medications are quite effective and should be administered to the afflicted fish in a bare hospital tank. Wounds should be treated topically with an antiseptic, and the fish should be watched for any signs of fungus, which if uncontrolled can consume the entire fish.

INTERNAL INFECTIONS

Fish are susceptible to many internal infections as well, but these are much more problematic in that they are usually noticed only when they have reached critical stages.

Stomach and intestinal worms are common in wild-caught or pool-raised fish and are best treated with a medicated food. Unfortunately, the first symptom of such infestations is often a lack of interest in food.

A particularly difficult to treat condition is dropsy, a catch-all term for infections which cause the abdomen to swell and the scales to protrude. This normally indicates some massive system failure, often kidney failure, and treatment is usually ineffective at this point. Heroic measures such as using a hypodermic needle to draw off the fluid are sometimes advocated, but the sad truth is that dropsical fish rarely survive. The best prevention is, as for most fish ailments, absolutely stringent cleanliness, stable temperature and chemistry, and frequent water changes.

The name of the affliction "Malawi bloat" indicates its provenance among mbuna, the mouthbrooding cichlids from Lake Malawi in Africa. The exact cause and nature of this disease is uncertain, but many cichlidophiles report avoiding it by feeding all new imports with food medicated to kill *Hexamita*. Also implicated is a diet too heavy on meat. Many of these cichlids are primarily vegetarian and are ill equipped to handle a lot of meat in the diet. Some of the species, however, are quite carnivorous and will not thrive on a vegetable-based diet. It is always important to match the food to the fish's needs.

HOLE-IN-HEAD

Hole-in-head disease is one of those controversial topics in aquarium science. Believed by some to be nutritional, others pathogen-based, and still others hygienic in origin, it is an affliction of large cichlids, who develop pits, usually on their head. Some believe it can be reversed with treatment (the target organism is usually considered to be the protozoan *Hexamita*), while others claim treatment can merely stop its spread.

Discus and Oscars are most often plagued by this malady, and most breeders will insist that fish kept in clean water which is regularly changed in massive amounts will not come down with the problem. While such a regimen may or may not address the cause of this affliction, there is no doubt that it is quite effective in preventing it.

VETERINARY CARE

While still not commonly available, veterinary care for exotic fishes is an option for valuable fish which have become ill or injured. Some veterinarians are even performing surgery on large fish such as Koi, Goldfish, and certain cichlids.

Very often sick fish are simply euthanized in recognition of the fact that treatment of fish diseases is uncertain at best and that most fish are more inexpensively replaced than treated. The increased availability of piscine
966

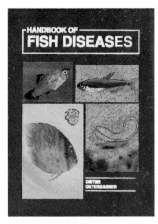

Dieter Untergasser's *Handbook of Fish Diseases* (style #TS-123 of T.F.H. Publications, publishers of this book) offers the most useful and easy-to-follow directions for diagnosing and treating the diseases of aquarium species.

veterinary care indicates both advancement in ichthyology and the trend among aquarists to keep and breed large, expensive species, which can most effectively make use of such medical care.

And, for the average aquarist, the benefits of ongoing veterinarian research into fish diseases are available in the form of constantly improved proprietary medications and in their included instructions for diagnosis and treatment.

EUTHANASIA

Although the "flush and forget" technique may be commonplace, such cruelty must be avoided. When a fish must be killed, it should be done in a humane manner. There is some controversy over the seltzer method, in which the afflicted fish is placed in a container of plain carbonated water, or club soda. The carbon dioxide rapidly puts the fish to sleep, but some aquarists report that the fish is obviously stressed, probably by the effervescence.

Often acclaimed is the freezer method, wherein the fish is placed in a small container of water, which is put into the freezer. Supposedly the fish becomes numb and unconscious quickly, then dies when the water actually freezes.

Undoubtedly the fastest way to put a fish to death is to drop it into very hot, even boiling, water. As with a lobster dropped into the steamer pot, death is instantaneous, and although we do not know the amount of pain registered in this manner, whatever discomfort the fish has lasts only a split second, as opposed to any of the other methods. This method necessarily is better used with small fish than large ones.

Scientific Names

Many new aquarists are frustrated and confused by the widespread use of scientific names for fish. These Latin and Greek names are hard to pronounce and remember at first. But they are extremely important. Every species in nature is given a two-part scientific name. Both are italicized, but the first is also capitalized. The first name is the *genus* name. A genus is a group of closely related species which share many common traits. The second name is the *species* name, which identifies individuals which belong to a common breeding population. The common Guppy is named *Poecilia reticulata*, which links it in its genus with the similar Sphenops Molly, for example. The popular Platy, *Xiphophorus maculatus*, and the Swordtail, *Xiphophorus helleri*, are two closely related species belonging to another genus. Both of these genera (the plural of "genus" is "genera," and the singular of "species" is "species"–"specie" refers to money, not living things) belong to the scientific family Poeciliidae, the group which contains the New World livebearers.

To complicate matters, taxonomists are always refining their classifications, meaning that names can be changed. Often these changes are on the genus level, so at least the species name stays the same. Thus we have the convict cichlid which has gone from *Cichlasoma nigrofasciatum* to *Herichthys nigrofasciatus*, and depending on which taxonomists one follows, may now be called *Archocentrus nigrofasciatus*. The ultimate result of all these changes, however, is a better classification.

But why bother, one might ask. Why not just use common names? Here are a few reasons:

1. There is no standard for common names. Even within one language, a fish may have several names, or several fish may have the same name. Going from one language to another it gets worse, since the names are not usually translations of one another, and the three or four different names a fish has in one language may be totally different from the two names it has in another. With worldwide trade of tropical fish, this would result in disastrous confusion. Wherever in the world a fish might travel, its scientific name remains the same.

2. Common names do not reliably indicate relationships. The use of genus names in particular indicates which species are most closely related,

which can be very useful information when considering the husbandry techniques to apply with an unfamiliar species. No, not all fishes in a given genus necessarily have the same requirements, but they are more likely to be more similar to each other than to more distantly related species. For example, hearing that a new cichlid in a dealer's tank has the genus name *Copadichromis*, one would surmise (correctly) that this was a mouthbrooding Malawi cichlid of the utaka type, needing hard, alkaline water. Hearing it was a *Pelvicachromis,* one would know that soft, acid water would probably suit this fish better, and that it would have a much smaller adult size. Such interpolations will not always succeed, but there is certainly much more information to be gained from this system than one in which the first was labeled a "blue African cichlid" and the second a "red-bellied African cichlid," but then, the name "cichlid" is itself an anglicization of the Latin family name Cichlidae, so even these names benefit from scientific naming systems.

3. The sheer number and variety of aquarium fish makes any other system unwieldy. Biological naming systems have already classified and named almost all of these fish, and as more are identified, they are added in a systematic way. Why *not* use such a useful system?

Serious hobbyists take scientific names seriously.

Index to Fish Catalog Section

The following is an index to the names of fishes covered in the Catalog of Fishes section of this book. Names are listed three separate ways to make it possible to find any fish covered in that section. The names are listed by scientific name according to genus and species (cross-referenced to common names) and also by common name (cross-referenced to the scientific name). Therefore it is possible to find a covered species even if only its common name is known. In addition, scientific names are listed separately by both generic and specific epithets, so it is possible to find covered species even if neither the common name nor the full scientific name is known, but only the specific name.

This book uses the most recently approved names for the fishes covered. Because many of the species discussed in the book have been reassigned to different genera recently and therefore have new generic names, this index also lists the older names for those species and provides the newer names under which they may be found in this book. In all such cases the older name appears in the index with the notation that the reader should refer to ("see") the fish under its newer name. This index therefore should be of special use in preserving a continuity of identification for hobbyists who want to use this book in conjunction with other fish books, many of which would of course contain only the older names.

The index to the **Plant Section** begins on page 1013.
The index to the **Aquarium Management Section** begins on page 1017.

Malawian Scale-Eater, *Genyochromis mento,* 296
Malayan Halfbeak, *Dermogenys pusillus,*258
Malayan Puffer, *Tetraodon cutcutia,* 689
Malpulutta kretseri, Malpulutta, 437
Malpulutta, *Malpulutta kretseri,* 437
managuensis, Herichthys (Nandopsis) 346
Many-Barred Tiger Fish, *Coius quadrifasciatus,* 196
Many-spotted Synodontis, *Synodontis multipunctatus,* 675
Marbled Catfish, *Leiarius marmoratus,* 413
Marbled Hatchetfish, *Carnegiella strigata fasciata,* 172
Marbled Hatchetfish, Carnegiella strigata pasciata,
Marbled Hatchetfish, *Carnegiella strigata strigata,* 170
Marbled Killifish, *Aphyosemion santaisabellae marmoratum,* 79
Marbled Swamp Eel, *Synbranchus marmoratus,* 671
marginatus, Hemigrammus 328
marginatus, Nannostomus 471
Maria's Cichlid, *Bujurquina mariae,* 153
mariae, Bujurquina 153
mariae, Tilapia 694
Mariae, Tiger Tilapia, *Tilapia mariae,* 694
Marlier's Julie, *Julidochromis marlieri,*387
marlieri, Julidochromis 387
marmoratus, Leiarius 413
marmoratus, Schilbe 646
marmoratus, Synbranchus 671
maroni, Cleithracara 194
marthae, Carnegiella 170
Masked Corydoras, Bandit Catfish, *Corydoras metae,* 212
Masked Juliochromis, *Julidochromis transcriptus,* 389
Masked Minnow, Star-Head Topminnow, *Fundulus notti,* 292
Mastacembelus armatus, White-Spotted Eel, 438
Mastacembelus erythrotaenia, Spotted Fire Eel, 438
Mastacembelus zebrinus: see Macrognathus zebrinus
Medaka, *Oryzias latipes,* 491
meeki, Herichthys (Thorichthys) 347

meeli, Lamprologus 408
Meeli, *Lamprologus meeli,* 408
megalopterus, Hyphessobrycon 369
megalotis, Lepomis 421
melanampyx, Barbodes 110
melanistius, Corydoras 211
Melanochromis auratus, Auratus, Malawi Golden Cichlid, 439
Melanochromis crabro, Chameleon Cichlid, Chameleo, 440
Melanochromis johanni, Johanni, 441
Melanochromis vermivorus, Purple Mbuna, 442
melanogaster, Poecilia 544
melanopleura, Leporinus 424
melanopterus, Balantiocheilos 108
melanospilus, Nothobranchius 485
melanotaenia, Cynopecilus 240
Melanotaenia boesemani, Boeseman's Rainbowfish, 442
Melanotaenia fluviatilis, Pink-Ear Rainbowfish, 443
Melanotaenia herbertaxelrodi, Lake Tebera Rainbowfish, 444
Melanotaenia maccullochi, Dwarf Australian Rainbowfish, 444
Melanotaenia nigrans, Dark Australian Rainbow, 44
Melanotaenia splendida, Pink-Tailed Australian Rainbow, 446
Melanotaenia trifasciata, Banded Rainbowfish, 447
melanurus, Bryconops 152
mento, Aphanius 56
mento, Catoprion 172
mento, Genyochromis 296
mento, Aphanius 56
Merry Widow, *Phallichthys amates,* 528
Mesonauta festivus, Flag Cichlid, 48
metae, Corydoras 212
metae, Hyphessobrycon 370
metallicus, Girardinus 300
Metynnis hypsauchen, Plain Metynnis, 448
Metynnis maculatus, Spotted Metynnis, 44
Mexican Rivulus, *Rivulus tenuis,* 638
Mexican Swordtail, *Xiphophorus montezumae,*714
mexicana, Poecilia 549
Mexicana Molly, Shortfin Molly, *Poecilia mexicana,* 549
micracanthus, Mystus 464

Index to Plant Section

Index to Aquarium Management Section

Notes

Notes

Notes